THE BLOOMSBURY RESEARCH HANDBOOK OF

CONTEMPORARY JAPANESE PHILOSOPHY

BLOOMSBURY RESEARCH HANDBOOKS IN ASIAN PHILOSOPHY

Series Editors:

Chakravarthi Ram-Prasad, Lancaster University, UK
Sor-hoon Tan, National University of Singapore

Editorial Advisory Board:

Bringing together established academics and rising stars, *Bloomsbury Research Handbooks in Asian Philosophy* survey philosophical topics across all the main schools of Asian thought. Each volume focuses on the history and development of a core subject in a single tradition, asking how the field has changed, highlighting current disputes, anticipating new directions of study, illustrating the Western philosophical significance of a subject and demonstrating why a topic is important for understanding Asian thought.

From knowledge, being, gender and ethics, to methodology, language and art, these research handbooks provide up-to-date and authoritative overviews of Asian philosophy in the twenty-first century.

Available titles:

The Bloomsbury Research Handbook of Chinese Philosophy and Gender, edited by Ann A. Pang White
The Bloomsbury Research Handbook of Chinese Philosophy Methodologies, edited by Sor-hoon Tan
The Bloomsbury Research Handbook of Indian Aesthetics and the Philosophy of Art, edited by Arindam Chakrabarti
The Bloomsbury Research Handbook of Indian Ethics, edited by Shyam Ranganathan

THE BLOOMSBURY RESEARCH HANDBOOK OF

CONTEMPORARY JAPANESE PHILOSOPHY

Edited by Michiko Yusa

BLOOMSBURY ACADEMIC
LONDON • NEW YORK • OXFORD • NEW DELHI • SYDNEY

BLOOMSBURY ACADEMIC
Bloomsbury Publishing Plc
50 Bedford Square, London, WC1B 3DP, UK
1385 Broadway, New York, NY 10018, USA

BLOOMSBURY, BLOOMSBURY ACADEMIC and the Diana logo
are trademarks of Bloomsbury Publishing Plc

First published in Great Britain 2017
This paperback edition published 2019

Cover design by Irene Martinez Costa
Cover image: Manyo gekkazu by Hirayama Ikuo (1930-2009). Used by kind
permission of the Hirayama Ikuo Silk Road Museum.

A catalogue record for this book is available from the British Library.

Library of Congress Cataloging-in-Publication Data
Names: Yusa, Michiko, editor.
Title: The Bloomsbury research handbook of contemporary Japanese
philosophy / edited by Michiko Yusa.
Description: New York : Bloomsbury Academic, 2017. |
Series: Bloomsbury research handbooks in Asian philosophy |
Includes bibliographical references and index.
Identifiers: LCCN 2017010882 | ISBN 9781474232685 (hardback) |
ISBN 9781474232708 (epdf)
Subjects: LCSH: Philosophy, Japanese–20th century. | Philosophy,
Japanese–21st century. | BISAC: PHILOSOPHY / Eastern. |
PHILOSOPHY / Social. | PHILOSOPHY / Political.
Classification: LCC B5241 .B59 2017 | DDC 181/.12–dc23
LC record available at https://lccn.loc.gov/2017010882

ISBN: HB: 978-1-4742-3268-5
PB: 978-1-3500-9695-0
ePDF: 978-1-4742-3270-8
eBook: 978-1-4742-3269-2

Typeset by Newgen Knowledge Works Pvt Ltd., Chennai, India.

CONTENTS

CHAPTER SUMMARIES

CHAPTER 1 PHENOMENOLOGY IN JAPAN: ITS INCEPTION AND BLOSSOMING

Keiichi Noe

The development of phenomenological studies in Japan can be viewed in three stages. The first stage is the period of the introduction of phenomenology from Germany by the Japanese graduate students who studied there. Representative scholars of this generation, Takahashi Satomi and Miyake Gōichi, both personally heard Edmund Husserl give lectures on his developing ideas at the University of Freiburg. On their return to Japan, each energetically introduced Husserl's philosophy to the intellectual public and the students of philosophy, disseminating a healthy interest in phenomenology as a new philosophical discipline. The second is the period of the burgeoning of phenomenology, primarily brought about by those who studied with Miyake Gōichi at Tōhoku University. Notable scholars and thinkers of this generation are Takiura Shizuo, Kida Gen, and Nitta Yoshihiro. Their effort led to what is known as the "renaissance of phenomenology in Japan" in the late 1960s and 1970s. These scholar-thinkers translated into Japanese Husserl's and Merleau-Ponty's writings one after the other. Tatematsu Hirotaka's contribution in this connection is noteworthy. The availability of important philosophical texts accessible in Japanese served as the springboard for the next generation of scholars to make a leap, ushering in the third stage of phenomenology. In this period, the discipline of phenomenology was transformed into diverse areas of research and reflections that have been carried out by the postwar generation of scholar-thinkers, whose major contributions include Washida Kiyokazu's "phenomenology of care," Murata Jun'ichi's "phenomenology of technology," and Noe Keiichi's "phenomenology of narration." In this way, phenomenology in Japan evolved into a multifaceted field. Today phenomenology with various orientations remains a vibrant philosophical field in Japan, and continues to develop new angles of research and reflections, as the new historical period generates new sets of philosophical issues.

CHAPTER 2 CONFUCIANISM IN MODERN JAPAN

Takahiro Nakajima

Japanese Confucianism, with the opportunities created by its popularization during the eighteenth-century *bakumatsu* period, turned into a modern moral ideology that supported the nation-state and its empire during the Meiji era. Its core teachings were those of modern Yōmeigaku (Wang Yangming Studies), and they were adopted to mold the hearts of the nation's subjects. The present chapter examines the structure of modern Yōmeigaku and its penetration in Taiwan by focusing on intellectuals such as Mishima Chūshū, an advocate of the doctrine of the unification of righteousness and economic profit; Shibusawa Eiichi, the father of Japanese capitalism; Inoue Tetsujirō, one of the founders of national morality; and Hattori Unokichi, the advocate of Kōshikyō (Confucian teachings). While this line of development of modern Yōmeigaku describes the aspect that was closely tied with the building of Japan's modern nation-state and its empire, there was another stream of development of Yōmeigaku within Japanese Confucianism. This is the tradition of populist or "grassroots" Confucianism, associated with Nakae Chōmin, a philosopher with a sharp, critical eye on the course of modern nation building, and Ishizaki Tōgoku, who sympathized with Chōmin and founded the Osaka Yōmei Gakkai. The latter progressively came to bear a religious characteristic. We analyze these two streams of Yōmeigaku in order to uncover the diverse realities of modern Japanese Confucianism.

CHAPTER 3 THE POLITICAL THOUGHT OF THE KYOTO SCHOOL: BEYOND "QUESTIONABLE FOOTNOTES" AND "JAPANESE-STYLE FASCISM"

Kenn Nakata Steffensen

This chapter is an exercise in the rectification of names, in the spirit of the Confucian epigram (*The Analects* 13.3). What the Kyoto School is understood to be today is a mental construction divorced from what it actually was when it flourished as a philosophical beacon in the "dark valley" of wartime Japan. Rectification of the name is what is needed to restore the Kyoto School to what it was in its original context, and to see how it has subsequently acquired other meanings. This kind of reorientation of perspective can contribute to the ongoing process of recovering and broadening of the concept of the Kyoto School, and its contribution to political thought. Revitalization of its original reality can in turn contribute to fulfilling what Ōhashi Ryōsuke calls its "intellectual potential." After an introductory section, the chapter will outline the post–Second World War creation of the image of the political thought of the Kyoto School; this genealogical exercise shows that the connotation of what the Kyoto School stood for in postwar Japan was largely defined by the perspective of the Marxist left wing, which was the main background of highly critical historians. The chapter moves on to a consideration of the wartime ambiguous strategy of "anti-systemic collaboration" pursued by most of the Kyoto School philosophers, and the interpretive problems that arise from it. The final section highlights a selection of political theoretical themes developed by the Kyoto School thinkers and discusses their relevance for contemporary theorizing in light of recent trends in the history of political thought, political theory, and international relations. The fulfillment of the intellectual potential of Kyoto School political thought requires breaking out of its relative isolation and being inserted into new, and arguably more relevant and hospitable, disciplinary fields, and also taking it out of the established traditions of the philosophy of religion and Japanese history.

CHAPTER 4 METANOETICS FOR THE DEAD AND THE LIVING: TANABE HAJIME, KARAKI JUNZŌ, AND MORITAKI ICHIRŌ ON THE NUCLEAR AGE

Nobuo Kazashi

In postwar Japan, Tanabe Hajime, who carried the living tradition of the Kyoto School of philosophy, first underwent a period of intense self-repentance (*zange*) for his wartime responsibility or inability. With the heightened sense of shared guilt as a survivor of the war, he turned to the analysis of technology, science, and the dialectic of death-qua-resurrection. Tanabe's students supplanted his logic of species, which was criticized as being laden with theoretical flaws. Those students, whose lineage may not be immediately apparent, actually constituted a continuation of the Kyoto School "on the side," into a different and lesser-known direction. One of them, Karaki Junzō, denounced the lack of the sense of responsibility on the part of scientists who were instrumental in creating the nuclear age; another student named Moritaki Ichirō, who was the leading figure of postwar antinuclear movement, came to advocate the philosophy of compassion as opposed to Tanabe's dialectic of death. His claim that humankind and nuclear power cannot coexist and that we must "absolutely negate" the nuclear energy, either employed to destroy or to generate energy, is a clear message that sounds even more convincing in the post-Fukushima period.

CHAPTER 5 IN THE WAKE OF 3.11 EARTHQUAKE: PHILOSOPHY OF DISASTER AND PILGRIMAGE

Cheung Ching-yuen

This chapter points to the possibility of developing a philosophy of disaster by engaging in the spiritual recovery and healing of the victims of the earthquake-tsunami disaster of March 11, 2011. This initiative at first led to an international conference, sponsored by the Japan Foundation, on "Disaster and the Creation of Value System." It was held in 2012 at the University of Tohoku in Sendai, on the day of the anniversary of the earthquake-tsunami; most significantly, a day after the conclusion of the official program of the conference, the participants made a pilgrimage to the disaster-stricken areas of Ishinomaki, Onagawa, and Arahama. This chapter examines the philosophical meaning of such a "pilgrimage" (and related activities such as holding a philosophical café, although it was not specifically developed in this chapter). It throws into question how philosophy, a discipline otherwise becoming progressively more theoretical and technical, may remain relevant to our everyday lives and make contributions to contemporary society. It is a call for enacting "engaged philosophy" in this day and age.

CHAPTER 6 THE AESTHETICS OF TRADITION: MAKING THE PAST PRESENT

Michael F. Marra

The theme of this chapter is that Japan continues to make its tradition in dialogue with the Other, and the West, as a case in point. The aesthetic discourses applied to the traditional Japanese arts are actually the invention of the twentieth-century academics in the field of aesthetics who were conversant with Western aesthetics. Such concepts as "*mono no aware*" (the pathos of things), "*yojō*" (overtone), and "*sabi*" (elegant simplicity, desolation) were newly introduced as "aesthetic categories" into the modern discourses. In this process, the Buddhist notion of paradoxical logic of the thirteenth century came to be interpreted to be grounded in the Buddhist logic of negation, and especially associated with the philosophical notion of "nothingness" (*mu*) that was developed in the twentieth century by Nishida Kitarō. Most aesthetic discussions on the nature of Buddhist *mu* are indebted to Nishida's thought.

While the creation of fictitious categories such as "the literature of recluse" (*inja bungaku*) went on, more serious philosophical interpretations of impermanence and nothingness have also been advanced by literary critics and philosophers. I single out Kobayashi Hideo on the notion of impermanence, and Nishitani Keiji on emptiness.

Nishitani's argument is especially eye opening, as he takes the concrete visible phenomenon of the "sky," and argues that phenomena are actually formless (or empty) just as the sky, and that knowledge is a transparent, formless space in the heart, which enables the transparent objects to be made into images and appear at the bottom of the heart. When these images develop and are filtered through the imagination, art is born. Hence, impermanence overcomes impermanence itself, and emptiness is understood as permanence in the midst of impermanence.

In short, Japanese traditions as we know them today would not have existed independent of the impact of the West (qua modernity), which has been felt since the latter half of the nineteenth century. Moreover, Nishitani's philosophy of emptiness actually turns out to be his response to existential nihilism out of a concern for the future that renders the past as the present.

CHAPTER 7 BODILY PRESENT ACTIVITY IN HISTORY: AN ARTISTIC STREAK IN NISHIDA KITARŌ'S THOUGHT

Enrico Fongaro

This chapter is a much-simplified introductory version of a larger chapter that aims to insert Nishida's aesthetic ideas into the horizon of contemporary aesthetics. Nishida's thought on artistic creativity may be divided into two phases: the first centered on the 1923 book *Art and Morality*, and the second on the 1941 essay *Artistic Creation as an Activity of History Formation*. Nishida's thought on aesthetics is significant because, on the one hand, it is rooted in the Japanese artistic tradition, for which I refer to the writings of Hisamatsu Shin'ichi (1889–1980). On the other hand, Nishida confronts himself with some of the most important Western aesthetic theories that appeared between the end of the nineteenth and the beginning of the twentieth centuries—in particular with those of Konrad Fiedler (1841–95) and W. Worringer (1881–1965). While drawing from these aesthetic works of Western scholars, Nishida continued to develop his own philosophical system.

Furthermore, it can be asserted that Nishida's philosophy itself possesses an "aesthetic" character ascribable to his personal experience as poet and calligrapher. The thesis that a creative act of artists must necessarily take place through their "bodily activity," which constitutes a "historical" action, seems to be at the core of Nishida's philosophy of creativity, which is intimately related to the concepts of praxis and of time that seem to have their origin in Zen Buddhism and share the common insight with the traditional *geidō*, or the "way of arts."

CHAPTER 8 IN SEARCH OF AN AESTHETICS OF EMPTINESS: TWO EUROPEAN THINKERS

Raquel Bouso García

This chapter deals with the reception of Japanese philosophy by two European thinkers, Giangiorgio Pasqualotto and Amador Vega. It is suggested that both philosophers practice a sort of intercultural philosophy since their works combine Eastern and Western sources with a special regard to Japanese thought. Moreover, in the case of the Italian thinker Pasqualotto, an important part of his contribution to philosophy throughout his career has been precisely his reflection on the need for opening Western philosophical tradition to non-Western philosophies and what it means to engage in comparative philosophy. The chapter focuses particularly on the role that Zen Buddhist tradition and the philosophy of the Kyoto School have played in the development of what can be called an "aesthetic of emptiness," which could be considered one of the main lines of research carried out by these two thinkers up to now.

CHAPTER 9 WATSUJI TETSURŌ: ACCIDENTAL BUDDHIST?

Steve Bein

Watsuji Tetsurō is widely thought to be Japan's most important secular philosopher of the twentieth century, held as equal in stature to the members of the Kyoto School's inner circle. This chapter raises the question of whether Watsuji should properly be thought of as a secular philosopher at all, or whether he is better described as an "accidental Buddhist," that is, a philosopher whose central ideas are so thoroughly informed by and infused with Buddhist thought that the Buddhism cannot be extracted from them. Buddhism was a wellspring to which he returned throughout his career, the double negation in the *Rinrigaku* and the *Fūdo* is structurally similar to the doctrine of dependent co-origination laid down by Nāgārjuna, and the theme of emptiness that pervades his work bears similarities to *śūnyatā*. I argue that he is not in fact a de facto Buddhist philosopher, though a survey of his life and work shows that his Buddhist influences are deep and lasting.

CHAPTER 10 ENCOUNTER IN EMPTINESS: THE I-THOU RELATION IN NISHITANI KEIJI'S PHILOSOPHY OF ZEN

Bret W. Davis

Nishitani Keiji (1900–90), the central figure of the second generation of the Kyoto School, argues that the I-Thou relation has been most deeply fathomed in the Zen tradition. The present chapter aims to elucidate and examine this crucial, yet heretofore insufficiently discussed dimension of Nishitani's philosophy of Zen. In addition to his *Religion and Nothingness*, it focuses on "The I-Thou Relation in Zen Buddhism" as well as on some later lectures Nishitani gave on this theme, most of which have not yet been translated. According to Nishitani, in order to understand the interpersonal encounter, one must think through a fundamental paradox. He gives two factors that must be borne in mind: "first, as subjectivities, both the I and the Thou are absolutes, each in its own respective subjectivity; second, I and Thou are absolutely relative to one another." The question is, how can the self be both absolutely independent and absolutely relative? Nishitani's answer lies in what can be called the irreducibly twofold nature of the self: on the one hand, the self is a relative being standing over against other relative beings; and yet, on the other hand, the ultimate "home-ground" of the self is the "field of emptiness" that engenders and encompasses such relations between relative beings. The last section of this chapter argues that Nishitani's final writings on this topic suggest that the proper attitude of the twofold self to other selves is a twofold love: a love that both dissolves a dualistic sense of separateness from others, and yet also respects the other's unfathomable alterity.

CHAPTER 11 CREATIVE IMAGINATION, *SENSUS COMMUNIS*, AND THE SOCIAL IMAGINARY: MIKI KIYOSHI AND NAKAMURA YŪJIRŌ IN DIALOGUE WITH CONTEMPORARY WESTERN PHILOSOPHY

John W. M. Krummel

This chapter examines the imagination, its relationship to "common sense," and the recent development of the notion of the social imaginary in Western philosophy and the contributions Miki Kiyoshi and Nakamura Yūjirō can make in this regard. I trace the historical evolution of the notion of the productive imagination from its seeds in Aristotle through Kant and into the social imagination or imaginary as bearing on our collective being-in-the-world, with semantic and ontological significance, in Paul Ricoeur, Cornelius Castoriadis, and Charles Taylor. Miki and Nakamura, when brought into dialogue with these contemporary Western thinkers, have much to add to and enrich the recent development of the imagination's creativity into the collective sphere. Miki shows a connection between the imagination and a certain form-formlessness dynamic he inherited from Nishida Kitarō. Nakamura in turn points to a connection between imagination and place via his development of the Aristotelian notion of *sensus communis* or *koinē aisthēsis*. Both have implications on how we understand the social imaginary.

CHAPTER 12 NISHIDA KITARŌ AS A PHILOSOPHER OF SCIENCE

Keiichi Noe

Nishida's philosophy of science constitutes an indispensable part of his later philosophy, but his achievements to ground sciences in philosophy have been largely neglected. In order to understand Nishida's philosophy as a whole, however, it is essential that we reevaluate his philosophy of science. Although Nishida Kitarō has often been considered as a philosopher of religion or a kind of metaphysician, the fact is that in the past ten years of his life, his speculation was devoted to the problems of the philosophy of science. The time when Nishida lived (1870–1945) corresponds to the period of "the crisis of science," marked by such events as the discovery of Russell's paradox in mathematics, the rise of quantum mechanics in physics, and the controversy between mechanism and vitalism in biology. Nishida took sides with heterodox positions in these scientific controversies—namely, Brouwer's intuitionism in mathematics, Bridgman's operationism in physics, and Haldane's organism in biology. Nishida's sympathy with these ideas was rooted in his philosophical view that was founded on the key concept of "action intuition"—the intuitive grasp of an object through the bodily action in *poiesis*. From this vantage point, Nishida criticized the law of excluded middle in logic following Brouwer's analysis of the π-sequence and evaluated the development of quantum physics as a "genuine return to the intuition of the bodily self."

We may generally classify Nishida's philosophy of science as "anti-realism," because his view of science does not presuppose an ideal scientific world independent of scientists' activities. Nishida was fond of quoting de Broglie who said, "Before analysis by prism there are seven colors in the colorless ray. But they exist in such a way that if we make an experiment, they come out." For Nishida, the structure of reality is closely tied with "action intuition" and bodily *poiesis* that are history-forming.

CHAPTER 13 JAPANESE AND WESTERN FEMINIST PHILOSOPHIES: A DIALOGUE

Erin A. McCarthy

This chapter explores the resonance between Japanese and Western feminist philosophies, and demonstrates that Japanese feminist philosophy has much to offer Western feminist philosophy. Drawing on recent translations, I introduce and analyze the work of Japanese feminist philosophers such as Yosano Akiko (1878–1942) and Hiratsuka Raichō (1886–1971), highlighting the themes of spirituality, embodiment, subjectivity, independence, and gender. I also investigate the ways in which Western feminist philosophy (such as the work of Luce Irigaray and Hélène Cixous) often struggles to find nondualistic frameworks for thinking about gender. Japanese feminist thought does not neatly fit inside Western feminist philosophies, and yet I argue that Japanese feminist philosophies, brought into dialogue with the Western counterparts, are a rich resource for the further development of feminist philosophies in a global age.

CHAPTER 14 AFFIRMATION VIA NEGATION: ZEN PHILOSOPHY OF LIFE, SEXUAL DESIRE, AND INFINITE LOVE

Michiko Yusa

Three thinkers who practiced Zen—Hiratsuka Raichō, D. T. Suzuki, and Nishida Kitarō—are brought together in this chapter to speak about their philosophies of life and sexual desire. The aim of such an arrangement is to articulate a possible Zen "philosophy of peace." The objective of this choice of topic is to delineate a *kataphatic* dimension of Zen-inspired philosophy, which is often overshadowed by its more familiar *apophatic* expressions of "emptiness," "*mu*," and "absolutely nothing."

First, the *kenshō* (Zen awakening) experience of these three thinkers is examined with the view that there seems to be a correlation between one's *kenshō* experience and one's gaining insight into what "life" (*seimei* or *inochi*) is. Treated next is their philosophies of life, including their discussions on sexual desire. Suzuki succinctly states that sexual desire arises from the very source that turns itself into great compassion; for Raichō women's sexuality leads her to formulate the view that woman has to be liberated qua sexed body, qua woman, and not just as an abstract "human being." Nishida takes the whole issue of the body as a fundamental philosophical problem, and places desire and the body within the wider dialectical framework of the individuals and the world. Desire, says Nishida, arises as the individual "mirrors" the world, and it spurs one into action (*praxis*) and production of things (*poiesis*). One's activities in turn shape the "world" one lives in. Human actions construct the world of history, while the world of history also shapes how one exists in the world.

Ultimately, Raichō, Suzuki, and Nishida each point to the reality of "love," or *mahākarunā* (great compassion), which, when applied as a *social constructive principle*, has the potential of building a philosophy that averts conflict and war. Moreover, what is meant in Zen by "dying" is far from the negation of life, but "dying" to the ego-centered mode of being. Understood as such, negation is a necessary step toward affirming life. Furthermore, mortality is cast in a spiritual framework of eternal life. Thus, in the radical turnabout of the individual self via "negation," a key may be found for us to envision a more caring and "grace-ful" society and world.

NOTES ON CONTRIBUTORS

Steve Bein (PhD University of Hawaii) is associate professor of philosophy at the University of Dayton, where he is a specialist in East Asian thought. His books include *Compassion and Moral Guidance* (2013) and *Purifying Zen: Watsuji Tetsurō's* Shamon Dōgen (2011). He is a regular contributor to the Blackwell's popular And Philosophy series and to various anthologies of Japanese philosophy.

Raquel Bouso Garcia is an associate professor at the Universitat Pompeu Fabra in Barcelona, Spain, where she received her PhD with a thesis on the notion of emptiness in the thought of Nishitani Keiji (1900–90). She has translated into Spanish works by Nishitani Keiji, Ueda Shizuteru, and Toshihiko Izutsu, along with other works in Japanese philosophy. Besides various articles, she has published *El zen* (Catalan, 2008; Spanish, 2012), coedited FJP vol. 6, *Cross-Currents and Confluences* (2009), and edited *La filosofía japonesa. En sus textos*, with J. W. Heisig, T. P. Kasulis, and J. C. Maraldo (2016). Her research interests include intercultural philosophy, aesthetics and religion, East Asian religions and thought, particularly Japanese Zen and Kyoto School. She is a member of the Research Group Bibliotheca Mystica et Philosophica Alois M. Haas, a board member of the European Network of Buddhist Christian Studies (ENBCS), and a cofounding member of the European Network of Japanese Philosophy (ENOJP).

Cheung Ching-yuen received his PhD from Tohoku University in Sendai, Japan, and is currently teaching in the Department of Japanese Studies, Chinese University of Hong Kong. His research interests include Japanese philosophy and Japanese literature. Among his numerous publications, the more recent ones are: "Educating Rita: The Case of Japanese Philosophy," in *Whither Japanese Philosophy? III: Reflections through Other Eyes* (2011), 55–67; "Abe Jirō," in JPS, 816–821; "Nishida Kitarō's Philosophy of Body," in *Dao: A Journal of Comparative Philosophy* 13 (2014), 507–523. He is an assistant editor of the *Journal of Japanese Philosophy*, and on the editorial team of the book series *Tetsugaku Companions to Japanese Philosophy*.

Bret W. Davis is professor of philosophy at Loyola University Maryland. He received a PhD in philosophy from Vanderbilt University, and spent thirteen years in Japan, during which time he studied Buddhist thought at Otani University, completed the PhD program in Japanese philosophy at Kyoto University, and also trained as a lay practitioner at Shōkokuji, a Rinzai Zen monastery. He has authored more than fifty articles in English and Japanese on Continental, Japanese, East Asian Buddhist, and comparative philosophy. He is the author of *Heidegger and the Will: On the Way to*

Gelassenheit (2007); translator of Martin Heidegger's *Country Path Conversations* (2010); and editor of *Martin Heidegger: Key Concepts* (2014) and *The Oxford Handbook of Japanese Philosophy* (forthcoming). He coedited *Sekai no naka no Nihon no tetsugaku* (Japanese philosophy in the world) (2005), *Japanese and Continental Philosophy: Conversations with the Kyoto School* (2011), and *Engaging Dōgen's Zen: The Philosophy of Practice as Awakening* (2017).

Enrico Fongaro is associate professor in the Art History Program in the Graduate School of Arts and Letters at Tohoku University in Sendai. After having studied philosophy at Padua University in Italy, he received the Japanese Ministry of Education, Culture, Sports, Science and Technology scholarship to study in Japan. He completed his PhD program in Japanese Philosophy at Kyoto Institute of Technology (with thesis in progress). His research interests are philosophy and aesthetics, and in particular his work is focused on Nishida Kitarō. His recent publications include: "*Nishida's Philosophy of Time and Hakuin's 'Guest,'*" in *Japanese Buddhism Seen from the Perspective of Comparative Thought* (2015). He is the editorial supervisor of the *Complete Works of Nishida in Italian* (Milan). His translations of Nishida Kitarō's include: *Uno studio sul bene* (*An Inquiry into the Good*) (2007, revised edition 2017); *Luogo* (*Place*) (2011); and *Problemi fondamentali della filosofia. Conferenze per la società filosofica di Shinano* (*Fundamental problems of philosophy. Lectures for the Shinano Philosophical Society*) (2014). He has also translated works by Max Weber and Martin Heidegger. He is on the editorial board of the European Network of Japanese Philosophy (ENOJP).

Nobuo Kazashi is professor of philosophy at Kobe University. Born in Shimizu City in 1953, he received a master's degree from Tokyo University of Foreign Studies in 1981, PhD from Yale in 1993, and taught at Hiroshima City University till 2001. He specializes in modern Japanese thought, comparative philosophy, and peace studies. Publications in English include "The Passion for Philosophy in a Post-Hiroshima Age: Rethinking Nishida's Philosophy of History" and "The Musicality of the Other: Schutz, Merleau-Ponty, and Kimura"; among those in Japanese are *Nishida's Philosophy of History* (editor) and *The Unending Iraq War: Questioning Anew from Fukushima* (coeditor). Based in Hiroshima, he has been engaged in peace activities; in 2015 he codirected the World Nuclear Victims Forum held in Hiroshima. He is the recipient of the sixth William James Prize from the American Philosophical Association (1991), and an award from Japanese Society for Science and Technology Studies (2012).

John W. M. Krummel was born and raised in Tokyo in a bilingual family. He moved to the United States to attend Earlham College in Richmond, Indiana, where he received his BA, majoring in philosophy. He then studied at the New School for Social Research where he received an MA in philosophy with a thesis on Heidegger and Foucault under Reiner Schürmann as advisor. Further, he conducted his doctoral work in philosophy with a dissertation on Heidegger's interpretation of Kant's concept of imagination, under Agnes Heller as advisor. He then attended Temple University and received a PhD in religion with a dissertation on Nishida Kitarō's dialectic under Shigenori Nagatomo as advisor. He teaches at Hobart and William

Smith Colleges in Geneva, New York, where he is currently associate professor in the Department of Religious Studies. He is also currently assistant editor of *The Journal of Japanese Philosophy* and coeditor of *Social Imaginaries*. He is also the author of *Nishida Kitaro's Chiasmatic Chorology: Place of Dialectic, Dialectic of Place?* (Bloomington, IN: Indiana University Press, 2015).

Michael (or Michele) F. Marra was professor of Japanese literature, aesthetics, and hermeneutics at the University of California, Los Angeles, from 1993 until his death in 2012. Before that, he taught at several universities in Japan. His publications include *The Aesthetics of Discontent: Politics and Reclusion in Medieval Japanese Literature* (1991), *Modern Japanese Aesthetics: A Reader* (1999), *A History of Modern Japanese Aesthetics* (2001), among others. His remarkable learning and achievements are warmly remembered by his friends and colleagues; one of his essays is included in this research handbook to pay tribute to his remarkable contribution to the field.

Erin A. McCarthy is professor and chair of the Philosophy Department at St. Lawrence University, New York, where she has taught since 2000. She teaches Asian, feminist, continental and comparative philosophy in the Philosophy Department, Gender and Sexuality Studies Program, and the Asian Studies Program. Author of the book *Ethics Embodied: Rethinking Selfhood through Continental, Japanese and Feminist Philosophies* (2010), her work has been published in several anthologies and journals in both French and English. She was an inaugural recipient of the "Frederick P. Lenz Foundation Residential Fellowship for Buddhist Studies and American Culture and Values" at Naropa University in 2009. She is on the editorial boards of the journals *Comparative and Continental Philosophy, Journal of Japanese Philosophy, Body and Religion*, and is coeditor of the *ASIANetwork Exchange: A Journal for Asian Studies in the Liberal Arts*. She has also served as chair of the Board of Directors of ASIANetwork (a consortium of over 170 North American colleges). In addition to her research in comparative feminist philosophy, she also works on contemplative education.

Nakajima Takahiro is professor of Chinese philosophy and comparative philosophy at the Institute for Advanced Studies on Asia, the University of Tokyo. He started his philosophical path by examining the "rectification of names" in Chinese philosophy. And he broadened his themes into the problem of "language and politics," the "evil and normativity," and "state and religion" in Chinese philosophy and Japanese philosophy. In this past decade, he devoted himself to the phenomenon of Confucian revival in East Asia. In the realm of Japanese philosophy, he has mainly focused on the intellectuals at the Imperial University of Tokyo who produced "National Philosophy" in modern Japan. His publications include *Cosmologia: Heaven, Transformation, and Time* (2015), *The Philosophy of Evil: Imaginations in Chinese Philosophy* (2012), *Praxis of Co-existence: Nation-State and Religion* (2011), *Deconstruction and Reconstruction: The Possibilities of Chinese Philosophy* (2010), *Humanities Philosophy* (2009), *The Zhuangzi: Announce the Hours with Becoming a Cock* (2009), and *The Reverberation of Chinese Philosophy: Language and Politics* (2007).

Keiichi Noe is currently the president-appointed extraordinary professor at the Institute for Excellence in Higher Education, Tōhoku University, in Sendai. He earned his BS in physics at Tōhoku University, and then studied Husserl's phenomenology under Shizuo Takiura for one year. After that, he moved to the University of Tokyo, where he worked under Ōmori Shōzō in analytic philosophy (1972–76), earning the master of science degree. He was a visiting fellow in the Department of Philosophy at Princeton University, 1979–80, where he worked with Richard Rorty on American pragmatism. He has published just about 200 articles and several scholarly books, including *Monogatari no tetsugaku* (*Philosophy of Narration*) and *Rekishi o tetsugakusuru* (*Philosophizing History*), among others. He is the winner of the twentieth Yamazaki Prize in 1994. Not only did he serve the position of the dean of the Faculty of Arts and Letters (2003–2006) and the vice president and director of the Library (2005–12) at Tōhoku University, he was the founding secretary-general of the Phenomenological Association of Japan (1999–2000), the president of the Philosophical Association of Japan (2003–2007), and the member of the Science Council of Japan, acting as the chairperson of the Philosophy Committee (2005–14).

Kenn Nakata Steffensen is a research fellow in the School of Philosophy at University College Dublin. He was educated in politics, anthropology, and philosophy at the University of Copenhagen, University of London School of Oriental and African Studies, and the National University of Ireland. He held the position of an Irish Research Council Marie Sklodowska Curie research fellow in the Department of Philosophy at University College Cork in Ireland and at the University of Tokyo Institute for Advanced Studies on Asia in Japan, 2015–16. His main research interest is modern Japanese political thought, particularly the political theories of the Kyoto School philosophers. He also has interests in the politics of language and translation, the political-theoretical and linguistic aspects of international relations, and audiovisual and philosophical translation. He has held research and teaching positions at the Universities of Winchester, Nottingham, and Roehampton in the United Kingdom, at the University College Cork in Ireland, and at Temple University and University of Tokyo in Japan. His publications include: *A Philosophy of East Asian Community: Miki Kiyoshi's Cooperative Communitarianism on the Scales of World History* (forthcoming) and "The Translation of Tosaka Jun's 'Philosophy of the Kyoto School'" in *Comparative and Continental Philosophy* (2016).

Michiko Yusa is a professor of Japanese thought and intercultural philosophy at Western Washington University in Bellingham, in the Department of Modern and Classical Languages, and the Center for East Asian Studies. She received her BA from the International Christian University in Tokyo (1974), and her MA (1977) and PhD (1983) from the Department of Religious Studies at the University of California Santa Barbara, where she worked closely with Raimon Panikkar and Ninian Smart. Her main focus of research is the philosophy of Nishida Kitarō, but her research interests extend to philosophical and religious writings East and West, women's spirituality in Japanese Buddhism and Western contemplative traditions, Raimon Panikkar's thought, among others. She has published over fifty articles and several books, including *Zen and Philosophy: An Intellectual Biography of Nishida Kitarō* (2002); *Japanese Religious Traditions* (2002), *Denki Nishida Kitarō* (A biography of Nishida Kitarō in Japanese) (1998), and *Basic Kanji* with Matsuo Soga (1989, fifth printing 2007); she also coedited the volumes *Isamu Noguchi and Skyviewing Sculpture: Proceedings of Japan Week 2003* (2004), and *CIRPIT Review 5* (2014), special issue of the symposium proceedings on Raimon Panikkar (2013). She is the past president of the Society for Asian and Comparative Philosophy, and is currently serving as its program chair for the American Academy of Religion. She was a recipient of the Japan Foundation Fellowship 1993–94; she is currently affiliated with the Nanzan Institute for Religion and Culture, 2016–17, as the Roche Chair visiting research fellow.

ABBREVIATIONS AND CONVENTIONS

1. The following abbreviations are employed throughout this volume, including the notes and the bibliographical information given by each author.
2. Works are cited using the abbreviation for the collection, followed by the volume number and the page number(s).
3. For the *Collected Works of Nishida Kitarō* and the *Collected Works of Suzuki Daisetz*, there are two different editions, the original and the new. The new edition is designated by an "N" following the abbreviation of NKZ, that is, as NKZ-N; likewise the new edition of SDZ is abbreviated as SDZ-N (see Introduction).
4. Japanese and Chinese names are listed with the family name first, followed by the personal (given) name. The names of the contemporary Japanese and Chinese thinkers and scholars are listed according to the preference of the individuals concerned (when necessary, the family names are capitalized).
5. *Kanji* is supplied sparingly in the text for proper nouns and for polyvalent words to clarify the meaning.

FJP	*Frontiers of Japanese Philosophy* (Nagoya: Nanzan Institute for Religion and Culture), 7 vols (2006–).
Vol. 2	"Neglected Themes and Hidden Variations," ed. Victor S. Hori & Melissa A.-C. Curley (2008).
Vol. 4	"Facing the 21st Century," ed. Cheung Ching-yuen & Kavin Lam (2009).
Vol. 6	"Confluences and Cross-Currents," ed. James Heisig & Raquel Bouso (2009).
Vol. 7	"Classical Japanese Philosophy," ed. James Heisig & Rein Raud (2010).
HRC	*Hiratsuka Raichō Chosakushū* 『平塚らいてう著作集』 [Collected works of Hiratsuka Raichō] 8 vols (Tokyo: Ōtsuki Shoten, 1983–84).
HRJ	*Hiratsuka Raichō Jiden: Genshi josei wa taiyō de atta* 『平塚らいてう自伝：原始女性は太陽であった』 [Autobiography: In the beginning woman was the sun], 4 vols (Tokyo: Ōtsuki Shoten, 1971–73).
HSC	*Hisamatsu Shin'ichi Chosakushū* 『久松真一著作集』 [Works of Hisamatsu Shin'ichi] (Tokyo: Risōsha, 1970–73).
ITZ	"The I-Thou Relation in Zen Buddhism," by Nishitani Keiji, reprinted in Fredrick Frank, ed., *The Buddha Eye: An Anthology of the Kyoto*

	School and Its Contemporaries (Bloomington: World Wisdom, 2004, revised ed.), 39–53.
JPS	*Japanese Philosophy: A Sourcebook*, ed. James W. Heisig, Thomas P. Kasulis, & John C. Maraldo (Honolulu: University of Hawaii Press, 2011).
KK	*Kyōtsū kankaku ron* 『共通感覚論』 [On common sense], by Nakamura Yūjirō 中村雄二郎 (Tokyo: Iwanami Shoten, 1983).
MKZ	*Miki Kiyoshi Zenshū* 『三木清全集』 [Collected works of Miki Kiyoshi] 20 vols (Tokyo: Iwanami Shoten, 1966–68, vol. 20, 1986).
NKC	*Nishitani Keiji Chosakushū* 『西谷啓治著作集』 [Collected writings of Nishitani Keiji] 26 vols (Tokyo: Sōbunsha, 1968–86).
NKZ	*Nishida Kitarō Zenshū* 『西田幾多郎全集』 [*Collected works of Nishida Kitarō*, 4th ed.], 19 vols (Tokyo: Iwanami Shoten, 1987–89).
NKZ-N	*Nishida Kitarō Zenshū, Shinpan* 『西田幾多郎全集・新版』 [*Collected works of Nishida Kitarō*, new ed.]. 24 vols (Tokyo: Iwanami Shoten, 2002–2009).
OB	*On Buddhism*, by Nishitani Keiji, trans. Seisaku Yamamoto & Robert E. Carter (Albany, NY: SUNY Press, 2006).
Rinrigaku	*Watsuji Tetsurō's Rinrigaku: Ethics in Japan*, trans. R. Carter & S. Yamamoto (Albany, NY: SUNY Press, 1996).
RN	Nishitani Keiji, *Religion and Nothingness*, trans. Jan Van Bragt (Los Angeles: University of California Press, 1982).
SDZ	Suzuki Daisetsu Zenshū 『鈴木大拙全集』 [*Collected works of Suzuki Daisetz*], 32 vols (Tokyo: Iwanami Shoten, 1968–71).
SDZ-N	*Suzuki Daisetsu Zenshū* 『鈴木大拙全集・新版』 [*Collected works of Suzuki Daisetz*, new ed.], 40 vols (Tokyo: Iwanami Shoten, 1999–2003).
THTS	*Tanabe Hajime Tetsugaku Sen* 『田辺元哲学選』 [Selected works of Tanabe Hajime], ed. Fujita Masakatsu 藤田正勝, 4 vols (Tokyo: Iwanami Shoten, 2010).
THZ	*Tanabe Hajime Zenshū* 『田邊元全集』 [Collected works of Tanabe Hajime], 15 vols (Tokyo: Chikuma Shobō, 1963–64).
TJZ	*Tosaka Jun Zenshū* 『戸坂潤全集』 [Collected works of Tosaka Jun], 6 vols (Tokyo: Keisō Shobō, 1966–67; vol. 6 1970).
WTZ	*Watsuji Tetsurō Zenshū* 『和辻哲郎全集』 [Collected works of Watsuji Tetsurō], 20 vols (Tokyo: Iwanami Shoten, 1961–63).

Introduction

MICHIKO YUSA

The year 2011 marked a watershed for the field of Japanese philosophy, when the wealth of writings of Japanese thinkers became accessible in English, thanks to the publication of the monumental work *Japanese Philosophy: A Sourcebook* (hereafter abbreviated as JPS) under the able editorship of James W. Heisig, Thomas P. Kasulis, and John C. Maraldo. Its publication irrevocably altered the academic perception of Japanese philosophy. Its Spanish translation, titled *La filosofía Japonesa. En sus textos*, was published in September 2016, which will no doubt disseminate the interest in Japanese philosophy even further among the Spanish reading public. At present (February 2017), two other anthologies are in the making: *The Oxford Handbook of Japanese Philosophy* (edited by B. W. Davis), and *The Dao Companion to Japanese Buddhist Philosophy* (edited by G. Kopf), each of which contains over thirty original essays that further explore in depth the thinkers introduced in the JPS. Another anthology of essays addressing Japanese philosophy as an academic discipline is published: Ching-yuen Cheung and Wing-keung Lam's *Globalizing Japanese Philosophy as an Academic Discipline* (Goettingen: V & R unipress; Taipei: National Taiwan University Press, 2017), which contains sixteen new essays. Adding to this dynamic scene, two new philosophical associations have been launched and have begun holding their annual meetings—the International Association of Japanese Philosophy (IAJP) and the European Network of Japanese Philosophy (ENOJP)—each with its own journal to publish current works in Japanese philosophy and related fields.

The present *Bloomsbury Research Handbook on Contemporary Japanese Philosophy* showcases philosophical discourses currently taking place in and outside Japan, with the hope of building a bridge from "both sides"— from the Western side and the Japanese side. Fourteen essays (with the exception of one which was reprinted with the permission of the publisher), written for this volume by specialists of their respective fields in Japanese philosophy, extend from the reception and the robust flowering of phenomenology in Japan to the philosophy of science, aesthetics, political thought, social philosophy, gender studies, and Zen-inspired philosophy. The time period covered by these essays is primarily from the late Edo period (ca. 1790) onward up to the present, although the texts these essays cite are by no means confined to it, as the contributors freely go back in time to tap philosophical thinking and cultural perceptions crystalized in the past. This kind of diachronic hermeneutic approach is adopted to reevaluate modern theories, as well as what traditional ideas and concepts originally meant. Also to be mentioned here is a feature of diatopical hermeneutics (or intercultural hermeneutics), as Japanese philosophy, by nature, cannot be discussed in isolation from the larger intellectual and aesthetic traditions of the world.

The guiding principles of this volume have been several: (1) to introduce philosophical writings by the contemporary Japanese thinkers who are actively engaged in their philosophical thinking; (2) to include philosophical works conducted outside Japan on Japanese philosophy, in close tandem with what is taking place in Japan; (3) to present a wide range of subjects that constitute the present-day Japanese philosophical discourse; (4) to face the critical issues of the day, such as the use of nuclear energy, and how philosophy remains relevant to the realities of post-Fukushima Japan (i.e. after March 11, 2011), in the face of catastrophic disasters—a self-critical reflection on the place and the role of philosophy and the act of philosophizing; and (5) to think about what contributions Japanese can make to promote mutually enriching global and intercultural philosophical engagements.

1. AN ORIENTATION CONCERNING "JAPANESE" PHILOSOPHY" (*TETSUGAKU*)

As is well known, the Japanese word "*tetsugaku*" 哲学 was coined by Nishi Amane (1829–97), who, even before the end of the Tokugawa Shogunate rule (1603–1867), was dispatched to the University of Leyden in 1863, where he studied philosophy. Upon his return to Japan, he introduced new ideas from his study in Europe. Inoue Enryō (1858–1919), the founding figure of the Philosophy Society ("Tetsugakukai") and its monthly publication, *The Journal of Philosophy* (*Tetsugaku zasshi*), at the Imperial University of Tokyo, obtained Nishi's support to galvanize this new professional society. In 1912 Enryō, recalling how he came to meet Nishi Amane, gave the following oral recollection:

> The late Professor Nishi Amane was the person who introduced philosophy to Japan for the first time and explained the outline of logic, psychology, and ethics. He not only coined the term "*tetsugaku*" for philosophy but also came up with technical terms, such as "*shukan*" 主観 for subject, "*kyakkan*" 客観 for object, "*en'eki*" 演繹 for deduction, and "*kinō*" 帰納 for induction ... I first saw Professor Nishi around 1879 or 1880, at a public lecture held at Asakusa Ibumurarō, where he presented the theory of evolution ... But the first time I actually came to meet him in person was in early 1884, when I wished to consult him about establishing the Philosophy Society. With his calling card in my hand, without following the usual protocol of having someone else introduce me to him, I visited him at his house in Kyōbashi Sanjukkenbori [present-day Ginza area]. He warmly received this unannounced caller, and we became befriended ever since.[1]

In the early days of the academic studies of philosophy in Japan, what constituted philosophy was broadly and generously defined, overarching a wide range of academic disciplines from natural sciences and social sciences to humanities. This opened the door of the Philosophy Society to practically every professor and student on the university campus. Then students at the Imperial University, such names as

Kiyozawa Manshi, Natsume Sōseki (known then as Natsume Kin'nosuke), Fujioka Sakutarō, and Matsumoto Bunzaburō, were all among its active members. The first meeting of the Philosophy Society took place on January 26, 1884, with twenty-nine members in attendance.[2] Incidentally, Nishida Kitarō, being enrolled at the university as a student in the "limited track" (*senka*), had to have his friend, who was in the "regular track," sponsor his application to join the society; his application was approved at the monthly meeting of November 5, 1891.[3]

That these accounts sound so antiquated today comes as a proof that the academic discipline of philosophy has taken root quite rapidly and firmly during the second half of the Meiji period onward, thanks to the energetic entrepreneurial activities of the first generation of Japanese philosophy students, such as Inoue Enryō. The publication in 1911 of Nishida Kitarō's *Zen no kenkyū* (*An Inquiry into the Good*) was generally considered by his peers as the real beginning of the robust burgeoning of Japanese philosophical endeavor, predating exactly 100 years of the publication of the JPS, in which some may find a symbolic significance.[4]

In view of the diverse topics younger scholars and students of Japanese philosophy and intercultural philosophies are working on today and which are presented at international conferences, it may be irrelevant or redundant to discuss what distinguishes Japanese philosophy as such. Nevertheless, some discussion is not out of the place. The JPS editors offer a cautionary remark in the JPS concerning the variety of texts compiled therein: "a catalogue of criteria for what is to count as philosophy cannot be drawn up in advance of an examination of the texts themselves,"[5] before they proceed to sketch out four "Japanese senses" of the word "*tetsugaku*" (i.e. philosophy). Namely, (1) the first sense of "*tetsugaku*" refers to Anglo-American European philosophical approach, with the view that Japan never had a philosophy of its own (this notion is espoused by the "professional philosophers in academic positions who work on the texts of Plato, Kant, Heidegger, James, Bergson, Rorty, Derrida," and so on); (2) the second sense is that one can find a philosophical tradition in classical Japanese philosophy (such as Inoue Tetsujirō finding Japanese Confucianism to have a comparable philosophical concern and fundamental questions as addressed in Western philosophy); (3) the third sense is that philosophical methods and themes are principally Western in origin but that they can be applied to premodern, pre-Westernized Japanese thinking (to uncover themes such as "Dōgen's philosophy of being and time, or Kūkai's philosophy of language"); and (4) the fourth sense is to assert that there is a "markedly Eastern or Japanese character in Japanese philosophy that explicitly sets it off from non-Japanese philosophy" (most prominently exemplified by Nishida's thought). The JPS editors comment as follows on these four senses: (1) the first view places too severe a limit on "*tetsugaku*"; (2) the second approach tends to drift away from critical awareness of the very constructive nature of "*tetsugaku*" itself; (3) the third approach they find favorable, as this view recognizes not only "the historical fact of the Greek origins of Western philosophy" but also it enriches the field of philosophy "by the incorporation of non-philosophical sources and resources; it also understands philosophy as an unfinished work of deconstruction and reconstruction"; (4) the fourth view can generalize certain fundamentally "Japanese" orientations, but this definition of "*tetsugaku*" "easily slides into neglect of the conditions for innovation and distinctive differentiation."[6]

Instead of producing a list of "characteristics of Japanese philosophy," the JPS editors outline a possible method of intercultural inquiry with these words: "if we are to sustain the defining bond between philosophy and thinking that reflects on its own assumptions and limitations, then the burden of studying other traditions is to uncover their own modes of critical thinking and self-understanding."[7]

One cannot help but notice that the JPS editors' observations, as nuanced and sensitive to interculturality as they are, are made from the vantage point of "outside Japan" in their effort to recognize the "modes of critical thinking and self-understanding" that may be found in Japanese thinking. To balance out the flow of the methodological movement, the present Bloomsbury volume contains works that suggest an approach "from within Japan." In this connection, what I find most helpful in bringing to the foreground the effort that formed the backbone of a subsequent robust modern Japanese philosophical tradition is Nishida Kitarō's plodding of what philosophy is, and what may be "uniquely Eastern or Japanese," in contrast to the Western philosophical enterprise, to which I shall return shortly. In this effort Nishida adopted the Western philosophical method of reasoning, analysis, and explanation, which he brought to Eastern experience—personal and collective—developed over time.

1.1 *Proximity and distance in hermeneutics*

One distinct advantage that non-native Japanese thinkers bring to the field of Japanese philosophy is precisely the perspective afforded by the distance, which allows for creative objectivity. T. Kasulis, for instance, maintains in a conversation with me that he, precisely as an outsider, can see more clearly the distinctiveness of modern Japanese philosophy, in contrast with, say, Indian or Chinese philosophy. The latter are primarily based on their set of classical texts, and the philosophy arises out of exegetical analyses. Kasulis finds in modern Japanese philosophy something familiar and yet different from Western philosophy (for after all, modern Japanese philosophers apprenticed themselves in Western philosophy in varying degrees to master it), which makes Japanese philosophy unique, fascinating, and challenging. The vibrancy of Japanese philosophy may indeed be attributable to this very interculturality.[8]

From the vantage point of "distance," Kasulis pays attention to the somewhat excessive Japanese focus on their "cultural or social character of personal identity" as a marked characteristic of Japanese philosophical discourse. Concerning the question of what is "lacking in the typical Western philosophical anthropologies," he points out three typical responses by the Japanese thinkers, which nicely capture the main point of these prominent thinkers' ideas:

> Some, like Tanabe Hajime, saw a flow in logic: standard western logic allowed only universals and particulars, but left out the mediate dimension—the

> specific. Nishida Kitarō, by contrast, thought it a side effect of the western tendency to see self-consciousness as the agent of an ego, instead of seeing the ego as a product of self-consciousness. Still others, such as Watsuji Tetsurō, focused more on the flawed philosophical anthropology that ignored the ethical "betweeness of person and person" as essential to personal identity. Although the differences among the Japanese philosophers are not trivial they share the goal of developing a corrective on the western understanding of cultural identity.[9]

This stress on one's own cultural context may be "frustratingly ethnocentric" to a Western reader, and yet Kasulis points out, from the Japanese point of view, it may be that "the western tradition is ethnocentric."[10] In this way, intercultural philosophical engagement opens up more inclusive and comprehensive new horizons of awareness, which allow us to listen and think more open-heartedly and less close-mindedly.

2. TWO WAYS OF "DEFINING" JAPANESE PHILOSOPHY

With a bold stroke, the diverse views concerning Japanese philosophy presented above can be grouped into two. The first is what may be called an "import" theory, which upholds that philosophy is a Western discipline (or Greek origin) and that it did not exist in Japan prior to its introduction in the 1860s by Nishi Amane et al. The second is a non-Eurocentric view that considers a philosophical tradition to exist in all cultures of the world, based on the assumption that there is philosophy where a people have nurtured their own worldviews and grappled with the meaning of life. According to this latter position, which may be called an "indigenous" view of philosophy, diverse philosophical traditions have been in existence everywhere, and in Japan at least since the seventh century, philosophical ideas have been formed under the nurturing influences of Buddhism, Confucianism, philosophical Daoism, Legalism, and a native Japanese sensitivity to natural, cultural, aesthetic, and ethical elements (a sensitivity that may be called the tradition of "proto-Shinto" or "*ko-shintō*"). According to this view, the introduction of the Western philosophical discipline in the nineteenth century shed new light on the wealth of existent indigenous philosophical thoughts, and critically brought out their relevance—and sometimes even formed a deeper backdrop for a new philosophical approach.

Both views ("import or indigenous") recognize that the intercultural philosophical encounter that has been taking place since the nineteenth century in Japan has certainly enriched modern Japanese philosophical tradition. Most importantly, this encounter of East and West gave rise to a new style of philosophical inquiry and discourse, under the influence of Western philosophical vocabulary and analytical method, which were applied to the explication of traditional Eastern worldviews. Let me comment here that this kind of creative intercultural philosophical exchanges have been taking place on a global scale, and the pace appears to be accelerating. Thinkers interested in Japanese philosophy outside Japan are finding new ways of bringing their own traditional views beyond the pale of "theo-logical" assumptions. In fact, intercultural or cross-cultural enrichment has been taking place in diverse philosophical circles for several decades now.

2.1 Revisiting Nakae Chōmin's statement

Before we move on to the discussion of Japanese philosophy as understood by Nishida, let me first make a comment on the statement that has perhaps uncritically dominated the definition of Japanese philosophy. I refer to Nakae Chōmin's (1847–1901) statement "Since ancient times, there was no philosophy in Japan,"[11] for it is possible to read these words as a *rhetorical* and *political* statement rather than a statement of fact based on a careful scholarly study. Nakae, one of the first generation of Japanese thinkers who were trained abroad, studied law, history, and philosophy in Lyons and Paris, during which time he translated the works of Jean-Jacques Rousseau into Japanese, including *Of the Social Contract*. After his return to Japan, he had an active career as a member of the lower house of the National Diet, but he grew increasingly dissatisfied with the policy of nation building implemented by the Meiji government; he was also critical of factionalism within the government and especially of those intellectuals who rendered their service by drafting and disseminating a state-building ideology. Questioning the presence (or lack thereof) of the "philosophical spirit" among his contemporary opinion leaders who fashioned themselves as "philosophers," Nakae lamented that he did not see "the needed qualification of a philosopher *who rationally exercises the power of reason to observe things as they are*," which for him constituted the "*solemn reality of philosophy*."[12] He thus made the famous remark:

> Since ancient times, there was no philosophy in Japan … Recently a certain Katō and an Inoue fashion themselves as the model of philosophers, and although society at large allows them to pass as such, the truth is that they merely *import* Western ideas and theories that they have studied … and thereby claim themselves to be philosophers.[13]

By the time he was composing the above passage, Nakae knew that his health was failing fast, leaving him only a little more than a year to live. His feisty tone and the mention of Inoue Tetsujirō (1855–1944) and Katō Hiroyuki (1836–1916)[14] by name are telling. As a thoroughgoing supporter of Rousseau's egalitarian and republican ideals and as the outsider of the ivory tower, Nakae engaged the social issues outright. He wanted to see Japan seize the opportunity and develop into a fair and just modern society, which would abolish old discriminations and superstitions, including the discrimination practiced against the "*buraku*" people.[15] In the last years of his life, Nakae had to admit the failure of the experiment of the Meiji government, which, in his view, had lacked critical (i.e. philosophical) spirit and squandered the opportunity to create a considerably different social system. Taking all these reasons into account, it is possible to read Nakae's words, "There was no philosophy in Japan," as a rhetorical and political statement, and not intended as the wholesale denial of the existence of philosophical traditions in Japan, voicing his cynical appraisal of the philosophy professors in academia. I offer this nuanced reading of Nakae's passage because often the art of interpretation rides much on the *context* of the statement.

2.2 *A view of "philosophy" as a Western import*

Among those who adhere to the view of philosophy as a Western import, a small group of Japanese intellectuals claims that philosophical discipline is a Western enterprise, *and therefore* there is no "philosophy" as such in Japan. The majority of those who endorse this view maintain, *however*, that the Western philosophical approaches and methods, once introduced to Japan, were internalized by the Japanese. This latter observation tallies nicely with how Husserl's phenomenology, introduced to Japan by Takahashi Satomi and Miyake Gōichi, gradually got assimilated and transformed by the Japanese scholar-thinkers to the robust state it is in today.[16] Also, those who claim that "philosophy did not exist in Japan prior to X" (X being often replaced with the name Nishida Kitarō, 1870–1945) adhere to the view of philosophy as a Western import but also believe that it eventually took root in Japan.

3. NISHIDA KITARŌ'S VIEW OF PHILOSOPHY AS AN INDIGENOUS CULTURAL ACTIVITY

Among those who upheld the second view, namely, that philosophy is indigenous to each culture, Nishida Kitarō stands out as the first articulate proponent of this view. His writings are the testimony of philosophizing that was taking place in Japan, and give us the view of Japanese philosophy "from within." For this reason, I shall dwell on his thought fully.

Nishida believed that each culture was unique and had its place in the world; he thus maintained that the cultures of the world can take different courses of development from those in Europe, and therefore to apply the way European cultures developed as *the sole* standard to measure the "maturity" of other non-European cultures and assign their place in the scale of "evolutionary development" was to miss the point. Accordingly, Nishida's understanding of philosophy departed from considering the European model as *the* only one. His stance was fundamentally pluralistic.[17] He understood philosophy to begin "with the historical life coming to its own self-awareness, which co-arises with one's existential endeavor to live one's life truly authentically."[18] As for the philosophical method, Nishida defined it simply as "*jikakuteki bunseki*,"[19] which is ambiguous enough to be read to mean both (1) the "analysis accompanied by critical self-awareness," and (2) the "analysis of self-consciousness." In the former sense, it is to grapple with a philosophical problem on one's own, and think it through, until the problem becomes clear. In the latter sense, it summarized Nishida's entire philosophical enterprise—to start out with the investigation of the phenomena of consciousness.

3.1 *Japanese philosophy, French philosophy, German philosophy . . .*

Is it meaningful to speak about philosophy in terms of such adjectives as Greek, French, German, British, Italian, Chinese, Indian, Persian, Japanese, and so forth? Nishida's essay "On French Philosophy"[20] answers this question with an unequivocal "yes." Therein he muses that the artistically minded French people philosophize by being incited by the intuition of things that appeal to their senses, and that the French thinkers find profound philosophical significance in things sensuous. Thus, Nishida writes: "the French word '*sens*' has a connotation that cannot be easily translated into English *sense* or German *Sinn*."[21] He concludes this essay somewhat poetically with this reflection: "Greek philosophy had a deeply contemplative and conceptual aspect, as well as the artistic intuitive aspect that responded to beauty. Could one say that the former found its way into the Germans, while the latter into the French?"[22]

How did Nishida characterize *Japanese* philosophy then? He saw that both the French and the Japanese people possess a keen sense of intuition (*chokkan* 直観), but the French intuition is related to "concrete things" (*mono* 物), while the Japanese intuition to "things as happening" (*ji* 事), that is, things come into being in one moment and disappear in the next. Nishida gives haiku poetry as a good example that illustrates this Japanese penchant, in which the poet grasps the ever-fleeting world from the vantage point of a split second (*setsuna* 刹那).[23]

3.2 *Cultural experience and philosophical formulation, or logic*

Initially, Nishida did not set out consciously to establish a "Japanese philosophy" that is distinct and different from Western philosophy, but along the way he realized that the Western philosophical paradigm did not fully explain the "Eastern" experience. He famously wrote:

> There is no denying that we have much to admire and learn from the brilliant developments of western cultures, which took form as the actual reality and becoming as good. At the same time, I think that at the depths of eastern cultures, which have nurtured our ancestors for thousands of years, there is the kind of awareness that "sees the form of the formless and hears the voice of the voiceless." Our hearts do not cease to yearn for this kind of reality. I want to attempt to give a philosophical foundation to such demand (*kakaru yōkyū*).[24]

What Nishida had in mind when he poetically described the quality "to see the form of the formless and hear the voice of the voiceless" may be illustrated by Matsuo Bashō's advice to his students as to how to write a good verse: "Learn about a pine tree from a pine tree, and about a bamboo from a bamboo," meaning that a poet must let go of his willfulness and follow the "inner light" of the "object" of his versification. Nishida himself referred to the art of *wabi-cha* (commonly known as the tea ceremony), for instance, and noted that the quality of "*sabi*" (subdued refinement) "cannot be placed under Kant's categories of beauty."[25] Again, the feeling of oneness of a black "*raku*" tea bowl held in one's palm, or the feeling of unity of oneself and a rustic tearoom are examples that appeal to the cultural sensitivity developed in Japan.[26]

Classical works of Japanese cinemas are permeated with the "voice of the voiceless," as actors portray deep emotions through their subtle gestures without many words.

3.3 Eastern and Western "accents" in logic

Nishida grappled with developing a logical formulation that does justice to the kind of experience of the world mentioned above. To get a general orientation of what he considered "logic," it is helpful to turn to *The Problem of Japanese Culture* (*Nihon bunka no mondai*, 1940). He starts out by saying that the Eastern worldview has its own "logic," just as the Western worldview does. What Nishida means by "logic" (*ronri* 論理) is the "ontological structure" of the actual everyday world.[27] Lest it be misunderstood that he is advocating two "kinds" of logic, he explains that "logic," although one, retains "*different accents*." He elaborates on this point as follows:

> I do not mean to say that there are two kinds of logic, eastern and western. Logic must abide by one and the same rule (*ronri wa hitotsu* 論理は一). But it developed into different directions in accordance with the respective [cultural] environment. Roughly speaking, the western logic is a logic that takes the material thing as its object (*mono o taishō to shita ronri* 物を対象とした論理), while the eastern logic is a logic that takes the workings of the mind (or consciousness) as its object (*kokoro o taishō to shita ronri* 心を対象とした論理).[28]

To distill the Eastern mode of experience into a "logical form" preoccupied Nishida for some time, since he saw that by putting through the filter of "logos," the Eastern experience gets crystalized in a logical form, and as such it becomes universally accessible.

It is fascinating that in this endeavor, it was Aristotle's definition of substance that gave Nishida a hint. Aristotle defined the substance as "that which becomes the subject but never the predicate." Gaining a clue from this formulation, Nishida took a step further in his reflection as follows:

> By transcending [the logical formula] in the direction of the subject-term [of judgment], Aristotle tried to arrive at the substance. All judgment is made up of the subject-term and the predicate-term, and takes the form of "A is B." If this is the case, unlike Aristotle who focused on the subject-term, i.e., the side of the individual, it is also possible to focus on the predicate-term, i.e., the side of the universal. By following Aristotle's definition of the substance, it is possible to think of that which becomes the predicate-term and not the subject-term. As such, the predicate-term cannot be predicated any further by another predicate—that is, it would be absolutely *nothing*. By turning the Aristotelian definition upside down and by transcending [the logical formula] on the side of the predicate-term, we can at the same time transcend [the logical formula] on the side of the subject-term and reach the true reality.[29]

In another place, moreover, Nishida mentioned that "the true reality (*jitsuzai*) resides neither in the direction of the subject term nor that of the predicate term, but in the direction of copula (*keiji* 繋辞)."[30] That is to say, the real existence is ontological. This kind of intuition led him to formulate his "logic of topos" (*basho no ronri*), with which he tried to explain how various modes of operation of consciousness give rise to, and construct, the multilayered and multifaceted actual reality. In the direction of the "subject-term oriented logic" (or, intellectual judgment, S is P) the mind bridges subject and object, and as such it is an essential component of practical daily life. This orientation of "S is P" stands on the dichotomy of subject and object, and forms the intellectual discrimination and makes calculation possible. The "predicate-term oriented logic" (S is in P), on the other hand, reveals the radical embeddedness of intellectual discrimination within the field of consciousness, and how the self in "positioned" or "situated" in the world, and how the self engages in expressive creative activities." In the field of consciousness, the individual reflects the environment (world of things, society, history, and spirituality), as one assumes various positions in such a world—in such manners as intellectually, politically, aesthetically, productively, and spiritually. Nishida's "logic of topos" explains the workings of the interpenetration of self-consciousness and the shape of the world. Reflexive consciousness emerges out of a horizon and submerges into it, as the individual self-awareness assumes various vantage points and standpoints within it. The logic of topos is therefore the outcome of Nishida's attempt at uncovering the intrinsic connection between philosophy and experience, or logic and life.

3.4 Theism, non-theism, worldview, and philosophy

Nishida attributed the basic difference of Eastern and Western worldviews to the differing relationships between the individual and the absolute (or "God"), and observed that the perception of how one is related to the absolute not only shapes one's worldview (*sekaikan*) but also determines the mode of one's self-awareness (*jikaku*). Nishida describes Western philosophy, which tended to be tied with Christianity and monotheistic traditions, considers the relationship between individual and absolute in terms of the opposition of the transcendent and the relative, and views the absolute to be "on the other side." So does the Western view of morality—the absolute moral ideal is set on the "other side," after which the individual strives but never reaches it. Nishida contends, moreover, that the absolute understood to stand against the relative is but a "relative absolute" and not real absolute.[31]

In contrast, in the Eastern worldview—shaped under the influence of Mahayana Buddhism, for instance—this reality is perceived to be absolute—Buddhists would speak of "*shohō jissō*" (諸法実相, all things are real as they are). This perception creates a worldview in which

> the real absolute is not something that just negates the individual but it is that which affirms the individual. The absolute transcends the opposition of relative and absolute and establishes this very opposition within it. We individuals exist in the absolute. We stand in a "contiguous way" with this absolute, which, however, we can never "touch" [as an object]. Eternity embraces time, and we touch eternity in the present moment—it is this type of awareness.[32]

To reiterate, the worldview is intrinsically related to the individual's perception of its relationship to the transcendent. In the West, Nishida noted that the individual stands "facing" the absolute; in the East the individual "returns" to the bosom of the absolute.[33] This is why for Nishida religion and philosophy originate from the same source, and the task of a philosopher is to *reflect critically on this fact* and examine it, while in religion one *thoroughly embraces* this fact.[34] This may also explain why Christian mystical tradition that embraces the experience of union with the divine, as well as the robust "trinitarian" understanding of unhindered interpenetration of the material, the divine, and the human dimensions finds the philosophical approach, especially carried out by some members of the Kyoto School thinkers, to be congenial.[35]

In reference to the connection between philosophy and Christian elements, K. Noe, a contributor to this volume, has the following observation concerning why phenomenology was favorably accepted by the Japanese thinkers. Noe writes:

> Takahashi Satomi, the first Japanese philosopher who studied under Edmund Husserl, was deeply impressed by the phenomenological maxim, "*zu den Sachen selbst*" [To the things themselves]! One can directly confront the "*Sache selbst*" [thing itself] and grasp the essence of the object without having a knowledge of Christianity. In terms of practice, to the Japanese philosophers the method of "phenomenological reduction" was understood synonymous with eliminating prejudices and making oneself empty (*onore o munashiku suru*), which attitude resonates with Zen practice. After WWII, phenomenology was eagerly embraced as the new methodology of humanistic science by the younger generations of the Japanese intellectuals including myself. We were fascinated by academic radicalism of phenomenology that boldly based all the sciences on the ultimate ground, i.e., that of the "life-world."[36]

3.5 Cultural boundaries can be transcended

Over against the model of classification based on the generic entity called philosophy and specific philosophies, such as French, Italian, Japanese, and so forth, Nishida's paradigm is one of interpenetration of the universal and the particular. According to this way of conceptualization, just as one can be "a human being" and "a Japanese" at the same time without a conflict, so are philosophy and Japanese philosophy not mutually exclusive. On the relationship between an individual and a people, Nishida upheld that "one does not exist as a species of a genus, or as a particular case of the universal, but each individual exists as *a* unique individual in this unique historical world."[37] That is, each individual is first and foremost a self-determining, self-forming independent being and creates one's own personality or individuality ("*kosei*" 個性). The implication here is that one is not fixed by such factors as race, culture, and nationality. An individual, understood thus, is a self-determining unique being (or "agent," in the sense of "*agere*"—that which acts), and each transcends one's own cultural environment and boundaries to the extent that one can actually *choose and create* the kind(s) of cultural environment one feels most congenial and comfortable; one can embrace multiple cultures as one's own, or even transcend any particular culture. In this day and age, many individuals freely create a unique cultural environment of their own, regardless of where they reside, or transcend their native cultural heritage.

3.6 *Cultural and intercultural sensitivity*

In reality, however, not everyone responds the same way to one's cultural environment, let alone to a cultural environment different from one's own. Nishida addressed it as follows:

> Different from the discipline of objective studies (*taishōteki gakumon*), philosophy takes as its foundation the actual experience of a people (*minzoku*) or an individual (*kojin*). This explains why to a certain individual, or to a certain people, only a certain kind of philosophy may make sense.[38]

The other side of this "coin" is the very possibility that one can actually understand and appreciate the other. In other words, Japanese cultural sensitivity can be learned, acquired, and lived by a non-Japanese person. For instance, out of his penetrating study of Western philosophical traditions, Nishida developed such appreciation of things Western that for him both the Eastern and Western cultural expressions complemented each other, and at the same time the distinct preciousness of each tradition could not be flattened out.[39] He repeated this sentiment often, as we read:

> While I appreciate eastern culture as profound and precious, I cannot deny my longing for western culture, which is a great development of rich and free humanity. Just as I derive pleasure from Sesshū's paintings or poetry in Chinese, so I cannot help but be moved by the paintings of Rembrandt or the poetry of Goethe.[40]

How does "Japanese" sensitivity coexist with the appreciation of other cultures? This question is related at once to how Nishida understood the self to be formed by experience. Over against the ego-centered view that it is the self that has the experience, he saw "without experience, there is no individual," or "experience makes an individual" (*kojin atte keiken aru no de wa naku, keiken atte kojin aru*).[41] He also noted that "[the experience of] emotions actually makes up the individual; for emotions are the naked facts (*jijitsu*) belonging to direct experience."[42]

Experiences are not uniform in kind but multifaceted, corresponding to the biological, cultural, intellectual, and spiritual aspects of human existence. The experience of hunger, thirst, fatigue, hotness or coldness, for instance, pertaining to the biological level, is transcultural at large. The emotions of sadness, joy, loneliness, and so forth pertain to the cultural environment, as these emotions are, to an extent, learned from the behavior of those around one, and in that sense it is conditioned by one's environment. When it comes to the aesthetic-spiritual experience, it is much more subtle and complex—the uplifting emotion the "Pastoral Symphony" arouses in one is quite different from the titillating emotion aroused by *nagauta* chanting accompanied by *shamisen* on a *kabuki* stage. These aesthetic experiences are closely tied with respective cultural and art forms. If experiences make up the individuals, then it follows that the cultural environments also make up the individuals. Indeed, to paraphrase Nishida, "life is inextricably bound with cultural awareness (*Kulturbewusstsein*)."[43] It follows then, direct experience and its interpretations can be *culturally colored*. In this historical world, individuals are culture-making (and also culture-destroying) first and foremost. Moreover, one is born in a certain culture, but in the activity of "from the created to the creating," one learns to create one's own cultural environment over and beyond what one is born into or has inherited.

3.7 Cultural "terroir"

In terms of the close connection between cultural environment and experience, the French word "*terroir*" strikes me as extremely suggestive. This word is used to describe the natural makeup of the soil (including its mineral contents), topography, and climate that produces a particular *wine*. *Mutatis mutandis* this term can be adopted to signify the conditions and components of a cultural environment that gives rise to certain specific and unique types of experience. The word "terroir," obviously related to the Latin word for earth, "*terra*," resonates with Watsuji's "*fūdo*," which positively acknowledges the climatic environment as constitutive of the ontological category, and as a defining cultural factor. We can talk about a "*cultural terroir*" to understand and appreciate unique worlds and environments that encompass complex realities of cultural, geographical, environmental, material, linguistic, and spiritual conditions; it also explains how one experiences a particular "world" and how one is a "product" of a particular world; but Nishida would add to this the other side of the cultural terroir—that is, how one creates a particular world, a particular cultural terroir. The most peculiar component of the cultural terroir is probably the specific languages spoken at specific places.

To digress slightly, the relationship between philosophy and a specific language was something Nishida did not touch on. Moreover, to speak about "Japanese philosophical expression" there is no denying that it is closely tied with the linguistic features (e.g. syntactical) and vocabulary (i.e. crystallization of experience in words) of the Japanese language. This feature of the connection between language and thought was taken up, among others, by Mori Arimasa (1911–76), who lived in France for almost two decades and taught in Paris, before he returned to Japan.[44]

3.8 A "semiotics" of "*semi*" (cicadas)

Let me digress further and dwell on the connection between direct experience and culture. If experience always takes place in some given environment and not in a vacuum, then it is open to the cultural environment. A good example that comes to my mind is the sound of cicadas. Cicadas ("*semi*" in Japanese) are insects that spend long years (as long as seventeen years!) underground as larvae, and when they finally emerge aboveground they live only for a single week. The loud noises the males make signal to the Japanese children the joy of the arrival of summer holidays and their temporary reprieve from schoolwork—or so it used to be. Hearing the cicadas make the sound of "*mii-n, mi-n, mi-n*" (or "*gii gii gii*" or "*si si si*" among many other songs—different kinds of cicadas make different sounds) comes to the Japanese with the association of hot and humid summer days, ripe and fresh vegetables that are in abundance, and pleasures of outdoor activities, and so on and so forth. The songs of cicadas may even conjure up a famous haiku or two by Bashō:

Yagate shinu 頓て死ぬ
keshiki mo miezu けしきも見えず
semi no koe 蝉の声

Soon you shall die
and yet without showing a hint of life's brevity,
you cicadas sing your loud songs.[45]

Or, the famous verse:

Shizukasa ya 閑かさや
iwa ni shimiiru 岩にしみ入る
semi no koe 蝉の声

Ah! Utter silence,
seeping into the rocks
are the loud songs of cicadas.[46]

Curiously, these noisy insects altogether escape the notice of my non-Japanese acquaintances and friends who may have lived in Japan for decades and yet do not know what cicadas are, or their iconic symbolism. The scope of one's experience is indeed determined by one's cultural awareness. This fact implies that by becoming familiar with the web of symbolic associations—by being introduced to these haiku poems by Bashō, for instance—the gate opens up to one who is interested in penetrating into the dimensions of Japanese culture that may have been closed hitherto. One can always learn a new "language."

3.9 Universality of a culture as the "public" property

As for the "contradictory self-identity" of the particular and the universal in Japanese culture, Nishida spoke about it in his essay "What it means 'to be Japanese'" (*Nihonteki to iu koto*, 1917). The gist of his argument is that for the Japanese culture to develop truly authentically so as to become a significant player and contributor in the global world, it has to develop its uniqueness, without compromise, to the point of it becoming universally viable. To achieve this end, not only self-confidence in the value of Japanese culture but also the generosity of open spirit is required. If the Japanese culture were to shut its door and remain self-conceitedly isolated, it would but be an "idiosyncratic" culture and not a genuinely universal one. The more the Japanese deepen and nurture their culture, the more universal and open it will become.

So is Japanese philosophy.[47] The dimension of particularity (or singularity) and universality belong together. Nishida maintained that if the uniqueness of Japanese culture is recognized and savored by every people in the world, it is proof that it has achieved its universal height (and depth). Anything universally valid, moreover, belongs to the world as its "public property" (*ōyake no mono*), and ceases to be a private possession. Nishida was expressing his caution over against the then rising trend of cultural (and national) exclusivism and chauvinism in Japan.[48] In short, according to Nishida, a genuinely unique culture is by definition a universal culture. He saw that different cultures, if allowed to develop authentically, would contribute to the making of a greater global culture, which will augment and enrich human spirit on a global scale as well. Nishida himself never travelled abroad and yet he developed his cultural sensitivity that enabled him to appreciate western philosophy and art (as we already saw above). He was also keenly aware of the contemporary political affairs of the world. He lived to prove that one could truly be a Japanese, truly be a global citizen, and truly be a unique individual all at once.

3.10 Philosophy as authentic praxis

To the "four Japanese senses of the word *tetsugaku*," as touched on in the beginning of this introduction, the fifth, sixth, and seventh sense of the word may be added. The fifth sense of the word "*tetsugaku*" is the perception that philosophizing is inseparable from how a thinker lives his or her own private life. The organic unity of being and action, words and action, thought and life is something deeply ingrained in the Japanese mind. One needs not quote Fichte's stance that "a philosophical system is not some sort of dead piece of furniture but is animated with the spirit of the person."[49] The vestiges of Wang Yangming's Confucian teaching of the unity of knowledge and action (*chigyō icchi*) and the Buddhist notion of authentic action, livelihood, and meditation (as in the eightfold path) inform the sense of *integrity* of personal action, thought, and the self. What you think, what you say (and write), and what you do are not separate.[50] Accordingly, the authenticity of one's philosophical activity is judged by the *integrity of the philosopher* as a person even by popular perception. This is a distinct sense of the word "*tetsugaku*."

The sixth sense is that "*tetsugaku*" implies the *dialogical* nature of Japanese philosophy, and especially of modern Japanese philosophy. For concrete evidence, the reader is referred to the Timeline in the end of this book, which demonstrates how modern Japanese thinkers have philosophized in dialogue with non-Japanese thinkers. The Japanese tradition has always remained open to other cultures. John Maraldo has the following to say about Nishida's philosophy: "it enriched the creative discipline of philosophy by infusing Anglo-European philosophy with Asian sources of thought," and "it produced novel theories of self and world with rich implications for contemporary philosophizing."[51]

In this connection, Nishida wrote in 1940 concerning the highly "porous" nature of the Japanese culture as follows:

> Japanese culture has no fixed "shape" of its own; if one is to compare it to a genre of art, it is similar to music [which moves on in time]. This is why the Japanese culture has taken in various foreign cultures. If it had a fixed content of its own, the choice would have been either to appropriate other cultures as its own or to be wiped out by the others. As I see it, the Japanese culture constantly takes in other cultures and in this process it undergoes change. This is the characteristic of the Japanese culture, which excels in synthetizing different cultures and creating

> a culture of its own. But it is also the vulnerable side of the Japanese culture that it does not have its own property ... Because its unique feature is to have no fixed shape, the danger is that the Japanese culture, if it errs, could become vacuous. To avert this pitfall and for the Japanese culture to become a real player in global history, it has to create a new expansive assimilative culture. This is where the Japanese culture may exercise its great flexibility.[52]

The seventh sense of "*tetsugaku*" is the unity of knowledge and being. Nishida wrote a short essay entitled "Knowledge and Love" ("*Chi to ai*," 1907),[53] which he appended to his *Inquiry into the Good* as its concluding chapter. He characterized intellectual knowledge (*chi*) as an impersonal way of knowing things, even if dealing with things alive, while love (*ai*) is a personalized way of knowing things, even if dealing with inanimate things, and accordingly he maintained that love is a deeper form of knowledge, because "love has the power to grasp the actual reality itself; it constitutes the deepest knowledge of things. Love is a supreme form of knowledge."[54] Taking from the title of this essay, I would like to suggest another softer word for philosophy, "*chi'ai*" 知愛 ("knowledge of love" and "love of knowledge") as an equivalent to the "love of wisdom" (*philo-sofia*). This, perhaps, is the seventh sense of the word "*tetsugaku.*"

4. CONCLUDING REMARKS

4.1 Language, philosophy, and translation

What is most helpful in carrying out an intercultural philosophical work is to be able to read the texts in the target language. I say this without making light of the inevitable fact that we are all indebted to translations. Even for a polyglot, it would be close to impossible to master all the major languages and classical languages of East and West, spanning from Sino-Japanese ideograph-based writings to Arabic script, to Cyrillic alphabet—just to list a few orthographic practices. Thus, the art of translation will always remain a necessary feature of intercultural philosophical studies. Moreover, translation is a funny animal. One day the translator reads what he or she has just translated and it makes sense; the next day, not quite so—and vice versa. Also, there is no one "correct" translation. At best, all translations are tentative "fingers" pointing to the moon, and some fingers point more beautifully and elegantly to the moon than some others, while a few other fingers might inadvertently miss the moon altogether.

This leads to the question of the necessity of learning the language in which the text is written (and in our case, it is the Japanese language). No doubt, there is a great advantage in being able to read the original text and translate it into another language. In this regard, one can set three different levels of "proficiency" in Japanese to be attained as one's goal. The first is to have the passive knowledge of the target language, so that one can compare the translation with the original. This is greatly helpful. The second level of proficiency is to be able to read the text accurately, even if one is not able to converse in the target language, let alone comprehend the spoken form. The third level of proficiency is to become fluent enough in the target language so that one can read, speak, listen, think, and write in it, and translate it into another language. This last stage is an endless road, the adventure of which many are finding personally satisfying.

4.2 Notes on the original textual sources

Writings by the Japanese philosophers are typically compiled into collected volumes—be it "*Zenshū*" ("collected works," typically compiled posthumously), "*Chosakushū*" ("collected writings," typically compiled while the author is still alive), or simply "*shū*" ("collection") and sometimes "*sen*" ("selection") or "*senshū*" ("selected collection"), attached to the name of the author. In order to streamline the bibliography and the notes, abbreviations have been adopted throughout this volume.

The *Collected Works of Nishida Kitarō* (NKZ) requires a special explanation, as it has two distinct editions. The original collection (19 volumes, the last edition, and supplements were published 1987–90) was practically overhauled when the new edition of NKZ in 24 volumes was published by the same publisher, 2002–2009. In this handbook, the original edition is simply referred to as NKZ. The new edition is specified as NKZ-N, "N" standing for "new edition."

In the case of the *Collected Works of Suzuki Daisetz* (SDZ), the new edition (40 volumes, published 1999–2003) diverges from the original edition (32 volumes, published 1968–71), starting with volume 26 and thereafter. Thus, only volumes 26–40 are designated as SDZ-N.

The index of original texts cited is added at the end of this volume, which should help those who are interested in locating the original texts in Japanese. Also the Timeline contains not only the dates but also the kanji for the names of the Japanese and Chinese thinkers and authors mentioned in this volume.

NOTES

1. Inoue Enryō's communication to Itō Kichinosuke, then editor of the *Tetsugaku Zasshi* [*The Journal of Philosophy*] (hereafter abbreviated as JP) 27.301 (1912), 121. The occasion was the celebration of the publication of the 300th issue. For an English translation of Enryō's statement on the Philosophical Society, see M. Yusa, "Inoue Enryō's 1887 Position Statement on Philosophical Studies in Japan," in the online *Kokusai Inoue Enryō kenkyū* [*International Inoue Enryo Research*] 2 (2014), 167–180.
2. Itō Kichinosuke, "*Tetsugakukai shiryō*" [Records of the Society of Philosophy], Part 1, JP 27.300 (1912), 196. See also *Tōkyō Daigaku hyakunenshi* [A history of the centennial of the University of Tokyo], *Bukyoku-shi* [History of colleges and departments], vol. 1 (Tokyo: Tokyo Daigaku, 1986), 500.
3. "*Kiji*" [Editors' notes], JP 6.57 (1891), 1300.
4. For a detailed and thorough exposition of the reception of academic philosophy in Japan, the "Overview to Modern Academic Philosophy" by John Maraldo and Nakajima Takahiro in the JPS is highly recommended. See JPS 553–582.
5. "Defining Philosophy" under "Framework," JPS 21.

6. Ibid., 19–21.
7. Ibid., 18–19.
8. This is the point strongly emphasized in B. W. Davis, B. Schroeder, and J. A. Wirth, ed., *Japanese and Continental Philosophy: Conversations with the Kyoto School* (Bloomington: Indiana University Press, 2011).
9. JPS 1007–1008.
10. Ibid., 1009.
11. For instance, Abe Masao quoted this passage as accurately portraying the state of Japanese philosophy, in his "Introduction" to the English translation of Nishida Kitarō's *An Inquiry into the Good* (New Haven and London: Yale University Press, 1990), vii–viii.
12. Nakae Chōmin, *Ichinen yūhan* [A year and a half; a sequel to a year and a half] (Tokyo: Iwanami Shoten, 1995), 114–115; emphasis added. See Chapter 2 for fuller references and further discussion.
13. Ibid., 155; emphasis added.
14. They were influential professors at the Imperial University, commanded the respect of the public, and defined the field of philosophical study as an academic discipline.
15. The specific group of Japanese people who used to be also called "*eta*" (defiled folks, or "untouchables") on account of their occupation of disposing dead horses and other large animals and engaging in the production of tanned leather and so forth. They were segregated from the rest of the society as quasi-outcasts.
16. See Chapter 1 in this volume.
17. Nishida Kitarō, "*Nihon bunka no mondai*" [The problem of Japanese culture] (1940), NKZ 12.287.
18. Nishida Kitarō, "*Chishiki no kyakkansei ni tsuite*" [On the objectivity of knowledge] (1943), NKZ 10.472.
19. Nishida Kitarō, "*Jikaku ni tsuite*" [On self-awareness] (1943), NKZ 10.564.
20. Nishida Kitarō, "*Furansu tetsugaku ni tsuite no kansō*" [On French philosophy] (1936), NKZ 12.126–130.
21. Ibid., NKZ 12.126–127.
22. Ibid., NKZ 12.130.
23. Nishida Kitarō, *Nihon bunka no mondai*, NKZ 12.372.
24. Nishida Kitarō, Preface to *Hataraku mono kara miru mono e* [*From that which works to that which sees*] (1927), NKZ 4.6.
25. Nishida Kitarō, *Nihon bunka no mondai* (1938), NKZ 14.403.
26. See, for instance, "*Rekishiteki keiseisayō to shite no geijutsuteki sōsaku*" [Artistic creation as an activity of history formation] (1941), NKZ 10.262–263; 10.241. Also see Chapter 7 in this volume.
27. The aspect of "*ri*" (理, also pronounced as "*kotowari*," meaning "the universal way, the principle") is stressed in this compound word; "ri" refers to the ultimate mode or the way of reality.

28. Nishida Kitarō, *Nihon bunka no mondai* (1940), NKZ 12.289.
29. Nishida Kitarō, *Tetsugaku gairon* [The outline of philosophy, university lecture notes] (ca. 1926), NKZ 15.171; emphasis added.
30. Ibid. (1924), NKZ 15.219.
31. Nishida Kitarō, "*Jissen to taishō ninshiki*" [Praxis and the recognition of the object] (1937), NKZ 8.423.
32. Ibid., NKZ 8.423–424.
33. Nishida Kitarō, *Chishiki no kyakkansei ni tsuite*, NKZ 10.473. As a parenthetical remark, it is not hard to see how the individual's worldview is formed in varying relationship to the "absolute" or the transcendent. Some embrace the absolute being positively (as affirming the presence of the divine), some negatively (as in atheism), skeptically (as in agnosticism), neutrally, or indifferently. And these convictions shape one's lifestyle as informing one's thinking, values, and conducts.
34. Nishida Kitarō, "*Jissen tetsugaku joron*" [Prolegomena to the philosophy of praxis] (1940), NKZ 10.121.
35. See, for instance, Raimon Panikkar, *The Rhythm of Being* (Maryknoll, NY: Orbis Books, 2010), who refers to Nishitani Keiji's thought on 314, 360–361. Also see Chapter 8 in this volume.
36. Email communication, from Keiichi Noe to Michiko Yusa, March 29, 2016.
37. Nishida Kitarō, "*Dekaruto no tetsugaku, furoku*" [On Descartes' philosophy, Appendix] (1944), NKZ 11.187.
38. Nishida Kitarō, *Chishiki no kyakkansei ni tsuite*, NKZ 10.472.
39. See, for instance, Nishida Kitarō, "*Tanka ni tsuite*" [On Japanese short poetry, "*tanka*"] (1933), NKZ 13.130–132; for an English translation, see appended, below.
40. Nishida Kitarō, Letter # 595, January 4, 1930, to Watsuji Tetsurō and his wife, NKZ 18.398. Translated in M. Yusa, *Zen and Philosophy: An Intellectual Biography of Nishida Kitarō* (Honolulu: University of Hawaii Press, 2002) (hereafter, *Zen and Philosophy*), 246. Also see Chapter 14 in this volume.
41. Nishida Kitarō, *Zen no kenkyū* [An inquiry into the good] (1911), NKZ 1.28; also see his preface (1911), ibid., NKZ 1.4.
42. Ibid., NKZ 1.62 (Book 2, chapter 3): "*Jōi ga kojin o tsukuru no de aru. Jōi wa chokusetsu-keiken no jijitsu de aru.*"
43. Nishida Kitarō, "*Batsu*" [postscript] to *Jikaku ni okeru chokkan to hansei* (1917), NKZ 2.349.
44. See JPS 1047–1052; he was the grandson of Mori Arinori, the first minister of education in the Meiji government and one of the Meirokusha thinkers.
45. Matsuo Bashō, "*Genjū'an no ki*" [A record of the hermitage, "Unrealistic Dwelling"], in N. Imoto et al., ed., *Matsuo Bashō-shū* [Collected works of Matsuo Bashō], vol. 2 (Tokyo: Shōgakukan, 1997), 295. The meaning of this verse is the brevity of life of cicadas, which, without knowing their imminent death, vigorously make loud sound, and this fact heightens the poet's sympathy for the little insects. The backdrop is the "brevity of human life."

46. Matsuo Bashō, "*Oku no hosomichi*" [A narrow road to the north], ibid., 103. The editors interpret this verse to mean that in the evening, the entire mountain temple complex is wrapped in deep silence, and only the songs of cicadas are audible—as noisy as they are, they only seep into the mountain rocks.
47. This would be Nishida's response to B. W. Davis, "'*Nihon tetsugaku' no teigi ni tsuite*" [On how to define "Japanese philosophy"], *Nishida Tetsugakukai kaihō* 13 (2015), 5–7.
48. Nishida Kitarō, "*Nihonteki to iu koto ni tsuite*" [On what is considered "Japanese"] (1917), NKZ 13.116–120.
49. Quoted in Yusa, *Zen and Philosophy*, xxi.
50. On a related topic, see John C. Maraldo, "An Alternative Notion of Practice in the Promise of Japanese Philosophy," FJP 4 (2009), 7–21.
51. John C. Maraldo, "Nishida Kitarō," *Online Stanford Encyclopedia of Philosophy*, http://plato.stanford.edu/entries/nishida-kitaro/, accessed November 1, 2016.
52. Nishida Kitarō, "*Nihon bunka no mondai*" [The problems of Japanese culture] (Monday Lecture series delivered at the University of Kyoto, April–May 1938), NKZ 14.416–417.
53. He composed this essay on August 3, 1907 (see his diary), for the journal *Seishinkai* [The spiritual world]; NKZ 1.196–200.
54. Nishida Kitarō, *Zen no kenkyū* (book 4, chapter 5) (1911), NKZ 1.196–200.

PART ONE

Making of Modern Japanese Philosophy: Phenomenology as a Case in Point

CHAPTER ONE

Phenomenology in Japan: Its Inception and Blossoming

KEIICHI NOE

1. THE FIRST GENERATION: THE INTRODUCTION OF PHENOMENOLOGY TO JAPAN

It is not overstating the case to say that the phenomenological studies began at the Imperial University of Tōhoku in Sendai. Husserlian phenomenology was formally introduced to the Japanese philosophical circle by Takahashi Satomi, who studied with Husserl in Germany.[1] Miyake Gōichi, his junior colleague, also went to Germany and studied with Husserl. Miyake formulated his philosophy of human existence based on the phenomenological method, while he also introduced Heidegger's philosophy to the Japanese students. Both Takahashi and Miyake taught for decades at Tohoku University,[2] and trained their students, who became the leaders of the postwar Japan's phenomenological studies, to bring about the "renaissance of phenomenology."

In stating this, certainly I am not neglecting the philosophers of the Kyoto School, for instance, who sustained the dawning period of Japanese academic philosophical studies, including such important thinkers as Nishida Kitarō, Tanabe Hajime, and Kuki Shūzō. Incidentally, they also studied phenomenology according to the dictates of their philosophical interests, and as such phenomenology can be said to have played an important formative role in their thinking. When we speak about the tradition of phenomenology in Japan that has survived into the post–Second World War period, however, we need to credit the thinkers in Sendai, rather than those in Kyoto or Tokyo. Based on this assessment of mine, I shall begin my essay by focusing on Takahashi and Miyake as the first generation of phenomenological studies in Japan.

1.1 *Takahashi Satomi (1886–1964) and the introduction of Husserl*

Takahashi Satomi 高橋里美 was born in 1886 (the nineteenth year of Meiji) in Yamagata Prefecture and studied philosophy at the Imperial University of Tokyo.

Soon after his graduation, he wrote an extensive review article, critiquing Nishida Kitarō's *Zen no kenkyū* (*An Inquiry into the Good*). Takahashi's essay, entitled "Facts and Meanings of the Phenomena of Consciousness" (*Ishiki genshō no jijitsu to sono imi*) was published in May and June 1912 issues of *Tetsugaku Zasshi* (*Journal of Philosophy*).[3] His bold challenge of Nishida's first book marked his debut in the world of academic philosophy. In meeting his astute criticism squarely, Nishida wrote his response entitled "My Response to Takahashi Satomi's Criticism of My Book, *An Inquiry into the Good*" (*Takahashi (Satomi) Bungakushi no seccho* Zen no kenkyū *ni taisuru hihyō ni kotau*). It was published in the October 1912 issue of *Tetsugaku Zasshi*. The philosophical exchanges that took place between the two stands out as the first full-fledged philosophical debate that took place in modern Japan. Takahashi was twenty-six years old then, and Nishida forty-three.

In 1915 Takahashi got a teaching position as a German-language teacher at the Sixth Higher School in Okayama, and it so happened that Miyake Gōichi was among his students there. In 1921 (the tenth year of Taishō), now thirty-five years old, he moved to Sendai, upon the invitation of the Faculty of Natural Sciences of the Imperial University of Tōhoku to join its faculty as an associate professor. From 1925 onward, for two years, he was granted a scholarship to study abroad in Europe under the auspices of the Ministry of Education. He went to the University of Freiburg to study with Husserl, which set the course of his subsequent philosophical career to specialize in phenomenology.

Takahashi took Husserl's seminar for two semesters, from fall 1926 through summer 1927. He attended the Winter Lecture on the "Introduction to Phenomenology" (*Einführung in die Phänomenologie*) and the Summer Lecture on "Nature and Mind" (*Natur und Geist*).[4] He also came to be intimately exposed to Husserl's phenomenological thinking through his seminars and private conversations. We may note here, however, that Husserl's lectures were far from riveting. Takahashi recalls in a matter of a fact fashion:

> One could more or less imagine from his writings that his lectures would not be lively or exciting. In fact, they were repetitive beyond one's imagination. It easily far surpassed the point of being boring. It was like an empty wheel rolling in the air. Day after day, he would repeat the same thing over and over again. Who could have foreseen that lectures that met four hours a week barely covered the topic of "phenomenological reduction" by the end of the semester? … The classroom, which was reasonably packed in the beginning of the semester, began to show deserted empty spots here and there, and these lonely holes became more and more conspicuous as the semester progressed. But nothing seemed to have bothered the professor. He simply continued the rotation of this empty wheel in the air without moving very much ahead.[5]

Indeed, we could sense how Husserl's belabored complex sentences must have been transposed to the lecture podium. Husserl by this time had already published his *Logical Investigations* (*Logische Untersuchungen*, 1900–1901) and the *Ideas* (*Ideen zu einer reinen Phänomenologie und phänomenologischen Philosophie*, vol. 1, 1913), secured his solid position within the German academic philosophical world, and was the torchbearer of phenomenology as a viable school of thought over against the neo-Kantian schools. But after his appointment at the University of Freiburg as full professor in 1916, he had published only several articles and no major book. He was going through an extended period of silence. Obviously, it was not that he had stopped thinking. Rather, as it became apparent from the posthumous publications of his work after the Second World War, he was groping as to how to make the transition from "constitutive phenomenology" to "generative phenomenology," and producing several pieces of writings, which gave rise to the "renaissance of phenomenology."

As a matter of fact, Husserl, after this period of silence, began to publish his work one after another, including the *Lectures on the Phenomenology of Inner Time-Consciousness* (*Vorlesungen zur Phänomenologie des inneren Zeitbewußtseins*, 1928), the *Formal and Transcendental Logic* (*Formale und transzendentale Logik*, 1929), and the *Cartesian Meditations* (*Méditations cartésiennes, Introduction à la phénoménologie*, 1931), signaling the opening of the curtain to the act two of his thinking, the so-called later Husserlian phenomenology. In this context, the year Takahashi studied at Freiburg falls right on the eve of Husserl's breaking his silence, and it was fortunate for Takahashi to have witnessed Husserl, who was at the very point of breaking the cocoon to fly out, the cocoon which he had been spinning until then.

Takahashi returned to Japan in February of 1928, and immediately in May of that year he gave a series of lectures on phenomenology upon the request of the Association of Educators of the city of Nagano. The content of the lectures were later published as an article in the journal *Risō*, in the October 1929 issue. This marked the beginning of Takahashi's introduction of phenomenology to Japan.[6] Takahashi's article drew on Husserl's lectures and seminars that he had personally attended in Freiburg, and as such it is an invaluable account of Husserl during this period of silence. To cite a few example, such key concepts as "passivity," "association," "body," "kinesthesis," "intersubjective reduction," "empathy," "appraesentation," and "monad"—the ideas that came to constitute the later Husserlian phenomenology—are already frequently mentioned in this article by Takahashi, bearing witness to the fact that generative phenomenology was already ripening in Husserl's mind.

What Husserl was grappling with by using these key concepts was the question of how to recognize the "other ego" (*alter ego*). Takahashi deftly summarizes what was behind this question as the task of "phenomenologically restoring the objectivity of nature that had been discarded by the theory of ego (*Egologie*), as well as to reduce (i.e. rehabilitate) social, historical and cultural world, which the theory of ego overlooked, and give such a world a phenomenological foundation."[7] This is actually the leitmotif of what Husserl was to study in a detailed analysis in his *Cartesian Meditations*, especially in the "Fifth Meditation."

We must remember, here, that Husserl's *Cartesian Meditations* in French was not yet published until 1931, and its German translation did not appear until after the Second World War in 1950. Therefore, Takahashi, at the time of penning this article, had no notion of what Husserl was to unfold in his forthcoming publications.

Interestingly, his work on Husserl's phenomenology entitled "Intersubjective Phenomenological Reduction" (which constitutes chapter 5 of his book) actually reads as an elegant summary of Husserl's "Fifth Meditation." This indicates how accurate Takahashi's grasp of Husserl's phenomenology was, to which he was exposed through the master's lectures at Freiburg. Takahashi also mentions that "Husserl considers the monad to have the body which acts as a window, through which it enters into reciprocal relationship with other monads," and he even infers the possibility of the establishment of the phenomenology of the body, anticipating later Husserl.[8]

It is remarkable that in 1929, when Takahashi published his work, his was the only academic paper in the world that described Husserl's theories of recognition of alter ego and intersubjectivity and even mentioned the body as a phenomenological problem. How remarkable this was becomes apparent when we read his German colleagues' works. For instance, Oskar Becker makes a brief mention of "intersubjective reduction" in his work "Edmund Husserl's Philosophy" (1930), but he never touched on the questions of the "body" or "empathy" (*Einfühlung*). Again, Husserl's beloved disciple Eugen Fink's well-known work, "Edmund Husserl's Phenomenological Philosophy and the Contemporary Critique" (1933), contains only several lines of reference to the description of "monad" in view of later Husserlian phenomenology. That Takahashi was able to introduce to the Japanese academic philosophers the later development of Husserl's phenomenology, even before it happened in Europe, is something I would like to underscore, when we speak about how phenomenology was introduced to Japan.

1.2 Miyake Gōichi (1895–1982) and the introduction of Heidegger and Merleau-Ponty

Miyake Gōichi 三宅剛一, who had the privilege of tutelage by Takahashi Satomi, became the bridge to the next generation of phenomenologists in Japan. Born in 1895 in Okayama Prefecture, he studied German under Takahashi at the Sixth Higher School, as mentioned above. After that, Miyake entered the Kyoto Imperial University and studied philosophy under Nishida Kitarō. In 1924, when he was twenty-nine years old, he was offered associate professorship in the Faculty of Natural Science at Tōhoku Imperial University. He, too, had the opportunity to study in Europe, 1930–32, under the auspices of the Ministry of Education, and naturally chose the University of Freiburg where Husserl was. He participated in Husserl's seminars held at the professor's home, and studied the phenomenological method. He was also closely acquainted with Eugen Fink and Martin Heidegger, and Oskar Becker was his private tutor with whom he went over Heidegger's *Sein und Zeit* (*Being and Time*, 1927).

Following his return to Japan in 1932, Miyake wanted to introduce Heidegger's philosophy to the Japanese academic philosophers. His article "Heidegger's Philosophical Position" (*Haideggā tetsugaku no tachiba*) was published in the 1934 issue of the journal *Bunka* (Culture), published by the Association of Humanities, a group that existed at Tōhoku University. This is one of the earliest academic works on Heidegger in Japan, and it bears a unique stamp as it contains the exchanges of ideas he personally had with Husserl, Heidegger, Fink, and Becker back in Freiburg.

Miyake considers "reflection" (*hansei* 反省) as the essence of philosophy, and at the same time asserts that any reflection cannot be free of historicity, and, therefore, even the method of phenomenological reduction cannot be absolutized. According to Miyake, Heidegger recognized innate historicity and the finitude of humanity, and he discovered a possibility of actively accepting the social milieu (*jidaiteki keikō*) of contemporary Europe in the phenomenological method. At that time, the structure of reflection (of consciousness) and the role of phenomenological reduction were the issues of the ultimate importance for phenomenology, which were hotly debated and being worked out by Husserl and Fink and were later coherently presented by Fink in his *Sixth Meditation* (1988). Here, again, one notices that Miyake's understanding of Heidegger came from the cutting-edge discussions held in common among his German colleagues concerning the promises and potentials of phenomenology.

The astute questioning Miyake pursued was crystalized in his book *On Human Existence* (*Ningen sonzairon*) (1966). In the preface, Miyake states that "what is fundamental in philosophy is to have an overarching perspective on human reality, without excluding any sort of possibilities."[9] In order to carry out this task, he adopts the phenomenological method, which he considers "open and a method-at-work."[10] However, this does not mean that Miyake simply adopts Husserl's or Heidegger's method as his own. Rather his attempt is to start out with the critical reflection on their methods. What he says about this point is rife with suggestions. Miyake writes, for instance:

> In Husserl's phenomenology, the actual existence of human beings is ultimately viewed from the perspective of the inner reflection of the subjective (conscious) life. In his philosophy of life, he does talk about "constitution" (*Konstitution*) or the "intentional work (*Leistung*)," but the aspects of the impotent, the deficient, the falsehood—which are also all uniquely present in human existence—are overlooked.[11]

And further,

> In Heidegger the actual existence (Dasein) is given the ontological significance in terms of the "understanding of existence." This is the characteristic feature of Heidegger's analysis of Dasein, but because his style of inquiry rests on "either this or that" as the guiding principle, his phenomenological investigation into human existence naturally tends lopsided. The question of the body drops out of the treatment of beings-in-the-world, and in his discussion of history, his viewpoint of "intrinsic (*eigentlich*) or not" ends up simplifying the historical reality.[12]

I submit that these are the kinds of criticisms that can be raised only by those who were intimately acquainted with Husserl and Heidegger, and had grasped the essence of phenomenology. Miyake himself proceeds to describe nature and history and how we are related to them not from the perspective of ontology in general but from the perspective of "human existence." In this undertaking, Miyake considers the body to be an important philosophical issue, and draws the attention of the Japanese academic philosophers to the ideas developed by Maurice Merleau-Ponty and Claude Lévi-Strauss quite early on. Miyake approaches the "self" (*jiko*), which forms the basis of the body and behavior, in its concrete reality, as he writes: "The human self is a corporeal subjectivity; there is no self that is devoid of the drive to fulfill desire. Fulfillment of desire is a given as the right to life, for the sake of self-preservation."[13] Miyake's philosophy of *human existence* (*Ningen sonzairon*) can be seen as the culminating point of the first generation of Japanese phenomenologists. The second generation of Japanese phenomenologists, nurtured by Miyake, flew out of the nest to make a big stir in the Japanese philosophical world.

2. THE SECOND GENERATION: THE BURGEONING OF PHENOMENOLOGY IN JAPAN

Being solicited by the Philosophy Department at Kyoto University, Miyake Gōichi left Tōhoku University in 1954, but until then he dedicatedly trained many able younger philosophers. Notable among them are Takiura Shizuo 滝浦静雄 (1927–2011), Kida Gen 木田元 (1928–2014), and Nitta Yoshihiro 新田義弘 (b. 1929)—all of them were students of Miyake, inherited the academic tradition of Takahashi and Miyake, and greatly contributed to generating the movement, which came to be known as the "renaissance of phenomenology" in Japan.

2.1 Human existence as corporeal and the discovery of Merleau-Ponty

In postwar Japan, Jean Paul Sartre held the position of the hero-philosopher as the flag-bearer of existentialism. Takiura and Kida, however, discovered Merleau-Ponty, who had been overshadowed by Sartre, and identified him as the real successor of the spirit of later Husserlian phenomenology. Thus, they began translating Merleau-Ponty's works into highly readable plain Japanese one after the other, starting with *The Structure of Behavior* (*Kōdō no kōzō, La Structure du comportment*, 1942), followed by *Eye and Mind* (*Me to seishin, L'Œil et l'esprit*, 1961). Obviously, one sees Miyake's influence in the background. In fact, Takiura and Kida paid the following tribute in the "Translator's postscript" of their translation of *The Structure of Behavior*:

> We thought about translating this book to express our deeply felt gratitude for Professor Miyake Gōichi, on the occasion of the upcoming celebration of his 70th birthday next spring. Professor Miyake, not only during his tenure at Tōhoku University but also after he left, continues to encourage us warmly.[14]

It has already been mentioned above that Miyake paid close attention to the importance of the body from early on; Takiura and Kida picked up this thread, and aside from translating the works of Merleau-Ponty, they developed on the concept of the body in their own philosophies. Two notable books on this topic by them are: Takiura's *Language and the Body* (*Gengo to shintai*, 1978), and Kida's *Merleau-Ponty's Philosophy* (*Merurō-Pontī no shisō*, 1984).

I hope it is now clear to the reader that seeds of the renaissance of phenomenology that blossomed in the 1960s and 1970s Japan were sown by Miyake. These seeds matured into such works as Nitta Yoshihiro's *What Is Phenomenology?* (*Genshōgaku to wa nani ka*, 1968) and *Phenomenology* (*Genshōgaku*, 1978); Kida Gen's *Contemporary Philosophy* (*Gendai tetsugaku*, 1969) and *Phenomenology* (*Genshōgaku*, 1970); and Takiura Shizuo's *Phenomenology of Imagination* (*Sōzō no genshōgaku*, 1972) and *Time* (*Jikan*, 1976).

2.2 *Kida Gen: The radical spirit of social and philosophical critique*

Among these excellent works, some technical and others more popular, Kida Gen's *Phenomenology* stands out to merit a special mention. Being published as a pocketbook-sized edition, easily obtainable and affordably priced, it was read widely by university students who were living the heydays of "student power," and who quickened the intellectual movement that led to the "phenomenology boom." Myself included, the university students of those days found many passages of Kida extremely provocative, and they felt they came upon a new kind of philosophy, going beyond the traditional old-fashioned discipline of "philosophy." To quote a passage from Kida, where he refers to Husserl, Heidegger, Sartre, and Merleau-Ponty:

> The efforts of these philosophers should be viewed to summarize and highlight the methodological innovations taking place in the various fields of humanistic sciences [such as the academic discipline of psychology, sociology, history, and linguistics] to overcome the method that were mechanistic and based on fragmented elements, the method which has dominated the fields up until now. In turn, the critical methodological reflections highlighted by these thinkers impart direct or indirect influence on the various fields of humanistic disciplines that relatively lagged behind. Thus, the phenomenological movement is not just *a* trend in philosophy, but more aptly it should be viewed as an encompassing larger movement that covers multiple fields of scholarly disciplines of this century, especially of humanities.[15]

Kida's statement such as this helped delineate the contribution of phenomenology as a philosophy that critiques modern natural sciences and modern rationalism. In short, my generation of university students understood phenomenology to stand for a new scientific methodology that would break new ground for the academic studies that had fallen into a state of impasse. It also accorded with the spirit of the day, in which the young generation was rebelling against the oppressive "regimented society" governed by technocrats. Kida emphasized that Husserl "saw the crisis of academic studies as the fundamental crisis of the life of European humanity—as the overall expression of the ontological crisis—and attempted to formulate his transcendental phenomenology as the very means to overcome this crisis."[16] Moreover, according to Kida, Husserl criticized the contemporary scholarly trend of entrusting its fundamental principle to other disciplines—such as was taking place in naturalism, psychologism, and historicism—to be irresponsible, looked for the foundation of their own scholarly disciplines in other academic fields; while likening the phenomenological reduction to Descartes's methodological doubt, he characterized the spirit of phenomenology as "a radical move," which assumes its own scholarly responsibility."[17] In this way, Husserl's scholarly radicalism and the radicalism of the spirit of that specific point in time in Japan coincided and resonated together.

Husserl wrote in his last book, *The Crisis of European Sciences and Transcendental Phenomenology* (*Die Krisis der Europäishen Wissenschaften und die transzendentale Phänomenologie*, 1936), the modern crisis of academic scholarship to have originated in the excess of positivistic science:

> The exclusiveness with which the total world-view of modern man, in the second half of the nineteenth century, let itself be determined by the positive sciences and be blinded by the "prosperity" they produced, meant an indifferent turning-away from the question which are decisive for a genuine humanity. Merely fact-minded sciences make merely fact-minded people.[18]

Certainly, positivistic sciences have enriched our lives and accelerated utility and efficiency. But positive sciences tell us nothing about what meaning scholarly learning may have for human existence. That is, we have forgotten to ask "questions of the meaning or meaninglessness of the whole of this human existence."[19]

Husserl thus inquires into the origin of this forgetfulness, traces it back in the stream of modern sciences, and arrives at the figure of Galileo Galilei, who was "at once a discovering and a concealing genius."[20] What Galileo concealed was the "lifeworld" (*Lebenswelt*). He put a veil over this lifeworld with mathematical formulae and philosophical ideals, thus concealing the fact that this lifeworld is the foundation of meaning underlying natural sciences.

2.3 Nitta Yoshihiro and Kida Gen: Philosophies of rudimentary nature

It was Nitta Yoshihiro's detailed and rigorous textual reading of Husserl's writings in his *What Is Phenomenology?* (*Genshōgaku towa nani ka*, 1968) that introduced Husserl's later thought focused on the lifeworld. Taking advantage of new materials that became available with the publication of the *Husserliana* series, Nitta was able to draw from many hitherto unknown texts of Husserl and brought to light the underappreciated dimensions of his phenomenological thinking. Nitta especially paid attention to the notion of "living present" ("*ikeru genzai*," *lebendige Gegenwart*) or "streaming (or flowing) present" ("*nagareru genzai*," *strömende Gegenwart*), which Husserl saw to constitute the steady feature of the function of ego-consciousness. Nitta recaptures this concept as the "force that works teleologically," and calls it "rudimentary" or "original nature" (*kongenteki shizen* 根源的自然). Nitta writes:

> This force that works teleologically reveals itself within my freedom, which allows me to feel that "I can"—a sense of kinesthesia—and constitutes our essence when we are moving towards a goal (*telos*). This force that comes to us, flows away, and urges us to make it firmly positioned (in our body) is the ultimate matter (*shitsuryō*); it is rudimentary nature in the fundamental sense … That we

> accept this rudimentary nature is something that we are demanded by rudimentary nature itself. In the movement of rudimentary nature, it sends itself into [our bodies] and thereby hides itself.[21]

Nitta, by taking this rudimentary nature as the basis of his philosophical thinking, moves closer to the "phenomenology of life." The key concept here is "mediality" (*baitaisei* 媒体性, *Medialität*). In terms of the relationship of the world and human beings, it is not that the world appears to the human beings, but rather, human beings are the negative medials (*baitai*) of the world for the world to manifest itself. Keeping this in mind, Nitta constructs his "phenomenology of transcendental mediality" based on the conscious apprehension of life as the goal of phenomenological knowledge.

Interestingly, Kida Gen, too, finds the breakthrough of phenomenology in the concept of rudimentary nature. (Kida, together with Nitta, led the post–Second World War studies on phenomenology; moreover both of them were disciples of Miyake as mentioned above.) In his 1980 article "World and Nature" ("*Sekai to shizen*"), while referring to Husserl and Heidegger's notions of "earth" (*Erde*) and Merleau-Ponty's idea of the "untamed wild existence" (*l'être sauvage*), Kida asks the following question:

> This kind of notion of rudimentary nature originated most likely outside the field of phenomenology, and to recognize the existence of such a notion may risk the bankruptcy of phenomenology itself. Then, why did all these thinkers end up arriving at this kind of nature? … It might be the unavoidable fate of western philosophy, or perhaps when we shift our focus and think from the perspective of radical nature, the essence of Western knowledge, which has been called philosophy, may become clearer.[22]

This kind of self-questioning prompts Kida to take a big stride beyond the pale of traditional phenomenology. He now turns to the inquiry into the tradition of "anti-" or "counter" philosophy (*han-tetsugaku* 反哲学). He sees this countermovement in the efforts made by Nietzsche and Heidegger, for instance, who attempted to "overcome the mainstream notion of what philosophy is," including the notion of existence in terms of "being made" that become prevalent after Plato, or the materialistic view of nature since Descartes with its presupposition of homo-centrism. Noting that the basis Nietzsche and Heidegger resorted to in order to criticize "Western philosophy" is the view of nature held by the pre-Socratic thinkers, Kida layers in his philosophical vista this pre-Socratic view of nature and the originally Japanese ancient view of rudimentary nature that permeates, for instance, *The Records of Ancient Matters* (*Kojiki*).

Granted, while they take "rudimentary nature" as the key concept, what Nitta attempts to do with it in his "phenomenology of mediality" and Kida in his "counter-philosophy" are greatly different in terms of goal and approach. There would be no opposition, however, to consider the achievements of these thinkers as the culminating points of the second generation of Japanese phenomenological studies.

2.4 *Tatematsu Hirotaka: Translations of Husserl's writings*

Not to be forgotten here concerning the momentous achievements the second generation of Japanese phenomenologists made are twofold: the establishment of the Phenomenological Association of Japan, and the publication of the *Lectures on Phenomenology* (*Kōza genshōgaku*) in four volumes, published by Kōbundō in Tokyo. Here, in this context, I must introduce one more figure, Tatematsu Hirotaka 立松弘孝 (1931–2016), besides the three disciples of Miyake, Takiura, Kida, and Nitta. The foremost contribution of Tatematsu's is his extensive translation of Husserl's writings into precise and accurate Japanese. The list of translated works (some are co-translated) includes: *Genshōgaku no rinen* (*Die Idee der Phänomenologie*, 1965); *Naiteki jikan ishiki no genshōgaku* ("Zur Phaenomenologie des inneren Zeitbewusstseins," 1967)[23]; *Ronrigaku kenkyū* (*Logische Untersuchungen*) in four volumes (1968–76); *Idēn II* (*Ideen zu reinen Phänomenologie und phänomenologischen Philosophie: Zweites Buch, Phänomenologische Untersuchungen zur Konstitution*) in two volumes (2001 and 2009); and *Keishiki ronrigaku to chōetsuronteki ronrigaku* (*Formale und. Transzendentale Logik, Versuch einer Kritik der logischen Vernunft*, 2015). Without these ambitious and painstaking undertaking, the handing-down of the baton to the third generation of Japanese students of phenomenology would have been greatly delayed, if not at least by a decade.

Concerning the establishment of the Phenomenological Association of Japan, it traces its inception to March 1979, when a call for a conference was circulated, tentatively titled "A Conference on Phenomenological Studies in Japan." The meeting was held in May 1979 at Sophia University in Tokyo, where Noe Keiichi and Washida Kiyokazu presented their papers on the conference theme of "Behavior and Communication," which were followed by lively debates among the conference participants. This conference led to the establishment of the Phenomenological Association of Japan. A year later, in 1980, on the occasion of the second meeting held at Nanzan University in Nagoya, the name of the group was officially declared as Phenomenological Association of Japan, and the bylaws were drawn up, with the association's office being set up at Nanzan University with Tatematsu Hirotaka as its director. The formation of this academic association laid the firm foundation for the third generation of Japanese phenomenologists to carry out their academic and philosophical activities.

3. THE THIRD GENERATION: THE TRANSFORMATION OF PHENOMENOLOGY

In discussing the third generation of phenomenological studies in Japan, I must emphasize the indispensable role played by the "Study Group on Phenomenology and Hermeneutics," which Nitta Yoshihiro personally organized and led. This study group crossed the boundaries of universities and localities, encouraged the exchange of views among younger academics, and reached outside academic philosophy into the fields of psychiatry, social sciences, and so forth, augmenting the interdisciplinary discussions. The three figures who represent the third generation of Japanese phenomenologists—Washida Kiyokazu 鷲田清一, Murata Jun'ichi 村田純一, and Noe Keiichi 野家啓一—all took part in this study group and expanded their realm of research. The third generation of thinkers was basically nurtured under the influence of the second generation of phenomenologists mentioned above. That when Kida Gen was asked to compile an *Encyclopedia of Phenomenology* (*Genshōgaku jiten*, published 1994),[24] he appointed Washida, Murata, and Noe, the younger academics, instead of scholars of his own generation, is a good illustration of how the generational change took place smoothly. This *Encyclopedia of Phenomenology* has been translated into Korean, and considered by those in the field as an indispensable research tool, it has been contributing greatly to the advancement of the study of phenomenology among Asian academics.

3.1 *Washida Kiyokazu's phenomenology of care and Murata Jun'ichi's phenomenology of technology*

In contrast to the second generation of Japanese phenomenologists, those who belong to the third generation are almost all born after the Second World War, and their philosophical interests are accordingly more widespread than those of the former generations. On the one hand, detailed analysis and reading of the original texts of Husserl, Heidegger, Merleau-Ponty, and so on continue, while on the other hand various original works have been produced, ever widening the scope of phenomenology.

Washida Kiyokazu (born in 1949) started out with the study of Merleau-Ponty, and cleared a new ground on the theory of corporeity; he later advocated "clinical philosophy" (*rinshō tetsugaku*) and opened up the academic study of philosophy to society at large. In concrete terms, he engaged in dialogue with those who actually face the daily challenges at their work—nurses, teachers, caregivers, and so on. His attempt has created a new field, which may be called a "phenomenology of nursing and caregiving," or a "phenomenology of care."[25]

Murata Jun'ichi (born in 1948), known for his careful reading of texts by Husserl and Brentano, has turned to his own phenomenological analyses, and contributed in the area of phenomenology of technology (*gijutsu*), and technological ethics.[26] At present, he is working to bridge ecological psychology and phenomenology by taking the concept of "affordance" as the common ground.

3.2 *Noe Keiichi's phenomenology of history as narration*

In response to the request of the volume editor of this present book, in the remainder of this essay, allow me to sketch out my current interest in a "history as narration" (or a theory of "history as narration"). What initially got me interested in phenomenology was Kida Gen's book *Phenomenology*, mentioned above. Accordingly, at first I understood phenomenology as a kind of scientific methodology, and I was especially influenced by Husserl's discussion of the criticism of modern natural sciences, which he carried out in his aforementioned *Crisis of European Sciences and Transcendental Phenomenology*. At graduate school I majored in the philosophy of science, and this led me to ask myself whether or not I might bring together the phenomenological method and analytical philosophy in the analysis of language.

Phenomenology and analytic philosophy in those days were considered something like water and oil repelling each other, and thus my audacious attempt was met, as expected, with many harsh criticisms, but what gave me a glimpse of the possibility of success was the essay written by Nitta Yoshihiro, "Concerning the Narrative Act in the Study of History" ("*Rekishi kagaku ni okeru monogatari kōi ni tsuite*") that appeared in the October 1983 issue of *Shisō*. Therein Nitta took up the debates on "explanation and understanding" that was taking place between the British and North American analytic philosophers and the German-language based group of hermeneutical philosophers, and moreover, treated A. Danto's *Analytical Philosophy of History* and J. G. Droysen's *Logic of History* on an equal footing. This fact greatly encouraged me when I was groping to bridge, in terms of methodology, phenomenology and analytic philosophy.

Another great encouragement that came to me was the essay, "*Poiesis* of the Past" (*Kako no seisaku*, 1985), written by my research advisor, Ōmori Shōzō 大森荘蔵. In this article Ōmori denied the "past-in-itself" which is comparable to a "thing-in-itself," unfolded his view that there is no independent past without experience of recollection, and advocated the "theory of the pastness of recollection" (*sōki-kakosetsu* 想起過去説). This gave me the theoretical backbone of my philosophy of narration. In this sense, my philosophy of narration has two main pillars—Nitta's phenomenology and Ōmori's analytic philosophy. Actually, there is a third pillar, Yanagida Kunio's theory of oral literature or folklore.[27] But here, I shall limit myself to the discussion pertaining only to phenomenology

The starting point of my philosophy of history as narration is very simple. That is, insofar as history is the description of the events of the past, no one can directly perceive these events, and we must resort to the "narratives" (*katari* 語り) in words as the medium (*baikai*). Now, as a "narrative" (*katari*) can also degenerate into a fraud (*katari* 騙り), so can words be both actual and non-actual reality, but it cannot be denied that the words point to a certain object when we speak. The fact that in Romance languages "history" is etymologically related to "story" seems to me to reveal this aspect.

Different from the description of a perception of things in front of one's very eyes, a historical narration cannot directly point out the things and events that are its objects. For instance, " 'this rose is red' as a fact" can be demonstrated simply by pointing to the rose in question, without having recourse to language. But before the withered rose, whose color has turned into brown, how can we describe its past reality of "this rose was red," except by relying on language? The characteristic of the past event is precisely this—that it has passed, and it is no longer "before our eyes" in terms of perception. That is, the prime feature of the past fact lies in its "absence" (*fuzai* 不在) in the present moment. Now, it is the most significant function of the language, in which words can freely "point their fingers" to these "absent things" and express them.

Moreover, the past may be the events presently absent, but different from dreams and fictions; the past events are accompanied by our strong sense (or awareness)

of their having been once in existence. This "awareness of (having been in) actual existence" (*jitsuzai ishiki*) permeates not only the past experiences that we have actually undergone, but also the entire historical past, which cannot be experienced firsthand, even if we want to. What sustains this awareness of actual existence of the past is the existence of historical sources, understood broadly, that form a connection with the presently actually existing human beings. If these historical sources *qua evidence* were to disappear, the past reality would accordingly lose its foothold, and its status would degenerate into one that is no different from dreams and fictions. This is the reason why historians pour their utmost energy in discovering, collecting, and preserving historical records and sources, and stake their scholarly lives on decoding and analyzing them.

Actually, however, only a tiny segment of the vast past events has been left behind to us as the historical sources qua evidence, while almost all the other past facts have sunk beneath the surface of the ocean into oblivion. Moreover, the historical sources as evidence, insofar as they are narrated or written, cannot be a faithful recapitulation of past reality. The ideologies of the narrator or writer may have distorted the historical records, and the selection process of what is to be included and what is to be left out reflects the value system of the narrator. That is to say, historical sources (qua evidence) come to us by already having been filtered through the process of selection and omission, as they are but the outcome of a certain mode of interpretation.

The manner in which historical records and sources exist, as I have described above, can be likened to "perspectival aspect"—the Husserlian term of *Abschattung* (*shaei* 射映). Husserl states that even God, the perfect cognitive subjectivity, cannot escape "this perspectival aspect" in spatial perception. Perspectival aspects of things are indeed the essential condition that accompanies the perception of things. For instance, we cannot perceive six faces of a die all at once. At best we can only see two or three faces from a certain angle. But, this perspectival aspect of things is not a mental image or a copy of the thing. In each case of the perspectival aspects what shows forth is the real die itself. Therefore, in having multiple perspectival aspects, it is impossible to say a certain one is correct and others wrong. The perception of spatial things is established by the intentional consciousness that unifies innumerable perspectival aspects. Moreover, because it is impossible to assume countless perspectival aspects all at once, our perception must always remain "incomplete" and an "undefined area" is left open. This "undefined area that is possible to be defined" is called "the horizon" in phenomenology.

This idea of "perspectival aspects" or "shading-off things" can be applied mutatis mutandis to the recollection of past events. Everyone has had the experience of a situation in which the contents of the recollection of the multiple individuals who underwent the same event differ subtly. The content of the memory of each individual corresponds to the "perspectival aspect" in recollection. That is to say, each recollection is not a mental image or a copy of the past event, but a manifestation of the past event itself. The only way to avoid evoking the ghost of the past-in-itself is to stop considering the past-in-itself as existence independent of recollection, and apprehend the various recollections-perspectival aspects in the intentional unification. This method can be expanded to treat the historical past. In other words, the "intentional unification" of various historical sources *is* the past event itself.

It is important to note, here, however, that there is a big difference between the perceptual perspectival aspects and the "retrieval" perspectival aspects (of recollection) in terms of how this intentional unification is carried out. That is, the perceptual perspectival aspect is the unification by way of consciousness, while the historical past events are the unification by way of language. In the case of perception, I can look at one and the same object by changing the angle and adopting various perspectives. That is, I alone can experience the variety of perspectival aspects. When it comes to the perspectival aspects of recollection, however, I cannot recall from the perspective of another person, and for this reason the various perspectival aspects of the past events must remain the recollections of others persons. And moreover, it is impossible for me to experience directly the content of the recollection of others. In order to bring these multiple recollections into an intentional unity, we must depend on linguistic means. This is what I meant by my earlier statement that the unification of the past events is not by consciousness but by language. Only by rendering the past events into propositions by using words can we examine "the truth or falsehood" of the past event. For "truth or falsehood" does not belong to the nature of things and events, but to the propositions. In this regard, we have much to learn from analytic philosophy.

What I have discussed thus far by the "intentional unification" of the perspectival aspect of recollections signifies, when applied to historical facts, that various historical sources, including testimonies and material evidences, are unified coherently without contradictions. Through this operation, the past events gain their "actual position" (*jitteisei* 実定性) as well as "intersubjectivity" (*kanshukansei* 間主観性), and become the past that is "publicly acknowledged" by society. In short, they become the "actually existing" (*jitsuzaisuru* 実在する), actually present, past. The meaning of the "thing actually existed in the past" is nothing more than this or less than this. The past is not something that "exists" anywhere independent of our recollection or sources qua evidence, but it is a thing that is "born and grows" by going through the socially acknowledged public procedures—something akin to the witness statements and the examinations of evidence in the court of law.

For this reason, if a new witness statement or evidence is discovered, even the past that is already "established as a fact" must be submitted to a retrial, just as in the legal trial. As already described above, just as perception is undetermined and has its horizon, so too the past is "unfinished" and has its horizon, and the confirmation and emendation of the past is actually open to a further future experience. In this sense, my philosophy of history as narration is an ideal atelier (or workshop) where phenomenology and analytic philosophy can work together and collaborate.

BY WAY OF CONCLUSION

In a bold stroke, I have described the reception and development of phenomenological studies in Japan in terms of three successive generations, but actually the time is right to hand over the baton to the fourth generation of thinkers. It is natural then that phenomenology must remain open to the influences of new movements of thoughts, such as feminism, postcolonialism, and cognitive science. Regardless of whatever transformation phenomenology will undergo in the future, we must not relinquish "the radical academic self responsibility" that Husserl upheld. It is after all the methodologically radical and thoroughgoing attitude that has drawn the young generations of able minds to phenomenology to start with.

NOTES

This chapter, originally written in Japanese, was translated by M. Yusa.

1. Takahashi was appointed as the dean of the Faculty of Law and Literature in 1928, following his return to Japan from Germany, and after his mandatory retirement from his teaching position, he was elected as the president of Tohoku University, 1949–57.
2. Takahashi was at the teaching position for twenty-seven years, and Miyake thirty years.
3. Cf. M. Yusa, *Zen and Philosophy* (Honolulu: University of Hawaii Press, 2002), 129.
4. S. Takahashi, "*Jo*" (Introduction) to *Husserl's Phenomenology*, in *Takahashi Satomi: Zentaisei no genshōgaku* [*Takahashi Satomi: Phenomenology of the whole*], ed. Noe Keiichi (Kyoto: Tōeisha, 2001), 6.
5. S. Takahashi, "*Fusseru no koto*" [About Husserl], in ibid., 82.
6. Takahashi Satomi, *Fusseru no genshōgaku* [Husserl's phenomenology]. This essay and other writings of his on Husserl were compiled into a single volume, published in 1931 and reprinted in 1946. It is now included in Takahashi Satomi, *Zentaisei no genshōgaku*, 6–94.
7. Ibid., 47.
8. Ibid., 48.
9. Miyake Gōichi, *Ningen sonzairon* [On the mode of human existence] (Tokyo: Kōdansha, 2008), 3.
10. Ibid.
11. Ibid., 44.
12. Ibid., 46.
13. Ibid., 198.
14. Merleau-Ponty, *La Structure du comportment*, Takiura Shizuo and Kida Gen, trans. into Japanese, *Kōdō no kōzō* (Tokyo: Misuzu Shobō, 1964), 368–369.
15. Kida Gen, *Genshōgaku* (Tokyo: Iwanami Shoten, 1970), 7–8.
16. Ibid., 58.
17. Ibid., 57.
18. E. Husserl, *The Crisis of European Sciences and Transcendental Phenomenology: An Introduction to Phenomenological Philosophy*, trans. David Carr (Evanston, IL: Northwestern University Press, 1970), 5–6.
19. Ibid., 6.
20. Ibid., 52.

21. Nitta Yoshihiro, *Genshōgaku towa nani ka* [What is phenomenology?] (Tokyo: Kōdansha, 1992 [1968]), 226–227.
22. Kida Gen, *Tetsugaku to hantetsugaku* [Philosophy and counter-philosophy] (Tokyo: Iwanami Shoten, 1996), 72.
23. It contains Husserl's 1905 lecture and related papers on "time," 1905–10.
24. Kida Gen, editor in chief, *Genshōgaku jiten* [An encyclopedia of phenomenology] (Tokyo: Kōbundō, 1994), 749 pp.; its compact edition was published in 2014.
25. Washida Kiyokazu, *Kikukoto no chikara [The power of "listening"]* (Tokyo: TBS Britannica, 1999).
26. Murata Jun'ichi, *Gijutsu no tetsugaku [Philosophy of technology]* (Tokyo: Iwanami Shoten, 2009).
27. See Noe Keiichi, *Monogatari no tetsugaku [Philosophy of narration]* (Tokyo: Iwanami Shoten, 2005).

BIBLIOGRAPHY

Becker, Oskar. "Die Philosophie Edmund Husserls." *Kant-Studien* 35 (1930), 119–150.

Fink, Eugen. "Die phänomenologische Philosophy Edmund Husserls in der gegenwärigen Kritik." *Kant-Studien* 38 (1933), 319–383.

Husserl, Edmund. *The Crisis of European Sciences and Transcendental Phenomenology*, trans. David Carr. Evanston, IL: Northwestern University Press, 1970.

Kida Gen 木田元. *Genshōgaku* 『現象学』 [*Phenomenology*]. Tokyo: Iwanami Shoten, 1970.

Kida Gen. *Tetsugaku to hantetsugaku* 『哲学と反哲学』 [*Philosophy and counter-philosophy*]. Tokyo: Iwanami Shoten, 1996.

Kida Gen, ed. *Genshōgaku jiten* 『現象学事典』 [*An encyclopedia of phenomenology*], 749 pp. Tokyo: Kōbundō, 1994; its compact edition was published in 2014.

Miyake Gōichi 三宅剛一. *Ningen sonzairon* 『人間存在論』 [*A philosophy of human existence*]. Tokyo: Kōdansha, 2008 (1966).

Murata Jun'ichi 村田純一. *Gijutsu no tetsugaku* 『技術の哲学』 [*Philosophy of technology*]. Tokyo: Iwanami Shoten, 2009.

Nitta Yoshihiro 新田義弘. *Genshōgaku towa nani ka* 『現象学とは何か』 [*What is phenomenology?*]. Tokyo: Kōdansha, 1992 (1968).

Noe Keiichi 野家啓一. *Monogatari no tetsugaku* 『物語の哲学』 [*Philosophy of narration*]. Tokyo: Iwanami Shoten, 2005.

Noe Keiichi. *Rekishi o tetsugakusuru* 『歴史を哲学する』 [*Philosophizing history*]. Tokyo: Iwanami Shoten, 2016.

Takahashi Satomi 高橋里美. *Fusseru no genshōgaku* 「フッセルの現象学」 [*Husserl's Phenomenology*]. In *Takahashi Satomi: Zentaisei no Genshōgaku* 『高橋里美—全体性の現象学』 [*Takahashi Satomi: Phenomenology of the whole*], ed. Noe Keiichi, 6–94. Kyoto: Tōeisha, 2001 (1931).

Takiura Shizuo 滝浦静雄 and Kida Gen 木田元, trans. *Kōdō no kōzō* 『行動の構造』 (translation of Merleau-Ponty, *La Structure du comportment* [*The structure of behavior*], 1942). Tokyo: Misuzu Shobō, 1964.

Washida Kiyokazu 鷲田清一. *Kikukoto no chikara* 『「聴く」ことの力』 [*The power of "listening"*]. Tokyo: TBS Britannica, 1999.

FURTHER READING

Blosser, Philip, Eiichi Shimomisse et al. eds. *Japanese and Western Phenomenology.* Dordrecht: Kluwer Academic Publishers, 1993.

Kadowaki Shunsuke 門脇俊介. *Husserl* 『フッサール』 [Husserl]. Tokyo: NHK Shuppan, 2004.

Kida Gen 木田元. *Genshōgaku* 『現象学』 [*Phenomenology*]. Tokyo: Iwanami Shoten, 1970.

Kida Gen, ed. *Genshōgaku jiten* 『現象学事典』 [*An encyclopedia of phenomenology*]. Tokyo: Kōbundō, 1994; compact edition published in 2014.

Moran, Dermot, and Joseph Cohen. *The Husserl Dictionary.* London: Continuum, 2012.

Nitta Yoshihiro 新田義弘. *Genshōgaku to wa nani ka* 『現象学とは何か』 [*What is phenomenology?*]. Tokyo: Kōdansha, 1992 (1968).

Nitta Yoshihiro, ed. *Japanische Beitraege zur Phaenomenologie.* Freiburg: K. Alber, 1984.

Nitta Yoshihiro, and Hirotaka Tatematsu, eds. *Japanese Phenomenology.* Dordrecht: D. Reidel, 1979.

Nitta Yoshihiro, and Tani Toru, eds. *Phaenomenologie in Japan.* Wuerzburg: Koenigshausen & Neumann, 2011.

Noe Keiichi 野家啓一. "*Husserl: Shintai to daichi no arukeorojii*" 「フッサール：身体と大地のアルケオロジー」 [Husserl: the archeology of body and earth]. In *Gendai shisō no genryū* 『現代思想の源流』 [The origin of contemporary thought], ed. Imamura Hitoshi 今村仁司 et al. Tokyo: Kōdansha, 2003.

Noe Keiichi, ed. *Tetsugaku no rekisi vol.10: Kiki no jidai no tetsugaku* 『哲学の歴史』第10巻 「危機の時代の哲学」 [History of philosophy, vol. 10: Philosophy in the age of crisis]. Tokyo: Chūōkōron Shinsha, 2008.

Ogawa, Tadashi, Michel Lazarin, and Guido Rappe, eds. *Interkulturelle Philosophie und Phaenomenologie in Japan.* Munich: Iudicium Verlag, 1988.

Spiegelberg, Herbert. *The Phenomenological Movement.* The Hague: Martinus Nijhoff Publishers, 1982.

Taguchi Shigeru 田口茂. *Genshogaku toiu sikō* 『現象学という思考』 [Phenomenology as a path of thinking]. Tokyo: Chikuma Shobō, 2014.

Takahashi Satomi 高橋里美. *Fusseru no genshōgaku* 「フッセルの現象学」 [*Husserl's phenomenology*]. 1931.

Takahashi Satomi, and Noe Keiichi, eds. *zentaisei no genshōgaku* 『全体性の現象学』 [*Takahashi Satomi: Phenomenology of the whole*], 6–94. Kyoto: Tōeisha, 2001.

Tani Toru 谷徹. *Kore ga gennshogaku da* 『これが現象学だ』 [This is phenomenology]. Tokyo: Kōdansha, 2002.

Yamaguchi Ichiro 山口一郎. *Genshogaku kotohajime* 『現象学ことはじめ』 [Introduction to phenomenology]. Tokyo: Nihon Hyōronsha, 2012.

PART TWO

Social and Political Themes

CHAPTER TWO

Confucianism in Modern Japan

TAKAHIRO NAKAJIMA

INTRODUCTION

When one crosses the Hijiri Bridge 聖橋 from the Ochanomizu station in Tokyo, one comes across the Yushima Seidō 湯島聖堂, a Confucian temple. It was first built in 1690 by the fifth Tokugawa Shōgun, Tsunayoshi 綱吉, and the eleventh Shōgun Ienari 家斉 installed an affiliated academy, known as the Shōheizaka Gakumonjo 昌平坂学問所, or Shōheikō 昌平黌, which served as the academic center of Confucian studies in Japan during the Edo period.

To this day this Yushima Seidō still celebrates the annual festival carried out in Confucius's honor, a ritual known as "Sekiten" 釈奠, on the fourth Sunday of April. The celebration that took place on April 26, 2015, was hosted by Tokugawa Tsunenari 徳川恒孝, the current head of the main branch of Tokugawa family and chair emeritus of the Shibunkai 斯文会, the arterial association that oversees the festival and conducts scholarly activities on Confucian studies. The annual event of 2015 was presided over by the head priest of the Kanda Myōjin Shrine 神田明神, and Zhu Wenqing 朱文清, advisor to the Tokyo branch of the Taipei Economic and Cultural Representative Office, gave a speech as the guest of honor. A student choir of Nishōgakusha High School 二松学舎大学附属高等学校, affiliated with Nishōgakusha University, sang songs in praise of Confucius. This format of the annual celebration retains many crucial elements that comprise Japanese Confucianism—namely, the flowering of Confucianism during the Edo period, the redefinition of Confucianism into its modern form during the Meiji period, and the colonial policies of the Japanese empire that transpired thereafter. With all these aspects in mind, I shall proceed to solve the puzzle of how to define Japanese Confucianism, and especially modern Confucianism.

1. TOKUGAWA CONFUCIANISM

In the eyes of the Tokugawa Bakufu (Shogunal government, 1603–1867), Confucianism was an ambivalent thing. On the one hand, the ethical and metaphysical worldview of Confucianism potentially functioned as an effective ideology in support of Japan's hierarchical system of social ranks with the Shōgun at its top. But on the other hand, its other political doctrines of the rectification of names and the debates on rulership insistently recalled the Emperor 天皇 as the ruler of Japan, raising fears that the legitimacy of the Shōgun 将軍 might be called into question. For that reason, Confucianism in the Edo period tended to be practiced with constraints, and entrusted to the handful of scholars as their responsibility to study it.

However, about two hundred years after the founding of the Shogunal government, great changes took place in society, and the system of social advancement based on a samurai ethos began to wane. This situation required a new group of talented men who possessed a Confucian worldview. In 1790 the senior councilor Matsudaira Sadanobu 松平定信 issued an edict called the "Kansei Edict" 寛政の改革, also known as the "Prohibition on Unorthodox Learning" 寛政異学の禁. This aimed at implementing a Chinese-style examination system that would produce a new crop of elite scholars conversant with the teachings of Zhu Xi. Specifically, in the ninth month of 1792, the Bakufu established an examination system called the *gakumon ginmi* 学問吟味, initiating a system of elite recruitment based on the Chinese state examination model, and made the collected commentaries of Zhu Xi the basis of examination questions. At this point, for the first time, Confucianism in Japan began to spread to provinces, taking on a distinctly popular cast. Miyagi Kimiko makes the following observations on this phenomenon:

> In the last part of the Edo period ("*bakumatsu*" 幕末), with the issuance of the Kansei Edict, the Yushima Seidō was refurbished, and the number of domain-operated schools ("*hankō*" 藩校) increased, as the examination system opened a way for the lower-level samurai to gain good prospective positions. This ignited a warm enthusiasm for Confucian education, which began to spread across the land. Commoners of the wealthy farmers and merchant class studied Confucianism with an eye towards acquiring a rank of warrior, and in this way Confucian learning became popular. Regardless of one's social status or family background, it became a path of upward mobility, albeit still narrow, for one to establish oneself in society. As such, Confucianism for the commoners was not a subject they chose out of free will. Instead it was a historically given situation, and therefore it did not come to constitute a consciously articulated paradigm of what learning was.[1]

The crucial point here is that the system of recruiting talented men to office in the Bakufu government spread to the local provinces, causing an increase in domain-operated schools, where the practice of appointing officials by examinations was implemented. In this way, the enthusiasm for Confucian education spread even among the common people. A growing number of rural schools and private academies were set up, and these institutions became the basic infrastructure of Confucian learning in commoners' society. Miyagi calls this phenomenon "the popularization of Confucianism."[2] Moreover, as striking examples of "rich peasants and merchants from the rank of common people" who successfully gained autonomy through studying Confucian teachings, Miyagi lists such names as Bitō Nishū

尾藤二洲 (1745–1813), Rai Shunsui 頼春水 (1746–1816), Fujita Yūkoku 藤田幽谷 (1774–1826), and Yamada Hōkoku 山田方谷 (1805–77).[3]

Through this so-called popularization of Confucian teaching, a new group of elites that broke across social ranks was created, and some of these elites came to shoulder the social changes that swept Japan from the latter Edo period to the Meiji period. We should especially note here that although these elite scholars were officially trained in Zhu Xi learning (Shushigaku 朱子学), Satō Issai 佐藤一斎 (1772–1859), the head of the Shōheikō, for instance, is said to have practiced "Zhu Xi's teaching in public, Wang Yangming's in private" 公朱私王—a stance also known as "the *yang* of Zhu and the *yin* of Wang" 陽朱陰王. This shows that along with the study of Zhu Xi, the study of Wang Yangming's teaching (Yōmeigaku 陽明学) formed another important source of the education of the elites. It is known that Yamada Hōkoku and his colleagues, mentioned above, took Yōmeigaku seriously. These men who embraced Yōmeigaku did not directly participate in the Meiji Restoration, however. The connections between the Restoration and Yōmeigaku would arise much later.

2. THE NISHŌGAKUSHA AND MODERN CONFUCIANISM—MISHIMA CHŪSHŪ AND THE DOCTRINE OF THE UNIFICATION OF MORALITY AND PROFIT

In the Meiji period (1868–1912), Confucianism became actively employed as the effective means for modernization. This occurred in such a way that one can talk about a Confucianized Japan for the first time, but it is more accurate to say that Confucianism was used as the indispensable constructing principle to building the modern nation-state of Japan. In concrete terms, Confucianism became the ethical and religious discipline that forged the Japanese people into national subjects.

In order to see how this took place, we may do well to take up the case of the school, Nishōgakusha 二松学舎. It was originally a private academy of Chinese learning founded in 1877 by Mishima Chūshū 三島中洲 (1830–1919). Mishima, a student at Yamada Hōkoku's academy in his boyhood, traveled to Edo to study at the Shōheikō in adolescence, and later apprenticed himself under Satō Issai. Mishima's learning revolved around Yōmeigaku, and he was one of the major figures in Tokyo's Yōmeigaku academic society; he gave private lectures on this subject to the then crown prince (who became Emperor Taishō) for twenty successive years. Judging from the names of students who enrolled at the Nishōgakusha—such as Nakae Chōmin 中江兆民 (in 1880) and Natsume Sōseki 夏目漱石 (in 1881)—we may surmise that Yōmeigaku captured the hearts of many young Japanese men.

Sōseki, for instance, wrote an essay in Chinese entitled "The Idea That the Dwelling Place Affects How One Feels" (居移気説), when he was a first-year student in the literature department of the First Higher School (the essay is dated June 3, 1889). He wrote therein that he desired the state of "clear mind empty of desires" (*kyorei fumai* 虚霊不昧), which remained unaffected by the external environment.[4] The concept of the "clear mind empty of desires" goes back to Zhu Xi, but Sōseki took this idea from the *Records of Wang Yangming's Teachings*: *Chuanxilu* 伝習録 (J. *Denshūroku*), a passage in which it reads: "The clear mind empty of desire contains all principles and everything comes out of it. Outside this mind there is no principle; outside this mind there is no thing."

Mishima Chūshū was not a mere conservative who dreamt of reviving Chinese learning. He was a specialist of jurisprudence, and studied with the French scholar G. E. Boissonade (who was in Japan 1873–95). Mishima served actively as an expert on modern civil law after the French model. He believed that Confucianism had to be modernized in order to unite Japan and Western modernity. The slogan he developed was the "doctrine of the unification of moral righteousness and profit" (義利合一論 *giri gōitsuron*). He explained this as follows:

> Certainly, the study of moral righteousness (*gi* 義) and the universal principle (*ri* 理) has constituted learning so much so that it has become a cliché in the extreme. But this definition of learning is guilty of one crime. That is, during the Song dynasty in China, the flourishing of the discourse on moral righteousness and the universal principle led to the neglect of discourse on profit and loss. This led the ordinary people to view Confucian scholars to be only concerned with moral righteousness and principle and indifferent to profit and loss. However, actually, the words of ancient sages have it that moral righteousness and the universal principle are not inimical to the discussion on profit and loss. Therefore, I propose the doctrine of the unification of moral righteousness and profit (*ri* 利), in the hope of redressing the oversight of the past.[5]

As seen from this excerpt, Mishima criticized the Confucianism of Song Dynasty, in particular Zhu Xi's thought, for having ignored the discussion on economic profit and having focused solely on morality and the universal principle. Mishima's strategy was to go back to the older Confucian texts, such as the words of Confucius and Mencius, to prove that the central tenets of Confucianism could be unified with economics without contradiction. Further:

> I firmly believe that just as in Heaven the universal principle and the vital force (*ki* 気) are one, so in the human realm the moral righteousness and profit are one; in Heaven the universal principle is the essential thrust of the vital force, while in the human realm moral righteousness is the essential thrust of profit. Because moral righteousness penetrates into the activity of making profit, depending on the interests in the situations and circumstances, it adopts itself in a myriad of ways and manifests its appropriateness in every situation. It is called "situational appropriateness" (*jichū* 時中) of Confucius. Thus if we wish to learn about it, we only need to bring together moral righteousness and profit.[6]

In short, by redefining moral righteousness as the integral principle of profit-making, Mishima sought to make clear that modern Western capitalism and the "original" Confucian teaching were not in conflict, but they may be deeply brought into one.

3. JAPANESE CAPITALISM AND CONFUCIANISM—SHIBUSAWA EIICHI

This timely interpretation of Confucianism was viewed as accommodating the emerging capitalism of Meiji Japan. In fact, Shibusawa Eiichi 渋沢栄一 (1840–1931), who was often called "the father of Japanese capitalism," was closely associated with Mishima Chūshū. Shibusawa's *Rongo to soroban* (*The* Analects *and the Abacus* 論語と算盤, 1916) is a book that symbolically represents the connection between Japanese capitalism and Confucianism. In the opening chapter, Shibusawa describes that he actually received encouragement from Mishima on the connection between the *Analects* and economic activities.

> One day the learned scholar Professor Mishima Ki [Chūshū] visited my house and saw the picture of the *Analects* and an abacus that hang on the wall. Being impressed by this, he said to me, "I'm a scholar of the *Analects*, while you are a specialist of abacus, and yet you so expertly discuss the *Analects*. It leads me to think that I, too, must endeavor to understand abacus. You and I should work together towards uniting the *Analects* and the abacus." … What constitutes the source of wealth must be the virtue of humanity, righteousness, and morality; if the wealth is devoid of moral principle, it will not endure long. For this reason, I take it our urgent task to unite these discrete subjects—the *Analects* and the abacus.[7]

As quoted above, Shibusawa noted that "what constitutes the source of wealth must be the virtue of humanity, righteousness, and morality; if the wealth is devoid of moral principle, it will not long endure"—a statement that argues strongly for moral virtue to support the economic activities. This line of thought takes the same track as Mishima's doctrine of "unity of moral righteousness and profit." Shibusawa formulated this idea into "the unity of morality and economic activities" 道徳経済合一説 (*dōtoku keizai gōitsusetsu*) and propounded it.

This idea developed by Shibusawa may remind us of Max Weber's monumental work *The Protestant Ethic and the Spirit of Capitalism* (1905), which featured Benjamin Franklin as the person who embodied secular asceticism in relation to American Protestantism. Shibusawa introduces a comparable "Japanese Benjamin Franklin," about whom he had heard from his father in his youth many a time.

> This is an anecdote that I heard from my father many times as a life's lesson in my childhood. It is about a most industrious old man who lived near my ancestor's home . . .
>
> This old man used to say: "Nothing delights me more than learning about things through my work and purifying myself into a better person. I consider my work the ultimate bliss in my life. While I engage in my work, 'leftovers' of my work pile up—what they call money and material possessions. But I do not necessarily work for the sake of accumulating the 'leftovers,' and in fact they do not occupy my mind … My father's point was that people in modern days pay attention only to success or failure, forgetting the far more important principle;

> they are unable to live a life dedicated to the principles in the world, and tend to consider the leftover stuff as wealth and the main goal of life. Should not they feel ashamed of themselves in the face of this simple old man?"[8]

While Franklin spoke of time as money, denied every kind of useless diversion, avoided idleness, and regarded his work as the vocation performed for the sake of receiving divine grace, the old man in Shibusawa's anecdote considered his labor as "purifying" himself, that is, his work improved him as a person in a moral and religious sense, and "wealth" was merely a secondary outcome of that process. With regards to "profit," Shibusawa's Protestant-sounding doctrine of "unification of morality and economic activities" is not completely in line with Mishima's "unity of moral righteousness and profit" that asserts that moral righteousness as the core principle of profit (economic gain). Even so, I have sought to draw attention to how the modern interpretation of Confucianism in Japan provided an economic ethics, or perhaps one could say that it functioned as a secular religion that supported capitalism.

4. INOUE TETSUJIRŌ AND MODERN YŌMEIGAKU

Mishima Chūshū with Shibusawa Eiichi were actually closely involved in the annual Sekiten celebration held at the Yushima Seidō. The Shibunkai, which has hosted this annual event for the past one hundred years, has the Shibun Gakkai 斯文学会 (established in 1880) as its predecessor. Mishima was one of its founders, and Shibusawa participated in it as an advisor. This group evolved into the Shibunkai in 1918 through the merger of the Kenkeikai 研経会, the Tōa Gakujutsu Kenkyūkai 東亜学術研究会, and the Kanbun Gakkai 漢文学会. In 1919, two more societies—the Kōshi Saitenkai 孔子祭典会 (funded in 1907) and the Kōshikyōkai 孔子教会—also came under its umbrella.

The revival of the Sekiten festival in modern Japan was actually initiated by the Kōshi Saitenkai, of which Mishima and Shibusawa were directors. This group revived the Sekiten celebration in 1907, after it had been discontinued since the last years of the Edo period. They continued to hold this annual event until 1919, when they merged with the Shibunkai, as mentioned above. During that time, Mishima served four times as the head priest of the rites, and Shibusawa lectured twice. The Shibunkai inherited the Sekiten festival from the Kōshi Saitenkai after their merger.

The Shibunkai boasted such core members as Inoue Tetsujirō 井上哲次郎 (1855–1944) and Hattori Unokichi 服部宇之吉 (1867–1939), who were the next generation to succeed Mishima and Shibusawa. An examination of Inoue and Hattori's thought will further clarify the unique characteristics of modern Japanese Confucianism.

Inoue Tetsujirō, a professor of philosophy at the Tokyo Imperial University, lectured on modern Western philosophy with a focus on Kant, but he also constructed a framework of interpretation of Confucianism to make it relevant to the modern period. Inoue authored the *Chokugo engi* 勅語衍義 (1891), the manual that commented on the *Imperial Rescript on Education* 教育勅語, which further shows his central role in establishing the moral foundations of modern Japan.[9] It was Inoue's view that Confucianism, in particular Yōmeigaku, could contribute significantly in formulating a modern moral foundation. He also wrote a three-part treatise on Edo-period Confucianism: the *Nihon Yōmeigakuha no tetsugaku* (日本陽明学派之哲学 or the "Philosophy of Japanese Wang Yangming Studies"), the *Nihon kogakuha no tetsugaku* (日本古学派之哲学 or the "Philosophy of Japanese Studies of Original Confucianism"), and the *Nihon Shushigakuha no tetsugaku* (日本朱子学派之哲学 or the "Philosophy of Japanese Zhu Xi Studies").[10] Let us look at the preface to the first of this trilogy, the *Nihon Yōmeigakuha no tetsugaku*:

> If one wishes to understand what the virtue of our country is, one must understand the spirit of moral teaching that have forged our national character. This treatise being on the philosophy of Japan's Yōmeigaku, one may ask what may be its contribution to the Japan's national moral character. The expression of our people's virtue may be witnessed in how our army behaves in China. Among the allied forces presently in China, what does distinguish the Japanese army from the rest? The Japanese army refrains from arbitrary plunder and wanton violence, keeps strict observance of military discipline, and is never motivated by the desire for private gain. If this is not the manifestation of our national character, what is it?[11]

Here Inoue argued that Japan's Yōmeigaku was in fact what had forged modern Japan's "national morality" (*kokumin-teki dōtokushin* 国民的道徳心), and spoke proudly of how it was clearly displayed by the actions of the Japanese army, which was then fighting in the Eight-Nation Alliance to suppress the peasant uprising of the Boxer Rebellion that erupted in June of that year, 1900. Furthermore, the preface closes with the statement: "The virtue of our people is nothing but the universal virtue of the mind (*shintoku* 心徳), and the universal virtue of the mind can be said to be precisely the essence of Oriental morality (*tōyō dōtoku* 東洋道徳)."[12] Inoue considered Japan's Yōmeigaku to have shaped Japanese moral character, and thereby it merited being accorded a universal dimension.

The emphasis Inoue gives to Yōmeigaku did not remain within the confines of building the foundations of national morality. In his work, Inoue delineates a genealogy of Japanese scholars belonging to the lineage of Yōmeigaku, starting with Nakae Tōju 中江藤樹 (1608–48) and Kumazawa Banzan 熊沢蕃山 (1619–91), moving on to Satō Issai (mentioned above), Ōshio Chūsai (Heihachirō) 大塩中斎 (平八郎) (1793–1837), Yamada Hōkoku (mentioned above), Kasuga Sen'an 春日潜庵 (1811–78), and concluding with Saigō Takamori 西郷隆盛 (1828–77), Yoshida Shōin 吉田松陰 (1830–59), and Takasugi Shinsaku 高杉晋作 (1839–67). It is of profound interest that Katsu Kaishū 勝海舟 (1823–99), who acted on behalf of the Tokugawa Shogunate at the time of the surrender of political power to the emperor, is mentioned as the final figure to complete this genealogy. In short, Inoue attempted to establish the connection between the Yōmeigaku of the latter Edo period and the Meiji Restoration by implying that the Meiji Restoration was actually the embodiment of the ideas developed by the thinkers belonging to Yōmeigaku.

This interpretation of Yōmeigaku as the true spirit of the Meiji Restoration spread widely, and became a view shared even by modern Chinese intellectuals. Ogyū Shigehiro sums it up as follows:

> After Japan's war with Qing China, the Qing imperial government implemented policies of modernization after the fashion of the Meiji Restoration, and many Chinese exchange students were sent to Japan. Moreover, exiled officials and revolutionaries also made Japan the base of their activities. Liang Qichao梁啓超, Zhang Binglin章炳麟, and even Sun Wen 孫文 (Sun Yat-sen), were examples of these people. They "discovered" Yōmeigaku, then popular in Japan, and brought home to China the view that Yōmeigaku constituted the driving force of the Meiji Restoration.[13]

According to Ogyū, the modern Japanese Yōmeigaku "discovered" by the Chinese exchange students can be described as "a modern ideology formulated in the environment of Japanese nationalist thought, as the backlash of two decades of Meiji government's policy of westernization. It was a political theory that was artificially constructed by reflecting the demands of the time in history."[14]

This interpretation of modern Japanese Yōmeigaku was most clearly demonstrated by two books, both published in 1893 (the twenty-sixth year of Meiji). One was entitled *Yoshida Shōin* (吉田松陰) by Tokutomi Sohō 徳富蘇峰 (1863–1957), and published by Min'yūsha; and the other was *Ō Yōmei* (王陽明) by Miyake Setsurei 三宅雪嶺 (1860–1945), and published by Seikyōsha. Also reflecting this trend, a journal, *Yōmeigaku* 陽明学, was serialized by the Tekka Shoin Company 鉄華書院 from 1896 through 1900; it was superseded by another journal, *Ōgaku zasshi* 王学雑誌 (published by Meizen Gakusha, 1906–1908), and finally by yet another journal, *Yōmeigaku* (published by Meizen Gakusha 明善学舎, which changed its name to Yōmei Gakkai 陽明学会, 1908–28). (Note: Shibusawa Eiichi was a sponsor of Yōmei Gakkai.) Each one of these publications was an attempt to position Yōmeigaku as the foundation of Japanese "national morality."[15] Inoue Tetsujirō's discourse is therefore to be situated within this genealogy of modern Japanese Yōmeigaku.[16]

5. HATTORI UNOKICHI AND KŌSHIKYŌ ("CONFUCIUS'S TEACHING")

Hattori Unokichi, like Inoue Tetsujirō, was a professor at the Tokyo Imperial University and lectured on Chinese philosophy. The role Hattori played within modern Japanese Confucianism is that he removed any religious elements from Confucianism to render it a purely moral code, fit not only for the nation-state but also for the Empire of Japan.

This attempt by Hattori is to be viewed in contrast to the opposite movement that was taking place in China, where Kang Youwei 康有為 and his colleagues were advocating Confucianism as a religion. Theirs was a movement to redefine Confucianism as a religion comparable to Christianity, and make it the spiritual backbone of modern China. Hattori was very aware of this, and took the exact opposite approach in promoting a Confucianism that was devoid of religiousness, by upholding Confucius's teaching as a doctrine of moral code. Hattori called his a-religious view as "Confucius's teaching" or "Kōshikyō 孔子教." These clashing approaches revolved around the interpretation of the following passage in *The Analects* (7.35):

> Confucius's illness grew worse. Zilu said that he would pray for him. Confucius said: "Was there such a thing as prayer?" Zilu answered: "Yes. The *Eulogies* say: 'I pray for you to the gods of heaven and earth.'" Confucius said: "Then I have long been praying."[17]

Some traditional commentaries on this passage interpret this passage to mean that Confucius's disciple Zilu 子路 attempted to offer a prayer to the gods to wish for his master's recovery, but Confucius rejected his offer. The problem is how to interpret the final line of Confucius, "I have long been praying."

Hattori, who promoted a specifically nonreligious interpretation in modern Japanese Confucianism, interpreted these words to mean that "because Confucius believed his conduct to have been constantly in accord with the morality of the deities of heaven and earth, he told Zilu that even though he was now ailing, there was no need to pray now."[18] In other words, this interpretation suggests that Confucius does not actually pray but takes the content of Zilu's offer to be that of "aligning oneself with the morality of gods," which was something he had already been doing for a long time. It is a reading tracing back to Kong Anguo's 孔安国 and Zhu Xi's 朱熹 commentaries, but Hattori adopted it in order to counter the interpretation taken by Kang Youwei and his colleagues who adhered to Confucianism as a religion and their Church of Confucius (孔教会).

According to Hattori, Kang Youwei and his colleagues had "twisted" this passage on prayer in order to give Confucianism a religious quality. That is, in order to elevate "prayer" as the central practice within the Church of Confucius,[19] they interpret the line on "I have long been praying" to mean that "Confucius actually prayed."[20] Over against this religious reading, Hattori upheld that "granted, almost all 'religions' of today contain prayer as their central praxis, but Confucius himself actually completely rejected prayer."[21] Hattori took the position strongly opposed to making Confucianism into a religion, based on the claim that Confucian teaching of moral code rejects the practice of prayer.

Thus, Kōshikyō (or "Confucius's Teaching") that Hattori advocated was the veneration of Confucius's teaching, strictly in its ethical and moral aspects and devoid of any religious overtone. Hattori elaborated on this point:

> Originally, Confucianism developed in tandem with the Chinese people's experiences, and its ethnic colouring was its most striking characteristic. Therefore it could not be extended to other peoples who had different historical experiences, as well as different customs and dispositions. An ethnic doctrine cannot be a universal doctrine. Now Confucius was active during the Spring and Autumn period, and through his work of assembling and organizing the teachings of ancient sages, he transformed the ethnic doctrines into a universal doctrine. What has spread to various parts of East Asia, and is on the verge of dissemination into Europe and America today, is actually this Confucius's Teaching and not the old Confucianism.[22]

In Hattori's view, Confucius transformed the old Confucianism, which was "an ethnic doctrine" or "folk doctrine," into Confucius's Teaching (Kōshikyō) as "a universal doctrine," and on account of its universality it spread to other parts of Asia. Be that as it may, how was this transformation of Confucianism possible? On this point, Hattori maintains that the old Confucianism was religious, but as Confucius's Teaching became more rational and ethical, as its religious elements disappeared."[23] Confucianism as "Confucius's Teaching" attained its universality through its philosophical and ethical contents. It follows then that religious elements such as prayer must be extricated from Confucianism by all means. In succeeding in this venture Kōshikyō will be accepted universally, and moreover it would allow non-Chinese people, such as the Japanese, to uphold and spread Confucius's teaching instead of China. Behind Hattori's emphasis on the philosophical and ethical dimensions of Confucius's Teaching, one notices that there was Japan's imperial ambition to elevate its presence to a universal height.[24]

Chen Wei-fen analyzes the consequences of Hattori's view of Confucianism as follows:

> One could say that he [Hattori] chose to court the political authority, passively because he did not want to deviate from the framework of the emperor system, and actively as an educator and intellectual who harbored the ardent sense of mission to uphold the spiritual identity of the people under the imperial system. That his thought had such a starting point can be seen in his formulation of Confucius's Teaching (*Kōshikyō*), which he advocated during the Taishō and Shōwa periods. But it was too narrowly constrained by the political realities of the time, so that it failed to develop into a system of thought that allowed plurality and diversity. Because he aligned himself too closely with the ideology of the emperor system of the [Japanese] nation-state, his assertions reveal a marked lack of flexibility as an intellectual construction. But Confucianism contains political and social elements, as it upholds the idea to "refine oneself to govern the people"; since its beginnings, Confucianism had always contained a deep link to socio-political affairs. In the face of this strong tradition of praxis, a Japanese approach to Chinese studies was indeed an alternate option from the Meiji period onwards.[25]

The most politically charged event that took place in connection with Hattori's interpretation of Confucian philosophy, which Chen points out as being too closely aligned with the ideology of the emperor system of the Japanese nation-state, is probably the "Great Symposium on Confucianism" (*Judō taikai* 儒道大会) held in 1935 at the Yushima Seidō.[26] Organized to commemorate the completion of the reconstruction of the Yushima Seidō destroyed in the Great Kantō Earthquake, scholars were invited from the Japanese colonies of Korea and Taiwan, but also from Manchuria and China, with the aim of building a theoretical apparatus of East Asian peace based on "the Confucian Way" (*judō* 儒道). At that time, Hattori was the vice president of the Shibunkai and also the director of the Japan-Manchuria Cultural Association, and he gave the following address at the closing ceremony:

> Enthusiastic interest in Oriental Studies, that got fermented during World War [I] and spread across various parts of the world following the conclusion of the war, is blossoming today. By the "Oriental culture" what is meant is the Chinese civilization as well as what was introduced to Japan and assimilated by the Japanese people and became the integral part of its culture. It is of common knowledge that Oriental culture has the Confucian Way (*judō* 儒道) at the foundation. Since the introduction of Confucian Way to Japan, it got blended with the Great Way of venerating the native gods 惟神の大道, nourished the foundation of the Japanese spirit, helped to give birth to great saintly figures, and contributed greatly to the three major political shakeups of the Taika Reforms [645 CE], the Kenmu Restoration [1333–35], and the Meiji Restoration [1868]. Presently, there are different views of what the Confucian Way is, when considering its historical importance in our country, and while looking to the future of the world, I believe that the specialists from different countries gathered here to freely exchange their views about the Confucian Way will transcend politics and economics issues and differences, and will no doubt contribute greatly to achieving world peace.[27]

For Hattori, the core parts of the Oriental cultures that became the subject of the Oriental studies borne of the First World War consisted of the "Chinese culture" and Japan's "ethnic spirit," and their fusion that created the "Confucian Way." This "Confucian Way" was not only effective in supporting the modern Japanese nation-state and the ideology of the emperor system but it was also expected to contribute greatly to the realization of world peace in the crisis-ridden period immediately following the First World War. The rhetoric here was that insofar as this "Confucian Way" was the conceptual achievement of the Japanese thinkers, world peace was also something that was rendered possible by the initiative of Japan as the empire.

6. TAIWAN AND JAPANESE CONFUCIANISM

The term "Confucian Way" (*judō*) is still in use today in the Sekiten festival celebrated at the Confucius Temple in Taipei. In the beginning of this chapter, I made a special reference to the fact that a Taiwanese representative was among those who took part in the Sekiten ceremony of 2015 at Yushima Seidō in Tokyo. This bespeaks the close connection that existed between the Japanese Empire of the pre–Second World War period and the colonial Taiwan; it also touches on the normalization of Mainland China-Japan relations of 1972 that broke up the formal ties with Taiwan, and its repercussions felt in various sectors in Japan.

As we saw above, modern Japanese Confucianism was an ideology closely tied with the pre–Second World War Japanese Empire. Let us consider this point via the case study of Taiwan.[28] At the Sekiten ceremony held on September 28, 2011, in the Confucius Temple in Taipei, important officials were in attendance, including the interior minister Jiang Yi-Huah 江宜樺 as the deputy of President Ma Ying-jeou 馬英九, the mayor of Taipei Hau Lung-pin 郝龍斌, with Kung Tsui-chang 孔垂長, the seventy-ninth direct descendent of Confucius, officiating the rites. It may appear that this guest list seems to violate the principle of the separation of church and state, but that was not the perception of the locals, who did not see it as a religious ceremony but as one that reflected the traditional practice. It can be readily discerned that this reasoning is identical with the one that supported the Sekiten ceremony in pre–Second World War Japan.

Confucius Temple in Taipei has a complicated history.[29] It was initially built under the auspices of the Qing Dynasty government from 1879 to 1884; but during the Sino-Japanese War of 1894, it was destroyed by the Japanese troops and the Sekiten festival was also discontinued. However, in January 1917, the Ying Society 瀛社, the association of Taiwanese poets, and the Taishō Kyōkai 大正協会, an organization established to promote the rapport between the peoples of Taiwan and Japan, together founded the Sūseikai 崇聖会 and began worshipping Confucius in schools. This was the result of the coming together of the interest of the Japanese colonial bureau and the Taiwanese power-holders. The chief architect of this movement was Kimura Tadashi 木村匡. Kimura was a colleague of Isawa Shūji 伊沢修二 working in the Taiwan government-general; Isawa was also a member of the aforementioned Kōshi Saitenkai, the organization that was absorbed into the Shibunkai. The restoration of the Taipei Confucius Temple began in 1927, and by 1930 it was almost complete. At that time the Sekiten ceremony was revived. In 1940, the Taiwan government-general issued the orders that the ritual procedures used at the Yasukuni Shrine in Tokyo be incorporated into the Sekiten ceremony.

In the post–Second World War period, the Sekiten ceremony continued under the auspices of the Sūseikai, sponsored by the mayoral office of the city of Taipei. In 1950, then president Chiang Kai-shek (or Jiang Jieshi) 蒋介石 presented them with a framed tablet of his own calligraphy. The basic ritual protocol was set in place at that time, but some elements from the pre–Second World War days remained. A fundamental change took place in 1972, when the relations between Japan and mainland China were normalized, which severed the official ties between Japan and Taiwan. This move displeased several private civil groups in Japan, and led them several years later to send their own delegates annually to the Taipei Confucius Temple.

One of these Japanese private groups is the Rongo Fukyūkai 論語普及会, spearheaded by Yasuoka Masahiro 安岡正篤 (1892–1983). Yasuoka, a scholar of modern Japanese Yōmeigaku, became well known for his thesis *Studies on Wang Yangming*, which he wrote before his graduation from the Department of Law at the Tokyo Imperial University. In the prewar period, he had exercised great influence on the group of officials called the "new bureaucrats" through his private school, the Kinkei Gakuin 金鶏学院, and the association called Kokuikai 国維会 (1932–34). After the war, Yasuoka formed close ties with Kung Te-cheng 孔徳成 (1920–2008), the seventy-seventh direct descendent of Confucius. In 1935 Kung Te-cheng had actually declined to attend the Symposium of the "Confucian Way" (*judō*) held in Japan because he eschewed to be politically manipulated, but after the Second World War, he enthusiastically cultivated the ties with Japan and attended the tercentenary festival at the Yushima Seidō in 1990.

The other group that sends delegation from Japan to the Confucius Temple in Taipei is the Institute for Moral Research 道徳科学研究所 associated with Hiroike Chikurō 廣池千九郎 (1866–1938), an educator who had promoted "scientific morality," or "Moralogy." Kung Te-cheng's first visit to Japan took place in 1957 at the invitation of this institute.

One must admit then that the legacy of pre–Second World War Japanese Confucianism that emphasized national morality and Yōmeigaku still remains robustly in Taiwan, the former Japanese colony. For instance, in 1966 Chiang Kai-shek launched a movement to revive the Chinese culture, in which he emphasized Confucian teachings and advocated that Taiwan is *the* legitimate heir of the authentic Chinese culture. It is interesting that the pre–Second World War imperial Japanese view of Confucianism was quite similar to this idea.

7. NAKAE CHŌMIN AND "RED YŌMEIGAKU"

As we have seen above, modern Japanese Confucianism envisioned by Inoue Tetsujirō and Hattori Unokichi constituted one "option" for Japan, mentioned by Chen Wei-fen. Yet there were other options for Japanese Confucianism. Apart from the possibility of building a national Confucian teaching that molded people's moral character into the subjects of the modern nation, another option was the promotion of a popular Confucianism rooted in the people, removing the boundaries imposed on them as subjects of a modern nation-state.

It was Nakae Chōmin 中江兆民 (1847–1901) who kept his spirit of criticism alive and was not afraid to remark: "I am constantly dissatisfied with the Meiji society."[30] He was unhappy with the kind of society that modern Japan was striving to build. In terms of generation, Nakae falls between Shibusawa Eiichi and Inoue Tetsujirō. Nakae in his youth studied Yōmeigaku from Okunomiya Zōsai 奥宮慥斎 (1811–77), who had known Ōshio Heihachirō (mentioned above). Nakae also studied Yōmeigaku with Mishima Chūshū at the Nishō Gakusha in Tokyo. Nakae's Confucianism was not the official learning propagated by the Meiji government, but the Confucian learning for the ordinary common people that was formed in the latter part of the Edo period.

Nakae's student Kōtoku Shūsui 幸徳秋水, and his friend, Okunomiya Kenshi (or Takeyuki) 奥宮健之 (the third son of Okunomiya Zōsai), were implicated in the Great Treason Incident 大逆事件 of 1910, and executed for their part in 1911. They were executed not simply because they were socialists but because they promoted "Red Yōmeigaku,"[31] which allegedly harbored the view of revolution by the commoners. Interestingly, Inoue Tetsujirō, who supported the ideology of Confucianism as the official governmental learning, in fact saw the spirit of Yōmeigaku could be connected to socialism.[32]

Nakae, having studied French philosophy and especially Jean-Jacques Rousseau, believed that a philosophy had to be linked to social concerns, to the Yōmeigaku of the populace. Therefore, in his indignation at social injustices of discrimination practiced against the "*buraku* people 部落民," he severely criticized the official Confucianism represented by Inoue Tetsujirō. In his *Ichinen yūhan* (A year and a half 一年有半),[33] he wrote:

> Since ancient times, there was no philosophy in Japan ... Recently a certain Katō [Hiroyuki] and an Inoue [Tetsujirō] fashion themselves as the model of philosophers, and although society at large allow them to pass as such, the truth is that they merely import Western ideas and theories that they have studied ..., and thereby claim themselves to be philosophers.[34]

Then what was "philosophy" for Nakae? For him its ideal form was *rigaku* 理学 (science of the principle), devoid of any religious elements. After the publication of his *Ichinen yūhan*, his *Zoku ichinen yūhan* 続一年有半 followed as a sequel to the former in 1901, with the alternate title of "No God, No Soul" (*mushin mureikon* 無神無霊魂). Therein Nakae asserted in the name of philosophy that he was advocating "purely material theory, which had nothing to do with Buddhas, Gods, and the spirit."[35]

> Notorious bandits like Dao Zhi 盜跖, who ravage people and run rampant in acts of cruelty, live long, while sages like Yan Hui 顔回 perish young. When I see gangster camouflaging as gentlemen thrive and prosper in this world, while those who keep to the ways of righteousness die without so much as the lees of wine, it is welcome news for the majority of the people that in the future we will have a court of justice that will meet out justice. For those of us like myself, who are so ill that whose time on earth is ticking every minute, to be able to believe in the existence of just God or the immortality of the soul would be a great comfort. But then, how would we justify the solemn reality of philosophy? What are we to do with the needed qualification of a philosopher who rationally exercises the power of reason and observe things as they are? I have lived for fifty-five years, and read a few books and understood a few principles, but unfortunately I do not have the luxury to indulge in sleep talking concerning the existence of God or the immortality of the soul.[36]

What Nakae meant by philosophy was the theory of the matter, or materialism. It aimed at attaining a view of thoroughgoing equality beyond the distinctions not only among people but also between human beings and animals. For Nakae, the official doctrine (*kangaku* 官学), as espoused by Inoue et al., attempted to link philosophy and religion surreptitiously. Even though they declared that their Confucianism was not a religion but a moral code, Nakae sensed that in that moral code lurked a religious character, one that deified the Emperor. In its stead, Nakae who had been influenced by French thought that protected civil rights, longed for a republican society made up of common ordinary people.

Accordingly, Confucianism, too, had to contribute to the civil ideology. It was Osaka Yōmei Gakkai that thoroughly pursued this direction under the helm of Ishizaki Tōgoku.

8. THE OSAKA YŌMEI GAKKAI AND THE "CIVIL FOUNDATION"

The Osaka Yōmei Gakkai was an academic society established by Ishizaki Tōgoku 石崎東国 (1873–1931) in June of 1907 with the official name of Senshindō Gakkai 洗心洞学会, taking after the name of the private school "Senshindō" run by Ōshio

Chūsai (Heihachirō). It changed its name to Osaka Yōmei Gakkai 大阪陽明学会 in December 1908. Its flagship magazine, *Yōmei* 陽明, was serialized from July 1910, and changed its name to *Yōmei-shugi* 陽明主義 in 1919.

The issue of *Yōmei* published on December 5, 1911, was devoted to the memory of Nakae Chōmin, and carried a photograph of him on its cover along with a reprint of chapter 6 of Nakae's *Min'yaku yakukai* 民約訳解 (The *Social Contract* translated into Japanese), with these words of Ishizaki:

> It has been a full ten years since the passing of Master Nakae Chōmin, the Meiji scholar of Yōmeigaku, who for fifty-five years fought so gallantly for the social welfare of the people. December 13 of this year marks the tenth anniversary of his death. Our association cannot help but express our admiration of the master in view of the present state of society. Therefore, we have put together this commemorative volume.[37]

To begin with, this issue was not intended simply to commemorate the tenth anniversary of Nakae Chōmin's death. It was Tōgoku's rebuttal against Inoue Tetsujirō, who had characterized him as harboring "dangerous thoughts." Tōgoku had expressed his concern for Kōtoku Shūsui and Okunomiya Kenshi, mentioned above, who had been arrested and imprisoned (in May 1910), with the alleged charge of the assassination plot of the emperor, an incident that came to be known as the "Great Treason Incident."[38] While these men were still in prison, Tōgoku wrote that his "sense of desolation is hard to bear" (July 29, 1910). At that time he also made a reference to Chōmin.[39] In this commemorative volume two full pages were dedicated to Chōmin's tract *Shinmin Sekai* 新民世界, which he wrote in 1889, assuming the vantage point a "new commoner," which was the Meiji term coined to designate those born into outcast communities (*hisabetsu burakumin* 被差別部落民). It was a strident declaration of Tōgoku that the Yōmeigaku he believed in belonged to Chōmin's lineage. Ogyū Shigehiro summarizes the situation as follows:

> The Osaka Yōmei Gakkai from its inception had been labeled by Inoue Tetsujirō as harboring a "dangerous ideology," which "while externally hoists [Wang Yangming's] 'putting conscience into action' (*chiryōchi* 致良知, ch. *zhiliangzhi*), inwardly promotes socialism." Tōgoku, however, turned the table around on Inoue, emboldened by the Great Treason Incident. He decided to make their journal available at regular bookstores, and reconstructed the genealogy of Nakae Chōmin and Kōtoku Shūsui as the genuine Meiji-era Yōmeigaku. He criticized the Yōmeigaku of Inoue and others as the "government learning" and "the government's ancillary," that deviated from the true spirit of Yōmeigaku. He actively promoted the association's activities that went against the current of the time.[40]

Ogyū Shigehiro finds the possibility of interpreting the position of Osaka Yōmei Gakkai in terms of the Confucianism of the people, in that "it took the daily problems of the masses as its main focus, and revived this focus in line with the modern rhetoric of international solidarity in pacifism, which transcended the parochial boundaries of nation-state."[41] His understanding sheds light on the existence of the civil foundation, different from that of the nation-state sought by Inoue Tetsujirō.[42] In short, the Osaka Yōmei Gakkai belonged to the stream of "popularization of Confucianism" that took place in the latter part of Edo period.

9. RELIGIOUS YŌMEIGAKU

Another thing I wish to note is that the Osaka Yōmei Gakkai progressively took on a religious characteristic. Already on June 13, 1909, Ishizaki had made the following "Declaration of the Yōmei Sect" 陽明宗宣言, which read:

> Our Yōmei Sect (*Yōmeishū* 陽明宗) is not a dead religion, but a living way of humanity. Yōmeigaku is no empty philosophy but is of action. Its direct simplicity shows the reason why it is a teaching based on the [lives of] common people. It, as a modern religion, worships labor.[43]

Here Ishizaki points out that in the post–Meiji Restoration period, the way of humanity dwindled and people were oppressed under a materialistic civilization, and he prophesized that a forthcoming revolution would be accomplished by the innate discernment of goodness (*ryōchi* 良知). His manner of speaking began to bear a Christian overtone. The opening of Ishizaki's address read as follows:

> This is the declaration of our Yōmei Sect. The reason why we, although unworthy, rely on the spirit of Heaven, honor the order of the master, and declare this Sect as a religion stems from the unceasing "innate discernment of goodness" that resides in our hearts. Now, in the following, I shall describe its founder, Wang Yangming, followed by a brief history and the basic tenet of our religion, the cruel hardships our apostles underwent as well as their glorious achievements. I shall also delineate the heavenly calling of the Yōmei Sect in the modern day, what apostles should and should not do. This is the declaration of the Yōmei Sect. Because this religion stands on the foundation of "innate discernment of goodness," this declaration is the outcry of this conscience. The outcry of this conscience is the gospel that comes from Heaven. Ah, how desolate the way of humanity has grown, but the revolution is approaching. Come together, you people, and listen to the heavenly tidings![44]

What the members of the Osaka Yōmei Gakkai aimed at was different from the actualization of Nakae Chōmin's republican society or socialism. Instead, they desired a society that was based on Yōmeigaku, while deeply influenced by Christianity. In such society people would attain self-awakening of their conscience, or innate discernment of goodness, and each would aspire to become a sage. Ishizaki continued:

> Human beings attain independence from machinery only when they become aware that they possess conscience, or innate discernment of goodness, and only then they become free from the prison of their habits. They can place material things under their own human control. Herein they find genuine life and freedom. If human beings attain freedom and independence, even if they are not sages, they can come close to being sages.[45]

Such a construction of society based on a religious interpretation of Confucianism would surely have posed troubles for those who wished to make the national morality out of Confucianism. Not only had Inoue Tetsujirō harshly criticized this kind of movement, but also Takase Takejirō 高瀬武次郎, a professor of Kyoto Imperial University, and who initially supported the Osaka Yōmei Gakkai as its core member, ended up breaking his association with Ishizaki.

Regardless of that, it is good to remember that modern Japanese Confucianism had the opportunity to embrace an alternate option. Alongside officially sanctioned Confucianism of the state, there also existed Confucianism that supported the ordinary people, even if its theoretical formulation was rather roughly hewn.

CONCLUDING REMARKS

Japanese Confucianism, galvanized by its popularization during the last part of the Edo period, developed into a moral ideology that supported the nation-state and the Empire of Japan during the Meiji period. Its core teachings were based on the Wang Yangming's branch of Confucianism (Yōmeigaku), which effectively cultivated and molded the hearts of the Japanese people into the nation's subjects. But at the same time, another alternative existed for Japanese Confucianism. This was the stream of populist or civil Confucianism, which tended to bear religious characteristics.

I have frequently cited Ogyū Shigehiro, who is one of the leading scholars of contemporary studies on Yōmeigaku. He is actually the descendant of Ogyū Sorai 荻生徂徠 (1666–1728), the prominent Confucian scholar of the mid-Edo period. It is interesting to learn that Sorai did discuss the religious character of Confucianism, and commented on the controversial passage that we saw above, dealing with the question of whether or not Confucius actually prayed (cf. *The Analects* 7.35: "I have long been praying"). On this point, Ogyū Sorai's commentary reads:

> Prayer issues forth from one's respect for Heaven. For a man of virtue to honor Heaven is like a filial son to honor his parents. A filial son apologizes if his parents get angry at him, but without asking whether or not he was at any fault, because he simply respects his parents. A man of virtue prays to Heaven when natural calamities occur, without questioning whether or not he was at fault, because he simply respects Heaven.[46]

From a larger perspective that transcends humanity, even if one feels that one has been virtuous, it still may be that one is in the wrong or one's deeds may be insufficient, and, moreover, in the case of natural disasters taken as the expressions of Heaven's wrath, there is nothing human beings can do but pray. This attitude of reverence for Heaven was the attitude Confucius always cultivated—such is Sorai's interpretation of this passage.

It goes without saying then that Hattori Unokichi rejected Sorai's reading of the *Analects* with these words: "I am of the opinion that Sorai tends to adopt strange examples in his commentary, and he has the penchant for idiosyncrasy."[47] Sorai's interpretation was banished by the Kansei Edict of 1790, and in the Meiji period his interpretation was banished again by elite scholars who upheld Confucianism as a governmental ideology.

The religious, populist, and socially critical aspects of Confucianism, however, cannot simply be suppressed and silenced for good. Reevaluation of Japanese Confucianism as intellectual heritage opens up this alternate possibility before us.

NOTES

1. Miyagi Kimiko, *Bakumatsuki no shisō to shūzoku* (Tokyo: Perikansha, 2004), 24.
2. Ibid. 27.
3. Ibid., 28.
4. Natsume Sōseki, "*Kyoikisetsu*," compiled in *Natsume Sōseki Zenshū* (Tokyo: Iwanami Shoten, 1995), 18.505.
5. Mishima Chūshū, *Chūshū kōwa* [Chūshū's lectures] (Tokyo: Bunkadō, 1909). This is his public lecture delivered on October 10, 1886, at the Tokyo Academy (*Gakushikaiin*).
6. Ibid., 20.
7. Shibusawa Eiichi, *Rongo to soroban* [The *Analects* and the Abacus] (Tokyo: Kokusho Kankōkai, 1985), 2–3.
8. Shibusawa, *Keizai to dōtoku* [Economy and morality] (Tokyo: Nihon Keizai Dōtoku Kyōkai, 1953), 66–67.
9. Winston Davis describes Inoue's idea of establishing the moral foundations of modern Japan as the "civil theology" that is the "articulation of civil religion by the elite." See Winston Davis, "The Civil Theology of Inoue Tetsujirō," *Japanese Journal of Religious Studies* 3.1 (1976), 5–6.
10. They were published by the publisher Fuzanbō in Tokyo in 1900, 1902, and 1905, respectively.
11. Inoue Tetsujirō, *Nihon Yōmeigakuha no tetsugaku* [The philosophy of the Japanese Yōmei school] (Tokyo: Fuzambō, 1900), 3.
12. Ibid., 6.
13. Ogyū Shigehiro, *Kindai-Ajia-Yomeigaku* [Modernity, Asia, Yōmei learning] (Tokyo: Perikansha, 2008), 400.
14. Ibid., 354–355.
15. Ibid., 356.
16. Tokutomi Sōhō defined Yoshida Shōin as "a revolutionary spearhead of the Meiji Restoration" (Tokutomi Sōhō, *Yoshida Shōin* [Tokyo: Min'yūsha, 1893], 3), linking the Meiji Restoration and Shōin's revolutionary thought. Inoue Tetsujirō in his *Nihon Yōmeigakuha no tetsugaku* described Shōin's thought as "not necessarily that of Wang Yangming but extremely close," and thereby drew in Shōin to the circle of Yangming thinkers (Inoue, *Nihon Yōmeigakuha no tetsugaku*, 606). In 1896 (the twenty-ninth year of Meiji), when the Imperial Council on Education held a commemorative symposium on the fiftieth anniversary of Shōin's death, Inoue Tetsujirō, Tokutomi

Iichirō 徳富猪一郎 (Sohō), Kanō Jigorō 嘉納治五郎, and others gave laudatory speeches, and furthered the image of Shōin as the Yōmeigaku scholar and the fighter for the Meiji Restoration.

17. See http://www.acmuller.net/con-dao/analects.html#div-8, translation by A. Charles Muller (accessed January 18, 2016).
18. Hattori Unokichi, *Kōshikyō taigi* [The main tenets of "the Confucius's teaching"] (Tokyo: Fuzambō, 1939), 11.
19. Ibid., 9.
20. Ibid., 11.
21. Hattori Unokichi, *Shina no kokuminsei to shisō* [The national character and thought of China] (Tokyo: Kyōbunsha, 1926), 187.
22. Hattori Unokichi, *Shinshū Tōyō rinri kōyō* [New edition of an outline of Eastern ethics] (Tokyo: Dōbun Shoin, 1938), 118.
23. Hattori Unokichi, Kōshikyō *taigi*, 32.
24. Watsuji Tetsurō 和辻哲郎 may have been aware of Hattori's interpretation of Confucianism. Watsuji, in his *Kōshi* [Confucius] (Iwanami Shoten, 1933), also discussed the same passage from the "Transmissions" chapter of the *Analects* discussed above, interpreting it to read that "Confucius did not pray to get well even when he was ill" (WTZ 6.331 and 337). This can be read as an argument to erase any religious elements associated with Confucius and the *Analects*, emphasizing that Confucius, as a teacher of humankind, taught the path of secular morality rooted in everyday ethical and moral conduct.
25. Chen Wei-fen 陳瑋芬, "Hattori Unokichi's 'Confucius's Teaching,'" (2001), 63–64.
26. For details, see Nakajima Takahiro, *Kyōsei no purakushisu—kokka to shūkyō* [The praxis of coexistence: Nation-state and religion] (Tokyo: University of Tokyo Press, 2011), especially chapter 8.
27. Hattori Unokichi, "*Heikai no ji*" [Closing remarks], in *Yushima Seidō fukkō kinen judō taikai shi*, ed. Fukushima (1938), 68.
28. For details, see the forthcoming article by Nakajima Takahiro, "Civil Spirituality in Confucian Piety Today: The Activities of Confucian Temples in Qufu, Taipei, and Changchun."
29. See http://www.tct.gov.taipei/ct.asp?xItem=1060114&CtNode=27764&mp=102141 (accessed May 4, 2015).
30. Nakae Chōmin, *Ichinen yūhan, zoku ichinen yūhan* (Tokyo: Iwanami Shoten, 1995), 76.
31. Kojima Tsuyoshi, *Kindai Nihon no Yōmeigaku* (Tokyo: Kōdansha, 2006), 132.
32. Ibid., 124.
33. Nakae's book title, *An Year and a Half*, refers to the advanced state of his illness and that he was expected to live only for a year and a half at the most.
34. Nakae Chōmin, *Ichinen yūhan*, 155.
35. Ibid., 115.
36. Ibid., 114–115.

37. Ishizaki Tōgoku, *Yōmei* 2.6 (Osaka: Osaka Yōmei Gakkai, 1911), 1.
38. Both these young men, together with nine others who were judged guilty, were executed on January 24, 1911.
39. Ishizaki, *Yōmei* 2.6, 3.
40. Ogyū Shigehiro, *Kindai-Ajia-Yōmeigaku*, 406.
41. Ibid., 409.
42. Ibid., 411.
43. Ishizaki Tōgoku,*Yōmei* 3.6 (Osaka: Osaka Yōmei Gakkai, 1914), 3.
44. Ibid., 2.
45. Ibid., 3.
46. Ogyū Sorai, *Rongochō* [Commentary on the *Analects*], vol. 1 (Tokyo: Heibonsha, 1994), 300.
47. Hattori Unokichi, *Kōshikyō taigi*, 11.

BIBLIOGRAPHY

Chen Wei-fen 陳瑋芬. "Hattori Unokichi no 'Kōshi kyō' ron: Sono 'jukyō hi shūkyō' setsu, 'ekisei kakumei' setsu oyobi 'ōdō rikkoku' setsu o chūshin ni" 服部宇之吉の「孔子教」論－その「儒教非宗教」説・「易姓革命」説・及び「王道立国」説を中心に」 [On Hattori Unokichi's "Confucius's teaching," with a focus on its theses of "areligious Confucianism," "change of dynasty" and "state-building by the way of the king"], *Kikan Nihon shisō shi* 『季刊 日本思想史』 [*Quarterly: The intellectual history of Japan*] 59 (Tokyo: Perikansha, 2001), 49–68.

Davis, Winston. "The Civil Theology of Inoue Tetsujirō." *Japanese Journal of Religious Studies* 3.1 (1976), 5–40.

Fukushima Kashizō 福島甲子三, ed. *Yushima Seidō fukkō kinen judō taikai shi* 『湯島聖堂復興記念 儒道大会誌』 [Commemorating the revival of Yushima Seidō Publication of the Symposium on Confucianism]. Tokyo: Shibunkai, 1938.

Hattori Unokichi 服部宇之吉. *Shina no kokuminsei to shisō* 『支那の国民性と思想』 [The national character and thought of China]. Tokyo: Kyōbunsha, 1926.

Hattori Unokichi. *Shinshū Tōyō rinri kōyō* 『新脩東洋倫理綱要』 [New edition of an outline of Eastern ethics]. Tokyo: Dōbun Shoin, 1938.

Hattori Unokichi. *Kōshikyō taigi* 『孔子教大義』 [The main tenets of the Confucius's teaching]. Tokyo: Fuzambō, 1939.

Inoue Tetsujirō 井上哲次郎. *Nihon Yōmeigakuha no tetsugaku* 『日本陽明学派之哲学』 [The philosophy of the Japanese Yōmei School]. Tokyo: Fuzambō, 1900.

Ishizaki Tōgoku 石崎東国. *Yōmei* 『陽明』 2.6 (Osaka: Osaka Yōmei Gakkai, 1911).

Ishizaki Tōgoku. *Yōmei* 『陽明』 3.6 (Osaka: Osaka Yōmei Gakkai, 1914).

Kojima Tsuyoshi 小島毅. *Kindai Nihon no Yōmeigaku* 『近代日本の陽明学』 [The Yōmei learning of modern Japan]. Tokyo: Kōdansha, 2006.

Mishima Chūshū 三島中洲. *Chūshū kōwa* 『中洲講話』 [Chūshū's lectures]. Tokyo: Bunkadō, 1909.

Miyagi Kimiko 宮城公子. *Bakumatsu ki no shisō to shūzoku*『幕末期の思想と習俗』[The thought and customs of the Bakumatsu Era]. Tokyo: Perikansha, 2004.
Miyake Setsurei 三宅雪嶺. *Ō Yōmei*『王陽明』[Wang Yangming]. Tokyo: Seikyōsha, 1893.
Nakae Chōmin 中江兆民. *Ichinen yūhan, zoku ichinen yūhan*『一年有半、続 一年有半』[A year and a half, a sequel to a year and a half]. Tokyo: Iwanami Shoten, 1995.
Nakajima Takahiro 中島隆博. *Kyōsei no purakushisu—kokka to shūkyō*『共生のプラクシス—国家と宗教』[The praxis of coexistence: Nation-state and religion].Tokyo: University of Tokyo Press, 2011.
Nakajima Takahiro. *Civil Spirituality in Confucian Piety Today: The Activities of Confucian Temples in Qufu, Taipei, and Changchun*. Forthcoming.
Natsume Sōseki 夏目漱石. "Kyoikisetsu"「居移気説」[The idea that the dwelling place affects how one feels]. In *Natsume Sōseki zenshū*『夏目漱石全集』[Collected works of Natsume Sōseki], vol. 18, 505. Tokyo: Iwanami Shoten, 1995.
Ogyū Shigehiro 荻生茂博. *Kindai-Ajia-Yōmeigaku*『近代・アジア・陽明学』[Modernity, Asia, Yōmei learning]. Tokyo: Perikansha, 2008.
Ogyū Sorai 荻生徂徠. *Rongo chō*『論語徴』[Commentary on the *Analects*], vol. 1, Ogawa Tamaki 小川環樹 trans. into Modern Japanese. Tokyo: Heibonsha, 1994.
Shibusawa Eiichi 渋沢栄一. *Keizai to dōtoku*『經濟と道徳』[Economy and morality].Tokyo: Nihon Keizai Dōtoku Kyōkai, 1953.
Shibusawa Eiichi. *Rongo to soroban*『論語と算盤』[The *Analects* and the Abacus]. Tokyo: Kokusho kankōkai, 1958.
Tokutomi Sōhō 徳富蘇峰. *Yoshida Shōin*『吉田松陰』. Tokyo: Min'yūsha, 1893.
Watsuji Tetsurō 和辻哲郎. *Kōshi*「孔子」[Confucius]. WTZ 6.257–357.

FURTHER READING

For an overall picture of Confucianism in modern Japan, I recommend Warren W. Smith, *Confucianism in Modern Japan: A Study of Conservatism in Japanese Intellectual History* (Tokyo: The Hokuseidō Press, 1959). It puts Japan's Confucianism in a wider colonial context including Korea and Manchuria.

As for modern *Yōmeigaku*, Ogyū Shigehiro, *Kindai-Ajia-Yōmeigaku* [Modernity, Asia, Yōmei learning] (Tokyo: Perikansha, 2008) is recommended. It not only deals with the detailed background of modern *Yōmeigaku*, but also has a wide perspective of critically examining Japanese modernity in East Asian context. Also recommended is Kojima Tsuyoshi, *Kindai Nihon no Yōmei-gaku* [The Yōmei learning of modern Japan] (Tokyo: Kōdansha, 2006). As a historian, he gives us a sharp contrast between red *Yōmeigaku* for the people and white *Yōmeigaku* for the nation-state.

CHAPTER THREE

The Political Thought of the Kyoto School: Beyond "Questionable Footnotes" and "Japanese-Style Fascism"

KENN NAKATA STEFFENSEN

> If names be not correct, language is not in accordance with the truth of things. If language be not in accordance with the truth of things, affairs cannot be carried on to success.
>
> —The Analects 13.3

INTRODUCTION

The Kyoto School of philosophy is a broad movement that originated at Kyoto Imperial University in the first decades of the twentieth century. Apart from the fact that Nishida Kitarō and Tanabe Hajime are considered its founding figures and that it drew creatively on and sought to combine insights from the East Asian and European traditions, there is little consensus as to who of Nishida and Tanabe's students should fall within its perimeter on what grounds they should be included or excluded, or what gives the group coherence as a school of thought, if such coherence can be found. One would argue that its most intellectually productive period was from around 1930 to 1945, thus coinciding with the political crises that eventually led Japan to the prolonged war-effort, subsequent defeat, and occupation by the Allied Powers.

The development of the Kyoto School and historical assessments of its legacy have in large part been shaped by the political situation it found itself embroiled in, and which its members attempted to address philosophically. The Kyoto School philosophers, in varying degrees of enthusiasm or reluctance, engaged in political theorizing aimed at resolving the problems faced by Japan and the world in the 1930s and first half of the 1940s. Although this aspect of political involvement was central to its identity, it has received relatively little serious attention, and their ideas have rarely been treated as political philosophy. However, at the present historical juncture, developments in the humanities and social sciences, combined with a renewed interest from new academic constituencies in both Japan and abroad, hold much promise for the study of the Kyoto School's political thought as political thought proper.

Much of the controversy has centered on the participation of the four major figures of second-generation thinkers—Kōsaka Masaaki, Kōyama Iwao, Nishitani Keiji, and Suzuki Shigetaka, who took part in the discussion on "The Standpoint of World History and Japan," on the eve and during the early months of the Pacific War, as well as on Nishitani's and Suzuki's contributions to the July 1942 symposium, entitled "Overcoming Modernity." (Little mention has been made that another member of the Kyoto School, Shimomura Toratarō, also took part in the "Overcoming Modernity" symposium.) Other areas of debate have been the nature of the political ideas espoused by Nishida and Tanabe and their political standpoints during the war. In all this, Miki Kiyoshi's thought and his role as a public intellectual and leading figure in the Shōwa Research Association has received less attention and has tended not to be framed as a Kyoto School problematic but as one of Marxism or fascism. Miki had the promise of becoming Nishida's intellectual successor and the main figure of the second-generation Kyoto School, but he has often been left out of conventional accounts, no doubt owing to how his life was tragically cut short. Exclusion of Miki and Tosaka Jun, another original mind, however, makes it "impossible to grasp the intellectual context and richness of the School."[1] Addressing the questions posed not only by the political theorizing of the wartime Kyoto School but by other related philosophical issues requires a broader and more inclusive perspective. It turns out that what has come to be known as the "Kyoto School" and the place of political thought within this group has largely been shaped by the members who survived the war and by the most influential postwar interpreters, and it is not always historically accurate.

Seven decades after the passing away of Nishida, Miki, and Tosaka, we finally arrive at the juncture in history when it appears to be an opportune time to consider the political thought and wartime political engagement of the Kyoto School philosophers. Contemporary trends in intellectual history, international relations scholarship, and political theory in particular facilitate the reorientation of the past assessment. The world seems to be ready to hear about it. For "an objective assessment of any thought, a certain distance of time is necessary," to "facilitate the task of scholarly assessment."[2] Even with the lifting of the fog of war, the debate concerning the real contribution of the Kyoto School thinkers has still only scratched the surface and many potentially fruitful areas remain relatively unexplored. We stand today at the point where we can challenge the stigma of the past, being able to engage in critical and appreciative research in both Japan and abroad, even if there may be some way to go before the Kyoto School can achieve the canonical status it arguably deserves in the history of political thought and as an integral part of the global conversation on political theory.

The argument for a reconsideration of political thought and an opening up to political studies will redress the one-sided view of the Kyoto School as Buddhist philosophy, with the new promise of recognizing its breadth and fully realizing its potential in hitherto less explored areas, including but not limited to political thought.

1. A SKETCH OF THE PAST SEVEN DECADES IN ACADEMIA IN JAPAN AND ABROAD

The political thought of the Kyoto School is undoubtedly the most controversial part of its legacy and has colored the postwar assessments of its character. The controversies tended to fall into two types of verdicts. One was to acknowledge that the political theorizing of its members was nationalistic and supportive of wartime Japanese government foreign policies; not having opposed nationalistic or patriotic sentiment unambiguously and to some degree having supported the idea of Japan-led East Asian liberation and regional integration are considered failings, but nevertheless their political theory does not invalidate the wider philosophical endeavors. There is a competing verdict, which has argued that the supposedly compromised nature of the political theories and war collaboration irredeemably tainted the entire school. In both cases, the intellectual framework of the argument has been one of moral history in which the series of interlinked political and military conflicts that took place during the Second World War have been cast as a confrontation between fascism and antifascism. The arguments have also conflated political ideas, behavior, and ethics under a simplistic lens of resistance or collaboration, where behavior considered to be ethically suspect has led to the dismissal of the ideas, often by retrospective application of ethical standards from a different place and later time.

In the immediate postwar years appreciative assessments of the recently deceased Nishida prevailed. These publications were mostly in the form of memoirs and sympathetic interpretations by friends and former students, such as Shimomura Toratarō's recollections of *The Young Professor Nishida Kitarō* (*Wakaki hi no Nishida Kitarō Sensei*) or Kōsaka Masaaki's *The Life and Thought of Nishida Kitarō* (*Nishida Kitarō Sensei no tsuioku*). Special issues of the journals *Tetsugaku Kenkyū* and *Shisō* were devoted to Nishida.[3] Exactly seventy years after the first memorial issue, an issue of *Shisō* dedicated to Nishida was published in November 2015.[4] Tosaka and Miki, both of whom perished as political prisoners in 1945, were commemorated to a lesser extent and with a longer delay.[5] The Iwanami journal *Sekai*, which became one of the main organs of left-wing political analysis and opinion, was specifically launched in memory of Miki.[6] A prominent structural feature of the Japanese debate has been a tendency to treat individual Kyoto thinkers and their philosophies as sui generis and in particular to disassociate thinkers considered left-wing from the school.[7] There has therefore been a stronger focus placed on individual members of the Kyoto School, and not so much on the general discussion of the school as a group.

At the same time, almost as soon as the war ended, a number of works appeared that were highly critical of the Kyoto School's conceptions of state and nation, its philosophies of history, and alleged war collaboration. These were often written from Marxist or otherwise left-leaning perspectives. Nagata Hiroshi's 1948 book *Philosophy and Democracy: Towards a Critique of Nishida and Tanabe Philosophy* set the tone for much of the postwar debate. Also published in 1948 from a Marxist perspective was Hayashi Naomichi's *A Critique of Nishida Philosophy*, which asserted that Kōsaka and the second generation had "glorified and sanctified a war of aggression and provided logical content to the aggressive scheme of the Greater East Asia Co-Prosperity Sphere."[8] Wholesale contemptuous dismissal of the Kyoto School was not limited to the Marxist left, however. Maruyama Masao's first postwar essay on "Modern Thought" (1946) had scathing remarks concerning "overcoming modernity." He held that there was nothing to overcome when the project was incomplete:

> When compared with the Japan of today, which General Douglas MacArthur is introducing to the "ABC" of modern civilization, mixed feelings of wretchedness and ridiculousness inevitably well up. Without themselves having the so-called "intrinsic" culture that Natsume Sōseki spoke about, these intellectuals were possessed by the vulgar historicist illusion that everything that temporally entered the scene later was more progressive, and thus bowed their heads before the "world-historical" meaning of fascism.[9]

Where Kyoto School philosophy of world history had sought to "provincialize Europe," Maruyama kept a low profile, but emerged as the leading postwar advocate of modernization as westernization. In the same vein as Fukuzawa Yukichi's thesis of "transcending Asia" (*datsua-ron*), Maruyama argued that Japan's political modernity was "not there yet" and still in "an imaginary waiting room of history."[10] Like the Kyoto School thinkers, Maruyama was steeped in European philosophy, but the crucial difference was that where the former "used their knowledge of European thought as a weapon to confront 'Europe,'" Maruyama used it to take "a sarcastic attitude" toward their "arrogance and conceit."[11]

With few exceptions, such as Takeuchi Yoshimi's highly critical yet more balanced view in "*What Is Modernity*" (1959)[12] and Ōshima Yasumasa's overlooked article on the political participation of the Kyoto School,[13] the view that held sway among both the liberal democratic modernizers and the Marxist left saw the Kyoto School as exponents of an unpalatable "philosophy of all-out war" and "ethno-national philosophy,"[14] with little or only negative significance for postwar thought. It was therefore an epistemic shock when the eminent Marxist Hiromatsu Wataru controversially began to revisit the idea of "overcoming modernity" and Miki's "East Asian cooperative communitarianism" in the late 1980s and 1990s. His aim was to mobilize Kyoto School insights and Asianism in order to claim "the idea of the Greater East Asian Co-prosperity Sphere" as "a slogan of the anti-establishment left wing, which calls for a radical inquiry of Japanese capitalism itself."[15] By the end of the Cold War, the previously hostile treatment was transformed into a Marxist "rediscovery of Japanese philosophy"[16] and resurrection of Miki's vision of East

Asian solidarity and political community in a multipolar world order, as well as of the Mahayana Buddhist relational conception of selfhood and the anti-Eurocentric Hegelian-influenced philosophy of world history that Maruyama had dismissed as a vulgar illusion.[17]

As Fujita argues, the passing of time seems indeed to make for more balanced and productive studies.[18] Through the efforts of Fujita and Ōhashi Ryōsuke over the past three decades, the Kyoto School has lost much of the stigma attached to it and largely been rehabilitated in Japan.[19] By 1995, Kyoto University inaugurated its first chair in the history of Japanese philosophy, signaling a sea change in the "normalization" of the Kyoto School, albeit in principle as an episode in the history of philosophy rather than as a living tradition. But rather than closure, the current wave of Asian interest and the work of such Japanese scholars as the political theorists Tobita Maiko at Waseda, Shimizu Kōsuke at Ryūkoku, and the social theorist Okumura Yūto at Keiō are resulting in a resurgence of social and political Kyoto School studies. These scholars are reading the Kyoto School corpus not as Buddhist philosophy but as what Nakajima Hirokatsu has called "a theory of modern civilization."[20]

A step toward the rehabilitation that is now evident in Japan has been the growing interest in the Kyoto School on the part of Western and Asian scholars.[21] The Western encounter with the Kyoto School took off in the 1980s and has tended to emphasize Buddhist elements, although this strand is by no means absent from the Japanese literature. Unlike in Japan, where much of the postwar engagement came from philosophy, political theory, and intellectual history, in the English-speaking world the study of the Kyoto School thinkers was pioneered by Christian theologians and specialists in religious studies. Some of the pioneers were theologians like Johannes Laube and missionary scholars like Heinrich Dumoulin and Jan van Bragt. Early Kyoto School studies hence displayed a strong interest in "the religious and soteriological aspects of the philosophy, and not in its political dimensions or implications."[22] This was also in part due to the influence of D. T. Suzuki in the United States,[23] and Tanabe's and Nishitani's refashioning of themselves as "post-philosophical" Buddhist thinkers. It has been observed that presenting the Kyoto School "as a philosophy of religion was a shortcut to further understanding by western intellectuals."[24] This has resulted in outstanding works but has also had the effect of somewhat limiting, and if I may say, "ghettoizing," the Kyoto School within the academic disciplines.

The political theoretical aspects have hence tended to be treated either as a series of "political ventures and misadventures"[25] that should not detract attention from the school's core philosophical contribution, or as unworthy of sustained study because of its allegedly nationalist or even fascist character. As James Heisig aptly summarized it, the debate has been between "side-stepper" and "side-swipers"—that is to say, between those who seek to defend the school in spite of its problematic political ideas and activities and those who base their rejection of the entire school on the very same ideas and political participation.[26] What has also characterized the debate until recently is that it has for the most part not included disciplinary specialists in political thought, be they philosophers, political theorists, or social scientists. The "side-stepping" end of the spectrum has been occupied by philosophers of religion, and the "side-swiping" end by a theoretically eclectic group of historians of Japan labeled as "neo-Marxists" by Graham Parkes and as "Chicago School" intellectual historians or "Najitunians" by John Lie.[27] The former have tended to be sympathetic to their conception of the Kyoto School as essentially apolitical "philosophers of nothingness" caught up in historical events that led them to make questionable decisions and theoretical pronouncements. For this grouping, the political theorizing may be objectionable, but there remains a philosophical core that is worthy of recognition and which can inspire contemporary philosophy. As one of the leading proponents advocates, we should see "the political misadventures of the Kyoto School as questionable footnotes to their central philosophical endeavors, rather than the other way around."[28] Some historians, however, have precisely approached matters "the other way around." For these "side-swipers," there is little, if anything, worth serious engagement in the Kyoto School as a whole. Rather than separating the political theory from the wider philosophy, their damning assessment of the political ideas leads them to a rejection of the whole body of thought as mere propaganda with no lasting philosophical value. As phrased by Najita and Harootunian:

> This group's central purpose was to construct what they called a "philosophy of world history" that could both account for Japan's current position and disclose the course of future action. But a closer examination of this "philosophy of world history" reveals a thinly disguised justification, written in the language of Hegelian metaphysics, for Japanese aggression and continuing imperialism. In pre-war Japan, no group helped defend the state more consistently and enthusiastically than did the philosophers of the Kyoto faction, and none came closer than they did to defining the philosophic contours of Japanese fascism.[29]

Such pronouncements have done untold damage, and amounted to reducing the Kyoto School to unsavory political propaganda, with the implication that it is "philosophically nugatory."[30] This thesis that the Kyoto School included "Japanese-style fascists"[31] is built on very weak textual and factual foundations, and the claims it makes of European fascist influences are demonstrably unsubstantiated. Parkes has shown these allegations to be "sadly short on facts and long on neo-Marxist jargon and deconstructionist rhetoric."[32] Williams has gone to further textual depths and expanded the scope to include considerations on the shortcomings as political philosophy (but not otherwise) of the "religious studies paradigm."[33] With the exception of Heisig's measured response,[34] Parkes's and Williams's interventions have not provoked responses but been greeted with a deafening silence.[35] There is little to add that could further discredit this corner of Kyoto School studies other than the often unacknowledged but very noticeable influence Miles Fletcher's work has had on authors like Harry Harootunian, Lesley Pincus, and Julia Adeney Thomas.[36] In this way, the "side-steppers" have attempted to navigate around the political ideas in order to salvage a religious-philosophical core, while the "side-swipers" have rejected the school as a whole on the basis of questionable interpretations of those ideas. In the former case, the problem is tackled by the steadfast assertion "that the political thought of the major figures of the School" is nowhere "near the core of their thinking"[37]; in the latter case by ignoring sound criticism and perpetuating that "the members of the Kyoto faction openly acknowledged their admiration for European fascism."[38] Both perspectives are vulnerable to the inconvenient facts presented by closer and more balanced scrutiny of the textual and historical material.

In the past decade and a half, new voices have made themselves heard, namely, scholars like Christopher Goto-Jones and David Williams who stand out by approaching the matter from the disciplinary perspective of political studies, albeit in very different ways and reaching very different conclusions. Goto-Jones has offered a persuasive interpretation of Nishida as a political thinker and intellectual,[39] while Williams has provided novel readings of Tanabe and *The Standpoint of World History and Japan*.[40] With admirable textual depth and rigor, Richard Calichman has contributed with translations and analytical commentaries of the Overcoming Modernity symposium and Takeuchi's associated theory of Asian modernity, published as *Takeuchi Yoshimi: Displacing the West* (2004); *What Is Modernity? Writings of Takeuchi Yoshimi* (2005); and *Overcoming Modernity: Cultural Identity in Wartime Japan* (2008). The full texts and rigorous philological and philosophical analyses of the two most controversial wartime Kyoto School texts are thus available in English for the first time, which is a major step forward.

The dividing lines between mutually opposed camps are changing, and English and German-using scholars with the necessary linguistic and "disciplinary preparedness" to engage responsibly with the primary texts are breaking significant new ground.[41] This coincides with growing interest across Asia as well as with more measured treatments among Japanese scholars. Still hoped for in this regard is much more integrated collaboration between Japan-based scholars working in Japanese and their colleagues abroad. It remains the case that Kyoto School political thought continues to have little impact on Japan studies, not to mention in the field of political theory and history of political thought. It is indeed "surprising that the debate on the Kyoto School remains for the most part confined to those scholars who deal explicitly with the topic of modern Japanese philosophy" and that it is "virtually unknown outside this small circle of scholars."[42] As already noted, it is only recently, and to a limited extent, that this field began to draw the attention of non-Japanese researchers with backgrounds in political studies or cognate fields. There has been hardly any interaction with Japan-related comparative and international politics, which tend to be dominated by more empirical concerns.[43] The impact on history of political thought and political theory has been even more negligible.

In light of some contemporary trends in these fields, history of political thought and political theory ought to be fertile grounds for attracting interest in the Kyoto School. Although Goto-Jones seems to suggest that dialogue with mainstream Cambridge School history is a lost cause due to its inherent ethnocentrism, this is not necessarily the case. Radicalizing the Cambridge School insistence on "seeing things their way" and careful contextualization ought—when taken to its logical conclusion and supplemented by more cross-culturally appropriate interpretation strategies—to enable it to deal with non-Western texts. In an age where Hiromatsu can draw on the wartime Kyoto School to imagine an emancipatory East Asian political community and post-Marxists like Chantal Mouffe can mine the oeuvre of Carl

Schmitt, there is an unprecedented climate of openness to revisiting and rethinking even controversial ideas from the early twentieth century. Political theory as such has become more open and pluralized, and one finds contributions on Chinese, South Asian, and Islamic themes in reflections of the state of the art like the *Cambridge History of 20th Century Political Thought*, and the Oxford and Sage handbooks of political theory.[44]

Since its emergence as a self-conscious field of inquiry in the late 1990s, comparative political theory has acquired "an increasingly visible presence in discourse and debate about the nature, scope, purpose, and methods of political theorizing."[45] Here, considerations of the Kyoto School contribution to political thought could prove critical as something more than "merely expanding the canon to include non-Western texts."[46] As some of the first and most sophisticated theorists of Orientalism, Eurocentrism, subjectivity, modernity, and liberalism, the Kyoto School thinkers could even be considered comparative political theorists themselves. Comparative political theory may be the field where the potential for Kyoto School political studies is the greatest and some recent publications indicate that it is beginning to find its way there.[47] Filling the "Japan-shaped hole" in this body of literature by inserting "something resistant and Oriental,"[48] requires building on and overcoming the previous seventy years of debate and approaching it from the disciplinary standpoints of political studies in dialogue with Western and postcolonial political theory.

2. THE KYOTO SCHOOL AS POLITICAL THOUGHT THEN AND NOW: BACK TO TOSAKA'S "PHILOSOPHY OF THE KYOTO SCHOOL"

What we understand by the term "Kyoto School" today has arguably become divorced from what it meant in its heyday. The first known publication to introduce this expression was Tosaka Jun's September 1932 article "The Philosophy of the Kyoto School."[49] The name itself thus came from the left wing of the school.[50] There is some disagreement surrounding who should be included in this notion of the Kyoto School and, related to this, what its defining features are. Tosaka, the originator of the term, was himself, first and foremost, a social and political thinker. The status of political thought in the formation and definition of the school stands at the center of this debate.

In the broadest sense, the term "Kyoto School" refers to those philosophers who were influenced by Nishida during and after his tenure at Kyoto Imperial University's Department of Philosophy from 1910 to 1928 (the Taishō to Shōwa periods). In the expansive sense, it can include such figures as Tosaka, as well as Watsuji Tetsurō and Kuki Shūzō. In the narrowest sense, it refers only to Kōsaka Masaaki, Kōyama Iwao, and Nishitani Keiji, which is to say those of Nishida's students "who tried to give a positive meaning to the Second World War."[51] Nishida joined Kyoto from Gakushūin University in 1910 as an associate professor and was promoted to a chair in humanities in 1913. He recruited Tanabe from Tōhoku Imperial University in 1919, and a number of talented scholars and students were attracted to the distinct intellectual environment around them. As Tosaka argued, without Tanabe there would have been no Kyoto School, only "Nishida philosophy." Nishida and Tanabe are thus considered the founding figures, and the disputes concerning its "boundary" are about who else should be included and on what grounds.[52]

The Kyoto School has been delimited in two principal ways: on philosophical, or on sociological-historical grounds. The first is represented by such authors such as James Heisig and Ōhashi Ryōsuke, the second by Fujita Masakatsu, Shimomura Toratarō, and Nakai Masakazu. For Heisig and Ōhashi, what makes the Kyoto School a school of philosophy is that its members took on Nishida's core concept of absolute nothingness. What is striking, especially in the accounts of those who insist that the Kyoto School should be understood as "philosophers of nothingness,"[53] is that their conception has little connection with how it was understood by contemporaries. A narrowly philosophical conception tends to focus attention away from political thought toward philosophy of religion as well as toward historically decontextualized "great text" readings. The "religious-philosophical paradigm"[54] has thus only partially addressed the Kyoto School's political theorizing as part of its engagement with "the historical world."[55] Given the importance paid to history by these philosophers, it is ironic that their leading interpreters today often operate as if Nishida, Tanabe, and Nishitani were "alive and well and working just down the corridor."[56] This has resulted in a picture of the Kyoto School as "onto-theological" in orientation, which is "not untrue, but also not unproblematic."[57] The problem is that an excessive focus on "explaining the precise nuance of Buddhist religious thought at the expense of historical context" has resulted in a relative neglect of the turn to philosophy of history and political theory that is evident in the writings of both Nishida and Tanabe in the 1930s, not to mention in that of their students. This goes along with a general neglect, with the exception of Nishitani, of the second generation represented by such figures as Miki Kiyoshi, Kōsaka Masaaki, and Kōyama Iwao. Also, much of the impetus toward political theorizing came from the younger scholars, Tosaka Jun and Miki Kiyoshi in particular, and out of debates with and about Marxism. Shortly after "The Philosophy of the Kyoto School," another article by Tosaka elaborated further on the Kyoto School, which was considered distinct from, and intellectually superior to, what he derisively called "the philosophical school of Yamato Spirit." The thinkers to whom he attached this label were principally Kuki Shūzō and Watsuji Tetsurō, whose "theory of national morality" he takes issue with. He censured these philosophers for their nationalism which was ultimately "nothing but some kind of fascism."[58] What Tosaka argued in this series of articles, to which should also be added the December 1932 publication "The Emergence of Tanabe Philosophy,"[59] was that by around 1930, the creative tensions between Nishida, Tanabe, and their junior colleagues had resulted in the formation of an identifiable school centered on Kyoto Imperial University.[60] What can also be discerned from Tosaka's naming of the school and the way he situated it in relation to contemporary currents of thought is that it was defined by its social and political stance of "bourgeois idealism" and should be understood in terms of its "social and political meanings." As Goto-Jones states, Tosaka "used the label Kyoto School politically" to distinguish a group who built critically on the pioneering work of Nishida.[61] To further underline the fact that social and political thought was considered central at the time of naming, in Tosaka's analysis, the work that secured Miki's position as Nishida's formidable successor was *The Philosophy of History*.[62]

Tosaka's "The Philosophy of the Kyoto School" and its companion pieces show that, like other Marxist critics of the time, he saw it as "neither fascistic nor reactionary, and even judged it positively."[63] He did, however, caution his readers not to be misled by Tanabe's superficial closeness to "left-wing thought" because he remained "a theoretically firm bourgeois philosopher."[64] The critical but respectful engagement by Marxist thinkers was reciprocated by Nishida and Tanabe, who both acknowledged the fruitful philosophical challenges posed by Marxism.[65] While reluctantly accepting the label of "Kyoto School philosopher" applied to himself, Miki believed in 1932 that "Professor Nishida and Professor Tanabe study Marxism from their own standpoints and try to incorporate it into their own philosophies."[66] Although Nishida found Marxism "one-sided," he felt a need to "understand the Marxists and basically take from them what should be taken."[67] Even though advocates of the comparative philosophy of religion approach would agree that Tosaka's perspective on the Kyoto School was political, it has been given short shrift, and views have been attributed to him that are at odds with his largely appreciative critique. Heisig thus tells us that "for Tosaka the term pointed to a 'hermeneutical, transhistorical, formalistic, romantic, phenomenological philosophy'—in short, a bourgeois ideology," adding that "the political ideology he wished to attach to the name was one of 'racial philosophy' and the 'philosophy of total war.'"[68] The words "ideology," "racial," or "total war," however, do not figure in Tosaka's text but come from a secondary source published in 1975—Yamada Munemutsu's *Shōwa Intellectual History*. And whether these words are adequate English translations is contestable.[69] The thinkers Tosaka first mentioned in regard to the Kyoto School were limited to the two major players, Nishida and Tanabe, but he further explains that apart from these representing figures, such as Miki, Yamanouchi Tokuryū, Ueda Juzō, Mutai Risaku, and even Takahashi Satomi (of Tohoku University) are intimately associated with the group.[70] Lacking from Tosaka's mention are Kōsaka, Kōyama, and Nishitani,[71] who were still young and on their way to securing their academic career. The main objective of his essay on the "philosophy of Yamato spirit" was to critique trends of thought other than the "Kyoto School," within the Japanese academy. Tosaka propounded that in order to situate the Kyoto School, "one would inevitably have to understand the social and political meaning" it espoused. He continues to say that:

> "Nishida philosophy" (originally so given the name by the late Dr Sōda Kiichirō) is thriving to form a "Nishida School," and is now on the brink of developing into a Kyoto School. It is now a perfectly formed socially existing entity. It would appear that Professor Tanabe should be credited in having made Nishida philosophy into a firm ground, resembling a school of thought. This is evident, if one looks at how Tanabe was able to make effective use of Nishida's philosophy (in his *Studies in the Philosophy of Mathematics*) and moreover how Tanabe's recent theories loyally organize and tie together the various theses of Nishida philosophy. (It also merits our attention that recently Miki Kiyoshi's thought is becoming

a formidable heir to the Nishida School—for instance, see his *Philosophy of History*.)[72]

The Kyoto School as defined by Tosaka thus comprises a narrower and more limited membership than the English and German-language literature has transmitted.[73] The most notable absence is Nishitani, who himself rejected the label as journalistic shorthand.[74] Elegantly "triangulating" the school around Nishida, Tanabe, and Nishitani,[75] or insisting on absolute nothingness as its indispensable *Grundbegriff*[76] is at variance with its original meaning as "the most rarefied phenomenology" and "the ultimate statement of bourgeois philosophy."[77] It also leads to the historically inaccurate inclusion of Nishitani as the "third man" rather than Miki, who is at best acknowledged as a "marginal" figure."[78]

Postwar conceptions of the Kyoto School tended to marginalize its philosophies of history and politics and promoted a certain "popular image" of it as "Zen Buddhists under the guise of Western philosophy." But this image is rejected by Nishida himself, who was ill at ease with the identity ascribed to him as a Zen philosopher.[79] To paraphrase Nishida's letter to Nishitani written in February 1943, it was absolutely the case that Zen was in the background of his philosophy as something which informed his grasp of reality. But the relationship between Zen and his philosophy had in essence been completely misunderstood. Although he held it was impossible, nevertheless it had been Nishida's earnest desire since he was in his thirties to somehow combine Zen with philosophy. But when people who do not know Zen impute Zen positions to him, he would vehemently oppose it. Those people understand neither Zen nor philosophy, say that X is Y, and they both misunderstand his philosophy and misunderstand Zen.[80] Nishida held that "religion" is "the end of philosophy,"[81] but this does not mean that the philosophy should be reduced to Buddhist metaphysics, nor should it mean that the Kyoto School should be reduced to Nishida. Tosaka also noted that there was "mysticism" and "elements of religious consciousness" in Nishida's philosophy.[82] By contrast, Tosaka's discussion of Tanabe does not mention Buddhism or religion but praises, among other things, his profound knowledge, his philosophy of mathematics, his original interpretation of Hegel, and his open-minded but firmly bourgeois stance toward Marxism and left-wing politics. The postwar Buddhist thinker Tanabe had yet to emerge. The Kyoto School may perhaps be better understood as embodying a particular standpoint toward philosophy, rather than any conceptual coherence as philosophy of nothingness, in which religion constitutes the ultimate beginning (*arche*) and the goal (*telos*) of their thought.[83] Although some argue that thinkers like Miki had very little concern for the religious content of Buddhism,[84] it did figure in the background of the Kyoto School as an element in a dialectical move toward a universal post-Western philosophy,[85] and Miki, in fact, was working on a manuscript on Shinran at the time of his death.[86] "To philosophize" in modern Japan has not meant (and does not do so even today) reconstructing the Buddhist or any other East Asian tradition of thought, even if it forms part of the enterprise to varying degrees; instead, it means to contribute to philosophy conceived of as a modern intellectual discourse and academic discipline, which is strictly demarcated from the wider category of thought, into which Buddhism and Confucianism fall.

While the motivations behind the urge to find a unifying conceptual core in absolute nothingness by triangulating Nishida, Tanabe, and Nishitani are understandable, reducing the Kyoto School to "religion and nothingness" may do it a disservice. Nishida had no intention of founding a school of philosophy in Ōhashi's sense of "a circle of philosophers who were animated by a common philosophical spirit shared with Nishida and who accepted certain fundamental concepts, such as 'nothingness.'" The "socially existing entity" that Tosaka defined in his 1932 articles emerged as a fortuitous, although explicable, cluster of genius in a particular place "reflecting the social condition of a Japan, which was gaining confidence at the time."[87] It included thinkers who do not fulfil Heisig and Ōhashi's requirements and excluded others who do. The historical reality may therefore be that the Kyoto School is made up of the very "mishmash" which Ōhashi is at pains to avoid.[88] It was first and foremost an intellectual network centered on Kyoto Imperial University, Nishida, and Tanabe. That is to say that it was a historical sequence of philosophers who influenced each other through debate without sharing a unifying doctrine, but whose intellectual problems, methods, and styles overlapped. One of the cross-cutting problems was precisely that most of the thinkers—some more reluctantly than others—felt a responsibility to respond philosophically to the critical political developments of their time. Some shared characteristics of Kyoto School were thus philosophy of history, theories of modernity, and the critique of Eurocentrism.[89] There was also a perceived urgency of theorizing political life, as expressed in the title of Tanabe's *The Urgent Task of Political Philosophy*.[90] That said, the various political theories are philosophically very diverse.

Returning to Tosaka and the original naming of the Kyoto School suggests that prevailing images of its political thought as either "some absent-minded lapse from Buddhism"[91] or as the ideologically charged outpourings of a nefarious "Kyoto faction" that defined "the philosophic contours of Japanese fascism"[92] are inaccurate. The "political dimension" of the Kyoto School should therefore not be considered "'just one of those things' that one is vaguely aware of but that somehow distracts from the main point"[93] but as a focal concern from the moment it acquired its name. It was named politically, it explicitly theorized political life in dialogue with itself and other bodies of thought, and it came under political attack for its wartime dissent and later for its supposedly compromised wartime activities. There is therefore more to the story than "religion and nothingness."[94]

3. THE ART OF WRITING UNDER WARTIME PERSECUTION: THE TWO-EDGED SORT OF ANTI-SYSTEMIC COLLABORATION

The questions surrounding the Kyoto School and politics can be broken down into, on the one hand, the nature of the political ideas espoused by its members and, on the other hand, their wartime political conduct. There has, however, been a tendency for both the school's defenders and detractors to not clearly separate the theoretical and historical aspects from the ethical, and in so doing to impose the "standards of American political correctness" retrospectively.[95] This conflation has led Williams to the assessment that for most Kyoto School scholars "politics means neither research on political institutions nor the study of political philosophy but something much narrower and less scientific: the ethical criticism of wartime Japan from an Allied perspective."[96]

It is hence necessary, as far as possible, to separate the political theory and any assessment of it from post-hoc moral judgments of the political behavior of its authors. This can at times be difficult, since the two elements interact: the political engagement of these philosophers stems from their identity as intellectuals and a sense of professional duty. As Miki Kiyoshi noted, they were forced by historical circumstances "to stand up assertively and participate in real-world issues" to ensure that "if Japan's conduct in China is to be different from the traditional methods and principles of European and American capitalist imperialism, then its characteristic behaviour must have a characteristic theory."[97] The political interventions could range from the outright collaboration and active legitimation of imperialism and ultranationalism claimed by their fiercest critics to the "philosophy of resistance" supposedly practiced by Miki and Tosaka.[98] In this scheme, Miki incongruously occupies both extremes. For John Dower, he "embodied qualities of independent thought and personal autonomy which appeared admirable in a country where most people had caved in completely, in many cases enthusiastically, to the authoritarian state,"[99] and in Hiromatsu's opinion he unsuccessfully sought to inject "Marxist socialism" into the policymaking mainstream.[100] Against this, others have seen his involvement with the Shōwa Research Association and resultant writings as providing such clear evidence of "fascist influence"[101] that "with Miki, a strand of Kyoto School is securely woven into fascist thread"[102] and that he "led the creation of a fascist movement."[103] While Miki provides the most extreme case of contradictory placements as either a despicable Kyoto School "fascist" or an exemplary Marxist martyr, the ambiguity and incongruous pigeonholing of Nishida, for instance, is also widespread. In all cases, both the demonologists and hagiographers rely on "random quotes chosen for purposes of moral critique."[104]

The repression and political crises of the 1930s and early 1940s required of intellectuals that they master the art of "writing between the lines" so as to be understood by their "reasonable friends."[105] Although it is questionable whether the political system of wartime Japan took a turn that can reasonably be classified as "fascist" or "totalitarian" in the sense these terms are applied to Germany, Italy, or the Soviet Union,[106] from 1930 onward public discourse was subject to gradually stronger governmental controls and reprisal by nongovernmental nationalist forces as well as direct action by radical elements of the military. Political life became increasingly dominated by illiberal and anti-intellectual nationalism and the military, but the scale of political repression was restrained by European and Soviet standards, with only around 5,000 prosecutions under Peace Preservation Law between 1928 and August 1945.[107] In spite of his secure sociological position as professor emeritus with personal links to the political elite and thus a member of the establishment, Nishida himself was at risk of arrest. Miki and Tosaka were in much more precarious positions as known dissidents and did perish in prison after due legal (but not necessarily legitimate) process; in fascist Europe they would have been summarily executed. It was in this radicalized political culture that the Kyoto School philosophers had to operate, and the options available were limited. The possible responses ranged from full collaboration and open resistance at the two extremes over withdrawal from public life, cultural commentary "with no overt claim to a political agenda,"[108] and the path of "anti-systemic collaboration."[109] An option, which very few exercised, was exile.[110] In this scheme, the political participation by the Kyoto School was mostly of the "anti-systemic collaboration" variety.[111] In spite of the heroic image of Miki as a "philosopher of resistance,"[112] his involvement with the Shōwa Research Association along with other leftists should also be understood as "anti-systemic collaboration" rather than outright resistance.[113] This choice by Nishida, Tanabe, Miki, and the distinguished second-generation disciples meant that they put themselves "in a dangerous place" and provoked censure and reprisals from both ends of the political spectrum, both during and after the war. Nishitani, describing it, said: "During the war we were struck on the cheek from the right; after the war we were struck on the cheek from the left."[114]

It has also left questions open as to whether it was characterized more by collaboration than resistance. It is certainly true that their attempts to avoid being silenced or imprisoned while instilling some rationality and "liberal direction" to policy[115] was ineffective and even counterproductive. The documentary record shows a strong commitment to political-philosophical reflection combined with "action in the world"[116] on the part of Tanabe, Nishitani, Kōsaka, Kōyama, Miki, and Tosaka, who were "clearly aware of the inseparability of politics, history, and culture."[117] It also shows that their aims must be reconstructed as on the whole more resistant than collaborative, even to the point of conspiring to topple the Tōjō government.[118] The outcomes, however, were more ambiguous because the demands of "anti-systemic collaboration" meant that certain elements lent themselves to propagandistic purposes, most evidently in the cases of Nishida, Tanabe, and the participants in the wartime symposia. But no matter how ineffective, the interventions sought to criticize rather than to legitimize the policies of the wartime government, the army in particular. Here Heisig is correct that "in the greatest bulk of their writings" there is nothing "approaching or supporting the imperialistic ideology of wartime Japan." This ideology therefore does not belong "to the fundamental inspiration of their thought."[119]

Their critical and politically transformative aims notwithstanding, the eventual outcome was that certain ideas were co-opted by the very nationalist forces they opposed. As Ōtsuka Katsura notes, the Kyoto School took a "liberal" stance in relation to the "totalitarian currents" of the time, but there was also content that could easily be used "to legitimise national policy." The three key characteristics of Kyoto School thought open to abuse, according to Ōtsuka, were absolute nothingness, the historical world, and the critique of Western modernity. Absolute nothingness was assumed to mean the imperial household as the center of nothingness and was employed to strengthen political control and mass mobilization. The idea of the historical world "developed into creative action and exalted *moralische Energie*." And the anti-Eurocentric critique of modernity became "linked with the theory of overcoming modernity" and thereby came to "guide anti-Europeanism, anti-Americanism and Greater East Asianism."[120]

Once a text is published and enters public discourse, its author is no longer the master of its interpretations. An analogous example of the unintended political uses to which certain Kyoto School statements were put is the fate of Benedict Anderson's 1972 essay "The Idea of Power in Javanese Culture." In spite of the fact that Anderson was a vocal critic of the Indonesian military government, his text nevertheless "inspired a trend" which aimed "to legitimise the country's authoritarian regime."[121] When examining the political record of the Kyoto School, careful distinctions must therefore be made between authorial intent and the political afterlife of a text, for which the author cannot be held responsible. Great care must also be taken to make the appropriate separation between normative political theory as expressed in writing, the political reality it addressed and interacted with, and any outcomes that cannot reasonably be attributed to the author. As far as possible, the interpreter must learn to contextualize and suspend any immediate rush to judgment in order to restore "the world in which his ideas were initially formed" and "with a commitment to trying to see things their way."[122]

4. OPENING UP BY WAY OF CONCLUSION: REALIZING THE INTELLECTUAL POTENTIAL OF KYOTO SCHOOL POLITICAL THOUGHT

It has been argued that the Kyoto School can neither be reduced to philosophy of religion nor to nationalist war propaganda. It ranged widely over philosophy of science, technology, aesthetics, education, language, history, politics, and religion. It also ranged "from Marxism to anti-Marxism" and "learned deeply from western studies" while trying "to construct their own thought from the oriental tradition." In this, the various members "are not necessarily fixated on Zen Buddhism and focus broadly on the oriental tradition."[123] This makes it difficult to posit any "essential similarity" between Hisamatsu Shin'ichi's Zen Buddhism, Hatano Seiichi's Christianity, Tanabe and Kōsaka's "nationalism," Miki and Tosaka's "Marxism," and Nishitani's existentialism.[124]

While recognizing this diversity and the variety of political views adopted by the school, it is nevertheless possible to identify certain shared themes. These can be seen as arising from the particular standpoint toward philosophy as the modern intellectual discipline of *tetsugaku*.[125] A further factor that lends some unity to the school's political theorizing is that it was a response to the political problems Japan faced in the 1930s and 1940s. The responses to nationalism, Eurocentric globalization, the militarization of politics, and the crisis of liberal modernity varied, but no matter how ineffective the strategy of "anti-systemic collaboration" turned out to be, there is sufficient evidence to dispel the myth of enthusiastic war collaboration. By exposing the philosophical, philological, and historical fallacies of it, Parkes, Ōhashi, Williams, and Goto-Jones have dealt a profound blow to the "side-swiping" side in the debate, from which it has not been able to recover nor even defend itself.[126] The research program of the more serious, linguistically competent, and philosophically literate "side-stepping" side, however, continues to maintain that whatever contributions the Kyoto School made to political philosophy, these are mere "footnotes" to the core contribution as philosophy of religion. As such it can neither effect a revision of their view of Kyoto School philosophy as "Zen thought expressed in the language of German philosophy"[127] nor bring it to a stage where it can contribute to the political studies disciplines. As noted above, from the beginning of the Western engagement with the Kyoto School, it found a more welcome reception among theologians and scholars of religion than in philosophy departments. Writing in 1997, Parkes attributed this state of affairs to the hegemonic status of analytic philosophy in the Anglosphere.[128] Today, when "Hegel no longer lives" in German universities, this dominance and resultant narrowing of philosophy has become a "global victory."[129] Academic political philosophy in the liberal analytic mode is consequently even more closed to comparative studies than when Parkes made his observation. A decade and a half into the twenty-first century, mounting competition for rankings and the nature of the assessment instruments employed have created another institutional barrier, which non-Western philosophy is finding even harder to break through.[130] Philosophy as an institutionalized academic discipline is increasingly becoming provincial and closed to alternatives; it is one of the least sociologically diverse academic professions,[131] and has problems of "bias and partiality in many of its theoretical outputs."[132] One of these biases with regard to non-Western philosophy is an "exaggerated focus on religiosity" and a concomitant neglect of social and political thought.[133] If the study of Kyoto School political thought is therefore to break out of its status as a sideline for scholars whose strengths and interests lie elsewhere, it would have to be positioned within disciplinary fields where it can be taken seriously as political thought. It might therefore find a more hospitable institutional environment in area studies and political studies, particularly in the emerging subdiscipline of comparative political theory. As we have also seen, the most innovative recent contributions have often come from scholars with strong political studies backgrounds based in area studies departments and in social science departments within Japan.

Comparative political theory has emerged in similar historical circumstances to those of the wartime Kyoto School and addresses similar concerns to those of the "20-years' crisis."[134] Then as now, a relatively stable international order is undergoing transformation, the future is uncertain, and a variety of theoretical responses are under elaboration. In fact, the Kyoto School philosophers were in some respects pioneers of what now travels under the name of comparative political theorizing. Faced with the crisis of the Taishō (1912–25) political order, a world economic crisis, and heightened regional and global tensions, they came up with a number of responses that prefigure and speak to contemporary concerns.

As both the domestic and international crises of the 1920s–1940s were crises of liberalism, it is no surprise that the critical response was targeted at what Tanabe called "old liberalism."[135] In this respect, the Hegelian meditations on the historical constitution of subjectivity in the Chūō Kōron symposia and in Miki's *Philosophy of History* (1932) and *Philosophical Foundations of Cooperative Communitarianism*

(1939) resonate with post-Rawlsian critics of liberalism like Charles Taylor. Like some of the critical reactions to Rawls, this phase of the Kyoto School was a Hegelian response to the previously dominant neo-Kantian liberalism. Tanabe's "experiment in metaphysical reasoning about the political-historical realm"[136] that began with "The Logic of Social Existence" (1934) was also a normatively and methodologically communitarian critical response to, on the one hand, Nishida's ahistorical individualism and, on the other hand, to Marxism. As evidenced by *The Urgency of Political Philosophy*, in the postwar and Cold War context this developed into clear-cut advocacy of a specifically Japanese version of social democracy as a "third way" between American liberalism and Soviet authoritarianism.[137]

Another Hegelian problematic explored by the Kyoto School and much misunderstood by its postwar Anglograph interpreters was that of "totality" and the alleged "totalitarianism" of, for instance, Nishida or Miki. As Traverso cautions, navigating through the "uses and abuses" of the idea of totalitarianism requires constant awareness of how its meanings have been shaped by the Second World War and the Cold War to make it "the antithesis of liberalism."[138] This means that a contemporary reader must, as far as possible, approach the term by setting aside what postwar scholarship by the likes of Adorno and Horkheimer, Hayek, Popper, Russell, Berlin, and Arendt have taught us. The "totality" the Kyoto School is referring to is Hegel's *das Ganze*, not Mussolini's and Gentile's idea of a totalitarian state. Bearing in mind that the postwar Western analysis of fascist and Stalinist totalitarianism was not on the intellectual horizon, the term *zentaishugi* covered a wider semantic spectrum, and the boundaries between political totalitarianism and methodological holism were more fluid than in postwar usage. And, as Yusa argues, Nishida resisted totalitarian trends and held that "any totalitarian system that negates outright the role of the individual is an anachronism."[139] Miki likewise, while recognizing the need to balance individual liberty with the social whole, sees political life as not simply reducible to securing individual autonomy. Like with most contemporary critics of liberalism, his structurationist and communitarian theory does not become illiberal:

> at the same time as being made by society, the individual as an autonomous entity conversely makes society. Individuals are autonomous of each other and thus discontinuous with each other, so while they are contradictory entities all individuals are enveloped by the whole and continuous with the whole, so that the whole as a coincidence of opposites is a true harmony. While being a tool of the whole because it is a component of the whole, the individual has self-purpose as an independent entity. The whole envelops all individuals and at the same time transcends them.[140]

While Kyoto School thinkers such as Miki and Tanabe, and to a lesser extent Nishida, found arguments in the European and East Asian traditions to question liberal individualism on ontological, methodological, and normative grounds, this did not amount to advocacy of totalitarian rule. Quite the contrary, their search for a theoretical standpoint "after liberalism"[141] distinguished the same problems of liberal modernity that Sandel, Taylor, Avineri, Etzioni, and MacIntyre have addressed, and their conclusions and prescriptions are far from illiberal. The "post-liberal" humanist standpoint that Miki was elaborating in the mid-1930s, in fact, deplored the compromises liberals were making with "Japanism" and "fascism." Miki called for imbuing humanism into liberalism and thus radicalize it.[142] As Kim argues for Tanabe and Miki, there is no doubt that they expressed a strong commitment to universal human emancipation, even if the effects in the context of empire were oppressive, as is equally the case for American liberalism today.[143] Identifying this liberal stance is complicated by the fact that Nishida, Nishitani, and Tanabe "took up the jargon and slogans of the day and sought to redeem from their petty provincialism by opening them up to a more universal perspective."[144] Nevertheless, Nishida's subtle inversion of terminology "represents his political engagement in the production of a counter-narrative to the dominant imperialist regime."[145] Miki was similarly engaged in a "tug of war over meaning,"[146] but tried to consciously avoid the more ideologically charged terminology. This signaled dissent to knowledgeable readers, who could distinguish between the army's co-prosperity sphere and his call for a pluralistic East Asian Cooperative Community. And not surprisingly, it was attacked from the right as a "red" and "federalist" cosmopolitanism that "lacked Japanese subjectivity."[147]

Yet another area that could benefit from engagement, and which speaks to contemporary concerns, is the distinctive anti-Eurocentrism of Kyoto School political thought and philosophy of history. As with other thematics of the school, it ranges widely from Nishitani's apparent "intrinsically nationalistic"[148] standpoint to the "imperial cosmopolitanism" of Miki and Tanabe,[149] and Nishida's "cultural constructivist" vision of an equitable, polycentric, and interdependent "global world."[150] Within this diversity, there is an underlying theme that self-universalizing Eurocentric thought, and European-derived forms of political organization had failed, combined with an optimistic sense that Japanese political agency could open up a new and post-hegemonic era in world history:

> Up to now Westerners thought that their culture was superior to all others, and that human culture advances toward their own form. Other peoples, such as Easterners, are said to be behind and if they advance, they too will acquire the same form. There are even some Japanese who think like this. However … I believe there is something fundamentally different about the East. They [East and West] must complement each other and … achieve the eventual realization of a complete humanity. It is the task of Japanese culture to find such a principle.[151]

But, in common with the postcolonial situation of thinking, their self-positioning in relation to the universal tradition of philosophy, which they sought to inscribe themselves into, made European ideas "both indispensable and inadequate" for their attempts "to think through the various life practices that constitute the political and the historical."[152] As Miki argued, "The prejudiced view of world history characterized by so-called Europeanism should be corrected" because "the world, in its ideal state, should not be unicentral but multicentral. If Europe is one centre, the Orient is another, and these centres, with their respective uniqueness, should be closely interrelated."[153] Like Okakura Tenshin, Miki and Nishida conceived of Japanese culture as occupying a world-historically privileged position that enabled it to mediate between the West and the non-West in order to reach a true universality. This has often been framed in terms of a contradiction between Japanese nationalism and universalism,[154] where nationalism has been interpreted as inherently conservative or reactionary and supportive of militarism and imperialism. This leaves no room for the possibility that, with various emphases, the thinkers of the Kyoto School were both "liberal nationalists" and anti-Eurocentric universalists.[155] In the same manner as Japan's war had a dual nature as "simultaneously a war of aggression and a war of imperialism against imperialism,"[156] nationalism is a "modern Janus" with intertwined progressive and regressive, oppressive and emancipatory aspects.[157] If the nationalism in question is compatible with or logically part of a conception that privileges universal humanity, it is mistaken to simply dismiss it as purely negative.[158] This theoretical universalism expressly sought to further the liberation of East Asia as a step toward an equitable world order but was a two-edged sword in political practice that could serve as an instrument of both liberation and oppression.[159] As such, this is not a particular feature of Kyoto School thought but one that characterizes modern political theory and political modernity in general, and similar contradictions plague liberalism. As one of the first and most rigorous formulations of an anti-Eurocentrism emerging out the particular standpoint taken toward philosophy and Western universalism, the Kyoto School has much to offer to—and can be fruitfully interpreted in the light of—postcolonial theory and the general post-Western and comparative "turns" in political theory and international relations, and the "international turn" in intellectual history.[160]

Other hardly explored areas of fruitful interaction between the Kyoto School, political theory, and other subdisciplines of political studies are, by way of example, their conceptions of international justice, nothingness and state sovereignty, the structure-agency problematic with both structure and agency as correlates of nothingness, monarchy and social democracy, economic ethics, citizenship, theories of the state, realism and idealism, and legitimacy. There is a wealth of unexplored books and articles. In addition to the three dozen titles listed by Williams,[161] as a representative sample, one can add many of Miki's prolific writings through the 1930s on such topics as Stalinism, humanism, and the logic of politics, Spinoza's theory of the state, the political role of intellectuals, ethnicity, political and intellectual crisis, nationalism, and cosmopolitanism. Other neglected works that merit reconsideration are Tanabe's *The Urgency of Political Philosophy*, or Kōyama's *The Realm of Japan and the Spirit of Culture* (1941) and *The Ideal of the Civilised State* (1946).

The study of Kyoto School political thought has far from reached its conclusion. In some respects, it is a disciplinary *terra nullius*, which has only recently come to be claimed by innovative scholars in both Japan and abroad. Most of the new voices have emerged from outside the traditional groupings of religious studies scholars and historians. This is decisively bringing the field beyond "side-stepping" and "side-swiping" and holds much promise for our understanding of Kyoto School political theory as something more than a series of "questionable footnotes." Although major steps have been taken, the task of taking the Kyoto School seriously as political thought is still in its infancy. It requires a more open and tolerant "broad church" conception of the historical Kyoto School *wie es eigentlich gewesen ist*—"how it actually was." Such an open stance ought to attract not only specialists in political thought and its history but also researchers in fields such as ecology, education, bioethics, philosophy of science, cognitive science, technology studies, and sociology.

To reiterate, the present historical conjuncture is an opportune time to reconsider the Kyoto School and to insert it into previously unexplored disciplinary contexts where its social and political thought may find a new and more comfortable home. Political studies is more welcoming to engagement with non-Western thought, both traditional and modern, than at any time in its history. This is reflected in the growth of such fields as "non-Western" or "post-Western" international relations theory and comparative political theory. The Kyoto School is gradually finding its way into both, the former in particular. The dominant tendency in history of political thought, as practiced by such scholars as Quentin Skinner, has so far remained remarkably Eurocentric, but there is no reason why in principle it cannot be opened to cross-cultural interpretations and to the investigation of ideas such as those of the Kyoto School. For this to finally materialize would be a fulfilment of the school's vision of a more balanced intellectual world order of mutual recognition.

NOTES

1. Nakaoka Narifumi, "*Kyōto Gakuha*" ["The Kyoto School"], in *Iwanami tetsugaku shisō jiten* [Iwanami dictionary of philosophy and ideas], ed. Hiromatsu Wataru, Koyasu Nobukuni, Mishima Ken'ichi, Miyamoto Hisao, Sasaki Chikara, Noe Keiichi, and Sueki Fumihiko (Tokyo: Iwanami Shoten, 1998), 347.
2. Fujita Masakatsu, "*Nishida Kitarō botsugo nanajū-nen o furikaeru*" ["Looking back 70 years after the death of Nishida Kitarō"], *Shisō* 1099 (November 2015), 2.
3. See Fujita Masakatsu, "Looking back 70 years," 2–6. The November 1945 memorial issue of *Shisō* (no. 270) had a preface by Suzuki Daisetz and articles by Amano Teiyū, Yanagida Kenjūrō, Suetsuna Joichi, Kimura Motomori, Satō Nobue, and Kōsaka Masaaki.
4. The 2015 issue was published exactly seventy years after the memorial issue of 1945.
5. It was, for instance, not until the early 1960s when a memorial to Miki was erected in his hometown of Tatsuno by the Miki Kiyoshi Society, which was at its most active throughout the 1960s.
6. On the train back from Miki's funeral service in Kamitakada, Iwanami Shigeo and Ōuchi Hyōe came up with the idea of a new journal to honor his memory. Iwanami had sponsored Miki's research fellowship in Europe, and Ōuchi, who befriended Miki in Heidelberg, oversaw the publication of Miki's complete works.
7. Fujita Masakatsu, "Introduction," in *Kyōto gakuha no tetsugaku* [*The philosophy of the Kyoto School*], ed. Fujita Masakatsu (Kyoto: Shōwado, 2001).
8. Cited in Fujita, "Looking back 70 years," 4.
9. Maruyama Masao, "*Kindaiteki shii*" [Modern thought] (a testimony written in 1946, January), compiled in Kawade Shobō, ed., *Maruyama Masao, Botsugo jūnen, minshushugi no 'shinwa' o koete* [Maruyama Masao: Commemorating the tenth anniversary of his death, trajectoring beyond the myth of democracy] (Tokyo: Kawade Shobō-shinsha, 2006), 136–137.

10. D. Chakrabarty, *Provincializing Europe: Postcolonial Thought and Historical Difference* (Princeton: Princeton University Press, 2007), 8.
11. Inukai Yūichi, "*Sezoku no Kyoto-gakuha?*" in *Kyōto Gakuha no shisō: shuju no zō to shisō no potensharu*, ed. Ōhashi Ryōsuke, 11.
12. See R. F. Calichman, *What Is Modernity? Writings of Takeuchi Yoshimi* (New York: Columbia University Press, 2005).
13. Ōshima Yasumasa, "*Daitōa sensō to Kyōto gakuha: chishikijin no seiji sanka ni tsuite*" ["The Greater East Asia War and the Kyoto School: On the political participation of intellectuals"], *Chūō Kōron* (August 1965), 125–143.
14. Yamada Munemutsu, *Shōwa no seishinshi: Kyōto gakuha no tetsugaku* [*Showa intellectual history: The philosophy of the Kyoto School*] (Kyoto: Jinbun Shoin, 1975), 280.
15. Hiromatsu Wataru, *"Kindai no chōkoku" ron—Shōwa shisōshi e no ichi shikaku* [*Theories on "overcoming modernity": A perspective on the history of ideas during the Showa period*] (Tokyo: Kōdansha, 1989). Cited in Takahiro Nakajima, *The Chinese Turn in Philosophy* (Tokyo: University of Tokyo Center for Philosophy, 2007), 116. Mentioned by Nakajima Hirokatsu, "*Kyōto gakuha to wa nan datta no ka—gendai bunmeiron toshite no Nishida tetsugaku*" ["What was the Kyoto School? Nishida's philosophy as a theory of modern civilization"] (Kyoto: Kyoto Academeia, 2010), online.
16. See Kobayashi Toshiaki, *Hiromatsu Wataru: Kindai no chōkoku (Saihakken Nihon no tetsugaku)* [*Hiromatsu Wataru: Overcoming modernity (the rediscovery of Japanese philosophy*)] (Tokyo: Kōdansha, 2007).
17. Hiromatsu did remain highly critical of Nishida and held him "theoretically responsible" for the uses his ideas were put to. But shortly before his death in 1994, he argued forcefully for reclaiming certain Kyoto School ideas for the left.
18. Fujita, "Looking back 70 years," 2.
19. Ōhashi Ryōsuke, ed., *Kyōto gakuha no shisō: shushu no zō to shisō no potensharu* [*The philosophical thought of the Kyoto School: Various images and their intellectual potential*] (Kyoto: Jinbun Shoin, 2004).
20. Nakajima Hirokatsu, "What was the Kyoto School?"
21. In his address at the memorial symposium to mark the seventieth anniversary of Nishida's death, Fujita noted that the East, Southeast, and South Asian scholars who had recently taken an interest in the Kyoto School approached it as a modern philosophy that was relevant to the problems of modernization their societies were undergoing.
22. G. Parkes, "The Putative Fascism of the Kyoto School and the Political Correctness of the Modern Academy," *Philosophy East & West* 47.3 (1997), 307.
23. Ibid.
24. Nakaoka Narifumi, "Kyoto School," 347.
25. B. Davis, "The Kyoto School," in *The Stanford Encyclopedia of Philosophy* (2014).

26. J. Heisig, "The Religious Philosophy of the Kyoto School: An Overview," *Japanese Journal of Religious Studies* 17.2 (1990), 53.
27. Parkes, "The Putative Fascism," and G. Parkes, "Heidegger and Japanese Fascism: An Unsubstantiated Connection," in *Japanese and Continental Philosophy: Conversations with the Kyoto School*, ed. Bret W. Davis, Brian Schroeder, and Jason M. Wirth (Bloomington: University of Indiana Press, 2011), 247–268. Also see D. Williams, *Defending Japan's Pacific War: The Kyoto School Philosophers and Post-White Power* (London: Routledge, 2004); J. Lie, "Enough Said, Ahmad: Politics and Literary Theory," *positions* 2.2 (1994), 421.
28. Davis, "The Kyoto School."
29. T. Najita and H. Harootunian, "Japanese Revolt against the West: Political and Cultural Criticism in the Twentieth Century," in *The Cambridge History of Japan*, vol. 6: The Twentieth Century, ed. Peter Duus (Cambridge: Cambridge University Press, 1989), chapter 14, 741.
30. Parkes, "The Putative Fascism," 305.
31. Najita and Harootunian "Japanese Revolt," 742–743.
32. Parkes, "The Putative Fascism," 347.
33. Williams, *Defending Japan's Pacific War*, 130.
34. See J. Heisig's review, "David Williams *Defending Japan's Pacific War: The Kyoto School Philosophers and Post-White Power*," *Japanese Journal of Religious Studies* 32.1 (2005), 163–166.
35. The closest to a response there has been from Harootunian was a vitriolic and ad hominem review of Williams's *Defending Japan's Pacific War* (Harry D. Harootunian, "Returning to Japan: Part Two," *Japan Forum* 18.2 [2006], 275–282), which failed to address the specific points raised about his own work.
36. M. Fletcher, "Intellectuals and Fascism in Early Shōwa Japan," *Journal of Asian Studies*, 39.1 (1979), 39–63; also M. Fletcher, *The Search for a New Order: Intellectuals and Fascism in Prewar Japan* (Chapel Hill: University of North Carolina Press, 1982).
37. Heisig, "David Williams *Defending Japan's Pacific War*," review, 165.
38. Najita and Harootunian, "Japanese Revolt," 742.
39. C. Goto-Jones, *Political Philosophy in Japan: Nishida, the Kyoto School, and Co-prosperity* (New York and London: Routledge, 2005); C. Goto-Jones, "The Kyoto School, the Cambridge School, and the History of Political Philosophy in Wartime Japan," *positions: east asia cultures critique* 17.1 (2009), 13–42.
40. Williams, *Defending Japan's Pacific War*; D. Williams, *The Philosophy of Japanese Wartime Resistance: A Reading, with Commentary, of the Complete Texts of the Kyoto School Discussions of "The Standpoint of World History and Japan"* (Abingdon and New York: Routledge, 2014).
41. N. Sakai, "Resistance to Conclusion: The Kyōto School Philosophy under Pax Americana," in *Re-politicizing the Kyōto School as Philosophy*, ed. C. Goto-Jones (London: Routledge, 2007), 190.

42. R. Calichman, "Guest Editor's Introduction," *positions: east asia cultures critique* 17.1 (2009), 1–2.
43. C. Goto-Jones, "Comparative Political Thought: Beyond the Non-Western," in *Ethics and World Politics*, ed. D. Bell (New York: Oxford University Press, 2010), 220.
44. See works such as B. Parekh, "Non-Western Political Thought," in *The Cambridge History of Twentieth-Century Political Thought*, ed. T. Ball and R. Bellamy (Cambridge University Press, Cambridge, 2003), chapter 26, 553–578; S. Ismail "Islamic Political Thought," in Ball and Bellamy, *The Cambridge History of Twentieth-Century Political Thought*, chapter 27, 579–601; D. Bell *China's New Confucianism: Politics and Everyday Life in a Changing Society* (Princeton: Princeton University Press, 2008).
45. D. von Vacano, "The Scope of Comparative Political Theory," *Annual Review of Political Science* 18 (2015), 2.
46. A. March, "What Is Comparative Political Theory?" *The Review of Politics* 71 (2009), 531.
47. C. Goto-Jones, "Comparative Political Thought: Beyond the Non-Western"; C. Goto-Jones, "When Is Comparative Political Thought (Not) Comparative? Dialogues (Dis) continuities, and Radical Difference in Heidegger and Nishida," in *Comparative Political Thought: Theorizing Practices*, ed. M. Freeden and A. Vincent (Abingdon and New York: Routledge, 2013), 158–180.
48. D. Williams, *Japan and the Enemies of Open Political Science* (London: Routledge, 2002), xiv, 261.
49. For its English translation, see K. N. Steffensen, "Tosaka Jun's 'The Philosophy of the Kyoto School,'" *Comparative and Continental Philosophy* 8.1 (March 2016), 54–73.
50. Hattori Kenji, "'Kyoto gakuha' to sono 'saha' no ningengaku no keifu: aru jidai *jyōkyō no naka de* ["On the 'Kyoto School' and the Genealogy of the Anthropology of Its 'Left Wing': In the Circumstances of the Time]", *Ritsumeikan Bungaku* 603 (2008), 263–279. As Goto-Jones has pointed out, "Searching for a political left in a non-European context is complicated by the profusion of other directions that are granted political significance," the main ones in Japan since the Meiji Restoration being the East-West and tradition-modernity dichotomies, with which the left-right scheme inherited from the French revolution intersects. See C. Goto-Jones, "The Left Hand of Darkness: Forging a Political Left in Interwar Japan," in *The Left in the Shaping of Japanese Democracy*, ed. D. Williams and R. Kersten (London, Routledge, 2004), 3. In *Japanische Philosophie nach 1868*, Junko Hamada also groups Kyoto School philosophers into left, right, and center, which Ōhashi objects to because distinguishing in this manner between "left" (Miki), "right" (Tanabe and Kōsaka), and "centre" (Nishida and Nishitani) is "often taken over by left-wing polemicists like e.g. Munemitsu Yamada with reference to their political (and not philosophical) orientations." See R. Ōhashi, "Zur Philosophie der Kyoto-Schule," *Zeitschrift für Philosophische Forschung* 40.1 (1986), 121.

51. See Iwamoto Noritaka, “The Kyoto School,” in *Nihon Shisōshi jiten [Dictionary of Japanese intellectual history]*, ed. Koyasu Nobukuni et al. (Tokyo: Perikansha, 2000), 124.
52. Nakai Masakazu has a somewhat different view on the scope of the Kyoto School, and includes Watsuji and Kuki, along with Tosaka and himself, in his wider conception of the Kyoto School as a “body of brilliantly scattered diversity” that did not coalesce into “a fixed entity, as some people like to believe.” According to Nakai, “it was like one gigantic comet, a shooting star with a shining tail.” Cited in M. Yusa, *Zen and Philosophy* (Honolulu: University of Hawaii Press, 2002), 233. As a prominent left-wing thinker and activist during and after the war, Nakai is another of the figures often written out of the standard accounts.
53. See J. Heisig, *Philosophers of Nothingness: An Essay on the Kyoto School* (Honolulu: University of Hawai’i Press, 2001).
54. Williams, *Defending Japan’s Pacific War*, 97.
55. Ōhashi, “Zur Philosophie der Kyoto-Schule,” 121–125.
56. I. Hampsher-Monk, “Speech Acts, Languages or Conceptual History?” in *History of Concepts: Comparative Perspectives*, ed. I. Hampsher-Monk, K. Tilmans, and F. van Vree (Amsterdam: Amsterdam University Press, 1998), 38.
57. Ōhashi, “Zur Philosophie der Kyoto-Schule,” 121.
58. Tosaka Jun, “*‘Yamato damashii’ gakuha no tetsugaku*,” *Keizai Ōrai* (October 1932), TJZ 5.88–94.
59. Tosaka Jun, “*Tanabe tetsugaku no seiritsu*” [“The emergence of Tanabe’s philosophy”], TJZ 3.177–184.
60. Yusa, *Zen and Philosophy*, 232–233; Heisig, *Philosophers of Nothingness*, 3–7; Ōhashi, “Zur Philosophie der Kyoto-Schule,” 122–124.
61. C. Goto-Jones, “The Kyoto School,” in *Encyclopedia of Political Theory*, vol. 2, ed. M. Bevir (London: Sage, 2010), 771.
62. Miki Kiyoshi, *Rekishi tetsugaku* [*The philosophy of history*] (1932), MKZ 6.1–288; See K. N. Steffensen’s translation of Tosaka’s “The Philosophy of the Kyoto School.”
63. R. Ōhashi, *Die Philosophie der Kyôto-Schule*, second ed. (Freiburg/Munich: Karl Alber, 2011), 13.
64. K. N. Steffensen, trans., Tosaka’s “The Philosophy of the Kyoto School,” 70.
65. Tosaka Jun, “*Kyōto gakuha no tetsugaku*” [“The philosophy of the Kyoto School”], TJZ 3.171–176.
66. Miki Kiyoshi, “*Setchō hihyō ni kotau*” 「拙著批評に答ふ」 [“Responding to my critics”] (1932), NKZ 10.229–254, 231.
67. K. Kracht, “Nishida und die Politik, Erster Teil,” *Japonica Humboldtiana* 5 (2001), 223.
68. Heisig, *Philosophers of Nothingness*, 52.
69. Usage of the term “philosophy of total war” would have been about a decade premature, as it first surfaces in connection with the World-Historical Standpoint and Japan symposium. Ōhashi somewhat summarily dismisses Yamada as a “left-wing

polemicist," and although Yamada's general view of the Kyoto School is uncharitable, he did not attribute the claims about "racial" philosophy (J. Heisig's translation of *minzoku*, which is more accurately rendered as "national" or "ethnic") and "philosophy of total war" to Tosaka. These were Yamada's own assessments. The translation of *kokka sōryokusen* as "total war" is also misleading because of the strong association it has with Goebbels's 1943 Sportpalast speech. The Japanese term appeared before Goebbels made it a household word and has its origins in Clausewitz and Ludendorf.

70. Tosaka Jun, "*'Yamato damashii' gakuha no tetsugaku*," TJZ 5.88.
71. See, for instance, Heisig, *Philosophers of Nothingness*, 52; Goto-Jones, "The Kyoto School," 771.
72. Tosaka Jun, "*Kyōto gakuha no tetsugaku*," TJZ 3.175: translation modified by M. Yusa.
73. J. Heisig, "The Religious Philosophy of the Kyoto School: An Overview," *Japanese Journal of Religious Studies* 17.2 (1990), 51–81; J. Heisig, *Philosophers of Nothingness*; Ōhashi, *Die Philosophie der Kyôto-Schule* .
74. In Heisig's translation: "The name 'Kyoto School' is a name journalists used in connection with discussions that friends of mine and I held immediately before and during the war" (NKC XI, 207). See Heisig, *Philosophers of Nothingness*,277; and Davis, "The Kyoto School."
75. Heisig, *Philosophers of Nothingness*.
76. Ōhashi, *Die Philosophie der Kyôto-Schule*.
77. Tosaka Jun, "The Philosophy of the Kyoto School," TJZ 3.171–176.
78. Ōhashi, *Die Philosophie der Kyôto-Schule*, 12: "As far as the concept of the Kyoto School means Nishida's circle of students or a salon centered on the group around Nishida, Miki ought to be considered a member of this school, since he was after all a favorite student of Nishida's. However, if the concept of the school should be understood not merely as a collegial circle around Nishida but as a circle of philosophers who were animated by a common philosophical spirit shared with Nishida and who accepted certain fundamental concepts, such as 'nothingness,' then Miki ought rather to be considered a marginal Kyoto School figure."
79. T. Asakura, "Converging East Asian Philosophies: New Confucianism and the Kyoto School," in *After New Confucianism: Whither Modern Chinese Philosophy?*, ed. T. Nakajima, W. Lam, and T. Baba (Tokyo: University of Tokyo Center for Philosophy, 2014), 113.
80. NKZ 19.225. This letter is translated and quoted in Yusa, *Zen and Philosophy*, xx.
81. Cited in J. Krummel, *Nishida Kitarō's Chiasmatic Chorology: Place of Dialectic, Dialectic of Place* (Bloomington: Indiana University Press, 2015), 165.
82. Tosaka Jun, "*Kyoto gakuha no tetsugaku*," TJZ 3.174.
83. The latter is the view advanced by Davis, in his "The Kyoto School."
84. J. Gonzalez Valles, *Historia de la Filosofia Japonesa* (Madrid: Tecnos, 2001), 362.

85. Fujita Masakatsu, "Editor's Introduction" to *Kyoto gakuha no tetsugaku* 『京都学派の哲学』 [*The philosophy of the Kyoto School*] (Kyoto: Shōwado, 2001), iii.
86. Miki had an unfinished manuscript on Shinran with him in his prison cell when he died on September 26, 1945. This has led Harootunian to conjecture that he was exhausted and seeking in vain for a way for a Buddhist "native home" that he "never quite got to." See H. D. Harootunian, *Overcome by Modernity: History, Culture and Community in Interwar Japan* (Princeton: Princeton University Press, 2001), 358. What Miki himself had stated three years earlier in the short autobiographical "My Youth" was that he was influenced by his Shin Buddhist upbringing and had an interest in clarifying the philosophical significance of popular traditions such as those represented by Hōnen and Shinran rather than the more elitist Zen (MKZ 1.383).
87. Nakajima Hirokatsu, "What was the Kyoto School?"
88. Ōhashi, "Zur Philosophie der Kyoto-Schule," 121.
89. Nakajima Hirokatsu, "What was the Kyoto School?"
90. The book was published in the liberal climate of 1946, but conceived and written during the war. It may be seen as disingenuous or as part of Tanabe's "repentance," but his advocacy of what he now openly thought of as a nonutilitarian social democratic theory reconciling liberty and equality can also be read as a continuation of his earlier work rather than a break with it (THZ 8.323–396).
91. Williams, *Defending Japan's Pacific War*, 176.
92. Najita and Harootunian, "Japanese Revolt," 741.
93. J. van Bragt, "Kyoto Philosophy—Intrinsically Nationalistic?" in *Rude Awakenings: Zen, the Kyoto School and the Question of Nationalism*, ed. J. W. Heisig and J. C. Maraldo (Honolulu: University of Hawai'i Press, 1994), 234.
94. J. van Bragt, translation of Nishitani Keiji's work, *Religion and Nothingness* (Berkeley: University of California Press, 1982).
95. G. Parkes, "The Putative Fascism of the Kyoto School and the Political Correctness of the Modern Academy," *Philosophy East & West* 47.3 (1997), 309.
96. Williams, *Defending Japan's Pacific War*, 154.
97. Miki Kiyoshi, "*Chishiki kaikyū ni atau*" ["To the intellectuals"], MKZ 15.238–239; "*Tōa Kenkyūjo*" ["The East Asia Research Institute"], MKZ 15.293–294.
98. Uchida Hiroshi, *Miki Kiyoshi: Koseisha no kōsōryoku* [Miki Kiyoshi: The imagination of the individual] (Tokyo: Ochanomizu Shobō, 2004), 129.
99. J. Dower, *Embracing Defeat: Japan in the Wake of World War II* (New York: W. W. Norton, 1999), 190–191.
100. Nakajima Takahiro, *The Chinese Turn in Philosophy* (Tokyo: University of Tokyo Center for Philosophy, 2007), 118.
101. See P. Lavelle, "The Political Thought of Nishida Kitarō," *Monumenta Nipponica* 49.2 (1994), 139–165.
102. C. Goto-Jones, *Political Philosophy in Japan: Nishida, the Kyoto School, and Co-Prosperity* (New York and London: Routledge, 2005), 106.

103. W. M. Fletcher, *The Search for a New Order: Intellectuals and Fascism in Prewar Japan* (Chapel Hill: University of North Carolina Press, 1982), 158.
104. Williams, *The Philosophy of Japanese Wartime Resistance*, xxii.
105. L. Strauss, *Persecution and the Art of Writing* (Westport, CT: Greenwood Press, 1973 [1952]).
106. P. Duus and D. I. Okimoto, "Fascism and the History of Pre-war Japan: The Failure of a Concept," *Journal of Asian Studies* 39.1 (1979), 65–76; also B. Shillony, *Politics and Culture in Wartime Japan* (Oxford: Clarendon, 1981).
107. Shillony, *Politics and Culture*, 12–13.
108. M. Silverberg, "War Responsibility Revisited: Auschwitz in Japan," *Review of Asian and Pacific Studies* 29 (2005), 43–63.
109. Ōhashi Ryōsuke, *Kyoto Gakuha to Nippon Kaigun* [*The Kyoto School and the Japanese Navy*] (Tokyo: PHP Shinsha, 2001), 120–121.
110. Ōyama Ikuo, though not a Kyoto School philosopher, was one of the few to leave Japan, spending 1933–46 at Northwestern University's Department of Political Science.
111. This term has also been translated as "anti-establishment cooperation" (Williams, *Defending Japan's Pacific War*, p. 73), "resistive cooperation" (C. Rigby, "Nishida on Heidegger," *Continental Philosophy Review* 42 [2010], 522 and 531), and as "cooperative resistance" (Davis, "Kyoto School"), with the latter reversing Ōhashi's emphasis.
112. Uchida Hiroshi, *Miki Kiyoshi*, 129.
113. Nozawa Toshiharu, "*Shohyō, Uchida Hiroshi Miki Kiyoshi, Koseisha no kōsōryoku*" [Review of Uchida Hiroshi's *Miki Kiyoshi: The imagination of the individual*], *Shakaikagaku Nenpō* 39 (2005), 201.
114. Cited in T. Horio, "The *Chūōkōron* Discussions, Their Background, and Meaning," in Heisig and Maraldo, *Rude Awakenings*, 291.
115. Sugiyama Masao, "*Daitōa kyōeiken no seitōka to ronri, Sekaishi no tetsugaku to Miki Kiyoshi*" ["The justification and logic of the Greater East Asia Co-prosperity Sphere: 'The philosophy of world history' and Miki Kiyoshi"], *Ningenkankei Ronshū* 21 (2004), 75.
116. Williams, *Defending Japan's Pacific War*, 69.
117. Chen-kuo Lin, "Nishitani on Emptiness and Historical Consciousness," *Dao* 13 (2014), 492.
118. See Williams *Defending Japan's Pacific War*; Ōhashi Ryōsuke, *Kyoto Gakuha to Nippon Kaigun.*
119. Heisig, *Philosophers of Nothingness*, 6. This said, the manner in which Heisig seeks to rescue Kyoto School philosophy by emphasizing philosophy of religion over philosophy of history and social and political theory is not entirely unproblematic, particularly with regard to the "middle phase" that Williams identifies as the time from around 1927 to August 1945, during which "the focal

concern was political philosophy" (Williams, *Defending Japan's Pacific War*, 30 and 179). As can also be said for Davis—B. Davis, "Turns to and from Political Philosophy: The Case of Nishitani Keiji," in *Repoliticising the Kyoto School as Philosophy*, ed. C. Goto-Jones (London: Routledge, 2009), 26–46, as well as his entry on "The Kyoto School," in *Stanford Encyclopedia of Philosophy*; Heisig's purpose is an assertion that the valuable *sophia perennis* in the Kyoto School corpus is in its philosophy of religion and that, whatever its flaws or merits, the political philosophy has little bearing on this. Williams, on the other hand, seeks "to squeeze maximum contemporary value" (Williams, *Defending Japan's Pacific War*, 202, n. 7) by treating the relevant texts from the "middle phase" as "political thought in the classic sense" (179).

120. Ōtsuka Katsura, *Daitōa sensō no seijigaku* [*Political studies during the Greater East Asia War*] (Tokyo: Seibundō, 2007), 58.

121. S. Eklöf, *Power and Political Culture in Suharto's Indonesia: The Indonesian Democratic Party (PDI) and the Decline of the New Order (1986–98)* (Abingdon and New York: Routledge, 2004), 5.

122. Q. Skinner, *Machiavelli: A Very Short Introduction* (Oxford: Oxford University Press, 1982), 2; and Q. Skinner, *Visions of Politics: Regarding Method* (Cambridge: Cambridge University Press, 2002), 6.

123. Ishige Tadashi et al., ed., *Nihon shisō-shi jiten* [*Dictionary of Japanese intellectual history*] (Tokyo: Yamakawa Shuppansha, 2009), 242–243.

124. Rigby, "Nishida on Heidegger," 519–520.

125. See Asakura, "Converging East Asian Philosophies."

126. In his vindication of Nishida, Goto-Jones's treatment of Tanabe and Miki, however, comes close to that of the "side-swipers" because of methodological inconsistency. Heisig noted in his review of *Political Philosophy in Japan*: as an ancillary thesis, Jones presents Tanabe and Nishitani (and to a lesser degree Miki) as having forfeited their philosophical souls to keep their public voices during the war years. The purpose of this argument is to support the exoneration of Nishida, but the results are less convincing than the other chapters for one important reason—Jones fails to apply the same method to their writings that he did to Nishida's. Gone are all echoes of Confucian and Buddhist thought. Gone is the wider context of thought against which to read their wartime statements. Gone, too, is any hint of a struggle for reclaiming a language wrenched from its context in service of the vilest of causes. See J. Heisig, review, "Christopher C.S. Goto-Jones, *Political Philosophy in Japan: Nishida, the Kyoto School and Co-Prosperity*," *Japanese Journal of Religious Studies* 32.1 (2005), 180.

127. Inukai, "*Sezoku no Kyoto gakuha?*" 5.

128. Significant contributions have also been made by scholars with less religious interests based in area studies departments, first and foremost by Naoki Sakai and Richard Calichman.

129. M. Frank, "*Hegel wohnt hier nicht mehr: Die kontintentale Philosophie verschwindet aus Europa*," *Frankfurter Allgemeiner Zeitung*, September 24, 2015.

130. B. Bruya, "Appearance and Reality in *The Philosophical Gourmet Report*: Why the Discrepancy Matters to the Profession of Philosophy," *Metaphilosophy* 46.4/5 (2015), 680.

131. M. Paxton, C. Figdor, and V. Tiberius, "Quantifying the Gender Gap: An Empirical Study of the Underrepresentation of Women in Philosophy," *Hypatia* 24.4 (2012), 949–957.

132. B. Baker et al., *Report to the Canadian Philosophical Association from the Committee to Study Hiring Policies Affecting Women* (Ottawa: Canadian Philosophical Association, 1991), 18.

133. A. Sen, *The Argumentative Indian: Writings on Indian History, Culture, and Identity* (London: Allen Lane, 2004), 25.

134. E. H. Carr, *The Twenty Years' Crisis, 1919–1939* (Basingstoke: Palgrave MacMillan 2001 [1939]).

135. Tanabe Hajime *Seiji tetsugaku no kyūmu* [*The urgent task of political philosophy*] (1946), THZ, 8.323–396.

136. Williams, *Defending Japan's Pacific War*, 97.

137. Shimohara Motoaki, "*Mujō to zettaimu, Tanabe Hajime no tetsugaku*" ["Indeterminacy and absolute nothingness: Tanabe Hajime's philosophy"], *Aida/Seisei* 5 (2015), 6–7; Gōda Masato, *Tanabe Hajime to Haidegā: fūin sareta tetsugaku* [*Tanabe and Heidegger: Sealed-off philosophies*] (Kyoto: PHP, 2013).

138. E. Traverso, "El Totalitarismo: Usos y Abusos de un Concepto," in *Las Escalas del Pasado: IV Congreso de Historia Local de Aragón*, ed. A. S. Alcutén and C. F. Alvarez (Huesca: IEA, 2005), 100.

139. Nishida Kitarō, "*Goshinkō sōan, Rekishi tetsugaku ni tsuite*" (A draft of the New Year's Lecture to His Majesty the Emperor, "On the Philosophy of History"), NKZ 12.271, cited in M. Yusa, "Nishida and Totalitarianism: A Philosopher's Resistance," in Heisig and Maraldo, *Rude Awakenings*, 111. The entire lecture is translated into English, "A New Year's Lecture to the Emperor: On the Philosophy of History," in Yusa, *Zen and Philosophy*, 314–318.

140. "*Shin nihon no shisō genri, zokuhen*" [The philosophical principle of new Japan, Part II], MKZ 17.552.

141. Miki Kiyoshi "*Jiyūshugi igo*" ["After liberalism"], MKZ 13.168–175.

142. He also analyzes the failure of self-undermining Japanese liberalism as stemming from its "cultural" rather than "political" orientation, which he attributes to its German rather than British and French sources.

143. J. N. Kim, "The Temporality of Empire: The Imperial Cosmopolitanism of Miki Kiyoshi and Tanabe Hajime," in *Pan-Asianism in Modern Japanese History: Colonialism, Regionalism and Borders*, ed. S. Saaler and J. V. Koschmann (Abingdon and New York: Routledge, 2007), 167.

144. Yusa, "Nishida and Totalitarianism," 131.

145. K. Shimizu, "Nishida Kitaro and Japan's Interwar Foreign Policy," *International Relations of the Asia Pacific* 11 (2011), 159.

146. Ueda Shizuteru, "Nishida, Nationalism, and the War in Question," in Heisig and Maraldo, *Rude Awakening*, 97.
147. Arai Masao, "*Nishida Kitarō to Miki Kiyoshi: Kindai chōkoku no tetsugaku (sekaiteki sekai, kyōdōshugi) o teishō*" ["Nishida Kitarō and Miki Kiyoshi: Advocating the overcoming of modernity (world of worlds/cooperative communitarianism)"], *Tetsugaku to Kyōiku* 60 (2013), 46.
148. Van Bragt, "Kyoto Philosophy—Intrinsically Nationalistic?"
149. Kim, "The Temporality of Empire," 151–167.
150. Shimizu, "Nishida Kitaro," 158; Y. Arisaka, "The Nishida Enigma: 'The Principle of the New World Order' (1943)," *Monumenta Nipponica* 51.1 (1996), 101.
151. Nishida Kitarō, "*Nihon Bunka no mondai*" [Questions concerning Japanese culture] (three-part lectures delivered at the Imperial University of Kyoto, 1938, Lecture 2), NKZ 14.404–405, cited in Y. Arisaka, "Beyond 'East and West': Nishida's Universalism and Postcolonial Critique," *The Review of Politics* 59.3 (1997), 545, translation by Arisaka.
152. Chakrabarty, *Provincializing Europe*, 6.
153. Miki Kiyoshi, "The China Affair & Japanese Thought" (in English), MKZ 20.12–13.
154. Arisaka, "Beyond 'East and West,'" 546–554.
155. Williams, *Defending Japan's Pacific War*, 152.
156. Takeuchi cited in Sugiyama Masao, "Tōa kyōeiken no seitoka to ronri: sekaishi no tetsugaku to Miki Kiyoshi" "The Justification and Logic of the Greater East Asia Co-Prosperity Sphere," 70; Calichman, *What Is Modernity?*,125.
157. T. Nairn, "The Modern Janus," *New Left Review* I/94 (1975), 3–29.
158. For instance, van Bragt, "Kyoto Philosophy—Intrinsically Nationalistic?"
159. Arisaka, "Beyond 'East and West,'" 551; Kim, "The Temporality of Empire"; N. Sakai, "Resistance to Conclusion: The Kyōto School Philosophy under Pax Americana," in Goto-Jones, *Re-politicizing the Kyōto School as Philosophy*, 183–198.
160. A. Acharya and B. Buzan, eds., *Non-Western International Relations Theory: Perspectives on and beyond* Asia (London and New York: Routledge, 2010); D. Armitage, "The International Turn in Intellectual History," in *Rethinking Modern European Intellectual History*, ed. D. M. McMahon and M. Moyn (New York: Oxford University Press, 2014), 232–252. See also K. Shimizu, "Reading Kyoto School Philosophy as a Non-Western Discourse: Contingency, Nothingness and the Public," Afrasian Research Centre Working Paper Series Studies on Multicultural Societies No. 31 (Kyoto: Ryukoku University, 2015).
161. Williams, *The Philosophy of Japanese Wartime Resistance*, 20.

BIBLIOGRAPHY

Acharya, Amitav, and Barry Buzan, eds. *Non-Western International Relations Theory: Perspectives on and beyond Asia*. London and New York: Routledge, 2010.

Arai Masao 荒井正雄. "*Nishida Kitarō to Miki Kiyoshi: Kindai chōkoku no tetsugaku (sekaiteki sekai, kyōdōshugi) wo teishō*" 「西田幾多郎と三木清—近代超克の哲学（世界的世界／協同主義）を提唱」 ["Nishida Kitarō and Miki Kiyoshi: Advocating the overcoming of modernity (global world/cooperative communitarianism)"]. *Tetsugaku to Kyōiku* 60 (2013), 41–56.

Arisaka, Yoko. "The Nishida Enigma: 'The Principle of the New World Order' (1943)." *Monumenta Nipponica* 51.1 (1996), 81–106.

Arisaka, Yoko. "Beyond 'East and West': Nishida's Universalism and Postcolonial Critique." *The Review of Politics* 59.3 (1997), 541–560.

Armitage, David. "The International Turn in Intellectual History." In *Rethinking Modern European Intellectual History*, ed. Darrin M. McMahon and Samuel Moyn, 232–252. New York: Oxford University Press, 2014.

Asakura Tomomi 朝倉友海. "'*Dōtoku' e no higashi ajiateki apurōchi: Kyōto gakuha to shinjuka no dōtokuron o tegakari to shite*" 「〈道徳〉への東アジア的アプローチ—京都学派と新儒家の道徳論をてがかりとして」 ["Morality and modernity in East Asia: Post-war Kyoto School and New Confucianism in the historical and social context"]. *Ōyō Rinri Tetsugaku Ronshū* 3 (2006), 74–87.

Asakura Tomomi. "Converging East Asian Philosophies: New Confucianism and the Kyoto School." In *After New Confucianism: Whither Modern Chinese Philosophy?*, ed. Takahiro Nakajima, Lam Wing-keung, and Tomokazu Baba, 111–132. Tokyo: University of Tokyo Center for Philosophy, 2014.

Baker, Brenda, et al. *Report to the Canadian Philosophical Association from the Committee to Study Hiring Policies Affecting Women.* Ottawa: Canadian Philosophical Association, 1991.

Bell, Daniel A. *China's New Confucianism: Politics and Everyday Life in a Changing Society.* Princeton: Princeton University Press, 2008.

Bragt, Jan van. *Religion and Nothingness*, trans. Nishitani Keiji. Berkeley: University of California Press, 1982.

Bragt, Jan van. "Kyoto Philosophy—Intrinsically Nationalistic?" In *Rude Awakenings: Zen, the Kyoto School and the Question of Nationalism*, ed. James W. Heisig and John C. Maraldo, 233–254. Honolulu: University of Hawai'i Press, 1994.

Calichman, Richard F. *Takeuchi Yoshimi: Displacing the West.* Ithaca, NY: Cornell University Press, 2004.

Calichman, Richard F. *What Is Modernity? Writings of Takeuchi Yoshimi.* New York: Columbia University Press, 2005.

Calichman, Richard F. *Overcoming Modernity: Cultural Identity in Wartime Japan.* New York: Columbia University Press, 2008.

Calichman, Richard F. "Guest Editor's Introduction." *positions: east asia cultures critique* 17.1 (2009), 1–12.

Carr, E. H. *The Twenty Years' Crisis, 1919–1939.* Basingstoke: Palgrave MacMillan, 2001 (1939).

Chakrabarty, Dipesh. *Provincializing Europe: Postcolonial Thought and Historical Difference*, second ed. Princeton: Princeton University Press, 2007.

Davis, Bret W. "Turns to and from Political Philosophy: The Case of Nishitani Keiji." In *Repoliticising the Kyoto School as Philosophy*, ed. Christopher Goto-Jones, 26–46. London: Routledge, 2009.

Davis, Bret W. "The Kyoto School." In *The Stanford Encyclopedia of Philosophy* (most recently updated 2014). http://plato.stanford.edu/entries/kyoto-school/

Dower, John. *Embracing Defeat: Japan in the Wake of World War II*. New York: W.W. Norton, 1999.

Duus, Peter, and Daniel I. Okimoto. "Fascism and the History of Pre-war Japan: The Failure of a Concept." *Journal of Asian Studies* 39.1 (1979), 65–76.

Eklöf, Stefan. *Power and Political Culture in Suharto's Indonesia: The Indonesian Democratic Party (PDI) and the Decline of the New Order (1986–98)*. Abingdon and New York: Routledge, 2004.

Fletcher, Miles. "Intellectuals and Fascism in Early Shōwa Japan." *Journal of Asian Studies* 39.1 (1979), 39–63.

Fletcher, Miles. *The Search for a New Order: Intellectuals and Fascism in Prewar Japan*. Chapel Hill: University of North Carolina Press, 1982.

Frank, Manfred. "Hegel wohnt hier nicht mehr: Die kontintentale Philosophie verschwindet aus Europa." *Frankfurter Allgemeiner Zeitung* (September 24, 2015). http://www.faz.net/aktuell/feuilleton/hegel-wohnt-hier-nicht-mehr-die-kontinentale-philosophie-verschwindet-aus-europa-13816301.html

Fujita Masakatsu 藤田正勝. "Introduction." In *Kyōto gakuha no tetsugaku* 『京都学派の哲学』 [*The philosophy of the Kyoto School*], ed. Fujita Masakatsu. Kyoto: Shōwado, 2001.

Fujita Masakatsu. "*Kindai nihon tetsugaku no potensharu: 'tetsugaku' no imi o megutte*" 「近代日本哲学のポテンシャル：「哲学」の意味をめぐって」 ["The potential of modern Japanese philosophy: Concerning the meaning of philosophy"]. *Tetsugaku* no. 57 (2006), 4–17.

Fujita Masakatsu. "'*Kyōto gakuha' towa nani ka: kin'nen no kenkyū ni furenagara*" 「〈京都学派〉とは何か：近年の研究に触れながら」 ["What is the 'Kyoto School': Touching on the research of recent years"]. *Nihon Shisōshigaku* no. 41 (2009), 35–48.

Fujita Masakatsu. "Logos and Pathos: Miki Kiyoshi's Logic of Imagination." In *Japanese and Continental Philosophy: Conversations with the Kyoto School*, ed. Bret W. Davis, Brian Schroeder, and Jason M. Wirth, 305–318. Bloomington: University of Indiana Press, 2011.

Fujita Masakatsu. "*Nishida Kitarō botsugo nanajūnen o furikaeru*" 「西田幾多郎没後七十年をふり返る」 ["Looking back 70 years after the death of Nishida Kitarō"]. *Shisō* 1099 (November 2015), 2–6.

Fujita Masakatsu. "*Nishida tetsugaku to Tanabe tetsugaku: sōzōteki taiwa no hitotsu nokatachi*" 「西田哲学と田辺哲学：創造的対話の一つの形」 ["Nishida's philosophy and Tanabe's philosophy: A form of creative dialogue"]. *Shisō* 1099 (November 2015), 8–26.

Gōda Masato 合田正人. *Tanabe Hajime to Haidegā: fūin sareta tetsugaku* 『田辺元とハイデガー　封印された哲学』 [*Tanabe and Heidegger: Sealed-off philosophies*]. Kyoto: PHP Shinsho, 2013.

Gonzalez Valles, Jésus. *Historia de la Filosofia Japonesa*. Madrid: Tecnos, 2001.

Goto-Jones, Christopher. "Ethics and Politics in the Early Nishida: Reconsidering *Zen no Kenkyū*." *Philosophy East & West* 53.4 (2003), 514–536.

Goto-Jones, Christopher. "The Left Hand of Darkness: Forging a Political Left in Interwar Japan." In *The Left in the Shaping of Japanese Democracy: Essays in Honour of J.A.A. Stockwin*, ed. David Williams and Rikki Kersten, 3–20. London: Routledge, 2004.

Goto-Jones, Christopher. *Political Philosophy in Japan: Nishida, the Kyoto School, and Co-prosperity*. New York and London: Routledge, 2005.

Goto-Jones, Christopher. "The Kyoto School, the Cambridge School, and the History of Political Philosophy in Wartime Japan." *positions: east asia cultures critique* 17.1 (2009), 13–42.

Goto-Jones, Christopher. "The Kyoto School." In *Encyclopedia of Political Theory*, ed. Mark Bevir, vol. 2, 771–773. London: Sage, 2010.

Goto-Jones, Christopher. "Comparative Political Thought: Beyond the Non-Western." In *Ethics and World Politics*, ed. Duncan Bell, 219–232. New York: Oxford University Press, 2010.

Goto-Jones, Christopher. "When Is Comparative Political Thought (Not) Comparative? Dialogues (Dis)continuities, and Radical Difference in Heidegger and Nishida." In *Comparative Political Thought: Theorizing Practices*, ed. Michael Freeden and Andrew Vincent, 158–180. Abingdon and New York: Routledge, 2013.

Hagiwara Minoru 萩原稔. "*Chōkokkashugi no shosō: Kita Ikki to Tachibana Shiraki o chūshin ni*" 「超国家主義の諸相：北一輝と橘樸を中心に」 [Various faces of ultranationalism: A study on Kita Ikki and Tachibana Shiraki as the main focus]. In *Nihon seiji shisōshi* 『日本政治思想史』 [*A history of Japanese political thought*], ed. Nishida Takeshi 西田毅, 231–267. Tokyo: Minerva Shobō, 2009.

Hamada, Junko. *Japanische Philosophie nach 1868*. Leiden: EJ Brill, 1994.

Hampsher-Monk, Ian. "Speech Acts, Languages or Conceptual History?" In *History of Concepts: Comparative Perspectives*, ed. Ian Hampsher-Monk, Karin Tilmans, and Frank van Vree. Amsterdam: Amsterdam University Press, 1998.

Harootunian, Harry D. *Overcome by Modernity: History, Culture and Community in Interwar Japan*. Princeton: Princeton University Press, 2001.

Harootunian, Harry D. "Returning to Japan: Part Two." *Japan Forum* 18.2 (2006), 275–282.

Hattori Kenji 服部健二. "*Kyōto-gakuha 'saha' zō*" 「京都学派《左派》像」 ["The image of the 'left wing' Kyoto School"]. In *Kyōto gakuha no shisō, shushu no zō to shisō no potensharu* [*The philosophical thought of the Kyoto School: Various images and their intellectual potential*], ed. Ōhashi Ryōsuke, 23–43. Kyoto: Jinbun Shoin, 2004.

Hattori Kenji. "*'Kyōto gakuha' to sono 'saha' no ningengaku no keifu ni tsuite: aru jidai jōkyō no naka de*" 「「京都学派」とその「左派」の人間学の系譜について: ある時代状況のなかで」 ["On the 'Kyoto School' and the genealogy of the anthropology of its 'left wing': In the circumstances of the time"]. *Ritsumeikan Bungaku* 603 (2008), 263–279.

Hayashi Naomichi 林直道. *Nishida Tetsugaku hihan* 『西田哲学批判』 [*A critique of Nishida's philosophy*]. Tokyo: Kaihōsha, 1948.

Heisig, James W. "The Religious Philosophy of the Kyoto School: An Overview." *Japanese Journal of Religious Studies* 17.2 (1990), 51–81.

Heisig, James W. *Philosophers of Nothingness: An Essay on the Kyoto School*. Honolulu: University of Hawai'i Press, 2001.

Heisig, James W. "David Williams *Defending Japan's Pacific War: The Kyoto School Philosophers and Post-White Power*." Review in *Japanese Journal of Religious Studies* 32.1 (2005), 163–166.

Heisig, James W. "Christopher C.S. Goto-Jones *Political Philosophy in Japan: Nishida, the Kyoto School and Co-prosperity*." Review in *Japanese Journal of Religious Studies* 32.1 (2005), 178–180.

Hiromatsu Wataru 廣松渉. *"Kindai no chōkoku" ron—Shōwa shisōshi e no ichi shikaku* 『〈近代の超克〉論、昭和思想史への一視覚』 [*Theories on "overcoming modernity": A perspective on the history of ideas during the Showa period*]. Tokyo: Kōdansha, 1989.

Hiromatsu Wataru. "*Tōhoku ajia ga rekishi no shuyaku ni: nicchū o jiku ni 'tōa' no shintaisei o*" 「東北アジアが歴史の主役に – 日中を軸に「東亜」の新体制を」 ["Northeast Asia taking a leading role in history: The new 'East Asian' system along a Japan-China axis"]. *Asahi Shinbun*, March 16, 1994. Reprinted in *Hiromatsu Wataru Chosakushū* 『廣松渉著作集』 [Collected writings of Hiromatsu Wataru] 14, 497–500. Tokyo: Iwanami Shoten, 1997. http://www.linelabo.com/touashintaisei.htm

Horio, Tsutomu. "The *Chuokoron* Discussions, Their Background and Meaning." In *Rude Awakenings: Zen, the Kyoto School, & the Question of Nationalism*, ed. James W. Heisig and John C. Maraldo, 289–315. Honolulu: University of Hawai'i Press, 1994.

Inukai Yūichi 犬飼裕一. "*Sezoku no Kyoto-gakuha?*" 「世俗の京都学派?」 [The revival of the Kyoto School? *Hokkai Gakuen Gakuen Ronshū* no. 126, December 2005, 263–279.

Ismail, Salwa. "Islamic Political Thought." In *The Cambridge History of Twentieth-Century Political Thought*, ed. T. Ball and R. Bellamy, chapter 27, 579–601. Cambridge: Cambridge University Press, 2003.

Jenco, Leigh, Murad Idris, and Megan Thomas, eds. *The Oxford Handbook of Comparative Political Theory*. New York: Oxford University Press, forthcoming.

Kim, John Namjun. "The Temporality of Empire: The Imperial Cosmopolitanism of Miki Kiyoshi and Tanabe Hajime." In *Pan-Asianism in Modern Japanese History: Colonialism, Regionalism and Borders*, ed. Sven Saaler and J. Victor Koschmann, 151–167. Abingdon and New York: Routledge, 2007.

Kobayashi Toshiaki 小林敏明. *Hiromatsu Wataru, Kindai no chōkou (saihakken nihon no tetsugaku)* 『廣松渉　近代の超克 (再発見 日本の哲学)』 [*Hiromatsu Wataru: Overcoming modernity (the rediscovery of Japanese philosophy)*]. Tokyo: Kōdansha, 2007.

Kōsaka Shirō 高坂史朗. "*Higashiajia no shiten kara mita Nishida tetsugaku (Nishida tetsugaku kenkyū no shatei: botsugo 70-nen ni yosete)*" 「東アジアの視点から見た西田哲学（西田哲学研究の射程：没後70年に寄せて）」 [Nishida philosophy seen from an East Asian perspective (the range of philosophical studies of Nishida 70 years after his death)]. *Shisō* 1099 (November 2015), 71–87.

Kracht, Klaus. "Nishida und die Politik. Erster Teil." *Japonica Humboldtiana* 5 (2001), 205–250.

Krummel, John W. M. *Nishida Kitarō's Chiasmatic Chorology: Place of Dialectic, Dialectic of Place*. Bloomington: Indiana University Press, 2015.

Lavelle, Pierre. "The Political Thought of Nishida Kitarō." *Monumenta Nipponica* 49.2 (1994), 139–165.

Lie, John. "Enough Said, Ahmad: Politics and Literary Theory." *positions* 2.2 (1994), 417–429.

Lin, Chen-kuo. "Nishitani on Emptiness and Historical Consciousness." *Dao* 13 (2014), 491–506.

March, Andrew F. "What Is Comparative Political Theory?" *The Review of Politics* 71 (2009), 531–565.

Maruyama Masao 丸山真男. "*Kindaiteki shii*" 「近代的思惟」 [Modern thought] (a testimony written in January 1946). In *Maruyama Masao, Botsugo jūnen, minshushugi no 'shinwa' o koete* 『丸山真男、没後十年、民主主義の〈神話〉を超えて』 [Maruyama Masao: Commemorating the tenth anniversary of his death, going beyond the "myth" of democracy], 136–137. Tokyo: Kawade Shobō-shinsha, 2006.

Miki Kiyoshi 三木清. *Rekishi tetsugaku* 『歴史哲学』 [*The philosophy of history*]. MKZ 6.1–288 (1932). Tokyo: Iwanami Shoten, 1967.

Miki Kiyoshi. "*Setchō hihyō ni kotau*" 拙著批評に答ふ ["Responding to my critics"]. MKZ 10.229–254 (1932).

Miki Kiyoshi. "*Chishiki kaikyū ni atau*" 「知識階級に与ふ」 ["To the intellectuals"]. MKZ 15.237–243 (1938).

Miki Kiyoshi. "*Jiyūshugi igo*" 自由主義以後 ["After liberalism"]. MKZ 13.168–175 (1935).

Miki Kiyoshi. "*Tōa kenkyūjo*" 「東亜研究所」 ["About the East Asia Institute"]. Originally in *Waseda Daigaku Shinbun*. MKZ 15.293–295 (1938, 9/14).

Miki Kiyoshi. "The China Affair & Japanese Thought." MKZ 20.1–13 (1938).

Miki Kiyoshi. "*Shin nihon no shisō genri, zokuhen*" 「新日本の思想原理、続編」 [The intellectual principle of new Japan, Part II]. MKZ 17.534–588 (1939).

Miki Kiyoshi. "*Waga seishun*" 我が青春 ["My youth"]. MKZ 1.353–368 (1942).

Nagata Hiroshi 永田広志. *Tetsugaku to minshushugi: Nishida-Tanabe tetsugaku hihan no tame ni* 「哲学と民主主義—西田・田辺哲学批判のために」 [*Philosophy and democracy: Towards a critique of Nishida and Tanabe's philosophy*]. Tokyo: Komeiji Shoten, 1948.

Nairn, Tom. "The Modern Janus." *New Left Review* 1.94 (1975), 3–29.

Najita, Tetsuo, and Harry Harootunian. "Japanese Revolt against the West: Political and Cultural Criticism in the Twentieth Century." In *The Cambridge History of Japan*, ed. Peter Duus, 6.711–774. Cambridge: Cambridge University Press, 1989.

Nakai Masakazu 中井正一. "*Kaiko jūnen: Omoiizuru mama ni*" 「回顧十年–思い出づるまゝに」 ["Random recollections of ten years ago"]. *Tetsugaku Kenkyū* 35.2 (February 1951), 108–112.

Nakajima, Takahiro 中島隆博. *The Chinese Turn in Philosophy.* Tokyo: University of Tokyo Center for Philosophy, 2007.

Nakajima Hirokatsu 中島啓勝. "*Kyōto gakuha towa nan datta no ka: Gendai bunmeiron toshite no Nishida tetsugaku*" 「京都学派とは何だったのか: 現代文明論としての西田哲学」 ["What was the Kyoto School? Nishida's philosophy as a theory of modern civilization"]. Kyoto: Kyoto Academeia, 2010. http://kyoto-academeia.sakura.ne.jp/index.cgi?rm=mode4&menu=mogi&id=71

Nakaoka Narifumi 中岡成文. "*Kyōto gakuha*" ["The Kyoto School"]. In *Iwanami Tetsugaku Shisō Jiten* [Iwanami dictionary of philosophy and ideas], ed. Hiromatsu Wataru, Koyasu Nobukuni, Mishima Ken'ichi, Miyamoto Hisao, Sasaki Chikara, Noe Keiichi, and Sueki Fumihiko, 347–348. Tokyo: Iwanami Shoten, 1998.

Nishida Takeshi 西田毅, ed. *Nihon seiji shisōshi* 『日本政治思想史』 [*A history of Japanese political thought*]. Tokyo: Minerva Shobō, 2009.

Nozawa Toshiharu 野沢敏治. "*Shohyō*, Uchida Hiroshi *Miki Kiyoshi: koseisha no kōsōryoku*" 「〈書評〉内田弘 『三木清 個性者の構想力』」 ["Review of Uchida Hiroshi's *Miki Kiyoshi: The imagination of the individual*]. *Shakaikagaku Nenpō* 39 (2005), 197–201.

Ōhashi, Ryōsuke. "Zur Philosophie der Kyoto-Schule." *Zeitschrift für Philosophische Forschung* 40.1 (1986), 121–134.

Ōhashi, Ryōsuke 大橋良介. "*Sengo nihon no shisō hyōshiki, Miki Kiyoshi to Nishida Kitarō*" 「戦後日本の思想標識 三木清と西田幾多郎 ["Intellectual markers of post-war Japan: Miki Kiyoshi and Nishida Kitarō"]. *Asuteion* 40 (1996), 194–210.

Ōhashi Ryōsuke. *Kyōto gakuha to Nippon kaigun* 『京都学派と日本海軍』 [*The Kyoto School and the Japanese Navy*]. Tokyo: PHP Shinsha, 2001.

Ōhashi, Ryōsuke, ed. *Kyōto gakuha no shisō, shushu no zō to shisō no potensharu* 『京都学派の思想 種々の像と思想のポテンシャル』 [*The philosophical thought of the Kyoto School: Various images and their intellectual potential*]. Kyoto: Jinbun Shoin, 2004.

Ōhashi, Ryōsuke. *Die Philosophie der Kyôto-Schule*, second ed. Freiburg/Munich: Karl Alber, 2011.

Ōshima Yasumasa 大島康正. "*Daitōa sensō to Kyōto gakuha: chishikijin no seiji sanka ni tsuite*" 「大東亜戦争と京都学派－知識人の政治参加について」 ["The Greater East Asia War and the Kyoto School: On the political participation of intellectuals"]. *Chūō Kōron* (August 1965), 125–143.

Ōtsuka Katsura 大塚桂. *Daitōa sensō no seijigaku* 『大東亜戦争の政治学』 [*Political studies during the Greater East Asia War*]. Tokyo: Seibundō, 2007.

Parekh, Bhikhu. "Non-Western Political Thought." In *The Cambridge History of Political Thought*, ed. T. Ball and R. Bellamy, chapter 26, 553–578. Cambridge University Press, Cambridge, 2003.

Parkes, Graham. "The Putative Fascism of the Kyoto School and the Political Correctness of the Modern Academy." *Philosophy East & West* 47.3 (1997), 305–336.

Parkes, Graham. "Heidegger and Japanese Fascism: An Unsubstantiated Connection." In *Japanese and Continental Philosophy: Conversations with the Kyoto School*, ed. Bret W. Davis, Brian Schroeder, and Jason M. Wirth, 247–268. Bloomington: University of Indiana Press, 2011.

Paxton, Molly, Carrie Figdor, and Valerie Tiberius. "Quantifying the Gender Gap: An Empirical Study of the Underrepresentation of Women in Philosophy." *Hypatia* 24.4 (2012), 949–957.

Rigby, Curtis A. "Nishida on Heidegger." *Continental Philosophy Review* 42 (2010), 511–553.

Sakai, Naoki. *Translation and Subjectivity: On Japan and Cultural Nationalism.* Minneapolis: University of Minnesota Press, 1997.

Sakai, Naoki. "Resistance to Conclusion: The Kyōto School Philosophy under Pax Americana." In *Re-politicizing the Kyoto School as Philosophy*, ed. Christopher Goto-Jones, 183–198. London: Routledge, 2007.

Sakai, Naoki. "Imperial Nationalism and the Comparative Perspective." *positions: east asia cultures critique* 17.1 (2009), 159–205.

Sen, Amartya. *The Argumentative Indian: Writings on Indian History, Culture, and Identity.* London: Allen Lane, 2004.

Shillony, Ben-Ami. *Politics and Culture in Wartime Japan.* Oxford: Clarendon, 1981.

Shillony, Ben-Ami. "Universities and Students in Wartime Japan." *Journal of Asian Studies* 45.4 (1986),769–787.

Shimizu, Kōsuke. "Nishida Kitaro and Japan's Interwar Foreign Policy: War Involvement and Culturalist Political Discourse." *International Relations of the Asia-Pacific* 11.1 (2011), 157–183.

Shimizu, Kōsuke. "Reading Kyoto School Philosophy as a Non-Western Discourse: Contingency, Nothingness and the Public." Afrasian Research Centre Working Paper Series Studies on Multicultural Societies no. 31. Kyoto: Ryukoku University, 2015.

Shimohara Motoaki 篠原資明. "*Mujō to zettai mu: Tanabe Hajime no tetsugaku*" 「無常と絶対無: 田辺元の哲学」 ["Indeterminacy and absolute nothingness: Tanabe Hajime's philosophy"]. *Aida/Seisei* 5 (2015), 1–13.

Shiozaki Hiroaki 塩崎弘明. "*Shōwa Kenkyūkai to Miki Kiyoshi no kyōdōshugi*" 「昭和研究会と三木清の協同主義」 ["The Shōwa Research Association and Miki Kiyoshi's cooperative communitarianism"]. *Nihon Rekishi* 542 (1993), 18–37.

Silverberg, Miriam. "War Responsibility Revisited: Auschwitz in Japan." *Review of Asian and Pacific Studies* 29 (2005), 43–63. Republished 2007 with an introduction by Ann Sherif in *The Asia-Pacific Journal: Japan Focus.* http://japanfocus.org/-Miriam-Silverberg/2470/article.html

Skinner, Quentin. *Machiavelli: A Very Short Introduction.* Oxford: Oxford University Press, 1982.

Skinner, Quentin. *Visions of Politics: Regarding Method.* Cambridge: Cambridge University Press, 2002.

Steffensen, Kenn Nakata, trans. "Tosaka Jun's 'The Philosophy of the Kyoto School.'" *Comparative and Continental Philosophy* 8.1 (2016), 54–73.

Strauss, Leo. *Persecution and the Art of Writing.* Westport, CT: Greenwood Press, 1973 (1952).

Sugiyama Masao 杉山雅夫. "*Daitōa kyōeiken no seitōka to ronri,* Sekaishi no tetsugaku *to Miki Kiyoshi*" 「大東亜共栄圏の正当化と論理—『世界史の哲学』 と三木清」 ["The justification and logic of the Greater East Asia Co-Prosperity Sphere: 'The philosophy of world history' and Miki Kiyoshi"]. *Ningenkankei Ronshū* 21 (2004), 69–91.

Tanabe Hajime 田辺元. *Seiji tetsugaku no kyūmu* 『政治哲学の急務』 [*The urgent task of political philosophy*]. THZ (*Tanabe Hajime Zenshū*) (1946), 8.323–396.

Tosaka Jun 戸坂潤. "*Kyōto gakuha no tetsugaku*" 「京都学派の哲学」 ["The philosophy of the Kyoto School"]. *Keizai Ōrai* (September 1932), TJZ3.171–176. Tokyo: Keisō Shobō, 1966.

Tosaka Jun. "*Tanabe tetsugaku no seiritsu*" 「田辺哲学の成立」 ["The emergence of Tanabe's philosophy"]. *Shisō* 128 (December 1932), TJZ 3.177–184. Tokyo: Keisō Shobō, 1966.

Tosaka Jun. "'*Yamato damashii' gakuha no tetsugaku*" 「〈やまと〉魂学派の哲学」 [The philosophy of Yamato Japanese spirit]. *Keizai Ōrai* (October 1932), TJZ 5.88–94. Tokyo: Keisō Shobō, 1967.

Traverso, Enzo. "El Totalitarismo: Usos y Abusos de un Concepto." In *Las Escalas del Pasado: IV Congreso de Historia Local de Aragón*, ed. Alberto Sabio Alcutén and Carlos Forcadell Alvarez, 99–100. Huesca: IEA, 2005.

Uchida Hiroshi 内田弘. *Miki Kiyoshi: Koseisha no kōsōryoku* 「三木清一個性者の構想力」 [Miki Kiyoshi: The imagination of the individual]. Tokyo: Ochanomizu Shobo, 2004.

Ueda, Shizuteru 上田閑照. "Nishida, Nationalism, and the War in Question." In *Rude Awakenings: Zen, the Kyoto School, & the Question of Nationalism*, ed. J. Heisig and J. Maraldo, 77–106. Honolulu: University of Hawaii Press, 1994.

Vocano, Diego von. "The Scope of Comparative Political Theory." *Annual Review of Political Science* 18 (2015), 465–480.

Williams, David. *Japan and the Enemies of Open Political Science*. London: Routledge, 2002.

Williams, David. *Defending Japan's Pacific War: The Kyoto School Philosophers and Post-White Power.* London: Routledge, 2004.

Williams, David. *The Philosophy of Japanese Wartime Resistance: A Reading, with Commentary, of the Complete Texts of the Kyoto School Discussions of "The Standpoint of World History and Japan."* Abingdon and New York: Routledge, 2014.

Yamada Munemutsu 山田宗睦. *Shōwa no seishin-shi: Kyōto gakuha no tetsugaku* 『昭和の精神史一京都学派の哲学』 [*Shōwa intellectual history: The philosophy of the Kyoto School*]. Kyoto: Jinbun Shoin, 1975.

Yusa, Michiko. "Nishida and Totalitarianism: A Philosopher's Resistance." In *Rude Awakenings: Zen, the Kyoto School and the Question of Nationalism*, ed. James Heisig and John Maraldo, 107–131. Honolulu: University of Hawai'i Press, 1994.

Yusa, Michiko. *Zen and Philosophy: An Intellectual Biography of Nishida Kitarō.* Honolulu: University of Hawaii Press, 2002.

FURTHER READING

Arisaka, Yoko. "Beyond 'East and West': Nishida's Universalism and Postcolonial Critique." *The Review of Politics* 59.3 (1997), 541–560.

Calichman, Richard F. *Overcoming Modernity: Cultural Identity in Wartime Japan.* New York: Columbia University Press, 2008.

Davis, Bret W. "The Kyoto School." In *The Stanford Encyclopedia of Philosophy* (most recently updated 2014). http://plato.stanford.edu/entries/kyoto-school/

Goto-Jones, Christopher. *Political Philosophy in Japan: Nishida, the Kyoto School, and Co-prosperity.* New York and London: Routledge, 2005.

Goto-Jones, Christopher, ed. *Repoliticising the Kyoto School as Philosophy.* London: Routledge, 2009.

Goto-Jones, Christopher. "The Kyoto School." In *Encyclopedia of Political Theory*, ed. Mark Bevir, vol. 2, 771–773. London: Sage, 2010.

Goto-Jones, Christopher. "Comparative Political Thought: Beyond the Non-Western." In *Ethics and World Politics*, ed. Duncan Bell, 219–232. New York: Oxford University Press, 2010.

Heisig, James, and John Maraldo, eds. *Rude Awakenings: Zen, the Kyoto School, and the Question of Nationalism*. Honolulu: University of Hawaii Press, 1994.

Parkes, Graham. "The Putative Fascism of the Kyoto School and the Political Correctness of the Modern Academy." *Philosophy East & West* 47.3 (1997), 305–336.

Parkes, Graham. "Heidegger and Japanese Fascism: An Unsubstantiated Connection." In *Japanese and Continental Philosophy: Conversations with the Kyoto School*, ed. Bret W. Davis, Brian Schroeder, and Jason M. Wirth, 247–268. Bloomington: University of Indiana Press, 2011.

Williams, David. *Defending Japan's Pacific War: The Kyoto School Philosophers and Post-White Power*. London: Routledge, 2004.

Williams, David. *The Philosophy of Japanese Wartime Resistance: A Reading, with Commentary, of the Complete Texts of the Kyoto School Discussions of "The Standpoint of World History and Japan."* Abingdon and New York: Routledge, 2014.

Yusa, Michiko. "Philosophy and Inflation: Miki Kiyoshi in Weimar Germany, 1922–1924." *Monumenta Nipponica* 53.1 (Spring 1998), 45–71.

CHAPTER FOUR

Metanoetics for the Dead and the Living: Tanabe Hajime, Karaki Junzō, and Moritaki Ichirō on the Nuclear Age

NOBUO KAZASHI

Japan's defeat in the Second World War in 1945 was the final cumulative consequence of its modern history that was punctuated with wars and imperialistic expansions, starting with the 1894 Sino-Japanese War, the 1904–1905 Russo-Japanese War, the 1910 annexation of Korea, the 1914–18 First World War, and the outbreak of the Fifteen-Year War triggered by the Manchurian Incident in 1931. Many Japanese intellectuals and writers became involved in it, willingly or unwittingly in one way or another, and philosophers were no exception. Most controversial cases were the round-table discussions, *Japan and the Standpoint of World-History* (1941–42) and *Overcoming Modernity* (1942), in which some of the central figures of the Kyoto School participated.[1] The controversies over their involvements are alive even to this day.[2]

Nishida Kitarō passed away in June 1945, just a couple of months before the end of the war, and Miki Kiyoshi (1897–1945) and Tosaka Jun (1900–45), Marxism-oriented and politically committed members of the Kyoto School, died a tragic death as political prisoners. Tanabe Hajime (1885–1962), successor to Nishida, remained highly productive until his last years—despite, or because of, his tormented years of crisis during the Pacific War and his subsequent postwar "seclusion" from the world.

In this chapter I will treat the lineage of Tanabe, Karaki Junzō, and Moritaki Ichirō, all of whom addressed the crisis of the nuclear age, first by sketching out what was at stake in Tanabe's endeavor to establish a viable "ontology of social existence" and its transformation during and after the war. I will focus particularly on his postwar thought on the nuclear age as the "age of death" in terms of its contemporary relevance, while I will also point out inherent problems in his thought.

Next, I will introduce the thought of Karaki Junzō, who remained a faithful correspondent of Tanabe's during the latter's seclusion years. I shall then introduce the idea of "joint struggles with the dead" advocated by a historian Uehara Senroku (1899–1975), which offers a way to develop Tanabe's "philosophy of death," and serves as a bridge to introduce the Hiroshima-based philosopher Moritaki Ichirō (1901–94). Though Moritaki was widely recognized as a leader of the antinuclear movement in postwar Japan, little attention has been paid to the fact that he studied philosophy, though briefly, under Nishida[3] and Tanabe at Kyoto Imperial University, and that we can notice, in his use of such terms as "place of nothingness" or "*zange*" (懺悔= repentance), some clear traces of the deep influences he received from them. Furthermore, what is of great significance for us today is that Moritaki, after having gone through deep self-critical repentance (*zange*), came to embrace the conviction of "absolute negation of the nuclear"—not only the military weapons but also the "peaceful" use of nuclear power. Although it took him almost three decades of scruples and considerations of scientific evidence before he finally came to pronounce this stance, it nevertheless turned into the powerful theoretical backbone for his political engagement. However, Moritaki's thought differs substantially from his teacher's "philosophy of death" because it urges that "human beings must live on." Thus, it would be legitimate for us to regard Moritaki's career and thought not only as belonging in the wake of the Kyoto School, but also as extending his teacher Tanabe's thought as a response to the nuclear age.

1. TANABE HAJIME (1885–1962): FROM THE "LOGIC OF SOCIAL EXISTENCE" TO "PHILOSOPHY OF DEATH"

After his critical departure from Nishida's philosophy in his essay "Requesting an Elucidation by Professor Nishida" in 1930,[4] Tanabe embarked on developing his "logic of species" (*shu no ronri* 種の論理, also translated as the "logic of specifics") in a series of articles published in 1934–35, one of which is entitled "The Logic of Social Existence—Essays in Philosophical Sociology."[5] At the outset Tanabe declares that the central task of contemporary philosophy consists in inquiring after the principles of society, and goes on to clarify what is at stake in such an agenda for "ontology of social existence" as follows:

> Unlike Comte who was concerned with the human race as a whole, sociology after Comte was concerned with partial specific societies and, not concentrating its attention on order and cooperation like him, paid the same degree of attention to *opposition and antagonism*. Meanwhile, theories of class society were developed as *theories of struggle*. These factors made the fundamental inquiry into social existence the principal task for contemporary philosophy.[6]

He also writes:

> Envisage a philosophy, the standpoint of which is one of *absolute affirmation transformed and mediated by absolute negation*, as it directly looks at the reality

> of evil in the eye and takes its standpoint out of the painful recognition of the finitude of evil—for such a philosophy, first of all, *social existence presents itself as the problem in terms of particular, finite, and relative societies*; the structure of social existence is defined in terms of confrontation and negation. It is here, then, that it becomes necessary that these societies be mediated, in the manner of absolute negation, to turn into human society as a whole. *This mediation is nothing other than the logic of species.* We begin, then, with a clear distinction between the *generic* society of the human race and particular *specific* societies.[7]

Thus we see that the objective of Tanabe's initial inquiry was mapped out clearly in terms of its axial themes—to address the aspects of opposition, struggle, and evil in social existence. Thus, one of the reasonable and necessary ways to assess the validity of Tanabe's philosophical inquiry is to examine the extent to which it can be considered faithful to its initial objective, and whether or not his ideas were adequate to deal with the concrete reality of social existence. In the late 1930s Tanabe continued to develop his logic of species (*shu no ronri*),[8] but after Japan's attack on Pearl Harbor in December 1941, he stopped publishing his works and kept silent, with the exception of giving some special lectures in addition to teaching classes, for more than three years until the end of the war.

The major cause for such silence was the intractable dilemma Tanabe faced as an intellectual amid the aggravating war. Reflecting on it, Tanabe wrote in his preface to *Philosophy as Metanoetics*, published in 1946:

> In such a critical situation, where there was not time for delay, would it not be disloyal to my country to keep silent and fail to express whatever ideas I had on reform? On the other hand, there seemed something traitorous about expressing in time of war ideas that, while perfectly proper in time of peace, might end up causing divisions and conflicts, among our people that would only further expose them to their enemies. Caught between these alternatives, I was unable to make up my mind and was tormented by my own indecision. In the impasse I even wondered whether I should go on teaching philosophy or give it up altogether, since I had not adequate solution to a dilemma that philosophically did not appear all that difficult.[9]

One might say that this is a very understandable characterization of the wartime situation in which many Japanese intellectuals found themselves. But Tanabe was encountering serious difficulties that were inherent in his logic of species. For one thing, as it was evidenced in the 1939 article entitled "The Logic of National Existence" (*Kokkateki sonzai no ronri* 国家的存在の論理), his thinking gravitated too much toward the actual nation-state despite the critical motif of the logic of species as a logic of perpetual mediation between individuals, the nation-state, and the universal.[10] For another related problem, Tanabe's view of the nation-state was, in a word, too idealistic in that he failed to recognize the "radical evil lying latent at the bottom of the state's existence just as the radical evil backing up the individual freedom"—as he came to criticize it himself in the *Dialectics of the Logic of Species* published in 1947.[11]

As early as February 1944 Tanabe began to talk about "repentance" (*zange*) in the lecture given at his alma mater First Higher School in Tokyo. He also gave his last university lecture course, starting in October 1944, entitled "*Zangedō*" (*Metanoetics*) at Kyoto Imperial University.[12] Regarding this early turn in Tanabe, Ienaga Saburō noted positively: "Tanabe accomplished his voluntary breakaway from the state absolutism before Japan's surrender and the democratization-demilitarization policies by the Occupation Forces that followed. This could be regarded as a result of the inner reflections guided by his conscience and reason, and I consider it worthy of a merit as a thinker."[13]

1.1 *Philosophy as Metanoetics*

Tanabe wrote in his *Philosophy as Metanoetics*:

> To practice *metanoia* (*zange*) means to be negated and transformed into such being-*qua*-nothingness. *The philosophical subject comes into being only after the self's direction has been changed in metanoia.*[14] This does not mean, however, that there is some special acting subject that turns us around and effects a conversion in us. When we speak of Other-power, the Other is absolute precisely because it is nothingness, that is, *nothingness in the sense of absolute transformation.* It is because of its genuine passivity and lack of acting selfhood that it is termed absolute Other-power. Other-power is *absolute Other-power only because it acts through the mediation of the self-power of the relative that confronts it as other.*[15]

Today the word "*zange*" may sound quite odd as applied to concrete social life, if not completely obsolete. But the double significance of "repentance" and the "critique of logocentrism," brought about by Tanabe's use of "metanoetik," contains contemporary relevance. Especially after the Fukushima nuclear disaster of March 2011, we are being forced to reconsider, with a heart-rending sense of repentance, the way of human civilization from the ground up. In Tanabe's tenacious inquiry we can hear foregoing questionings related to the core of our own self-questionings regarding the environmental issues.

First of all, the proposition that the "philosophical subject becomes possible only after the self's direction has been changed in metanoia" urges us to overturn the modern view of the "subject that is reliant on one's reason-based autonomy," which has been taken for granted as the legitimate ideal in the post-Enlightenment era. This is a highly arresting thesis even reminiscent, in its fundamental nature, of Plato's understanding of philosophy's mission as "*periagoge*" (turning around) of the soul toward the world of ideas. In other words, a new "subject of philosophy" can begin to be at the very limit where the ordinary "subject" is abandoned and dismantled.

Second, Tanabe is not exhorting simply to abandon reason or self-power; he emphasizes that the "absolute other-power" is mediated by the so-called self-power. He sees the workings of the absolute in the mediating relationships themselves both at individual and collective levels, as well as among the "relative beings" that have to live as self-reliant beings, which exist as "others" for the absolute.

And yet one might feel it difficult to see what sorts of state of affairs are being assumed as concrete historical realities due to the abstract and general nature of Tanabe's language. Tanabe writes, for instance: "In terms of its concrete content, metanoetics is a radical historicism in that the continuous *zange* provides basic principles for the circular development of history."[16] However, if we may talk about such historicism in reference to any historical time, would it not end up turning into, so to speak, a supra-historical historicism? Tanabe writes in the opening paragraph of the preface to *Philosophy as Metanoetics*:

> The only thing for me to do in the situation was, first of all, to persist in doing *zange* and look squarely at my self, and, turning my eyes, which are directed toward everything outside, to my own inside, and to explore the depth of my powerlessness and lack of freedom; would not this mean a new task for me as it replaces conventional philosophy?[17]

But the problematic implications of such concentration on one's interior to the neglect of critical consideration of external realities would stand out clearly, when brought into contrast, for instance, with *Dialectic of Enlightenment*, a contemporary work of philosophical reflection on the failure of enlightenment project.[18]

1.2 *Philosophy of death*

In the last years of his life Tanabe's philosophical inquiry made another turn in the name of "philosophy of death," which can be regarded as another seminal contribution by Tanabe to contemporary philosophy. In addition to his critical engagement with what he regarded as Heidegger's "ontology of life," there were three moments occasioning this last turn: his realization of the nuclear age as the "age of death," the passing away of his long-beloved wife Chiyo in 1951, and the sense of his own impending death. Tanabe's "Philosophy of death" was formed out of these interrelated motifs of different orders, and herein lies, it seems, its characteristic appeal as well as its internal difficulty. Thus, we first clarify the relationships between these motifs, before we try to bring into relief their features, both seminal and problematic, by shedding light on them from the perspectives held by some significant thinkers who were related to his thought or career in one way or another.

1.3 *Existential collaboration with the dead*

Tanabe's earliest reference to A-bombs was already made in his *Philosophy as Metanoetics*, which he finished writing in October 1945. In its last chapter, entitled "Metanoetics as a Religious View of Society," we read: "The horrendous power of A-bombs consists, not in the material, but in the absolute reality mediated by the subject" (主体 *shutai*). However, it took a decade for his meditations on the nuclear age to form his "philosophy of death." The catalytic moment was the death of his wife on September 17, 1951. Four days after her death Tanabe wrote: "the feared catastrophe has arrived at last"[19]—in his letter to Karaki Junzō, who as an undergraduate student studied under Nishida and Tanabe, and who became Tanabe's faithful supporter and correspondent throughout the latter's postwar years of seclusion. Tanabe's marriage to Chiyo took place in 1916, when he was thirty-one years old. It is said that although Chiyo was sickly and they had no children, she supported Tanabe's strenuous career throughout her life. The following are two short *waka* poems Tanabe included in his letter to Karaki about a month after the death of his wife:

kanashimi no
soko no soko made
ajiwan to
kokoro sadametsu
mo ni komori ori

Resolving to taste the sorrow
to the bottom of its bottom,
I remain withdrawn in mourning.

And another:

shin'nai ni
akishi utsuro no
kagiri nasa
sabishisa ni
koe hariagete
na o yobau

Emptiness
opened up in my heart
its boundlessness.
Out of loneliness,
Screamed and called her name.[20]

These confiding utterances convey straightforwardly the poignancy of Tanabe's grief of being bereaved of his lifelong companion.

Ten months later, however, he writes to Karaki: "I have gone beyond *Einsamkeit* (loneliness); now it has become natural for me to live always in *Zweisamkeit* (two-someness)."[21] Here we notice that Tanabe's companionship with the deceased wife is beginning to transform into what he will call the "existential collaboration with the dead." Sueki Fumihiko highly values the later Tanabe's thought and considers his "thematization of the dead" to have carried out an "unprecedented Copernican turn from 'death' to the 'dead'" in philosophy.[22] Sueki argues that the question regarding the dead has not been taken up seriously in philosophy although the question of death has always been pivotal in philosophy as it is symbolized in Plato's well-known definition of philosophy as "practice of death" in *Phaedo*. Our life cannot be grasped fully without our relationships with the dead in spite of the fact that we cannot be sure if the dead exist or not in a clear-cut ontological frame; the dead are the real "others" in the sense that we have to live and associate with them even if they remain incomprehensible to us.[23]

1.4 The nuclear age as the age of death

Meanwhile on the international scene, the Cold War was assuming the perilous aspect of nuclear proliferation with the Soviet Union succeeding in the nuclear test in 1949 and the hydrogen bomb test in August 1953. It was in response to the end of the US monopoly of nuclear capability that President Eisenhower gave his "Atoms for Peace" speech at the UN General Assembly in December 1953. The United States aimed to keep its political power over its allies by promoting nuclear power generation among them; building and maintaining nuclear plants would necessitate the US allies to depend on the United States for its most advanced technology. This was the ulterior motive behind the "Atoms for Peace" speech. In March 1954, however, the Japanese tuna-fishing boat *Daigo Fukuryū-maru* (Lucky Dragon No. 5) was exposed to the nuclear fallouts of the "Castle Bravo," the hydrogen bomb testing conducted by the United States near the Bikini Atoll in the South Pacific. The news of the "contaminated tuna" landed at various ports around Japan ignited the antinuclear sentiment especially among housewives raising small children,[24] and led to the First World Conference against Atomic and Hydrogen Bombs held in Hiroshima in 1955.

It was amid such a heightened sense of crisis that Tanabe started to talk about the nuclear age as the "age of death." His letter to Karaki, dated February 5, 1956, reads:

> Reading through Eckhard's work and going ahead with my thinking while aided by it, at last I've come to the stage where I can take up my pen. The theme is the "philosophy of death." The "philosophy of life" of the preceding generation was applied to science-technology for the sake of life, ending up as its slave. The tendencies manifested in the impasse of poetry composition of Valérie and Rilke in the early years of this century turned into the fashion of British poets' interest in death due to two World Wars. The present-day atomic and hydrogen bombs are surely making the present age the "century of death." It is quite obvious to me that philosophy should be overturned from the "philosophy of life" to the "philosophy of death." Though it is questionable to what extent I can effect this overturning, I wish to carry it out and prepare for death.[25]

With the fear of nuclear doom rising around the world, it was not only Tanabe who felt it incumbent on the philosophers to take on the nuclear issues as a pressing and fundamental problem. As is well known, among those who engaged the question were Bertrand Russell (1872–1970), Michel Serres (b. 1930), and Karl Jaspers (1883–1969), whose works Tanabe followed closely alongside Heidegger's. Therefore, we would need to look into Tanabe's thought more closely in order to bring out the distinctive features of his philosophical prescriptions in the nuclear age.

As already mentioned above, the death of his wife left Tanabe in trying loneliness, but he came to find himself living in a state of "*Zweisamkeit*" (twosomeness) with his dead wife. In a letter dated February 12, 1956, addressed to Nogami Yaeko, a renowned writer who became an invaluable confidante and correspondent after his wife's death, Tanabe explains the unexpected experience of such transformation in reference to the "age of death" as follows:

> Now I'm envisaging a "philosophy of death." ... Such "philosophy of death" should not be a philosophy only for my humble self, but a philosophy for everybody as a philosophy of the present age, which is the "century of death." What I have to elaborate here is the notion of "resurrection." It would be inevitable that, when uttered by my humble self who is not a Christian, you should suspect that it would remain a totally empty word... . But the death of my wife has made this possible. Resurrection is witnessed, no longer as an objective natural phenomenon, but as a spiritual experience (reiteki-keiken 霊的経験), that is, as an existential content which appears in the subjecthood (*shutaisei* 主体性) of the personalities united by love... . For my humble self as well, the dead wife has been resurrected and is always living in the inside of my humble self.[26]

Though one may wonder how the Christian notion of "resurrection" can be related to the basically Buddhist stance of Tanabe's thought,[27] we can sense keenly the "spiritual" reality of his wife's presence after death for him. However, what is problematic is the relevance of such "resurrection" for the macro-level question of the nuclear age as the "age of death." Although its relevance seems to be taken for granted by Tanabe himself, we would need to call it into question since it concerns the core of the later Tanabe's philosophy of death.[28]

1.5 Dialectics of death

Let us look closely at one of the most crucial passages in Tanabe's "An Ontology of Life, or a Dialectics of Death?" (1959), an essay he contributed to the *Festschrift* commemorating Heidegger's seventieth birthday.[29] It reads as follows:

> The nuclear age is, so to speak, the "age of death." We have to say that now we are facing the end of the life-centered modern age with its faith placed in the almighty power of science and technology. The teleology of life, which is the seedbed for science and technology, cannot possibly control science-technology in order to avoid death as long as it remains in its idealist stand. *To follow the contradiction of its consequence to its bottomless bottom*, and to endure obediently and affirm freely at the abyss of downfall-extinction due to it, that to die is life's fate, and, at the same time, *to enjoy and appreciate the differential joy of getting converted-resurrected at eternity's moments*, and furthermore *to realize-prove it integrally in the simultaneous collaboration with one's own beloved others*; this would be nothing less than the welfare of absolute security going beyond the teleology of life.... *Even if a collective death of the species occurs as a result of nuclear war, there will still remain a possibility that a few people would escape death and survive.* In such a case, we cannot say that it should be impossible for bodhisattva-acts by one or a few persons to realize the above-stated collaboration union of the human species. Of course, *this does not mean to affirm the genocide by a nuclear war; we must doggedly oppose to it and endeavor to eradicate war*. But there is neither guarantee nor promise that

> such efforts would bear fruits. If the subjective idealism (*kan'nen-ron* 観念論) must be renounced in the face of human contradictions in order for teleological idealism (*risōshugi* 理想主義) to be preserved, there can be no hope remaining for human liberation, except the love of existential collaboration. With this love, it cannot be said that it is impossible to renew the human group as a species. We cannot seek the realization of these hopes through no other way but the death-resurrection dialectics of the bodhisattva way. This is my conviction.[30]

As usual, Tanabe's style is highly abstract and convoluted, but with regard to this particular passage, with its abstruseness pregnant with metaphors, parallelisms, and double negatives, we may say that it betrays the difficulty of the matter Tanabe was struggling with, or rather the tensions inherent to the relations between his motifs on different orders. For one thing, we notice that the notion of "death-resurrection dialectics" is used here quite differently from the case of his wife's "resurrection." And, concretely speaking, it is difficult to understand what sort of "bodhisattva acts" Tanabe was envisioning as achievable by "one or a few persons" after a "collective death of the species."

For another, Tanabe seems to have leaned toward, and focused more on, the "collective death of the species" despite his additional concession that "we must doggedly oppose to any nuclear war and endeavor to eradicate war." I consider that herein lies the most problematic tendency of Tanabe's meditations on the age of death, which is revealed conspicuously in the following passage in Tanabe's letter to Karaki, dated January 7, 1955:

> Since I employ such "*Dialektik*" (dialectical thinking) as mediation, I cannot agree with philosophical view of science-technology including Heidegger's.[31] I think it is no use trying to stop the pursuit of science-technology on the ground of the paradox of human self-destruction, and to replace it with another worldview. *We have no choice but to accept it if self-destruction is our fate*. Religion will not be established unless we obtain a stance in which we should have no regrets or anxiety even if we ruin ourselves.[32]

It sounds as if Tanabe has already accepted our collective fate of self-destruction for the reason that it is what "*Dialektik*" should lead us to. One suspects that Tanabe's thinking is under the sway of the "rhetoric" of dialectics here. We recognize the critical implication of Tanabe's "dialectical" thinking style over the movement of his discourse itself.[33]

2. KARAKI JUNZŌ (1904–80): SOCIAL RESPONSIBILITIES OF SCIENTISTS

Karaki left many works on Japanese literature and aesthetics, but his last work, posthumously published in 1980, was *The Notes on "the Social Responsibilities of Scientists,"*[34] in which he denounced nuclear scientists for not expressing their repentance for their involvement in inventing atomic bombs. One might say there is nothing particular about calling into question the social responsibilities of scientists nowadays. However, Karaki's last work invites our reflection for the following reasons.

First of all, the theme itself should appear quite unusual for Karaki as a literary critic known for his works such as *A Genealogy of the Useless People* (*Muyōsha no keifu*, 1960) and *Impermanence* (*Mujō*, 1964). Even Kasuya Kazuki, a lifelong colleague in editorial work, considered this work to be a "deviation" from Karaki's whole career.[35] However, we can recognize an essential relation between Karaki's devotion to the medieval thought and literature and his concern for nuclear issues. In one of his letters to Tanabe, Karaki wrote about his concerns for the nuclear crisis as the utmost manifestation of "nihilism inherent in the modern worldview" and he relates it to the need he felt to go back to the medieval thought centering around the notion of nothingness in order to seek a way to tackle this nihilism.[36] Thus, Usui Yoshimi, another lifelong friend of Karaki, stated in his "Postscript" to *The Notes*, as if addressing Karaki directly, as follows:

> Naturally, doubts and mistrust toward modernity cannot help leading on to critique and accusation of contemporary age. It was these raging flares of accusation against contemporary age that continued searing your heart, though you appeared almost like a hermit who could have been invited to join the seven wise men of the bamboo forest.... It truly was a symbolic event that you put a period to his life and work with the cry to condemn contemporary physics.[37]

Furthermore, Usui declares: "I consider it to be the role of my afterword also to take back Karaki Junzō from the hands of those insensitive and smug commentators who talk about his immersion in the medieval times and what not."

Second, what Karaki does in this work to call into question the social responsibilities of scientists was what Tanabe did not do in his reflection on the nuclear age as the age of death because of his "dialectical" understanding of technology and the human destiny. How can one call the scientists' responsibilities into question if it was a matter of "dialectical necessity"? For his part, Karaki denounced nuclear scientists for their lack of repentance for having been involved in inventing atomic bombs. The very last sentences he jotted down in a hospital room read as follows:

> This "absolute evil" and the advancement of physics, on the one hand, and, on the other hand, the bliss one feels at finding what has not been discovered or invented yet—where and how can they be connected? In the case of Yukawa [Hideki], they are not connected in him; that is to say, there is no "*zange*" in him. There is no base or bottom from whence "zange" comes out; there is no self-repentance, no self-criticism. Even if we cannot conclude decisively, we can at least say that it is very tenuous.
>
> In this point, Yukawa differs from Einstein, and also from Tomonaga Shin'ichirō;[38] in a nutshell, this is the question of one's awareness of "guilt."[39]

Third, one might be struck by the vehement tone of Karaki's critique targeted on Yukawa Hideki, the first Japanese to receive the Nobel Prize in 1949, who played a leading role at the Pugwash Conference held in Kyoto in 1975; Yukawa himself drafted the statement that condemned nuclear weapons as "absolute evil." For Karaki, however, such a statement was not sufficient without calling into the individual responsibilities of those scientists involved in the development of contemporary physics.

But what is to be emphasized is the fact that Karaki's critique is directed not only against Yukawa as a responsible individual physicist. Karaki writes: "There is no base or bottom from whence 'zange' comes out; there is no self-repentance, no self-denunciation." Karaki was also calling into question what seemed to him the absence of cultural and philosophical base for "*zange*." As seen above, his critique of contemporary technology and civilization was, at least in part, what motivated him to reflect back on the medieval Japanese thought centering in nothingness and impermanence.[40]

Fourth, we can see that, compared to Tanabe's vision of nuclear catastrophe, Karaki harbors a much more realistic and dismal understanding about the possible consequences of nuclear doom. Referring to Rachel Carson's *Silent Spring* (1962) and Helen Caldicott's *Nuclear Madness: What You Can Do!* (1978), he concludes that we cannot believe any longer, unlike Heisenberg, that "the fields would be filled with flowers after springs" or "towns would be rebuilt after each war" and that it is not possible any longer to differentiate between the acceptable "peaceful" use of nuclear energy and the unacceptable nuclear weapons.[41] Such realization shares the same axis with Moritaki Ichirō's stance of "absolute negation of the nuclear energy."[42]

3. UEHARA SENROKU (1899–1975): JOINT STRUGGLES WITH THE DEAD

Before we move on to the discussion of Moritaki's thought proper, we shall briefly touch on the idea of "joint struggles with the dead," an idea first pronounced by Uehara Senroku. It serves as a bridge to proceed from Tanabe's thought to Moritaki's antinuclear thought. With regard to Tanabe's philosophy of death, a critical but constructive observation has been offered by Sueki as follows:

> He [Tanabe] regards human existence as monad-like being, and recognizes therein its ambiguity of "having exclusivity toward, and cooperativity with, others." But for Tanabe, exclusivity and hostility become sublated by higher love that loves one's enemies. Should we not reconsider the problem anew today, however, as we become aware of the difficulty of too optimistic an ideal of "existential collaboration"?[43]

And further:

> In Tanabe, the nuclear age was viewed from the pessimistic prospect toward the future, that is, the possibility of human extinction, and "existential collaboration" had rather a strong soteriological significance. In contrast, Uehara Senroku tried, through "joint struggles with the dead (*shisha tono kyōtō* 死者との共闘)," to confront actively the problems in the world of the living. Uehara's thought contributed to expanding greatly the range of thinking on the dead.[44]

We must admit that our relationships with the dead can be varied and entangled just like those with the living—they can be troubled by lingering regret or unexpressed gratitude, or even tormented by pent-up indignation. The "existential collaboration united by love" as described by Tanabe is, we have to say, a very fortunate one. There are innumerable people who had to die a tragic and unreasonable death because of an unjust act or negligence; in such cases we often feel obliged to fight for and with them to restore their honor or not to repeat the same instance again.

Uehara Senroku was a specialist of medieval European history and produced many progressive scholarly works in that field. The collection of his works comprises some twenty volumes. He was politically active and protested against the revision of the Japan-US Security Treaty in 1960. Shortly thereafter, he abruptly resigned from Hitotsubashi University, where he had served as president and established the department of sociology. After the death of his wife, which he suspected to have been caused by a medical malpractice, Uehara began to engage the question of the dead and came to foster the idea of "joint-struggles with the dead" as part of the whole idea of "co-existing, co-living, co-fighting" with the dead. Thus, his thought opens up an alternative vista, widening Tanabe's thought, in such a way as to connect one's personal experience of bereavement to social and political problems more directly and critically.[45]

Now we may recall that Tanabe's initial inquiry into "an ontology of social existence" was focused on opposition, struggle, and evil in social existence. Thus, the idea of "joint struggles with the dead" could be regarded as a perspective in which Tanabe's initial project can be developed further in much more concrete and public ways. Along this line, I hope that the thought and career of Moritaki Ichirō will appear more than appropriate for our attempt to draw a new genealogy of thought in the nuclear age. Moritaki Ichirō was exactly one of those who committed themselves to joint struggles with the dead (the A-bomb victims in his case), for the sake of the living and the future generations to come.

4. MORITAKI ICHIRŌ (1901–94): "STEPS TOWARD THE ABSOLUTE NEGATION OF NUCLEAR POWER"

When we reflect back on the trajectory of philosopher Moritaki Ichirō, we notice some distinctive features, such as that he entered the Philosophy Department at Kyoto Imperial University in 1927, a year before Nishida was to retire.[46] Moritaki was of the same generation as Nishitani Keiji (1900–90), Kōsaka Masaaki (1900–69), and Kōyama Iwao (1905–93), but because he entered the university at the age of twenty-seven, after having taught for two years at Miyoshi Junior High School (north of Hiroshima) immediately following his graduation from Hiroshima Higher Normal School, and because he finished his undergraduate studies in three years and his master's program in one year to assume his teaching position at his alma mater, Hiroshima Higher Normal School, it seems that he was not on close terms with those disciples of Nishida's who formed the core group of the Kyoto School.

The field Moritaki chose as a philosophy student was the British ethical thought. It was rather a minor research field when German idealism was the mainstream in Japanese academia. The compelling reason why he chose this field was that English was his first foreign language, and this choice was of decisive significance in view of his later career as an antinuclear advocate. His doctoral dissertation submitted in 1950 to Hiroshima Bunri University is entitled "A Study on the British Ethical Thought."[47] It consisted of 535 handwritten pages, and structured as follows:

1. Introduction
2. A Study of Hobbes's Leviathan
3. A Study of Butler's Theory of Conscience: Conscience and Self-Love
4. Central Problems in Sidgwick's Ethical Theory: Self-Interest and Obligation

As a study on British ethical thought, the structure of his dissertation is both orthodox and modern, but there is no direct reference to the nuclear problem or his own personal A-bomb experience. But Moritaki added an appendix to his dissertation, entitled "The Fundamental Problems of Social Ethics: Public Mind and Self-interest," which was "one of the practical lessons [he] could learn from British ethics." Moritaki expressed his resolve to look squarely at the postwar reality in order to explore practical visions toward "just society" amid the utmost social confusion that ran over postwar Japan.

4.1 In the wake of the Kyoto School: Traces of Nishida and Tanabe

In Moritaki's thought, one recognizes undeniable traces of influences he received from Nishida and Tanabe, and in this sense, he can be considered to belong to an extended Kyoto School. Also by juxtaposing his thought along with social-oriented thinkers such as Nakai Masakazu (1900–52),[48] a new perspective emerges that brings to light "hidden" genealogies of philosophical thought in postwar Japan.[49] For example, Moritaki's thoughts immediately after August 15, 1945, are recorded in *Witness of Moritaki's Diary: 40 Years of Hiroshima*, edited on the occasion of the fortieth anniversary of the A-bombing in 1985, as follows:

> A-bomb and the end of the war. At this watershed in history, Moritaki's days and the inquiries and values he espoused as a professor of Hiroshima Higher Normal School were cut off sharply:
>
> "Once Professor Nishida Kitarō told me that those engaged in ethics and philosophy have got to have the resolve of self-negation. It may happen that you have to negate all of your views just before entering your coffin. In the aftermath of the bombing of Hiroshima I was painfully reminded of these words."
>
> The articles written and the contents of the ethics lectured to the students before and during the war. . . . Were they wrong? I felt as if part of my soul had been wrenched off.[50]

The diary of February 20, 1965, when Moritaki gave his last lecture before retiring from Hiroshima University, reads as follows:

> Cloudy and drizzling rain. I gave my last lecture in the large lecture hall, filled with many memories. The title: "The Way I Came." I started my talk with the

teachings I received from my three professors, Nishi,[51] Nishida, and Tanabe, and about the outlines of my ideas on ethics, and then about how I came to criticize the "civilization of power" after the war in order to emphasize the importance of the "civilization of love." Then I talked about my experience with the A-bomb that forced me to proceed from the stand of "species [race]" of Nishi's ethics to the stance of "genus [human species]," and talked about my inquiry of peace ethics based on the supreme imperative that "human species must live on" and my hope to stay engaged in praxis until the last day of my life.[52]

4.2 Postwar turn: The public mind and a "culture of compassion"

Moritaki's indebtedness to Nishida and Tanabe is evident in his use of such notions as the "place of nothingness" and "*zange*"(metanoia-repentance) in his essay entitled "Culture of Compassion," which concisely summarizes Moritaki's postwar thought. The very expression "absolute negation," used in the title of his book *Kaku-zettai-hitei e no ayumi* (*Steps toward the Absolute Negation of the Nuclear*)[53] can be taken as a symbol of Moritaki's connection to the Kyoto School. To cite a passage from this posthumously published collection:

> Having arrived at the apex of power, we are now finding ourselves in the destruction of power. Only after facing the crisis of self-destruction, we seek the principle of salvation in what transcends the power of one's self. If the work of negating oneself and letting others live can be called love, what negates itself absolutely must be absolute love. The place of nothingness, which is absolute nothingness itself but lets all beings be, is, as it is, the world of absolute compassion.[54]

However, Moritaki's notion of absolute "negation" of the nuclear power differs substantially from the notion of negation in Tanabe's "death-resurrection" dialectics, let alone that in the Hegelian "dialectics." He simply maintains: "The impossibility of co-existence of the human race and the nuclear power means: either human species negates the nuclear, or the nuclear negates the human species. There is no other way. After all, we must live on by absolutely negating the nuclear."[55] Moritaki urges, in a straightforward way, to make a Kierkegaardian "either-or" choice with regard to nuclear power.

Thus, the thought of Moritaki goes far beyond in its concrete urgency and resoluteness that of his mentor Tanabe, who had also written about the "nuclear age as the age of death" in the postwar period. What was spurring Moritaki to such contemplation and action to the point of no return was his personal experience of losing his right eye due to a piece of glass that injured it in the explosion caused by the A-bomb, as well as his painful realization that he had "led many students into a wrong direction" as a head teacher in charge of dispatching them to the battlefields at the Eba shipyard operated by the Mitsubishi Heavy Industries in Hiroshima.

While convalescing from his injury in his mountainous hometown of Futami (today's Miyoshi) to the north of Hiroshima, he realized through his body and soul that human species will tread the path of self-destruction, if left to the "civilization of power" with nuclear weapons as its culminating point. Instead, he sought a "single path (*hitosujino michi* ひとすじの道)" to overcome it. Moritaki's "Notes Written during Convalescence" contains a section entitled "thinking," which lists such themes as "the world of sorrowful prayer" (*hinen* 悲念), "being and indebtedness" (*on* 恩), "culture of compassion" (*ji* 慈), "state of compassionate love" (*jiai* 慈愛), "politics and religion" (*seikyō* 政教), and "recovery of faith" (*shin* 信).[56]

Within only half a year of his A-bomb experience, Moritaki began talking about the need for a "culture of compassion." The first occasion was on February 25, 1946, at the request of the teaching staff of the Kimita Elementary School, where he had studied as a child; soon afterwards on March 14, he "talked long into the night huddling around a brazier in the teachers' office" of the Higher Normal School's Kamo branch.[57] One of his former students recalls: "It was in the April of 1947 that I entered the Hiroshima Higher Normal School… . Professor Moritaki gave his 'overview of ethics' under the title of 'culture of compassion.' … I feel that the lectures given around that time became the point of departure for his later peace movement to ban nuclear weapons."[58]

It seems, however, some of his students could not follow Moritaki's swift philosophical turn propelled by his deep repentance and the consciousness of the impending crisis. One of them reflects: "We were filled with rancor against the A-bomb and chagrin at the defeat. We even wanted to retaliate upon America. When Professor Moritaki lectured for peace after returning to the school the year after, we could not listen to him obediently."[59]

4.3 *"Peaceful Use": Struggle with the magical power of words*

In July 1958 Moritaki contributed a short essay to the *Chugoku Shimbun*, a Hiroshima-based newspaper, declaring his stance that "the human race must live on," which would become widely known. The core of Moritaki's thought anticipated almost by two decades the book by Hans Jonas (1903–93), *The Imperative of Responsibility* (originally in German, 1979), which advocated the permanence of human life as the new supreme principle in the contemporary world, in which it has become a real possibility for humankind to perish because of science and technology. In response to the 1955 controversy over the United States' plan for "constructing a nuclear power plant as a gift to Hiroshima," and the US-initiated exhibition on "Peaceful Use of Nuclear Power" held in Hiroshima the following year, Moritaki expressed strong concerns about the questions of nuclear waste and the exposure to low-level radiation.

Even on the twentieth anniversary of the A-bombing in 1965, however, the "absolute negation of the nuclear" (*kaku-zettai-hitei*) was still used simply as an abbreviation for the negation of nuclear weapons.[60] Why? In his essay "The Human Species Must Live On" published in 1979—coincidentally the same year when Jonas's *Imperative of Responsibility* was published—Moritaki wrote: "I consider the magical power of the word truly terrifying. But at that time I thought *peaceful use* might be acceptable while *military use* was not."[61]

Indeed, this was the core of the whole problem. Yoshioka Hitoshi (1953–), a historian of science, points out a similar binary framework of thinking even in the arguments presented by Taketani Mitsuo (1911–2000), a famous physicist who wrote many significant works in the philosophy of science and civil movements. Yoshioka critically analyzes Taketani's writing "The Direction of Nuclear Research in Japan" (1952) in the following manner:

> Based on the simple and clear dichotomy of "peaceful and civil use" as nuclear power's light and the "military use" as its shadow, it argues that Japanese people have a special right and obligation to receive benefit because of the depth of the shadows they have endured... . Taketani's argument, which claimed for the promotion of the "peaceful use" of nuclear power on the ground of the existence of the "*hibakusha*" (A-bomb survivors), was not a heretical but rather a familiar one. However, this argument is not appropriate in many regards. First of all, since the military use and the civil use mostly overlap with each other, the major premise itself that we can separate the two uses is not tenable.[62]

This is a point of fundamental significance that concerns the present situation in which catchwords such as "*positive peace*" or "*peace security* legislation" have been employed by Japanese politicians with completely opposite implications. In this connection, we may recall Shūnsuke Tsurumi's critical assessment of "talisman-like use of words"—the use of grandiose but empty slogans that were employed during the Fifteen-Year War—such as "*kōdō*" (imperial way 皇道) and "*kokutai*" (national polity 国体).

4.4 *Looking for theories to oppose nuclear power*

In May and June of 1971, Moritaki embarked upon a trip around the world; one of its major objectives was to "interview scientists about their views on nuclear power generation and to gather materials on the issue." He became firmly convinced that the expression "peaceful use of the nuclear" was a horrendous deception and a mistake, having confirmed the risk of low-level radiation, through his interviews with foreign scientists, including L. C. Pauling, a professor at Stanford University, and a physicist Patricia Lindop of St. Bartholomew's Medical College in London. In "Conscience of Scientists" in *Steps toward the Absolute Negation of the Nuclear* Moritaki writes:

> On an airplane from San Francisco to Washington, D.C., I read passages from a short article given to me by Dr. Pauling.[63] ... Therein he argues that there cannot be a "threshold" for acceptable level,[64] *at least concerning the questions of genetics* ... Through this trip I came to know directly that conscientious scientists in the West are beginning to think and act seriously with regard to the environmental contamination accompanying the peaceful use of nuclear power.[65]

Also in the following section, "The Reasoning behind Opposing Nuclear Power," he wrote:

> On the occasion of the 28th anniversary in 1973, Dr. Arthur Tamplin came to Japan on behalf of his collaborator friend, Dr. Gofman.[66] ... What he emphasized was the problem of huge amounts of nuclear waste produced by the nuclear plants; the problem of how to dispose nuclear waste was unresolved; and the most serious problem was not only the military conversion of plutonium and nuclear proliferation, but also the toxicity of nuclear waste as a burden to our posterity. *Basic reasons for opposing nuclear power have been clarified for me almost entirely*.[67]

Thus, finally at the thirtieth anniversary conference held by *Gensuikin* (Japan Congress Against Atomic and Hydrogen Bombs) in 1975, Moritaki came to uphold, in his keynote speech, the stance of the "absolute negation of the nuclear" including power generation. But it was with the deep, tormenting sense of "*zange*" as Moritaki would write later as follows: "'What a wonderful future will be opened up if the power of that horrible magnitude can be utilized peacefully?'—Even we, radiation-exposed survivors of Hiroshima and Nagasaki, who have undergone those harrowing experiences because of the military use of nuclear power, that is, A-bombs, were entertaining such a fantasy, which I find unbearably shameful now."[68]

4.5 Galileo Galilei's lament in the nuclear age

In his 1979 memorial lecture entitled "Human Species Must Live On—From My Personal A-Bomb Experience," Moritaki reflected on the Matsuyama District Court's "decision to give their wholesale approval to the safety of nuclear generation" in the Ikata Nuclear Plant Lawsuit. The Ikata Nuclear Plant, located in the Ehime Prefecture on the Shikoku Island roughly on the opposite side of Hiroshima across the Seto Inland Sea, started its operation in 1977, although the local inhabitants had brought a suit against its safety as early as in 1973. The above court decision was issued in 1978. Moritaki writes:

> I cannot possibly forget the pathetic feeling I experienced at that time... . Galileo Galilei was put on a religious trial because he advocated that the earth is moving. He was ordered not to assert the heliocentric theory any longer. The moment the trial was over, however, he murmured to himself: "Still it moves."
>
> Even though the court has given the wholesale guarantee for safety, people in Ikata will continue to oppose the decision, murmuring: "Still, nuclear plants are dangerous." Leaving such words, I came back to Hiroshima. . . .[69]
>
> ... In any case, although the court gave a wholesale guarantee that nuclear generation was safe, what the people's side claimed about its danger did happen at Three Mile Island[70] exactly as they apprehended, didn't it? Hasn't it been verified? Although it is a very unfortunate verification, it has been indeed verified.[71]

It was in the 1970s, more than forty years ago from now, that Moritaki came to make a "*zange*" ashamed of his own naïve ignorance that constrained him within the one-sided stand of "absolute negation of *nuclear weapons*." If Moritaki had encountered the Fukushima nuclear disaster, how much more tormenting would his sense of repentance have been? The contemporary significance of Moritaki's thought of "absolute negation of the nuclear" seems to be only increasing, unfortunately.

IN PLACE OF A CONCLUSION—"THINGS THAT ARE NEAR YET FAR: THINGS THAT ARE FAR YET NEAR"

Katō Shūichi (1919–2008) was a widely known critic who wrote about an extremely diverse range of themes and issues; among his major works are his autobiography, *A Sheep's Song* (*Hitsuji no uta*『羊の歌』; 1966–68) and *A History of Japanese Literature* (『日本文学史序説』; 1980). Actually, however, the nuclear issue was one of his deep concerns running all through his career. Katō was a medical doctor by training and witnessed the devastation of Hiroshima firsthand when he stayed there for two months in the fall of 1945 as a member of the Joint US-Japan Investigation Team on the Effects of Atomic Bomb. Most significant is the fact that Katō directly talked to the people and children who survived the A-bomb but were suffering from what came to be known as the "A-bomb sickness" (*genbaku-byō*).[72]

His experience and intuition were condensed in his essay entitled "Things That Are Near Yet Far: Things That Are Far Yet Near" (*chikōte tōki mono, tōkute chikaki mono*「近うて遠きもの・遠くて近きもの」),[73] an expression he borrowed from the famous *Pillow Book* (*Makura no sōshi*『枕草子』), written around the year 1000 by a Heian court-lady-in-waiting who served Empress Teishi. According to Sei Shōnagon the author, "things that are near yet far" are, for example, siblings and relatives; and among "things that are far yet near" are the Buddhist paradise (*gokuraku* 極楽) and human relations particularly between men and women.

For his part, Katō wistfully imagines that had Sei Shōnagon been alive today, she would have found "things that are near yet far" and "things that are far yet near" both in reference to the nuclear issues.[74] First, as for "things that are far yet near," it is exactly what Moritaki came to realize, as seen above, the relationship between nuclear weapons, as the military use of nuclear energy, and the so-called peaceful use of nuclear energy. Katō explicitly confirms that there is no essential difference between the two in terms of the basic scientific principles utilized, and the radioactive damage that they can cause, and ends the essay by warning:

> Although the probability of a nuclear war is small, it will bring horrendous damage if it occurs. The probability of a serious accident at a nuclear plant is small but not nil, and, if it ever occurs, it is difficult to predict the scale of its disaster. If one were against the nuclear weapons, would it not be natural to reconsider the policy of nuclear power generation? I think it natural to be reminded of "Hiroshima," when the accident occurred [in 1999] at Tōkaimura.[75]

However, Katō called into question the symbolism of Hiroshima; often one talks about a "peaceful world without nuclear weapons" as if a "peaceful world" is equivalent to a "world without nuclear weapons." Actually, even if abolition of nuclear weapons should be a necessary condition for establishing a peaceful world, it is far from a sufficient condition. In this sense, although "pacifism" and "anti-nuke" sound very near from each other and almost overlapping with each other in the symbolism of Hiroshima, actually a "world without nuclear weapons" is very far from a "peaceful world" without war, injustice, and poverty. With this sobering confirmation, we shall continue our reflections on our nuclear age.

NOTES

1. See JPS, "Chūōkōron Discussion" and "Overcoming Modernity, A Symposium," 1059–1084.
2. See J. W. Heisig and J. C. Maraldo, eds, *Rude Awakenings* (Honolulu: University of Hawaii Press, 1995).
3. Nishida Kitarō was to retire at the end of the academic year that Moritaki entered the university.
4. J. W. Heisig, *Philosophers of Nothingness* (Honolulu: University of Hawaii Press, 2001), 109.
5. Tanabe Hajime, "*Shakai sonzai no ronri: tetsugakuteki shakaigaku shiron*," THZ 6 (Chikuma Shobō, 1963), 51–167.
6. Tanabe Hajime, THZ 6.58; THTS 1.19; emphases added.
7. THZ 6.70; THTS 1.37; JPS 671; translation modified; emphasis added.
8. These essays, including the immediate postwar writings on the same theme, are contained in THZ 7.
9. Tanabe Hajime, *Philosophy as Metanoetics*, trans. Takeuchi Yoshinori et al. (Berkeley and London: University of California Press, 1986), il–l.
10. See Nakazawa Shin'ichi, *Firosofia Yaponika* (Tokyo: Shūeisha, 2001), which presents one of the most theoretical attempts to draw out and develop further the initial motif of Tanabe's logic of species in relation to contemporary ideas.
11. Tanabe Hajime, THZ 7.253–254. For an overview of Tanabe's thought, see the well-balanced explications given by Fujita Masakatsu, who edited the four-volume paperback series of Tanabe's essential works, THTS.
12. For a detailed study of the itinerary of Tanabe's wartime thought toward metanoetics, see Chin Ping Liao, "Zangedō to shite no Tetsugaku," *Tetsugaku shisō ronsō* 24 (Tsukuba University, 2006), 51–65.
13. Ienaga Saburō, *Tanabe Hajime no shisōshiteki kenkyū* (Tokyo: Hōsei University Press, 1974), 186.
14. In the published translation this sentence is rendered as "The philosophical subject comes into question only after one has been converted in metanoesis."
15. Tanabe Hajime, *Philosophy as Metanoetics*, 18; translation modified; emphasis added.
16. Ibid., lii.
17. Ibid., l; translation modified to make it more literal.

18. See Kazashi Nobuo, “Tanabe Hajime, zangedō to shite no tetsugaku ni okeru tenkai, risei hihan no shatei,” in *Ajia diasupora to kindai shokuminchi shugi*, ed. Ogata Kō (Tokyo: Bensei Shuppan, 2013), 263–289. John C. Maraldo expresses similar concerns in his article “Metanoetics and the Crisis of Reason: Tanabe, Nishida, and Contemporary Philosophy,” in *The Religious Philosophy of Tanabe Hajime*, ed. T. Unno and J. Heisig (Berkeley: Asian Humanities Press, 1990), 248–249, as follows: “I have wanted Tanabe’s work to speak to philosophers today and to their present concerns, world or not. Ultimately, however, the removal of philosophy as metanoetics from its concrete historical situation in wartime Japan raises the specter of massive deception and betrayal,” and “ordinary reason cannot guide us through such crises with impunity, but neither can Tanabe’s reason transformed, for it is transformed only after one’s total submission. Is metanoesis possible as repentance for the past?”
19. Tanabe Hajime and Karaki Junzō, *Tanabe Hajime, Karaki Junzō ōfuku shokan* (Tokyo: Chikuma Shobō, 2004), 266.
20. Ibid., 271.
21. Ibid., 297.
22. Sueki Fumihiko, “Shisha no hakken: Tanabe Hajime no shi no tetsugaku to gendai,” in *Tasha, shisha, watashi: tetsugaku to shūkyō no ressun* (Tokyo: Iwanami Shoten, 2007), 63. If we take into account relevant works in other fields such as religious studies and ethnology, particularly those by Yanagita Kunio and Origuchi Shinobu, we would need to qualify Sueki’s evaluation as applicable only to philosophy in the narrow sense.
23. Sueki Fumihiko, “*Shisha to tomoni*,” in *Tetsugaku no genba: nihon de kangaeru to yū koto* (Tokyo: Transview, 2011), 108.
24. Now it is known that the total of 856 Japanese fishing boats brought back “contaminated fish” to their homeports by the end of 1954. See Daigo Fukuryu Maru Exhibition Hall at http://d5f.org/about.html/
25. Tanabe and Karaki, *Tanabe Hajime, Karaki Junzō ōfuku shokan*, 385–386.
26. Tanabe Hajime and Nogami Yaeko, *Tanabe Hajime, Nogami Yaeko ōfuku shokan* (Tokyo: Iwanami Shoten, 2012), 2.17–19. Quoted in Sueki, “*Shisha no hakken*,” 64.
27. It is noteworthy that for Tanabe Christianity remained a significant source of inspiration along with Buddhism.
28. A similar concern has been expressed by Ienaga Saburō in his pioneering work on Tanabe’s philosophy, *Tanabe Hajime no shisōshiteki kenkyū*, 312: “Tanabe’s heart-rending realization of the ‘existential collaboration’ with his dead wife was the major condition for the establishment of his ‘philosophy of death’; it would entail that the response to the global nuclear situation be a secondary factor and that his ‘philosophy of death’ become, rather than a public reasoning with a world-historical background, something tinged with sensible elements strongly dominated by private moments. Wouldn’t this lead to a conclusion that the universalism Tanabe pursued consistently began to crumble in his last years? Because this point cannot be lightly thought of in evaluating ‘dialectics of death,’ which was Tanabe’s last stand, we need to give it a close scrutiny.”

29. "Todesdialektik," in *Festschrift Martin Heidegger zum 70. Geburtstag*, ed. Günther Neske (Tübingen: Pfullingen, 1959), 93–133.
30. THTS 4.250–251; emphasis added.
31. Tanabe subsequently read Heidegger's "The Question concerning Technology" (Die Frage nach der Technik, 1953) included in *Vorträge und Aufsätze* (1954), and changed his view to a highly positive and admiring one.
32. Tanabe and Karaki, *Tanabe Hajime, Karaki Junzō ōfuku shokan*, 353; emphasis added.
33. A similar observation is given by Tachibana Fuhito, "Issai no jitsuzai ga tokesaru harō" in *Kindai no chōkoku, Fukushima ikō*, ed. Ishizuka Masahide (Tokyo: Risōsha, 2013), 137: "Rather than seeking a meaningful critique against the nuclear, Tanabe was attached to the 'dialectical' view that we have no choice but to push ahead the nuclear technology, which cannot be pushed back once invented. Thence, he started advocating the way of self-renunciation that affirms willingly even the destruction by nuclear war. And the very notion of self-renunciation, which must have originally referred to altruistic acts (利他行 ritagyō) became radicalized toward literal self-sacrifice. The impression of somberness and narrowness the 'philosophy of death' gives us seems to come largely from these aspects."
34. Karaki Junzō, *Kagakusha no shakaiteki sekinin ni tsuite no oboegaki* (Tokyo: Fujiwara Shoten, 2012).
35. See Kasuya Kazuki, *Han-jidaiteki shisakusha: Karaki Junzō to sono shūhen* (Tokyo: Chikuma Shobō, 2005), 254, 310.
36. It was in response to this statement that Tanabe expressed his "dialectical view" of the human fate bound up with technology and science.
37. Usui Yoshimi, "Postscript" to Karaki Junzō, *Kagakusha no shakaiteki sekinin*, 193.
38. Tomonaga Shin'ichirō (1906–79), a graduate of Kyoto University, was the second Japanese physicist to receive the Nobel Prize in 1965.
39. Karaki Junzō, *Kagakusha no shakaiteki sekinin*, 98–99. His note to this paragraph reads: "This much I finished writing at around 1:15 a.m., March 8, 1980."
40. Karaki's vehement questioning of what he regarded as the absence of thorough "zange, repentance" in Yukawa might be related to Karaki's ambivalent and tension-filled relationship with Tanabe, which Karaki revealed in an essay entitled "Tanabe Hajime sensei" (Professor Tanabe Hajime). Karaki confesses that at the funeral of Tanabe he chose to read passages from Tanabe's "Memento Mori" instead of reading a message of condolence because of the fear that he might not be able to contain his ambivalent feelings toward Tanabe, and poses a fundamental question: "Was Tanabe-sensei really a practitioner of metanoetics?" See Karaki Junzō, "Tanabe Hajime sensei," in *Karaki Junzō Zenshū* (Tokyo: Chikuma Shobō), 10.412.
41. Karaki, *Kagakusha no shakaiteki sekinin*, 53.
42. Although this present chapter presents a critical assessment of Tanabe's philosophy of death particularly with regard to his views on the nuclear age as the age of death, we should note the heightened and widespread interest in Tanabe philosophy, as is shown, for instance, in the issue of *Shisō* journal featuring Tanabe's thought on the occasion of the fiftieth anniversary of his death in 2012. This issue contains about

a dozen significant contributions drawing out various features and potentialities of Tanabe philosophy; the contributors include Fujita Masakatsu, Kobayashi Toshiaki, Koizumi Yoshiyuki, Hayashi Susumu, Gōda Masato, Kakuni Takashi, Higaki Tatsuya, Sugimura Yasuhiko, Murai Norio, Taguchi Shigeru, and Takehana Yōsuke.

43. Sueki Fumihiko, "*Shisha no hakken,*" in *Tasha, Shisha, Watashi* (Iwanami Shoten, 2007), 74.
44. Sueki Fumihiko, "*Shisha to tomoni*," in *Tetsugaku no Genba* (Tokyo: Transview, 2011)," 112–114.
45. Uehara Senroku, *Shisha, seija: Nichiren nin'shiki e no hassō to shiten* (Tokyo: Miraisha, 1974), 5.
46. This section is based partly on my article "Genten kara toinaosu hankaku-heiwa shisō: Hiratsuka Raichō, Maruyama Masao, Moritaki Ichirō," in *Heiwa kenkyū* [Peace studies], 45 (Nihon Heiwa Gakkai, Waseda University, 2015), 23–41.
47. Moritaki Ichirō, *Eikoku rinri kenkyū [A study on the British ethical thought]*, doctoral thesis submitted to Hiroshima Bunri University (1950).
48. Nakai, a native of Hiroshima like Moritaki, engaged in critical journalism in the 1930s and involved in cultural activities for citizens as director of Onomichi City Library soon after Japan's defeat in the Second World War. His pioneering works on media, film, and sports are drawing renewed interest recently, just as the works by Marxist Tosaka Jun, who died a political prisoner. A book in French on Nakai is recently published: Michael Lucken, *Nakai Masakazu, Naissance de la théorie critique au Japon* (Dijon: Les Presses du Réel, 2015).
49. For example, Maruyama Masao (1914–96), a representative historian of political thought in postwar Japan, highly evaluated, in his book review of *Shakai sonzai-ron* [*Social ontology*] (1939) by Mutai Risaku (1890–1974), one of Nishida's earliest students, the fact that "the interest of the pure philosophers [such as Nishida and Tanabe] came to concentrate on the concrete historical-social existence," although he expressed dissatisfaction because their views "appeared still transcendent and as if descending from above." Maruyama Masao, *Senchū to sengo no aida: 1936–1957* (Tokyo: Misuzu Shobō, 1976), 43–48.
50. Moritaki Ichirō, *Hiroshima yonjūnen: Moritaki nikki no shōgen*, ed. Chūgoku Shinbun (Tokyo: Heibonsha, 1985), 17. Moritaki's own words are quoted together with the editor's comments.
51. "Nishi" refers to Nishi Shin'ichirō (1873–1943), who left behind many works in the field of "Kokumin-dōtoku-ron" (national moral theory). Sometimes he was referred to as "Two Nishis" together with Nishida Kitarō. Moritaki received Nishi's close guidance since his higher school days and married Nishi's second daughter, Shige. The Confucian culture Moritaki acquired through Nishi retained great significance in the postwar period as well. Moritaki also appreciated the emperor under the new constitution in terms of the "symbol of 'nothingness-qua-love' as the unifying principle of truth"; therein we can recognize a fundamental problem common in the Kyoto School. See Moritaki Ichirō, "Genka dōtoku kyōiku no konpon mondai: ningenzō, tokumoku, ningensei," in *Gakkō kyōiku* 402 (1951), 7.

52. Moritaki Ichirō, *Hiroshima yonjūnen.*
53. Moritaki Ichirō, *Kaku-zettai-hitei eno ayumi* (Hiroshima: Keisuisha, 1994). This is a collection of writings by Moritaki that was posthumously published in 1994. Its enlarged second edition was published under the title of *Kaku to jinrui wa kyōzon dekinai: Kaku-zettai-hitei e no ayumi* [The nuclear and human species cannot co-exist: steps toward the absolute negation of the nuclear] in 2015.
54. Moritaki, *Kaku zettai hitei*, 103–106.
55. Moritaki, *Kaku zettai hitei*, 36.
56. Moritaki, *Hiroshima yonjūnen*, 23.
57. Ibid., 26.
58. Ebita Terumi, "Memories of Moritaki-sensei's Lectures on Ethics and Morals" in *Moritaki Ichirō sensei no sotsuju o kinen shite*, ed. Yukiyasu Shigeru (Okayama: Daigaku Kyōiku Shuppan, 1991), 70.
59. Moritaki, *Hiroshima yonjūnen*, 18.
60. Ibid.
61. Ibid., 12; emphases added. "There was a fixed pattern of thinking; that is, while atomic and hydrogen bombs are "evil" and "death," "peaceful use" is "good" and "life."
62. Yoshioka Hitoshi, *Genshiryoku no shakaishi, sono nihonteki tenkai* (Tokyo: Asahi Shinbunsha, 2011), 77.
63. Linus Carl Pauling (1901–94) received the Nobel Prize twice, first in 1954 in chemistry and in 1964 for his activities against the aboveground nuclear testing.
64. It refers to the so-called linear no-threshold (LNT) theory.
65. Moritaki Ichirō, *Kaku zettai hitei*, 21–23; emphases in the original.
66. See John W. Gofman and Arthur R. Tamplin, *Poisoned Power: The Case against Nuclear Power Plants before and after Three Mile Island* (Emmaus, PA: Rodale Press, 1971). Its Japanese translation was published in 1974 entitled *Genshiryoku kōgai: jinrui no mirai o obiyakasu mono* [Nuclear power pollution: What threatens the future of human beings] (Tokyo: Agune, 1974); its new Japanese translation by Kawamiya Nobuo was published in March 2016 by Akashi Shoten, Tokyo.
67. Moritaki Ichirō, *Kaku zettai hitei*, 25–27; emphasis added.
68. Ibid., 11.
69. Moritaki Ichirō, "*Kinen kōen, jinrui wa ikineba naranai—watakushi no hibaku-taiken kara*," in *Buraku Liberation*, 139 (Kaihō Shuppansha, 1979), 33.
70. The Three Mile Island accident broke out on March 28, 1979.
71. Ibid., 34.
72. Katō Shūichi, "Hiroshima," in *A Sheep's Song: A Writer's Reminiscences of Japan and the World*, trans. Chia-ning Chang (Berkeley: University of California Press, 1999), chapter 22, 223–226.
73. Katō Shūichi, "*Chikōte tōki mono, tōkute chikaki mono*" [What is near yet far; what is far yet near], in *Katō Shūichi Jisen-shū* [Katō Shūichi: collection of self-selected essay] (Tokyo: Iwanami Shoten, 1999), 10.41–45.

74. Cf. Ōe Kenzaburō's reference to this essay (Kanno Akimasa, *Chi no kyoshō Katō Shūichi* [Tokyo: Iwanami Shoten, 2011], 40–44). Ōe points out Katō's characteristic style, exhibited in this essay, of combining his critical mind with his wide literary culture.
75. Katō wrote this essay in the wake of the nuclear accident at the Tōkaimura Uranium Processing Facility in Ibaraki Prefecture, not far from Tokyo, on September 30, 1999. It was the worst accident until the Fukushima Daiichi nuclear disaster of March 2011 took place. Two workers died of the exposure to high radiation. Katō passed away in 2008, without witnessing the Fukushima Daiichi disaster.

BIBLIOGRAPHY

Gofman, John W., and Arthur R. Tamplin. *Poisoned Power: The Case against Nuclear Power Plants.* Emmaus, PA: Rodale Press, 1971.

Gofman, John W., and Arthur R. Tamplin. Trans. into Japanese, Kawamiya Nobuo 河宮信郎, *Genshiryoku kōgai: jinrui no mirai o obiyakasu mono* 『原子力公害—人類の未来を脅かすもの』. Tokyo: Akashi Shoten, 2016.

Heisig, James W. *Philosophers of Nothingness.* Honolulu: University of Hawaii Press, 2001.

Heisig, James W., Thomas P. Kasulis, and John C. Maraldo. *Japanese Philosophy: A Sourcebook* (2011).

Heisig, James W., and John Maraldo, eds. *Rude Awakenings: Zen, the Kyoto School, & the Question of Nationalism.* Honolulu: University of Hawai'i Press, 1995.

Ienaga Saburō 家永三郎. *Tanabe Hajime no shisōshiteki kenkyū: sensō to tetsugakusha* 『田辺元の思想史的研究—戦争と哲学者』 [An intellectual-historical study of Tanabe Hajime: War and philosopher].Tokyo: Hōsei University Press, 1974.

Jaspers, Karl. *The Future of Mankind* (German original in 1958 under the title of *Die Atombombe und die Zukunft des Menschen. Politisches Bewusstsein in unserer Zeit*). Chicago: University of Chicago Press, 1961.

Jonas, Hans. *The Imperative of Responsibility: In Search of an Ethics for the Technological Age*, revised ed. Chicago: University of Chicago Press, 1984; German original, 1979).

Kanno Akimasa 菅野昭正, ed. *Chi no kyoshō Katō Shūichi* 『知の巨匠　加藤周一』 [Intellectual master Katō Shūichi]. Tokyo: Iwanami-shoten, 2011.

Karaki Junzō 唐木順三. "*Tanabe Hajime sensei*" 「田邊元先生」 [Professor Tanabe Hajime]. In 『唐木順三全集』 [Collected works of Karaki Junzō], vol. 10, 407–415. Tokyo: Chikuma Shobō, 1968.

Karaki Junzō. *Kagakusha no shakaitei sekinin ni tsuite no oboegaki* 『「科学者の社会的責任」についての覚え書』 [Notes about "social responsibilities of scientists"]. Tokyo: Fujiwara Shoten, 1980, 2012.

Kasuya Kazuki 粕谷一希. *Han-jidaiteki shisakusha: Karaki Junzō to sono shūhen* 『反時代的思索者—唐木順三とその周辺』 [An untimely thinker: Karaki Junzō and his surroundings].Tokyo: Chikuma Shobō, 2005.

Katō Shuichi 加藤周一. *A Sheep's Song: A Writer's Reminiscences of Japan and the World.* Berkeley: University of California Press, 1999.

Katō Shuichi. "*Chikōte tōki mono, tōkute chikaki mono*" 「近うて遠きもの・遠くて近きもの」 [What is near yet far; what is far yet near]. In *Katō Shūichi Jisen-shū* 『加藤周一自選集』 [Katō Shūichi: Collection of self-selected essays], vol. 10, 41–45. Tokyo: Iwanami Shoten, 1999.

Kazashi Nobuo 嘉指信雄. "*Tanabe Hajime,* Zangedō to shite no tetsugaku, *ni okeru tenkai, risei hihan no shatei: Horukuhaimā-Adoruno's keimō no benshōhō tono hikau shiron*" 「田辺元『懺悔道としての哲学』における転回・理性批判の射程：ホルクハイマー／アドルノ『啓蒙の弁証法』との比較試論」 [The range of critique of reason in Tanabe Hajime's *Philosophy as Metanoetics*: In contrast to *Dialectic of Enlightenment* by Horkheimer and Adorno]. In *Ajia diasupora to kindai shokuminchi-shugi* 『アジアディアスポラと近代植民地主義』 [Asian diaspora and modern colonialism], ed. Ogata Kō 緒形康, 263–289. Tokyo: Bensei Shuppan, 2013.

Kazashi Nobuo. "*Genten kara toinaosu hankaku-heiwa shisō: Hiratsuka Raichō, Maruyama Masao, Moritaki Ichirō*" 「原点から問い直す反核・平和思想—平塚らいてう・丸山眞男・森滝市郎」 [Radical reassessment of anti-nuclear pacifist thought: Hiratsuka Raichō, Maruyama Masao, & Moritaki Ichiro]. In *Heiwa kenkyū* 『平和研究』 [Peace studies] 45, 23–41. Nihon Heiwa Gakkai, Waseda University, 2015.

Liao, Chin Ping. "'*Zangedō to shite no tetsugaku': haisen zengo no zange to sangan-ten'nyū o megutte*" 「『懺悔道としての哲学』—敗戦前後の懺悔と三願転入をめぐって」 [Tanabe's *Philosophy as Metanoetics*: "Repentance" and "three vows of Amida" in and around the end of WWII]. In *Tetsugaku-shisō ronsō* 24, 51–65. Tsukuba University, 2006.

Moritaki Ichirō 森瀧市郎. *Eikoku rinri kenkyū* 『英國倫理研究』[*A study on the British ethical thought*]. Doctoral thesis submitted to Hiroshima Bunri University, 1950.

Moritaki Ichirō. *Genka dōtoku kyōiku no konpon mondai: Ningenzō, tokumoku, ningensei* 「現下道徳教育の根本問題—人間像・徳目・人間性」 [Fundamental problems of moral education today: Ideal human image, virtues, humanity]. In *Gakkō kyōiku* 『学校教育』[School education] 402, 3–9. Hiroshima Daigaku fuzoku shōgakkō kyōiku kenkyūkai, 1951.

Moritaki Ichirō. "*Kinen kōen, jinrui wa ikineba naranai: watakushi no hibaku taiken kara*" 「記念講演 人類は生きねばならない—私の被爆体験から」 [Memorial lecture: Human species must live on—from my personal A-bomb experience]. In *Buraku kaihō* 『部落解放』 [Buraku liberation], 139, 24–37. Kaihō Shuppansha, 1979.

Moritaki Ichirō. *Hiroshima yonjūnen: Moritaki nikki no shōgen* 『ヒロシマ四十年—森瀧日記の証言』 [Hiroshima forty years: Witnesses of the Moritaki diary], ed. Chūgoku Shinbun. Tokyo: Heibonsha, 1985.

Moritaki Ichirō. *Kaku zettai hitei e no ayumi* 『核絶対否定への歩み』 [Steps toward the absolute negation of the nuclear]. Hiroshima: Keisuisha, 1994.

Moritaki Ichirō. *Kaku to jinrui wa kyōzon dekinai: kaku zettai hitei e no ayumi* 『核と人類は共存できない—核絶対否定への歩み』 [The nuclear and human species cannot co-exist: Steps toward the absolute negation of the nuclear], revised and enlarged ed. Tokyo: Nanatsumori Shokan, 2015.

Nakazawa Shin'ichi 中沢新一. *Firosofia Yaponika* 『フィロソフィア・ヤポニカ』 [PhilosophiaJaponica]. Tokyo: Shūeisha, 2001; Tokyo: Kōdansha, 2011.

Sueki Fumihiko 末木文美士. "*Shisha no hakken: Tanabe Hajime no 'shi no tetsugaku' to gendai*" 「死者の発見—田辺元の「死の哲学」と現代」 [Discovery of "the dead": Tanabe Hajime's philosophy of death and the modern period]. In *Tasha, shisha, watashi: tetsugaku to shūkyō no ressun* 『他者／死者／私—哲学と宗教のレッスン』 [The other, the dead, the I: Lessons of philosophy and religion]. Tokyo: Iwanami Shoten, 2007.

Sueki Fumihiko. "*Shisha to no kyōtō*" 「死者との共闘」 ["Joint struggles with the dead"]. In *Tasha, shisha tachi no kindai* 『他者・死者たちの近代』 [The other and the dead in modernity]. Tokyo: Transview, 2010.

Sueki Fumihiko. *Tetsugaku no genba: Nihon de kangaeru to iu koto* 『哲学の現場—日本で考えるということ』 [The actual field of philosophy: What it means to think in Japan]. Tokyo: Transview, 2011.

Tachibana Fuhito 立花史. "*Issai no jitsuzai ga tokesaru harō: Tanabe Hajime 'shi no tetsugaku' no shatei*" 「いっさいの実在が溶け去る波浪—田辺元 「死の哲学」の射程」 ["Ocean waves whereby all reality melts away: The parameter of Tanabe Hajime's 'philosophy of death'"]. In *Kindai no chōkoku: Fukushima ikō* 『近代の超克：フクシマ以降』 [Overcoming modernity: Post-Fukushima], ed. Ishizuka Masahide 石塚正英. Tokyo: Risōsha, 2013.

Tanabe Hajime 田辺元. "*Todesdialektik*." In *FestschriftMartin Heidegger zum 70. Geburtstag*, ed. Günther Neske, 93–133. Tübingen: Pfullingen, 1959.

Tanabe Hajime. THZ 7 (1963).

Tanabe Hajime. *Philosophy as Metanoetics*, trans. Takeuchi Yoshinori, with Valdo Viglielmo and James Heisig. Berkeley and London: University of California Press, 1986.

Tanabe Hajime. THTS 1, *Shu no ronri* 『種の論理』 [Logic of Species] (2010).

Tanabe Hajime. THTS 2, *Zangedō to shite no tetsugaku* 『懺悔道としての哲学』 *Philosophy as Metanoetics*, trans. by Takeuchi Yoshinori (Berkeley: University of California Press, 1990; Nagoya: Chisokudo Publications, 2016).

Tanabe Hajime. THTS 4, *Shi no tetsugaku* 『死の哲学』 [Philosophy of death] (2010).

Tanabe Hajime and Karaki Junzō (2004). *Tanabe Hajime-Karaki Junzō ōfuku shokan* 『田辺元・唐木順三往復書簡』 [Correspondence between Tanabe Hajime and Karaki Junzō]. Tokyo: Chikuma Shobō, 2004.

Tanabe Hajime, and Nogami Yaeko 野上弥生子. *Tanabe Hajime-Nogami Yaeko ōfuku shokan* 『田辺元・野上弥生子往復書簡』 [Correspondence between Tanabe Hajime and Nogami Yaeko], 2 vols, ed. Takeda Takeda 竹田篤司 and Uda Takeshi 宇田健. Tokyo: Iwanami Shoten, 2012; original ed. 2002.

Uehara Senroku 上原専禄. 『死者・生者—日蓮認識への発想と視点』 [The dead and the living: Ideas and perspectives for understanding Nichiren]. Tokyo: Miraisha, 1974.

Unno, Taitetsu, and J. Heisig, eds. *The Religious Philosophy of Tanabe Hajime*. Berkeley: Asian Humanities Press, 1990.

Yoshioka Hitoshi 吉岡斉. *Genshiryoku no shakaishi: sono nihonteki tenkai* 『原子力の社会史 その日本的展開（新版）』 [Social history of nuclear power: Its Japanese unfolding (new edition)]. Tokyo: Asashi Shinbunsha, 2011.

Yukiyasu Shigeru 行安茂, ed. *Moritaki Ichirō sensei no sotsuju o kinen shite* 『森瀧市郎先生の卒寿を記念して』 [Commemorating the ninetieth birthday of Professor Moritaki Ichirō]. Okayama: Daigaku Kyōiku Shuppan, 1991.

FURTHER READING

Chūgoku Shimbun Online, Hiroshima Peace Media Center. http://hiroshimapeacemedia.jp

Karaki Junzō 唐木順三. "*Baikai to shōchō: Tanabe ni tsuite*" 「媒介と象徴—田辺について」 [Mediation and symbol: On Tanabe philosophy]. In *Gendai-shi e no kokoromi: sōshitsu no jidai* 『現代史への試み—喪失の時代』 [An attempt toward the history of modernity: The age of loss], 234–252. Tokyo: Chūōkōron Shinsha, 2013.

Schroeder, Brian. "Other-Power and Absolute Passivity in Tanabe and Levinas." In *Japanese and Continental Philosophy: Conversation with the Kyoto School*, ed. B. W. Davis, B. Schroeder, and J. M. Wirth, 193–211. Bloomington: Indiana University Press, 2011.

CHAPTER FIVE

In the Wake of 3.11 Earthquake: Philosophy of Disaster and Pilgrimage

CHEUNG CHING-YUEN

INTRODUCTION

Without doubt, 3.11 was a catastrophe that shocked the world. It was a complex disaster including earthquake, tsunami, and nuclear plant incidents. My experience of having been a PhD student at Tohoku University from 2000 to 2007 returned vividly to me, as I recognized on television in Hong Kong most of the coastal cities and towns damaged by earthquake and tsunami such as Yuriage, Watari, Shiogama, Ishinomaki, Onagawa, and Ōfunato. To aggravate my shock, I had just been in Sendai for an international conference a month ago in February. It was hard to believe that a month later the Sendai International Airport would be flooded by a tsunami. Later, there were uncensored scenes from various media showing the explosions, caused by hydrogen, at Fukushima Daiichi Nuclear Plant, but at that time the real problem was yet to be "seen" as meltdowns were occurring inside three nuclear reactors of the Fukushima Nuclear Plant.

Naturally, many people tried to contact their families and friends living in affected areas, but it was impossible to contact immediately those who were in the areas without electricity. Suddenly, the world was no longer connected. While I was checking emails and following the latest developments on the Internet day and night, I, a teaching staff at the Department of Philosophy, began to think about what philosophy could offer in a major disaster like this. Could philosophy, as a reflective thinking, solve actual problems in human life? Could philosophers offer relief to those who are suffering? Could philosophy help those who lost their family members? Why is philosophy useless in the real world? What is the relationship between our existence and the philosophical arguments in academic journal articles? What is philosophy?

These doubts and anxiety of mine were heightened when three days after the earthquake I received the following e-mail from a professor whom I had met in a philosophical conference in Japan in 2010. He wrote:

> Dear Mr. Cheung,
>
> Thank you for your kind email. The situation in Wakabayashi Ward of Sendai, where you have lived, is really bad. I believe it is a huge shock to you. I am praying for our friends, but most of us are fine right now. I am now staying in the rural area of Chiba Prefecture. There is no severe damage here, so please do not worry. Definitely, we have just witnessed one of the biggest earthquakes and tsunami in the history of Japan. We realized finally how weak human beings are under this tremendous power of nature. Nevertheless, it is our responsibility as survivors to overcome the disaster. This fact is not going to be changed. Although the North-Eastern Japan is still unsettling, the other part of Japan is physically safe. There are some worrying factors related to the incidents in Fukushima, but I am still looking forward to my future and my life, even though I am an old man! I wish you further success, and reply with thanks.
>
> Best regards,
> W. K.[1]

The message is clear. Although we are not directly the victims of this particular disaster, it is our responsibility to think philosophically about the problem of disaster as such. Philosophy has always been dealing with disasters, as well as other contemporary issues such as wars and calamity. Indeed, it would be unthinkable if philosophers were not responding to wars in Syria and disasters in Japan.

This chapter is an attempt to philosophize on 3.11, and to unfold a "philosophy of disaster" and a "philosophy of pilgrimage." In this attempt, a possibility of a new direction of the post-3.11 Japanese philosophy will be addressed, with ideas borrowed from the post-3.11 Japanese literature.

1. PHILOSOPHY OF DISASTER

We shall begin with the following question: how do we explain a disaster? Taking earthquake as an example, one may explain the phenomenon in terms of myths. According to Lévi-Strauss, in Japan as well as in some parts in South America, earthquake is explained as a result of the movement of a gigantic fish underground. Lévi-Strauss observes:

> The *namazu* is the cause of the earthquakes in Japan; in America, or at least in certain corners of America, the cause is a fish that belongs to the Scorpaenides family. And that family is represented in Japan by the *okoze* fish, which is an offering to the god of the mountains.[2]

It is rather interesting that different cultures associate earthquake with imaginary beings. However, can it be regarded as a philosophical explanation? Many philosophers argue that it is a fallacy to explain natural disasters in supernatural terms.

Nature philosophers, in the age of ancient Greek, tried to explain earthquake as a natural phenomenon. For examples, Anaximenes believed earthquake as a result of the change in the moisture in the soil; Democritus suggested that earthquake is a result of the movement of water; and Anaxagoras reckoned that air is the cause of earthquakes. These theories were rejected by Aristotle, who argued that the wind is the cause of earthquakes. In *Meteorology*, he wrote:

> Water has been known to burst out during an earthquake. But that does not make water the cause of the earthquake. The wind is the cause whether it exerts its force along the surface or up from below: just as winds are the causes of waves and not waves of winds. Else we might as well say that earth was the cause; for it is upset in an earthquake, just like water (for effusion is a form of upsetting). No, earth and water are material causes (being patients, not agents): the source is the wind.[3]

A more famous figure for his philosophical approach to the cause of the earthquake is Immanuel Kant. We known him for his three *Critiques*, but Kant is also the author of three essays on earthquakes written after the Lisbon earthquake and the tsunami of November 1, 1755.[4] Kant delivered lectures on geography, and natural disaster was one of the topics he was interested in. More importantly, he was a philosopher not impressed by "divine punishment theory", by which it was suggested that thousands of Portuguese had to be punished for their evil acts in trade and colonial activities. Opposing the theory that appeals to the will of monotheistic God, Kant proposed that earthquake should be understood as a natural phenomenon caused by explosion of natural gas in the depths of the earth. It was unreasonable to "justify" earthquake or tsunami by resorting to supernatural explanations.

From the standpoint of modern seismology, Kant and the philosophers mentioned above are all wrong. Scientifically speaking, we should explain earthquake as a result of the pressure released along the earth's plates. However, philosophers and semiologists share the same reasoning, which may be described as "naturalism." That is, natural phenomena should be explained in natural terms. Even in the twenty-first century, however, some may still believe in divine punishment. Ishihara Shintarō, the former mayor of Metropolitan Tokyo, said, right after 3.11, that the disaster was a "*tenbatsu*"—heaven's punishment. He went on to say: "Japanese politics is tainted with egoism and populism. We need to use the tsunami to wipe out egoism, which has attached itself like rust to the mentality of the Japanese people over a long period of time."[5] Following Kant and other naturalistic philosophers, we should strongly disagree with Ishihara's position. Many people have been suffering in the aftermath of 3.11, which came to be known as "the Great East Japan Earthquake," and yet they also suffered from the humiliation of the fallacious claims that the family members and friends who had perished in the disaster deserved to be punished by heaven or god(s).

Thus, philosophy can be regarded as a critique, a critical approach to claims unfounded by reason. Critical thinking is essential not only in philosophical discussions but also in debates related to our daily life. For instance, philosophical training is necessary for us to analyze arguments for or against nuclear power after the Fukushima Nuclear Plant incidents. What is the reasoning for Japan to continue using nuclear power? What is the rhetoric in suggesting that nuclear power is a "green" energy? Is it ethical to use a technology which could cause disasters that will take many generations to redress?

Needless to say, however, philosophy offers more than critical thinking. For example, philosophy of death is important for us to rethink about the different ways of dealing with life and death. Moreover, Japanese philosophy would offer crucial clues for us to understand the Japanese culture: how the Japanese react to natural disasters and why.

Be that as it may, philosophy cannot be regarded as an almighty "cure" to all kinds of pains and sufferings. Likewise, one cannot heal or eliminate fear or anger by just reading philosophical works by Descartes or Hegel. Armchair philosophers or professors of philosophy can philosophize in their own office, but post-3.11 philosophy is not just about philosophizing theoretically about disaster. Above all, before making any speculation about disaster, it is important for us to visit the actual areas devastated by the disaster (*hisaichi*). In other words, the place (*basho*) or "locus" of philosophizing is not only in an office or a lecture hall, but also includes the very spot (*genba*) where the disasters took place in our contemporary world.

I managed to visit Ishinomaki in December 2011, several months after the disaster struck. Located in Miyagi Prefecture, Ishinomaki is a port city which saw the most damage. Before the disaster, one could travel to Ishinomaki from Sendai by a local train in one hour. But since some parts of the train rails and stations were damaged by the tsunami, when I visited it, it was necessary to change to shuttle bus between Takagimachi and Yamoto stations. It took almost two hours to arrive at Ishinomaki. With the suspension of the direct train service between Sendai and Ishinomaki, life was clearly inconvenient for commuters and to a visitor like myself.[6] The trip was made even more unbearable as there were many shocking scenes along the coastline still untouched after the disaster—spotted with flooded farmlands and abandoned skeleton-like remains of houses. Obviously, there had been some clearance of tsunami wreckage, but one saw only a wasteland of ruins.[7]

Upon arriving in Ishinomaki, I immediately went to the Ishinomori Manga Museum, a major attraction of the city. It was closed due to the damage caused by the tsunami.[8] There stood some buildings next to the museum, but most of them had been washed away and only their foundations remained. It crossed my mind that the concept of foundation, "that which is certain and unshakable," is one of the most important concepts of modern philosophy. Descartes in the *Second Meditations* wrote:

> So serious are the doubts into which I have been thrown as a result of yesterday's meditations that I can neither put them out of my mind nor see any way of resolving them. It feels as if I have fallen unexpectedly into a deep whirlpool which tumbles me around so that I can neither stand on the bottom nor swim up to the top. Nevertheless I will make an effort and once more attempt the same path

> which I started on yesterday. Anything that admits of the slightest doubt I will set aside just as if I had found it to be wholly false; and I will proceed in this way until I recognize that there is no certainty. Archimedes used to demand just one firm and immovable point in order to shift the entire earth; so I too can hope for great things if I manage to find just one thing, however slight, that is certain and unshakeable.[9]

Philosophers are searching, or perhaps are obsessed with, the Archimedean point as the starting point of philosophy. All can be doubted but still there is an unshakable ground, as Descartes demonstrated in his path to "*ego sum ego existo*" (I am, I exist) in his *Second Meditations*. However, it seems to me that the very idea of foundation has lost its meaning. In Ishinomaki as well as in many other disaster-stricken areas (*hisaichi*), it is reported that the ground level has dropped by 50–80 centimeters. Areas that used to be living spaces in the past will now be flooded during high tide. The so-called certain and unshakable foundation, which had been safeguarded in our lifeworld or remained immune to catastrophes, has become inhabitable, and hence meaningless.

What is the meaning of philosophy? I may not have had my answer before my visit to Ishinomaki, but now it is clear that philosophy is something that can develop new ideas and approaches beyond foundationalism. To be precise, philosophy is not about the idea of a meaningless foundation, but an act for us to live in the world with some sense of meaning, even when we are still in the process of recovery after a major disaster like 3.11. Here, "recovery" does not mean the physical restoration of damaged buildings and cites or towns, but the true revitalization of a community which suffered from the catastrophe and was desperately in need of new values.

2. PHILOSOPHICAL REFLECTION ON 3.11

Driven by a strong sense of need to philosophize on the meaning of "recovery," my colleagues and I organized an International Conference on "Disaster and the Creation of Value System" in Tohoku University on March 9 and 10, 2012—exactly one year after the 3.11 disaster. The program of this conference included a keynote speech by Augustin Berque (an expert on Watsuji Tetsurō's philosophy), special lectures by Takeuchi Seiichi (Japanese thought) and Suzuki Iwayumi (religious studies), a keynote discussion by Noe Keiichi (philosophy of science) and Kawamoto Takashi (political philosophy), as well as other individual presentations.[10]

"Why people did not evacuate?" This was the title of my presentation given at this conference. Over the past year following the disaster, there had been reports of what people did immediately after the earthquake. Most Japanese knew from their ancestors' experience that a tsunami will follow a very strong earthquake, and they were educated to evacuate to safe places such as the hillside or schoolyard. However, it came to be known that some people actually went back to the coastal area after the earthquake. Hirose Hirotada, an expert in the psychology of disaster, explained that these people fell into three psychological traps: normalcy bias, synching bias, and altruistic action.[11] Normalcy bias is the feeling that one is safe without any reason, such as those people who tried to tidy up their homes after the earthquake. Synching bias is the tendency to follow the mass. If many people do not evacuate, one would prefer not to evacuate either. These two biases are common in many disasters as well as accidents. Although some might not be affected by these two biases, they may risk their lives because of altruistic action. For example, a TV program called "NHK Special" analyzed the data from the car navigators, and it turned out that some people actually went back to the coastal area. Mr and Mrs Hashiura were among those people. In their case, they had the time to go into an inland area, but they chose to visit an old lady living in a fishing village called Yuriage and tried to persuade her to evacuate. At first the old lady refused to go, but she finally changed her mind after they negotiated with her for more than twenty minutes. By then, it was too late. They faced the tsunami attack, and, unfortunately, Mrs Hashiura and the old lady died.[12] It is a tragedy for Mr Hashiura, but Hirose suggests this is a typical case of altruistic action.

Why does one choose to help the other, instead of oneself? Hirose notices that in many coastal regions along the Sanriku area, there is a traditional expression, "*tsunami-ten-den-ko*" (津波てんでんこ). "*Ten-den-ko*" literally means "individuals separately," that is "take your own way." It conveys the instruction that one should run for safety first before helping others in the case of tsunami. Hirose argues that this traditional teaching is not plausible, for human beings are social beings. Although Mr and Mrs Hashiura should have been able to evacuate themselves, they decided to risk their lives to take care of the old lady. This, however, is but a psychological "trap," says Hirose, and from the viewpoint of disaster prevention, altruistic action will only increase the number of casualties. I argue, however, that we should not accept Hirose's narrative. Mr Hashiura demonstrated a moral action. Even though Mr and Mrs Hashiura did not bring a positive consequence, their action remains morally justified. Philosophy should remain critical of the opinions of psychologists or government officials, who may put too much emphasis on the numbers and rational view of disaster prevention, and forget the importance of moral action.

My emphasis of the moral action is in fact related to an accident that happened in Foshan, PRC, in 2011. Wang Yueyue, a two-year-old Chinese girl, was hit by two different vehicles, but was ignored by eighteen passers-by. Finally, the nineteenth person (reported as a homeless woman) picked her up, but it was too late. Chinese netizens made comments such as follows:

> "Now people have become so selfish. So many people walked by but no one helped her because they didn't want to get into trouble."
> "I hope that this little angel who was discarded by society can act as a wake-up call to the nation about the importance of moral education."
> "Hope you can find some love in heaven. This world is full of apathy."[13]

It may not be easy to encourage people to be good Samaritans, but it is important to promote altruistic action. Even though there is no law to fine people who do not help others in need, one should be able to act morally when called into action. This was the conclusion of my presentation.

3. A VISIT TO THE DISASTER-STRICKEN AREAS

Following the two-day conference in Sendai, the Department of Philosophy at Tohoku University arranged a day excursion for the conference attendees to visit the earthquake-tsunami hit areas, and it was on March 11, 2012, exactly the day of the first anniversary of the Great East Japan Earthquake. In a hired bus, we visited Onagawa, a town that saw heavy destruction due to the tsunami. Upon arriving there, we went up to a terrace about 16 meters high, but were told that the tsunami waves rose higher than 20 meters and the terrace was washed out. We also saw a large concrete building pulled down by the tsunami. It was a place for us to feel and recognize the destructive power of nature and the powerlessness of human beings.

Next we visited Ishinomaki, as I had arranged a meeting with Richard Halberstadt, an English teacher at Ishinomaki Senshu University. Mr. Halberstadt's story was reported by many media in the world, for he refused to go back to United Kingdom after the UK government announced an evacuation scheme.[14] He explained to us that he was not injured in the disaster, and was well cared for by his friends after 3.11. As a foreigner living in Japan for many years, he would have felt extreme remorse had he left Ishinomaki during the difficult time. That is why he did not even think of leaving his friends and students. One year after the earthquake, he noticed that student enrolment had dropped significantly due to the suspension of train service. He also mentioned the strong wish of Japanese people to return to "everydayness" (*nichijō* 日常). However, there were too many TV programs that triggered trauma for the survivors. For those who have lost their family members, jobs, and homes, what does "everydayness" mean? We did not come to any conclusion during this conversation, but we observed a minute of silence at 2:46 pm (the time the M9 earthquake hit Japan a year ago).

After the meeting with Mr. Halberstadt, we paid a special visit to Arahama, which is located in the coastal area of the city of Sendai. The tsunami in this area was about 6 meters high, but it proves to be even more fatal. Unlike Onagawa, the Sendai plain is an area without any hills or slopes, and hence there was no place to take refuge in during the tsunami attack. Fortunately, the movement of the tsunami was blocked by a highway as its structure functioned as a wall. The highway protected many houses and farmlands, as well as a small Shinto Shrine named *Namiwake Jinja* (浪分神社). It was Augustin Berque who insisted that we pay a visit to the shrine. It is a very small shrine, built in 1611 after a great tsunami had devastated the area. The shrine was built precisely at the spot where the tsunami stopped, and served as a reminder to the local residents that one must not build anything beyond the shrine toward the ocean. The name of the shrine is composed of "*nami*," meaning waves, and "*wake*," meaning division or separation. However, if there had been no highway to block the tsunami, the shrine would have been destroyed in the 2011 tsunami.

4. TOWARD CONSTRUCTING A PHILOSOPHY OF PILGRIMAGE

On our way back in the bus, one of conference participants M. Yusa described our excursion as a sort of "pilgrimage."[15] It struck me to be a very profound observation. The word "pilgrimage" has this original meaning of going to a "foreign" (strange, alien) place. As noted by Ian Reader:

> The English words "pilgrimage" derives, via the French *pèlerinage*, from the Latin terms *peregrinus*, "foreign," and *per ager*, "going through the fields." Thus it indicates the idea of journeys, travelling, leaving the comforts of home, and being a stranger in the lands through which one journeys.[16]

Although the origin of the word "pilgrimage" is closely associated with Christianity, pilgrimage is practiced widely. Reader observes that the "concepts of searching for ultimate meaning" are also present in the terms equivalent to "pilgrimage." He points out that in Japanese, "[a word] *junrei*, for example, is commonly used for one of the most prevalent forms of pilgrimage in Japan, visiting circuits of Buddhist temples, and it combines the notion of 'going around' (*jun*) and worshipping (*rei*)."[17]

Here, I would like to further develop the idea as a philosophy of pilgrimage with insights borrowed from Watsuji Tetsurō (1889–1960). One of the beloved books Watsuji wrote, demanded by the readers to republish it from its state of being out of print, was titled *Koji-junrei* (*A Pilgrimage to Ancient Buddhist Temples* 古寺巡礼). According to Watsuji's introduction we learn that it was an account of a trip he took with several friends to ancient temples in Nara and its vicinity in May 1918.[18]

Surprisingly, Watsuji begins his book with a chapter on neither Nara nor Kyoto; rather, with his experience of seeing an excellent reproduction of the Ajanta wall paintings done by his university friend at the latter's home. There are also side stories about his conversations with his father, a medical doctor dedicated to the mission which believes that "treating a sick person is an humane art" (*I wa ninjutsu nari* 医は仁術なり), who asked the young Watsuji whether his way of life was contributing to the general welfare of humankind; he also reflects on the different effects of Japanese and Western style baths on the mind and the body; and he even goes in detailed and colorful observations of foreign guests, whom he saw in the hotel restaurant—male and female, young and old, a family party and single travelers, some extremely attractive to Watsuji—all staying at the same hotel in Nara where he and his party were staying. All these sidelines seem to be irrelevant to his pilgrimage or to his book, but Watsuji explains:

> You might feel strange about my taking interest in these scenes that are international, while I am on a trip to Nara to visit temples, but I can say that I did not feel misgivings at all about how I felt. After all, we are the pilgrims of art, and not of Buddha the benevolent savior of all beings. Even if we were to feel like bowing down from the depths of our hearts in front of a statue of Buddha or be stricken by the bolt of Buddha's mercy, which would make us feel so deeply that we were reduced to tears, it would only be because we were overwhelmed by the art, which made use of Buddhist power, not because we converted to Buddhism

> in a strict religious sense. After all, we have not forsaken the senses of flesh to the degree that we can overcome every temptation and act only according to Buddhist precepts. So, in the dining hall, we let ourselves enjoy not only the culinary pleasure but also the visual pleasures of the world.[19]

It is worth noting that Watsuji claims himself to be a "pilgrim of art, not of Buddha." By art, he meant anything appealing to the senses (aesthetics), and honing his pen was equal to sharpening his senses to strengthen his power of observation. Inner reflections must be clear before they are made into linguistic expressions. Also, his approach in this book is one of finding a connection between the ancient Japanese art and the continental (Chinese, Korean, Indian, and Central Asian, including Persian) art. Nara used to be the capital city and cultural center of Japan in the eighth century, but it was in ruins by the time of Watsuji's visit. "We followed the narrow road that made me think of the old capital of Nara, now dilapidated, more and more."[20] He mentions his disappointment of seeing the destruction of Buddhist temples, a result of the national policy to promote Shinto as the religion of modern Japan in the early years following the Meiji Restoration (1867). Watsuji also wrote about the history of the now-treasured eleven-faced Kannon (Avalokiteśvara) statue that had been abandoned on the roadside fifty years earlier;

> The statue was apparently the main object of worship at a temple called Jingūji of Miwayama in the city of Sakurai, Nara. When the government attempted to separate Shinto from Buddhism at the time of the Meiji Restoration, the statue, sadly, was abandoned at the roadside, at the insistence of the believers of ancient Shinto. There was no benevolent taker of this statue in the neighborhood. In the end, this noble Kannon lay covered with dirt in tall grass day after day. One day, the abbot of a small temple called Shōrinji, a temple of the Pure Land sect, happened to walk by it and discovered it. "How precious," he thought. "If there is no one to take it, I will take it back to the temple." So the Kannon was brought to the Shōrinji temple.[21]

In stark contrast to the image of Watsuji, associated with a certain degree of nationalism, in his prewar writings we find him embracing the diverse roots of Japanese culture. He suggests, for instance, that the Japanese have borrowed many things from China, including the writing system, out of which the Japanese invented the syllabary (*kana*) system and architectural techniques. He argues,

> Hence, we should regard these changes and developments as uniquely Japanese developments, only if we acknowledge that they were based on the foundation of foreign cultures. In other words, it is not that a culture specific to Japan embraced foreign culture, but that characteristics of the Japanese people developed in this particular way in a society where the air was thick with foreign cultures. This viewpoint is different from the one that contends that foreign cultures were simply inserted into existing Japanese culture. I argue, rather, that foreign cultures provided the soil for the development of native Japanese culture. If one takes this point of view, we may say that Japanese creativity is not something that stands opposed to foreign cultures but that it was actually born out of foreign cultures.[22]

Watsuji made various pilgrimages not only within Japan but also in Italy. His pilgrimages were not for a specific religious purpose to visit Christian or Buddhist sacred places. He reiterated that pilgrimage for him was *not* a religious act, but an experience to understand art. This point is highly suggestive to my interest, as the philosophy of pilgrimage is not about religious pilgrimage or artistic pilgrimage, but a *philosophical practice* which focuses on the recollection of the forgotten history. Noe Keiichi, a contemporary Japanese philosopher (whose work is found in this Handbook), argues that "history" has a twofold meaning.[23] He writes,

> On the one hand, historians have to choose valuable events for description out of enormous historical materials. On the other hand, they have to exclude, delete, or forget insignificant events. In this sense, "history" is a ceaseless struggle between memory and oblivion. Preserved memories from oblivion are organized into a historical narrative.[24]

Here, Noe goes on to suggest the twofold meaning of "narrative." It can be "that which is narrated, a story," or "the act of narrating." Stories are being told, but we are the one who narrates. We are *homo narrans*. In this sense, pilgrimage can be regarded as an act similar to historical narratives. To give an example, Noe mentions Matsuo Bashō's famous work *Oku no Hosomichi* (published posthumously in 1702). During his pilgrimage to Hiraizumi, Bashō recalls a celebrated poem by the Chinese Tang Dynasty poet Tu Fu (Du Fu 杜甫, 712–770):

> The country has fallen but its rivers and mountains remain;
> When spring comes to the city its grass turns green again.[25]

Now Bashō writes his own haiku:

> The summer grasses—
> For many brave warriors
> The aftermath of dreams.[26]

There is another important message about pilgrimage in Bashō's writing. In the preface to *Oku no Hosomichi*, he wrote:

> Many of the men of old died on their travels, and I, too, for years past have been stirred by the sight of a solitary cloud drifting with the wind to ceaseless thoughts of roaming. Last year I spent wandering along the seacoast. In autumn I returned to my cottage on the river and swept away the cobwebs. Gradually the year drew to a close. When spring came and there was mist in the air, I thought of crossing the Barrier of Shirakawa into Oku. Everything about me was bewitched by the travel gods, and my thoughts were no longer mine to control. The spirits of the road beckoned, and I could do no work at all.[27]

Noe explains:

> Here, we notice, Bashō was recollecting the tragic narrative concerning young general Minamoto no Yoshitsune, who was killed by his elder brother's army. At the same time, he overlapped the ruins before his eyes with the images of war in

> ancient China through citing Tu Fu's poem. This double image is none other than the effect of narrative. Under the power of narrative, just an ordinary landscape wears collective memories and historical significance.[28]

Bashō, recalling the famous poem by Tu Fu and composing his haiku, is not merely a poet, but a true practitioner of the philosophy of pilgrimage. Indeed, Bashō writes about the very essence of the philosophy of pilgrimage as follows:

> Many are the names that have been preserved for us in poetry from ancient times, but mountains crumble and rivers disappear, new roads replace the old, stones are buried and vanish in the earth, trees grow old and give way to saplings. Time passes and the world changes. The remains of the past are shrouded in uncertainty. And yet, here, before my eyes, was a monument that none would deny had lasted a thousand years. I felt as if I were looking into the minds of the men of old. "This," I thought, "is one of the pleasures of travel and living to be old." I forgot the weariness of the journey and was moved to tears of joy.[29]

Yanagita Kunio (1875–1962), a famous Japanese folklore scholar and travelogue writer, explains that travel "is not the *tabi* (trip) of ancient times, nor the *ryokō* (sightseeing tour) of the present."[30] Traveling is a way for us to reconnect the past with the present, as an old idiom suggests that traveling ten thousand miles is better than reading ten thousand books.[31]

5. CONSTRUCTING POST-3.11 LITERATURE AND PHILOSOPHY

In her book entitled *Post-Earthquake-Disaster Literature*, Japanese author Kimura Saeko suggested that there are three kinds of noticeable approaches to 3.11 disaster in the literary circles of Japan. The first approach is the attitude of "must do something" (何かをしなければならない), the second is marked by "avoidance" or "escapism," and the third is the attitude succumbing to a social pressure, expressed as "self-restraint" (*jishuku* 自粛), which is nothing but a kind of self-censorship.

Those who adhere to the first approach advocate a creation of new literature. As in the case of postwar literature, post-disaster literature is something new, because "something got lost, and something new was born" out of the disaster. People are promoting new literary theories as well as producing new poems, novels, music, movies, manga, and performing arts. This feeling of need to develop "something new" is a response supported by concrete reality.[32]

The second approach can be understood as something akin to escapism, as people try to escape from reality. Kimura quotes Don DeLillo's *Falling Man*, a post-9.11 novel in this context:

> People read poems. People I know, they read poetry to ease the shock and pain, give them a kind of space, something beautiful in language … to bring comfort or composure. I don't read poems. I read newspapers. I put my head in the pages and get angry and crazy.[33]

People may read novels for an escape from reality, but Kimura suggests that we read poems or novels not because of hoping for a kind of escape, but out of the desire to read something written that has strong impacts.[34] In this sense, the mission of literature remains the same even after a disaster. But we may see that some Japanese novelists disagree with the special need to develop a new kind of literature after a disaster. For examples, Nakamura Fuminori argues, "Literature as such in essence does not change ... In this country, we have 30,000 people committing suicide every year. This is an internal tragedy, or a certain state of war. I have always been writing literature with this in mind."[35] Matsuura Rieko writes, "As far as I am concerned, the core of my views on the world, life and literature remained almost the same after the earthquake."[36] She admits that her daily life has changed because of the nuclear incident, but many Japanese suffered from compassion fatigue in watching scenes on television. Another novelist Satō Yūya writes,

> Praying for the victims, being angry about the reaction of the government, fearing about radioactive substances, emphasizing on the importance of human life and economy, but remaining silent on the nuclear policy as there is no "common consensus" about nuclear energy—this is the general attitude of Japanese people in spring 2011.[37]

Kimura suggests that this wishy-washy attitude widely shared among the Japanese people is due to the fact there nuclear-related issues have become a taboo in Japan to discuss and seriously confront.[38]

The third response, according to Kimura, is self-restraint. This is a social behavior of restraining from doing anything different to draw the attention of others after a scandal or an accident. In the case of 3.11, it took the form of a taboo to mention "death" in the disaster. This taboo was, however, shuttered in Itō Seikō's novel *Imaginary Radio*, which is about a DJ receiving phone-in from tsunami victims at a radio station. Itō's novel was nominated for the Akutagawa Prize in literature, but was criticized by the judges as "cashing in on" the voices of the dead.[39] Here, Itō's intention is summarized by Kimura as follows:

> This country [Japan] is not listening to the voices of the dead, and is marching on while forgetting the wars and the atomic bombs in Hiroshima and Nagasaki. Therefore, after this earthquake we have to start listening continuously to the voices of the dead. We need to restore our path from a wrong direction. The voices of the dead are the memories of tragedy and traumatic history. We have totally forgotten these memories, and it seems that we are going to forget this earthquake as well.[40]

Based on these literary outputs of post-3.11, Kimura concludes: "Post-earthquake-disaster literature does not merely mean works written after the earthquake, but works written in the dire situations in which writing about disaster itself has become a taboo."[41] One of the most difficult challenges is the theme related to nuclear issues and radiation pollution.[42]

By taking after Kimura's project in literature to embrace the voices of the dead, I propose the need to develop a post-3.11 philosophy. Philosophy could be radically changed or unchanged after a disaster, but it is important for us to philosophize on disaster in general, as well as on more specific issues such as pilgrimage, technology, and the use of nuclear energy. These are issues we cannot ignore any longer in the contemporary lifeworld. Kōno Tetsuya observes in a phenomenological language of 3.11 and notes:

> The life-world is the background environment of our competences, practices, and attitudes. Because all of our practices and attitudes have to be changed according to safety conditions, whether it is safe or risky constitutes a fundamental meaning of the lifeworld.[43]

To be sure, antinuclear movement in Japan has been led not just by philosophers such as Karatani Kōjin but also by novelists such as Ōe Kenzaburō and Setouchi Jakuchō. Setouchi is among those who repeatedly visited Tohoku. During a hunger strike demonstration (May 2, 2012) held in Tokyo against the reopening of the Ooi Nuclear Plant, she said: "In my life, nothing more scary than Fukushima has happened apart from WWII. I wonder why Japanese government is in such a hurry to restart Ooi nuclear plant. Nuclear disaster is a human-made disaster. I'm so sorry for children and young people, if we are to repeat the same thing."[44] Facing the crisis of humanity in Japan, Japanese philosophy can no longer remain a mere theory but is becoming a practice or even a social engagement.

CONCLUDING REMARKS

In this chapter, I have delineated a possibility that Japanese philosophy should face the reality of contemporary Japan, and that pilgrimage stands out to be one of the keywords in understanding the Japanese culture as well as our lifeworld. Saulius Geniusas, a colleague of mine and a phenomenologist, observed during our pilgrimage of 2014 to Fukushima Prefecture:

> Here we are near the nuclear power plant. I am probably the first Lithuanian to come here, and you would think we came to see this gorgeous nature around us. But this is a heavily polluted place. So the contrast is remarkable … I keep on thinking about the contrast between the beauty of the place and the severity of the disaster. I know many people who would come here and say this is at least one of the most beautiful places they have visited. The roads are remarkable. Here you can see the Pacific Ocean. The villages we passed are old and seem to be well kept. And even now you can see so few people, and everything is so clean and in order. This contrast is very hard to comprehend. How a place can be so beautiful and could be so unsafe and unlivable at the same time? The only way for the people to live here is to exercise self-forgiveness and the denial of everything that is happening. You have to somehow deceive yourself. "Everything is okay. Nothing is really taking place." Because if you do not do that, you will not be here.[45]

Japanese philosophy is powerless if it cannot face the reality of Japan after Fukushima. With a contemporary reading of Watsuji's idea of pilgrimage, we can conclude that pilgrimage is no mere traveling or a visit; it is an act to rescue and preserve memories from oblivion; as such, it should be regarded as a way of doing philosophy. One may argue that this "non-theoretical" approach is not philosophy *proper*, but as suggested by John Maraldo, it can be regarded as a kind of philosophy of practice. Practice is not the "secondary philosophy." Rather, this can be seen as the very promise of Japanese philosophy. I quote Maraldo by way of my conclusion: "My hope is ultimately to transform the arena in which philosophy is practiced. In the case of practice, the potential of the alternative is to heal the divide between theory and practice and make philosophy, traditionally a very theoretical discipline, more relevant to everyday life in society."[46]

NOTES

1. Originally written in Japanese; translation mine.
2. C. Lévi-Strauss, *The Other Face of the Moon* (Cambridge, MA: Belknap Press of Harvard University Press, 2013), 139.
3. Aristotle, *Complete Works of Aristotle, Volume 1* (Princeton, NJ: Princeton University Press, 1984), 595.
4. Some of Kant's essays on earthquake can be found in Kant, *Natural Science* (Cambridge: Cambridge University Press, 2012).
5. *The Guardian*, March 15, 2011.
6. In May 2015, the Senseki Line (the railroad line that connects Sendai and Ishinomaki) was reopened, with a new line called Senseki-Tohoku Line. The new and improved line takes only forty minutes from Sendai to Ishinomaki.
7. See my video: https://www.youtube.com/watch?v=Ygikh9PTzFo
8. The museum reopened in November 2012.
9. Descartes, *Meditations on First Philosophy* (Cambridge: Cambridge University Press, 1996), 16.
10. For details of this conference, refer to the following website: https://sites.google.com/site/tohokuconference311/Home
11. H. Hirose, *Kyodai Saigai no Seiki wo Ikinyku* [Survival in the century of gigantic disasters] (Tokyo: Shueisha, 2011), 181.
12. http://www.nhk.or.jp/special/onair/111002.html
13. http://www.reuters.com/article/us-china-girl-idUSTRE79K0HM20111021
14. For example: http://in.reuters.com/video/2011/04/05/briton-helps-rebuild-japan?videoId=200552562
15. What she meant, she told me later, was that we had just visited a place that defied any human imagination and provoked a profound sense of awe in the visitors. Such a place has the power to shake and transform the visitor from the ground level up. If it was not a "pilgrimage," what was it?
16. I. Reader, *Pilgrimage: A Very Short Introduction* (New York: Oxford University Press, 2015), 20.

17. Ibid., 21–22.
18. Watsuji Tetsurō, *Pilgrimages to Ancient Temples in Nara* (Honolulu: University of Hawaii Press, 2011), 1. The book was first published in 1919, and twenty-eight year later in 1946, it was republished with slight revisions made to the text.
19. Ibid., 19; translation slightly altered.
20. Ibid., 21.
21. Ibid., 38; translation slightly altered.
22. Ibid., 110; translation modified.
23. This speech was delivered in a 2012 conference, "Heritage and Societies: Toward the 20th Anniversary of the Nara Document and Beyond." A report of the conference can be found here: http://www.academia.edu/3626272/_Heritage_and_Societies_Toward_the_20th_Anniversary_of_the_Nara_Document_and_Beyond_Conference_Report
24. Quoted from the unpublished speech mentioned in n. 23.
25. D. Keene, *Travelers of a Hundred Ages* (New York: Columbia University Press, 1999), 316.
26. Ibid.
27. Ibid., 309.
28. See 2012 conference, "Heritage and Societies: Toward the 20th Anniversary of the Nara Document and Beyond," cited above in n. 23 and 24.
29. Keene, *Travelers of a Hundred Ages*, 316–317.
30. Quoted in Melek Ortabasi, *The Undiscovered Country: Text, Translation, and Modernity in the Work of Yanagita Kunio* (Cambridge: Harvard University Press, 2014), 81.
31. Japanese: 百聞は一見に如かず; Chinese: 百聞不如一見.
32. Kimura Saeko, *Shinsaigo Bungakuron* [Post-3.11 earthquake theory of literature] (Tokyo: Seidosha, 2013), 9.
33. Don DeLillo, *Falling Man* (New York: Scribner, 2007), 42. Quoted by Kimura, *Shinsaigo Bungakuron*, 13–14.
34. Ibid., 14. Kimura comments that Don DeLillo's novel has far more "real power" than newspapers.
35. Ibid., 117.
36. Ibid., 117–118.
37. Ibid., 118–119.
38. Ibid., 119.
39. Ibid., 40–41.
40. Ibid., 48.
41. Ibid., 59.
42. In April 2016, there were earthquakes in Kumamoto and Oita Prefectures. Although many people were worried about the situation of Sendai Nuclear Plant in Kagoshima Prefecture, nuclear issues remain a taboo in the media.

43. T. Kōno, "The Disastrous Lifeworld: A Phenomenological Consideration of Safety, Resilience, and Vulnerability," in *Philosophy Study* 3.1 (January 2013), 58.
44. From the *Fukushima Diary*, May 3, 2012. See: http://fukushima-diary.com/2012/05/90-years-old-nun-joined-hunger-strike-to-be-against-restarting-ooi-nuclear-plant/
45. The Chinese Translation of the message is published in *Kitetsu: A Chinese Philosophical Magazine for Everyone* (2014), supported by knowledge transfer fund of Chinese University of Hong Kong. Details of the project can be found here: http://www.orkts.cuhk.edu.hk/knowledge-transfer-initiatives/project-highlights/228-restoration-after-3-11-pain-suffering-memory-and-trauma-kpf13icf18
46. J. Maraldo, "An Alternative Notion of Practice in the Promise of Japanese Philosophy," in Kevin Lam Wing-keung and Cheung Ching-yuen, ed., FJP 4 (2009), 21.

BIBLIOGRAPHY

Aristotle. *Complete Works of Aristotle, Volume 1*. Princeton, NJ: Princeton University Press, 1984.

DeLillo, Don. *Falling Man*. New York: Scribner, 2007.

Descartes, René. *Meditations on First Philosophy*. Cambridge: Cambridge University Press, 1996.

Hirose Hirotada 広瀬弘忠. *Kyodai saigai no seiki o ikinuku* 『巨大災害の世紀を生き抜く』 [Survival in the century of gigantic disasters]. Tokyo: Shūeisha, 2011.

Kant, Immanuel. *Natural Science*. Cambridge: Cambridge University Press, 2012.

Keene, Donald. *Travelers of a Hundred Ages*. New York: Columbia University Press, 1999.

Kimura Saeko 木村朗子. *Shinsaigo Bungakuron* 『震災後文学論』 [Post-earthquake theory of literature]. Tokyo: Seidosha, 2013.

Kōno Tetsuya 河野哲也. "The Disastrous Lifeworld: A Phenomenological Consideration of Safety, Resilience, and Vulnerability." *Philosophy Study* 3.1 (2013), 52–63.

Lévi-Strauss, Claude. *The Other Face of the Moon*. Cambridge, MA: Belknap Press of Harvard University Press, 2013.

Maraldo, John. "An Alternative Notion of Practice in the Promise of Japanese Philosophy." In *Frontiers of Japanese Philosophy 4*, ed. Kevin Lam Wing-keung and Cheung Ching-yuen, 7–21. Nagoya: Nanzan Institute for Religion and Culture, 2009.

Ortabasi, Melek. *The Undiscovered Country: Text, Translation, and Modernity in the Work of Yanagita Kunio*. Cambridge: Harvard University Press, 2014.

Reader, Ian. *Pilgrimage: A Very Short Introduction*. New York: Oxford University Press, 2015.

Watsuji Tetsuro. *Pilgrimages to Ancient Temples in Nara*. Honolulu: University of Hawaii Press, 2011.

FURTHER READING

Hutchinson, Rachael, and Marks Williams, eds. *Representing the Other in Modern Japanese Literature: A Critical Approach*. London: Routledge, 2007.

Karatani Kōjin 柄谷行人. *Yanagita Kunio ron* 『柳田国男論』 [Essays on Yanagita Kunio]. Tokyo: Inscript, 2013.

Karatani Kōjin. *Yūdōron: Yanagita Kunio to yamabito*『遊動論、柳田国男と山人』 [On mobility: Yanagita Kunio and the mountain people]. Tokyo: Bunshun, 2014.

Karatani Kōjin. "Two Types of Mobility" [Appendix to *Yūdōron*], trans. Cheung Ching-yuen. *Journal of Japanese Philosophy* 4 (2016), 3–15.

Nagashima Yoichi, ed. *Return to Japan: From "Pilgrimage" to the West*. Aarhus: Aarhus University Press, 2001.

Noe Keiichi 野家啓一. *Monogatari no Tetsugaku* 『物語の哲学』 [Philosophy of narration]. Tokyo: Kōdansha, 2005.

Yanagita Kunio. *Folk Legends from Tono: Japan's Spirits, Deities, and Fantastic Creatures*. Lanham, MD: Rowman & Littlefield, 2015.

PART THREE

Aesthetics

CHAPTER SIX

The Aesthetics of Tradition: Making the Past Present

MICHAEL F. MARRA

1. MEDIEVAL AESTHETICS OF YŪGEN

Fujiwara no Teika (1162–1241), one of Japan's most distinguished poets, composed the following poem in 1186:

Miwataseba
Hana mo momiji mo
Nakarikeri
Ura no tomaya no
Aki no yūgure

Looking far, I see
No sign of cherry blossoms
Or crimson leaves.
A reed-thatched hut on a bay
On an evening in autumn.[1]

It is not an easy task to ascertain how the poem was interpreted at the time Teika composed it. We can be sure, however, that the reception by Teika's contemporaries was far from flattering. As Teika himself acknowledged in his collection of poems *Shūi gusō*, critics challenged his work of that time as "nonsensical": "During the Bunji and Kenkyū eras (1185–1198) I was criticized by all levels of society for writing faddish, Zen-nonsense poetry. I seriously considered giving up *waka* composition."[2] Teika was criticized for creating a style that was a poetic translation of the paradoxical statements then in vogue among monks of the Zen sect. Critics disparagingly called Teika's poetry *darumauta*, or "poems of Bodhidharma"—Bodhidharma being regarded as the founder of Chan (J. Zen) Buddhism. The criticism addressed matters of style, especially the technical language of poetics. Teika's alleged obscurities, which critics compared to the paradoxical structure of a Zen dialogue (*mondō*), resulted from a peculiar use of the so-called *yūgen* style (the style of profundity). This term was used in Daoism and Buddhism to indicate a religious depth which the mind finds difficult to grasp; it entails the presence of something that is hard to perceive. In Chan Buddhism, *yūgen* came to express "the profundity within the awareness of non-presence (Ch. *wu*; J. *mu*)."[3] Teika skillfully voiced this non-presence by stressing the absent seasonal marks: cherry blossoms and maple leaves.

Kamo no Chōmei (1153–1216), a contemporary of Teika, acknowledged the difficulty of describing the "*yūgen* style" by resorting to the use of a series of negatives in what is perhaps the *locus classicus* of definitions of *yūgen* in the thirteenth century. Chōmei explained this term in a text on poetics, the *Mumyōshō* (*Nameless Treatise*, 1209–10), as follows:

> Since I do not understand it very well myself, I am at a loss as to how to describe it in a satisfactory manner, but according to the views of those who have penetrated into the realm of *yūgen*, the importance lies in overtones (*yojō*), which are not stated in words and an atmosphere that is not revealed through the form of the poem. When the content rests on a sound basis and the diction excels in lavish beauty, these other virtues will be supplied naturally. On an autumn evening, for example, there is no color in the sky, nor any sound, and although we cannot give a definite reason for it, we are somehow moved to tears. A person lacking in sensitivity finds nothing particular in such a sight, he just admires the cherry blossoms (*hana*) and scarlet autumn leaves (*momiji*) that can be seen with his own eyes.[4]

Chōmei included this comment in a chapter in which he discussed a controversy between ancient and new poetic styles. According to Chōmei, *yūgen* is a style (*yūgen-tai*) that is expected to bring about a change in the quality of poetry at a time when poetry had reached a dead end in expression and content. The repetitiveness of verses, images, and associations between words had become so stifling that poets felt a need to turn once again to ancient poems for help in creating new, original verses. Chōmei points out the difficulty in following the new "*yūgen* style" in the composition of poetry unless one has already mastered poetic techniques, and has already entered the realm of poetry. Otherwise, Chōmei continues, the effect will be vulgar, like a low-class woman who applies powder to her face without knowing the technique of proper make-up. The simple repetition of "original" verses in the *yūgen* style will lead to nonsense (*mushin shojaku*, literally "there is no place to settle for the mind"),[5] and to the composition of what Chōmei called "Bodhidharma's poems"—the antithesis of *yūgen*.

Teika developed a technique of composition based on a stylistic predilection for making the negative effectual (there are no cherry blossoms), a possibility of being caught in the negative moment. It stands opposed to earlier styles that used negative forms in conjunction with conditional clauses in order to express wishful thinking, an impossibility devised in order to appease the turmoil of the heart (at the view of the scattering cherry blossoms). We see the latter approach, for example, in the following poem composed three centuries earlier:

Yo no naka ni
Taete sakura no

Nakariseba
Haru no kokoro wa
Nodokekaramashi

Ah, if in this world
There were only no such thing
As cherry blossoms—
Then perhaps in the springtime
Our hearts could be at peace.[6]

The same conditional clause that begs nature to stop its course was applied to the maple leaves (*momiji*) in the following poem written a few decades after the one mentioned above. Here, the logic of the poem is reversed: the poet yearns for the maple leaves to continue to linger rather than to disappear. The style, however, remains the same.

Ogura yama
Mine no momijiba
Kokoro araba
Ima hitotabi no
Miyuki matanan

You autumn leaves
On the slopes at Ogura—
If you have a heart,
Put off your falling this once:
Till the Emperor's visit.[7]

Teika does not simply omit the seasonal marks from his poem. This omission becomes the topic of the poem from which a new perception of reality is born and an unfamiliar rhetorical *topos* is evoked: the quietness of humble dwellings fading in the twilight as distinctive marks of autumn.

I stress the attention that Teika's contemporaries paid to the rhetorical elements of poetic composition since most poetic treatises (*karon*) and judgments at competitive poetry-composing gatherings (*uta-awase*) centered on the propriety of vocabulary, expressive skills, and all sorts of rhetorical devices in the formulation of poetic discourses. With a few exceptions aimed at explaining poetry in terms of religious significance, mainly fragments of Buddhist thought,[8] we seldom see medieval poets engaged in the discussion of broader issues which explain their rhetorical choices in terms of what we would call "aesthetic discourses" today. Even when we might think that the poet is genuinely concerned with descriptions of Buddhist worldviews, in most cases, he simply reduces complicated doctrinal points to rhetorical *topoi*. For example, the discussion that Teika's father Fujiwara Shunzei (1114–1204) gave of poetry, in light of the doctrine espoused in the *Makashikan* (Ch. *Mohe Zhiguan*) (*Great Concentration and Insight*) in his treatise *Korai fūteishō* (*Essays on Ancient and Modern Styles*, 1197), is a revitalization of an ancient rhetorical *topos* centered around the challenge that Buddhist monks posed to poetry in their critique of a secular language that was not directly subordinated to religious concerns. Shunzei, who was preceded and followed by a line of famous poets, searched for an answer to the monks' criticism by creating the rhetoric of a "poetic path of composition" (*kadō*) modeled after and running parallel to the "Buddhist path of practice" (*butsudō*). The *topos* became a kind of exorcism, a magic formula that all poets had to follow in order to dispel the possible evil consequences that might come from an improper use of words, that is, a use removed from religious practice, which was directly linked to the praise of the Buddha. The poets' actual concern was mainly *poetic* in the sense that they aimed at creating the language of poetry, and making poetic language work differently from other types of language.

2. THE TWENTIETH-CENTURY CREATION (OR INVENTION) OF "TRADITIONAL AESTHETICS"

When we look at modern interpretations of Teika's poem by Japanese scholars of medieval Japanese literature, we cannot avoid being perplexed by the disappearance of the preeminent emphasis on the rhetoric of the poem in favor of adherence to alleged "aesthetic discourses," which came into being at least six centuries after the time of the poem's composition. Historically speaking, however, these "aesthetic discourses" became theoretical bodies only in the twentieth century, no earlier than the 1920s. There seems to be unanimous agreement among leading scholars of Japanese literature on the fact that Teika's poem stands for more than it was intended to accomplish. This "more" is actually the product of the creation and development in Japan of the field of aesthetics that began in the late 1870s and had an enormous impact on the creation of what goes in Japan today under the label of "tradition." Teika's poem came to be read in light of a series of aesthetic discourses that have transformed words—which originally came from the field of poetics and were associated with poetic styles—into local expressions of aesthetic experiences. The "*yūgen* style," one among several styles from which the poet could choose in order to give the poem a lofty, melancholy, or comic tone, became the "aesthetics of *yūgen*," a complex world of experience, perception, and communication related to a series of other aesthetic discourses, such as the aesthetics of *mono no aware, yojō, sabi, wabi, mujō*, and so on.

Once we look at Teika's poem, we notice that aesthetic concerns are shared by all of the editors of the major collections of the *Shinkokin waka-shū* in which the poem was anthologized in 1205. Hisamatsu Sen'ichi (1894–1976), who edited the collection for Iwanami Publishing (first series), explains what he construes as the mood of the poem by saying that despite the absence of the marks of beauty (cherry blossoms and maple leaves) which are replaced by the thatched roofs of the fishermen's humble dwellings, the poet interestingly displays a taste for *mono no aware*.[9] Here, we are confronted with a series of concepts which would have puzzled, and maybe even amused, Teika, had he been given the opportunity to follow Hisamatsu's hermeneutics: mood, beauty, taste, and the idea of *mono no aware* (the pathos of things) seen as an aesthetic category. At the very least, Teika would have needed a crash course on the genealogy of *Stimmung*, Western debates on the notion of taste, the ideas of

Kantian judgment and Aristotelian catharsis, as well as Ōnishi Yoshinori's systematization of Japanese aesthetic categories (*biteki hanchū*).

Along similar lines, Kubota Utsubo (1877–1967) explains Teika's poem in terms of a paradox: despite the sadness elicited by the absence of the marks of seasonal beauty (cherry blossoms in spring and maple leaves in autumn) and the presence of a simple, poignant, moving architecture (the straw roofs of humble workers), the poet sings the "pleasure" or "joy" (*yorokobi*) of such a view. Kubota arrives at this conclusion by referring to the antithetical technique of contrast used by the poet: since cherry blossoms and maple leaves elicit a sense of joy on the part of the observer, such a joy is suggested by referring to the markers of pleasure in absentia. Kubota calls such a suggestion *yojō* (overtones). He then proceeds with a further explanation of the poem in terms of the vocabulary of Japanese aesthetics. The fact that the poet makes the silence of an autumn evening with a hamlet of fishermen in the background a reason for a greater rejoicing (*yorokobashii*) than the view of cherry blossoms and maple leaves points to a progression of aesthetic feelings: from *en* (charm) to *aware* (pathos), and from *aware* to *sabi* (elegant simplicity, desolation).[10] Teika might have understood Kubota Utsubo's comment were he given some instruction on the notion of "aesthetic pleasure," which he undoubtedly conceived differently.

In his commentary of Teika's poem, Kubota Jun (b. 1933) adds another aesthetic term. He argues that this poem "symbolizes the spirit of *wabi*-tea (*wabicha*) in the tea ceremony." Kubota adds *wabi* (quiet elegance) to *sabi*.[11] The major problem with this interpretation is that the ritual of tea ceremony postdates Teika's poem.

The notion of "overtones" is carried over in the commentary appended to the poem in the new Iwanami series of the Japanese classics, which has been recently published and in which we read that the term of "negation '*nakarikeri*' does not extinguish the image of the cherry blossoms and the maple leaves." They remain as an "afterimage of desolation" (*sabireta*) in the reader's mind. Again, the aesthetic notions of *yojō* and *sabi* are invoked in the interpretation of this poem, together with the suggestion that Teika's use of the negative, rather than dissolving the object of observation, produces a positive image, that is to say that being or presence (*u*) results from nonbeing or non-presence (*mu*).[12]

This last comment takes us to the complex philosophy of "nothingness" (*mu*) developed in the early twentieth century by Nishida Kitarō (1870–1945) and his followers of the Kyoto School. Most discussions on the nature of Buddhist *mu* are indebted to Nishida's thought and are grounded in the belief that the concern for "being" shown by ancient Greek philosophers found a counterpart in Japan in the Buddhist concern for "nonbeing" (*mu*), "emptiness," and "void."

To summarize the hermeneutical strategies followed in the past and in the present to explain Teika's verse, we can say that in the past, a rhetoric was discovered in the poem that reminded readers of the paradoxical logic of a developing Buddhist school which was struggling for recognition at a time when the literati in the capital were not particularly impressed with the antics of Zen masters. In the present, the vocabulary of aesthetics is consistently used to talk about the poem in terms of aesthetic categories while, at the same time, grounding local aesthetic categories in the

Buddhist logic of negation—a logic that came to structure the philosophy of "nothingness" proposed in Japan in the twentieth century.

3. THE BUDDHIST NOTIONS OF NOTHINGNESS AND IMPERMANENCE ADOPTED AS MODERN AESTHETIC TERMS

When we look at the responses of twentieth-century interpreters to Teika's poem we realize that the construction of Teika's poetic discourse was molded by the interpreters' aesthetic and philosophical concerns. First of all, we must remember that the introduction to Japan of the field of aesthetics was contemporaneous with the introduction of Japan to the West as an aesthetic product. Whereas Japan had to struggle to obtain recognition from the West as an economic and industrial power, it easily capitalized on its exoticism and foreignness thanks to the avid demand in European markets for cultural products that could be vaguely associated with the current of "Japanese taste" (*Japonisme*). By responding to the Western desire for the "mysteries" of a recently "discovered" land, Japan aggressively moved to present itself as a repository of Asian culture and beauty, and to satisfy the demands of its Western customers. Within a few years of the opening of the country to Western nations, Japan was able to set itself up as "a museum of Asiatic civilization," to use a well-known motto from Okakura Tenshin's *The Ideals of the East*.[13] In Japan survived the vestiges of an Indian and Chinese past that had vanished from its countries of origin. Not only had Japan assured the world with the preservation of Buddhism and the Confucian world of rituals, it had also improved upon them by adding the aesthetic dimension, the urge for beauty that Okakura saw exemplified in the tradition of Japanese painting (*Nihonga*), which he helped to construct.[14]

As a result, today it is difficult to approach Teika's poem without inscribing it in an aesthetic discourse that brings into relationship one of the basic tenets of Buddhism, "impermanence" (*mujō*), with the notions of "art" (*geijutsu*) and artistic "beauty" (*bi*). The vocabulary of aesthetics and the configurations of knowledge that this vocabulary has created have become so intrinsically tied to modern subjectivity that it is very difficult to look at the past without making it speak the language of aesthetics. We can see this, for example, in the argument, widespread among scholars, that in classical times (the Nara and Heian periods), the relationship between a person and his changing natural surroundings was essentially an aesthetic relationship, in the etymological sense of *aisthesis* or a "feeling for" external reality. For example, Karaki Junzō (1904–80), a major scholar of Japanese literature and intellectual history, begins his book on "Impermanence" (*Mujō*) by locating the genealogy of the concept in an alleged "feeling for impermanence" (*mujō-kan*, where *kan* is indicated by a character meaning "to feel") which characterized the response of the inhabitants of the Heian court, especially female subjects, to the dreadfulness that the anxiety of change (changing relationships, changing political and familial circumstances, and so on) brought to their lives. According to Karaki, the encounter of these subjects with the "nothingness" of existence (death and change) began as a simple perception, a feeling that was not theorized until the thirteenth century when Dōgen (1200–53) transformed the "feeling for impermanence" into a philosophy, a "view on impermanence" (*mujō-kan*, where *kan* is indicated with a character meaning "to see," "to contemplate," "a view," and we could also add "a worldview").[15]

The argument for an emotional response to impermanence that reduces the perception of change to an exclamation of awe (*eitanteki*) on the part of the people of the Heian period is also made by Kobayashi Tomoaki (b. 1911) in his book *Mujōkan no bungaku* (*The literature of the feeling of impermanence*).[16] Kobayashi argues that since literature is a vehicle for the expression of what one feels while confronting change, the notion of impermanence came to be tied to the aesthetic components of the literary work, mainly the notion of "beauty." This point was echoed by Karaki Junzō who later added to his explanation of the genealogy of "impermanence" the extended sense of aesthetics as "a discourse on beauty" by arguing that "the feeling for impermanence" was actually a "feeling for the beauty of impermanence" (*mujōbi-kan*). The arts which expressed the author's feelings toward change actually mediated the passage from the notion of "impermanence" to the idea of "beauty" conveyed by the arts.

Literary historians of Japan transformed the aesthetic categories related to change, impermanence, and "nothingness" into a literary genre that in the twentieth century came to be known as "the literature of recluse" (*inja no bungaku*). This genre wrought together the separate threads of "detachment" (*ridatsu*), "vision" (*me*), "nature" (*shizen*), "existential sadness" (*sonzai no kanashimi*), and the "arts of the recluse" (*injakei geijutsu*) into a single pattern that synthesized 600 years of literary history.[17] Scholars such as the influential Ishida Yoshisada (1890–1987) grouped together in this category writers and poets whose literature stressed the paradoxical desire to abandon worldly desires and to become recluses. Their love for nature and power of observation led to the formulation of a literary discourse praising the values of detachment from worldly ties, and displacing the threat of change and impermanence into the consoling stability of the literary product. Historical details were bracketed and reduced to a common love for a reclusive lifestyle, half monk-half layman (*inton*), that distinguished such vastly different and contextually mutually contradictory literary figures as Saigyō (1118–90), Kama no Chōmei (1153–1216), Yoshida Kenkō (ca. 1280–1352), masters of linked verse poetry (*renga*) such as Kyūsei (1283?–1376?), Shinkei (1403–75), and Sōgi (1421–1502), and the master of *haikai* Bashō (1644–94). A false impression was created that in premodern Japan an "aesthetic and a tradition of reclusion" existed from the twelfth to the seventeenth century, together with a literature that sang the beauty of the negative—an impression which is heavily at work in the commentaries on the poem by Teika mentioned above. As a matter of fact, the term "*inja bungaku*" and the discourse surrounding it were created in 1927 by the folklorist Orikuchi Shinobu (1887–1953) in an article titled "From the Literature of Court Ladies to the Literature of Reclusion" (*Nyōbo bungaku kara inja bungaku e*).[18] The heading "literature of reclusion" did not appear in any history of Japanese literature prior to the publication of Orikuchi's article, although since then, no history of Japanese literature has failed to include a lengthy chapter on it.

4. A PHILOSOPHICAL INTERPRETATION OF IMPERMANENCE (*MUJŌ*): KOBAYASHI HIDEO

While literary historians have approached the issue of impermanence from the perspective of folklore and literary genres, literary critics and philosophers have given more genuinely philosophical interpretations to the concept. The literary critic Kobayashi Hideo (1902–83), for example, attempted an existential reading of the relationship between impermanence and art in an essay titled "*Mujō to iu koto*" (On Impermanence).[19] Kobayashi interprets the Japanese concern for impermanence as the result of a search for permanence in a life characterized by change and contingency. This search aims at rising above the unsettledness of *mujō* in an effort to withstand it. According to Kobayashi, the ideal of permanence—the impossible victory over death—can only be found amid impermanence itself. Art would correspond to such permanence: an art that takes form by making into an image the emptiness found in the storage of emotions. Art manifests itself from a place of formlessness and blooms amid mortal history like the flower (*hana*) which the medieval playwright Zeami (1364?–1443) took to represent the mastery of technique on the part of a Nō actor.[20] By blooming in the world of impermanence (*mujō*), the beauty and reality of a flower possess a permanence and unchangeable form; and yet, such a form cannot be separated from its origin, from impermanence. For Kobayashi, eternity presents itself in the human world in the "flower," the most weak and fragile thing in the whole world. Reality takes on a special strength by manifesting itself in what is most frangible—a truth teaching the following lesson: that *mujō* is the form taken by eternity to show itself to us. The eternity, which we can neither see with our eyes nor touch, appears in the form of *mujō*. Man's finiteness and sorrow lie in the fact that eternity takes the form of *mujō* in this world. This explains why *mujō* was linked to beauty. Unable to make itself discernable directly, eternity shows itself to mankind in the form of beauty within *mujō*. Art provides emptiness with an image, a form.

5. EMPTINESS (*ŚŪNYATĀ*) ACCORDING TO NISHITANI KEIJI

The field of aesthetics mediates the articulation of the notions of "finiteness" and "eternity" in discussions on this subject by members of the Kyoto School of philosophy. Concerned with the issue of Western nihilism and the question of how to overcome it, Nishitani Keiji (1900–90), a leading member of the school, developed an entire metaphysics of *aisthesis* beginning from the Chinese character indicating the sky (Japanese *sora* 空). The same character was used in the past to denote emptiness (Japanese *kū* 空). The poets' use of this character made the sky a popular metaphor to indicate the notion of emptiness. A famous example comes from the poetry of Saigyō, who was canonized among the leading voices of the literature of recluse:

Yami harete
Kokoro no sora ni
Sumu tsuki wa
Nishi no yamabe ya
Chikaku naruran

The mind is a sky
Emptied of all darkness,
And its moon,
Limpid and perfect, moves
Closer to mountains in the west.[21]

In an essay titled "*Kū to soku*" (Emptiness and identity) Nishitani calls the view of a blue sky—the infinite visible to the naked eye—a "metaphysical feeling" (*keijijōteki kankaku*).[22] Nishitani posits a direct linkage between the visible sky (*sora*) and the invisible " 'doctrine' of emptiness" (*kū no oshie*). He stresses the fact that the image (*Build, keishō*) of the sky is more than a simple metaphor pointing at emptiness. The degree of closeness between the concrete sky and the invisible concept is greater than is required by metaphor. In fact, the visible sky, which we call an "image," has no form (*katachi naki mono*) and therefore, in a strict sense, cannot be called an image. Nishitani can, then, argue that the concrete, visible phenomenon (the sky) is actually formless. At this point, the relationship between visible and invisible becomes less clear. According to Nishitani, the sky that we see with our eyes is actually the infinite, unlimited world that cannot be seen with the eye. The sky is emptiness (*kū*).[23]

Descending to earth, the sky permeates the world and sustains the invisible atmosphere surrounding man. It also opens up at the bottom of the heart of man who responds emotionally to this atmosphere. This opening is what Nishitani calls "the formless place at the bottom of the heart that comes into appearance by taking different forms." Such a place cannot be seen by the naked eye; rather it is seen by the eye of the heart. The sky that opens at the bottom of the heart comes into view within knowledge (*shiru*), within the working of a heart which is made, first of all, of feelings (*kankaku*), intellect (*chisei*), and will (*ishi*). Knowledge is a transparent, formless space in the heart, the most profound essence of the heart. Accordingly, "to know" could be called "the sky within the heart." By feeling, we become one with objects and we directly live/experience the objects. Feelings, however, are also endowed with knowledge. Moreover, the most original form of knowledge is the senses/feelings (*kankaku*). The "sky" is the space prior to our living together with objects in feelings. A knowledge within feelings (or the knowledge possessed by feelings) develops. When the objects are transparent to us and are made into images, the transparent sky at the bottom of our heart appears. Several images and forms develop from our heart through the mediation of the power of conceptualization or imagination (*kōsōryoku*). Then, white clouds start trailing through the sky. Once images develop from the bottom of a formless heart, thanks to the imagination, art (*geijutsu*) is born. Religion, however, makes transparent the images that have developed in the process, and enables man to see the formless blue sky.

Emptiness is not a place external to *mujō* that overcomes *mujō*; it is the opening of a path that overcomes *mujō* from *mujō* itself. To transcend *mujō* means to leave *mujō*. But the problem is: how can we find a place outside *mujō* from which to transcend it? The main characteristic of the thought of emptiness is that emptiness is not a different world from *mujō* but is *mujō* itself. *Kū* is permanence amid impermanence; it is the place of the transformations of *mujō*. *Kū* is not the other bank of the river of impermanence; it is the overcoming/transcendence of impermanence on the same bank of the same river. The transformations occurring in emptiness are not products of mediations; they are "equalities/identity" (*soku*) as when we say "death-qua-life" (*shi-soku-sei*), or "cravings-qua-enlightenment" (*bonno-soku-bodai*), or "impermanence-qua-Buddha nature" (*mujō-soku-busshō*).

Nishitani Keiji developed similar arguments in his works *Shūkyō to wa nani ka* (*What Is Religion?* also translated as *Religion and Nothingness*) and *Zen no tachiba* (*The Standpoint of Zen*). Here, he argued that *kū* and *mu* are not objects that can be looked at. They actually disappear if we take such an objectifying attitude. Therefore, *kū* has no form that can be pointed out to others. It is the absolute bank from the midst of *mujō*, and it opens as a transcendence of this world. This transcendence, however, does not have the religious meaning of transcendence. It is not a permanence against an impermanence, an immortality or spirit against death as in Western metaphysics and other religious systems that posit a God at the end. *Kū* does not partake of a structure in which a lower being destined to die and disappear is placed in relation to a higher Being that is permanent, eternal, and unchangeable. Absolute emptiness (*zettai kū*) is "things as they are" (*ari no mama*). Things are not metaphors of the absolute; they are an absolutization of themselves.

Nishitani calls the Buddhist "metaphors" of Zen "ultimate nature bereft of a specific character" (*enjō jisshō*; Sanskrit *parinishpanna-svabhāva*).[24] These "metaphors" make absolute the relativity of what is permanent and what is eternal. The transcendence that is found in *kū* is essential in order to solve the anxiety of nihilism and meaninglessness, since there is no way we can overcome both by taking a path outside such anxiety. The anxiety of nihilism and meaninglessness has already penetrated the presences of permanence (God, man), which were entrusted with the task of overcoming impermanence in the first place. We find a confirmation of this truth in the inability of technologies related to the natural sciences to cope with such anxieties. Contemporary nihilism has reached and engulfed notions of permanence such as God and progress. According to Nishitani, *kū* (emptiness) is an indicator of the way to transcend nihilism from inside nihilism itself. Here lies the possibility of a philosophy of emptiness for the modern age.

CONCLUSION

Nishitani reminds us that a powerful event has taken place in the creation of the Japanese traditions of "emptiness" and "nothingness." Rather than looking at Teika's poem mentioned at the beginning of the chapter as a source of the "literature of recluse," an "aesthetic of impermanence," and "a philosophy of negation," we might want to see it as the result of a modern process of interpretation which has called Teika into a dialogue with existentialism, phenomenology, and other philosophical currents. Then can we actually understand the enormous role played by Western thought in the creation of the so-called Japanese traditions—preeminently ideas related to nihilism, which sparked in Japan discourses on the need to overcome it, particularly after the ultimate destruction of the Second World War. In 1949, Nishitani wrote a popular book on the subject, *Nihirizumu* (*Nihilism*), which stands as a monument to the fact that "Japanese traditions" would not exist without the impact that modernity (the West) has had on Japan since the latter half of the nineteenth century. Japan's encounter with the Other (the West) prompted Japanese thinkers to ponder over the notion of the self—a process that led to the creation of a series of traditions. The so-called tradition of emptiness is less a continuation of an alleged discourse on issues related to Buddhist thought than a response to a suffocating reality that the philosophy of nihilism had portrayed so powerfully. Nishitani's hermeneutic response to existential nihilism highlights the dialogical nature of Japanese traditions, which came into being out of a concern for the future rather than for the past, as we can see from Nishitani's discussion of the meaning of nihilism for Japan:

> Creative nihilism in Stirner, Nietzsche, Heidegger and others was an attempt to overcome the nihilism of despair. These attempts, conducted at varying depths, were efforts (in Nietzsche's words) "to overcome nihilism by means of nihilism." The tradition of oriental culture in general, and the Buddhist standpoints of "emptiness," "nothingness," and so on in particular, become a new problem when set in this context. Herein lies our orientation toward the future—Westernization —and at the same time our orientation toward the past— reconnection with the tradition. The point is to recover the creativity that mediates the past to the future and the future to the past (but not to restore a bygone era). The third significance of European nihilism for us is that it makes these things possible.[25]

Although in the quotation above, Nishitani still maintained a strong notion of "tradition," in this chapter I have tried to dilute the weighty presence of tradition by showing it is a modern construct in a process of continuous making.

NOTES

This essay originally appeared in *Asian Aesthetics*, edited by Ken'ichi Sasaki (National University of Singapore Press and Kyoto University Press, 2010), 41–55. Section headings are newly added; further reading was also supplied by the volume editor.

1. Hisamatsu Sen'ichi, Yamazaki Toshio, and Gotō Shigeo, eds, *Shinkokin waka-shū*, Nihon Koten Bungaku Taikei 28 (Tokyo: Iwanami Shoten, 1958), 101, poem 363. The English translation is by Steven D. Carter, *Traditional Japanese Poetry: An Anthology* (Stanford: Stanford University Press, 1991), 197.
2. Jin'ichi Konishi, *A History of Japanese Literature*, vol. 3 (Princeton: Princeton University Press, 1991), 189.
3. Ibid., 186.

4. Hilda Katō, trans., "*The Mumyōshō* of Kama no Chōmei and Its Significance in Japanese Literature," *Monumenta Nipponica* 23.3–4 (1968): 408, with a slight change in the translation; emphasis added. The original text appears in Yanase Kazuo, *Mumyōshō Zenkō* (Tokyo: Katō Chūdōkan, 1980), 387–390.
5. *Mushin shojaku* 無心所着 refers to poems that make no sense, because the words do not cohere or hang together to form an imagery.
6. The English translation is by Steven D. Carter, *Traditional Japanese Poetry*, 77. This poem by Ariwara no Narihira (825–880) is included in the first imperial anthology, *Kokinshū* 1.53.
7. The English translation is by Steven D. Carter, *Traditional Japanese Poetry*, 214. The poem is by Fujiwara no Tadahira (880–949).
8. See William R. LaFleur, "Symbol and *Yugen*: Shunzei's Use of Tendai Buddhism," in *The Karma of Words: Buddhism and the Literary Arts in Medieval Japan* (Berkeley: University of California Press, 1983), 80–106.
9. Hisamatsu Sen'ichi, Yamazaki Toshio, and Gotō Shigeo, eds, *Shinkokin waka-shū*, 101.
10. Kubota Utsubo, *Kanpon Shin kokin waka-shū hyōshaku*, "*Jo*" (Tokyo: Tōkyōdō, 1964), 323–324.
11. Kubota Jun, ed., *Shinkokin waka-shū*, Jo, Shinchō Nihon Koten Shūsei 24 (Tokyo: Shinchōsha, 1979), 133.
12. Tanaka Yutaka and Akase Shingo, eds, *Shinkokin waka-shū*, Shin Nihon Koten Bungaku Taikei 11 (Tokyo: Iwanami Shoten, 1992), 117.
13. Kakuzō Okakura, *The Ideals of the East with Special Reference to the Arts of Japan* (London: John Murray, 1903), 5. See also Karatani Kōjin, "Japan as Art Museum: Okakura Tenshin and Fenollosa," in *A History of Modern Japanese Aesthetics*, ed. and trans. Michael F. Marra (Honolulu: University of Hawaii Press, 2001), 43–52.
14. See Satō Dōshin, *Nihon bijutsu tanjō: kindai nihon no "kotoba" to senryaku* (Tokyo: Kōdansha, 1996).
15. Karaki Junzō, *Mujō* (Tokyo: Chikuma Shobō, 1965), 5–10.
16. Kobayashi Tomoaki, *Mujōkan no bungaku* (Tokyo: Kōbundō, 1965).
17. All these topics are the actual headings in the first chapter of Ishida Yoshisada, *Inja no bungaku: kumon suru bi* (Tokyo: Hanawa Shobō, 1969).
18. The essay is included in Orikuchi's *Kodai kenkyū* [A study of antiquity]. See *Orikuchi Shinobu Zenshū*, vol. 1 (Tokyo: Chūō Kōronsha, 1975), 265–320.
19. Kobayashi Hideo, "*Mujō to iu koto*" (Tokyo: Kadokawa Shoten, 1954), 55–113.
20. "Thus an actor who has mastered every aspect of his art can be said to hold within him the seeds of flowers that bloom in all seasons, from the plum blossoms of early spring to the chrysanthemums of the fall. As he possesses all the Flowers, he can perform in response to any expectations on any occasion." From Zeami's "Fūshikaden" [Teachings on style and the flower], in *On the Art of the Nō Drama: The Major Treatises of Zeami*, trans. J. Thomas Rimer and Yamazaki Masakazu (Princeton: Princeton University Press, 1984), 53.

21. William R. LaFleur, trans., *Mirror for the Moon: A Selection of Poems by Saigyō (1118–1190)* (New York: New Directions, 1978), 45.
22. See Nishitani Keiji, *NKC*, vol. 13 (Tokyo: Sōbunsha, 1987), 111–160. For an English translation, see Michele Marra, *Modern Japanese Aesthetics: A Reader* (Honolulu: University of Hawaii Press, 1999), 179–217.
23. Here I follow a reading of Nishitani's essay by a contemporary member of the Kyoto School, Hase Shōtō, "*Kū to mujō*," in *Nihon bungaku to bukkyō*, vol. 4 (Tokyo: Iwanami Shoten, 1994), 299–333.
24. *Enjō jisshō* 円成実性 is the third of the "three nature theory," which describes the progressive stages of awareness from delusion to clarity, developed by the Yogācāra school of Indian Buddhism.
25. Nishitani Keiji, *The Self-Overcoming of Nihilism*, trans. Graham Parkes with Setsuko Aihara (Albany: SUNY, 1990), 179.

BIBLIOGRAPHY

Carter, Steven D. *Traditional Japanese Poetry: An Anthology*. Stanford: Stanford University Press, 1991.

Hase Shōtō. "*Kū to mujō*" [Emptiness and impermanence]. In *Nihon bungaku to bukkyō*, vol. 4, 299–333. Tokyo: Iwanami Shoten, 1994.

Hisamatsu Sen'ichi, Yamazaki Toshio, and Gotō Shigeo, eds. *Shinkokin waka-shū*, Nihon Koten Bungaku Taikei 28. Tokyo: Iwanami Shoten, 1958.

Ishida Yoshisada. *Inja no bungaku: kumon suru bi* [Writings of hermits: The "agonizing" beauty]. Tokyo: Hanawa Shobō, 1969.

Karaki Junzō. *Mujō* [Impermanence]. Tokyo: Chikuma Shobō, 1965.

Karatani Kōjin. "Japan as Art Museum: Okakura Tenshin and Fenollosa." In *A History of Modern Japanese Aesthetics*, trans. and ed. Michael F. Marra, 43–52. Honolulu: University of Hawaii Press, 2001.

Katō, Hilda, trans. "*The Mumyōshō* of Kama no Chōmei and Its Significance in Japanese Literature." *Monumenta Nipponica* 23.3–4 (1968), 321–349.

Kobayashi Hideo. *Mujō to iu koto* [What is called impermanence]. Tokyo: Kadokawa Shoten, 1974.

Kobayashi Tomoaki. *Mujōkan no bungaku* [Literature imbued with the sensibility of impermanence]. Tokyo: Kōbundoō, 1965.

Konishi, Jin'ichi. *A History of Japanese Literature*, 3 vols. Princeton: Princeton University Press, 1991.

Kubota Jun, ed. *Shinkokin waka-shū*, Shinchō Nihon Koten Shūsei 24. Tokyo: Shinchōsha, 1979.

Kubota Utsubo. *Kanpon Shinkokin waka-shu hyōshaku* [Unabridged commentary on the *Shinkokin Poetry Collection*]. Tokyo: Tōkyōdō, 1964.

LaFleur, William R., trans. *Mirror for the Moon: A Selection of Poems by Saigyō (1118–1190)*. New York: New Directions, 1978.

LaFleur, William R. *The Karma of Words: Buddhism and the Literary Arts in Medieval Japan*. Berkeley: University of California Press, 1983.

Marra, Michele. *Modern Japanese Aesthetics: A Reader.* Honolulu: University of Hawaii Press, 1999.

Nishitani Keiji. "*Kū to soku*" [Emptiness and identity]. *NKC*, vol. 13, 111–160. Tokyo: Sōbunsha, 1987; trans. into English, Michele Marra, *Modern Japanese Aesthetics: A Reader*, 179–217. Honolulu: University of Hawaii Press, 1999.

Nishitani Keiji. *The Self-Overcoming of Nihilism*, trans. Graham Parkes with SetsukoAihara. Albany: SUNY, 1990.

Okakura, Kakuzō. *The Ideals of the East with Special Reference to the Arts of Japan.* London: John Murray, 1903.

Orikuchi Shinobu. "*Kodai kenkyū*" [A study of antiquity]. *Orikuchi Shinobu Zenshū*, vol. 1, 265–320. Tokyo: Chūō Kōronsha, 1975.

Satō Dōshin. *Nihon bijutsu tanjō: kindai Nihon no "kotoba" to senryaku* [The birth of Japanese fine arts: "Words" and strategies adopted by modern Japan]. Tokyo: Kodansha, 1996.

Tanaka Yutaka, and Akase Shingo, eds. *Shinkokin waka-shū*, Shin Nihon Koten Bungaku Taikei 11. Tokyo: Iwanami Shoten, 1992.

Yanase Kazuo. *Mumyōshō zenkō* [Lectures on the *Mumyōshō* of Kamo no Chōmei]. Tokyo: Katō Chūdōkan, 1980.

Zeami Motokiyo. "Fūshikaden" [Teachings on style and the flower]. In *On the Art of the Nō Drama: The Major Treatises of Zeami*, trans. J. Thomas Rimer and Yamazaki Masakazu, 3–63. Princeton: Princeton University Press, 1984.

FURTHER READING

Marra, Michele (Michael) F., ed. *Modern Japanese Aesthetics: A Reader* (Honolulu: University of Hawaii Press, 1999). This volume contains the English translation of Japanese writings by prominent philosophers and authors: Nishi Amane, Tsubouchi Shōyō, Okakura Kakuzō, Ōnishi Hajime, Takayama Chogyū, Ōnishi Yoshinori, Kusanagi Masao, Nishitani Keiji, Imamichi Tomonobu, Sakabe Megumi, and Karatani Kōjin.

Marra, Michele (Michael) F., ed. *A History of Modern Japanese Aesthetics* (Honolulu: University of Hawaii Press, 2001). This volume contains the English translation of essays by the leading Japanese scholars and authors of aesthetics: Karatani Kōjin, Kaneda Tamio, Bruno Lewin, Watanabe Kazuyasu, Yamamoto Masao, Kambayashi Tsunemichi, Imamichi Tomonobu, Yamamoto Masao, Sasaki Ken'ichi, Koyasu Nobukuni, Hijikata Teichi, Hirata Toshihiro, Yoshioka Kenjirō, Iwaki Ken'ichi, and Tanaka Kyūbun.

Marra, Michele (Michael) F., ed. *Japanese Hermeneutics: Current Debates on Aesthetics and Interpretation* (Honolulu: University of Hawaii Press, 2001). This volume contains philosophical essays on hermeneutics by Gianni Vattimo, Sasaki Ken'ichi, Ōhashi Ryōsuke, Amagasaki Akira, Graham Parkes, Mark Meli, John Maraldo, Hamashita Masahiro, J. Thomas rimer, Kambayashi Tsunemichi, Inaga Shigemi, Stefan Tanaka, Otaba Tanehisa, Haruo Shirane, Suzuki Sadami, Thomas LaMarre, and Haga Tōru.

CHAPTER SEVEN

Bodily Present Activity in History: An Artistic Streak in Nishida Kitarō's Thought

ENRICO FONGARO

INTRODUCTION: THE CENTRAL RELEVANCE OF ART IN NISHIDA'S THOUGHT

At a first glance, Nishida Kitarō (1870–1945) may appear to have written relatively little on art, but this impression gives away as soon as one approaches his works by paying close attention to his references to art, artists, and artistic creativity. In fact, it may be asserted that the artistic insight formed an integral part of his philosophical reflection, even from the very beginning. This aspect of Nishida's thought has received some attention thus far.[1] The fact is that already in his first book *An Inquiry into the Good* (1911),[2] there are ample references to art and artists—primarily to illustrate the points he is making. In his later works, however, artistic activities became more an integral part of his philosophical worldview, and sometimes help Nishida to explain the paradigm of how we live in and give shape to this "historic world," and how the ongoing process of the self-formation of this historic world takes place.

To find "the land of knowledge through the morning door of beauty"—to paraphrase the poet Friedrich Schiller, whose line was fondly quoted by a German philosopher-sociologist Georg Simmel[3]—may not have been so unique to philosophers East and West. A scholar of aesthetics Iwaki Ken'ichi observes that for Nishida artistic activities provided "an evidence" or "a proof" (*reishō*) of his philosophical thinking, and that "Nishida's philosophy of art is intertwined with his entire philosophical project."[4] One could go a step further here to suggest that for Nishida art presented a concrete paradigm of "expressions" "life" (*seimei*) can take, and that Nishida the philosopher and Nishida the artist mutually deepened their insight into the reality of creativity. In short, artistic elements appear to have played an essential role in the development of Nishida's philosophy proper.

What makes Nishida unique in this respect is that he himself engaged in poetry composition and calligraphy. He turned to the composition of "*waka*" poems (or *tanka*, the thirty-one-syllable traditional Japanese poetic form), when he encountered the excruciating circumstance of his eldest son dying of illness at a young age of twenty-two in 1920 (Nishida was then fifty years old). His interest in calligraphy (*kigō* 揮毫), however, got kindled following his mandatory retirement from his teaching position at the Imperial University of Kyoto in 1928, which afforded him the luxury of time.[5] His broad interest in art went hand in hand with his philosophical style, which was open to the vital realm beyond a narrowly circumscribed realm of "*logos*."

Endearing to the nonspecialist of philosophy, Nishida's artworks offer enjoyment to everyone, as they easily transcend the confines of the "ivory tower philosophy." His "*waka*" poems, for instance, are often done in his own calligraphy and inscribed on monuments. For instance, a well-known poem,

The others are the others	人は人
I am I	吾は吾なり
Be that as it may,	とにかくに
I go the way	吾ゆく道を
I go.	吾はゆくなり[6]

is inscribed on a stone monument, which is placed along the path Nishida used to take while absorbed in his philosophical ideas—the path known as "the philosopher's path"[7] or "*tetsugaku no michi*," which connects the Buddhist temples of Nanzenji and Ginkakuji (the Silver Pavilion) in the northeastern section of Kyoto. Aside from his *waka* poems, his key philosophical concepts, rendered into pithy phrases, are sometimes made into calligraphy. One such example is: "Thinking by becoming a thing, acting by becoming a thing" (*mono to natte kangae, mono to natte okonau*).[8]

It is not because his philosophy is a "philosophy of art," but because philosophical thought and artistic activities originate from the same deep source of life-experience for Nishida, to focus on the elements of art enables one to sketch out the fundamental features of his thought more concretely in its various phases of development. His essays contained in the *Art and Morality* (1923)[9] as well as his later essays such as the "*Artistic Creation as an Activity of History Formation*" (1941) will be introduced into the present discussion.

1. "ABOVE THE SADDLE NO RIDER, UNDER THE SADDLE NO HORSE"

Before going into Nishida's thought proper, a brief mention will be made of the aesthete-philosopher-religionist scholar Hisamatsu Shin'ichi 久松真一 (1889–1980), who started out his career as a student of Nishida at the Imperial University of Kyoto. Hisamatsu became interested in Zen under Nishida's influence, and began the *zazen* practice under Master Ikegami Shōsan (1856–1928) at the Myōshinji Temple in Kyōto. His breakthrough experience (*kenshō* 見性) followed in the early days of the beginning of his practice. He remained a lay Zen adept (*koji* 居士) instead of going into the monastic way of life and in 1944 established a small group for the university students who were interested in Zen meditation. In 1958 he gave this group the name of "FAS Association," "FAS" standing for the first letter of the three guiding tenets of this group:

Formless self,
All humankind,
Superhistorical history.

For the members of the FAS, Zen practice and intellectual scholarly engagements were mutually integral. Hisamatsu was also an expert in the art of tea (*cha no yu*), and a gifted calligrapher and scholar of Zen art and aesthetics. His scholarly works on Zen painting and tea ceremony[10] are just the tip of the iceberg of his extensive scholarly writings on Zen and arts.

Hisamatsu writes in his short essay entitled "*Koshō*" (己象) or "The Self-Image" (1962)[11] that calligraphy as a form of art is ultimately none other than the "self-image" of the artist. In order to explain this point, he refers to the traditional tip for how to master the art of horseback riding: "In perfect horseback riding, there is no rider on the saddle nor a horse under the saddle" (*anjō hito naku, anka uma nashi*). That is to say, as long as the rider is conscious of being on the saddle and the horse under it, the rider and the horse are two separate entities and the rider cannot command the horse. The more the rider and the horse become "one body," the more perfect the riding will be.[12] Thus, "only when there is no rider up on the saddle and no horse down the saddle, and the rider and the horse are 'one body, not two' (*ittai funi*), does the rider acquire the genuine skill of horseback riding."[13] The main objective here is to overcome the "dualism" of subjective and objective consciousness of the rider and the horse, in order to attain perfect reality of riding. Hisamatsu notes that the same goes with any other forms of art, such as the traditional Japanese archery, and then he turns to the art of calligraphy to explain it further.

In the art of calligraphy, it is only when the calligrapher, the brush, and the paper form one unbroken unity that the art reaches its ultimate height. The paper is not just a dead "passive" material, but forms a living space which transforms itself into a calligraphy together with the brush, and the calligrapher is not just a technician but is one with the brush, engaging his or her entire soul and imbuing the *paper* with *life*, and expresses himself or herself thereby. A calligraphic work produced in this manner is none other than "the form of oneself," or the "image of oneself" (*koshō* 己象), and reveals itself as a "shape of life" (*seimei no katachi* 生命の形).[14]

Nishida's calligraphy works, too, are open to the enjoyment of the viewer as that which captured the whole engagement of the artist, the instrument, and the material, and in its dynamic activity life is given a certain expression of form or shape. Moreover, Hisamatsu's explanation of calligraphy and horseback riding nicely illustrates Nishida's philosophical notion of the unity of subject and objet (*shukyaku gōitsu* 主客合一), which Nishida eventually develops into the key concept of "action-intuition" (or *kōiteki chokkan* 行為的直観).

2. CASTIGLIONE: THE GRACE OF THE COURTIER

What Hisamatsu writes about the unity of practical art contains an insight similar to what an Italian courtier-ambassador Count Baldassare Castiglione (1478–1529) wrote in his *Il Cortegiano*, or *The Book of the Courtier*.[15] It concerns the aesthetic quality of "*sprezzatura*," which is an air of perfect naturalness or spontaneity acquired through discipline. According to Castiglione, this unaffected naturalness should be the property of any physical movement that flows with grace and elegance. He writes:

> I have discovered a universal rule which seems to apply more than any other in all human actions or words: namely, to steer away from affectation at all costs, as if it were a rough and dangerous reef, and (to use perhaps a novel word for it) to practice in all things a certain *sprezzatura* [nonchalance] which conceals all artistry and makes whatever one says or does seem uncontrived and effortless.[16]

Beauty and elegance arise from *sprezzatura* or"spontaneity"—that is, from a physical movement that is unaffected, even if this "naturalness" is the result of artistry acquired after assiduous training. This echoes Hisamatsu's notion of art as "the self-image of the artist." It also reminds one of the passage of *An Inquiry into the Good*, where Nishida mentions an episode quoted by Vasari of Giotto, who painted his famous "O," upon the papal request for a specimen of his work.[17] Nishida quoted this episode to emphasize the spontaneous simplicity of Giotto's unaffected response.[18] Had he known the notion of *sprezzatura*, so essential to Castiglione,[19] and possibly perfectly executed by Giotto, one wonders what else Nishida might have added to his remark of Giotto's action.[20]

Castiglione, who wrote two centuries before Charles Batteux[21] invented the system of fine arts, does not restrict himself to painting, singing, or dancing, and he is able to find *sprezzatura* even in fencing, and should have found no difficulty in ascribing *sprezzatura* to horseback riding as well—to refer back to Hisamatsu's example above—something which the courtier certainly should have been able to stand out in. In fact, this quality of *sprezzatura* may be seen as the basic aesthetic thread of the Japanese traditional "fencing"—be it *kendō* (剣道) or *iaidō* (居合道)—in which "natural bodily posture" (*shizentai* 自然体) is derived from the state in which "sword and mind are one" (*kenshin ittai* 剣心一体). Such unity of sword, body, mind, and technique is an essential precondition for the fulfillment of the "beautiful" movement and also for the "efficient" action.

What distinguishes Hisamatsu's notion from Castiglione's *sprezzatura* is that Castiglione's "graceful" movement is primarily an aesthetic category because its aim is solely to realize physical grace (or elegance), whereas in Hisamatsu, it emphasizes the immediate experience of "non-duality" of the artist and any instrument or material involved in the creation of work of art, and ultimately it presents the "image of the artist." In this sense a Zen work of art, or any other creative act for that matter, becomes an image of the self, which Ryōsuke Ōhashi calls the "*auto-bio-graphy*" or self-expression of life.[22] On this point, we are reminded of the passage in *An Inquiry into the Good*, where Nishida mentions the manifestation of the true personality (*jinkaku no hatsugen* 人格の発現) of an artist: "When does the true personality or originality of the painter appear? Insofar as the painter consciously intends various things, we cannot yet truly see the painter's personality. We first see it only when, after long years of struggle, the painter's skills mature and the brush follows the will."[23]

3. *AN INQUIRY INTO THE GOOD* AND ART

It is well known that in *An Inquiry into the Good*, Nishida explored the concept of *pure experience*. The intent of Nishida is to "explain all things on the basis of pure experience as the sole reality."[24] Different from William James (1842–1910), who developed the notion of "pure experience" as a multiple stream of consciousness, what Nishida calls "pure or immediate experience" is the unified experience of reality. Defining "pure experience," Nishida writes:

> The moment of seeing a color or hearing a sound, for example, is prior not only to the thought that the color or sound is the activity of an external object or that one is sensing it, but also to the judgment of what the color or sound might be. In this regard, pure experience is identical with direct experience. When one directly experiences one's own state of consciousness, there is not yet a subject or an object, and knowing and its object are completely unified.[25]

Starting from this position of pure experience, Nishida tries to elucidate the entire activity of consciousness (sensation, perception, thought, will, and intellectual intuition) on the basis of which he develops his ontology, ethics, and philosophy of religion.

Nishida's full-fledged discussion on the feeling (*kanjō* 感情) appears in his later work, *The Problem of Consciousness* (1920), but already in *An Inquiry into the Good*, the "aesthetic" references—understood in terms of unmediated self-expression—are evident and abundant throughout his inquiry. In order to give a concrete example of "pure experience," Nishida gives the examples of "a cliff-climber's determined ascent of a cliff and a musician's performance of a piece that has been mastered through practice."[26] In this fusion, "there is simply one world, one scene," and not the self and the object.[27] Nishida calls this "state of subject-object oneness and a fusion of knowing and willing" an "intellectual intuition." Examples of intellectual intuition thus understood are most clearly found, according to Nishida, "in the intuition of artists and people of religion. With respect to the process of intuiting, intellectual intuition is identical to ordinary perception, but with respect to content, intellectual intuition is far richer and more profound."[28] Nishida displays his penchant for treating art and religion in their close affinity—art and spiritual awareness constituting for him the two most marked experiences of reality.[29] Nishida in his later works, however, moves away from this view and distinguishes them, by taking religious dimension to be more fundamental and comprehensive than artistic expressions.[30]

4. "SESSHŪ PAINTED NATURE OR NATURE PAINTED ITSELF THROUGH SESSHŪ"

In *An Inquiry into the Good*, Nishida mentions along with such Italian Renaissance masters as Giotto, Michelangelo, and Raphael, a Japanese painter and Zen monk Sesshū (雪舟, 1420–1506). In the section on the "Good," where Nishida discusses the motivation of good conduct, he writes:

> We reach the quintessence of good conduct only when subject and object merge, self and things forget each other, and all that exists is the activity of the sole reality of the universe. At that point we can say that things move the self or that the self moves things, *that Sesshū painted nature or that nature painted itself through Sesshū*. There is no fundamental distinction between things and the self, for just as the objective world is a reflection of the self, so is the self a reflection of the objective world.[31]

This passage seems rife with meaning, because it not only summarizes the development of Nishida's approach to art thus far, but also suggests the future direction of his philosophical inquiry. I see here that in Sesshū, the transition took place from "nature" as the object of the artistic praxis to "naturalness" as the principle of praxis, in which the self and nature are inseparably fused.

Looking ahead a little: although it is not until around 1925 that Nishida formulates the important notion of "*place*" (*basho* 場所), his thinking is already given to the mode of *consciousness in its relation to the world*. In a certain sense, Nishida first having assumed the point of view of "Sesshū painting nature," later moves on to the perspective of "nature painting through Sesshū." Being facilitated by the notion of "place," Nishida's focus of inquiry shifts from the "self" (*jiko* 自己) and "self-consciousness" (*jikaku* 自覚) to the "world" (*sekai* 世界) and "environment" (*kankyō* 環境). But I shall return to the present discussion.

5. FROM PURE EXPERIENCE TO THE STRUCTURE OF SELF-CONSCIOUSNESS

In his philosophical contemplation that followed *An Inquiry into the Good*,[32] Nishida tries to overcome the ambiguities of his concept of pure experience, which came under the criticisms of his younger colleagues.[33] In order to refine his point of experience and cognition, his next step is to examine self-consciousness (*jikaku* 自覚), especially in its aspects of intuition and reflection. Calling it "a phase of philosophical apprenticeship," he read extensively the works of J. G. Fichte (1762–1814), Henri Bergson (1859–1941), Josiah Royce (1855–1916), Richard Dedekind (1831–1916), works by Neo-Kantian thinkers, Wilhelm Dilthey (1833–1911), as well as Edmund Husserl (1859–1938).

Nishida finds in Royce and Dedekind a description of consciousness in terms of the infinite reflexive creative movement. Dedekind defined an "infinite system" as: "A system S is said to be infinite when it is similar to a proper part of itself," whose salient example is "my own realm of thoughts."[34] Royce illustrates this "self-representative system of consciousness" with an example of a person drawing a perfect map of England while residing within England.[35] Nishida appropriates these ideas and develops his understanding of *self-consciousness* (*jikaku* 自覚). The motive for this choice of word, as opposed to more literary "*jiko ishiki*" 自己意識 for self-consciousness may be argued that Nishida wants to underline that it is not just that the subject objectifies itself into an object in the reflexive consciousness, but that the *self actively mirrors itself and sees itself*. The crucial point is for Nishida that all this happens "in the self," and in this way the self becomes really "infinite," in Dedekind's sense. Going back to the example of Royce, it is not enough that a person draws a map of England, but this person must carry out this activity "inside" England in order for the image of this process to be self-mirroring.

6. THE BODY-MIND UNITY IN THE ARTISTIC CREATION

It was in the aesthetic theory of Konrad Fielder (1841–95) that Nishida found the bridge that enabled the transition from the epistemological non-duality of subject-object to the experiential unity of the body and the mind.[36] Nishida's first mention of Fiedler and his *Der Ursprung der künstlerischen Tätigkeit* (*The Origin of the Artistic Activity*, 1887) is found in Section 19 (published June 1915) of his serialized work, *Intuition and Reflection in Self-Consciousness*, which was written over the period of five years, 1913–17,[37] and in it he focused on Fiedler who analyzed the sense of vision (*Sichtbarkeit*) and advanced a theory of visual art in which the act of seeing, which is normally thought to be passive, becomes active as converted into the expressive bodily movement of an artist. In this way, new visual materials are created and expand the horizon of the knowledge of the real.

Nishida concluded his detailed study of self-consciousness focusing on intuition and reflection only to emphasize the primacy of the self that is endowed with absolute free will (*zettai ishi* 絶対意志) and moves of its own accord. In the next phase of his philosophical investigation, he treats consciousness in relation to the senses, feeling, the mental act of symbolization, and the will (see *The Problem of Consciousness* or *Ishiki no mondai*, 1920). Here, we have a more upfront treatment of artistic activities as offering concrete evidences to support the formulation of his systematic understanding. We read, for instance, his treatment of the feeling (*kanjō* 感情): "Artistic activities in particular confer a clear content to our feelings. A Raphael deprived of his hands would most likely harbor nothing more than a vague feeling. Feeling that has no external outlet would probably be no different from a nebulous sensation of comfort and discomfort. Artists produce their works in order to articulate their feeling."[38] Nishida also notes that what is considered contradictory in cognition may have a positive content in the realm of feeling. In this sense, feeling is the "content of the will as the activity of activities"; it is "the content of imagination (fantasy)," if we postulate the function of imagination between the will and cognition.[39] He analyzes the vision thus: the color as a series or a continuum gets connected to the activities of the absolute will (i.e. an individual person), and each sensation of color is understood to contain the whole color, because each point of a series or a continuum implies the rest (or the whole). Thus, "In the 'forming activity' (*Gestaltungstätigkeit*) of pure vision, the whole experience of vision is contained. We think of the visual sensation to be accompanied by activities is because the vision transcends the world of cognitive objects, and enters into the world of symbols where 'the mind and the body are one.' "[40]

In his next work, *Art and Morality* (1923), Nishida discusses "feeling" (*kanjō* 感情), and attributes it the position of the fundamental condition for the establishment of consciousness (*ishiki seiritsu no konponteki jōken*). Feeling is more than just one aspect of mental phenomena (*seishin genshō* 精神現象).[41] Staying close to the ideas developed by Bergson and Fiedler, Nishida muses:

> The content of knowledge does not determine the quality of feeling; rather knowledge exists within feeling (*chishiki wa kanjō no naka ni aru*). The new synthesis of intellectual content means the birth of the new emotional content ... that which creates new intellectual content is not knowledge but feeling. In other words, it is the dynamic content of consciousness. As Bergson says, our consciousness is the center that glows within the clouds and mist . . . .
>
> Holding onto this concept of feeling, I maintain that pure feeling is nothing but pure consciousness; it is not the case that there is a specific artistic consciousness or feeling within feeling. I maintain that pure feeling, or pure consciousness, is always aesthetic ... When there is immediate synthesis of the activity of the color distinguishing itself within the person (the *absolute will*), that is, when we assume the standpoint of pure visual perception, colors all of a sudden gain life and become alive—that is, colors becomes the aesthetic objects. When our entire body becomes our eye and ear, feeling passes over into things, which bear aesthetic gestures of themselves in terms of the expressive movement.[42]

The content of feeling has its organic unity, and cannot be dissected into objectified bits, just as Bergson held in his notion of *élan vital* or a physical unitary "motion" (*mobilité*). Nishida traces the source of artistic creation to *élan vital* and writes:

> That which flows forth from the tip of Phideas' chisel and from the tip of Leonardo's brush is the "flow of life" that has flowed within their bodies from the past of the past. The surge of life that overflows within them can no longer remain within the environment centered around their bodies but creates a new world in their art.[43]

Nishida continues further:

> Bergson states that even though the human personality, when young, is extremely rich in potential, it must lose such abundance as it grows up. But the rich life of a genius, which instead of being discarded, finds its venue in artistic creation. It might be merely an illusion, but "the great breath of life" (*le grand souffle de la vie*) is in it. In such an instance, what units the artist and the artist's work is

> internal muscular perception (*naimenteki kinkaku* 内面的筋覚). Through this a single life force courses through.[44]

The point Nishida wants to make, together with Fiedler, is that "artistic creation is the expressive movement."[45] He also finds crucial Fiedler's observation that "where the eye stops the hand takes over the work of the eye, or the vision incites the body's extremities, and make it possible for what was formerly within to be expressed outwardly."[46] To quote Nishida on these crucial points:

> The visual act, which is part of the flow of the *élan vital*, demands infinite development as the basic act underlying all acts. Here the hand of the artist assists at those places where the eye is unable to function. Fiedler also states that *the hand, taking over after the work of the eye* is finished, causes further development. At this time, the hand becomes one with the eye; *the entire body becomes the eye, as it were*. The world of visual perception that has been perfected in this way is the objective world of art. Sculpture and painting are the reality that have been disclosed by the eyes and hands of the artist becoming one.
>
> Thus, when the sculptor is sculpting and when the painter is painting, each becomes a process of seeing. Plotinus states that nature does not create by seeing, but, rather, that nature's seeing is creation.[47] In this respect, the artist is nature itself. If we consider that the visual act itself is the flow of one great *élan vital*, then art is the overflow of the surge of that greater life that cannot flourish completely within the channels of the ordinary eye.[48]

What is at the heart of Nishida's discussion on Fiedler's aesthetics and Bergson's observation is the reality of the mind and the body working in unison, which is most clearly exemplified in the immediate, creative, non-dual, and bodily experience of artists. In Fiedler's thought Nishida finds the moment of oneself becoming totally fused with the act of seeing, and the entire body of the artist turning into an "eye." Nishida had in fact written on this point in his early essay:

> Sensory activities such as seeing and hearing are not mere passive activities, as normally taken to be. As Fiedler shows, total absorption in vision is an infinite development, leading to artistic creation, and the same may be said, I think, for all other sensations. Perception, thought, or any other activity developing itself from one a priori, is in itself infinite self-development, and the unity of all of them is our will or personality.[49]

Nishida has always maintained that if we are to clarify philosophically the reality of artistic creation, we must start out with the investigation into the relationship of body and mind (or the spirit) in any activity. The position of the unity of the body and mind is connected with the standpoint of "absolute will." When one totally embraces this standpoint, "there is no inside or outside of the mind. There is only the activity produced out of the oneness of mind and body." This reality stands beyond the category of cognition and cannot be explained objectively, but only can be understood by experiencing and moving with it. If we move our body by totally becoming one with the mind (and vice versa), we understand this realty. Here again, we are reminded of Hisamatsu's example of calligraphy or horseback riding. To go back to Nishida's text:

> Spiritual activities (*seishin sayō* 精神作用) do not stop as events within the mind but must seek expression in the body (*nikutai* 肉体). Expressive movements are not external signs of spiritual phenomena but are states of their development and completion. The spiritual act and the expressive movement are internally one act. Thus, our language is not a sign of thought but is an expressive movement of thought. Thought perfects itself through language. Our 'world of reality' is nothing more than the world that has been expressed through language. Our spiritual acts are infinite activities, and each possesses its own world of expression. As the act of pure visual perception develops into language, it naturally moves our body (*shintai* 身体) and develops into a kind of expressive movement. This is the creative act of the artist (*künstlerische Tätigkeit*).[50]
>
> . . .
>
> However, to clarify the true aspect of artistic creation in the above sense, we must proceed from a profound consideration of the relationship between spirit and body. In the standpoint of absolute will, there is no distinction between the interior and the exterior of the mind. There is only the activity of mind and body as one living reality (心身一如の活動 *shinshin ichinyo no katsudō*). The content of internal unity of acts—that is, of pure consciousness—which appears in this plane, transcends the categories of thinking and is not reducible to the realm of cognitive objects, for we can understand it only by acting in unison with it. In self-consciousness, acting is knowing.[51]

7. BEINGS IN THE ENVIRONMENT: LOCATEDNESS OF BEING

Nishida's attempt to move beyond the neo-Kantian orbit resulted in his gradual abandonment of the emphasis given to self-consciousness, and led him to the formation of the individual existence in terms of "*place*." We saw the budding of the notion of place in the quotation above, where Nishida mentions "the *place* where the self knows itself." It was Nishida's genius to pay attention to this aspect of "located-ness" of consciousness. This "topological" perspective allows Nishida to shift the focus from the individual self of self-consciousness to the wider world, in which the individual exists, and of which each individual is a constituent. He accordingly attempts to reorganize his ontology, ethics, religion, and aesthetics anew.

The emergence of the hallmark notion "basho" is already detectible in Nishida's analysis of self-consciousness. For example:

> How does the content of self-consciousness develop? [The answer is that it takes place as] the self reflects the self within itself. The mirror that reflects the content of one's self is also nothing but the selfsame self. It is not that the self projects its image onto some external thing. Some may argue that the self-consciousness

develops within the category of "time." But actually, it is not in "time" that self-consciousness gets established but "time" gets established in self-consciousness. Ordinarily, "self-consciousness" is understood merely to refer to the oneness of the knower and the known. But I consider that the genuine form of self-consciousness to be "I know myself within myself." If we simply take it as the oneness of subject and object, it may be considered something like the so-called "intuition" prior to reflection. For the establishment of self-consciousness, the factor of "in the self" must be added. In "self-consciousness," the self that knows, the self that is known, and the *place* where the self knows itself are one.[52]

8. GLOBAL CULTURE AND THE FORMATION OF HISTORIC WORLD

In his 1941 essay *Artistic Creation as an Activity of History Formation*,[53] Nishida looks to the ancient Greek religious rituals, out of which art is observed to have evolved. Nishida finds in the writings of Jane Harrison (1850–1928)—The *Ancient Art and Ritual* and The *Themis*—to give fascinating evidences of how a certain worldview gets shaped in history through ancient ritual activities, which were performed (and not merely contemplated). Harrison uncovers the origin of art in "a ritual" (δρώμενον, *drōmenon*),[54] which gradually differentiated itself into "the artist, the work of art, and spectator or art lover."[55] Ritual performance (*dromenon*) also developed into a *drama* made up of the story tellers (i.e. actors) and the audience.[56] Both words are derived from the verb "*draō*" (δράω, "to do"); *dromenon*, the present passive participle, means "a thing done."[57] Nishida observes that in the rituals, if they are to have the quality of "sacred," there had to be a strong emotion that excites the participants. According to Harrison, these rites had leaders who "officiated" the ritual activities. For instance, the spring festival dedicated to Dionysius was led by a young man (κοῦρος, *kouros*), whose image was overlapped with that of the god, and in this way god was created out of ritual. Rituals which were performed with strong communal emotion appears to Nishida as the early phase of the self-formation of the historic world. He writes:

> The self-formation of the historic world takes place as the self-determination of the *place* (*basho*) ... The ritual dance of the primitive people in the sense Harrison describes is the primordial momentum of the process of the self-formation of the historic world. Gods are born out of rituals. Not only religion and art get shaped out of this, but also scholarly activities.[58]

Nishida reiterates that "whatever appears in the historic world" is not an objectively laid out phenomenon but a "dromenon" acted out, which is fueled by strong and shocking emotions.[59] We notice here, going back to his earlier works such as *Art and Morality*, Nishida considers feeling and emotions as the driving force of artistic expressions, but now it is no longer a matter of psychological or individual feelings. As Harrison's work on ritual and the genesis of gods indicates, the self-formation of the world itself is based on the "emotion." This is possible because the self-formation of the world is "topological," involving the dialectical interaction of the human beings and their environment. As such, "the *pathos* must be the content of the activities of historic formation,"[60] as Nishida is dearly in agreement with the view that "without passion (*Leidenschaft*) nothing great is achieved."[61]

In this essay, Nishida also clarifies the relationship among religion, art, and scholarly engagements. Religion stands at the opposite end of art and scholarly engagements. For "religion" concerns the very existence of humanity, and it is the question of life itself. To quote his words: "Religion is the exact opposite direction of action-intuition. It being the relationship of the self to the Absolute, *it concerns very existence, the question of life itself.* Religion is the fundamental standpoint that establishes everything else. Religion does not share the same soil with art, contrary to Harrison's conjecture."[62]

Also in this essay, Nishida considers the works of art in terms of "the activity of history creation (*rekishiteki sōzō sayō*)," instead of approaching it from the perspective of "the subjective conscious-self (*shukanteki na ishikiteki jiko no tachiba*)."[63] In this context, although Nishida expresses his appreciation of Fiedler as someone who "thought in the deepest way the artistic creation as an act of expressive formation," he finds Fiedler to have approached "the expressive formation" simply from the perspective of the conscious self, and thus the scope of his investigation was limited.[64]

Nishida then turns his discussion to the latest development in Western art history, which began to open up to non-Eurocentric view of art, as heralded by Alois Riegl (1858–1905), Wilhelm Worringer (1881–1965), and others. Nishida welcomes the pluralistic paradigm of art history, as he is convinced that each culture has its own sociocultural environment and develops accordingly. Their findings, which broaden the source of Western art to Greco-Roman classical art, can be employed, mutatis mutandis to the appreciation and assessment of non-Western art and cultural forms, independent of European paradigms. To Japanese thinkers, including Nishida, it was often a source of wonder as to how even a great thinker as Hegel could maintain a naïve view on this matter, which may be paraphrased as "when the oriental culture develops fully, it becomes the western culture." In a lecture of 1935, Nishida expounds on this point:

> It can be said, in a broad stroke, that the oriental culture developed having subjectivity as its central focus, while objectivity was the central focus of the western culture. Western culture has the horizontal extension, while the oriental culture a vertical extension. Where these two paradigms get unified we can think about a global culture. The future of the culture will probably be heading in this direction. The idea that the oriental culture is not yet fully developed, and that when it will have fully developed it will grow into western culture is a wrong way to approach this question of human cultures. Each culture stands on an independent footing and develops accordingly.[65]

In order to illustrate his point, he chooses the Asian ink painting and Western painting:

> If we look at paintings, we understand that Western and Eastern paintings are fundamentally different. Eastern ink painting does not "mature into" Western

> painting, but they are two fundamentally different things. Likewise, it would be absurd to argue reversely that Western painting would mature into Eastern painting. Western painting concentrates on the form (*katachi*), while Eastern painting pays attention to the formless (*katachi no nai mono*).[66]

Based on this was his conviction that different cultures develop differently, and their "maturity" cannot be measured by one yardstick. Thus, for Nishida, the importance of works carried out by Riegl and others in the area of art history was promising.[67]

CONCLUSION

A working hypothesis of this chapter was that Nishida's philosophical thinking drew much from the experience of artists (including his own), as well as from his study of the scholarly works on aesthetics. By reading Nishida in this manner—by giving attention to his mention of art—a more concrete and colorful path of his thought emerges. It may be argued that in fact a more comprehensive understanding of Nishida's philosophy may be had by our being encouraged to approach his thought in such a creative manner.

Art, Nishida defines, is the expression of life. History is not an abstract unfolding of the "absolute spirit" to the omega point, or the linear flow of time from the past to the future. Rather, in each present moment past and future are co-present, and "time" determines itself in this manner. Artists embody this intuition of "absolute present" (*zettai genzai* 絶対現在) in their productive work, which shows how each moment comes about as the self-determination of the absolute present, or more poetically the self-determination of "Eternal Now" (*eien no ima* 永遠の今).

Nishida's reflection on the nature of temporality gets sharpened in his analysis of the essence of what makes Japanese art Japanese. "We should not call Japanese art mystical or symbolic and done away with it. Rather, its essence lies in grasping the world in the instant of absolute present."[68] Concerning the unique property of short Japanese poetry (*waka* or *tanka*), he writes: "it consists in grasping one's life centering in the present moment,"[69] or from the "vantage point" of the present moment. It is significant that Nishida's aesthetics leads to the very present moment, here and now. We read:

> In the world of the self-determination of the absolute present, past and future are simultaneously co-present in the present, and the past and future are "erased" in a way in the present moment, or the past and future are contained in the present moment. At the same time, this present moment is that which continuously disappears; it is a present that cannot stop and linger on even for a moment.[70]

One could say that freshness, surprise, and some sort of timelessness (as in Bashō's haiku poems) mark Japanese artistic expressions—as they spring forth out of this dynamic momentariness, which constitutes the historic reality, as Nishida says. Considering the unique features of Japanese art, Nishida muses that just as there is a way to find the expression of ardent spiritual yearning in the soaring tip of the Gothic spire, the human spirit can also "hold the entire universe" as one caresses a black *raku* (黒楽) tea bowl in one's hands.[71] Nishida is advocating the possibility of not collapsing the East-West differences but rather cultivating a cultural sensitivity to the unfamiliar ways of artistic appreciation, so that human beings may enrich their human cultures, which in turn can thrive as a more encompassing global culture with their diversity and hidden potentials intact. Nishida's philosophical works intimate this direction of globalization. There is no wonder then that his philosophical contemplation gave the nutrition to his successors such as Hisamatsu Shin'ichi.

NOTES

In this chapter, the new edition of NKZ has been used. It is abbreviated as NKZ-N (see Abbreviations and Conventions).

1. See Asakura Yūichirō, "*'Basho' no tachiba ni okeru geijutsu no igi*" [*The meaning of art in the perspective of "place"*], *Nishida Tetsugakukai Nenpō* 2 (2005), 110–127; also by Asakura, "*Nishida tetsugaku to geijutsu: K. Fīdorā o chūshin ni*" [*Nishida philosophy and art—Focus: K. Fiedler*], *Nishida Tetsugakukai Nenpō* 6 (2009), 83–92.
2. Nishida Kitarō, *Zen no kenkyū* (1911). An English translation, *An Inquiry into the Good*, M. Abe and C. Ives (New Haven: Yale University Press, 1990).
3. "Editors' Introduction" to Georg Simmel, *Rembrandt, an Essay in Philosophy of Art*, trans. and ed. Alan Scott and Helmut Staubmann (New York and London: Routledge, 2005), xi–xii. The notes provided by the editors identify this poem by Schiller: "*Durch das Morgentor des Schönen drangst Du in der Erkenntnis Land*" in *Die Künstler* (1789). Ibid., 167.
4. Iwaki Ken'ichi, "*Nishida Kitarō to geijutsu*"」 [Nishida Kitarō and art)], in *Nishida Tetsugaku Senshū* [Collected philosophical works of Nishida], vol. 6, ed. Iwaki Ken'ichi (Kyoto: Tōeisha, 1998), 409.
5. See M. Yusa, *Zen and Philosophy: An Intellectual biography of Nishida Kitarō* (Honolulu: University of Hawaii Press, 2002), 175–176, 220. Also see Nishida's essay, "*Sho no bi*" [*The beauty of calligraphy*] (May 1930), NKZ-N 7.331–332, and "Tanka ni tsuite" ["On the *Tanka* poetry"] (1933), NKZ-N 11.162–164.
6. The poem (1934) speaks about Nishida's way of philosophizing, or philosophy as his way of life.
7. The appellation was taken after the *Philosophenweg* (philosophers' path) in Heidelberg on the northern bank of Neckar river, where Goethe, Hölderlin, and others fondly strolled, while overlooking the charming old city.
8. Nishida Kitarō Ibokushū Henshū-iinkai, ed., *Nishida Kitarō ibokushū* [A collection of Nishida Kitarō's calligraphic works] (Kyoto: Tōeisha, 1977), 67.
9. Nishida Kitarō, *Geijutsu to dōtoku* [*Art and morality*] (1923), NKZ-N 3.1–247; translated into English by D. A. Dilworth and V. H. Viglielmo, *Art and Morality* (Honolulu: University of Hawaii Press, 1973).
10. For his writings on tea ceremony, see *Chadō no tetsugaku* [Philosophy of the art of tea ceremony], HSC vol. 4.

11. Hisamatsu Shin'ichi, "*Koshō*" in HSC 5.246–248.
12. Ibid., 5.246.
13. Ibid., 5.246.
14. Ibid., 5.247.
15. B. Castiglione, *The Book of the Courtier*, trans. George Bull (Harmondsworth: Penguin Books, 1967).
16. Ibid., 67.
17. Giorgio Vasari, *The Lives of the Artists*, selected and trans. George Bull (Harmondsworth: Penguin Books, 1965), 64–65.
18. NKZ-N 1.134. *An Inquiry into the Good*, 145. On this topic, see E. Fongaro, "*The Giotto's O—Some Considerations about the Reception of the Italian Translation of* Zen no kenkyū," *Nishida Tetsugakukai Nenpō* 9 (2012), 174–186.
19. B. Castiglione, *The Book of the Courtier*, 70: "Then again, in painting, a single line which is not laboured, a single brush stroke made with ease, in such a way that it seems that the hand is completing the line by itself without any effort or guidance, clearly reveals the excellence of the artist, about whose competence everyone will then make his own judgment. The same happens in almost every other thing."
20. On this topic, see E. Fongaro, *The Giotto's O—Some Considerations about the Reception of the Italian Translation of* Zen no kenkyū, *Nishida Tetsugakukai Nenpō* 9 (2012), 174–186.
21. Charles Batteux (1713–80) is usually considered the one who created the notion of "fine arts."
22. R. Ōhashi, "Philosophy as Auto-bio-graphy: The Example of the Kyōto School," in *Japanese and Continental Philosophy: Conversations with the Kyōto School*, ed. B. W. Davis, B. Schroeder, and J. M. Wirth (Bloomington: Indiana University Press, 2011), 71–81.
23. NKZ-N 1.124; *An Inquiry into the Good*, 134. Nishida wrote this section of the book as early as in 1906; therein one sees that it is an idea that goes back to the very beginning of his philosophical career.
24. NKZ-N 1.6; *An Inquiry into the Good*, xxx.
25. NKZ-N 1.9; *An Inquiry into the Good*, 3–4.
26. NKZ-N 1.11; *An Inquiry into the Good*, 6.
27. NKZ-N 1.34; *An Inquiry into the Good*, 32.
28. NKZ-N 1.33; *An Inquiry into the Good*, 30.
29. In his essay "Various Kinds of Continuation of the Experiential Content" (*Keiken naiyō no shushunaru renzoku* 「経験内容の種々なる連続」), compiled in *The Problem of Consciousness*, Nishida referring to Schopenhauer writes: "The perspective of art is the religious perspective, but in a partial experience. As Schopenhauer said, artists in the moment of inspiration, are religious." NKZ-N 2.381–382.
30. Nishida's remark in Section 42 of *Intuition and Reflection in Self-Consciousness*, trans. V. H. Viglielmo with Y. Takeuchi and J. S. O'Leary (Albany: State University of New York Press, 1987), intimates this later position: "The standpoint of the absolute will is the standpoint of religion." NKZ-N 2.240. Religious world is a more

comprehensive dimension where absolute will finds its most complete expression, whereas art, in comparison, remains always partial.

31. NKZ-N 1.125; *An Inquiry into the Good*, 135; emphasis added.

32. These essays are compiled in *Shisaku to taiken* [*Philosophical contemplation and experience*] (1915), NKZ-N 1.161–337.

33. Takahashi Satomi (1886–1960), for instance, wrote his detailed critique of Nishida's notion of pure experience. See "*Ishikigenshō no jijitsu to sono imi*" [*The factual reality of phenomena of consciousness and its meaning*], in *Takahashi Satomi Zenshū* [*Collected works of Takahashi Satomi*] (Tokyo: Fukumura Shuppan, 1973), 4.153–182. Takahashi pointed out the theoretical fragility of deriving every activity of consciousness in terms of "pure experience." Nishida wrote his response to this critique, and clarified his position in "*Takahashi (Satomi) Bungakushi no seccho, Zen no kenkyū ni taisuru hihyō ni kotau*" [My response to Mr. S. Takahashi's critique of *An Inquiry into the Good*] (August 1912), NKZ-N 1.240–253. This kind of fruitful exchanges further pushed Nishida to proceed deeper and further in his inquiry of consciousness.

34. R. Dedekind, *Essays on the Theory of Numbers*, trans. Wooster Woodruff Beman (Chicago: Open Court Publishing Company, 1901), 31.

35. NKZ-N 1.212–213. Also NKZ-N 2.14: "Introduction" to *Jikaku ni okeru chokkan to hansei* [Intuition and reflection in self-consciousness].

36. Fiedler remains important for Nishida, who quotes him in *The Problem of Consciousness* (1920, NKZ-N 2.273–462), in the *Art and Morality* (1923), and again in his 1941 essay on art and the formation of the historical world.

37. NKZ-N 2.1–272; *Intuition and Reflection in Self-Consciousness*. (Note by the editor: although the collected essays were published in book form in 1917, its forty-four sections were written over the period of four years, starting in 1913 and published in instalments.)

38. NKZ-N 2.324. "Kanjō" ["Feeling"] (1918), in *The Problem of Consciousness*.

39. Ibid.

40. NKZ-N 2.368. "*Keiken naiyō no shushunaru renzoku*" ["Various modes of continuations of the experiential content"] (1919) in *The Problem of Consciousness*.

41. The following discussion is based on Nishida's essay "*Bi no honshitsu*" ["The essence of beauty"] (originally published in March–April 1920), and compiled in his *Geijutsu to dōtoku* 『芸術と道徳』 [Art and morality] (1923), NKZ-N 3.15; for English translation, see Dilworth and Viglielmo, *Art and Morality*, 14.

42. NKZ-N 3.17; *Art and Morality*, 15; translation modified.

43. NKZ-N 3.27–28; *Art and Morality*, 25.

44. NKZ-N 3.29; *Art and Morality*, 25.

45. NKZ-N 3.29, "*geijutsuteki sōsaku wa hyōshutsu undō de aru.*"

46. NKZ-N 3.29.

47. Cf. Plotinus, *Enneades* III, 8, "On Nature and Contemplation."

48. NKZ-N 3.29; *Art and Morality*, 26–27; emphasis added.

49. NKZ-N 2.224–225, *Intuition and Reflection in Self-Consciousness*, Section 41 (1917), 144.
50. NKZ-N 3.26; "The Essence of the Beautiful," *Art and Morality*, 23–24; emphasis added.
51. NKZ-N 3.27; *Art and morality*, 24; translation slightly altered.
52. NKZ-N 3.350, "*Naibu chikaku ni tsuite*" [On the inner perception] (1924); emphasis added.
53. "*Rekishiteki keiseisayō to shite no geijutsuteki sōsaku*" [Artistic creation as an activity of history formation] (1941), NKZ-N 9.233–300.
54. Ibid., NKZ-N 9.237.
55. Jane E. Harrison, *Ancient Art and Ritual* (London, New York, and Toronto: Oxford University Press, 1951 [1913]), 204; also NKZ-N 9.244. *Rekishiteki keiseisayō to shite no geijutsuteki sōsaku.*"
56. See "*Rekishiteki keiseisayō to shite no geijutsuteki sōsaku*," NKZ-N 9.243.
57. Harrison, *Ancient Art and Ritual*, 35; also Nishida, *Rekishiteki keiseisayō to shite no geijutsuteki sōsaku*," NKZ-N 9.237 and 247.
58. Ibid., NKZ-N 9.245.
59. Ibid., NKZ-N 9.255.
60. Ibid., NKZ-N 9.251.
61. Ibid.
62. Ibid., NKZ-N 9.264; emphasis added. Here, we clearly see how Nishida moved away from his initial conception of the kinship of religion and art to the distinction between them.
63. Ibid., NKZ-N 9.234.
64. Ibid., NKZ-N 9.235–236.
65. "*Genjitsu no sekai no ronriteki kōzō*" [The logical structure of the actual world] (1935), NKZ-N 12.337.
66. Ibid., NKZ-N 12.338.
67. *Nihon bunka no mondai* [The problem of Japanese culture] (1940), NKZ-N 9.11.
68. "*Rekishiteki keiseisayō to shite no geijutsuteki sōsaku*." NKZ-N 9.300.
69. "*Tanka ni tsuite*" ["On the *Tanka* poetry"] (January 1, 1933), NKZ-N 11.163.
70. "*Rekishiteki keiseisayō to shite no geijutsuteki sōsaku*," NKZ-N 9.271.
71. NKZ-N 9.298. "*Rekishiteki keiseisayō to shite no geijutsuteki sōsaku*."

BIBLIOGRAPHY

Asakura Yūichirō 浅倉祐一朗. "'*Basho' no tachiba ni okeru geijutsu no igi*" 「『場所』の立場における芸術の意義」 [The meaning of art in the perspective of "place"]. *Nishida Tetsugakukai Nenpō* 2 (2005), 110–127.

Asakura Yūichirō. "Nishida tetsugaku to geijutsu: K. Fīdorā o chūshin ni" 「西田哲学と芸術 K.フィードラーを中心に」 [Nishida philosophy and art—focus: K. Fiedler]. *Nishida Tetsugakukai Nenpō* 6 (2009), 83–92.

Castiglione, Baldassare. *The Book of the Courtier*, trans. George Bull. Harmondsworth: Penguin Books, 1967.

Dedekind, Richard. *Essays on the Theory of Numbers*, trans. Wooster Woodruff Beman. Chicago: Open Court Publishing Company, 1901.

Fongaro, Enrico. "The Giotto's O—Some Considerations about the Reception of the Italian Translation of *Zen no kenkyū*." *Nishida Tetsugakukai Nenpō* 9 (2012), 174–186.

Harrison, Jane E. *Ancient Art and Ritual*. London, New York, Toronto: Oxford University Press, 1951 (1913).

Hisamatsu Shin'ichi久松真一. "*Koshō*" 「己象」 [Self-image], HSC, vol. 5, 246–248. Tokyo: Rishōsha, 1970.

Hisamatsu Shin'ichi. *Chadō no tetsugaku* 『茶道の哲学』 [Philosophy of the art of tea ceremony], HSC vol. 4. Tokyo: Rishōsha, 1973.

Iwaki Ken'ichi 岩城見一. "*Nishida Kitarō to geijutsu*"「西田幾多郎と芸術」 [Nishida Kitarō and art]. In *Nishida Tetsugaku Senshū* 『西田哲学選集』 [Collected philosophical works of Nishida], vol. 6, ed. Iwaki Ken'ichi. Kyoto: Tōeisha, 1998.

Nishida Kitarō Ibokushū Henshū-iinkai 西田幾多郎遺墨集編集委員会, ed. *Nishida Kitarō ibokushū* 『西田幾多郎遺墨集』 [A collection of Nishida Kitarō's calligraphic works]. Kyoto: Tōeisha, 1977.

Nishida Kitarō 西田幾多郎. *Zen no kenkyū* 『善の研究』 [An inquiry into the good] (1911). An English translation, M. Abe and C. Ives, *An Inquiry into the Good*. New Haven: Yale University Press, 1990.

Nishida Kitarō. "*Takahashi (Satomi) Bungakushi no seccho, Zen no kenkyū ni taisuru hihyō ni kotau*" 「高橋（里美）文学士の拙著『善の研究』に対する批評に答ふ」 [My response to Mr. S. Takahashi's critique of *An Inquiry into the Good*] (August 1912). NKZ-N 1.240–253.

Nishida Kitarō. *Shisaku to taiken* 『思索と体験』 [Philosophical contemplation and experience] (1915). NKZ-N 1.161–337.

Nishida Kitarō. *Intuition and Reflection in Self-Consciousness*, trans. Valdo H. Viglielmo with Takeuchi Yoshinori and Joseph S. O'Leary. Albany: State University of New York Press, 1987 (1917).

Nishida Kitarō. "Kanjō" 「感情」 [Feeling] (1918), in *The Problem of Consciousness*. NKZ-N 2.313–334.

Nishida Kitarō. "*Keiken naiyō no shushunaru renzoku*" 「経験内容の種々なる連続」 ["Various kinds of continuation of the experiential content"] (1919), compiled in *The Problem of Consciousness*.

Nishida Kitarō. "*Bi no honshitsu*" 「美の本質」 ["The essence of beauty"] (1920), and compiled in his *Geijutsu to dōtoku* 『芸術と道徳』 [Art and morality] (1923).

Nishida Kitarō. *Geijutsu to dōtoku* 『芸術と道徳』 [*Art and morality*](1923), NKZ 3.1–247; translated into English by D. A. Dilworth and V. H. Viglielmo, *Art and Morality*. Honolulu: University of Hawaii Press, 1973.

Nishida Kitarō. "*Naibu chikaku ni tsuite*" 「内部知覚について」 [On the inner perception], (1924). NKZ-N 3.311–356.

Nishida Kitarō. "*Sho no bi*"「書の美」 [*The beauty of calligraphy*] (1930). NKZ-N 7.331–332.

Nishida Kitarō. "*Tanka ni tsuite*" 「短歌について」 ["On the *Tanka* poetry"] (1933). NKZ-N 11.162–164.

Nishida Kitarō. "*Genjitsu no sekai no ronriteki kōzō*" 「現実の世界の論理的構造」 [The logical structure of the actual world] (1935). NKZ-N 12.293–341.

Nishida Kitarō. *Nihon bunka no mondai* 『日本文化の問題』 [The problem of Japanese culture] (1940). NKZ-N 9.1–94.

Nishida Kitarō. "*Rekishiteki keiseisayō to shite no geijutsuteki sōsaku*" 「歴史的形成作用としての芸術的創作」 [Artistic creation as an act of history formation] (1941). NKZ-N 9.233–300.

Ōhashi, Ryōsuke. "Philosophy as Auto-bio-graphy: The Example of the Kyōto School." In *Japanese and Continental Philosophy: Conversations with the Kyōto School*, ed. B. W. Davis, B. Schroeder, and J. M. Wirth, 71–81. Bloomington: Indiana University Press, 2011.

Plotinus. *Enneads* III (Loeb Classical Library), an English trans. by A. H. Armstrong. Cambridge: Harvard University Press; London: William Heinemann, 1967.

Simmel, Georg. *Rembrandt, an Essay in Philosophy of Art*, trans. and ed. Alan Scott and Helmut Staubmann. New York and London: Routledge, 2005.

Takahashi Satomi 高橋里美. "*Ishikigenshō no jijitsu to sono imi*" 「意識現象の事実とその意味」 [*The factual reality of phenomena of consciousness and its meaning*]. In *Takahashi Satomi Zenshū* 『高橋里美全集』 [*Collected works of Takahashi Satomi*]), 4.153–182. Tokyo: Fukumura Shuppan, 1973.

Vasari, Giorgio. *The Lives of the Artists*, selected and trans. George Bull. Harmondsworth: Penguin Books, 1965.

Yusa, Michiko. *Zen and Philosophy: An Intellectual Biography of Nishida Kitarō.* Honolulu: University of Hawaii Press, 2002.

FURTHER READING

Nishida Kitarō's writings in English translation

An Inquiry into the Good, trans. Masao Abe and Christopher Ives. New Haven and London: Yale University Press, 1990.

Intuition and Reflection in Self-Consciousness, trans. V. H. Viglielmo, with Y. Takeuchi and J. S. O'Leary. Albany: State University of New York Press, 1987.

Art and Morality, trans. D. A. Dilworth and V. H. Viglielmo. Honolulu: University Press of Hawaii, 1973.

Place & Dialectic, Two Essays by Nishida Kitarō, trans. J. W. M. Krummel and S. Nagatomo. New York: Oxford University Press, 2012.

Fundamental Problems of Philosophy: The World of Action & the Dialectical World, trans. D. Dilworth. Tokyo: Sophia University, 1970.

Last Writings, Nothingness and the Religious Worldview, trans. D. Dilworth. Honolulu: University of Hawaii Press, 1987.

"The Logic of *Topos* and the Religious Worldview," trans. M. Yusa. *Eastern Buddhist* 19.2 (1986) 1–29 and 20.1 (1987) 81–119.

On aesthetics and related topics

Castiglione, Baldassare. *The Book of the Courtier*, trans. George Bull. Harmondsworth: Penguin Books, 1967.

Harrison, Jane Ellen. *Ancient Art and Ritual*. London: Williams and Norgate, 1913.

Hisamatsu, Shin'ichi. *Zen and the Fine Arts*, trans. Tokiwa Gishin. Tokyo: Kodansha International, 1971.

Marra, Michael E., trans. and ed. *A History of Modern Japanese Aesthetics*. Honolulu: University of Hawaii Press, 2001.

Riegl, Alois. *Late Roman Art Industry*, trans. Rolf Winkes. Rome: G. Bretschneider, 1985.

Worringer, Wilhelm. *Abstraction and Empathy*, trans. Michael Bullock. Cleveland, OH: Meridian Books, 1967.

CHAPTER EIGHT

In Search of an Aesthetics of Emptiness: Two European Thinkers

RAQUEL BOUSO GARCÍA

INTRODUCTION: JAPANESE PHILOSOPHY IN DIALOGUE

In recent years the encounter with Japanese experience has been especially fertile for Western (European) thinkers in the field of aesthetics and religion. This intercultural encounter has widened the scope of philosophical discourse and has effected other subtle changes, thereby lowering the barriers that had previously separated different modes of experience and articulation.

I will discuss two case studies of European thinkers, who in conversation with Japanese philosophy have developed significant works of intercultural enrichment. Italian philosopher Giangiorgio Pasqualotto has made an important contribution in the field of study of Japanese aesthetics with his works on "intercultural aesthetics" focusing on Japanese philosophy. Spanish thinker Amador Vega has been working in the field of aesthetics in dialogue with Western mysticism and Japanese philosophy; although his basically hermeneutic approach does not focus on interculturality per se, his thought moves quite comfortably in this terrain.

These two distinct approaches show us the kinds of possibilities that relate aesthetics and spirituality. Both disciplines involve a particular mode of experience or feeling and generate a type of knowledge which has often been stigmatized as "intuitive." In the Western philosophical tradition rationalism has tended to draw a dividing line between aesthetic experience and religious experience, relegating feeling to a secondary role. By contrast, in Japan, at least up until the development of modern academic philosophy, the need to clearly separate aesthetics from spirituality seems not to have arisen. It is even suggested that traditional Japanese thought was expressed more in artistic and literary works than in philosophical systems. From this conception comes the idea that Japanese culture has traditionally valued emotion, the concrete, and the absence of a systematic approach more highly than logic, abstraction, or systematization.[1] It is therefore not surprising that the alleged role of feeling in the Japanese approach to the cultivation and appreciation of art has led to Japanese art being qualified as essentially poetic-aesthetic, contemplative, and centered on nature.[2]

It could be argued that it was in fact Japanese arts and spirituality that first attracted Europeans to Japan and that European interest in Japanese is relatively recent. We think of the phenomenon of Japanism as arising from factors such as the discoveries of *ukiyo-e* prints in nineteenth-century European artistic circles[3] or the attraction of Zen Buddhism in the 1950s and 1960s.[4] The aesthetic and religious dimension of Japanese thought would seem, then, to eclipse the logical, conceptual, and rational dimension of traditional Western thought. There is a need for modern academic philosophy to work further, if the intellectual history of premodern Japan is to be known, so that it can reconstruct it and present it to Western philosophers.

So then, we are left with a paradox. In modern Japan, under the influence of European and North American academia, aesthetics and spirituality have been separated out as two distinct areas of study. Meanwhile, largely inspired by the Japanese tradition, the European philosophers examined in this study choose to explore the close links between the dimensions of aesthetics and spirituality. When using the term "aesthetics" in relation to Japanese philosophy it is useful to remember the caution raised by Michele Marra in the introduction to his *Modern Japanese Aesthetics*. Marra observes that the very expression "modern aesthetics" is a tautology, given that aesthetics is, by nature, a product of modernity, born in Europe in the mid-eighteenth century. Thus, he suggests that to apply this term to Japan is an act of hermeneutic hegemony, whether we apply it to premodern Japan or to the works of modern Japanese thinkers educated in Western philosophy. And yet Marra finds that this term is actually useful. His reasoning is as follows: "The expression 'Japanese aesthetics' … refers to a process of philosophical negotiation between Japanese thinkers and Western hermeneutical practices in the creation and development of images of Japan. Inasmuch as we consider it the work done in Japan on the topic of the philosophy of arts, 'Japanese aesthetics' does indeed exist as a field."[5] According to this, when discussing "Japanese aesthetics," Europeans have to be aware not only that they project their own categories onto another culture that has traditionally expressed itself in different terms, but also that many of the images that reach European scholars come from Japanese authors who "speak a foreign (most of the time German) idiom."[6]

The two authors that we are examining here have developed what we could call an "*aesthetics of the emptiness*" in that intercultural terrain where the intellectual and spiritual traditions of the two cultures shed light on each other. Pasqualotto conceives intercultural philosophy as being like an ethical philosophical practice, transformative in that the understanding of the other forms of philosophical expression to which it gives voice, in turn transform the conception of the philosophy itself. Amador Vega's conception of hermeneutical practice also goes beyond the theoretical to incorporate the value of transformation. In the positions of both Pasqualotto and Vega the transformative element of the philosophical practice, characteristic of the understanding of philosophy as a way of life, finds a reference point in traditional Japanese aesthetics, which is understood as an artistic training and an art of living.

1. AN AESTHETICS OF EMPTINESS

Two books by Pasqualotto are of special relevance in understanding the relation between the mode of thinking and artistic expression in East Asia. They are *Estetica del vuoto: Arte e meditazione nelle culture d'Oriente* (Aesthetics of Emptiness: Arts and Meditations in the Oriental Cultures, 1992)[7] and *Yohaku: Forme di ascesi nell'esperienza estetica orientale* (*Yohaku*: Forms of Asceticism in the Eastern Aesthetic Experience, 2001).[8] They demonstrate how his study of Asian philosophies has evolved and matured since the publication of his early work, *Il Tao della filosofia* (The "Dao" of Philosophy, 1989)[9] that marked a turning point in his philosophical journey. As Pasqualotto explains in an interview, his journey began with analytical philosophy and led him to Hegel and Marx. For more than ten years, he concentrated on Nietzsche, writing a long commentary on *Thus Spoke Zarathustra* (1985) and publishing a series of essays called *Saggi su Nietzsche* (Essays on Nietzsche, 1988). Although interested in the Frankfurt School, he felt that he was unable to get beyond Hegel and Nietzsche by way of Adorno and Horkheimer. He also experimented with Italian neo-idealism and Heidegger but his initial passion for this line of inquiry ended in disappointment as he found that it did not offer him a language capable of saying something new that was percolating inside his consciousness. Pasqualotto explains:

> At the point where poetic, philosophical, and literary languages exhaust their function, what do we have left? For me what's left is the gesture, the action … I thought that art as an action in its pure state should be reduced to its absolute essence. And I noticed that in Japan especially the essential reduction of all that is artistic had been made.[10]

Thus, with his work, *Il Tao della filosofia*, Pasqualotto began his first "experiment in a philosophy" understood as a comparison of Eastern and Western thought. He has continued with this approach until now, although considerably broadening the sources, the presuppositions, and methods employed.[11] The need to clarify his own point of view has led him to redefine what he understands by "comparative philosophy" and "philosophy as comparison." On this point, he discovers that even before trying to find correspondences among different systems of thought, philosophical activity already involves the act of comparison—whether comparing concepts and words or propositions and arguments. This comparative approach should not be seen as a new branch of philosophy within the academic discipline but rather as a development that throws into relief the idea that "the activity of comparison is at the root of thinking itself."[12]

The same critical revision of his ideas and methods has led Pasqualotto in recent years to orient his research in the direction that he defines as "intercultural." This orientation starts out with the premise that Asia and Africa constitute an important presence in the West and that the processes derived from the migratory flows should be understood as being integral rather than parallel.[13] He argues that in the current debate about the possibility of intercultural philosophy, a paradigm shift has taken place. Pasqualotto writes that "a space has opened up in which to recognize the *need* for intercultural philosophy, a paradigm shift. For the first time in history, the conditions for intercultural communication are so widely spread and this trend is accelerating so quickly that they define a situation in which no culture can legitimately attempt to establish itself in a position of hegemony."[14] For Pasqualotto the intercultural perspective provides an alternative to monocultural thinking, as it recognizes that cultural identities are always the result of the interaction of diverse cultures. An intercultural approach is interested in "not only studying but also promoting experiences, whether theoretical or practical, of interaction between different cultures."[15] In an age defined by globalization, he opts for a philosophy that examines the real possibility of an encounter among philosophical perspectives that proceed from diverse cultures. Thanks to this diversity, understanding and transformation are possible without diluting the diversity into one homogeneous mass, and also avoids the subordination of one perspective to another.

Within the context of this intellectual challenge, Pasqualotto's book *Estetica del vuoto* (*Aesthetics of Emptiness*) is the result of an inquiry into traditional Japanese arts that he undertook in search of a new language. The philosophical interest of his approach lies in the way he deals with the Daoist and Buddhist experiences of emptiness, which he argues is at the core of all Japanese arts. Emptiness here is understood as the very object of practice rather than as a mere conceptual basis.

What stands out in the *Aesthetics of Emptiness* is the emphasis on meditation practice as part of aesthetic training, to allow both the execution of art and the enjoyment of the artistic work. Pasqualotto is conversant with religions and a wide range of works on art and oriental aesthetics, including Buddhism and Daoism, while remaining in dialogue with philosophers. Among them we find Japanese philosophers such as D. T. Suzuki, Toshihiko and Toyo Izutsu, Hisamatsu Shin'ichi, and Yuasa Yasuo. But without doubt, one of the main merits of his book is that it offers a guide to interpreting traditional Asian arts as well as clarifying ideas that underlie them, and along the way it discloses deep-rooted misunderstandings of Daoism and Buddhism held in the West.

Pasqualotto clarifies the notion of "identity" in Buddhist epistemology by taking the *Prajñāpāramitā* texts as his source. According to the Mahayana teaching on "no-self" and "dependent co-arising," contingent beings are empty since they are without their "own nature" or "own being." That all things are empty does not mean that they do not exist. This means that we cannot think of anything in terms of existence, nonexistence, both existence and nonexistence, or neither existence nor nonexistence. Things in themselves exist in a conditional, provisional, and interrelated way. Therefore, we could say that things (including our own selves) exist and do not exist at the same time, since they do not persist nor are they annihilated. Their identity is thought of as self-contradictory. Because this Buddhist notion of "identity" contradicts the Aristotelian principle of noncontradiction, and could be stigmatized as illogical or irrational, Pasqualotto turns to the dialectical tradition of Heraclitus and Plato to pre-empt such criticism. Following this approach, the work shows specifically how emptiness in Asian traditions should not be understood as mere nihilistic negation, but rather it should be taken as the condition without which nothing—no event—is possible. The traditional arts are presented as the ideal place in which to understand how this emptiness—as experienced by the artist—is manifested through form. For Pasqualotto, the merely aesthetic aspect, that is to say relating to feeling, acquires a wider sense in the cultivation of the arts because it involves all the phenomena of life, both subjective and objective. Here aesthetics refers to a training, an ascetic practice, which becomes a way of life. Thanks to meditation, through attention to breathing—which would imply a bodily experience or feeling of the emptiness—aesthetics is understood to be a quality that is not merely individual but rather universal to the world and to existence. This dialectic of empty and full experienced by the artist is recreated and captured in the work of art. Specific art forms explored by Pasqualotto are tea ceremony, *sumie* (ink) painting, haiku, *ikebana* (flower arrangement), *karesansui* (dry landscape gardens), and noh plays.

In his more recent work *Yohaku: Forme di ascesi nell'esperienza estetica orientale*, Pasqualotto continues his research into traditional Japanese philosophy of artistic practices this time centering on architecture, painting, haiku, calligraphy, and *bonsai*. His analysis fixes on elements such as the rustic and ephemeral materials used in traditional Japanese constructions; the transitional spaces which favor the relation of interior and exterior in architecture; the dialectic of form and background created by a stroke of ink from a brush on a white background in calligraphy and painting; the syncopated rhythm and conciseness of poetic compositions where all trace of the subject disappears and the fullness of a fleeting moment is captured; and the constant "care" that the practice of *bonsai* requires of a gardener to have respect for the plant, which transforms the artist, who shapes the miniature tree. These and other elements analyzed by Pasqualotto express the perfect interweaving of spirituality and feeling which underlies the aesthetic experience entailed in the practices mentioned. The thread that runs through this book is the word used as the title, "*yohaku*," which means "blank space," an "empty space," or "margin." Through this aesthetic quality, which simultaneously indicates simplicity and depth, the author shows how in his search for a reduction to the essential, he finds the artistic paths to form true *askesis* or"asceticism." He uses the Greek word "*askesis*" as a technical term to convey the meaning of a training that is carried out with the purpose of "giving form" to life. Concerning this aspect of traditional Japanese aesthetics, he observes:

> In general, if we want to talk about "aesthetics" with reference to the Japanese cultural tradition, it is useful above all to keep in mind that this term is not used to indicate a "theory of beauty" but rather to refer to a realm of practice and sensibility characterized by the activity of *giving form to experience*. Aesthetics is certainly a discipline, although not in the scientific or academic sense of being a particular branch of knowledge. Rather it is a *discipline* in the sense of *training* or *askesis*. This does not imply that aesthetics is an artistic burden but rather a way of giving form to life, or even the *art of living*.[16]

Some of the themes that he examines through this lens of *giving form to experience* are "vanguard and tradition," "emptiness," "the body and nature," "the mountain asceticism." In this way the possibility implicit in the positive vision of emptiness leads him to reflect on the need to continually produce new forms derived from a groundless ground. So he raises the idea that the artistic avant-garde of the twentieth century can also serve as examples for rethinking the relation between a sign and its condition of possibility. This same line of thought affirms the need for artists to achieve an emptiness within, thereby making them able to generate form. From this idea stem the psychophysical techniques developed by Asian spiritual traditions to encourage harmony between the body (microcosm) and nature (macrocosm). The mountain is presented as a privileged space for putting this ascetic-spiritual dimension into practice, as reflected in the Japanese tradition of mountain asceticism or *shugendō*, which, according to Pasqualotto, finds its most artistic expression in the symbolism of the garden. Resorting to his characteristic comparative-intercultural approach, Pasqualotto is able to relate concepts that seem radically incongruous at first. For instance, he takes Paul Klee's attempt to reveal the vital connections that have been obscured by our habit of perceiving reality only from an "optical" perspective, and links it with the Buddhist notion of *pratītyasamutpāda*—the "universal concatenation of all things." As we saw before, this notion emphasizes the interrelation that exists between all beings. If no being is self-generated, none is self-sufficient. Rather, all beings are the products of a causal chain and are therefore interdependent. In other words, "all being is in reality an *event,* that is to say, a process whose birth, development, and end are determined by conditions which do not depend on itself."[17] This leads us to think about reality in terms of process rather than essence and objects. Elsewhere Pasqualotto draws upon the "Mondrian's space," which resists objectification but rather sheds light on subjectivity: Malevic's determination to make visible the background which lies behind every form; the "positive nothingness" of the Neo-Platonist and the mystical traditions; the *basho* (*topos*) of the absolute nothingness in Nishida; and emptiness understood as a pure space present in all canonical Buddhist writings. In all these cases, which are "homeomorphic equivalents" (or "functional equivalents"), to use Raimon Panikkar's term, the background is an element which allows the relation and emergence of forms and beings in a way that they form a constituent part of the being (although they are not the being in and of themselves).[18]

The intercultural approach to philosophy undertaken by Pasqualotto responds to the contemporary need to find new modes of expression, and to widen the horizons of philosophy. It is also an ethical positioning in the face of a social reality that has become increasingly diverse and complex. We should not forget that "comparison" here does not mean the mere categorizing and cataloguing of philosophical "objects" in terms of their analogy or difference according to a neutral, disinterested, external observer. Rather, Pasqualotto understands comparison to be a philosophical practice "through which the subject is transformed. Comparison, therefore, is *askesis.*"[19]

2. AN APOPHATIC AESTHETICS

Three guiding elements constitute the philosophical journey of Amador Vega, namely (1) the internal unity of art and religion suggested by Nishida's work, (2) the search for new philosophical languages, and (3) an interest in modern art. Vega is an expert in European mysticism, who began his philosophical career with a doctoral thesis at the University of Freiburg on the Majorcan thinker Ramon Llull.[20] His edition of the Sermons of Meister Eckhart has made the work of Eckhart widely known to Spanish reader, and took him beyond the circle of specialists in medieval philosophy. In his teaching, lectures, and writings, Vega relates Eckhart's philosophy with modern art as well as the philosophy of the Kyoto School. Vega is currently at the forefront of studies in mysticism in Spain, while introducing analysis from a philosophical perspective into the rich heritage of traditional literary studies of the spiritual writings of the sixteenth and seventeenth centuries.

The novelty of Vega's approach is that he raises the possibility of a hermeneutical philosophy by bringing together aesthetic experience and mystical experience. The exploration of this possibility leads him to underline just how indebted certain twentieth-century artists were to mystical currents: poets such as Paul Celan, writers such as Robert Musil, painters such as Rothko, and the Basque sculptor Jorge Oteiza—just to name a few. The medieval European mystical tradition of "apophatic" or "negative theology" left the greatest mark on the work of these artists. To describe this confluence of apophatic religious ideas with art, Vega coined the expression "*apophatic aesthetics*." Despite its ascetic character, Vega notes that this apophatic aesthetics does not negate the perceptive character of sensitivity but rather it gives full expression to the senses.

Exploring the different hermeneutics concerning modernity, which is often interpreted in negative terms, Vega proposes a dialogue between the Western tradition and Japanese philosophy, especially Zen Buddhism and the Kyoto School, for example: "We can say that the negative way finds itself at the root of 'religious nihilism' or what Nishitani called an 'absolute nihilism'—to distinguish it from the 'relative nihilism' of Nietzsche. This fundamental perspectives of Zen can be adopted in our attempt to understand the German mystics."[21] And moreover,

> From the Eckhartian perspective, it is the experience of *kenosis* [i.e. emptying] represented by the gospel image of the "empty tomb" that comes closest, despite important differences, to the Buddhist experience of emptiness and nothingness (*śūnyatā*). This experience of the pouring out of the self, of humility, and of extreme poverty chosen freely, which the Son of God assumes, is the model for a life which rejects any form of idolatry in order to reach a place in which the essence of the divine resides. In Nishida, the analogy would be to transcend the realm of consciousness in order to reach a more rudimental self.[22]

In his work "Mystical Experience and Aesthetic Experience in modernity," Vega clearly details the hermeneutical approach of his research. He argues that the context for understanding the sacred has been lost from the representational languages in the modern world, and therefore, the sacred cannot be sought using the traditional religious languages.[23] But neither can we turn solely to the profane; without the criteria for truth and in the absence of spiritual authority we could fall into sacralizing the banal. Today, drawing a line clearly demarcating the sacred and the profane seems no longer feasible. As an alternative approach, Vega suggests that the creative potential of images in modern art represents and appropriates the sphere of investigation, not just in terms of aesthetic expression or the intention of the artist, but also regarding the capacity of art to embrace ritual processes and the modes of language involved in these processes. According to Vega, the twentieth-century avant-garde experimentation with the abstract has lent a greater versatility to the manifestations of the sacred.

As a clear example of this capacity of art to embrace art as the ritual process, Vega centers on the work of Russian America artist Mark Rothko. His findings are collected mainly in the volume *Sacrificio y creación en la pintura de Rothko: La vía estética de la emoción religiosa* (Sacrifice and Creation in the Painting of Rothko: The Aesthetic Way of Religious Emotion, 2010), although it does not explicitly address intercultural instances of the East.

In Vega's undertaking, the language of negativity in Nishida (in terms of no-self and self-contradictory identity) finds a correspondence in the mystical Christian tradition and in particular that of Meister Eckhart. As already mentioned, he finds analogies between Nishida's ideas and the kenotic experience of the gospels regarding the conception of the ultimate reality and an ascetic path which leads to spiritual death. For Vega, however, Nishitani is the key Japanese thinker who offers the working interpretation of the notion of nothingness. He finds that Nishitani's work *Religion and Nothingness*,"in a genuinely surprising way, appeals to the nihilist presuppositions of the Christian gospels—the negation of the world and of the self, as well as the conception of life through death."[24] Nishitani's philosophy helps him to widen the scope of "religious nihilism" both Eastern and Western.

It is of interest here to mention the lively philosophical engagement that took place among artists and scholars in an academic context. In the 1997–98, together with a specialist of mysticism Victoria Cirlot, Vega organized a course entitled "Nothingness and Poetic Experience," in which he explored poetry and mysticism as the "two forms of nihilistic expression."[25] Japanese philosophical ideas were part of the reading materials. Many illustrious scholars and artists attended the course, including the well-known poet José Ángel Valente (1929–2000).[26] Valente reflected on the various nuances of the notion of nothingness, both biblical and Greek, and looked to the Kyoto School thinkers as well. By way of his conclusion he turned to the words of the Catalan painter Antoni Tàpies (1923–2002):

> Perhaps the supreme and the only radical practice of art is that of retraction. To create is not an act of power (power and creation negate each other): it is an act of acceptance or recognition. Creativity bears a feminine trait. It is not an act of penetrating a subject but rather a desire to be penetrated by it. To create is to generate a state of availability in which the first thing created is emptiness, an empty space. And in the space of creation there is nothing (so that something may be created in it). The creation of nothingness is the absolute principal of all creation. And God said:
>
> *Let there be Nothing.*
> *And raised his right hand*
> *to cover his gaze*
> *And so there was Nothingness.*[27]

It is in the experience of artists that the Eastern idea of artistic life resonates most clearly with the Western experience of artistic life as a process of "dis-identification," a shedding of the ego-self that allows the artists to liberate in themselves a space for creation, a space through which art will express itself. The notion of nothingness, then, appears as a question that can bring closer together distinct cultural traditions. It prompts us to rethink the influence that mystical currents exercise on philosophical speculations in the West. It is the hermeneutical key with which to interpret both artistic works and the creative process.

In Vega's work we do not find a direct theoretical construction of intercultural philosophy, because he is already enacting intercultural philosophy. In his references to Zen Buddhism, Nishida, Nishitani, Tanabe, and Ueda are fully integrated and make their appearance in his argument alongside the traditional sources of Western philosophy. In "Iniciación y hermenéutica: estudios sobre mística comparada" (Initiation and Hermeneutics: Studies on Comparative Mysticism], he proposes an approach to the hermeneutics of religion in which the Asian traditions find a place. He advocates a comparative approach to different religious traditions and proposes the transformation of the individual into a totality to form the background for the aesthetic understanding to take place in this hermeneutical exercise. He explains this point as follows: "The 'hermeneutics of religions' is an aspect that remains underdeveloped in our studies, but is valuable for its ability to transform a person, as the mode of understanding (*modus intelligendi*) is subject to mode of being (*modus essendi*). To put it in a Heideggerian term, the mode of understanding (*Verstehen*) presupposes a way of 'being-in-the-world.' "[28] Similar to what we saw above in reference to Pasqualotto's conception of intercultural philosophy as a transforming philosophical practice, here Vega's idea of hermeneutical practice goes beyond its theoretical realm and incorporates a moment of transformation.

3. REFLECTIONS

The kind of "aesthetics of emptiness" examined here leads me to develop an aspect of thought that the Western apophatic tradition does not seem to have emphasized sufficiently but is embodied in Japanese aesthetics. Ueda Shizuteru draws special attention to this in a written piece on silence and words:

> *"What we cannot speak about we must consign to silence."*[29] Perhaps we humans, being endowed with language, cannot or do not want to remain silent so long as we are not made speechless. When we are rendered speechless, silence is not the end. For we would put into words what causes us to remain silent. It just is not true that there exists somewhere and somehow some unspeakable reality. What is real is the event that stirs us into moving from language toward language.[30]

Ueda observes that the phenomena of silence and of speech are connected through a particular experience of reality. Not all silence possesses the same quality. In fact, Ueda distinguishes three kinds of silence: (1) mere silence of not speaking, (2) meditative quietude, which refrains from speech in order to immerse oneself in a more profound silence, and (3) entering "silently the absolute realm of infinite stillness, which is not disturbed by speaking and cannot be broken, but rather endows speaking with a depth of meaning."[31] The quality of the word depends, then, on the kind of silence from which it arises. In this way both in Zen and in Christian mysticism, when negation is employed, it is not the last word. It will be followed by an affirmation which springs up out of the event that has left us speechless. Therefore the affirmation cannot be said to proceed directly from the speaker, as the speaker has not included a reflection upon it in what has been spoken. Instead, affirmation is the spontaneous self-expression of that which has left us speechless (the very withdrawal of that which is expressed, i.e., nothingness) that moves us toward language. Although expression is produced through words or simple images, they are not mere words or images, in terms of the way they relate to the experiential background from which they proceed.

Here we see clearly the sense in which Ueda's philosophy links the two lines of research by Pasqualotto and Vega that we have described and represented, namely, the study on the creative processes in certain types of arts that shed light on it. Ueda, Pasqualotto, Vega—all of them offer a reevaluation of nothingness or emptiness. As Pasqualotto mentions in his essay on the painter Tàpies, this reevaluation is important not only from a general philosophical point of view but also from a practical perspective, "in the sense that it possesses a specific artistic *efficacy* and a strong ethical resonance."[32] Artistic efficacy could be said to lie in not representing the power of emptiness in a direct way but rather though an indirect evocation, through signs that demonstrate its strength and that through the subject of art makes it possible and visible. The ethical resonance lies "in knowing how to live in *innocence* and *poverty*," in reference to Tàpies who once wrote that artistic expression is not about representing emptiness, which cannot be represented; nor is the purpose of the experience to seek emptiness for its own sake and settle down inside it.[33] If emptiness is the origin of all determinations and all possible relation between determinations, each new work must "return to its origin" and recognize this process, which requires of the artist a constant detachment from and negation of the self, as Nishida understood when he spoke of the continuity of art and religion. Creation and destruction are basic elements in every work of art—as Vega reminds us in a text which is also dedicated to Tàpies.[34] The nihilistic language of destruction and of negativity in the work of artists preserves "the religious element of human consciousness" within the profane forms. As shown by his study on the survival of mysticism in art and contemporary thought, one must think of religion (understood here as "religiousness," which is "distinct from idolatrous cults") as "a necessary space separating us from the divine, a path that leads us to the abyss of nothingness, to silence and night, as powerful images of that emptiness and nakedness that transform a person into a creator."[35]

CONCLUSIONS

In recent years we have seen the publication of new interdisciplinary studies on aesthetics and religion and different works that explore the relation between aesthetics and notions such as negativity, nothingness, and emptiness. They are tapping into rich stream of research in which the intercultural approach has undoubtedly opened up new perspectives. In this manner, the studies that we have explored by Giangiorgio Pasqualotto and of Amador Vega on the possibility of "aesthetics of emptiness" or "apophatic aesthetics" may be preparing the way ahead. The elements shared by their works—their concern with aesthetics, spirituality, and interculturality—find a common counter-axis in Japanese culture with its notion of emptiness, both artistic and philosophical.

As gleaned from Ueda's quoted passage above, emptiness does not reduce the being to nothing, words to silence, or meaning to nihilism. While the Christian apophatic tradition culminates in the ineffable, the artists, by contrast, set out on a path that seems to lead in the opposite direction and yet has a way back; they engage with a silence that is teeming with words. The reflections of Pasqualotto and Vega around this question show the fullness of meanings which are generated from the original open space of emptiness and how the process of capturing in gestures, forms, and figures is not exempt from a transformative spiritual value.

As we are dealing with active authors whose thought, although already mature, does not stop evolving or being expressed in new works, it is too early to assess the repercussions of their ideas. However, it is possible to argue that they have played a pioneering role in having introduced Japanese philosophy, in particular that of the Kyoto School, into their philosophical reflections.

Pasqualotto is one of the first intercultural thinkers in Europe who engaged the East. From his first comparative studies in which Daoism and Buddhism are in dialogue, he went on to become one of Italy's greatest experts on Nishida Kitarō. From among the numerous students he has taught at the University of Padua have emerged various specialists in Japanese philosophy, some of them translators of Nishida into Italian.

Vega, for his part, became more familiar with intercultural philosophy through his association with the Catalan philosopher Raimon Panikkar (1918–2010),[36] and wrote one of the first essays about philosophers of the Kyoto School published in Spain.[37] We can say that the thought of Nishitani Keiji significantly influenced his philosophical journey and from his first reading of Nishida, Nishitani, Tanabe, and Ueda these sources have been ever present in his writings. Ueda, whose dissertation was on Meister Eckhart, established a fruitful venue of dialogue and himself participated in the various activities of the Bibliotheca Mystica et Philosophica Alois M. Haas,[38] a Barcelona-based research group coordinated by Vega. This group explores the relationships between art and spirituality, with a particular focus on mysticism in the European tradition. One of the initiatives of the research group was indeed the first translation into Spanish of a selection of essays by Ueda.[39] The dialogue established by Vega in some of his writings between the aesthetic experience, European mysticism, and Japanese philosophy has opened new lines of research which have come together in a significant number of doctoral theses, and its impact is being felt more recently outside of Spain.

Pasqualotto's intention, meanwhile, to open up Western philosophies to dialogue with other sources coming from Asian thought has had a certain impact in Italian academia which tends to be cautious about introducing changes and new specialties.

While Asian studies have a strong tradition in Italy they have rarely ventured outside the ambits of philology or history, and into the faculties of philosophy. Dialogue between philologists and philosophers is lacking. Neither are there many Italian philosophers engaged in studying philosophies from outside of Europe.

Across Europe, however, academic programs with an interdisciplinary or global character that include Asian thought (such as the degree in "World philosophies and religions") are being introduced in response to a demand among young people that seems to be growing rapidly. But despite all this we should not overlook the fact that comparative or intercultural philosophy still lacks a significant resonance in philosophical debate as lamented by Pasqualotto in the preface to his 2012 edition of *Il Tao della filosofia*, written twenty-five years ago.[40] The reasons for this lack of emphasis on intercultural philosophy, Pasqualotto reflects, are diverse but probably stem from a certain rigidity endemic in academic disciplines. Besides, despite the efforts made by intercultural studies, xenophobic attitudes continue to surface both within Europe and beyond.

Despite challenges and difficulties, however, Pasqualotto's impressive trajectory and the novelty of his work have won him a prominent place in the panorama of Italian philosophy. The scarcity of translations of his works into other languages has meant that the impact of his work outside of Italy is not yet considerable as might be expected. But over the years he has established a network of working relationships with philosophers, such as François Jullien and Rolf Elberfeld, thereby demonstrating the affinity for his type of approach in other parts of Europe. Judging from the slowness of academia to incorporate non-European philosophers into humanistic studies and the current rise of xenophobic political parties in Europe, the examples of intercultural philosophy that we have examined might have fallen largely on deaf ears. The phenomenon has yet to generate the wide academic debate it deserves, nor has it tempered the mistrust still felt in society toward what is perceived to be foreign. Despite all these, however, the undeniable fact remains that these studies have opened up a new path of thinking for the new generations of students, among whom some have already made important academic contributions to intercultural philosophy in dialogue with Japanese traditions.

NOTES

Research for this chapter was supported by the Spanish Ministry of Economy and Competitiveness, Grant FFI2015-65662-P and FEDER, UE.

1. See, for example, Shūichi Katō, *A History of Japanese Literature*, vol. 1, trans. D. Chibbett (Tokyo, New York, and San Francisco: Kōdansha, 1979), 1–2: "The undeniable tendency of Japanese culture is to avoid logic, the abstract and systematization, in favor of emotion, the concrete and the unsystematic."
2. Toyo Izutsu, *The Theory of Beauty in the Classical Aesthetics of Japan* (The Hague: Martinus Nijhoff, 1981), 7.
3. On Japanism, see: Colta F. Ives, *The Great Wave: The Influence of Japanese Woodcuts on French Prints* (New York: The Metropolitan Museum of Art, 1974);

S. Wichmann, *Japonismus. Begengungen in der Kunst des 19. Und 20. Jahrhunderts* (Herrsching: Schuler Verlagsgesellschafts, 1980); *L'Âge du japonisme: la France et le Japon dans la deuxième moitié du XIXe siècle* (Tokyo: Société franco-japonaise d'art et d'archéologie, 1983); Jan Walsh Hokenson, *Japan, France, and East-West Aesthetics: French Literature, 1867–2000* (Madison, NJ: Farleigh Dickinson University Press, 2004).

4. For more on how much Europeans knew about Buddhism, particularly Zen, in the sixteenth and seventeenth, centuries, see Urs App, *The Cult of Emptiness: The Western Discovery of Buddhist Thought and the Invention of Oriental Philosophy.* (Kyoto: University Media, 2012). Regarding knowledge of Asia in the German tradition and in English Romanticism, see Arthur Versluis, *American Transcendentalism and Asian Religions* (New York and Oxford: Oxford University Press, 1993), 16–36. Regarding the progression of encounters between Buddhism and the West, see: Frédéric Lénoir, *El budismo en Occidente* [La rencontré du Bouddhisme et de l'Occident, Librairie Arthème Fayard, 1999], trans. Vicente Villacampa (Barcelona: Seix Barral, 2000).
5. Michele Marra, "Introduction," in *Modern Japanese Aesthetics: A Reader* (Honolulu: University of Hawai'i Press, 1999), 2.
6. Ibid., 7.
7. G. Pasqualotto, *Estetica del vuoto: Arte e meditazione nelle culture d'Oriente* (Venice: Marsillo, 1992).
8. G. Pasqualotto, *Yohaku: Forme di ascesi nell'esperienza estetica orientale* (Padua: Esedra Editrice, 2001).
9. G. Pasqualotto, *Il Tao della filosofia* (Milan: Luni Editrice, 1989).
10. G. Pasqualotto, "Il mondo dove l'estetica è alla base dell'etica. Intervista di Antonio Gnoli" [The world where aesthetics is the base of ethics: An interview by Antonio Gnoli], in *Tra Oriente ed Occidente. Interviste sull'intercultura ed il pensiero orientale* [Between East and West: Interviews of thinkers and oriental thought], ed. Davide De Pretto (Milan: Mimesis, 2010), 64. (Otherwise indicated, all the translations from Italian are mine.)
11. We should highlight the initiative, described by Pasqualotto as "a comparative and intercultural adventure" of publishing *Simplègadi. Rivista di filosofía orientale e comparata* (1996–2009). This journal served as a platform in Italy to promote theoretical and practical work in comparative philosophy undertaken by Italian researchers such as Pasqualotto but also renowned authors such François Jullien, Raúl Fornet Betancourt, Graham Parkes, and Raimon Panikkar.
12. G. Pasqualotto, "Oltre la filosofia comparata: filosofia come comparazione" [Beyond comparative philosophy: Philosophy as comparison], in *East and West: Identità e dialogo interculturale* [East and West: Identity and intercultural dialogue] (Venice: Marsilio, 2003), 48.
13. G. Pasqualotto, "Premessa," *Il Tao della filosofia* (Milan: Luni Editore, 2012), 8–9. Some representative publications of this new direction are *East and West* (2003), *Per una filosofía interculturale* (Milan, 2008), and *Filosofia e globalizzazione* (Milan, 2011).

14. G. Pasqualotto,"Nota introduttiva: Cultura, multiculturalismo, intercultura," in *Per una filosofía interculturale*, ed. G. Pasqualotto (Milan, Mimesis, 2008), 10; emphasis in the original.
15. Ibid., 9.
16. Pasqualotto, *Yohaku*, 57; emphases in the original.
17. Ibid., 14.
18. Raimon Panikkar, *La experiencia filosófica de la Índia* (Madrid: Trotta, 2000), 73–75.
19. Pasqualotto, *Il Tao della filosofia*, 26.
20. Among his numerous published writings, his *Ramon Llull y el secreto de la vida* (Madrid: Siruela, 2002) has been translated into English by James Heisig, *Ramon Llull and the Secret of Life* (New York: Herder & Herder, 2002).
21. A. Vega, "Estética apofática y hermenéutica del misterio: elementos para una crítica de la visibilidad" [Apophatic and hermeneutical aesthetics of mystery: Elements for a criticism of visibility], *Diánoia* 54.62 (2009), 7.
22. A. Vega, "*Experiencia mística y experiencia estética en la modernidad*" [Mystical experience and aesthetic experience in modernity], in *La experiencia mística. Estudio interdisciplinar* [The mystical experience: Interdisciplinary study], ed. Juan Martín Velasco (Madrid: Trotta, 2004), 258.
23. A. Vega, "Mystical and Aesthetic Experiences in Modernity," in *Naming and Thinking God in Europe Today: Theology in Global Dialogue*, ed. Norbert Hintersteiner (Amsterdam: Rodopi, 2007), 233–246.
24. Vega, "Estética apofática y hermenéutica del misterio: elementos para una crítica de la visibilidad," 257.
25. A. Vega and V. Cirlot, "*Nada, mística y poesía*" [Nothingness, mysticism, and poetry], *Er: revista de filosofía* 24/25 (1999), 11. This volume brings together the reading materials of the course, at the Institute of Humanities, Barcelona, 1997–98. Alois M. Haas, Blanca Garí, Raffaele Pinto, Christine Kaufmann, Berta Meneses, Félix Duque, Alfonso Alegre, and Enrique Granell also participated in this course.
26. As well as being a poet, Valente was the author of an important essay in which he deals with the painting and mysticism of Saint Teresa, St. John of the Cross, and Miguel de Molinos, among other subjects.
27. Quoted in Valente, "La experiencia abisal" [The abysmal experience], in Vega and Cirlot, "*Nada, mística y poesía*," 236; emphases in the original.
28. A. Vega, "Iniciación y hermenéutica: estudios de mística comparada" [Initiation and hermeneutics: Studies of comparative mysticism], *Revista de la Sociedad Española de Ciencias de las Religiones* (1996), 282.
29. This is a quote from L. Wittgenstein, *Tractatus Logico-Philosophicus*, trans. D. F. Pears and B. F. McGuinness (London: Routledge & Kegan Paul, 1961), 151; emphasis in the original.
30. Shizuteru Ueda, "Silence and Words in Zen Buddhism," 5. For the text, see online at www.thezensite.com/ZenEssays/Philosophical/Silence_and_Words. The translation is slightly modified.
31. Ibid., 8.

32. G. Pasqualotto, "L'arte di Tàpies tra Oriente e Occidente," in *East and West*, 200; emphasis in the original.
33. Ibid.; emphases in the original.
34. A. Vega, "Antoni Tàpies: 'negatio negationis'. Un espacio de meditación y silencio" [Antoni Tàpies: Negation of negations: space of meditation and silence], in *Mística y creación en el siglo XX* [Mysticism and creation in the 20th century], ed. V. Cirlot and A. Vega (Barcelona: Herder, 2012), 265.
35. Ibid.
36. After his retirement from his teaching at the UC Santa Barbara in 1986, he returned to his native Catalonia and established the Vivàrium Academy, 1988–2006. He personally knew members of the Kyoto School, Nishitani Keiji, Takeuchi Yoshinori, Ueda Shizuteru, and Abe Masao. The first studies on Nishitani in Spain was by Ignasi Boada-Sanmartín, "Keiji Nishitani: religió i nihilisme, el final de la metafísica a la llum de l'escola de Kyoto," *Revista catalana de teología* 23.1 (1998), 85–107, who worked closely with Panikkar.
37. Amador Vega, "Experiencia mística y mundo modern," in *Modernitat i Religió* (Andorra: Annals Universitat d'Estiu. Government of Andorra, 1996), 109–126; later published as "Nihilisme d'Orient, nihilisme d'Occident," in *Passió, meditació i contemplació, Sis assaigs sobre el nihilisme religiós* (Barcelona: Empúries, 1999), 61–83 (new ed., Barcelona: Fragmenta, 2012) and in Spanish, *Zen, mística y abstracción* (Madrid: Trotta, 2002), 49–64. Amador Vega, "Als jardins de Kioto: breu notícia sobre el pensament religiós modern al Japó," in *Passió, meditació i contemplació, Sis assaigs sobre el nihilisme religiós*, 15–60 (republished in Barcelona: Fragmenta, 2012); in Spanish: *Zen, mística y abstracción* (Madrid: Trotta, 2002), 19–48.
38. Vega cites Ueda in his 1997 edition of the sermons of the medieval mystic Meister Eckhart and how the mystic had been received by scholars of the Kyoto School. Maestro Eckhart, "Introducción," in *El fruto de la nada y otros escritos*, ed. and trans. Amador Vega (Madrid: Siruela, 1997), 27–30. In 2000, Ueda gave a lecture entitled "In Search of the True Self" at the Universitat Pompeu Fabra, Barcelona, in the seminar on "The Theory and Practice of Meditation." In 2004, he gave another lecture entitled "Mysticism and Zen" as part of a series called "Silence and Form: Religion and Art in Asian Thought: India and Japan." In 2006 he participated in the second Alois M. Haas lecture series, "West Is East: European Mysticism and Zen Buddhism," giving a presentation on "Mysticism and Logic in Zen Buddhism."
39. *Zen y filosofía*, ed. Raquel Bouso (Barcelona: Herder, 2004). Ueda wrote a prologue to this edition and attended the book launch in Barcelona in 2004.
40. Giangiorgio Pasqualotto, "Premessa," *Il Tao della filosofia* (Milan: Luni Editore, 2012), 10.

BIBLIOGRAPHY

App, Urs. *The Cult of Emptiness: The Western Discovery of Buddhist Thought and the Invention of Oriental Philosophy*. Kyoto: University Media, 2012.

Boada Sanmartín, Ignasi. "Keiji Nishitani: religió i nihilisme, el final de la metafísica a la llum de l'escola de Kyoto." *Revista catalana de teología* 23.1 (1998), 85–107.

Colloque franco-japonaise d'art et d'archéologie, ed. *L'Âge du japonisme: la France et le Japon dans la deuxième moitié du XIXe siècle*. Tokyo: Société franco-japonaise d'art et d'archéologie, 1983.

Franke, William. "Apophatic paths." *Angelaki* 17.3 (2012), 7–16.

Ghilardi, Marcello. *Una lógica del vedere. Estetica ed ética nel pensiero di Nishida Kitarō.* Milan: Mimesis, 2009.

Ghilardi, Marcello. *The Line of the Arch: Intercultural Issues between Aesthetics and Ethics*. Milan: Mimesis International, 2015.

González Vallés, Jesús. "Filosofía y religión en el pensamiento japonés moderno. 'Absoluto' by Kitarō Nishida." *Studium* 33 (1993), 437–481.

González Vallés, Jesús. *Historia de la filosofía japonesa*. Madrid: Tecnos, 2000.

Heisig, J. W. *Filósofos de la nada*. Barcelona: Herder, 2002.

Heisig, J. W., T. P. Kasulis, and J. C. Maraldo, eds. JPS.

Hokenson, Jan Walsh. *Japan, France, and East-West Aesthetics: French Literature, 1867–2000*. Madison, NJ: Farleigh Dickinson University Press, 2004.

Ives, C. F. *The Great Wave: The Influence of Japanese Woodcuts on French Prints.* New York: The Metropolitan Museum of Art, 1974.

Izutsu, Toyo. *The Theory of Beauty in the Classical Aesthetics of Japan*. The Hague: Martinus Nijhoff, 1981.

Katō, Shūichi. Trans. D. Chibbett, *A History of Japanese Literature*, vol. 1. Tokyo, New York, and San Francisco: Kōdansha, 1979.

Lénoir, Frédéric. *El budismo en Occidente* [La rencontré du Bouddhisme et de l'Occident, Librairie Arthème Fayard, 1999], trans. V. Villacampa. Barcelona: Seix Barral, 2000.

Marra, Michele. *Modern Japanese Aesthetics: A Reader.* Honolulu: University of Hawai'i Press, 1999.

Masiá, Juan. "K. Nishida y su filosofía de la religion." *Miscelánea Comillas* 48 (1990), 427–440.

Masiá, Juan. "Filosofía del absoluto en K. Nishida." In *Cuestiones epistemológicas: materiales para el estudio de la religion*, ed. José Gómez Caffarena and Jose Mª Mardones, 137–147. Barcelona, Madrid: Anthropos, 1992.

Onyós, Joaquim. "Vivàrium, Centre d'Estudis Interculturals, Fundació Privada." *Ausa* 13.122–123 (1989), 437–440.

Pasqualotto, Giangiorgio. *Il Tao della filosofia*. Milan: Luni Editrice, 1989.

Pasqualotto, Giangiorgio. *Estetica del vuoto: Arte e meditazione nelle culture d'Oriente.* Venice: Marsillo, 1992.

Pasqualotto, Giangiorgio. "Post fazione, Nishida: dialettica e buddhismo." In *L'io e il tu*, trans. Renato Andolfato, 151–207. Padua: Unipress, 1996.

Pasqualotto, Giangiorgio. *Yohaku: Forme di ascesi nell'esperienza estetica orientale.* Padova: Esedra Editrice, 2001.

Pasqualotto, Giangiorgio. *East & West: Identità e dialogo interculturale.* Venice: Marsilio, 2003.

Pasqualotto, Giangiorgio. "L'arte di Tàpies tra Oriente e Occidente." In *East and West. Identità e dialogo interculturale*, 197–202. Venice: Marsilio, 2003.

Pasqualotto, Giangiorgio. "Oltre la filosofía comparata. Filosofia come comparazione." In *East and West. Identità e dialogo interculturale*, 39–61. Venice: Marsilio, 2003.

Pasqualotto, Giangiorgio. "Introduzione al pensiero di Nishida Kitaro." In *Uno studio sul bene*, trans. E. Fongaro. Torino: Bollati Boringhieri, 2007.

Pasqualotto, Giangiorgio, ed. *Per una filosofía interculturale*. Milan: Mimesis, 2008.

Pasqualotto, Giangiorgio. "Nota introduttiva: Cultura, multiculturalismo, intercultural." In *Per una filosofía interculturale*. Milan: Mimesis, 2008.

Pasqualotto, Giangiorgio. "Il mondo dove l'estetica è alla base dell'etica. Intervista di Antonio Gnoli." In *Tra Oriente ed Occidente. Interviste sull'intercultura ed il pensiero orientale*, ed. Davide De Pretto, 63–68. Milan: Mimesis, 2010.

Ueda Shizuteru. "Sein, Nichts, Weltverantwortung im Zen-Buddhismus," In *Die Verantwortung des Menschen für eine bewohnbare Welt im Christentum, Hinduismus und Buddhismus*, ed. R. Panikkar and W. Strolz, 37–58. Freiburg, Basel, Wien: Herder, 1985.

Ueda Shizuteru. "Silencio y habla en el budismo Zen." In *Las palabras del silencio*, in collaboration with the Ávila Council International Studies Centre, 2006, ed. Óscar Pujol and A. Vega, 13–38. Madrid: Trotta, 2006.

Ueda Shizuteru. *Zen y filosofía*, ed. Raquel Bouso. Barcelona: Herder, 2004.

Ueda Shizuteru. "Silence and Words in Zen Buddhism." Online at www.thezensite.com/ZenEssays/Philosophical/Silence_and_Words

Valente, José Ángel. "La experiencia abisal," In "*Nada, mística y poesía. Er*," ed. A. Vega and V. Cirlot. *Revista filosófica, número especial* 24/25 (1999), 223–236.

Vega, Amador. "Iniciación y hermenéutica: estudios de mística comparada." *Revista de la Sociedad Española de Ciencias de las Religiones* (1996), 279–283.

Vega, Amador. *Ramon Llull and the Secret of Life*, trans. J. W. Heisig. New York: Herder & Herder, 2002.

Vega, Amador. "Experiencia mística y experiencia estética en la modernidad." In *La experiencia mística. Estudio interdisciplinar*, ed. Juan Martín Velasco, 247–264. Madrid: Trotta, 2004.

Vega, Amador. "Mystical and Aesthetic Experiences in Modernity." In *Naming and Thinking God in Europe Today: Theology in Global Dialogue*, ed. Norbert Hintersteiner, 233–246. Amsterdam: Rodopi, 2007.

Vega, Amador. "Estética apofática y hermenéutica del misterio: elementos para una crítica de la visibilidad." *Diánoia* 54.62 (2009), 3–25.

Vega, Amador. "Antoni Tàpies: 'negatio negationis.' Un espacio de meditación y silencio." In *Mística y creación en el siglo XX*, ed. Victoria Cirlot and A. Vega, 241–266. Barcelona: Herder, 2012.

Vega, Amador, and V. Cirlot, "*Nada, mística y poesía.*" *Er: Revista de filosofía* 24/25 (1999), 11.

Vega, Amador, and V. Cirlot, eds. *Mística y creación en el siglo XX*. Barcelona: Herder, 2012.

Versluis, Arthur. *American Transcendentalism and Asian Religions*. New York and Oxford: Oxford University Press, 1993.

Wichmann, S. *Japonismus. Begengungen in der Kunst des 19. Und 20. Jahrhunderts*. Herrsching: Schuler Verlagsgesellschafts, 1980.

FURTHER READING

Franke, William. *A Philosophy of the Unsayable*. Notre Dame, IN: University of Notre Dame, 2014.

Ghilardi, Marcello. *Una logica del vedere. Etica ed estetica nel pensiero di Nishida Kitarô* Milan: Mimesis, 2009.

Jullien, François. *La Grande Image n'a pas de forme. Ou du non-objet par la peinture.* Paris: Seuil, 2003.

Liu, Jee Loo, and Berger, Douglas, eds. *Nothingness and Asian Philosophies.* New York: Routledge, 2014.

Magno, Emanuela, and Marcello Ghilardi, eds. *La filosofia e l'altrove. Festschrift per Giangiorgio Pasqualotto*. Milan: Mimesis, 2016.

Marra, Michael. *Modern Japanese Aesthetics: A Reader.* Honolulu: University of Hawaii Press, 1999.

Panikkar, Raimon. *Pluralisme i interculturalitat. Opera Omnia* 6.1. Barcelona: Fragmenta, 2010.

Pasqualotto, Giangiorgio. *Filosofia e globalizzazione.* Milan: Mimesis, 2011.

Sasaki, Ken'ichi, ed. *Asian Aesthetics.* Kyoto: Kyoto University Press; Singapore: National University of Singapore Press, 2010.

Taylor, Mark C. *Disfiguring: Art, Architecture, Religion.* Chicago: University of Chicago Press, 1992.

Valente, José Ángel. *Obra completa*, vol. 2. Barcelona: Galaxia Gutenberg, 2008.

Vega, Amador. *Zen, mística y abstracción. Ensayos sobre el nihilismo religioso.* Madrid: Trotta, 2002.

Vega, Amador. *Ramon Llull y el secreto de la vida.* Madrid: Siruela, 2002; English translation by J. W. Heisig, *Ramon Llull and the Secret of Life*. New York: Herder and Herder, 2004.

Vega, Amador. *Tratado de los cuatro modos del espíritu.* Barcelona: Alpha Decay, 2005.

Vega, Amador. *Arte y santidad. Cuatro lecciones de estética apofática.* Pamplona: Cátedra Jorge Oteiza, Universidad Pública de Navarra, 2005.

Watson, Gay. *A Philosophy of Emptiness.* London: Reaktion Books, 2014.

PART FOUR

Some Prominent Twentieth-Century Thinkers

CHAPTER NINE

Watsuji Tetsurō: Accidental Buddhist?

STEVE BEIN

INTRODUCTION

Watsuji Tetsurō (1889–1960) is widely regarded as Japan's most important secular philosopher of the twentieth century. Of all the many volumes of nineteenth- and twentieth-century Japanese philosophy, almost everything to reach Western audiences is Buddhist philosophy. This is for at least two reasons: (1) Western audiences have long been fascinated by Japanese Buddhism—particularly Zen—and the fact that Zen has been so fashionable would naturally tend to bring Buddhist philosophy to the fore; (2) the Buddhist philosophers of nineteenth- and twentieth-century Japan produced important, insightful, groundbreaking work, work that was worthy of the attention of a global readership regardless of any preexisting interests. It is fair to say, however, that this newer body of work is but a recent addition to a long tradition of Japanese Buddhist philosophy, a tradition dating back at least as far as Kūkai (774–835) and proceeding all the way up to the storm over Critical Buddhism in the twentieth and twenty-first centuries. By contrast, secular philosophy did not really come into prominence in Japan until the Edo period (1603–1868) at the earliest, and (as we shall see) there were those who denied that there had ever been any Japanese philosophy at all. More than anyone else it is Watsuji who has been credited with bringing secular Japanese philosophy to the global stage—that is, a Japanese philosophy that is not also a Japanese Buddhist philosophy.

Watsuji himself was well versed in Buddhism, and indeed it was Nishida Kitarō (1870–1945), a founder of the Kyoto School, who recruited him to join the faculty at Kyoto Imperial University in 1925. That said, Watsuji has only been considered an "associate member" of the school (or, as Robert E. Carter and Erin McCarthy describe him, an "honorary member"[1]), for his work was, as Bret Davis puts it, "too independent to count [him] among the inner circle of the School."[2] Watsuji's philosophy was not religious in nature, as was that of Nishida and the others, and Watsuji did not remain in Kyoto long enough to develop a closer association with the group. However, the concept of emptiness (a topic to which the Kyoto School philosophers return time and time again) is central to Watsuji's philosophy as well, and his interest in absolute emptiness probably results at least in part from Nishida's influence.

Despite his "honorary" or "associate" status, in the annals of Japanese philosophy Watsuji is held to be equal in stature to that "inner circle" (viz., Nishida, Nishitani Keiji, and Tanabe Hajime), as these were the figures who ushered Japanese philosophy onto the global stage. In this chapter we will situate him historically, lay out the fundamental elements of the body of his work that is accessible to an English readership, and examine whether or not his philosophy amounts to a de facto Buddhist philosophy.

1. EARLY LIFE

Watsuji was born in Nibuno, a small town in Hyogo Prefecture, in 1889.[3] It was a tumultuous time in Japanese history, just twenty-one years after the Meiji Restoration and thirty-six years since Japan had opened her borders to foreigners for the first time in over two centuries. The opening was forced at gunpoint, but Japan quickly came not to welcome many strains of foreign influence but to voraciously absorb them. The motivation to transform was obvious: the Japanese had only to look around, see virtually every nation in Asia under the yoke of European colonization, and refuse such a fate for themselves. The best defense was to absorb European culture, including its technology, science, art, literature, and philosophy. It is little wonder, perhaps, that the generation tasked with this absorption should produce such radically innovative thinkers as Nishida Kitarō, Nishitani Keiji, Tanabe Hajime, and Watsuji Tetsurō.

Throughout his career Watsuji would show a taste for defying convention and expanding the accepted boundaries of philosophy. Furukawa Tetsushi has remarked on Watsuji's early interest in the "poet-philosophers," an interest that nearly cost him his graduation.[4] In 1912, the year he was to matriculate, his thesis on Nietzsche was rejected (though it was published under the title *A Study of Nietzsche* (*Niiche no kenkyū*) just one year later). He completed a second thesis, "Schopenhauer's Pessimism and Theory of Salvation," barely in time to graduate. His next publication was *Søren Kierkegaard* (1915), and as Robert E. Carter and Yamamoto Seisaku note, "At that time, neither Nietzsche nor Kierkegaard were studied as a part of the philosophical canon in Japanese universities."[5]

In Watsuji's day the difference between Japanese culture and that of the major European and North American powers was stark, observable, and the subject of much thought. A major issue at the time was whether the Japanese did philosophy at all, or whether philosophy was solely a Western endeavor. The philosopher Inoue Tetsujirō (1855–1944) argued that Japan had a long tradition of philosophy, dating at least as far back as the Confucian thinkers of the Edo period.[6] On the other hand, Nakae Chōmin (1847–1901) took Inoue (among others) to task, insisting that "over the ages in our country, Japan, there has been no philosophy."[7] Watsuji sided with Inoue, and as early as *Shamon Dōgen* (1926) he made the case that Japan's philosophical tradition extends at least as far back as the Kamakura period (1192–1333) with Dōgen and Shinran.

Watsuji harbored a deep interest in his own cultural heritage from the outset of his career. He began his university life by immersing himself in the Romanticism and individualism of European philosophy and literature, but a book written by one of his professors piqued his interest in Japanese thought: namely, Nitobe Inazō's *Bushidō: Soul of Japan* (1899). Nitobe (1862–1933) was the headmaster when Watsuji studied at the First Higher School of Tokyo, and according to James Kodera, *Bushidō* "began to awaken [Watsuji] not only to the Eastern heritage but also to the study of ethics."[8] This sprout found further nourishment when Watsuji encountered Natsume Sōseki (1867–1916), one of Japan's most acclaimed writers. He would later write at length about Sōseki, ultimately publishing his reminiscences in *Revival of Idols* (*Gūzō saikō*, 1918).

Sōseki's work involved the complexities of individuals in social relationships, lamenting the stark egoism and loneliness of life in an increasingly Westernized Japan.[9] Later in his career Watsuji would make a careful study of the relationship of individuals to the communities in which they find themselves—namely, in the three-volume *Rinrigaku* (*Ethics*, 1937, 1942, 1949)—but the immediate effect of Nitobe and Sōseki's influence was to turn Watsuji away from the poet-philosophers of Europe and toward his own country. After *Revival of Idols* he published *Koji junrei* (*A Pilgrimage to Ancient Temples*, 1919), followed shortly by his three-volume *Nihon kodai bunka* (*Ancient Japanese Culture*, 1920, 1926, 1934). From 1920 to 1923 he published a series of papers later collected to comprise *Shamon Dōgen* (*Dōgen the Monk*, 1926). There would be a long series of other works on Japanese culture, philosophy, and history, including an edited translation of Dōgen's *Shōbōgenzō* in 1929.[10]

In 1927 he took a leave of absence from his teaching position at Kyoto University to study in Europe on a three-year scholarship. He arrived in Berlin in 1927, even as Heidegger's *Being and Time* was released. *Fūdo: ningengakuteki kōsatsu* (*Climates: An Anthropological Study*), one of Watsuji's best-known works, was a direct response to Heidegger. *Fūdo* is also a reflection on Watsuji's European travels, and that fact, plus the climatological determinism he seems to advocate in the book, has drawn the criticism that *Fūdo* is a philosophical lightweight.[11] Nevertheless, it does contain some significant ideas about the nature of culture and climate (Watsuji says they mutually define each other) and about Heidegger's notion of *Dasein* (which Watsuji argues ought to have more to do with our being ontologically grounded in space than being ontologically grounded in time, as Heidegger has it).

Watsuji returned to Japan after only fourteen months, drawn home by the death of his father in 1928. He returned to Kyoto Imperial University, where he was promoted to professor in 1931. In 1934 he took the prestigious position of professor in the faculty of literature at Tokyo Imperial University, where he would teach until his retirement in 1949. In the interim, of course, was the Second World War, and this would radically change his stature in the annals of Japanese philosophy.

2. THE WAR AND ITS AFTERMATH

Watsuji's reputation would see significant damage after war, some of it arguably deserved, much of it not. According to William LaFleur, "One cannot ignore how controversial Watsuji's ideas have been in post-war Japan. From 1945 until fairly recently he was condemned by Japan's Marxist intellectuals as 'conservative,' nothing more than a provider of ideological struts for the chrysanthemum throne."[12]

On this point it must be pointed out that the specter of nationalism loomed large in Japanese memory following the Second World War. Anyone and anything connected to it was held in suspicion, to the point that Japan would have neither a national flag nor a national anthem until 1999.[13]

Watsuji's critics drew an association between him and the Imperial government during the war. The work he is best known for, the *Rinrigaku*, was published on the brink of, during, and in the wake of the war, and in the third volume he is accused of defending nationalism and Japanese elitism.[14] His critics used another of his wartime works, *Sonnō shisō to sono dentō (The Idea of Reverence for the Emperor and the Imperial Tradition*, 1943), as fodder to build a reputation for Watsuji as a reactionary. This is a misreading of the text (perhaps even a deliberate misreading), for Watsuji's intent was to write a work of intellectual history, not a right-wing screed. He argues that the feeling of reverence for an idealized humane leader, which successive emperors were to attempt to embody, was originally only an ethical ideal. Over time the Imperial lineage gradually took on the status of divinity, attaining its apotheosis in the Kamakura period. Watsuji says that during the Edo period the Confucian ideal of the "Way of the Sages" (*seijin no michi* 聖人の道) was superimposed on "reverence for the emperor" (*sonnō* 尊皇), which in turn became the ideological backbone of those who supported the emperor and opposed the Tokugawa shogunate. Their movement was ultimately successful, of course, bringing about the Meiji Restoration and restoring political power to the emperor.[15] But *sonnō jōi* ("revere the emperor and expel the barbarians") is indelibly marked in Japanese memory as the slogan of the xenophobic anti-shogunate movement, and Watsuji's detractors associated his essay with that movement.[16]

His critics cite one more essay as evidence that he was a propagandist and ultranationalist: *Amerika no kokuminsei* ("The National Character of the Americans"), which Watsuji delivered as a lecture to Japanese naval commanders in 1943.[17] Watsuji's detractors would describe it as a piece of anti-American propaganda, and the fact that he delivered it to the naval high command is taken as further evidence that he was an Imperial loyalist. It is true that there are passages that smack of propaganda: he writes of the "American ambition for world conquest," says the Americans "ventured into the Pacific with the attitude of gambling scoundrels," and predicts that the Americans, being "impudent and self-righteous" and lacking the moral fortitude of the Japanese people, could only "[cling] to the might of their machines for their sole support."[18] But to focus on these passages misses the forest for the trees. The purpose of the essay was not to whip its audience into a patriotic fervor (it is safe to assume the naval commanders' patriotism was fervent enough) but rather to present an analysis of what Watsuji calls the American "pioneer spirit." He traces this back to the empiricism of Thomas Hobbes and Francis Bacon. Hobbes theorized the "war of all against all" in a hypothetical state of nature, and Watsuji says it was Hobbesian rationalizations that allowed Europeans to justify their brutal treatment of Native Americans and African slaves.[19] (The historical truth is more complex than this, but Watsuji is off to a good start.) Bacon established the scientific method, and with it a mechanistic worldview that ultimately promoted a mechanistic civilization.[20] (Again, the truth is more complex than this, but it is hard to say Watsuji is wrong as far as he goes.) Watsuji contends that Hobbesian pessimism about human nature and Baconian mechanistic empiricism mutated in North America into an "American spirit" that thrives on taking risks, being audacious, and taking pleasure in doing one's utmost.[21] This is hardly a right-wing rant; these very qualities are deemed praiseworthy in the United States. One can hardly blame Watsuji—or any Japanese person, for that matter—for finding these qualities more than a little intimidating as American forces drew ever nearer in 1943.

It is certainly possible to interpret these two essays as rightist propaganda, but that is not the only interpretation, and there are good reasons not to interpret them that way. For one thing, in *Amerika no kokuminsei* Watsuji advised *restraint*, not further expansionism. But the broader truth is that Watsuji's position was far more nuanced than his critics let on. In about 1920 Watsuji was encouraged by his friend, the folklorist Yanagita Kunio, to read the literature of Anatole France. Watsuji was taken with France's pacifism—so persuaded, in fact, that he wrote an essay disparaging Japan's imperialism in the Russo-Japanese War. Indeed, in 1925—perhaps because of that essay and Watsuji's other studies of Romantic individualism and European philosophy—Watsuji was targeted for attack by the ultranationalist Japan Principle Society as being "liberal, pro-democracy, and pro-individualism, and thus 'dangerous' in the eyes of the ultranationalists."[22]

During the Second World War Watsuji would continue to anger the far right, defending fellow scholars like historian Tsuda Sōkichi, who was forced into retirement and saw his books banned (a fate many others suffered during the war).[23] Starting in 1935, Watsuji served briefly (along with Tanabe Hajime) on the Ministry of Education's Committee for the Renewal of Education and Scholarship. In his tenure there, Watsuji and Tanabe were the lone defenders of Nishida Kitarō, who argued that if the Committee wanted to advance the study of "the history of Japan and things Japanese," it would have to "give first-rate scholars the freedom to engage in basic research," which he found to be "still in its infancy" in Japan.[24] "Without laying a solid foundation for scholarship in Japan," he said, "we have no more hope of diverting the radical infiltration of foreign ideas than the Yellow River has of becoming clear blue."[25] But this reference to the "radical infiltration of foreign ideas" was clearly tongue in cheek. Nishida found the committee to be a farce and could not even bring himself to attend in person; he submitted a written opinion instead.[26]

Like Nishida, Watsuji was arguably neither an ultranationalist nor a reactionary, though such charges have been leveled against both of them.[27] That said, it is true that Watsuji turned away from European philosophy and from individualism. This, coupled with his brief governmental service, was evidently enough for his critics; they tarred him with the same brush, associating him—loosely at best, spuriously at worst—with the militaristic aggression, the expansionism, and the human rights abuses carried out by the Imperial government during the war.

Not long after Watsuji's death, Robert Bellah suggested that one of Watsuji's crimes may simply have been writing in the wrong place at the wrong time: "The humane and gracious figure of Watsuji Tetsurō would not be problematic for modern Japan were it not for the fact that partly behind the cloak of just such thinking as his, a profoundly pathological social movement brought Japan near to total disaster."[28] Watsuji's philosophy is not totalitarian but it is totalizing: for him, individuals are always embedded in the totality that is their family, their community, their nation-state, and these in turn are always embedded in the totality that is their geography and historicity. Put simply, "individuals" do not exist in any meaningful ontological, phenomenological, or ethical sense; they can only ever be facets of a totality. But it is all too easy to overlook or misunderstand the philosophical nuance there, and the oversimplified version, "individuals do not exist; they are only facets of the totality," is the very basis of totalitarianism. This is the "profoundly pathological social movement" that "brought Japan near to total disaster."

Watsuji took steps to understand and avert this social pathology. In the spring of 1945, he organized a group of scholars to study the isolationist policy of the Tokugawa period, ultimately publishing his thoughts from their meetings in 1950 as *Sakoku: Nihon no higeki* (*Closed Nation: Japan's Tragedy*). According to William LaFleur, Watsuji's argument in *Sakoku* and elsewhere is that Japan's imperialism in the Second World War was the direct result of the Tokugawa policy that closed the nation to the outside world for over two hundred years. His argument was quite critical of the nationalists and the militarists in their prosecution of the war given the country's limited resources.[29] LaFleur even suggests that Watsuji's 1943 lecture to Imperial Navy officers, in which he warned the command staff that their strategies were dangerous, may have been the reason he felt no need to apologize after the war: he advised restraint, and it is hard to see what more an intellectual could reasonably expect to accomplish.[30]

Whatever his reasons may have been for refusing to recant, Watsuji paid the price of his reputation. According to Yuasa Yasuo, after the war there was an "attack from the left" against "the emperor-system" of government, an attack Watsuji strongly opposed. He held that the emperor-system was a unifying force for the country—a rare one in those days, we might well guess—and that the people should therefore support it. Yuasa suggests, "This act is the primary reason why Watsuji came to be seen as a conservative who could not be easily reclaimed by the liberal intellectuals with whom he had been associated."[31]

Watsuji would not see his reputation recover within his lifetime (though his stance may have earned him the emperor's favor: after the war he served as a lecturer to Crown Prince Akihito—now Emperor Akihito—on the history of Japanese culture and thought). He died on December 26, 1960, after a long bout with illness. He left behind an impressive legacy, including a *zenshū* (complete works) that runs twenty volumes. He is also succeeded by his students, of whom the best known is his former graduate assistant Yuasa Yasuo (1925–2005), one of the most significant Japanese philosophers of the twentieth century.

3. MAJOR WORKS

The perennial frustration for Watsuji scholars outside of Japan is the paucity of translations of his work in Western languages. Only three of his philosophical books have been translated into English: *Climate and Culture* (1961), Geoffrey Bownas's translation of the *Fūdo*; *Rinrigaku: Ethics in Japan* (1996), Yamamoto Seisaku and Robert E. Carter's translation of the first volume of the *Rinrigaku*; and *Purifying Zen* (2011), my own translation of *Shamon Dōgen*. Let us examine each of these in turn, in the order Watsuji wrote them.

3.1 Shamon Dōgen

Shamon Dōgen (*Dōgen the Monk*, 1926) is a remarkable text for three reasons. First, it breathed new life into a very important figure on the brink of philosophical extinction. Dōgen Kigen (1200–53) ranks among Japan's greatest Zen masters. He is the founder of Sōtō Zen in Japan (which to this day remains the largest religious sect in the country), yet despite his widespread following the Sōtō sect actively discouraged the greater public from studying Dōgen's many works for nearly 700 years.[32] The motivations for this are not entirely clear, but whatever they may have been, Watsuji thought their effect was plain to see: "I think that up until now Dōgen has been killed within the sect."[33] Thus *Shamon Dōgen* was a revolutionary book—"a bombshell," as Hee-Jin Kim describes it, which sparked off a new age of Dōgen studies.[34] Were it not for this book, it is entirely possible that no one outside of the Sōtō sect would be reading Dōgen today.

Second, *Shamon Dōgen* is one of the few monographs *by* one of Japan's greatest philosophers *about* one of Japan's greatest philosophers. It is Watsuji's only monograph on a Japanese philosopher, and it is the only monograph on Dōgen by a philosopher of Watsuji's stature. This alone makes the book worthy of study. Furthermore, a central premise of the book is that Dōgen is "our Dōgen"—that is, not merely a Zen master but a *Japanese* Zen master, one who, Watsuji contends, is the equal of China's more famous Chan masters. This places this book at the heart of Watsuji's *Nihon seishinshi kenkyū* (*A Study of the History of the Japanese Spirit*, 1925, 1935), and marks *Shamon Dōgen* as one installment in a series of volumes by Watsuji on the religions and religiosity of his motherland.

Third, in *Shamon Dōgen* we see the first traces—little more than a palimpsest, really—of Watsuji's later thought. One important example is the word *jinkaku* (人格), which appears over fifty times in this slim seventy-page volume, and which Watsuji would return to later in his career, most notably in his book *Jinkaku to jinruisei* (*Personality and Human Nature*, 1938). It was a term of art among Japanese philosophers of the early twentieth century. According to T. P. Kasulis, "*Jinkaku* had a specific philosophical use in Japan: it translated the Western idea of 'person' (or sometimes 'personality')."[35] Abe Jirō, the founder of the Japanese "personalist" movement (*jinkakushugi* 人格主義), held that "the meaning of 'person' lies in its distinction from 'thing'" and that "there is nothing that can take the place of the value of the person; at the same time, the value of all other things is assigned in terms of how the value of the person is served."[36] (The comparison to Kant's distinction between rational beings, which have dignity, and everything else, which merely has value, is readily apparent.[37]) According to Cheung Ching-yuen, Abe proposed personalism as an alternative to radical capitalism or communism,[38] but Watsuji finds deeper meaning in *jinkaku*—or rather, four meanings.

In *Shamon Dōgen* one function of *jinkaku* is to serve as the ground of moral accountability. In his chapter on Shinran and Dōgen, Watsuji takes Shinran to task for his apparent fatalism: "But what is the meaning of responsibility if people 'attribute all acts, whether good or bad, to causality' and simply *cling devotedly to Amida*? Are we to believe that one's actions do not arise out of one's personality [*jinkaku*] but are rather imposed from outside? No, this is not the case."[39] Watsuji does not deny that many of our decisions are subject to our baser instincts, our animalistic cravings and aversions, our cultural and ancestral mores. He even grants the assumption that our behavior is rooted in karmic dependency. However, he says that we are capable of rising above all of that due to the uniqueness of our *jinkaku*—not how it manifests at any given time but what it truly is, right down to its roots: "The foremost root quality of our personality is existence above and beyond karmic dependency. Therefore, acts dictated by karmic dependency do not arise out of *this* root quality of our personality. Even if our personality manifests itself as being wrapped up in karmic dependency, this root quality of our personality denies those deeds and seeks forgiveness for them."[40] In Shinran's defense, it is worth noting that Shinran himself would not deny this. (Indeed, this sums up the essence of the *Nembutsu* rather neatly.) But regarding Watsuji's understanding of *jinkaku*, it is clear that this "root quality of our personality" (*jinkaku no honshitsu* 人格の本質) is the basis of moral accountability.

A second meaning of *jinkaku* is the exceptional charisma of certain individuals, fully in keeping with the English term "cult of personality." Watsuji does not mean this in any pejorative way; throughout the book (indeed, from the very first sentence) he expresses great admiration for Dōgen's personality. Clearly this sense of *jinkaku* is intertwined with the previous one: those whose force of personality is so strong that they can found a religious sect must take their moral responsibility seriously, and they are ideally placed to encourage their followers to do the same.

The third sense of *jinkaku* operates almost on the level of a soul. The Dharma transmission in Zen Buddhism—that is, the transmission of enlightenment—supersedes verbal communication, and Watsuji describes it as being transmitted from one *jinkaku* to the other.[41] (This idea of transmission has found its way into modern conversation: in Japanese people still speak of an *ishin-denshin* (以心伝心), or what we might call a "heart-to-heart talk" in English. The *den* of *ishin-denshin* means "transmission" and originates in the Buddhist idea of Dharma transmission.) In *Shamon Dōgen* Watsuji highlights the importance of a topic that rarely reaches the spotlight in Zen scholarship outside of Japan: the selection of a master, the responsibility for which Dōgen places firmly on the shoulders of the student. One ought to select a guru only when that teacher's *jinkaku* is so strong that it beckons the student. This is the first moment of *ishin-denshin*, and it was the search for it that—according to Watsuji, at any rate—drove Dōgen to abandon his life in Japan and travel China in search of a "true person" to guide his study of the Buddha-Way.[42]

Watsuji's fourth sense of *jinkaku* has to do with the character of enlightenment itself. In chapter 4 Watsuji writes of Dōgen's realization that he must abandon his old ways and cleave to the ways preached by his master. There Dōgen says, "Throwing out all your own thoughts and views and listening to your teacher is the most important point to watch while studying the way." To this Watsuji adds the following commentary:

> Clearly there is no concern at all for individuality here. Whether or not one imitates, whether or not one follows, grasping the eternal truth is the only important thing. This does not mean the disposal of individuality but rather the exultation of it. The possibility of imitating and following exists only along the path of self-cultivation; it has no relation to the realization of truth itself. Realization of the truth has its own distinctive personality (*jinkaku*). Only in the moment of realization does that individuality shine out as unique in all the universe.[43]

Watsuji seems to be working with two distinct types of individuality in this passage, both against a backdrop of Buddhist thought. One is the egocentric individuality most people experience on a day-to-day basis, since they do not understand the central insight Dōgen would have them understand: namely, that all beings are but manifestations of a unified whole. In other words, this everyday brand of individuality includes the belief that one exists as a distinct entity, independent of all others. The second type of individuality we might label "authentic individuality." In this state of awareness the individual can see that individuality is nothing but a singular manifestation of the Buddha-Dharma, which is the universe and all that is in it. Authentic individuality is the individuality of waves in the ocean: though one can discern one wave from the others, one recognizes that no wave has a claim to existence independently of the ocean, nor indeed of any other wave.

When Watsuji writes of both disposing of individuality and exulting it, it is egocentric individuality that is cast off and authentic individuality that is lifted up. He speaks of the patriarchs taking hold of self-cultivators and carrying them to enlightenment. When this happens, egocentric individuality disappears and the practitioner realizes authentic individuality. All the buddhas and patriarchs participate in and are a part of this authentic individuality, the individuality that transcends the particular human form. As we shall see, this transcendence from the egoistic to the authentic bears a certain resemblance to the process of double negation Watsuji lays out in the *Rinrigaku*. His rejection of unfettered individualism there parallels his rejection of egocentric individuality here. Here, authentic individualism eclipses and ultimately erases egocentric individualism; there, the socialized individual trumps the radical egoist. But there remains a significant difference between the two: in *Shamon Dōgen* his claim is that the *jinkaku* of enlightenment itself fuels the transcendence from the egocentric to the authentic, whereas in the *Rinrigaku* no appeal is made to anything transcendent.

3.2 *Fūdo*

Of central importance in Heidegger's *Being and Time* is the concept of being-in-the-world, which stipulates that there is no Cartesian ego, no tabula rasa, no independently existing mind. Phenomenologically speaking, human experience is always "worlded," so to speak: it always takes place in a "referential totality" in which things have meaning only in relation to other things.[44] For instance, a hammer is a hammer only in a world with nails. Nails and hammers each have their own in-order-to (*das Um-zu*), both perfectly suited to fit not only each other but also the human hand, the lumber, and so on. If a naked Cartesian ego were somehow to spring into being ex nihilo, it could not experience a hammer as a hammer; in the absence of the referential totality, there is only a heavy, awkwardly weighted *je ne sais quoi*.

Watsuji felt strongly that Heidegger did not go far enough, for despite the latter's efforts to escape the specter of Cartesian solipsism, his vision of Dasein's being-in-the-world is still too solitary. The referential totality of the hammer ought also to include the culture in which the carpenter hammers the nail. Carpenters build roofs, among other things, and a Norwegian carpenter must build a steeply sloped roof if it is to shed the heavy snows. Carpenters in Watsuji's low-lying hometown of Nibuno need not share this concern, but they need to know a good deal more about earthquakes and typhoons than their Scandinavian counterparts. In the opening of the *Fūdo* (1935) Watsuji says, "All of us live on a given land, and the natural environment of this land 'environs' us whether we like it or not."[45] Clothing, architecture, and even basic vocabulary are all cultural responses to climatic conditions. In fact, the linkage is so tight that he says it is nonsensical to speak of culture and climate as if they exist independently of one another: "From the very first, climate is historical climate. In the dual structure of man—the historical and the climatic—history is climatic history and climate is historical climate. History and climate in isolation from each other are mere abstractions."[46]

This is the ground of Watsuji's first model for understanding human existence (*ningen sonzai* 人間存在): we are "worlded" beings who always discover themselves in a particular geohistorical context. This context affects our identity through and through. Watsuji's chief criticism of *Being and Time* was that Heidegger devoted too much attention to our being in *time* and not enough attention to our being in *space*. In the concept of *fūdo*, time corresponds to history and space corresponds to geography, but both of these exist in a mutually defining, mutually transformative interplay with one another. Cultures arise in response to the environments in which they find themselves, and so when human beings engage in self-discovery, they always find themselves in a culture that has already been acclimatized, and a climate that has already been acculturated.

Just how to translate the word *fūdo* has been somewhat controversial. A literal translation—"wind and earth"—clearly falls short of the mark. Augustin Berque argues that Geoffrey Bownas's translation, "climate" or "climates," is also unsuitable, and goes so far as to say that this translation is indicative of the fact that Bownas has misunderstood the concept entirely.[47] Berque translates *fūdo* as "milieu" but devotes greater focus to *fūdosei* (風土性), which Bownas translates as "the function of climate" and Berque translates as "mediance."[48] I would argue that mediance is no clearer than *fūdosei*; as a neologism it is just as foreign, and therefore in just as much need of translation (though it must be noted that *fūdosei* itself is a neologism first coined by Watsuji, and in that sense Berque's approach is elegant, albeit unclear). This point is not lost on Berque: he initially translates "mediance" as "the sense of a milieu; at the same time, objective tendency, sensation/perception, and signification of this medial relationship."[49]

What makes "milieu" a strong choice, and "climate" not as viable, is that *fūdo* has the connotation of being highly localized. A *fūdobyō* (風土病), for instance, is an endemic disease specific to a particular location. As he was writing Watsuji had the *fudoki* (風土記) in mind, "regional reports" once collected by the central government detailing a specific province's agricultural output, meteorological records, public works, and even its folklore and tall tales.[50] At the close of the Meiji period Japan had sixty-eight provinces, and therefore at least sixty-eight potential *fudoki*, though of course the largest of these might well deserve more than one. (For instance, Tokyo's neighborhoods are both numerous and distinct. Many of these might well warrant *fudoki* of their own.)

Elsewhere I have suggested "acclimatized culture" and "acculturated climate" as interchangeable translations of *fūdo*, as these capture Watsuji's assertion that "in the dual structure of man—the historical and the climatic—history is climatic history and climate is historical climate."[51] (In reading *fūdo* this way, we must still keep in mind that cultures include subcultures and climates include microclimates. *Fūdo* remains highly localized and highly specific.) *Fūdosei*, then, is the sense of acculturated acclimatization. Consider, for example, stepping outside into the cold. Whether or not -1°C counts as "cold" depends in part on one's subjective experience but in larger part on where one is, where one is from, and how everyone else there reacts. In Sapporo, on Japan's north island of Hokkaido, winter temperatures routinely dip below freezing. In tropical Kagoshima, far to the south on Kyushu, subzero temperatures are rare in the extreme. With the lone exception of the actual reading on the thermometer, a -1°C day in Sapporo is in no way similar to a -1°C day in Kagoshima. In one city it is cause to play outside in the snow; in the other it is cause to close down schools. Watsuji puts the point this way:

> We feel the same cold in common. . . . The fact that the feeling of cold differs between us is possible only on the basis of our feeling the cold in common. Without this basis it would be quite impossible to recognise that any other "I" experiences the cold. Thus, it is not "I" alone but "we," or more strictly, "I" as "we" and "we" as "I" that are outside in the cold.[52]

Individuals discover themselves in the cold, and discover their neighbors too. But *fūdo* is also the ground of an entire culture's self-discovery, even including its most basic moral values. Watsuji cites diet as a case in point:

> It is not that man made the choice between stock-raising and fishing according to his preference for meat or fish. On the contrary, he came to prefer either meat or fish because climate determined whether he should engage in stock-raising or fishing. In the same way, the predominant factor governing the choice between a vegetable or a meat diet is climate, rather than the vegetarian's ideology.[53]

This, then, is world-in-the-being: *fūdo* is the very ground of human experience, the mirror that serves as "a means for man to discover himself."[54]

It was mentioned earlier that the *Fūdo* is widely regarded as a philosophical featherweight. This is because while the first chapter is primarily about *fūdo* and *fūdosei*, the next four chapters have more to do with ***kokumin jikaku*** (国民自覚 national character). To put it frankly, ***kokumin jikaku*** is a half-baked idea. As Bruce B. Janz observes, the idea that cultures have a specific character is not only a "vast over-generalization" but also falsely "sees those cultures as largely self-contained and self-sustaining over time."[55] Some of Watsuji's political opponents dubbed him as a rightist because of his advocacy of ***kokumin jikaku***, which is fundamentally conservative in nature. David Dilworth points out that the idea of national character crops up elsewhere in Watsuji's thought, most importantly in *Nihon rinri shisōshi* (*History of Japanese Ethical Thought*, 1952), a distillation of some of Watsuji's more propagandistic wartime and prewar writings.[56] Dilworth argues that "there is therefore a consistent thread of thought stretching over twenty years that climaxed with the appearance of the *Nihon rinri shisōshi*," and this is one of the main premises of his argument that Watsuji was a right-wing ultranationalist.[57]

As we have already seen, Watsuji's political position was not quite so straightforward or univocal, but setting politics aside it remains that the idea of national character fails to reflect what we know about social science. It may be that a later translator will find hidden wisdom in the later chapters of the *Fūdo*—Augustin Berque suggests that Geoffrey Bownas has missed a great deal[58]—but for the present, it is reasonable for Watsuji scholars to treat the first chapter of the *Fūdo* more seriously than the rest.

3.3 Rinrigaku, volume one

Only the first volume of the *Rinrigaku* (*Ethics*, 1937) has been translated into English, and the translators, Yamamoto Seisaku and Robert E. Carter, drew criticism for omitting the latter two, which are the most controversial.[59] There, at least in the earlier editions, Watsuji is accused of defending Japanese exceptionalism (though as William LaFleur observes, "Watsuji seems to have happily excised the jingoism from it once the war was over"[60]). For the present, we will set all that aside and speak of the *Rinrigaku* in the form that is accessible to an English readership: that is, as a single volume.

The *Rinrigaku* does not appear to be a book on ethics—at least not in the sense that Jeremy Bentham, John Stuart Mill, Immanuel Kant, and Aristotle write on ethics, not in the sense that fits the standard Introduction to Ethics syllabus, not in the sense that most academic ethics journals understand ethics. Watsuji offers no formula for determining right from wrong, no abstract universal principles, no virtues to inculcate, no criteria for defining moral and immoral behavior. We can ask, therefore, why the book is titled *Ethics* at all.

Watsuji's answer is audacious: Kant and Mill, Bentham and Aristotle, introductory ethics courses and top-ranked ethics journals, all misunderstand the subject of ethics itself. The first chapter of the *Rinrigaku* is called "The Significance of Ethics as the Study of Man," and there Watsuji lays the groundwork for the second of his models for understanding human existence. (The first, you will remember, is that of human beings embedded in *fūdo*—that is, in acculturated climates.) His primary criticism of the moral traditions of the Western canon is that they all begin with a faulty assumption about the moral agent—namely, that there exists an autonomous, independently existing consciousness that "does" ethics. After Descartes this could be called the Cartesian assumption, but something like it dates back at least as far as Plato (whose model of the *psyche*, tripartite though it may be, was still *one* entity with three parts) and pervaded Christian moral doctrine (damnation and salvation being distinctly private phenomena: there is no amount of sin *I* can commit that will condemn *you* to hell) more than a millennium before Descartes was born. Watsuji thinks this is fundamentally wrongheaded, and he says a more accurate, more elegant, more satisfying understanding of the moral agent is latent in the word *ningen* (人間), the ordinary Japanese word for "human being."

The two characters that comprise *ningen* capture the oppositional, dialectical nature of our being. *Nin* (人 person) represents the private, the personal, the individual, and the autonomous, while *gen* (間 between) represents the public, the communal, the societal, and the cooperative. These two sets of drives are engaged in a creative tension born out of a "dialectic of double negation": each negates the other in order to assert itself.[61] The collective naturally quashes the desires of egoistic individuals, and individuals naturally resist the desires of a collectivizing society. Yet at the same time the individualistic aspect of our being cries out for independence while the sociable aspect cries out for community. Thus *nin* works to subvert *gen* just as *gen* works to subvert *nin*, and from this conflict emerges the socialized individual, a *nin* that has negated *gen* just as it was first negated by *gen*.

Like Aristotle, Watsuji contends that we are social creatures, and in this respect *ningen* is not so different from the *zōon politikon*. But where Aristotle says this communality is rooted in our *ergon*, the characteristic function of our being, Watsuji says we discover it in absolute negation, i.e., emptiness. There is no *nin* without *gen*; in declaring autonomy, *nin* must have someone to defy. Similarly, there is no *gen* without *nin*, no collectives without members. This is the essence of what Watsuji calls "the negative structure of a human being."[62] In and of themselves, both *nin* and *gen* are empty (and here we see one facet of Watsuji's loose association with the Kyoto School). This means ethics *cannot* take place in the kind of atomic, self-contained, radically individuated mind that Descartes imagines, for there are no such minds. Rather, ethics takes place in the emptiness or betweenness (*aidagara* 間柄) between *ningen* and *ningen*:

> The context of ethical problems is not to be found within the consciousness of the isolated individual, but rather within the mediating space or "betweenness" that exists between one person and another. Ethics thus is none other than what could be called the study of human being. Without seeing ethics as the study of this dynamic mediating space, which exists between one person and another, we will not be able to unravel the nature of virtue, responsibility, obligations, and of the good and the bad within human actions.[63]

At last we may return to the question of ethics. In the above passage, Watsuji makes reference to the very things we study in an introductory ethics course or write about in academic ethics journals: virtue, responsibility and obligation, good and bad actions. This comes in the first chapter of the *Rinrigaku*, so it is clear that he has these ideas in mind from the outset, but in the subsequent chapters his efforts are mostly in metaethics, punctuated by long excursions into existentialism and the spatiality and temporality of human existence. We must ask, then, what he means by ethics in the first place.

Three kanji comprise the word *rinrigaku*: *rin* (倫), which Watsuji reads as "fellows" (*nakama*) and which also entails fellowship; *ri* (理), which means "reason" or "principle" and which—being etymologically associated with a unit of linear measurement (*ri* 里), which in turn is etymologically rooted in a rice field (*ta* 田)—strongly connotes organization or pattern; and *gaku* (学), meaning "study of" (closely analogous to the suffix "-ology"). Thus, Watsuji says, "*rinri*, that is, ethics, is the order or the pattern through which the communal existence of human beings is rendered possible. In other words, ethics consists of the laws of social existence."[64] Notice, then, that for Watsuji ethics is *ontological*.

Thus there is an enormous gulf between Watsuji's basic project and the basic project of, say, Bentham and Mill. The utilitarians are perfectly content to leave metaphysics to its own domain and to concern themselves with ethics as a standalone discipline. We cannot quite say the same of Kant and Aristotle—they are well known for their work in metaphysics—but we can say that they tend to separate metaphysics and ethics (and other topics too: epistemology, etc.) into separate works. And this, of course, is how modern university courses in philosophy were first constructed, along the same lines drawn by the first great philosophical taxonomer, Aristotle.

Watsuji, on the other hand, straddles these lines. (He is hardly alone, of course, and in fact many of the subjects of his monographs—Dōgen, Nietzsche, Confucius—do the same. So did Heidegger, who is perhaps Watsuji's greatest influence.) The frustration with Watsuji as an ethicist is that it is not clear what he actually stands for. It is clear that he thinks of human beings as having a "negative structure"—that is, our structure as the ongoing double negation of *nin* and *gen*—but he gives us nothing like a utility principle or a categorical imperative. Instead he gives us "the fundamental law of human being," which he also calls "the basic principle of ethics": "The negative structure of a human being is … the fundamental law that renders a human being capable of continuously forming itself. Were we to deviate from this law, we would cease to exist."[65] And again: "We can describe the basic principle of ethics in terms of 'the movement in which absolute negativity returns back to itself through negation.' "[66]

The former seems to merely reiterate *ningen*'s dialectic of double negation, which he also calls *ningen*'s "dynamic structure of reciprocal transformation."[67] The latter seems like more of the same, lacking as it is in any kind of overtly moral language. (Surely there ought to be an *ought* in there somewhere.) He does say that Jesus and the Buddha engaged successfully in this movement but that their later adherents fell short of it, so that is an implicit moral endorsement. However, if *ningen* is absolutely empty by nature, and if by nature it is engaged in this constant self-abnegation, then he has only described the "is," not the "ought." That means we are still stuck in his ontology and have not yet reached his ethics.

We must read him very carefully indeed if we are to find his ethics. Here is as close as he gets to defining moral wrongness:

> In revolting against one community or another, one revolts against one's own foundation. As an act, the movement of this rebellion is toward the destruction of community as well as being a revolt against one's own foundation. This is why this movement is not approved of by the other participants in the community, any more than it is approved by one's innermost essence. This movement is called *badness*.[68]

What is at stake here is the distinction between what I have called "creative tension" and "destructive tension."[69] "Revolting against one community or another" indicates *nin* negating *gen* in an effort to assert itself, and in this passage Watsuji makes it clear that this "revolt" and "rebellion" is destructive (hence the disapproval not only of the community but also of the very person engaged in rebellion). If this is badness, and if it is true that the reciprocal, dialectical struggle between *nin* and *gen* is the very nature of our being, then either all of our behavior is bad (in which case badness means nothing at all) or there is some way to engage in this struggle that is not destructive, not rebellious, and not disingenuous to oneself.

Watsuji has already described what such creative tension would look like: it is "the movement in which absolute negativity returns back to itself through negation."[70] That is, it is not *nin* negating *gen*, but rather *ningen* itself engaging in the double negation of both *nin* and *gen*—negating not rebelliously but selflessly, not destructively but creatively. (This was foreshadowed in *Shamon Dōgen*: *nin*, the person as against the community, is egocentrically individual. *Ningen*, the socially contextualized person, is authentically individual.) For *nin* to negate *gen* purely out of egoism is inauthentic, disingenuous to the individual, and unwanted by the community. If that is moral badness, then moral goodness is the opposite: *nin* and *gen* engaged in a creative, productive, altruistic transformation, one that is harmonious with both the community and the individual's own authentic self-expression.

Now what would this look like in practice? Watsuji does not tell us. His principle says nothing definitive about the permissibility of abortion, stem cell research, eating meat, exploiting ecosystems, or any of a host of other ethical problems. There are some debates on which we can infer a clear pronouncement—for instance, it is hard to see how torture could be genuinely authentic, selfless, and productive for all parties involved—but in most respects his moral philosophy (such as it is) has little light to shed in the field of applied ethics.

That said, if we take the *Rinrigaku* in the context of the *Fūdo* we can get closer to filling out a Watsujian environmental ethics. *Ningen* and *fūdo* share a dynamic, reciprocal, mutually transformative relationship that is quite similar to *nin* and *gen*'s. The *Fūdo* is not generally categorized as a work of ethics, but since Watsuji did not observe hard and fast distinctions between the philosophical disciplines, we can hardly say that the metaphysics and phenomenology he develops there are without moral implications. Given the parallel structures of the individual/

communal relationship and the culture/climate relationship, we can make stronger Watsujian claims in environmental ethics than perhaps any other area within moral philosophy.[71]

CONCLUSION: THE ACCIDENTAL BUDDHIST?

It was claimed from the outset that the majority of Japanese philosophy in the last two centuries to reach a Western readership has been Buddhist philosophy, and that Watsuji is widely regarded as Japan's most important secular philosopher. There is a caveat, however: scholars who do not read Japanese currently have no access to his Buddhist corpus aside from *Shamon Dōgen* and a handful of references within the *Rinrigaku*. In point of fact, Buddhist thought was a wellspring to which Watsuji would repeatedly return throughout his career. His early work, *The Practical Philosophy of Primitive Buddhism* (1927), is as yet untranslated, as are the lecture notes published in his *Zenshū* as "The History of Buddhist Ethical Thought" (1963), to say nothing of his various treatises on the history of Japanese thought and culture, which are (necessarily) suffused with Buddhism.

Of course a Buddhologist need not be a Buddhist. Watsuji's deep familiarity with Buddhist philosophy in no way implies that he is a Buddhist philosopher—certainly not in the sense that Nishida and Nishitani are. That said, one cannot ignore that Buddhist metaphysics are at the very heart of Watsuji's most important ideas. William LaFleur argues that Watsuji's ethics and aesthetics are ultimately grounded in the Buddhist conception of emptiness (*śūnyatā*). As LaFleur puts it, "The understanding of emptiness here is entirely consistent with Nāgārjuna's exposition of it; it is co-dependent origination."[72] Notice, for example, the way Watsuji explains the emptiness of *ningen*:

> Individuals are empty in themselves; only the negation of their respective community establishes them. If so, then we can say that before the individuality of the subject is discarded in the associative collectivity, this individuality was already established through the negation of the community. Therefore, association is "the discarding of individuality that appears in the form of the discarding of the community." This is double negation.[73]

What Watsuji calls "double negation" is exactly what Nāgārjuna calls "dependent co-origination." Nāgārjuna uses numerous examples to demonstrate the principle, some of which can be quite abstruse, so LaFleur humanizes them by grounding the principle in the most fundamental of social relationships: the relation of parent and child. It is not simply that parents bring children into being; children bring parents into being. A woman becomes an expectant mother the moment the existence of the embryo is known, and in that sense the embryo "creates" her as an expectant mother. Because neither the child nor the parent has any independent existence, because each exists only if the other exists, LaFleur says neither one has ontological priority over the other. He goes on to say,

> The ascription of *priority* is what, in Watsuji's view as well, misrepresents reality and, in addition, puts philosophy off balance. In keeping with the tradition of

Buddhism derived from Nāgārjuna, Watsuji holds that every trace of the notion of independent existence must be voided. The negations themselves are mutual and it is only in this kind of dialectic that an adequate understanding of man can, he holds, emerge.[74]

One might suggest, then, that if Watsuji's philosophy is not openly and explicitly Buddhist, it might still be *accidentally* Buddhist—that is, it might be so heavily influenced by Buddhism that the Buddhism cannot be extracted from it. (There is no shortage of philosophers in the Western canon who are accidentally Christian in just this way.) One might then ask is it *matters* whether or not Watsuji is accidentally Buddhist, and if so, whether an accidental Buddhist is properly counted among Japan's most influential *secular* philosophers.

I would argue that it does matter. It was inevitable that a boy born in Meiji era Japan would be heavily influenced by Buddhism; we cannot escape our milieux. Perhaps it was something close to inevitable that a Meiji-era Japanese university student who became acquainted with Nietzsche (whose philosophy is sympathetic to Buddhist thought in many respects) and Schopenhauer (who was himself deeply influenced by Buddhist philosophy) would find himself drawn to study Buddhism in greater detail. And given that background, it should certainly come as no surprise if a newly minted professor recruited by Nishida Kitarō himself took his abiding interest in Buddhism to a deeper level. Where Watsuji differs from Nishida and the Kyoto School—or one place where they differ, at least—is in their understanding of what Buddhism is, and of what religion is in general. As Kōsaka Masaaki puts it, "The difference is that while for Watsuji religion, just like scholarship and the arts, is to be included within 'culture,' for Nishida religion is not considered to be something simply cultural."[75]

At the outset the question was posed: is Watsuji's philosophy a de facto Buddhist philosophy? The answer is no. As William LaFleur observes, "It was in the Buddhist notion of emptiness that Watsuji found *the* principle that gives his system … coherence."[76] Nevertheless, Buddhism is not simply *śūnyatā*, and so while it is certain that Watsuji and his Buddhist contemporaries largely agree on the *importance* of this principle, they do not necessarily agree on the *nature* of the principle, and they certainly do not agree on its religious significance (or lack thereof). If Watsuji's philosophy takes emptiness as its cohering principle, it is in the end a Watsujian emptiness, not necessarily a Buddhist one.

NOTES

1. Robert E. Carter and Erin McCarthy, "Watsuji Tetsurō," *Stanford Encyclopedia of Philosophy*, http://plato.stanford.edu/entries/watsuji-tetsuro/#Not (accessed June 14, 2016).
2. Bret Davis, "The Kyoto School," *Stanford Encyclopedia of Philosophy*, http://plato.stanford.edu/entries/kyoto-school/ (accessed June 13, 2016).
3. Sections of this biography appeared in similar form in my *Purifying Zen* (Honolulu: University of Hawai'i Press, 2011).

4. Furukawa, "Watsuji Tetsurō, the Man and His Work," in Watsuji, *Climate and Culture: A Philosophical Study*, trans. Geoffrey Bownas (Tokyo: Hokuseido Press, Ministry of Education, 1961), 219.
5. Carter and Yamamoto, *Watsuji Tetsurō's* Rinrigaku*: Ethics in Japan* (Albany: State University of New York Press, 1996), 1; hereafter referred as *Rinrigaku.*
6. John A. Tucker and Chun-chieh Huang, *Dao Companion to Japanese Confucian Philosophy* (Dordrecht: Springer, 2014), 6–10.
7. *Nakae Chomin Shū*, 168, quoted by Abe Masao (*An Inquiry into the Good*, vii). Abe points out that to answer whether or not the Japanese did philosophy, one must first ask what is meant by "philosophy." Abe Masao and Christopher Ives, trans., *An Inquiry into the Good* (New Haven, CT: Yale University Press, 1990), viii–xi.
8. James Kodera, "The Romantic Humanism of Watsuji Tetsurō," *Dialogue & Alliance* 1.3 (1987), 6.
9. Ibid.
10. Others include *Practical Philosophy of Primitive Buddhism* (*Genshi bukkyō no jissen tetsugaku*, 1927), *National Seclusion: Japan's Tragedy* (*Sakoku: Nihon no higeki*, 1950), the two-volume *History of Japanese Ethical Thought* (*Nihon no rinri shisōshi*, 1952), *A Study of Japanese Arts* (*Nihon no geijutsu kenkyū*, 1955), and the work he is best known for in philosophical circles, the three-volume *Ethics* (*Rinrigaku*, 1937, 1942, 1949).
11. Augustin Berque argues that he does not—and in fact could not—advocate climatological determinism. See Berque, "Offspring of Watsuji's Theory of Milieu (Fūdo)," *GeoJournal* 60 (2004), 391.
12. *Rinrigaku*, viii.
13. The *hi no maru*—a red disc on a white field—is recognizable to nearly everyone, but legally speaking, from 1945 to 1999, it was merely emblematic, not official.
14. Even Watsuji's translators have drawn criticism on this count: in reviewing Yamamoto and Carter's translation of the Rinrigaku, David Gordon takes the translators to task for only translating the first two volumes. See "Rinrigaku: Ethics in Japan," *Philosophy East and West* 49.2 (1999), 216–218.
15. Watsuji Tetsurō, "*Sonnō shisō to sono dentō*," WTZ 14.7–294.
16. I am indebted to Michiko Yusa for these observations about *Sonnō shisō to sono dentō*.
17. See, for example, Peter Dale, *The Myth of Japanese Uniqueness* (New York: St. Martin's Press, 1986), and for an example of a similar (though less acerbic) indictment among Japanese philosophers. Also see Sakabe Megumi, "Watsuji Tetsurō—Case of Philosophical Thinking in Modern Japan," in *Traditional Thought and Ideological Change: Sweden and Japan in the Age of Industrialization*, ed. Seung-bog Cho and Nils Runeby (Stockholm: University of Stockholm Press, 1988), 155–167. According to William LaFleur, "This view of things ... is the almost universally accepted interpretation." "Reasons for the Rubble: Watsuji Tetsurō's Position in Japan's Postwar Debate about Rationality," *Philosophy East and West* 51.1 (2001), 5.
18. Watsuji Tetsurō, "*Amerika no kokuminsei*," WTZ 17, 481.
19. Ibid., 459–461.

20. Ibid., 457–459.
21. I am indebted to Michiko Yusa for this observation about *Amerika no kokuminsei*.
22. Michiko Yusa, "Nishida and Totalitarianism: A Philosopher's Resistance," in *Rude Awakenings: Zen, the Kyoto School, and the Question of Nationalism* (Honolulu: University of Hawai'i Press, 1995), 119–120.
23. Minamoto Ryōen, "The Symposium on 'Overcoming Modernity,'" in *Rude Awakenings*, ed. James W. Heisig and John C. Maraldo (Honolulu: University of Hawaii Press, 1995), 201.
24. Yusa, "Nishida and Totalitarianism," 116.
25. Ibid.
26. Ibid.
27. I will not develop a full case for or against them here, but see Heisig and Maraldo, *Rude Awakenings*; Graham Parkes, "The Putative Fascism of the Kyoto School and the Political Correctness of the Modern Academy," *Philosophy East and West* 47.3 (1997); and Robert N. Bellah, "Japan's Cultural Identity: Some Reflections on the Work of Watsuji Tetsurō," *The Journal of Asian Studies* 24.4 (1965).
28. Bellah, "Japan's Cultural Identity," 593.
29. LaFleur, "Reasons for the Rubble," 3.
30. Ibid., 5–8, 10.
31. Watsuji, *Rinrigaku*, 313.
32. See Steve Bein, *Purifying Zen: Watsuji Tetsurō's* Shamon Dōgen (Honolulu: University of Hawai'i Press, 2011), 28–29. For a study of the modern repercussions, see Ian Reader, "Zazenless Zen? The Position of Zazen in Institutional Zen Buddhism," *Japanese Religions* 14.3 (1986) 7–27.
33. Bein, *Purifying Zen*, 28.
34. Kim, *Dōgen Kigen*, 2.
35. Bein, *Purifying Zen*, 139.
36. Abe Jirō, "A Critique of Human Life," JPS 817; italics removed.
37. Immanuel Kant, *Grounding for the Metaphysics of Morals* (Indianapolis: Hackett, 1981), 434.
38. Cheung, "Abe Jirō," JPS 816.
39. Bein, *Purifying Zen*, 63; emphasis in the original.
40. Ibid., 64.
41. Ibid., 106.
42. This is the subject of *Shamon Dōgen*, chapter 2; see Bein, *Purifying Zen*, 34–44.
43. Bein, *Purifying Zen*, 57.
44. Heidegger, *Being and Time*, trans. Joan Stambaugh (Albany: State University of New York Press, 1996), 76.
45. Watsuji, *Climate and Culture*, 1.
46. Ibid., 10.

47. A. Berque, "Offspring of Watsuji's Theory of Milieu (*Fūdo*)," 390.
48. Ibid., 389–390.
49. A. Berque, *Mediance: de milieux en paysages* (*Mediance: From Milieux to Landscapes*), 48, cited in Berque, "Offspring of Watsuji's Theory of Milieu," 391. In the latter essay he branches away from this initial definition and comes to define "mediance" in entirely non-Watsujian terms as the coupling of the human "social body" and "animal body" (392, 394).
50. John C. Maraldo, "Between Individual and Communal, Self and Other, Subject and Object: Mediating Watsuji Tetsurō's Hermeneutics," in Michael F. Marra, *Japanese Hermeneutics: Current Debates on Aesthetics and Interpretation* (Honolulu: University of Hawai'i Press, 2002), 85, 76–86.
51. Watsuji, *Climate and Culture*, 1. My translations as "acculturated climate" and "acclimatized culture" appear in J. Baird Callicott and James E. McRae, eds, *Japanese Environmental Philosophy* (Oxford University Press, 2017).
52. Ibid., 4.
53. Ibid., 10.
54. Ibid., 8.
55. Bruce B. Janz, "Watsuji Tetsurō, Fūdo, and Climate Change," *Journal of Global Ethics* 7.2 (2011), 180.
56. D. Dilworth cites *Nihon seishin* (The Japanese Spirit, 1934) and "*Nihon shindō*" (The Way of the Japanese Subject, 1943), to which I would add some of the more egregious passages from the latter chapters of *Fūdo* and the third volume of the *Rinrigaku*.
57. D. Dilworth, "Guiding Principles of Interpretation in Watsuji Tetsurō's *History of Japanese Ethical Thought*: With Particular Reference to the Tension between the Sonnō and Bushidō Traditions," FJP (2008), 107.
58. Berque, "Offspring of Watsuji's Theory of Milieu," 390–391.
59. David Gordon, "*Rinrigaku*: Ethics in Japan," *Philosophy East and West* 49.2 (1999), 216–218.
60. William LaFleur, "Buddhist Emptiness in the Ethics and Aesthetics of Watsuji Tetsurō," *Religious Studies* 14.2 (June 1978), 241.
61. Watsuji, *Rinrigaku*, 22–24.
62. Ibid., 119.
63. Watsuji, "The Study of Human Being," JPS 860.
64. Watsuji, *Rinrigaku*, 11.
65. Ibid., 119.
66. Ibid.
67. Ibid., 124.
68. Ibid., 133; emphasis in the original.
69. I draw this distinction in "Climate Change as Existential Threat: Watsuji, Greimas, and the Nature of Opposites," in *Japanese Environmental Philosophy*, ed. J. Baird Callicott and James McRae (Oxford University Press, 2017).
70. Watsuji, *Rinrigaku*, 119.

71. James McRae develops an argument more fully along these lines in “Triple Negation: Watsuji Tetsurō on the Sustainability of Ecosystems, Economies, and International Peace,” in *Environmental Philosophy in Asian Traditions of Thought*, ed. J. Baird Callicott and James McRae (Albany: State University of New York Press, 2014), 359–376.
72. LaFleur, “Buddhist Emptiness in the Ethics and Aesthetics of Watsuji Tetsurō,” 247.
73. Watsuji, *Rinrigaku*, 115.
74. LaFleur, “Buddhist Emptiness in the Ethics and Aesthetics of Watsuji Tetsurō,” 245; emphasis in the original.
75. Kōsaka Masaaki, *Nishida Kitarō to Watsuji Tetsurō* (Tokyo: Shinchōsha, 1964), 109–110.
76. LaFleur, “Buddhist Emptiness in the Ethics and Aesthetics of Watsuji Tetsurō,” 239.

BIBLIOGRAPHY

Abe Jirō. “A Critique of Human Life,” JPS 816–821.

Bein, Steve. *Purifying Zen: Watsuji Tetsurō’s* Shamon Dōgen. Honolulu: University of Hawaii Press, 2011.

Bein, Steve. “Climate Change as Existential Threat: Watsuji, Grimas, and the Nature of Opposites.” In *Japanese Environmental Philosophy*, ed. J. Baird Callicott and James McRae. Oxford University Press, 2017.

Bellah, Robert N. “Japan’s Cultural Identity: Some Reflections on the Work of Watsuji Tetsurō.” *The Journal of Asian Studies* 24.4 (1965), 573–594.

Berque, Augustin. “Offspring of Watsuji’s Theory of Milieu (Fūdo).” *GeoJournal* 60 (2004), 389–396.

Callicott, J. Baird, and James McRae. *Environmental Philosophy in Asian Traditions of Thought*. Albany: State University of New York Press, 2014.

Callicott, J. Baird, and James McRae. *Japanese Environmental Philosophy*. Oxford: Oxford University Press, 2017.

Carter, Robert E., and Erin McCarthy. “Watsuji Tetsurō.” *Stanford Encyclopedia of Philosophy*, http://plato.stanford.edu/entries/watsuji-tetsuro/#Not (accessed June 14, 2016).

Carter, Robert E., and Yamamoto Seisaku. *Watsuji Tetsurō’s* Rinrigaku*: Ethics in Japan*. Albany: State University of New York Press, 1996.

Dale, Peter. *The Myth of Japanese Uniqueness*. New York: St. Martin’s Press, 1986.

Davis, Bret. “The Kyoto School.” *Stanford Encyclopedia of Philosophy*, http://plato.stanford.edu/entries/kyoto-school/ (accessed June 13, 2016).

Dilworth, David A. “Guiding Principles of Interpretation in Watsuji Tetsurō’s *History of Japanese Ethical Thought*: With Particular Reference to the Tension between the Sonnō and Bushidō Traditions.” FJP (2008), 101–112.

Furukawa, Tetsushi. “Watsuji Tetsurō, the Man and His Work.” In *Watsuji, Climate and Culture: A Philosophical Study*, trans. Geoffrey Bownas. Tokyo: Hokuseido Press, Ministry of Education, 1961.

Gordon, David. “Watsuji Tetsurō’s *Rinrigaku*: Ethics in Japan.” *Philosophy East and West*

49.2 (1999) 216–218.

Heidegger, Martin. *Being and Time*, trans. Joan Stambaugh. Albany: State University of New York Press, 1996.

Heisig, James W., and John C. Maraldo, eds. *Rude Awakenings*. Honolulu: University of Hawaii Press, 1995.

Janz, Bruce B. "Watsuji Tetsurō, Fūdo, and Climate Change." *Journal of Global Ethics* 7.2 (2011) 173–184.

Kant, Immanuel. *Grounding for the Metaphysics of Morals*. Indianapolis: Hackett, 1981.

Kim, Hee-Jin. *Dōgen Kigen: Mystical Realist*. Tuscon: University of Arizona Press, 1987.

Kodera, James. "The Romantic Humanism of Watsuji Tetsurō." *Dialogue & Alliance* 1.3 (1987), 4–11.

Kōsaka Masaaki. *Nishida Kitarō to Watsuji Tetsurō* [Nishida Kitarō and Watsuji Tetsurō]. Tokyo: Shinchōsha, 1964.

LaFleur, William. "Buddhist Emptiness in the Ethics and Aesthetics of Watsuji Tetsurō." *Religious Studies* 14.2 (1978), 237–250.

LaFleur, William. "Reasons for the Rubble: Watsuji Tetsurō's Position in Japan's Postwar Debate about Rationality." *Philosophy East and West* 51.1 (2001) 1–25.

Maraldo, John C. "Between Individual and Communal, Subject and Object, Self and Other: Mediating Watsuji Tetsurō's Hermeneutics." In *Japanese Hermeneutics: Current Debates on Aesthetics and Interpretation*, ed. Michael F. Marra, 76–86. Honolulu: University of Hawaii Press, 2001.

Minamoto, Ryoen. "The Symposium on 'Overcoming Modernity.'" In *Rude Awakenings*, ed. J. W. Heisig and J. C. Maraldo, 197–231. Honolulu: University of Hawaii Press, 1995.

Nakae, Chōmin. *Nakae Chōmin Shū* [Collected works of Nakae Chōmin]. Tokyo: Misuzu Shobō, 1984.

Nishida, Kitarō. *An Inquiry into the Good*, trans. Abe Masao and Christopher Ives. New Haven: Yale University Press, 1990.

Parkes, Graham. "The Putative Fascism of the Kyoto School and the Political Correctness of the Modern Academy." *Philosophy East and West* 47.3 (1997), 305–336.

Reader, Ian. "Zazenless Zen? The Position of Zazen in Institutional Zen Buddhism." *Japanese Religions* 14.3 (1986) 7–27.

Sakabe, Megumi. "Watsuji Tetsurō—A Case of Philosophical Thinking in Modern Japan." In *Traditional Thought and Ideological Change: Sweden and Japan in the Age of Industrialization*, ed. Seung-bog Cho and Nils Runeby, 155–167. Stockholm: University of Stockholm Press, 1988.

Tucker, John A., and Chun-chieh Huang. *Dao Companion to Japanese Confucian Philosophy*. Dordrecht, NL: Springer, 2014.

Watsuji, Tetsurō. *Climate and Culture: A Philosophical Study*, trans. Geoffrey Bownas. Tokyo: Hokuseido Press, 1961.

Watsuji, Tetsurō. WTZ. Tokyo: Iwanami Shoten, 1961–63.

Watsuji, Tetsurō. *Rinrigaku: Ethics in Japan*, trans. by Yamamoto Seisaku and Robert E. Carter (Albany: State University of New York Press, 1996).

Watsuji, Tetsurō. "Watsuji Tetsurō." JPS 850–869.

Yusa, Michiko. "Nishida and Totalitarianism: A Philosopher's Resistance." In *Rude Awakenings: Zen, the Kyoto School, and the Question of Nationalism*, ed. J. W. Heisig and J. C. Maraldo, 107–131. Honolulu: University of Hawaii Press, 1995.

FURTHER READING

Bein, Steve. *Purifying Zen: Watsuji Tetsurō's* Shamon Dōgen. Honolulu: University of Hawai'i Press, 2011.

Callicott, J. Baird, and James E. McRae, eds. *Japanese Environmental Philosophy*. Oxford: Oxford University Press, 2017.

Carter, Robert E. *Encounter with Enlightenment*. Albany: State University of New York Press, 2001.

Heisig, James W., T. Kasulis, and J. C. Maraldo, eds. JPS.

Heisig, James W., and John C. Maraldo, eds. *Rude Awakenings: Zen, the Kyoto School, and the Question of Nationalism.* Honolulu: University of Hawaii Press 1995.

Watsuji Tetsurō. *Climate and Culture: A Philosophical Study*, trans. Geoffrey Bownas. Tokyo: The Hokuseido Press, Ministry of Education, 1961.

Watsuji Tetsurō. *Rinrigaku: Ethics in Japan*, trans. Yamamoto Seisaku and Robert E. Carter. Albany: State University of New York Press, 1996.

CHAPTER TEN

Encounter in Emptiness: The I-Thou Relation in Nishitani Keiji's Philosophy of Zen

BRET W. DAVIS

Since Nishida Kitarō's pivotal essay of 1932, "I and Thou" (*Watashi to nanji* 私と汝),[1] the question of what it means for one individual to relate to another has been a recurrent topic among modern Japanese philosophers associated with the Kyoto School. In part, this no doubt reflects contemporaneous attention given to this question in the West, especially in the wake of Martin Buber's *Ich und Du*.[2] Yet the relation between persons has of course always been a central concern of East Asian thought. Nishitani Keiji (1900–90), Nishida's student and the central figure of the second generation of the Kyoto School, demonstrates how the I-Thou relation has been deeply—he argues *most* deeply—fathomed in the Zen tradition.[3] The present chapter aims to elucidate and examine this crucial, yet heretofore insufficiently discussed, dimension of Nishitani's philosophy of Zen.[4]

1. THE TWOFOLD SELF AND ITS ENCOUNTER WITH OTHERS

The relation between persons is frequently at issue in Nishitani's magnum opus *What Is Religion?* (*Shūkyō to wa nanika* 宗教とは何か, translated into English as *Religion and Nothingness*),[5] and is also the focus of several of his lectures and essays, including a talk given to the emperor and empress of Japan in 1969 entitled "The Human Relation as 'I and Thou'" (*Ware to nanji to shite no ningen kankei* 我と汝としての人間関係).[6] Yet Nishitani's most concise and penetrating—if also perhaps most difficult—treatment of this topic is surely his 1961 interpretation of a Zen dialogue or "*mondō*" (問答),[7] a text that Nishitani himself co-translated into German as "Vom Wesen der Begegnung,"[8] and which has been translated into English by Norman Waddell as "The I-Thou Relation in Zen Buddhism."[9] Near the beginning of this text Nishitani writes that the investigation into the interpersonal encounter one finds in Zen is distinct from "all biological, sociological, anthropology, ethical and other kinds of explanations that are made from a distance, from somewhere outside the encounter itself. Such explanations attempt to explain the entirety of the encounter without having reached into it depths." "After Martin Buber," Nishitani goes on to write, "this encounter has been emphatically characterized as the 'personal' relation between 'I and Thou.' This characterization is accurate enough, yet a great problem lies unrecognized precisely at the bottom of this 'personal' relation of 'I and Thou.' And it is with this problem that the investigation of Zen begins."[10]

According to Nishitani, in order to understand the interpersonal encounter one must think through, rather than evade, a fundamental paradox. "Two factors must be thoroughly, and without compromise, borne in mind," he writes. "First, as subjectivities, both the I and the Thou are absolutes, each in its own respective subjectivity. And second, I and Thou are absolutely relative to one another."[11] Elsewhere Nishitani says that "the basic structure of human existence," which "may at first appear contradictory," is that a human being is both "a singular absolute individual" and a being that "coexists" together with others.[12] The question is, how can the self be both absolutely independent and entirely relative? As we shall see, Nishitani's answer lies in what I will call "the irreducibly twofold nature of the self": on the one hand, the self is a relative being standing over against other relative beings; and yet, on the other hand, the ultimate "home-ground" (*moto* もと) of the self is the "field of emptiness" (*kū no ba* 空の場) that engenders and encompasses such relations between relative beings. In order to understand the I-Thou relation in all its dimensions, neither aspect of the self can be neglected.

Catching sight of the absoluteness of the self, while at the same time maintaining a sense of its relativity vis-à-vis other selves, entails nothing short of a religious awakening. And yet, the sense of "religion" is here significantly different from Middle Eastern and Western conceptions of transcendent theism. Nishitani agrees with such Western philosophers as Scheler, Buber, and Levinas that the I-Thou relation can only be fathomed by taking into account its religious background or context. Yet Nishitani understands this religious context in terms of Zen Buddhism rather than Abrahamic monotheism.

2. THE RELIGIOUS BACKGROUND, OR FIELD, OF THE I-THOU RELATION

Nishitani understands the religious background of the I-Thou relation as the "field" (*ba* 場) on which this relation takes place. He writes: "The 'absolute' is in fact the basis of the field in which the I-Thou relation is established; it is ... the fundamental field itself [*konpon-teki na ba sono mono* 根本的な場そのもの], that is, the field of the higher dimension" in which the I-Thou relation takes place.[13] "The 'I-Thou' relation," Nishitani says elsewhere, "harbors the potential to unfold into a relation with a great force that gives life to both the I and the Thou. In other words, the I-Thou relationship contains a pathway that leads to religion."[14] Here as elsewhere in his later writings, Nishitani understands "religion" in terms of "the awareness that one lives by being given life" (*jibun ga ikasarete ikiteiru no da to iu jikaku* 自分が生かされて生きているのだという自覚).[15] The finite and relative self is given life, literally "enlivened," not only by other finite and relative entities (persons, animals, plants, inanimate things), but also and ultimately by "something absolute" (*zettai-tekina mono* 絶対的なもの), something "infinite" (*mugen* 無限), which Nishitani refers to in these lectures as "a great force" (*ōkina chikara* 大きな力).[16]

Yet this "something absolute," this "great force"—or, as he refers to it in *Religion and Nothingness*, "nature" as a "field of force" (*chikara no ba* 力の場) that lets the finite and relative self live in interdependence with all other finite beings[17]—is not simply something outside the self. Like Nishida, Nishitani thinks of God or Buddha, not as an otherworldly being, nor as an *externally transcendent* infinite Other that is "beyond being," but rather as an *immanently transcendent* source of individual freedom and compassion as well as an *encompassing "place"or "field"* that enables ethically responsible relations between individuals to take place. The absolute, for Nishitani, as for Nishida, is thus not ultimately to be addressed as "the Eternal Thou" (*das ewige Du*), as it is for Buber.[18] Nor is God a transcendent Father, an "absolute exteriority" to be approached by means of what Levinas calls "trans-ascendance" (*transascendance*).[19] Rather, God or Buddha is found directly underfoot, in the bottomless depths of the self, by way of what Nishitani calls "trans-descendence."[20] In contrast to an Abrahamic theism that pursues a path of external transcendence, Nishida suggests that "Buddhism is characterized by an orientation toward immanent transcendence."[21] Similarly, Nishitani writes that "the distinguishing feature of Buddhism consists in its being a religion of the absolute near side."[22]

Nishitani understands the absolute as "the field of emptiness" which "opens up on the absolute near side of what is spoken of as our ego or subjectivity."[23] Indeed he thinks of God or Buddha in terms of the "Buddha-nature" or "original face" of the true self; it is the "radical subjectivity of non-ego" (*muga no kongen-teki shutaisei* 無我の根源的主体性)[24] which lies beneath the strictures of egoistic subjectivity. Moreover, this Buddha-nature is not only the source of the self's individual freedom and compassion but also the encompassing place or "field of emptiness" in which relative beings interrelate.

In *Religion and Nothingness*, after saying this field of emptiness is a "field of force" in which things have their being in "mutually circulating interpenetration" (*ego-teki sōnyū* 回互的相入) with other things, Nishitani goes on to say that

> this field opens up in the self when the self is truly in the self's home-ground. . . . The roothold of the possibility of the world and of the existence of things, namely, the place where the world and the existence of things "take hold of their ground," can be said to lie in the home-ground of each person, underfoot and right at hand.[25]

The "field of emptiness" is the ultimate "home-ground" of each and every human being. It is both the source of their individual absoluteness and the abode of their nondual or "mutually circulating" relativity. And yet, most humans most of the time remain oblivious to this as their "Buddha-nature" or "original face"; most humans most of the time falsely identify themselves with an egoistic subjectivity standing in dualistic opposition to other egoistic subjectivities. Hence, one ego clashes with another and a struggle ensues that is defined by what Nietzsche calls "the will to power."[26] In brute form, this struggle takes the form of a battle in which, as the Latin proverb puts it, "man is a wolf to man" (*Homo homini lupus*).[27] In the process of civilization, this struggle may pass through Hegel's "dialectic of master and slave" to a contractual society in which laws are enforced so as to restrict the violent clash of egos, or in which this clash is refashioned into athletic, economic, and other "civilized" forms of competition.[28] And yet, even in the most democratically administered societies, human relations can remain fundamentally characterized by a struggle for privilege and power between mutually antagonistic subjectivities. According to Nishitani, externally imposed universal laws can regulate, but cannot fundamentally alter, the "the so-called 'state of nature' in which humans are wolves to one another." "The original basis of the encounter between one individual and another remains concealed, even under the laws of the state, the rules of morality, or the commandments of God."[29] In order to reveal this original basis of human relations, it is necessary to undergo an existential or religious conversion, namely, a trans-descendence to the field of emptiness as a self-awakening to the home-ground of self and other.

3. A DHARMA BATTLE BETWEEN MASTERS OF ABSOLUTE SUBJECTIVITY

What would an encounter be like between two persons who had in fact awakened to their home-ground on and as the field of emptiness? This is what happens in the *mondō* Nishitani explicates in "The I-Thou Relation in Zen Buddhism." This *mondō*, which appears as case sixty-eight in *The Blue Cliff Record*, takes place as the following enigmatic exchange between Kyōsan Ejaku (Ch. Yangshan Huiji) and Sanshō Enen (Ch. Sansheng Huiran).

> Kyōsan Ejaku asked Sanshō Enen, "What is your name?"
> Sanshō said, "Ejaku!"
> "Ejaku!" replied Kyōsan, "that's my name."
> "Well then," said Sanshō, "my name is Enen."
> Kyōsan roared with laughter.[30]

As we reflect on this dialogue, the main points to bear in mind are the following: (1) Kyōsan asks Sanshō for his name, even though he must have already known it; (2) Sanshō responds with Kyōsan's name rather than his own; (3) Kyōsan says, "that's my name!"; (4) Sanshō then declares his own name; and finally (5) the dialogue ends with Kyōsan's roaring laughter.

According to Nishitani, if understood in all its competitive, playful, masterful, and compassionate dimensions, this *mondō* "shows the true significance contained in the encounter of one person with another."[31] The encounter between Sanshō and Kyōsan reveals not only "that it is impossible for two persons to live under the same sky," but also that "in everyday reality this nevertheless becomes possible,"[32] and moreover that "absolute opposition [can] be at the same time absolute harmony."[33]

Nishitani sets out to show how this *mondō* is a condensed demonstration of the fact that this apparently "blatant contradiction" can be our most concrete reality.

The encounter between Kyōsan and Sanshō is said to reveal both the "boundless terror" and the "boundless beauty" that lie at the bottom of the interpersonal encounter.[34] To begin with, we need to understand the "boundless terror" by looking at the "eat or be eaten" contest that "naturally occurs" when one master of absolute subjectivity encounters another.

Kyōsan's initial question, "What is your name?" can be understood as asking Sanshō to objectify himself and thus be appropriated into the world of Kyōsan's absolute subjectivity. To understand why this is so, we need to reflect on the significance of "names." In the past, Nishitani notes, the name "symbolized the reality of something; it became a manifestation of the thing itself; it gradually became united with the reality of the thing."[35] This is why, says Nishitani, if "a woman disclosed her name to a man, it meant that she had disclosed herself to him, had already given herself to him."[36] Even today, when we introduce people to each other, we generally start by giving the name of the person of inferior status to the person of superior status. A policeman or a border guard demonstrates his or her authority when he or she demands that someone show an ID or passport (though in a democratic society, one has the right, i.e., legal power to demand that the policeman show his ID in turn). In fact, with regard to Kyōsan's query, "What is your name?" Hakuin remarks that "it is like a policeman interrogating some suspicious fellow he has found loitering in the dark." In short, as Engo (Ch. Yuanwu) puts it, when Kyōsan asks for Sanshō's name, "He robs at once the name and the being (*meijitsu sōdatsu* 名実相奪)" of his interlocutor.[37]

Yet what is being demonstrated in the *mondō*, Nishitani tells us, is not simply an attempt by one relative ego to willfully usurp the name and being of another. It is rather the natural result of one who has experienced the absoluteness of the true self, the self who has realized that he is "of one body with all things," the self who can say, in the words attributed to the newborn Śākyamuni Buddha, "I alone am holy throughout heaven and earth."[38] Nishitani writes: "When that which has the nature of an absolute operates in the relative world, its operation, naturally of itself, disallows all relativity. That which opposes the self as 'other' must be stopped short in its tracks, taken into the self and appropriated."[39] Unlike the willful struggle for domination between relative egos, however, in this case, that is, "insofar as the self is its own master and maintains its full subjectivity—which is to say, insofar as it is in a true sense a 'self'—this will happen of itself, naturally [*onozukara* おのづから]."[40] Just as, mythologically speaking, when a Buddha appears in the world, he spontaneously turns that world into his own Buddha Land, so it is that when a Zen master arrives on the scene, he naturally becomes the center of attention, the leading actor (*shujinkō* 主人公) in the surrounding play of life.

But then, does that mean that two Buddhas could not coexist in the same land? Could two Zen masters not live in the same monastery? These questions are not as rhetorical or as flippant as they might seem. Indeed, the encounter between Kyōsan and Sanshō reveals to us the terrifying difficulty involved in two persons living under the same sky. For, just as the I, as absolute subject, naturally appropriates all others, "from the side of the Thou as subject, the same could be said to hold true." And so, "the I-Thou relation is, in an essential sense, a relation of 'either eating or being eaten.'"[41] The willful battle between unenlightened egos could thus be said to be rooted in an essential truth of human subjectivity that is in a sense magnified, not eradicated, upon enlightenment. The self, in its absolute subjectivity, naturally appropriates others.

Nevertheless, such natural appropriation of others is not the only manner in which the enlightened self operates. According to the "four classifications" of Linji, it is one of four ways. Specifically, it corresponds to the second of these, namely: "taking away the surroundings and not taking away the person" (*dakkyō fudatsunin* 奪境不奪人). Linji metaphorically describes this as a military conquest: "The rule of the sovereign prevails throughout the land; the general has laid to rest the dusts of battle beyond the frontiers."[42] A monadic master rules over his world, which has become an environment encircling his throne, a "universe" wherein everything turns around and is turned toward him as the sovereign center. The sovereign self brings peace to the world by allowing nothing and no one to oppose his rule. Of course, although Linji uses such military and political metaphors, and although he famously urges us to "just make yourself master of every situation, and wherever you stand is the true [place],"[43] he is not counseling a self-assertion of one's own relative ego over others. On the contrary, the true sovereign is one who has undergone the "great death," one who has died to the egoistic will to power and cares only for the welfare of all in the world, because he or she identifies with everything and everyone rather than with his or her own relative ego set in dualistic opposition to others.

4. SEPARATE MOUNTAIN PEAKS GREETING ONE ANOTHER

Still, the question remains: Can there be "others" in such a nondualistic universe? Could there be a relation between absolute masters, and, if so, could this relation be other than that of a fight to the death? How could there be more than one sovereign center of the universe? Nishitani notes how this question is raised in the Zen tradition metaphorically in terms of the experience of what Engo calls "wonderous mountain peaks of solitude" (*myōbukochō* 妙峰孤頂) where "each one is the whole" (*ichi ichi kaizen* 一一皆全). The question is, as Nishitani puts it: What does it mean for "an absolute 'single person' to encounter another absolute 'single person'"? For example, how can one encounter the monk Tokuun if he does not descend from his solitary mountain peak? Hakuin answers: By way of realizing that "I am originally of one body (*dōtai* 同体) with Tokuun; this is precisely a matter of 'separate mountain peaks greeting one another' (*beppō-shōken* 別峰相見)."[44] The metaphor is revealing. On the one hand, each of the two mountain peaks is unique and the two are separated by the deep valley that lies between them. On the other hand, the two mountains are both rooted in, and are each literally expressions of, the same earth; they are "originally of the same body." Each is both absolute, as a single focal point gathering the whole earth, and relative, as one focal point among other focal points. Thus, for Zen, the "mountain peak" not only refers to the attainment of absolute solitude, but also signals the "turning point" to a most profound relation with others: "the marvelous mountain peak is also the place of a Zen *Communio* (i.e., religious interrelation)."[45]

Echoing expressions used by Cusanus and Nishida,[46] Nishitani speaks of the field of emptiness as a "circumferenceless sphere whose center is everywhere."[47] This field is discovered through immanent transcendence through the depths of one's self, and indeed discovered *as* the very basis of one's true self. The self thus has both infinite and finite dimensions: it is both absolute and relative. On the one hand, the self is the "field of emptiness" itself as a "field of force" that engenders and gathers all things. "As a being in unison with emptiness, then, the self is one absolute center, and, to that extent, all things are in the home-ground of the self."[48] "Every human being in its selfness contains the field of that force by virtue of which the selfness of all things is gathered into one as a world."[49] On the other hand, "each human being is at the same time one 'thing' in the world among others."[50] The self is thus what I am calling a *twofold self*: it is both absolute and relative; on the one hand, it is the field of emptiness that engenders and embraces both the relative self and the relative other, and on the other, it is a singular focal point of this field, a unique focus that stands over against other unique foci.[51]

In a foreword to a collection of articles on his philosophy, Nishitani relates a personal episode of watching the sunrise from a hotel balcony, and having the "overwhelming experience that the radiance of the sun was focused on me and that the whole world was opening brightly, concentrated on myself alone." And yet, he goes on to say, this experience of "the whole is myself" does not exclude an openness to the fact that a person on the next balcony may be enjoying the same experience.[52] Indeed, although legend has it that *at the time of his birth* Śākyamuni Buddha said, "*I alone* am holy throughout heaven and earth," there is also a legend that, *at the time of his enlightenment* upon seeing the morning star, he said rather, "*All beings* have the wisdom and virtues of the Tathāgata."[53]

5. THE MUTUAL EXCHANGE OF HOST AND GUEST

As we have seen, not only the I but also the Thou, as absolute subject, naturally becomes the center of the universe, absorbing the I along with everything else into his or her environment.[54] From the perspective of the self, this could be said to correspond to the first of Linji's classifications: "taking away the person and not taking away the surroundings" (*datsunin fudakkyō* 奪人不奪境). In this case, the "surroundings" into which the self is taken away is the world of another person.

What would it mean to experience another person as the center of the universe? Buber well illustrates such an experience in his account of what it means to address another authentically as Thou: "He is no longer He or She, limited by other Hes or Shes, a dot in the world grid of space and time.... Neighborless and seamless, he is Thou and fills the firmament. Not as if there were nothing but he; but everything else lives in *his* light."[55] In the language of Huayan Buddhism, which both Linji and

Nishitani employ, the other is granted the role of "host" or "master" (*shu* 主) and all the rest of the world, including oneself, are relegated to the role of "guest" or "servant" (*hin* 賓, *kyaku* 客, or *jū* 従).[56] However, whereas Levinas might say that one should always remain a guest, that the ethical subject remains always "subjected" and even held "hostage" to the other,[57] for Zen the ideal is a mutual exchange, an appropriate circulation, of the roles of guest and host. As Ueda Shizuteru writes, "The free exchange of the role of host is the very core of dialogue."[58] "On the ethical plane," Ueda writes elsewhere, "the emphasis, obviously, falls on the moment of self-negation when the role of host or master is surrendered to the other. But this does not mean a one-sided sacrifice of self. At bottom it is a question of reciprocal exchange in 'giving priority to the other.'"[59]

Similarly, in *Religion and Nothingness* Nishitani depicts the field of emptiness as a "system of mutual circulation" in which "all things are in a process of becoming master and servant to one another."[60] In the concluding paragraph of the book, Nishitani writes: "True equality ... comes about in what we might call the reciprocal interchange of absolute inequality, such that the self and the other stand simultaneously in the position of absolute master and absolute servant with regard to one another. It is an equality in love."[61]

In such a relationship, "giving priority to the other" does not always mean to stand in the relative position of guest or servant. In a dialogue, sometimes it is proper to speak, while at other times it is proper to listen; and in cooperative activity with others, sometimes it is proper to lead and give orders, while at other times it is proper to follow and obey. The true "master" of which Linji speaks when he urges one to "become a master wherever you are"—in other words, the "true person of no rank" (*mu-i no shinnin* 無位の真人)—should thus not be understood as one who insists on occupying the *relative* standpoint of the "master" or "host" as opposed to the relative standpoint of the "guest," but rather as one who is rooted in the absolute "standpoint of emptiness" (*kū no tachiba* 空の立場). Nishida calls this standpoint of emptiness the "standpointless standpoint, wherein all standpoints are negated, and wherefrom all standpoints arise."[62] It can be understood in terms of what Zhuangzi calls the "pivot of the Way,"[63] that is, the empty hub that allows the wheel of the self to freely and responsively circulate between the relative roles of host and guest. When Nishitani says that "the self and the other stand simultaneously in the position of absolute master and absolute servant with regard to one another," this can be understood to mean that self and other are both rooted in this "locationless location [*shozai naki shozai* 所在なき所在],"[64] this empty hub that allows a free and responsive circulation among relative roles of host and guest, master and servant.

With Nishitani's notion of a "reciprocal interchange of absolute inequality," we have reached, at least in a preliminary form, an answer to the question of what it would mean for one "master" to meet another, as in the case of the *mondō* between Kyōsan and Sanshō. Although at first it seems that this meeting between masters stages a battle between subjects attempting to subdue and objectify one another—a battle to determine who is master and who is servant—to determine who gets devoured by whom, who gets relativized and objectified by whose absolute subjectivity, this is not in fact what ultimately occurs. As Zen master Ōmori Sōgen comments, in this *mondō* we witness rather "an exceptional dynamic of 'the exchange of host and guest' [*hinju gokan* 賓主互換]."[65] Let us return to Nishitani's account to see how the *mondō* unfolds.

6. WHENCE AND WHITHER KYŌSAN'S LAUGHTER: THE LOCATIONLESS LOCATION

Kyōsan begins the "Dharma battle," as we have seen, by asking for Sanshō's name. But then, when Sanshō responds to Kyōsan's request for his name with Kyōsan's own name, to his astonishment Kyōsan discovered that he had "caught a thief" who "turned the tables on him and robbed him of everything he owned." By responding to Kyōsan's demand for his name with Kyōsan's own name, "Sanshō actually took over for himself, as it were, Kyōsan's absolute nature," that is, the nature of "the one who will not allow any 'Thou' to stand in opposition to him and who would take all others into his 'self.' "[66]

But the *mondō* does not end there. Kyosān then says "Ejaku, that's my name!" How should we understand this? It could be thought that Sanshō's surprise counter-attack startled Kyōsan into declaring—and identifying himself with—his own name, such that he *inadvertently* becomes an object absorbed into Sanshō's world. This interpretation seems to be suggested in Nishitani's comment: "Skirting Kyōsan's defenses and attacking him from behind under the banner or his own self, Sanshō pulls the rug from under Kyōsan's feet, and seizes his very existence."[67] However, as is reflected in Engo's and Hakuin's comments, Kyōsan—who was already a great master and senior to Sanshō—is traditionally understood to have *freely* confessed his name, thus voluntarily descending (*kōge* 向下) into the realm of relativity. Sanshō is then understood to have accepted the invitation when he in turn declares his own name. Hence, rather than vying over the position of the absolute subject by "holding fast" (*hajō* 把定), they each "let go" (*hōgyō* 放行) in order to harmoniously coexist in the realm of relativity.

Whereas the first half of the *mondō* seems—at least on one level—to reveal the "unbounded horror" of the "absolute opposition" of "eating or being eaten," "devouring or being devoured," that underlies "the reality of the I-Thou encounter in everyday life," the latter half demonstrates the "infinite beauty" of the "harmony and concord" achieved in a true I-Thou relation.[68] This mutual letting-be on the plane of relativity corresponds to Linji's fourth classification: "taking away neither person nor surroundings" (*ninkyō gufudatsu* 人境俱不奪), here implying the harmonious coexistence of self and other.

This harmonious coexistence is not simply a contractual regulation of the battle between self-assertive egos, but rather a free circulation of host and guest, that is, a reciprocal exchange of the role of host or master (as we have seen depicted in Linji's second classification) and the role of guest or servant (as we have seen depicted in Linji's first classification). Moreover, this circulation is made possible in the first place by way of the realization of the state depicted in Linji's third classification: "taking away both person and surroundings" (*ninkyō gudatsu* 人境俱奪), a state radically before and beyond the appearance of either self or other.

The *mondō* ends, we recall, with Kyōsan's laughter. Nishitani writes:

> The tale of this encounter, which comes to a close with Kyōsan giving his name and Sanshō giving his, ends with Kyōsan's roaring laughter. This roaring laughter is the point of the whole tale. It is at this point that the struggle—which is really a "playful *samādhi*"—and with it all the singing and clapping, drumming and dancing, comes to an end. What was once battleground and the place where men sang in unison has now turned back to the place of origin.... The men who stood face to face in confrontation, relative to one another, are now gone. Kyōsan and Sanshō too are no longer there. All that remains is the resonance of Kyōsan's laughter.[69]

With reference to this *mondō*, Zen masters Setchō and Daitō prod us with the question: "To what place does this laughter go?" We could equally ask: "From what place does this laughter come?" Nishitani suggests that Kyōsan's laughter expresses "the ultimate conjunction of *Mahāprajñā* (great wisdom) and *Mahākarunā* (great compassion)."[70] This conjunction would take place precisely at "Kyōsan's locationless location,"[71] that is to say, at the null point, the standpointless standpoint of emptiness. It is this null point, this empty hub, which allows for a wise and compassionate circulation between roles of host and guest, master and servant. Only by radically stepping back to this absolute null point prior to the emergence of either self or other can one freely and responsibly reenter a relation of mutual circulation in which I and Thou are "not one and not two."

7. MUTUAL CIRCULATION: HARMONY OF COMPASSIONATE LOVE AND COMPETITIVE PLAY

The relation between persons can be harmonious rather than merely combative on account of the compassion or "other-centeredness" involved in this relation of mutual circulation. We have seen how the first half of the *mondō* between Kyōsan and Sanshō exposes the "unbounded horror" of "absolute opposition" that underlies the everyday encounter between persons, insofar as each person tends to reduce the other to an object in the universe of his or her own absolute subjectivity. Indeed, on one level, Kyōsan's asking for Sanshō's name and Sanshō responding with Kyōsan's name epitomize this existential struggle of "eat or be eaten." And yet, Kyōsan's query can be understood, not just as a "natural" assertion of the appropriating powers of his absolute subjectivity, but also as a sportive test of the newly arrived Sanshō. Moreover, as Nishitani suggests, Sanshō's response, in which he identifies himself with Kyōsan's name, can be understood, not simply as a passing of this test by means of appropriating the would be appropriator, but also, and on a deeper level, as a natural manifestation of Sanshō's compassion, in which he "absolutely empties himself and puts Kyōsan in his own place."[72] Whereas in the battle between self-centered egos each attempts to appropriate the nondifferentiation of self and other into his or her own absolute subjectivity, here Sanshō freely expropriates this nondifferentiation and grants it to Kyōsan. In other words, Sanshō abnegates his own "name" and hands his "being" over to Kyōsan.

The "absolute negation of self-love," Nishitani writes in *Religion and Nothingness*, opens up a "non-differentiating love where all others are loved individually 'as oneself.'"[73] "Hence," he goes on to say,

> the standpoint on which one sees oneself in others and loves one's neighbor as oneself means that the self is at the home-ground of every other in the "nothingness" of the self, and every other is at the home-ground of the self in that same "nothingness." Only when these two are one—in a relationship of mutually circulating interpenetration—does this standpoint come about.[74]

As we have seen, Nishitani suggests that the harmony of a relation of true "equality in love" comes about by means of "the reciprocal interchange" of such freely bestowed "absolute inequality."[75] "On the field of emptiness," writes Nishitani, "all things are in a process of becoming master and servant to one another in a system of mutual circulation. In this system, each thing is itself in not being itself, and is not itself in being itself."[76] That is to say, the true self is able to serve as the host or master of all other beings precisely because it can subordinate itself as guest or servant of all other beings.[77] Indeed, Nishitani claims that the "nonduality of self and other" realized here entails that "absolute subordination and absolute autonomy come about in unison."[78] This entails that "true self-centeredness" is realized precisely in breaking through egocentricity. Nishitani writes:

> True self-centeredness is a selfless self-centeredness: the self-centeredness of a "self that is not a self." It consists of … "mutually circulating interpenetration" on the field of emptiness. The gathering together of the being of all things at the home-ground of the being of the self can only come about in unison with the subordination of the being of the self to the being of all things at their home-ground.[79]

In "The I-Thou Relation in Zen Buddhism," Nishitani elaborates on this relationship of "mutually circulating interpenetration" as follows:

> Where the other is at the center of the self, and where persons become mutually "other-centered," absolute harmony reigns. This might be called "love" in the religious sense… . Absolute harmony is not simply nondifferentiation. Self and other are not one, and not two. To be not one and not two means that each self retains its absoluteness while still being relative, and that in this relativity the two are never for a moment separated.[80]

The I seeing itself in the Thou and the Thou in itself, on the one hand, and the Thou seeing itself in the I and the I in itself, on the other, together create a "harmony" that is "not one and not two" in the sense that it is neither a "relation" between two essentially separate beings, nor the "absolute identity" of a monistic One that prevents or abolishes differences. As we have seen, the *mondō* reveals the twofold nature of the self, which is on the one hand *absolute*, embracing all others, and on the other hand *relative*, standing over against others. Indeed, even my identification with you is not identical with your identification with me, and so, even in our mutually absolute nondifferentiation with one another, we are "not one and not two."

Moreover, the relation of mutual circulation is not merely that of reciprocal deference to the other; it also involves playful opposition and complementary competition. In their playful exchange, in their circulating roles of host and guest, and in their assuming absolute and relative stances, Kyōsan and Sanshō act out a dynamically harmonious relation in which self and other freely circulate between roles of host and guest in a kind of playfully competitive as well as compassionate give and take. In their dialogical exchange, "the condition of eat or be eaten [is] penetrated to the condition of at once eating and being eaten, until the little self of each one dissolves, and they are returned to the place where self and other are not one and not two, and where strife is transformed into sport."[81] Here oppositional relativity between individuals takes on a new meaning: it is a celebration of complementary diversity by way of playful competition, rather than a struggle for mastery between egocentric wills to power. In a poetic analogy, Hakuin compares this to "flowers competing with their reds and purples in the spring warmth"—a harmonious and complementary competition between individual forms of life which are irreducibly different from one another even as they are rooted in the same earth and interrelate in the same open sky.

Analogously, human beings can be understood as irreducibly unique expressions of the same field of emptiness. Moreover, humans have the ability and the responsibility to awaken to this shared origin of differences, and thereby to become ethically other-centered as well as self-expressively engaged in the oppositional interplay or complementary competition among individual and communal forms of existence. And, Nishitani concludes, "Unless the relations between individual and individual, between nation and nation, between all factions, all groups, return to this condition, there remains only the battle between wolves in the wild."[82]

8. AFTERWORD: SOMETHING THOROUGHLY HIDDEN, REQUIRING A TWOFOLD LOVE

The first four chapters of *Religion and Nothingness* were initially published separately in 1954–55; the final two chapters were added when the complete volume reached print in 1961, the same year that Nishitani's interpretation of the *mōndo* between Kyōsan and Sanshō first appeared. We have seen how in both texts he affirms what I have called "the twofold nature of the self." On the one hand, the self is but one finite, relative being among other finite, relative beings. On the other hand, the self is absolute insofar as it can awaken to its ultimate "selfness" or "home-ground," which is none other than the field of emptiness that embraces all relative beings.[83] Kyōsan and Sanshō can thus alternate between being interdependent beings standing over against one another and being absolute subjects encompassing one another.

However, in both of these texts, which seek to bring the standpoint of Zen to bear on contemporary philosophical issues, including the I-Thou relation, it could be said that there is a tendency to stress the absolute aspect of the self. By contrast, when he addresses the I-Thou relation in lectures over the course of the following decade—including a 1967 lecture at Otani University as well as in the 1969 talk given to the emperor and empress referred to earlier—it could be said that Nishitani stresses instead the relative aspect of the self. We can read these later texts as a kind of *afterword* to his treatment of the interpersonal relation in *Religion and Nothingness* and in "The I-Thou Relation in Zen Buddhism," especially with regard to the question of to what extent the self can identify with and know the other, or to what extent there is an inassimilable and unknowable alterity to the other.

In *Religion and Nothingness*, Nishitani speaks of three "standpoints" or modes of existence, corresponding respectively to the three fields of consciousness, nihility, and emptiness. On the field of consciousness (by which he means subjective, dualistic consciousness), we purport to know other persons and things; but in fact what we know are merely our own subjective representations of them. On the field of nihility, however, we realize that, "at his home-ground, [even] our closest acquaintance remains originally and essentially a stranger, an 'unknown.'"[84] In other words, on the field of nihility one realizes that there is an "absolute breach" between one's subjective consciousness and the things or persons it purports to represent. However, on the field of emptiness, one realizes that this "absolute breach" that distances one person or thing from another at the same time "points directly to a most intimate encounter with everything that exists."[85] This "intimate encounter" is possible because underneath the abyss of nihility that separates subjective consciousness from everything else lies the field of emptiness that unites things in their differences.

The question is, in what sense, and to what extent, does this "intimate encounter" on the field of emptiness enable the self to know the other? Nishitani defines "emptiness" as "the field of possibility of the world and also the field of possibility of the existence of things." He then goes on to say, "'Emptiness is self' means that, at bottom and in its own home-ground, the self has its being as such a field."[86] He emphasizes that the self has its being not just *on* this field but indeed "*as* that field."[87] Thus, "in truly returning to our own home-ground, we return to the home-ground of things that become manifest in the world." This return or "trans-descendence" to the field of emptiness, moreover, is said to enable a kind of non-representational "knowing of non-knowing" (*muchi no chi* 無知の知) that is a "knowledge of things in themselves."[88] By way of negating the ego and its mode of representational knowing, we are said to be able to "revert to the 'middle' of things themselves," and thereby enter "the realization (manifestation-*qua*-apprehension) of 'things' in themselves [*'mono' jitai no riarizēshon (genjō-soku-etoku)* 「もの」自体のリアリゼーション, 現成即会得], which cannot be grasped by sensation or reason."[89] On the field of emptiness, "there is no distinction between the phenomenon and the thing-in-itself. The original thing is the thing that appears to us as what it is, without front side or back."[90]

By contrast, in a lecture course on Buddhism given roughly a decade later in 1972, Nishitani questions the extent to which the self can ever fully know the other. There he writes:

> There is something at the basis of the mind to which no one else has access, except the person concerned. . . . The reason for this is that each person exists as an individual, . . . an absolutely singular self. This is manifest in the fact of embodiment. . . . A human being appears on the scene while at the same time leaving

> something thoroughly hidden. With something truly hidden, the self reveals itself to others. Without this hidden something, one's self would disappear. The human being harbors a contradiction in itself insofar as it reveals itself at the same time as it maintains something hidden that simply cannot be revealed. If this were not the case, it could not be said that an I-Thou relation is established, as self and other appear to one another through their bodies.[91]

Whereas in *Religion and Nothingness* and in "The I-Thou Relation in Zen Buddhism" Nishitani had stressed the ability of individuals to transcend (or trans-descend) their relative identities in order to identify with the field of emptiness and thereby with others on that field, here Nishitani stresses rather the mutually concealed dimension of embodied individuals, which is said to be necessary for the I-Thou relation to be established. This "something hidden that simply cannot be revealed" would presumably remain concealed even from the "knowing of non-knowing" of the enlightened self who has awakened to his or her home-ground as the field of emptiness. This "something thoroughly hidden"—something "to which no one else has access, except the person concerned"—would presumably remain impenetrable even in a relation of mutually circulating interpenetration. In the words of another of Nishitani's later essays, we could say that, in the midst of the nondual mutual circulation of self and other, there would remain a " 'stubborn' self-identity" to the other that is "non-mutually circulating."[92]

In *Religion and Nothingness*, Nishitani says that it is necessary for the self to "kill the 'self' by killing every 'other,' " thereby "breaking through the field where self and other are discriminated from one another and made relative to one another."[93] An experience of such a breakthrough beyond all relativity may indeed be possible; it may even be a precondition for entering a "most intimate encounter" which enables a nondualistic, that is to say, a nonsubjective and nonrepresentational, understanding of others. Yet insofar as this remains an encounter with a Thou, that is, with an other individual who is allowed to be as an other individual, he or she would "maintain something hidden that simply cannot be revealed." In the radical trans-descendence into the depths of "the equality of one taste" (*ichimi byōdō* 一味平等), in bowing down into absolute nothingness, there would indeed be neither self nor other. Yet as soon as one stands up on the plane of relativity, the Thou appears as Thou, the other appears as other, only by reserving an impenetrable dimension of alterity.[94] As Nishitani stresses in a lecture at Ōtani University in 1967, the I-Thou relation entails "a kind of independence" of the other, that is to say, it entails that the other "has the nature of being utterly not the self, of being something other than the self."[95]

In "The I-Thou Relation in Zen Buddhism," Nishitani says that "the absolute nondiscrimination of I and Thou belongs to both the I and the Thou." On the one hand, "the Thou is in the home-ground of the I, and moreover in such a manner that is absolutely undifferentiated from the I." On the other hand, "the I is absolutely undifferentiated from the Thou in the home-ground of the Thou."[96] And yet, is it not rather the case that the other is discovered *as other* in the home-ground of the self? As Nishida puts it, "The self includes an absolute other in itself," such that self-awareness is not a matter of realizing a nondifferentiated self-identity, but rather a matter of "seeing the absolute other in the self."[97] The other is a stranger who nonetheless dwells in my home, and I am a stranger who nonetheless dwells in the home of the other. Precisely because the self is an irreducibly twofold self,[98] this paradoxical relation of "not one and not two" is in fact our most concrete reality.

As we have seen, already in *Religion and Nothingness* and in "The I-Thou Relation in Zen Buddhism," Nishitani had understood the self in an irreducibly twofold sense as both relative and absolute. On the one hand, the self is a relative being standing over against other relative beings; and yet, on the other hand, the home-ground of the self is the place in which this relation between relative beings takes place.[99] Nishitani had accordingly seen the I-Thou relation as a "contradictory" relation wherein "the I and the Thou are absolutes [and] at the same time absolutely relative."[100] Moreover, he had already understood interpersonal relations to be characterized by Daitō Kokushi's saying, "For countless eons separated from one another, yet not divided for a moment. Standing opposite one another all day long, yet not opposed for an instant."[101] Accordingly, Nishitani's increasing stress on the unknowable alterity of the other can be understood as a shift of emphasis that balances out—rather than as a significant alteration of—his conception of the genuine I-Thou relation.

Nevertheless, this shift does add an important clarification of—and even necessary supplement to—his earlier account of the nature of the "religious love" that enables the genuine I-Thou relation. This "other-centered" love would need to entail not only a kenotically empathetic "absolute nondifferentiation" with the other, but also a recognition of "something truly hidden" that is essential to the other as a singular, finite, and embodied individual with a mind that is never fully accessible to the self. This love would, to be sure, dissolve a dualistic sense of separateness from others, insofar as it would entail a realization of the shared field of emptiness as the ultimate home ground of both self and other. But it would at the same time involve a letting-be of the alterity that is essential to others as irreducibly singular "self-expressions" (*jiko-hyōgen* 自己表現) or "self-localizations" (*jiko-kyokusho-ka* 自己局所化) of this field.[102] Ideally, then, the twofold self encounters a twofold other in the harmony engendered by a twofold love. This love is twofold insofar as it involves *both* a radical undermining *and* a respectful preservation of the borders between us, borders that separate as well as connect us insofar as we are interrelated yet irreplaceably unique forms of the same encompassing field of emptiness.

NOTES

In this chapter, existing English translations have been frequently modified by B. Davis. In places where translations were entirely redone, note of this is made.

1. NKZ 6.341–427. On Nishida's account of the I-Thou relation, see the following articles of mine: "Das Innerste zuäußerst: Nishida und die Revolution der Ich-Du-Beziehung," trans. Ruben Pfizenmaier, Eberhard Ortland, and Rolf Elberfeld, *Allgemeine Zeitschrift für Philosophie* 36.3 (2011), 281–312; "*Nijū naru 'zettai no ta e no naizai-teki chōetsu': Nishida no shūkyō-tetsugaku ni okeru tasharon*" [Twofold

"immanent transcendence to the absolute other": Alterity in Nishida's philosophy of religion], *Nihontetsugakushi Kenkyū* [Studies in Japanese philosophy] 9 (2012), 102–134; and "Ethical and Religious Alterity: Nishida after Levinas," in *Kitarō Nishida in der Philosophie des 20. Jahrhunderts*, ed. Rolf Elberfeld and Yōko Arisaka (Freiburg/Munich: Alber Verlag, 2014), 313–341.

2. Martin Buber, *Ich und Du*, in *Das dialogische Prinzip*, ed. Lambert Schneider (Heidelberg: Gütersloher Verlagshaus, 1986), 7–136. *Ich und Du* was originally published in 1923, though Nishida had apparently not yet read it when he wrote *Watashi to nanji*. Nishida does refer to the dialectical theologian Friedrich Gogarten's book, *Ich glaube an den dreieinigen Gott* (1926), which was influenced by Buber. For Buber's account of previous European reflections on the I-Thou relation, see Buber, "Zur Geschichte des dialogischen Prinzips," in *Das dialogische Prinzip*, 299–320.
3. Nishitani's successor and the current central figure of the Kyoto School, Ueda Shizuteru, has also developed at length a Zen interpretation of the I-Thou relation. See my "*Jiyū-na hinjugokan: Ueda Shizuteru no Zen-tetsugaku kara mita taiwa no kakushin*" [The free exchange of host and guest: The core of dialogue according to the Zen philosophy of Ueda Shizuteru], in *Nihon hatsu no sekai shisō* 『日本発の世界思想』 [Global thought from Japan], ed. Tōgō Kazuhiko, Mori Tetsurō, and Nakatani Masanori (Tokyo: Fujiwara Shoten, 2017), 104–124; and my "Conversing in Emptiness: Rethinking Cross-Cultural Dialogue with the Kyoto School," in *Philosophical Traditions* (Royal Institute of Philosophy Supplement 74), ed. Anthony O'Hear (Cambridge, UK: Cambridge University Press, 2014), 171–194.
4. The content of this chapter draws in part on an earlier article of mine written and published in Japanese: "*Kū ni okeru deai: Nishitani Keiji no Zen tetsugaku ni okeru 'ware to nanji' no ego-teki kankei*" [Encounter in emptiness: The mutually circulating I-Thou relation in the Zen philosophy of Nishitani Keiji], *Risō* 689 (2012): 114–131.
5. NKC 10.3–315. See Abbreviations and Conventions. Nishitani Keiji, *Religion and Nothingness*, trans. Jan Van Bragt (Los Angeles: University of California Press, 1982). *Religion and Nothingness* will hereafter be cited as RN.
6. NKC 20.68–74.
7. NKC 12.276–289.
8. Ryōsuke Ōhashi, ed., *Die Philosophie der Kyôto-Schule: Texte und Einführung*, second edition (Freiburg: Verlag Karl Alber, 2011), 242–257. It is noteworthy that Ōhashi chose this text (along with one other) to represent Nishitani's philosophy in his anthology of the Kyoto School. Ōhashi Ryōsuke also focused on this text in his chapter on Nishitani in *Hi no genshōron josetsu: Nihontetsugaku no roku teeze yori* [Prolegomenon to a phenomenology of compassion: From six theses of Japanese philosophy] (Tokyo: Sōbunsha, 1998), chapter 5.
9. First published in *The Eastern Buddhist* 2.1 (1969), 71–87; reprinted in *The Buddha Eye: An Anthology of the Kyoto School and Its Contemporaries*, ed. Frederick Frank (Bloomington: World Wisdom, 2004, revised ed.), 39–53. The latter will hereafter be cited as ITZ.
10. NKC 12.277/ITZ 41, translation by Davis.

11. NKC 12.277–278/ITZ 41.
12. NKC 17.198. Keiji Nishitani, *On Buddhism*, trans. Seisaku Yamamoto and Robert E. Carter (Albany: SUNY Press, 2006), 83. Hereafter abbreviated as OB.
13. NKC 24.108.
14. NKC 20.72.
15. NKC 20.72; see also NKC 16.81.
16. NKC 20.72; NKC 24.108–109.
17. NKC 10.169, 179, 183/RN 150, 159, 163.
18. Buber, *Ich und Du*, 76, 100–102, 113, 133.
19. Emmanuel Lévinas, *Totalité et infini: Essai sur l'extériorité* (Dordrecht: Kluwer Academic, 1971), 5; *Totality and Infinity: An Essay on Exteriority*, trans. Alphonso Lingis (Pittsburgh: Duquesne University Press, 1979), 35.
20. On Nishitani Keiji's employment of this neologism, and for his interpretation of Buddhism as "a religion of the absolute near-side," see Bret W. Davis, "The Step Back through Nihilism: The Radical Orientation of Nishitani Keiji's Philosophy of Zen," *Synthesis Philosophica* 37 (2004), 139–159.
21. NKZ 11.434.
22. NKC 10.112/*RN* 99.
23. NKC 10.112/RN 99–100. See also Nishitani Keiji, "Religious-Philosophical Existence in Buddhism," trans. Paul Shepherd, *The Eastern Buddhist* 23 (1990): 9–10.
24. NKC 1.88.
25. NKC 10.179/RN 159.
26. See my "Nishitani after Nietzsche: From the Death of God to the Great Death of the Will," in *Japanese and Continental Philosophy: Conversations with the Kyoto School*, ed. Bret W. Davis, Brian Schroeder, and Jason Wirth (Bloomington and Indianapolis: Indiana University Press, 2011).
27. Nishitani mentions Hobbes's use of this proverb; see NKZ 12.277.
28. See G. W. F. Hegel, *Phenomenology of Spirit*, trans. A. V. Miller (New York: Oxford University Press, 1977), 111–19.
29. NKC 12.279/ITZ 43.
30. NKC 12.276/ITZ 40. For an alternative translation of this dialogue, see *The Blue Cliff Record*, trans. Thomas Cleary and J. C. Cleary (Boston: Shambhala, 1992), 381. Since in this chapter I am discussing Nishitani's interpretation of the Zen tradition, I will generally use the Japanese pronunciation of Chinese names, except in cases, such as Linji (Jp. Rinzai), where the Chinese name is well known.
31. NKC 12.277/ITZ 40.
32. NKC 12.282–283/ITZ 46.
33. NKC 12.281/ITZ 45.
34. NKC 12.277/ITZ 40.
35. NKC 12.282/ITZ 45.
36. Ibid.

37. NKC 12.282/ITZ 46.
38. *The Blue Cliff Record*, Case 57.
39. NKC 12.283/ITZ 46.
40. Ibid.
41. NKC 12.283/ITZ 46–47.
42. *The Record of Linji*, trans. Ruth Fuller Sasaki, ed. Thomas Yūhō Kirchner (Honolulu: University of Hawai'i Press, 2009), 7, 151.
43. Ibid., 12, 186.
44. NKC 12.261–262.
45. NKC 12.262–263.
46. NKZ 7.208; NKZ 11.130, 423.
47. NKC 10.164, 178, 290/RN 146, 158, 263.
48. NKC 10.178/RN 158; see also NKC 10.170–171/RN 151–152.
49. NKC 10.186/RN 166.
50. Ibid.
51. See Nishitani, "Religious-Philosophical Existence in Buddhism," 16–17.
52. Nishitani Keiji, "Encounter with Emptiness," in *The Religious Philosophy of Nishitani Keiji*, ed. Taitetsu Unno (Berkeley: Asian Humanities Press, 1989), 2–3.
53. NKC 12.262.
54. NKC 12.283/ITZ 46.
55. Buber, *Das dialogische Prinzip*, 12; *I and Thou*, trans. Walter Kaufmann (New York: Charles Scribner's Sons, 1970), 59; emphasis in the original.
56. See Fa-tsang (Fazang), "Cultivation of Contemplation of the Inner Meaning of the Hua-yen: The Ending of Delusion and Return to the Source," trans. Thomas Cleary, in *Entry into the Inconceivable: An Introduction to Hua-Yen Buddhism* (Honolulu: University of Hawaii Press, 1983), 168. For Linji's uses of the language of host and guest, in which he tends to stress the importance of being capable of assuming the role of host or master, see *The Record of Linji*, 133–134, 232, 245–246. Yet, as a recent Zen master points out, Linji's famous injunction to "become master wherever you are" (*The Record of Linji*, 186) is "not a matter of selfishly asserting 'me, me' all the time, but rather quite the opposite." Ōmori Sōgen, *Rinzairoku kōwa* [Lectures on *The Record of Linji*] (Tokyo: Shunjūsha, 2005), 95. The true master has undergone the "great death" of the ego, and is hence able to naturally take on the role of servant when and where appropriate. See my "Zen's Nonegocentric Perspectivism," in *Buddhist Philosophy: A Comparative Approach*, ed. Steven M. Emmanuel (West Sussex: Wiley-Blackwell, 2017).
57. See Emmanuel Lévinas, *Autrement qu'être ou au-delà de l'essence* (Dordrecht: Kluwer Academic, 1978), 176–187; *Otherwise Than Being or Beyond Essence*, trans. Alphonso Lingis (Pittsburgh: Duquesne University Press, 1998), 111–118.
58. Ueda Shizuteru, "'Tomo-ni' to 'hitori'" ["Together" and "alone"], in *Ueda Shizuteru shū* [Ueda Shizuteru collection], vol. 10 (Tokyo: Iwanami, 2002), 281.

59. Shizuteru Ueda, *Wer und was bin ich? Zur Phänomenologie des Selbst im Zen Buddhismus* (Freiburg/München: Verlag Karl Alber, 2011), 36; Ueda Shizuteru, "Emptiness and Fullness: Śūnyatā in Mahāyāna Buddhism," trans. James W. Heisig and Frederick Greiner, *The Eastern Buddhist* 15.1 (1982), 37.
60. NKC 10.167/RN 149.
61. NKC 10.315/RN 285.
62. NKZ 11.454.
63. "Zhuangzi," in *Readings in Chinese Philosophy*, ed. Philip J. Ivanhoe and Bryan W. Van Norden, second ed. (Indianapolis: Hackett Publishing, 2005), 213.
64. NKC 12.288/ITZ 53; translation by Davis.
65. Ōmori Sōgen, *Hekiganroku* (Tokyo: Tachibana Shuppan, 1995), vol. 2, 133–134.
66. NKC 12.283/ITZ 47.
67. NKC 12.283/ITZ 47.
68. NKC 12.284–285/ITZ 48–49.
69. NKC 12.288/ITZ 52.
70. NKC 12.289/ITZ 53.
71. NKC 12.288/ITZ 53; translation by Davis.
72. NKC 12.285/ITZ 48.
73. NKC 10.308/RN 279.
74. NKC 10.308/RN 279.
75. NKC 10.315/RN 285.
76. NKC 10.167–168/RN 149.
77. See NKC 10.304–305/RN 275–277.
78. NKC 10.304/RN 275.
79. NKC 10.274/ RN 249.
80. NKC 12.285/ITZ 48–49.
81. NKC 12.286/ITZ 49.
82. NKC 12.286/ITZ 49–50.
83. NKC 10.186/RN 165–166.
84. NKC 10.113/RN 100.
85. NKC 10.115/RN 102.
86. NKC 10.170/RN 151.
87. NKC 10.171/RN 152; emphasis added.
88. NKC 10.183/RN 163.
89. NKC 10.157–158, 174/RN 139–140, 154–155.
90. NKC 10.156/RN 138.
91. NKC 17.196–197/OB 82; translation by Davis. Nishida also insists that "there must be understood to be an absolute alterity between my consciousness and the consciousness of another" (NKZ 6.392–393).

92. NKC 13.141.
93. NKC 10.290/RN 263.
94. On bowing down into, and standing back up out of, absolute nothingness, see *Ueda Shizuteru shū*, vol. 10.107–108. Ueda also writes elsewhere that "insofar as the other is an other, he or she is essentially untransparent" (*Ueda Shizuteru shū*, vol. 10.291).
95. NKC 24.111.
96. NKC 12.285/ITZ 48; translation by Davis.
97. NKZ 6.380, 407.
98. The identity of the self is, as Nishida says, an "absolutely contradictory self-identity," insofar as the self is an irreducibly "self-contradictory being" (NKZ 11.445).
99. In the final image of the *Ten Oxherding Pictures*, for instance, we could say that the true self is *both* the old recluse greeting the boy *and* the empty circle enveloping this encounter; the difference between the old man and the boy is that the former has awakened to this twofold nature of the self, while the latter presumably still restricts his self-awareness to his relative aspect. See my comments and Ueda Shizuteru's response in *Kyōto Sangyō Daigaku Nihonbunka Kenkyūsho Nenpō* [The bulletin of the Institute of Japanese Culture, Kyoto Sangyō University] (2012), 320–321.
100. NKC 12.77–278/ITZ 41.
101. NKC 10.115/RN 102; translation by Davis. NKC 11.59–60.
102. NKC 13.137.

BIBLIOGRAPHY

Buber, Martin. *I and Thou*, trans. Walter Kaufmann. New York: Charles Scribner's Sons, 1970.

Buber, Martin. *Ich und Du*. In Martin Buber, *Das dialogische Prinzip*, ed. Lambert Schneider, 7–136. Heidelberg: Gütersloher Verlagshaus, 1986.

Cleary, Thomas, and J. C. Cleary, trans. *The Blue Cliff Record*. Boston: Shambhala, 1992.

Davis, Bret W. "The Step Back through Nihilism: The Radical Orientation of Nishitani Keiji's Philosophy of Zen." *Synthesis Philosophica* 37 (2004), 139–159.

Davis, Bret W. "Das Innerste zuäußerst: Nishida und die Revolution der Ich-Du-Beziehung," trans. Ruben Pfizenmaier, Eberhard Ortland, and Rolf Elberfeld. *Allgemeine Zeitschrift für Philosophie* 36.3 (2011), 281–312.

Davis, Bret W. "Nishitani after Nietzsche: From the Death of God to the Great Death of the Will." In *Japanese and Continental Philosophy: Conversations with the Kyoto School*, ed. Bret W. Davis, Brian Schroeder, and Jason Wirth, 82–101. Bloomington and Indianapolis: Indiana University Press, 2011.

Davis, Bret W. ブレット・デービス. "Kū ni okeru deai: Nishitani Keiji no Zen tetsugaku ni okeru 'ware to nanji' no ego-teki kankei" 「空における出会い——西谷啓治の禅哲学における〈我と汝〉の回互的関係」 [Encounter in emptiness: The mutually circulating I-Thou relation in the Zen philosophy of Nishitani Keiji]. *Risō* 『理想』 689 (2012), 114–31.

Davis, Bret W. "*Nijū naru 'zettai no ta e no naizai-teki chōetsu': Nishida no shūkyō-tetsugaku ni okeru tasharon*" 「二重なる〈絶対の他への内在的超越〉——西田の宗教哲学における他者論」 [Twofold "immanent transcendence to the absolute other": Alterity in Nishida's philosophy of religion]. *Nihontetsugakushi Kenkyū* 『日本哲学史研究』 [Studies in Japanese philosophy] 9 (2012), 102–134.

Davis, Bret W. "Conversing in Emptiness: Rethinking Cross-Cultural Dialogue with the Kyoto School." In *Philosophical Traditions*, ed. Anthony O'Hear, 171–194. Royal Institute of Philosophy Supplement 74; Cambridge, UK: Cambridge University Press, 2014.

Davis, Bret W. "Ethical and Religious Alterity: Nishida after Levinas." In *Kitarō Nishida in der Philosophie des 20. Jahrhunderts*, ed. Rolf Elberfeld and Yōko Arisaka, 313–341. Freiburg/Munich: Alber Verlag, 2014.

Davis, Bret W. "*Jiyū na hinjugokan—Ueda Shizuteru no Zen-tetsugaku kara mita taiwa no kakushin*" 「自由な賓主互換——上田閑照の禅哲学から見た対話の核心」 [The free exchange of host and guest: The core of dialogue according to the Zen philosophy of Ueda Shizuteru]. In *Nihon hatsu no sekai shisō* 『日本発の世界思想』 [Global thought from Japan], ed. Tōgō Kazuhiko, Mori Tetsurō, and Nakatani Masanori, 104–124. Tokyo: Fujiwara Shoten, 2017.

Davis, Bret W. "Zen's Nonegocentric Perspectivism." In *Buddhist Philosophy: A Comparative Approach*, ed. Steven M. Emmanuel, 123–143. West Sussex: Wiley-Blackwell, 2017.

Fa-tsang (Fazang) 法藏. "Cultivation of Contemplation of the Inner Meaning of the Hua-yen: The Ending of Delusion and Return to the Source." In *Entry into the Inconceivable: An Introduction to Hua-Yen Buddhism*, trans. Thomas Cleary, 147–169. Honolulu: University of Hawaii Press, 1983.

Hegel, G. W. F. *Phenomenology of Spirit*, trans. A. V. Miller. New York: Oxford University Press, 1977.

Lévinas, Emmanuel. *Autrement qu'être ou au-delà de l'essence*. Dordrecht: Kluwer Academic, 1978.

Lévinas, Emmanuel. *Totalité et infini: Essai sur l'extériorité*. Dordrecht: Kluwer Academic, 1971.

Lévinas, Emmanuel. *Otherwise Than Being or Beyond Essence*, trans. Alphonso Lingis. Pittsburgh: Duquesne University Press, 1998.

Lévinas, Emmanuel. *Totality and Infinity: An Essay on Exteriority*, trans. Alphonso Lingis. Pittsburgh: Duquesne University Press, 1979.

Linji 臨済. *The Record of Linji*, trans. Ruth Fuller Sasaki, ed. Thomas Yūhō Kirchner. Honolulu: University of Hawai'i Press, 2009.

Nishida Kitarō 西田幾多郎. "*Watakushi to nanji*" 「私と汝」 ["I and Thou"] (1932). NKZ 6.341–427.

Nishida Kitarō. "*Bashoteki ronri to shūkyōteki sekaikan*" 「場所的論理と宗教的世界観」 [Topological logic and the religious worldview] (1945). NKZ 11.371–464.

Nishitani Keiji 西谷啓治. "*Ware to nanji to shite no ningen kankei*" 「我と汝としての人間関係」 (New Year lecture to the Emperor & Empress, 1969), included in *Kaze no kokoro* 『風のこころ』 [The heart of the wind], 82–89. Tokyo: Shinchōsha, 1980; reprinted in NKC 20.68–74.

Nishitani Keiji. *Religion and Nothingness*, trans. Jan Van Bragt. Los Angeles: University of California Press, 1982.

Nishitani Keiji 西谷啓治. *Nishitani Keiji chosakushū* [Collected works of Nishitani Keiji], 24 vols. Tokyo: Sōbunsha, 1986–95.

Nishitani Keiji. "*Shige, Daitō*" 『詩偈』「大燈」 [Zen poems, "Daitō Kokushi"]. In *Nishitani Keiji chosakushū* 『西谷啓治著作集』 [Collected works of Nishitani Keiji]. Tokyo: Sōbunsha, 1987 (1961). See below for translation as "The I-Thou Relation in Zen Buddhism."

Nishitani Keiji. *Shūkyō to wa nanika* 『宗教とは何か』 [What is religion?]. Reprinted as vol. 10 of *Nishitani Keiji chosakushū* 『西谷啓治著作集』 [Collected works of Nishitani Keiji]. Tokyo: Sōbunsha, 1987 (1961).

Nishitani Keiji. "*Kū to soku*" 「空と即」 [Emptiness and identity] (1979). NKC 13.111–160.

Nishitani Keiji. "Encounter with Emptiness." In *The Religious Philosophy of Nishitani Keiji*, ed. Taitetsu Unno. Berkeley: Asian Humanities Press, 1989.

Nishitani Keiji. "Religious-Philosophical Existence in Buddhism," trans. Paul Shepherd. *The Eastern Buddhist* 23 (1990), 9–10.

Nishitani Keiji. "The I-Thou Relation in Zen Buddhism," trans. Norman Waddell. *The Eastern Buddhist* II.2 (1969): 71–87; reprinted in *The Buddha Eye: An Anthology of the Kyoto School and Its Contemporaries*, ed. Frederick Frank (Bloomington: World Wisdom, 2004, revised ed.), 39–53.

Nishitani Keiji. *On Buddhism*, trans. Seisaku Yamamoto and Robert E. Carter. Albany: State University of New York Press, 2006.

Nishitani Keiji. "*Vom Wesen der Begegnung.*" In *Die Philosophie der Kyôto-Schule: Texte und Einführung*, ed. Ryôsuke Ohashi, second ed., 242–257. Freiburg: Verlag Karl Alber, 2011.

Ōhashi Ryōsuke 大橋良介. *Hi no genshōron josetsu: Nihontetsugaku no roku teeze yori* 『悲の現象論序説、日本哲学の六テーゼより』 [Prolegomenon to a phenomenology of compassion: From six theses of Japanese philosophy]. Tokyo: Sōbunsha, 1998.

Ōhashi Ryōsuke, ed. *Die Philosophie der Kyôto-Schule: Texte und Einführung*, second ed. Freiburg: Verlag Karl Alber, 2011.

Ōmori Sōgen 大森曹玄. *Hekiganroku* 『碧巌録』. Tokyo: Tachibana Shuppan, 1995.

Ōmori Sōgen. *Rinzairoku kōwa* 『臨済録講話』 [Lectures on *The Record of Linji*]. Tokyo: Shunjūsha, 2005.

Ueda Shizuteru 上田閑照. "Emptiness and Fullness: Śūnyatā in Mahāyāna Buddhism," trans. James W. Heisig and Frederick Greiner. *The Eastern Buddhist* 15.1 (1982) 9–37.

Ueda Shizuteru. "'*Tomo-ni' to 'hitori*'" 「『共に』と『独り』」 ["Together" and "alone"]. *Ueda Shizuteru shū* 『上田閑照集』 [Ueda Shizuteru collection], vol. 10, 269–298. Tokyo: Iwanami, 2002.

Ueda Shizuteru. *Wer und was bin ich? Zur Phänomenologie des Selbst im Zen Buddhismus.* Freiburg/München: Verlag Karl Alber, 2011.

Ueda Shizuteru 上田閑照, and Bret Davis. ブレット・デービス. On the "Ten Oxherding Pictures." *Kyōto Sangyō Daigaku Nihonbunka Kenkyūsho Nenpō* [The bulletin of the Institute of Japanese Culture, Kyoto Sangyō University] (2012), 318–321.

"Zhuangzi." In *Readings in Chinese Philosophy*, ed. Philip J. Ivanhoe and Bryan W. Van Norden, second ed., 208–250. Indianapolis: Hackett Publishing, 2005.

FURTHER READING

Translations

Nishitani Keiji. *Religion and Nothingness*, trans. Jan Van Bragt. Berkeley: University of California Press, 1982.

Nishitani Keiji. "The Standpoint of Zen," trans. John C. Maraldo. *The Eastern Buddhist* 18.1 (1984), 1–26.

Nishitani Keiji. "Religious-Philosophical Existence in Buddhism," trans. Paul Shepherd. *The Eastern Buddhist* 23 (1990), 1–17.

Nishitani Keiji. *The Self-Overcoming of Nihilism*, trans. Graham Parkes with Setsuko Aihara. Albany: State University of New York Press, 1990.

Nishitani Keiji. *Nishida Kitarō*, trans. Yamamoto Seisaku and James W. Heisig. Berkeley: University of California Press, 1991.

Nishitani Keiji. "Emptiness and Sameness," trans. Michele Marra. In *Modern Japanese Aesthetics*, trans. and ed. Michele Marra, 179–217. Honolulu: University of Hawai'i Press, 1999.

Nishitani Keiji. "Science and Zen." In *The Buddha Eye: An Anthology of the Kyoto School and Its Contemporaries*, ed. Frederick Franck, 107–136. Bloomington: World Wisdom, 2004.

Nishitani Keiji. "The I-Thou Relation in Zen Buddhism." In *The Buddha Eye: An Anthology of the Kyoto School and Its Contemporaries*, ed. Frederick Franck, 39–54. Bloomington: World Wisdom, 2004.

Nishitani Keiji. *On Buddhism*, trans. Seisaku Yamamoto and Robert E. Carter. Albany: State University of New York Press, 2006.

Nishitani Keiji. "My Views on 'Overcoming Modernity,'" trans. Richard Calichman. In *Overcoming Modernity—Cultural Identity in Wartime Japan*, ed. Richard Calichman, 51–63. New York: Columbia University Press, 2008.

Secondary sources

Davis, Bret W. "The Step Back through Nihilism: The Radical Orientation of Nishitani Keiji's Philosophy of Zen." *Synthesis Philosophica* 37 (2004), 139–159.

Davis, Bret W. "Turns to and from Political Philosophy: The Case of Nishitani Keiji." In *Re-politicising the Kyoto School as Philosophy*, ed. Chris Goto-Jones, 26–45. London: Routledge, 2008.

Davis, Bret W. "Nishitani after Nietzsche: From the Death of God to the Great Death of the Will." In *Japanese and Continental Philosophy: Conversations with the Kyoto School*, ed. Bret W. Davis, Brian Schroeder, and Jason Wirth, 82–101. Bloomington: Indiana University Press, 2011.

The Eastern Buddhist New Series 25.1. A special edition, "In Memoriam Nishitani Keiji 1900–1990." 1992.

Heisig, James W. *Philosophers of Nothingness: An Essay on the Kyoto School.* Honolulu: University of Hawai'i Press, 2001.

Parkes, Graham. "Nishitani on Practicing Philosophy as a Matter of Life and Death." In *The Oxford Handbook of Japanese Philosophy*, ed. Bret W. Davis (online version 2015), DOI: 10.1093/oxfordhb/9780199945726.013.25.

Unno, Taitetsu, ed. *The Religious Philosophy of Nishitani Keiji.* Berkeley: Asian Humanities Press, 1989.

Zen Buddhism Today 14. A collection of articles on the theme: "Religion and the Contemporary World in Light of Nishitani Keiji's Thought." 1997.

Zen Buddhism Today 15. A collection of articles on the theme: "Nishida's Philosophy, Nishitani's Philosophy, and Zen." 1998.

Japanese sources

Kyōto Shūkyō-tetsugakkai [Kyoto Society for the Philosophy of Religion], ed. *Keisei Nishitani Keiji*, vol. 2 (His Thought). Kyoto: Tōeisha, 1993.

Nishitani Keiji. *Nishitani Keiji chosakushū* [Collected works of Nishitani Keiji], 24 vols. Tokyo: Sōbunsha, 1986–95.

Nishitani Keiji. *Shūkyō to hi-shūkyō no aida* [Between religion and non-religion], ed. Ueda Shizuteru. Tokyo: Iwanami, 1996.

Nishitani Keiji, and Yagi Seiichi. *Chokusetsu keiken: Seiyōseishin-shi to shūkyō* [Direct experience: The intellectual history of the West and religion]. Tokyo: Sōbunsha, 1989.

Sasaki Tōru. *Nishitani Keiji: Sono shisaku e no dōhyō* [Nishitani Keiji: Signposts on the way to his thought]. Kyoto: Hōzōkan, 1986.

Ueda Shizuteru, ed. *Jōi ni okeru kū: Nishitani Keiji sensei tsuitō* [Passions in emptiness: In memory of Professor Nishitani Keiji]. Tokyo: Sōbunsha, 1992.

CHAPTER ELEVEN

Creative Imagination, *Sensus Communis*, and the Social Imaginary: Miki Kiyoshi and Nakamura Yūjirō in Dialogue with Contemporary Western Philosophy

JOHN W. M. KRUMMEL

INTRODUCTION

The faculty of the imagination has long been recognized as playing a role in our interaction with the world, both in its creativity and in its relation to a communal sensibility—what has been called *sensus communis* or "common sense." This recognition however has a long and precarious history in Western philosophy, which eventually led to the development of the notion of the social imaginary in the twentieth century. In modernity it is Immanuel Kant who develops the productive role of the imagination in positive terms, first in cognition and in aesthetics, and this creativity of the imagination subsequently becomes developed further in communal terms as ontological and semantic. This recent development of the imagination as not merely creative but social and constitutive of collective significations or shared meanings can be found in thinkers such as Paul Ricoeur, Cornelius Castoriadis, and Charles Taylor, each of whom has developed independently analogous but distinct notions. One finds a comparable but likewise independent line of development of the notion of the imagination across the Eurasian continent in the Far East, in modern and contemporary Japanese philosophy in the thinking of Miki Kiyoshi 三木清 and Nakamura Yūjirō 中村雄二郎. All of them, both the Western and the Japanese philosophers, are working upon a common heritage of Western philosophy, the concept of the imagination and its creativity traceable to Kant in modern times and further back to Aristotle. Especially in Nakamura's case, the notion of common sense or *sensus communis* is not only traceable to early modern times but also further back to Aristotle. In the following I would like to trace the unfolding of this contemporary understanding of the imagination as the "social imaginary" constitutive of the horizon of shared meaning,[1] and how the thinking of both Miki and Nakamura may provide unique contributions that shed new light upon this contemporary issue of the creative social imagination in Western philosophy. What we can draw from Miki's and Nakamura's discussions of the imagination and common sense is the connections between form and formlessness on the one hand and place on the other hand in the construction of the world or web of meanings.

I will begin by discussing the history of this concept within Western philosophy from the premodern period to Kant in the 1700s and finally Ricoeur, Castoriadis, and Taylor in recent decades. I shall follow this with discussions of Miki's and Nakamura's developments of the imagination and common sense, respectively, in Japan from prewar to postwar periods, and conclude with a discussion of how their theories tie into contemporary debates on the imagination.

1. FROM THE PRODUCTIVE IMAGINATION TO THE SOCIAL IMAGINARY IN WESTERN PHILOSOPHY

We might trace the historical inception of the concept of the imagination to Aristotle, for whom, the imagination (*phantasia*) is passive (*pathos*) vis-à-vis the faculty of sensation[2] but is nonetheless a requirement for thought. Mental images (*phantasma*) first emerge through the gathering or synthesis of particular sense impressions (such as sound, sight, touch, etc.) in a *common* sense (*koinē aisthēsis*)—the sense that unifies the various senses, compares and distinguishes them, and is self-aware of that act of sensation. On that basis the imagination (*phantasia*) reproduces the unified senses as mental images (*phantasma*), which remain even once the sensory object has departed.[3] As a consequence of this Aristotelian understanding, the Greek tradition has taken the imagination to be fundamentally imitative or reproductive of the senses. But at the same time due to the sensory mediation of the sensible object's activity upon the imagination, the imagination is given some creative leeway in (re) producing their images. This is why later at the dawn of modernity René Descartes, having inherited this conception, devalues the imagination as the source of error in its potential deviance from the source of sensation. And yet it is precisely this creativity of the imagination—an implicit *poiesis*—that later thinkers of modern and contemporary times have taken in a more positive light and eventually as socially significant even if it has never really won a proper place for a long time within Western history.

In the development of modern epistemology, it is Immanuel Kant who picks up on that potential creativity of the imagination as essential for cognition. The creativity of the imagination now becomes pronounced to the extent that it can no longer be confined to God as it was in medieval times. Creativity (or "production") at least in its epistemic significance for Kant—but eventually in its ontological significance for the Romantic tradition and the German idealists after Kant—becomes a function of the human mind.[4] For Kant, who jumpstarts this move, the imagination (*Einbildungskraft*) is not passive but an a priori faculty of intuition that is productive (*produktive*) or active (*tätiges*) (A118, A120).[5] In the first edition of the first *Critique* Kant describes the imagination as one of the original sources of experience that cannot "be derived from any other faculty of the mind" (A94). Its a priori transcendental synthesis precedes all experience, "conditioning the very possibility of all experience" (A101) and allowing for the empirical application of the categories of the understanding to the received sense impressions (A125). In doing so, it brings sensibility and understanding, intuitions and concepts together, and on this basis Kant makes the implicit suggestion that the imagination is actually the "common, but to us unknown, root" of sensibility and understanding (B29, B863). As the power of synthesis in general, the imagination as such is "a blind but indispensable function of the human soul" necessary for cognition (A78/B103). This power of synthesis, however, entails creativity. Kant thus also defines the imagination as "the faculty of representing in intuition an object that is *not itself present*" (B151; emphasis in the original). While this can refer to its *reproductive* sense when one has an image of what one has seen, it can *also* refer to its *productive* aspect if what is produced is something one has not perceived. There is here an active-creative component belonging to the side of spontaneity.[6] In the second edition of the *Critique* it is the schematism—in its provision of rules for image-production for concepts—that underscores this a priori formative feature of the imagination as "an art concealed in the depths of the human soul" (B180). For example, with the concept of "dog," or "triangle," the schematism delineates its figure in a general manner without delimiting it to the determinate image a particular experience (of a dog or a triangle) might present (B180). Thereby it represents that which is not itself present, not an image—*the schema*.[7]

What was circumscribed within cognitive bounds in the first Critique is given an even looser rein in the third Critique (*Critique of Judgment*), wherein Kant gives the imagination, in its "free activity"[8] or "free play,"[9] an artistic role. This is first apparent in its role in the productive capacity of the genius to create the unseen and thus reorder reality.[10] Exceeding the bounds of conceptuality, the aesthetic product of genius cannot be fully translated into language or symbols and induces in its audience an experience that likewise exceeds linguistic and conceptual boundaries. Kant problematizes that unconstrained creative activity of the imagination further with the introduction of the *sublime*. In the experience of the sublime one experiences awe and anxiety before the powers of nature externally or humanity within that transcend the bounds of any purposiveness. The imagination's creative dimension is here expanded in pursuit of reason's idea of infinity, but which, moving "beyond *reasonable* limits," moves to inevitably exceed any sense of purpose that reason assigns to things—whether to our own humanity or to nature.[11] The sublime points to the creative unboundedness of the imagination perceived externally while genius is the bearer of that creativity within to give it aesthetic expression. Both the sublime and genius underscore the imagination's creativity irreducible to the terms of reason and understanding in the cognitive or theoretical sphere, while problematizing its communicability.

Kant, however, attempts to fetter that creativity with his notion of *taste* as socialized for "universal approval" under the faculty of judgment[12]—even while recognizing the plurality and diversity of taste that assumes their articulation within a public sphere free from domination[13]—and subordinates it to the criterion of instrumentality or reason's purposive order.[14] For Kant this self-legislating use of reason central to communicability is what he calls "common sense" (*sensus communis*), involving the critical ability to think for oneself but also to think from the standpoint of an *other* beyond the parameters of one's own perspective, and the capacity to think in a consistent manner while combining the first two capacities.[15] The *sensus communis* here is the public sphere wherein unconstrained and unprejudiced critical reflection can occur.[16] With this notion Kant searches for a certitude to ground judgments of taste amid the plurality of tastes, a certitude he finds in the free harmonization of the imagination—the faculty of intuition—to the understanding—the faculty of conception—in the lawfulness of its concepts.[17] On this basis Kant claims that judgments of beauty can be shared and are "universally communicable."[18] The *sensus communis* in Kant thus becomes the "universal communicability" of the experience of harmonization, that is, it participates in a horizon of value that is universalizable.[19] Nevertheless this, in turn, opens the question of historicity and contingency underlying such alleged universalizability of value or universal communicability of taste and reason's purposiveness. John Rundell remarks in his analysis of Kant's notion of the *sensus communis* that judgments have recourse to values which in themselves are neither transcendental nor teleological nor secure and which themselves are historical creations—what later in the twentieth century, as we shall see shortly, Castoriadis comes to call "imaginary significations"[20] or for Ricoeur are "the living and received tradition in which one lives and with which the imagination's creativity is in dialectical tension."[21] Thus even after that creativity of the imagination had become further linked with the notion of community through German Romanticism and Idealism, in the twentieth century it becomes increasingly seen as no longer independently transcendental.[22]

The recognition of this *creative yet contingent*, and no longer transcendental, nature of the imagination blossoms in the twentieth century with thinkers like Ricoeur, Castoriadis, and Taylor. For Paul Ricouer (1913–2005) the imagination through the "symbolic function of the image *per se*" is an "indispensable agent in the creation of meaning."[23] He argues in *The Rule of Metaphor* for the imagination's generation and regeneration of meaning through metaphor. Adapting Kant's notion of the schematism, Ricoeur in *Time and Narrative* also speaks of a "schematism of the narrative function," but which, in distinction from Kant's schematism, has "the characteristics of a tradition," and thus is *culturally bound* and "constituted within a history."[24] But this "poetic" function of the imagination, by orienting us, can also manifest externally and concretely in human action.[25] In fact the imagination as such cannot be separated from the *practice* of being human. As social, it unfolds a complex cultural symbolic framework for providing us with a concrete sense of existence, fundamental to our practical life. On the one hand it plays a fundamental role in the elaboration of symbols, myths, metaphors, narratives, and so on, giving meaning to the world and to history, and on the other hand guides and orients human beings within their lifeworld.[26] In this function the imagination for Ricoeur is constitutive of human social reality and the world as such.

But its creativity also means that it can play a critical role, along with a conservative one, that leads to the (re)making of the social world. In his *Lectures on Ideology and Utopia*, Ricoeur discusses this dialectic between the given and its remaking, construction and destruction, prefiguration and transfiguration, confirmation and contestation of the present, and so on, in terms of ideology and utopia, as both imaginative endeavors (*pratiques imaginatives*) of the social imagination (*l'imaginaire social*)—whereby *ideology* on the one hand reenacts the contextual platform of social practices as "culture," preserving an order through integration or identity; and *utopia* on the other hand imagines another society or another reality with the function of contesting or critiquing the given lived sociocultural reality, serving to disrupt and break through the old to produce the new.[27] In this context, the social imaginary (*imaginaire social*) for Ricoeur would be the ensemble of stories, "symbolic discourses," that mediate human activity, bounded by ideology and utopia, and mediate reality as lived in all societies.[28]

Cornelius Castoriadis (1922–97) has also thematized the creativity of the imagination in its ontological significance, while developing the concept of the social imaginary. Taking off from Kant's understanding of the imagination and building on Freud's theory of the unconscious, Castoriadis defines the imagination as "the power to make that which 'realiter' *is not*"[29] or "the capacity to give rise to something that is not the 'real' "[30]—that is, what is not given in perception or previously constituted thought. The *radical* imagination (and imaginary)—taking *radical* in its root sense, *radix*, as originary—is the elementary creative force that creates figures, forms, images, meanings or significations, institutions, worlds, ex nihilo,[31] a representational spontaneity at the root of the human psyche that escapes subordination to any predetermined end, a "spontaneous, creative, afunctional force,"[32] "the unceasing and essentially *undetermined* (social-historical and psychical) creation of figures/forms/images … 'reality' and 'rationality' are its works."[33] The creative imagination encompasses both the more specific radical imagination of the psyche on the one hand and the radical imaginary of the social-historical (as social imaginary significations) on the other. What it creates are *images*, but which are *forms*—forms of being, whether language, institutions, art, and so on.[34] And the role of these imaginary significations is to provide answers to fundamental questions about our identity, origin, place, purpose, needs, relationship to the world, and so on—questions that neither "rationality" nor "reality" can answer.[35] With their function of valuing and devaluing, these imaginary significations provide society with an *orientation*, a *Stimmung* or mood.[36] They "construct (organize, articulate, vest with meaning) the world of the society considered,"[37] hence create for that society a *proper* world (*Eigenwelt*) and *are* this world.[38] The world is thus no longer chaos but an ordered plurality, an organized diversity, whereby value and non-value arise and a distinction is made between true and false, permitted and prohibited.[39] On this basis Castoradis states that the imagination/imaginary, encompassing both the social imaginary and the psychical imagination, is the logical and ontological condition of the "real."[40]

But in order to realize this ordering or formation the imaginary contains within it "an initial and infinitely fertile indistinction."[41] Its ordering is thus never functionalist or completely "rational" or "strictly utilitarian."[42] While its afunctional spontaneity needs to be tamed, the taming is never fully accomplished and never brought under complete control. The forms it creates then are never complete but allow for alteration and novelty. While the radical imagination, for Castoriadis, thus precludes reduction to functionality and escapes predetermination, it also permits creativity, novelty, and breaks. Hence the radical imaginary as such deploys itself through the two dimensions of the *instituting* and the *instituted, as* both society and history, as the *social-historical.*[43] In other words, it is social but the social is historical, it is never stabilized and thus changes.

Charles Taylor (1931–) more recently has developed an understanding of the social imaginary as a kind of "background" or "framework" informing all thought and action, so that it "enables, through making sense of, the practices of a society."[44] He defines social imaginary as the ways in which people collectively imagine their social existence or life pre-theoretically—their social surroundings often carried in images, stories, legends; how they fit together with others, how things go on between them, the expectations normally met, and the deeper norms underlying these expectations.[45] The social imaginary as such is shared in common by a group and is "the common understanding that makes possible common practices and a … shared sense of legitimacy,"[46] incorporating a sense of normal expectations of one another, the sense of how we all fit together through our common practices. It is thus constitutive of the world in which we live.[47] But this understanding, Taylor adds, is both factual and normative, involving the sense of how things *usually* go but also how they *ought* to go, a sense of moral order, presupposing a wider grasp of what makes our norms realizable, images through which we understand human life and history, how we stand to each other, our communal origins, and how we relate to others beyond our group.[48] This wider grasp of our "background" has no clear limits and is an "unstructured and inarticulate understanding of our whole situation," an indefinite something that can never be adequately articulated in explicit doctrines.[49] But it is precisely this broad indefinite scope of the social imaginary that enables a social theory then to be "schematized" in the sphere of common practice analogous to how an abstract category becomes "schematized" in application to sensible reality for Kant.[50] Moving beyond Taylor for a moment, this indefinition is analogous to what Castoriadis spoke of as the *nihil* or chaos out of which—ex nihilo—the imagination creates forms or in terms of the Kyoto School philosophy of Japan, the nothing that determines itself into beings or formlessness that forms itself into forms. This notion of the indefinition or the nothing behind—or at the root of—the imaginary or imagination is a point we need to keep in mind in the following as we now turn to the Kyoto School philosopher who takes Nishida's notion of the self-determining nothing as a starting point in developing his understanding of the creative imagination beyond the epistemic scope of Kant.

2. THE IMAGINATION IN JAPANESE PHILOSOPHY: MIKI KIYOSHI

While Ricoeur and Castoriadis were developing the concept of the creative imagination to encompass the social and the historical, the power of the imagination as creative and constitutive of human social existence was already recognized and articulated some decades earlier in the works of the Japanese philosopher Miki Kiyoshi (1897–1945). Miki was a student of the central figure of the Kyoto School, Nishida Kitarō, and like his mentor was concerned with the issue of transcending the subject-object dualism of Neo-Kantian epistemology. Miki articulated this in terms of the issue of the synthesis of the objective and the subjective, rational and irrational, intellectual and emotional, and ultimately in terms of the dialectical unity of *logos* and *pathos* in history.[51] Miki's attempt to solve this issue led him to the notion of the (creative) imagination (*kōsōryoku* 構想力), borrowing the concept from Kant, who recognized in the first Critique the imagination's synthetic function of bringing together sensibility and understanding[52] along with its creativity. Jean-Luc Amalric's reading of Ricoeur's imagination, whereby man is a "desire to be" (*désir d'être*) involving the ever-renewed mediation—a dialectic—between the finitude of his state and the infinitude of his act of existing, *bios* and *logos*, being and doing,[53] some decades later may perhaps be comparable. And perhaps analogous to Ricoeur's emphasis upon the practical dimension through which the imagination becomes manifest, Miki in developing his philosophy of the imagination aims to take the standpoint of the actor acting *within* history as opposed to the philosopher who merely theorizes about facts from outside of their historical happenings. The point is that the practical and historical dimension is essential in Miki's understanding of the imagination. For Miki, the creation of images out of emotion, passion, or impulse—what he calls *pathos*—through synthesis with the intellectual, culminates externally in the production—*poiesis*—of "formed images" (*keizō* 形像) (from the Greek *eidos* and German *Bild*).[54] He understands human technical production accordingly as creation via the imagination uniting *logos* and *pathos*. And he takes myth, technics, and institutions to be examples of such forms or the media of such forms, all of which undergo change through the history of human action. The imagination as such expresses the human impulse to act and produce by inventing, constructing, and altering reality. He expounds this in *The Logic of the Imagination*, which he begins writing in 1937 and continued working on until 1943.[55]

In opposition to Hegel's claim that the real is the rational, Miki's claim is that the real is imaginary (*sōzōteki* 想像的) in that it follows the "logic of the imagination" (*kōsōryoku (sōzōryoku) no ronri* 構想力(想像力)の論理).[56] That is, the real, similar to how it is the product of the social imaginary for Castoriadis, unfolds for our being-in-the-world according to the imagination's structuring activity, involving the ambiguities between subjectivity and objectivity, ideality and reality, interiority and exteriority, intellectual and emotive, time and space.[57] Miki's thesis thus is that the imagination is the formless source that creates forms in the unfolding of its logic. The imagination as such is a primordial creative power not confined to artists—as in Kant's understanding of genius—but lying in the depths of human nature itself, common to all human beings,[58] more primal than reason itself.[59] We may recall here how the etymology of the German word for imagination, *Einbildungskraft*, encompasses the sense of "formation" (*Bildung*), and how the German for image also means "form" (*Bild*). In Kant, the imagination produces "schemata" (*zushiki* 図式), which serve as rules indicating the scope or range for the production of the image (*Bild*). Miki takes this to mean that the imagination's originary activity of mediating sensibility and understanding—in Miki's terms, *pathos* and *logos*—is possible because it is their originary root. In Miki's reading of Kant, concepts of the understanding are only abstractions of schemata as such, which make possible "formed images" (*keizō* 形像).[60] But we also need to remember here that form and formation for Miki extend beyond the mere epistemic or cognitive domains as simply mental or ideal to also take concrete shape in what environs us as communal beings. The images the imagination produces are ultimately created as *formed* images (*keizō*), images embodied in forms, so that its logic is a logic of formed images (*keizō no ronri* 形像の論理)[61] and a logic of production (*seisaku no ronri* 制作の論理),[62] the creation of new forms. Objects are worked upon, trans-formed, and given new form[63] so that the forms thus produced are not merely ideal in the Platonic sense but *embodied*. In Plato, the *idea* as *eidos* has the significance of *form*, but in Miki's case the forms are not only ideal but include embodied and physical forms, whereby we give shape to our environment. In other words, what the imagination gives birth to is not imaginary in the sense of fanciful fictions but the very reality of the world in which we dwell.[64] Furthermore, they are historical: *forms* unfolding reality through history. Human history involves the trans-*formations* of forms in the logic of forms (*katachi no ronri* 形の論理) rooted in the imagination.[65] Several decades later Castoriadis will also speak of the products of the imagination as *forms*—forms of being, including language, institutions, art, and so on.[66] As Miki develops his concept of the imagination through the chapters on myth, institution, and technics, in his *Logic of the Imagination*, the embodied, practical, and concrete reality of the forms of the imagination becomes more and more apparent.

This logic of the imagination as it involves human embodied activity through history is a logic of *praxis*, a logic of action (*kōi no ronri* 行為の論理).[67] And this *praxis* is necessarily technical and productive. Miki describes this productivity as giving form to the formless, a movement from chaos to form, darkness to light (*yami kara hikari*), indetermination to determination (*mugentei kara gentei*), nothing to being (*mu kara yū*).[68] In the face of the nothing of indeterminacy and disorder, man is driven by a "demonic"—he uses the German word *demonisch*[69]—urge to give order, determine, form, to thus produce a new world and reality, a *cosmos* in the sense of *order* or *culture* in the sense of *cultivation*. The root of creation is this inner *pathos* of man, an indetermination demanding determination.[70] The imagination attempts to give form to that *pathos* affecting us within. So it unifies that *pathos* with *logos*, gathering or "raking together" (*kakiatsumeru* 掻き集める) the chaos to give it form or order.[71] This activity unfolds the process of human history as the formation and transformation of forms. And as forms undergo change through history,[72] the logic of the imagination that is a logic of forms is also a logic of historical creation (*rekishiteki sōzō no ronri* 歴史的創造の論理).[73] This activity mediates the subject and the environment, transforming the latter into culture that is a *world*. The world as such provides human beings with their environment, not just the natural environment but the cultural and social environments with their institutions. And thereby the imagination gives birth to the very reality of our world.[74]

Institutions (*seido* 制度) are therefore prime examples of what Miki means by forms. As forms created by the imagination but constituting our world, they possess "reality" despite being "fictions." As such institutions provide an "objective expression" to what otherwise is the "subjective expression" of the imagination.[75] What he calls "institutions" here includes "language, custom, morality, law, politics, art, etc." and signifies "culture" as a whole,[76] and in a certain sense also includes myth.[77] What they all have in common is that (1) they possess a fictional character in that they are *conventions*, thus having a social character that assembles a group of people (*convenio = to come together*); (2) they are endowed with the character of being customary (from custom, *coustume*) or traditions, whereby their fictionality is forgotten and they are seen as natural or necessary, as "second nature"; and (3) they have the character of *nomos* or normativity in that they become constraining and authoritative vis-à-vis the individual.[78] Despite being fiction, the normativity or imperative character of an institution constitutes its reality. Miki provides the example of ritual blood mixing to create artificial blood relations in ancient periods when blood relations were morally and socially necessary.[79] A more current example would be greeting customs, which are inventions rather than being based on nature or instinct.[80] This is analogous to how for Castoriadis institutions incarnate the imaginary and become autonomous in their functioning and how the "real" in the human world is thus not merely a possible object of knowledge but what becomes categorized by the imaginary in its meaningfulness.[81] For Castoriadis, the imaginary "institutes" or sets up institutions—for example, of government, laws, customs, norms, morality, sensibility, taste, judgment, and so on—for its own functioning and maintenance. The social imaginary manifests itself and brings itself into being in and through such social-historical institution, presenting its significations.[82] Society for Castoriadis is thus the institution of meanings, that is, social imaginary significations.[83] In Ricoeur, the cultural imagination facilitates the creation of "cultural patterns" that "provide templates or blueprints for the organization of social and psychological processes," that is, the sociocultural formation of reality in all of its forms.[84] Such patterns, Miki calls "forms" and in the concrete cultural sphere, they are "institutions." And he thinks, agreeing with Ricoeur, that it is not instinct but rather the imagination that is at work behind the production of such institutions.[85]

Institutions as such emerge in the human being's active relationship with the environment as adaptations.[86] It involves the habituation or customization of non-instinctive acts, making them second nature, which help us to adapt to the environment. Through custom and convention, the fiction of the institution becomes real and authoritative for the collective and operates as a powerful myth.[87] Moreover, as "working adaptations" (*sagyōteki tekiō* 作業的適応),[88] they are not fixed but variable and similar to how in Ricoeur, the imagination remains unceasingly dynamic in the dialectical tension between the given, its remaking, and the newly given, between prefiguration and transfiguration.[89] Once institutions as such are set up and become operative in adapting to the environment, they in turn constitute a new environment for us,[90] our "world" as the historically formed sociocultural environment.[91] Nevertheless despite Miki's recognition of the embodied nature of the products of the imagination and practice that actualize its creativity, in comparison to Ricoeur or Castoriadis, Miki still seems to be caught in a residual transcendentalism inherited from Kant when he emphasizes the transcendentality of the imagination[92] and uses the terminology of German transcendentalism.

The very actions whereby human beings transcend their environment to change it and create a new one are technical. Technics or technology (*gijitsu* 技術) as such is a productive activity of the imagination that gives birth to new forms (*katachi* 形) by structurally assimilating existent elements in new syntheses. Man transcends his environment from which he is alienated to reconstruct it through technics into an environment better suited to him. The imagination imagines what is not to thus generate being out of nothing, ex nihilo, via technics. More specifically technics produces new forms by synthesizing two moments: cognition of laws of nature (the objective) and the postulation of goals (the subjective)—another example of the imagination's synthesis of the objective and the subjective, *logos* and *pathos*. Resulting from that synthesis is the third moment, the creation of newly defined forms through the actual alteration of things.[93] The subjective expression of the imagination is thus given objective expression via institutions and made practical via technics.

Initially, at least for the majority of the chapters of the *Logic of the Imagination*, the imagination, whereby human beings transcend their environment to reconstruct it through technics, is what distinguishes the human from other living beings. Yet by the end of Miki's composition of the book, the tone changes as he begins to claim that the creative logic of the imagination is *already* operative *within nature itself*, prior to the rise of humanity, so that natural life can also be viewed to be technical and form-creating.[94] In another work, *Philosophy of Technics* (*Gijutsu tetsugaku*), published during the same period (1942) when he was composing the second part of the *Logic of the Imagination*, he defines the essence of technics common to both nature and humanity in terms of "transformation" (*tenkei* 転形) as the fundamental act in both.[95] And to the extent that there is the altering of forms in nature, nature has a kind of history as well. Miki thus states that natural history and human history *both* involve trans-*form*ation (alteration of forms) and are thus united in the history of *transformation* (*katachi no henka no rekishi* 形の変化の歴史).[96] And where there is transformation, there is technics. While human technics was born of man's struggle with his environment, it reconnects man estranged from nature thus back to nature. Human technics is an extension of the technics of nature. Man plays a particular role within the broader history of nature to bring it to completion by imitating and extending nature's technics, whereby human technics participates in the transformation of historical nature[97]: it "takes up the construction of the universe at the point it has been abandoned by nature."[98] The broader category here is history itself—the unfolding of the historical world—in which both man and nature, human culture and biological nature, are encompassed and participate through the foundational act of transformation (*tenkei*), the incessant history of the transformation of forms by means of technics. One might recognize here something similar to Nishida's notion of man as a creative element of the world, especially when Miki says in *The Philosophy of Technics*, "The historical world is creative and human being is a creative element of the creative world"[99] and that "as formative elements of the formative world, we participate in the self-formation of the historical world"[100] although it is up to debate in regard to the question of who influenced whom with this idea between Miki and his mentor Nishida.[101] In any case commentators like Nakamura—whom we shall discuss in the following section—have argued that Miki, at least, has begun the process of rendering certain ideas of Nishida that otherwise seem abstract into formulations that are more concrete and tangible.

Miki pursued the theme of the logic of the imagination consistently throughout the later years of his life. Yet he also admitted that his writings on the topic were still research notes and that he had not yet arrived at a systematic narrative of the issue that he hoped to complete. He passed away before he was able to bring Part Two of *The Logic of the Imagination* to completion. Nevertheless there is still much worth unpacking out of what Miki had left with us today, especially of his "logic of the imagination."

3. COMMON SENSE AND THE IMAGINATION IN JAPANESE PHILOSOPHY: NAKAMURA YŪJIRŌ

In postwar Japan, Nakamura Yūjirō (1925–) has taken up Miki's legacy in discussing the implications of the collective creativity of human nature constitutive of the world. But rather than focusing on the imagination, Nakamura explicates this creativity through the concept of "common sense" (*kyōtsū kankaku* 共通感覚), taking off from his readings of Aristotle's *koinē aisthēsis* and Giambattista Vico's *sensus communis*, in his book *On Common Sense* (*Kyōtsūkankakuron*, hereafter abbreviated as KK).[102] He does however admit to a connection between his notion of common sense and Miki's concept of the imagination, and between the common sense as first discovered by Aristotle and then developed and occluded through the history of Western philosophy and the imagination as developed by Kant and beyond.

Nakamura begins with the point that human beings exist not only as individuals but always within a "world," that is, a meaningful framework of social relationships assumed in all of their perceptions (see KK 1–4). The world that is assumed as a whole in our day-to-day activities provides the necessary context to make our perceptions meaningful—an intersubjective horizon of experience that is the working of "common sense." *Common sense* usually has this meaning of a faculty of judgment—a *sense*—that people possess *in common* within a society (KK 7). This for the most part is how we ordinarily use the term in English today, which in Japanese is *jōshiki* (常識). Common sense in this significance is our common understanding based on what has become self-evident or obvious within the common semantic field of a particular society or culture, but which we hardly ever notice (KK 5).

In turn it provides the horizon of further self-evidence that shapes a certain layer of thought and behavior within a given time, society, culture, and so on (KK 280). Yet in enveloping us in this unassailable horizon of self-evidence, it can also block our view of what is not obvious or self-evident.

In addition to that current and popular meaning of *common sense*, however, Nakamura reminds us of the original meaning of the term, that is, a *sense* that is *common* to, and coordinates and integrates the various sensations (*sense*), a synthetic or synthesizing sense that gathers and arranges the so-called five senses (seeing, hearing, smelling, tasting, and touching) (KK 7). When we plumb the depths of *common sense (kyōtsū kankaku* 共通感覚*)*, its originary sense reemerges with significance (KK 279–280). Nakamura traces the currently more popular meaning of common sense, its social sense, on the one hand, back to the lineage of the Humanists stemming from the Roman classics, including Cicero, and extending up to the Renaissance (KK 7, 152–153). He traces the older and more originary sense, on the other hand, to Aristotle's *koinē aisthēsis* or what in medieval times became known in Latin as *sensus communis*. Common sense in this latter significance is what is in phase with, and required by, the faculty of the imagination as its "seat," and serves as the contact point between sensitivity and reason (KK 199). According to Nakamura, Aristotle in *On Sleeping and Waking* understood common sense as such a primordial sensible faculty that compares, distinguishes, and coordinates the distinct senses (KK 8, 306 n.3).[103] The connection to the imagination here is that mental images (*phantasma*) are the affection or passive state (*pathos*) of common sense (*koinē aiesthēsis*) and first emerge when sense impressions are gathered through the common sensory faculty. Once the particular sense impressions are gathered and produce the *pathos* of common sense, the imagination (*phantasia*) reproduces that gathered and common sensory impression as mental images even in the absence of the sensory object (KK 228).[104]

At the dawn of modernity, René Descartes inherited this Aristotelian notion of common sense through the medieval Scholastics. He refers to the *sensorium commune* as the seat of the *sensus communis* (or *sens commun*) connecting reason and sensation (in *Meditations* IV, *On Man*, and *On the Passions* I) (KK 174–176). But at the same time he distinguishes *sens commun* as sensible and bodily from conceptual thought and reason. Taking it as the principle of the imagination, he devalues both imagination and common sense as the cause of error (KK 178–179). Thus rejecting *sens commun*, Descartes establishes *bon sens* (good sense) instead, identifying it with reason (KK 344). According to Nakamura, the understanding of common sense that had occupied the main current of the West from ancient and medieval times up to the Renaissance, through the lineage from Aristotle to the Scholastics (KK 152–153), became forgotten in this way with the beginning of modernity, or at least submerged under the more current social significance of the term and today remains only as an undercurrent.

In Nakamura's analysis of the history of this concept, the two meanings of "*sensus communis*" constitute two distinct lineages: on the one hand as the faculty of receptivity within the individual human being that integrates the various senses, and on the other hand, as the faculty of judgment held in common among a people.

Each significance has been the focus of one or other of two distinct intellectual streams in the history of Western thought, the Aristotelian-Scholastic line for the former and the line from the Roman classics (Cicero) to Renaissance Humanism for the latter. But Nakamura adds here that it is not always easy to separate the two as they have crisscrossed and intermingled within the history of ideas (KK 153). The two lineages cross at the point when Cicero took Aristotle's *sensus communis* and changed its meaning from the integration of the five senses to the faculty of sound judgment common to a people. Accompanying this change in meaning was Cicero's emphasis on ceaseless inquiry, open debate, the value of probability in the pursuit of truth, and the importance of agreement among a people—*consensus*—concerning public issues (KK 240–241). Appealing to common sense in this social sense, Cicero moreover proposed a *rhetorical* form of knowledge that deals with concrete practice in contrast to logic or dialectics (KK 288–289). Much later after the beginning of modernity, Giambattista Vico (in his *Scienza Neuova* or *New Science* of 1725) inherits this notion of *sensus communis* from Cicero. In his anti-Cartesian stance, Vico advances his understanding of common sense as the criterion of practical judgment over which a community is in consensus, supporting their sense of certitude. Parallel to this, Vico also advocates rhetoric as the form of knowledge that takes this significance of common sense as its standpoint. It is rhetorical knowledge as the knowledge of probable truths stemming from Vico's version of *sensus communis* that inspires Wolfgang Blankenburg's understanding of common sense as what facilitates the integration and interpretation of meanings within a given society, serving as the logic of the "life world"[105] (KK 42–43). Nakamura also here refers to Kant's notion of common sense (*Gemeinsinn*) developed in the third Critique, which in Blankenburg's reading assumes an intersubjective understanding of the world that is so familiar and elemental, hence "ordinary," yet so difficult to objectify (KK 43, 309 n.22). But eventually this meaning of common sense within Western modernity became separated from rhetoric and instead became associated with reason (KK 171).

The two meanings of common sense as analyzed by Nakamura may remind one of how Castoriadis's concept of the radical imaginary covers both the sociohistorical and the psychic-somatic dimensions. Nakamura suggests that the two senses making up aspects of common sense *are meant* to correspond in a way that leaves room for critique and change for better correspondence (KK 10). That is, the synthetic integration of the various senses ought to found the communal standards of a society and the latter ought to be an externalization of the former. But the commonly accepted ideas of society are related to our mode of integrating the various senses in reverse order as well. On the basis of our everyday perception of the world, common sense operates selectively in its integration of the senses. In other words, on the basis of common sense (*jōshiki*) as socially habituated and accepted ideas taking root at the unconscious level, our common sense (*kyōtsū kankaku*) becomes habituated in its mode of integrating the five senses so that its selection in perception becomes congealed (KK 28–29). Habituation as such on some level is certainly convenient and necessary—indeed indispensable for social life—for example, in the act of buying a ticket to ride public transportation or waiting for the green light to cross a cross-walk (KK 29, 32). Its "logic" in Husserlian terms is the logic of the "life world"

(KK 40). Yet such habituation can become congealed and fixed as what is merely "common place," mere convention, through captivation to invisible institutions, to the extent that it loses—and even obstructs—the ability to correspond and deal with the abundant diversity and alterations of reality (KK 30, 188). In such situations common sense—as the "commonly and socially accepted"—becomes something that needs to be questioned as inadequate in its grasp of reality. We then need to attend to the faculty of common sense itself so that we can grasp not only the affairs of everyday experience, but the very horizon for that inter-subjective experience that establishes and shapes their self-evidence (KK 11). We need to attend to the operation of common sense in both significances—"*jōshiki*" and "*kyōtsū kankaku*" (KK 280). For it is not simply social convention that becomes congealed but, even deeper, the integration of the senses, so that one no longer grasps reality in its diverse nature, and it becomes necessary to rearrange the senses in a way that would reactivate them and retrieve the original activity of common sense (see KK 30).

At this point, we might recall Kant's own discussion of the *sensus communis*, central to his notion of communicability in the third Critique. For Kant this "sense" involves three capacities: (1) the capacity for critical thinking in relation to both the everyday "common sense" that is taken-for-granted and the specialized forms of knowledge and opinion; (2) the capacity to think from the standpoint of an *other* or to think from a standpoint broader than one's own; and (3) the capacity to think in a consistent way while combining the first two capacities.[106] According to Rundell the *sensus communis* as such, within the context of the third Critique, operates as a public sphere wherein critical reflection occurs without preconditions and constraints.[107] Nakamura understands common sense in a similar fashion while distinguishing it from reason's analytic capacity. But it has been argued that what makes a judgment rational and hence successful for Kant in his third Critique is when it is derived not simply from a set of principles—hence reason—but also from a universalizable value horizon related to a specific human self-image, that is, autonomous freedom. In Rundell's reading of Kant, the *sensus communis* is the participation in this universalizable value idea, an orientating value that is neither transcendental nor teleological. And neither are they secure as they are historical creations—in Castoriadis's terms, "imaginary significations."[108] This again points back to Nakamura's understanding of common sense constitutive of a world horizon, which however is flexible and never stable and certainly capable of self-reflection. At the same time he has dropped the residue of German transcendentalism in his conception of common sense that still lingered in Miki's discussions of the imagination.

In distinction from reason's ability to analyze, divide, and partition, common sense in its ideal and healthy function, for Nakamura, is the ability to take the whole picture into view and respond spontaneously to the ever-changing demands of the real world and its concrete and diverse situations. This in a certain sense takes off from Kant's notion of the *sensus communis* in the third Critique. But Nakamura refers to Hannah Arendt,[109] according to whom common sense originally meant the sense that adapts each of the five senses to the world common to everyone (KK 151, 324 n.11). It fits the "five strictly individual senses and their strictly particular data" into reality as a whole—the common world—so that the senses can be understood as disclosing reality.[110] For Arendt, a noticeable decrease in common sense as such—what Nakamura would call *kyōtsū kankaku*—in any given community and a noticeable increase in superstition and gullibility—which often become a part of what Nakamura calls *jōshiki*—would therefore be "almost infallible signs of alienation from the world."[111] Nakamura thus believes it desirable to retrieve this original sense to shed new light on what we mean by common sense for the various contemporary issues surrounding the grounding of perception and cognition—body, identity, language, the ground of critique, lived time and space, landscape, institution, false consciousness, and so on—all of which relate to, and converge on, this issue of common sense (KK 9).

A related issue in contemporary times is the disintegration of the senses when the inherited social paradigm no longer seems applicable. When the ground assumed by common sense in its social significance begins to shake, fragment, and become overtly diverse, we lose our sense of normality and are overcome with anxiety as we come in touch with the *not* self-evident, *non*-ordinary (KK 280) chaos. Nakamura refers to Kimura Bin 木村敏 (1931–),[112] for example, who takes both schizophrenia and depersonal neurosis to be such pathologies, whereby common sense as the faculty orienting us to the world as a whole is no longer at work (see KK 44–46). Although this horizon formed by common sense is not unchanging and relative to time and place, epoch and society, it fundamentally shapes our reality. In periods of crisis when this horizon of self-evidence is disrupted—and Nakamura thinks this is the contemporary situation—a rearrangement or recomposition of "knowledge" becomes necessary (KK 280). And for this Nakamura seems to be suggesting that an acknowledgment of the rhetorical form of knowledge in association with the reassessment of common sense is necessary (see KK 301). By a "rhetorical form of knowledge" Nakamura means precisely a kind of knowledge that appeals to common sense and deals with concrete practice rather than logic. This would be prudential, situational knowledge such as of contexts, and can also include the knowledge of probabilities.

For Nakamura it is common sense that constitutes and perceives that horizon of the world along with rhetoric as a form of knowledge that cognizes the possibilities of that horizon. For it is common sense, not pure reason, that is the faculty for making practical decisions within specific communal contexts, and it is also common sense that comprehends language in its natural use with all of its logical ambiguity or polysemy of words, metaphorical expressions, and contextuality. And it is also common sense that in its relation to our body orients us within a place, connecting us to our environment. Taylor had spoken of our "implicit grasp of social space" that enables us to get around a familiar environment without having to adopt the overview standpoint of a map, and how our implicit grasp of "the common repertory" enables us to function likewise without a theoretical overview, both cases involving the social imaginary permitting human beings to operate pre-theoretically.[113] Nakamura's common sense in this regard is quite similar to Taylor's social imaginary. Common sense, in its intimacy with the imagination, is very much involved in the contextualizing interrelationality of body, language, and place, for Nakamura. For example, it is very much a part of collective memory as a social act involving the act of linguistic narration (KK 210). It is also attuned to time in the sense of the sociocultural rhythm of a nation or region—a people—formed historically (KK 254–256). Lived multilayered time as such is on the one hand an object of common sense as *kyōtsū kankaku*, but on the other hand what establishes common sense as *jōshiki* (KK 257). And common sense is also involved in the constitution and perception of a meaningful place whether as ground, symbolic, somatic, or linguistic and discursive (see KK 266–270).[114]

For example, linguistic or discursive place ties into rhetorical knowledge in its recognition of the contextual *topos* of an issue. Here Nakamura refers to Vico's view (in his *New Science* of 1744) that common sense is the sense that provides (contextual) places—*topoi*—for our common understanding, for "*sensus communis* is a judgment without reflection, shared by an entire class, an entire people, an entire nation, or the entire human race"[115] (KK 165–166). Vico incorporates Bacon's *topics* (*topica*) in his *On Method in Contemporary Fields of Study* (1709). Therein Vico states that without common sense, we can neither make accurate practical judgments nor sufficiently communicate to others what we want to say. As a clue to such practical judgment and oratory, Vico raises *topica* in its concern for the discovery of probable truths and issues based on the multi-sidedness of human existence (KK 164–165, 272). Nakamura makes the point that within the lifeworld, a concrete issue possesses a coherence of its own for which we need to discover its *topos*—the context wherein it coheres—while avoiding a quasi- or abstract universal explanation on the one hand and utter individualism that would abandon all explanation on the other hand (KK 275, 301). We can only grasp the meaning of history in the form of an *approximate sense* possessed by the assemblage of facts of the past, an approximate sense belonging to the multi-sided consideration of concrete issues (KK 276). Nakamura's point seems to be that common sense is very much involved in the uncovering of these *topoi* or *loci* of implicit and multilayered meanings. All of this in turn might also be rephrased in terms of the social imaginary or imagination.

Nakamura himself makes a connection between his understanding of common sense and the imagination as developed by Miki Kiyoshi. Like Nakamura, Miki was also interested in rhetoric, which he found to have been ignored by modern philosophy with its exclusive focus on logic.[116] Nakamura claims that we are now in a position to develop Miki's critique on the basis of an even broader setting (see KK 301–302). Nakamura thus views himself as standing in the same current of awareness of issues as Miki but that while Miki, borrowing Kant's terminology, proposed a "logic of imagination," he himself, borrowing Aristotle's terminology, proposes a "theory of common sense."[117] As Nakamura shows, the concept of common sense has been closely connected to—at times, even identified with—the imagination since Aristotle (see KK 176). In Aristotle's *On the Soul*,[118] perception given by the five senses and brought together by common sense is worked upon by the imagination, mediating perception and thought, producing mental images (*phantasma*) with which the soul can think (KK 217–218, 229). But, in turn, in founding memory and recollection with its mental images, imagination at the same time informs common sense. At the contact point between sensitivity and reason, common sense is thus in phase with the imagination. Operating on the collective level among people sharing cultural values, it motivates the socioculturally endorsed way of interpreting meaning and nurtures their communal emotions. Here we find possible resonances and points of contact with contemporary European notions of the social imaginary.

In Nakamura's view we ought not to forget common sense when thinking about how our senses can be recomposed or rearranged in shaping our concrete perception. This is relevant to contemporary theories of the social imaginary. Nakamura finds contemporary significance in the issue of whether we exclude the imagination as the cause of error as Descartes did or take it as something positive. From the invention of the printing press to the recent emergence of the electronic media, our central nervous system has come to receive increasingly irresistible stimuli. What was at first an expansion of the self through new media of communication has, in Nakamura's view, led to a sensory paralysis, resulting in the amputation of the self. We might add that this condition has intensified since Nakamura's formulation of this theory in the late 1970s and is even more conspicuous today with the Internet and World Wide Web. What is necessary then is the rearrangement or recomposition of the senses and—borrowing Marshall McLuhan's terms—the discovery of a "new sense ratio" for the distribution of the various senses[119] (KK 59) that would allow us to overcome the paralysis or closure of perception caused by technological media. As each new media invention—such as the radio or photography and now YouTube, Facebook, and Twitter, and so on—changes the distribution ratio of sensation, altering our whole sensory experience, we need a method for managing, from a psychological and social perspective, the alteration of that distribution ratio (KK 61). For this, common sense along with the imagination, in its constitution of the horizon of meaning, cannot be ignored as an issue of inquiry.

CONCLUSION

One common thread throughout these thinkers, East and West, is a recognition of an abyss at the heart of creation, that is, an indeterminacy behind determination, formlessness behind form. While what Miki in *Tetsugakuteki Ningengaku* (*Philosophical Anthropology*) called *pathos* meant the receptivity (*judō* 受動) of human existence as being situated in its embodied nature by certain dispositions or affects, it also involved a dynamic impulsive power of self-expression aimed outward, urging us to action.[120] Finding oneself passively faced with the nothing (*mu* 無) from deep within oneself, a human being in turn creatively determines this into something, a being.[121] And so all creation is a "creation from nothing" (*mu kara no sōzō* 無からの創造).[122] Standing upon nothing, human existence can transcend its concrete situatedness and create out of nothing or ex nihilo.[123] Similar to Castoriadis's notion of the radical imagination/imaginary as a creative force that creates forms, figures, meanings, worlds ex nihilo,[124] to account for the undeterminable, unpredictable alterities and alterations of the sociohistorical, the nothing as the ground of existence in Miki as well allows for novelty and creativity that breaks through determinacy. Both here recognize how meanings are brought into being, reproduced, displaced, altered, transformed, in the social construction of the world, from out of a nothing. The images that the imagination produces ex nihilo, the radical abyss of the formless, are *forms* for *both* Castoriadis and Miki. Through this creation ex nihilo are constructed the world vis-à-vis nature and the self vis-à-vis others. On the basis of this *creative nothing*, the environment becomes object and man becomes subject.[125] We can say that the imagination as this faculty of formation from the formless was the result of Miki's development of the notion of his mentor, Nishida Kitarō, of the place of nothing (*mu no basho* 無の場所) as a self-forming formlessness. Yet in Miki's view, Nishida's notion of this self-forming formlessness in terms of the "self-determination of the eternal now" was too abstract, lessening the significance of the dialectical process itself,[126] and in its transcendence may tend toward the exclusion of the relative dimension, its historicity and practical temporality.[127] For Miki, right before he began working on his *Logic of the Imagination*, Nishida's philosophy, even with its notion of acting-intuition, neglects a view to process, time, and history and fails to adequately take up the standpoint of action.[128]

Nakamura views Miki's theory as providing a more concrete expression for Nishida's theory of place that was lacking in Nishida's own formulations by tying it to the concrete structures and institutions of society and history. Nakamura takes off from Miki's critique of Nishida here, finding Nishida's notion of "absolute nothing" (*zettai mu* 絶対無) as inadequate in addressing the dimension of relativity, closing the path to unfolding various concrete issues belonging to place.[129] So here Nakamura sees his own project as inheriting Miki's legacy by attempting to shed new light on Nishida's theory of place through his own theory of common sense and by unfolding the various ways in which place becomes an issue for us today (see KK 258, 295).[130] The different senses of place that Nakamura analyzes—as ontological ground, somatic, symbolic space, linguistic or discursive *topos* as contextual locale—involve common sense for Nakamura.[131] But in turn this also implies that the imagination is meant to be in tune with place in its various significances. Imagination—the faculty of formation (*Bildung*)—would have to be that faculty that recognizes, or co-participates in, the differing, differentiation, determination of place—or in Greek terms the *chōrismos* of the *chōra*[132]—in its manifold sense to institute the world, the web of imaginary significations.

Resonating among the thinkers we have examined above is the sense that the imagination is the capacity to make images, pictures, forms, constructions (*Bilder*)—not only mental but social, cultural, and even physical. It constructs an alternative to the mere *thatness* of the real to invest the real with meaning—meaning concretized in institutions making up our environment, our world. Thinkers like Castoriadis, Ricoeur, and Miki thus extend the term imagination beyond its merely epistemological or aesthetic significances and apply it to the human social collective. Ricoeur, Castoriadis, and Taylor speak of the social imagination or social imaginary as responsible for the network of (social imaginary) significations (or meanings). Parallel to this, Nakamura building upon Miki's sense of the creative imagination as a collective faculty speaks of the significance of common sense in constituting our world. The web of meanings that parallels—corresponds with and co-constitutes—the network of human relations and constructions constitute our world.

Furthermore we can add here that this "world" in its turn is supported by what in Heideggerian terms would be "the earth." That is to say that the social imaginary, as the framework for the sum total of significations that interpret and create the world, entails an indeterminacy that escapes reduction and cannot be grasped as a whole. The web of meanings—our world—is contingent, it is in flux. And at its indeterminate and altering margins there are *other* imaginaries and beyond other imaginaries there is *nature*, our environing *other*. The "earth" as such is what implies *withdrawal*, an abyss, in Nishida's terms *nothing* (*mu*), or in Ueda Shizuteru's terms, the nothing that implaces the world beyond its horizon,[133] in Castoriadian terms, *chaos*. So the nothing that is the inner *radix*, root, of the imagination's creativity is also an exteriority *beyond* the horizon of constituted world. In Miki *mu* is both within but also outside; in Castoriadis, chaos is within the psyche but also in nature. The question that arises then is: To what extent are we in control of the imagination? To what degree is its forming act transparent? Can we speak of autonomy here vis-à-vis the unpredictability and contingency of events that unfold and spur the imagination to give shape to the world? Where do we stand in the building of our world? The chaos or indeterminacy is not only beyond, outside, the world but also within the inner depths of our selves that moves the imagination to construct a world. The depth of the imagination that opens up in its creative significance for the human experience uncovers the grounding of the transcendental upon the unground that is the unsayable, the non-objectifiable, the unpredictable, within and without.

Miki's discussion of the imagination contributes to an understanding of the creative imagination by underscoring and developing its sense as the formation of the formless. This is similar to Castoradis's sense of creation ex nihilo that acknowledges an indeterminacy in the historical processes of determination, but in Miki's case what is made explicit is that this is an act of the imagination forming forms out of the formless, a formlessness that is both within and outside. In both Castoriadis and Miki, that formlessness or chaos or nothing is internal as well as environmental, but what seems significant in Miki is an implicit reference to Nishida's notion of place. For Miki is taking off from Nishida's notion of the self-forming formlessness that is a self-determining place of nothing. The connection between imagination and place is here a key that is implicit but which can and ought to be drawn out. In Nakamura this is played out in the more concrete terms of common sense as constitutive of a communal horizon or world. Nakamura discusses this world-constituting function of common sense more directly in relation to place, developing Nishida's notion of place in the concrete terms, broadly, of a sociocultural world, but also specifically as somatic or symbolic or discursive, and so on. This is his development of Nishida's notion that the place of nothing unfolds a place of being, that a formless place becomes a formed place through common sense. In such ways Nakamura's investigations captures some of the unique ways in which modern and contemporary Japanese philosophy might contribute to the discussions of the social imaginary and creative imagination. In light of the globalization of the world, with its multiple modernities, that social theorists are attempting to understand, an awareness of some of the non-Western theories concerning this and related phenomena is indispensable. In Nakamura's examinations of both Nishida's notion of place *and* Miki's notion of the imagination, what Nakamura notices is an holistic image—a horizon constitutive of the world (or "world picture")—that while being in itself unobjectifiable and unsayable must be assumed by every knowledge of an object and in every utterance of the sayable. The arrangement of the senses, working in consort with collective understanding, into a coherent and meaningful picture of the world and Miki's notion of the imagination (*Einbildung*) that collectively gives shape to the human world in the formation (*Bildung*) of forms (*Bilder*, "images"), taking off from Nishida's notion of the place of nothing whose activity is the formation of the formless, indeed resonates to some extent with, and underscores suggestive ideas that can contribute to an understanding of, the social imaginary in the constitution of a meaningful world for a collective, in Ricoeurian terms, the constitution of a social reality in the creation of meaning and, in Castoriadian terms, the undetermined self-constituting function of society. Both Nakamura's theory of common sense and Miki's discussion of the creative imagination contribute suggestive ways of approaching the social imaginary and imagination by underscoring the connections between form, formlessness, and place. A dialogue between these thinkers of East and West would indeed be fruitful.

NOTES

The citations from Kant's *Critique of Pure Reason*, and Nakamura Yūjirō's *Kyōtsūkankaku* (abbreviated as KK) are directly inserted in the test.

1. For a good introduction to the topic of the social imaginary, see Suzi Adams, Paul Blokker, Natalie Doyle, John Krummel, and Jeremy Smith, "Social Imaginaries in Debate," *Social Imaginaries* 1.1 (2015), 15–52. This particular issue of the *Social Imaginaries* is dedicated to the topic of imaginary.
2. See Aristotle, *De Anima* (*On the Soul*), Book III, chapter 3, for example, in Aristotle, *The Basic Works of Aristotle*, ed. Richard McKeon (New York: Random House, 1941), 586–589.
3. Aristotle, *De Memoria et Reminiscentia* (*On Memory and Reminiscence*) I, 449b30–450a13 in Aristotle, *The Basic Works of Aristotle*, 608; and also *De Somniis* (*On Dreams*) II, 459b6–8, 460b1–9 in Aristotle, *The Basic Works of Aristotle*, 620 and 621.
4. See Richard Kearney, *The Wake of the Imagination: Toward a Postmodern Culture* (London: Routledge, 1988), 155–156.
5. Yet it is *also* the case that Kant subsequently reduces and submerges in the second edition of the *Critique of Pure Reason* the centrality of the imagination's creativity he underscored in the first edition. Numbers followed by "A" refer to pagination from the German original of the first edition of Kant's *Critique of Pure Reason* and those followed by "B" refer to pagination from the second edition. Citations of this work are based on the English translation by Norman Kemp Smith, *Critique of Pure Reason* (New York: St. Martin's Press, Macmillan, 1929).
6. Wayne Waxman, for example, reads Kantian imagination as a nondiscursive form of spontaneity in contrast to the understanding that is the discursive form of spontaneity. See Wayne Waxman, *Kant's Model of the Mind: A New Interpretation of Transcendental Idealism* (New York: Oxford University Press, 1991), 285–286.

7. Kant calls this creative act of the productive imagination in the schematism, "figurative synthesis" (B151).
8. Immanuel Kant, *The Critique of Judgment*, trans. James Creed Meredith (Oxford: Oxford University Press, 1952), General Remark, 122–123.
9. Ibid., Remark 1, 212.
10. Ibid., §§46–47, 168–172; and §49, 175–182.
11. Ibid., §§23–28, 90–114. On this, see John Rundell, "Creativity and Judgement: Kant on Reason and Imagination," in *Rethinking Imagination: Culture and Creativity*, ed. Gillian Robinson and John Rundell (London: Routledge, 1994), 87–117, 103–104; emphasis added.
12. Kant, *The Critique of Judgment*, §50, 183.
13. On this, see Rundell in Robinson and Rundell, *Rethinking Imagination*, 106–107 and 116 n.66.
14. Cornelius Castoriadis, *World in Fragments: Writings on Politics, Society, Psychoanalysis, and the Imagination*, ed. and trans. David Ames Curtis (Stanford, CA: Stanford University Press, 1997), 214.
15. See Kant, *The Critique of Judgment*, §40, 151–153.
16. Rundell in Robinson and Rundell, *Rethinking Imagination*, 107.
17. See Kant, *The Critique of Judgment*, §35, 143.
18. Ibid., §40, 153.
19. See Rundell in Robinson and Rundell, *Rethinking Imagination*, 108 and 112.
20. Ibid., 113.
21. See Paul Ricoeur, "Ethics and Culture: Habermas and Gadamer in Dialogue," in *Political and Social Essays*, ed. S. Stewart and J. Bien (Athens: Ohio University Press, 1974), 243–270.
22. María Avelina Celia Lafuente, "Social Imagination and History in Paul Ricoeur," *Analecta Husserliana: The Yearbook of Phenomenological Research* vol. XC (90): Logos of Phenomenology (2006), 195–222 and 197–198, quoting A. T. Tymieniecka, "Imaginatio Creatix," *Analecta Husserliana* vol. III (1974), 39. Tymieniecka speaks of it here as "a novel orchestration of man's functioning."
23. Richard Kearney, *Poetics of Imagining: Modern to Post-modern* (New York: Fordham University Press, 1998), 142 and 152.
24. Paul Ricoeur, *Time and Narrative vol. 1*, trans. Kathleen McLaughlin and David Pellauer (Chicago: University of Chicago Press, 1984), 68.
25. See Ricoeur's discussions of the imagination also in *Freedom and Nature: The Voluntary and the Involuntary*, trans. Razim V. Kohák (Chicago: Northwestern University Press, 1966); and *Fallible Man: Philosophy of the Will*, trans. Charles Kelbley (Chicago: Henry Regnery Co., 1965).
26. See Lafuente, "Social Imagination and History in Paul Ricoeur," 196–197, 217.
27. Paul Ricoeur, *Lectures on Ideology and Utopia*, ed. George H. Taylor (New York: Columbia University Press, 1986), 3; George Taylor, "Editor's

Introduction," in Ricoeur, *Lectures on Ideology and Utopia*, xxviii, xxxii–xxxv; and see Lafuente, "Social Imagination and History in Paul Ricoeur," 202.

28. Paul Ricoeur, "The Creativity of Language: Interview with Richard Kearney," in *A Ricoeur Reader: Reflection and Imagination*, ed., M. J. Valdes (Toronto: University of Toronto Press, 1991), 463–481, 470, 475.
29. Cornelius Castoriadis, "Radical Imagination and the Social Instituting Imaginary" in Robinson and Rundell, *Rethinking Imagination*, 136–154, 139; emphasis in the original. This article also appears in Castoriadis, *The Castoriadis Reader*, trans. and ed. David Ames Curtis (Oxford, UK: Blackwell, 1997), 319–337.
30. Castoriadis, *World in Fragments*, 181. Also see Castoriadis, *The Imaginary Institution of Society*, trans. Kathleen Blamey (Cambridge, MA: MIT Press, 1987), 388 n.25.
31. See Castoriadis, *Figures of the Thinkable*, trans. Helen Arnold (Stanford, CA: Stanford University Press, 2007), 73; also *Imaginary Institution of Society*, 127, 388 n.25.
32. Castoriadis, *Figures of the Thinkable*, 205.
33. Castoriadis, *Imaginary Institution of Society*, 3; emphasis in the original.
34. Castoriadis in Robinson and Rundell, *Rethinking Imagination*, 140; *Figures of the Thinkable*, 73.
35. Castoriadis, *Imaginary Institution of Society*, 146–147.
36. Ibid., 150; Castoriadis in Robinson and Rundell, *Rethinking Imagination*, 152.
37. Castoriadis, *Philosophy, Politics, Autonomy: Essays in Political Philosophy*, ed. David Ames Curtis (New York: Oxford University Press, 1991), 42.
38. Castoriadis in Rundell, 143, 152.
39. Castoriadis, *Imaginary Institution of Society*, 162–163.
40. Ibid., 336.
41. Ibid., 163.
42. See ibid., 149–150. Castoriadis reminds us here that in fact there is no society in which food, dress, dwellings, and so on obey strictly "utilitarian" or "rational" considerations.
43. Castoriadis, *Philosophy, Politics, Autonomy*, 143.
44. Charles Taylor, *Modern Social Imaginaries* (Durham: Duke University Press, 2004), 2. See also his *A Secular Age* (Cambridge: Harvard University Press, 2007), 387, where he speaks of "frameworks" and "complex environing backgrounds of our thought and action."
45. Taylor, *Modern Social Imaginaries*, 23, 50.
46. Ibid., 23.
47. See ibid., 30.
48. Ibid., 24, 25, 28.
49. Ibid., 25.
50. See ibid., 29–30.
51. Miki Kiyoshi, "*Kōsōryoku no ronri*" [The logic of the imagination] (1939), MKZ 8.4.
52. Ibid., MKZ 8.5.

53. Jean-Luc Amalric, "Affirmation originaire, attestation, reconnaissance: Le cheminement de l'anthropologie philospohique ricoeurienne." *Études Ricoeuriennes/ Ricoeur Studies* 2.1 (2011), 12–34, 16.
54. Miki, "*Kōsōryoku*," MKZ 8.46.
55. They were published as *Kōsōryoku no ronri* 『構想力の論理』 Part I (1939) and Part II (1946) by Iwanami Shoten. For my English translation of chapter 1, "Myth," of Part I, see *Social Imaginaries* 2.1 (forthcoming).
56. Miki, "Kōfuku ni tsuite" [On happiness] in his *Jinseiron nōto* [Notes on human life] (1938–41). MKZ 1.209.
57. See Miki, "*Kōsōryoku*," MKZ 8.7.
58. Miki Kiyoshi, "*Bungeiteki ningengaku*" [*Literary anthropology*] (1942). MKZ 11.477.
59. Miki, "*Kōsōryoku*," MKZ 8.40. Also see Tanaka Kyūbun, *Nihon no "tetsugaku" o yomitoku: "mu" no jidai o ikinukutame ni* [*Reading the "philosophy" of Japan to survive the epoch of the "nothing"*] (Tokyo: Chikuma Shobō, 2000), 199; and Akamatsu Tsunehiro, *Miki Kiyoshi: tetsugaku shisaku no kiseki* [*Miki Kiyoshi: The traces of philosophical speculation*] (Kyoto: Mineruva Shobō, 1994), 256–257.
60. On this, see Tanaka, *Nihon no "tetsugaku" o yomitoku*, 195–196. This seems to make sense if we take the schema created by the imagination as the scope or horizon within which a concept is applicable to something sensed, for it provides the range within which the heterogeneous faculties of conception (understanding) and sensation (sensibility) can work together. Phenomenologically we might then take that horizon as originary in relation to the concept and the sensation that are dichotomized in abstraction from that originary horizonal (nondualist) experience.
61. Miki, "*Kōsōryoku*," MKZ 8.46.
62. Ibid., MKZ 8.7.
63. Ibid.
64. Ibid., MKZ 8.41.
65. Ibid., MKZ 8.6.
66. See Castoradis in Rundell, 140; *Figures of the Thinkable*, 73.
67. Miki, "*Kōsōryoku*," MKZ 8.15.
68. Miki, "*Bungeiteki ningengaku*," MKZ 11.473.
69. Ibid.
70. Miki, "*Kōsōryoku*," MKZ 8.72.
71. See Tanaka, *Nihon no "tetsugaku" o yomitoku*, 193.
72. Miki, "*Kōsōryoku*," MKZ 8.7.
73. Ibid., MKZ 8.18.
74. Ibid., MKZ 8.41.
75. See Kosaka Kunitsugu, *Nishida Kitarō o meguru tetsugakusha gunzō* [*The group of philosophers surrounding Nishida Kitarō*] (Kyoto: Minerva Shobō, 1997), 222–223.
76. Miki, "*Kōsōryoku*," MKZ 8.102.
77. Ibid., MKZ 8.97.

78. Ibid., MKZ 8.102–103. Also see Tanaka, *Nihon no "tetsugaku" o yomitoku*, 203–204; and Akamatsu, *Miki Kiyoshi* 262–265.
79. Miki, "*Kōsōryoku*," MKZ 8.106–107.
80. Ibid., MKZ 8.107–108.
81. See Castoriadis, *Imaginary Institution of Society*, 160–161.
82. See ibid., 237–238, 369.
83. Castoradis in Rundell, 146.
84. Ricoeur, *Lectures on Ideology and Utopia*, 12.
85. Miki, "*Kōsōryoku*," MKZ 8.112.
86. Ibid., MKZ 8.158, 159.
87. Ibid., MKZ 8.99, 135.
88. Ibid., MKZ 8.159.
89. See Taylor in Ricoeur, *Lectures on Ideology and Utopia*, xxxii–xxxv.
90. Miki, "*Kōsōryoku*," MKZ 8.160, 180.
91. Miki, "*Tetsugakuteki ningengaku*" [*Philosophical anthropology*], MKZ 18.248.
92. Miki, "*Kōsōryoku*," MKZ 8.63ff.
93. Miki, "*Gijutsu tetsugaku*" [Philosophy of technics] (1941–42). MKZ 7.226; "*Kōsōryoku*," MKZ 8.241–243. Also see Kosaka, *Nishida Kitarō o meguru tetsugakusha gunzō*,226; and Akamatsu, *Miki Kiyoshi*, 276–277.
94. Miki, "*Kōsōryoku*," MKZ 8.236.
95. Miki, "*Gijutsu tetsugaku*," MKZ 7.253–254.
96. Miki, "*Kōsōryoku*," MKZ 8.237.
97. Miki, "*Gijutsu tetsugaku*," MKZ 7.254.
98. Miki, "*Kōsōryoku*," MKZ 8.237.
99. Miki, "*Gijutsu tetsugaku*," MKZ 7.223.
100. Ibid., MKZ 7.236.
101. For example, Funayama suggests that the influence between Nishida and Miki was reciprocal and that Miki's logic of imagination appears to have in turn influenced Nishida's logic of *poiesis*. See Funayama Shin'ichi, *Hēgeru tetsugaku to Nishida tetsugaku* [Hegelian philosophy and Nishida's philosophy] (Tokyo: Miraishia, 1984), 284. Miki himself allegedly felt that he had been approaching Nishida's philosophy with its notion of the self-formation of the formless. See Nakamura Yūjirō, "*Nishida tetsugaku to nihon no shakai kagaku*" [Nishida's philosophy and the social sciences of Japan], *Shisō* (*Thought*) (November 1995), 5–22, 7, 10. While he drew much from Nishida, his focus was on concrete phenomena, such as institutions and technics, and the logic of their unfolding.
102. Nakamura Yūjirō, *Kyōtsū kankaku ron* 『共通感覚論』 [*On common sense*] (Tokyo: Iwanami Shoten, [1979] 1983).
103. For example, this explains our ability to apply adjectives descriptive of particular senses to other sensory domains (e.g. "the *sweet sound* of a mandolin") as well as

our ability to perceive movement, rest, figure, magnitude, number, unity, and so on, which cannot be perceived by any particular sense alone. Aristotle, *De Anima* (*On the Soul*) III, 425a14–19 in Aristotle, *The Basic Works of Aristotle*, 582.

104. Aristotle, *De Memoria et Reminiscentia* (*On Memory and Reminiscence*) I, 449b30–450a13 in Aristotle, *The Basic Works of Aristotle*, 608; and also *De Somniis* (*On Dreams*) II, 459b6–8, 460b1–9 in Aristotle, *The Basic Works of Aristotle*, 620 and 621. In discussing the various sensory phenomena related to Aristotelian common sense, Nakamura (KK 43, 309–312 n.12) refers to a number of other authors, most notably Japanese psychopathologist and philosopher Kimura Bin as well as to Maurice Merleau-Ponty, who grasped man as a single *sensorium commune*, an organ of common sense.
105. Nakamura borrows this Husserlian term "life-world" (*Lebenswelt*) in explicating Blankenburg's understanding of common sense. He seems to mean the world that we live in and as shaped by our common sense.
106. Kant, *The Critique of Judgment*, §40, 152.
107. Rundell in Robinson and Rundell, *Rethinking Imagination*, 107.
108. Ibid., 112 and 113.
109. Hannah Arendt, *The Human Condition* (Chicago: University of Chicago Press, 1998), 283.
110. Ibid., 208–209. And this for Arendt was the meaning of the older German term "*Gemeinsinn*" as opposed to the more recent expression replacing it, *gesunder Menschenverstand* (283 and n.44).
111. Ibid., 209.
112. For example, in his *Jikaku no seishinbyōri* [*The pathology of self-awareness*], chapter 1, section 3.
113. Taylor, *Modern Social Imaginaries*, 25–26.
114. And for more on Nakamura's development of the notion of place, including his reading of Nishida's concept of *basho* (place), see my translation of his essay, "'The Logic of Place' and Common Sense," *Social Imaginaries* 1.1 (2015), 83–103, along with my "Introduction to Nakamura Yūjirō and his Work" in the same issue, 71–82.
115. Vico, *Scienza Neuova* (*The New Science*), §142 in Giambattista Vico, *The New Science of Giambattista Vico*, trans. Thomas Goddard Bergin and Max Harold Fisch (Ithaca, NY: Cornell University Press, 1968), 63.
116. See Miki Kiyoshi, *Retorikku no seishin* ["The spirit of rhetoric"]. MKZ 12.133–134.
117. Nakamura Yūjirō, *Nishida Kitarō II* (Tokyo: Iwanami Shoten, 2001), 58.
118. See Aristotle's *De Anima* (*On the Soul*) III, vii, 431b2-432a17 in Aristotle, *The Basic Works of Aristotle*, 594–596.
119. Marshall McLuhan, *Understanding Media: The Extensions of Man* (New York: McGraw-Hill, 1964), 45.
120. Miki, "*Tetsugakuteki ningengaku*" [Philosophical anthropology], MKZ 18.152. Fujita Masakatsu, "*Logos* and *Pathos*: Miki Kiyoshi's Logic of the Imagination," in *Japanese and Continental Philosophy: Conversations with the Kyoto School*, ed. Bret

Davis, Brian Schroeder, and Jason Wirth (Bloomington: Indiana University Press, 2011), 305–318, 311.

121. Miki, "*Tetsugakuteki ningengaku,*" MKZ 18.348–49.

122. Ibid., MKZ 18:340.

123. Miki, "*Kōsōryoku,*" MKZ 8.245; "*Tetsugakuteki ningengaku,*" MKZ 18.340.

124. Castoriadis, *Figures of the Thinkable*, 73.

125. Miki, "*Tetsugakuteki ningengaku,*" MKZ 18.266–267.

126. Miki, "*Nishida tetsugaku no seikaku nit suite*" [On the character of Nishida's philosophy], MKZ 10.433. It was published in 1936, a year before he began working on the *Logic of the Imagination.*

127. On this, see Kosaka, *Nishida Kitarō o meguru tetsugakusha gunzō*, 219, 248–249; and Nakamura, "*Nishida tetsugaku to nihon no shakai kagaku,*" 20.

128. Nishida himself develops his philosophy in response to his critics, including Miki, and Miki, for his part, comes to acknowledge that his philosophy has come to approach Nishida's thought.

129. See Nakamura, "*Nishida tetsugaku to nihon no shakai kagaku,*" 20.

130. See Nakamura Yūjirō, *Nishida Kitarō I* (Tokyo: Iwanami Shoten, 2001), 68; *Nishida Kitarō II*, 30.

131. In relation to this connection between the notion of place obtained from Nishida and the notion of common sense, it might be interesting to note that Nakamura acknowledges that his own theory of common sense owes much to *Aristotle Studies* (*Aristoteresu ronkō*) by Nishida's pupil Nishitani Keiji. His critique of Nishitani however is that the latter's study did not touch upon the development of common sense at the level of finite and relative things. See Nakamura Yūjirō, "'Absolutely Contradictory Self-Identity' and Japanese Culture" ["*Zettai mujunteki jiko dōitsu*" *to nihon bunka*], in *Nishida Kitarō II* (Tokyo: Iwanami, 2001), 97–131, 130.

132. By *chōra* I am referring to the Greek sense of place or region that also appears in Plato's *Timaeus*. By *chōrismos* I understand "difference" but as the process of differentiation whereby beings emerge in mutual differentiation from one another. In this I am inspired by Heidegger's reading of the Greek term. See Martin Heidegger, *Gesamtausgabe 19: Platon: Sophistes* (Frankfurt: Vittorio Klostermann, 1992), 476; and Heidegger, *Plato's Sophist* (Bloomington: Indiana University Press, 1997), 329.

133. See Ueda Shizuteru, *Basho: Nijūsekainai sonzai* [*Place: Twofold being-in-the-world*] (Tokyo: Kōbundō, 1992).

BIBLIOGRAPHY

Adams, Suzi, Paul Blokker, Natalie Doyle, John Krummel, and Jeremy Smith. "Social Imaginaries in Debate." *Social Imaginaries* 1.1 (2015), 15–52.

Akamatsu Tsunehiro 赤松常弘. *Miki Kiyoshi: tetsugaku shisaku no kiseki* 『三木清—哲学思索の軌跡』 [*Miki Kiyoshi: The traces of philosophical speculation*]. Kyoto: Minerva Shobō, 1994.

Amalric, Jean-Luc. "Affirmation originaire, attestation, reconnaissance: Le cheminement de l'anthropologie philospohique ricoeurienne." *Études Ricoeuriennes/Ricoeur Studies* 2.1 (2011), 12–34.

Arendt, Hannah. *The Human Condition*. Chicago: University of Chicago Press, 1998.

Aristotle. *The Basic Works of Aristotle*, ed. Richard McKeon. New York: Random House, 1941.

Castoriadis, Cornelius. *The Imaginary Institution of Society*, trans. Kathleen Blamey. Cambridge, MA: MIT Press, 1987.

Castoriadis, Cornelius. *Philosophy, Politics, Autonomy: Essays in Political Philosophy*, ed. David Ames Curtis. New York: Oxford University Press, 1991.

Castoriadis, Cornelius. "Radical Imagination and the Social Instituting Imaginary." In Robinson and Rundell, *Rethinking Imagination*, 136–154.

Castoriadis, Cornelius. *The Castoriadis Reader*, trans. and ed. David Ames Curtis. Oxford & London: Blackwell, 1997.

Castoriadis, Cornelius. *World in Fragments: Writings on Politics, Society, Psychoanalysis, and the Imagination*, ed. and trans. David Ames Curtis. Stanford, CA: Stanford University Press, 1997.

Castoriadis, Cornelius. *Figures of the Thinkable*, trans. Helen Arnold. Stanford, CA: Stanford University Press, 2007.

Fujita Masakatsu. "*Logos* and *Pathos*: Miki Kiyoshi's Logic of the Imagination." In *Japanese and Continental Philosophy: Conversations with the Kyoto School*, ed. Bret Davis, Brian Schroeder, Jason Wirth, 305–318. Bloomington: Indiana University Press, 2011.

Funayama Shin'ichi 船山信一. *Hēgeru tetsugaku to Nishida tetsugaku* 『ヘーゲル哲学と西田哲学』 [Hegelian philosophy and Nishidian philosophy]. Tokyo: Miraishia, 1984.

Heidegger, Martin. *Gesamtausgabe 19: Platon: Sophiste*. Frankfurt: Vittorio Klostermann, 1992.

Heidegger, Martin. *Plato's Sophist*. Bloomington: Indiana University Press, 1997.

Kant, Immanuel. *Critique of Pure Reason*, trans. Norman Kemp Smith. New York: St. Martin's Press, Macmillan, 1929.

Kant, Immanuel. *The Critique of Judgment*, trans. James Creed Meredith. Oxford: Oxford University Press, 1952.

Kant, Immanuel. *Kritik der reinen Vernunft*. Hamburg: Felix Meiner Verlag, 1993.

Kearney, Richard. *The Wake of the Imagination: Toward a Postmodern Culture*. London: Routledge, 1988.

Kearney, Richard. *Poetics of Imagining: Modern to Post-modern*. New York: Fordham University Press, 1998.

Kosaka Kunitsugu 小坂国継. *Nishida Kitarō o meguru tetsugakusha gunzō* 『西田幾多郎をめぐる哲学者群像』 [*The group of philosophers surrounding Nishida Kitarō*]. Kyoto: Mineruva Shobō, 1997.

Krummel, John W. M. "Introduction to Nakamura Yūjirō and his Work." *Social Imaginaries* 1.1 (2015), 71–82.

Lafuente, María Avelina Celia. "Social Imagination and History in Paul Ricoeur." *Analecta Husserliana: the Yearbook of Phenomenological Research* 90: "Logos of Phenomenology" (2006), 195–222.

McLuhan, Marshall. *Understanding Media: The Extensions of Man.* New York: McGraw-Hill, 1964.
Miki Kiyoshi. "*Tetsugakuteki ningengaku*" [Philosophical anthropology] (1933–37, unfinished MS), MKZ 18.125–419.
Miki Kiyoshi 三木清. "*Retorikku no seishin*" ["The spirit of rhetoric"] (1934), MKZ 12.131–147.
Miki Kiyoshi. "*Nishida tetsugaku no seikaku ni tsuite*" [On the character of Nishida's philosophy] (1936), MKZ 10.410–434.
Miki Kiyoshi. "*Kōfuku ni tsuite*" [On happiness] later compiled in his *Jinseiron nōto* [Essays on life] (1938–41), MKZ 1.204–212.
Miki Kiyoshi. "*Kōsōryoku no ronri*" [The logic of the imagination] (1939), MKZ 8.3–509.
Miki Kiyoshi. "*Gijutsu tetsugaku*" [Philosophy of technics] (1941–42), MKZ 7.195–329.
Miki Kiyoshi. "*Bungeiteki ningengaku*" [Literary anthropology] (1942), MKZ 11.464–478.
Miki Kiyoshi. "Myth," trans. John Krummel. *Social Imaginaries* 2.1 (2016), 25–69.
Nakamura Yūjirō中村雄二郎. *Kyōtsū kankaku ron* 『共通感覚論』 [*On common sense*]. Tokyo: Iwanami Shoten, (1979) 1983.
Nakamura Yūjirō. "Nishida tetsugaku to nihon no shakai kagaku" 「西田哲学と日本の社会科学」 ["Nishidian philosophy and the social sciences of Japan"]. *Shisō* 『思想』 [*Thought*] (November 1995), 5–22.
Nakamura Yūjirō. *Nishida Kitarō I* 『西田幾多郎　一』. Tokyo: Iwanami Shoten, 2001.
Nakamura Yūjirō. *Nishida Kitarō II* 『西田幾多郎　二』. Tokyo: Iwanami Shoten, 2001.
Nakamura Yūjirō. " 'The Logic of Place' and Common Sense," trans. John Krummel. *Social Imaginaries* 1.1 (2015), 83–103. Japanese original "*Basho no ronri to kyōtsūkankaku, Gendai nihon tetsugaku no ichikadai*" 「「場所の論理」と共通感覚　現代日本哲学の一課題 」 [The logic of "basho" and common sense: A project for modern Japanese philosophy] (1984), compiled in *Nishida Tetsugaku no datsu-kōchiku*『西田哲学の脱構築』 [Deconstruction of Nishida philosophy]. Tokyo: Iwanami Shoten, 1987; and in *Nishida Kitarō II* 『西田幾多郎　二』, 37–66. Tokyo: Iwanami Shoten, 2001.
Ricoeur, Paul. *Fallible Man: Philosophy of the Will*, trans. Charles Kelbley. Chicago: Henry Regnery Co., 1965.
Ricoeur, Paul. *Freedom and Nature: The Voluntary and the Involuntary*, trans. Razim V. Kohák. Chicago: Northwestern University Press, 1966.
Ricoeur, Paul. "Ethics and Culture: Habermas and Gadamer in Dialogue." In *Political and Social Essays*, ed. S. Stewart and J. Bien, 243–270. Athens: Ohio University Press, 1974.
Ricoeur, Paul. *The Rule of Metaphor: Multi-disciplinary Studies of the Creation of Meaning in Language*, trans. Robert Czerny with Kathleen McLaughlin and John Costello. Toronto: University of Toronto Press, 1981.
Ricoeur, Paul. *Time and Narrative vol. 1*, trans. Kathleen McLaughlin and David Pellauer. Chicago: University of Chicago Press, 1984.
Ricoeur, Paul. Lectures on Ideology and Utopia, ed. George H. Taylor. New York: Columbia University Press, 1986.
Ricoeur, Paul. "The Creativity of Language (Interview with Richard Kearney)." In

A Ricoeur Reader: Reflection and Imagination, ed. Mario J. Valdés, 463–481. Toronto: University of Toronto Press, 1991.
Robinson, Gillian, and John Rundell, eds. *Rethinking Imagination: Culture and Creativity*. London: Routledge, 1994.
Rundell, John. "Creativity and Judgement: Kant on Reason and Imagination." In Robinson and Rundell, *Rethinking Imagination*, 87–117.
Tanaka Kyūbun 田中久文. *Nihon no "tetsugaku" o yomitoku: "Mu" no jidai o ikinukutame ni* 『日本の「哲学」を読み解く—「無」の時代を生き抜くために』 [*Reading the "philosophy" of Japan to survive the epoch of the "nothing"*]. Tokyo: Chikuma Shobō, 2000.
Taylor, Charles. *Modern Social Imaginaries*. Durham: Duke University Press, 2004.
Taylor, Charles. *A Secular Age*. Cambridge: Harvard University Press, 2007.
Ueda Shizuteru 上田閑照. *Basho: Nijūsekainai sonzai* 『場所 二重世界内存在』 [*Place: Twofold being-in-the-world*]. Tokyo: Kōbundō, 1992.
Vico, Giambattista. *The New Science of Giambattista Vico*, trans. Thomas Goddard Bergin and Max Harold Fisch. Ithaca, NY: Cornell University Press, 1968.
Waxman, Wayne. *Kant's Model of the Mind: A New Interpretation of Transcendental Idealism*. New York: Oxford University Press, 1991.

FURTHER READING

Primary sources

Castoriadis, Cornelius. *The Imaginary Institution of Society*, trans. Kathleen Blamey. Cambridge, MA: MIT Press, 1987.
Castoriadis, Cornelius. "Radical Imagination and the Social Instituting Imaginary." In Robinson and Rundell, *Rethinking Imagination*, 136–154.
Miki Kiyoshi. *Kōsōryoku no ronri* [*Logic of the imagination*], MKZ 8.
Miki Kiyoshi. "Myth," trans. John Krummel. *Social Imaginaries* 2.1, 25–69.
Nakamura Yūjirō. *Kyōtsū kankaku ron* [*On common sense*]. Tokyo: Iwanami Shoten, 1983.
Nakamura Yūjirō. "'The Logic of Place' and Common Sense," trans. John Krummel. *Social Imaginaries* 1.1 (2015), 83–103.
Ricoeur, Paul. *Time and Narrative vol. 1*, trans. Kathleen McLaughlin and David Pellauer. Chicago: University of Chicago Press, 1984.
Ricoeur, Paul. *Lectures on Ideology and Utopia*, ed. George H. Taylor. New York: Columbia University Press, 1986.
Taylor, Charles. *Modern Social Imaginaries*. Durham: Duke University Press, 2004.

Secondary sources

Adams, Suzi, Paul Blokker, Natalie Doyle, John Krummel, and Jeremy Smith. "Social Imaginaries in Debate." *Social Imaginaries* 1.1 (2015), 15–52.
Akamatsu Tsunehiro. *Miki Kiyoshi: tetsugaku shisaku no kiseki* [*Miki Kiyoshi: The traces of philosophical speculation*]. Kyoto: Minerva Shobō, 1994.

Fujita Masakatsu. "*Logos* and *Pathos*: Miki Kiyoshi's Logic of the Imagination." In *Japanese and Continental Philosophy: Conversations with the Kyoto School*, ed. Bret Davis, Brian Schroeder, and Jason Wirth, 305–318. Bloomington, IN: Indiana University Press, 2011.

Kearney, Richard. *The Wake of the Imagination: Toward a Postmodern Culture.* London: Routledge, 1988.

Krummel, John W. M. "Introduction to Nakamura Yūjirō and His Work." *Social Imaginaries* 1.1 (2015), 71–82.

Krummel, John W. M. "Introduction to Miki Kiyoshi and his Logic of the Imagination." *Social Imaginaries* 2.1, 13–24.

Robinson, Gillian, and John Rundell, eds. *Rethinking Imagination: Culture and Creativity.* London: Routledge, 1994.

CHAPTER TWELVE

Nishida Kitarō as a Philosopher of Science

KEIICHI NOE

INTRODUCTION

Many excellent studies have been done on Nishida Kitarō's philosophy of religion and history, but when it comes to his philosophy of science, the situation is quite different. It may even seem strange that I speak about Nishida as a philosopher of science. However, there is probably very little objection to calling Tanabe Hajime or Shimomura Toratarō philosophers of science. They were close associates of Nishida and belonged to the Kyoto School of philosophy. Nevertheless, a closer study of Nishida's works, especially the *Philosophical Essays I–VII*, published in the last decade of his life, reveals that Nishida grappled with the fundamental questions of mathematics, logic, physics, and biology. If we are to have a well-rounded picture of Nishida's philosophical work, we cannot and should not overlook the fact that he increasingly poured his philosophical energy into the field of philosophy of science. It is the aim of this chapter to redress this oversight by demonstrating that Nishida's philosophy of science indeed constitutes an integral part of his philosophical endeavor.

Nishida's thought may be tentatively divided into three phases, namely:

Phase 1 (early period), which corresponds to the time when he was developing his ideas of "pure experience" and "self-consciousness" (*jikaku*); representative works are *An Inquiry into the Good* (1911), and the *Intuition and Reflection in Self-Consciousness* (1917).

Phase 2 (mid-period), when he was developing the idea of "the theory of *basho*" (topos); representative works are *From the Acting to the Seeing* (1927), and *The System of Self-Consciousness of the Universal* (1930).

Phase 3 (later period), when he was developing his idea of "action-intuition"; Representative works are the *Philosophical Essays*, volume 1 (1930) through volume 7 (1945).

The last phase of his philosophical thinking, extending from mid-1930s to mid-1940s, overlaps the time period when Japan became increasingly entangled in war-efforts, which began with the Manchurian Incident of 1931 and ended in the Pacific War. I personally do not think that this overlapping was a coincidence. Rather, I read

Nishida's interest in science as a form of "passive resistance" against the political-social current of the day, when the entire nation was progressively preoccupied with war-related efforts. I am suggesting that Nishida *chose* to grapple with the problems fundamental to natural science—which does not lie—in his criticism of the trend of the day that was overridden by warmongering propagandas. This is not to say, however, that Nishida withdrew from the political reality of his day, as his writings such as *The Problem of Japanese Culture* (1940) and "The Principle of the New Global Order" (1943) bear witness to the contrary. Certainly, his responsibility for having engaged in the political affairs of the time is something we must not dismiss, but one thing is clear—that his resistance against the prevailing social and political current made him focus his attention more and more on the investigation of the foundations of natural science.

Actually, Nishida's interest in natural science did not emerge only in the last decade of his life but goes back much earlier. For instance, a year after the publication of his first book, *An Inquiry into the Good*, he published three essays in succession entitled "Laws," "Logical Understanding and Mathematical Understanding," and "Henri Poincaré as an Epistemologist"—all in 1912. Moreover, his interest in natural science goes back even further to his teens. When young Nishida had to decide on his academic major, he was in a quandary as to whether to choose mathematics or philosophy. He recalled this dilemma in the speech he gave on the occasion of the retirement reception his colleagues held for him in 1929:

> The time came when I had to decide on my major. Just as many young boys wondered about this question, so did I. It was very hard for me to choose between mathematics and philosophy. A certain professor, whom I respected greatly, recommended that I should go into mathematics. His argument was that "in philosophy, not only logical ability, but a poetic imagination is necessary," and he was not sure I had it. It was certainly reasonable advice, and I didn't have enough confidence in myself to challenge it. Yet I did not feel like spending the rest of my life studying cut-and-dried mathematics. Although I did have some misgivings, I decided on philosophy.[1]

"The professor" that Nishida mentions above is Hōjō Tokiyuki (1858–1929), who later became the second president of the Imperial University of Tohoku, 1913–17. Hōjō had a BA in mathematics from the Imperial University of Tokyo, and therefore for him to recommend Nishida to major in mathematics meant that he recognized in young Nishida a genuine mathematical talent. Indeed, as for Nishida, even after he made up his mind to major in philosophy, he actively stayed abreast of the current developments in mathematics and physics abroad. I wonder if Nishida dedicated the last ten years of his life to the philosophy of science in order to follow his unfulfilled desire and returned to the "original starting point" of his career to engage anew the studies that he was yet to carry out to his satisfaction. Regardless, in the very last days of his life Nishida began working on an essay titled "Concerning My Logic." It opens with these words:

> As a result of many years of my philosophical inquiry, I believe I was able to clarify, from the standpoint of historically active self, the form of thinking which

> I call the "logic of history formation." My logic is to be distinguished from traditional forms of logic, which stand on the abstractly conceived conscious self. I also grappled with fundamental problems of various natural sciences, as well as those of morality and religion from my own logical standpoint.[2]

This passage makes amply clear that Nishida's lifelong philosophical project was dedicated to the "fundamental problems of natural science, as well as those of morality and religion." For him, then, philosophy of science and philosophy of religion were by no means two separate incompatible fields, like water and oil. Rather, they were "front" and "back" panels of the door, as it were, with his own "logic" functioning as the hinge. Because of these reasons, I am compelled to think it is incumbent on us to reevaluate Nishida's achievements in the field of philosophy of science, in order to gain a proper overall understanding of Nishida the thinker.

1. NISHIDA'S EARLY VIEW OF SCIENCE

First, I will give a brief account of Nishida's early view of natural science. Even though the main tenor of *An Inquiry into the Good* is ethics, metaphysics, and religion, he does mention natural science therein. Nishida's attempt in this book was to explain actual reality with the notion of "pure experience" or "direct experience"—the concept he borrowed from William James's radical empiricism. The accent of *An Inquiry into the Good* heavily falls on the unity of consciousness before its bifurcation into subject and object. His early view on natural science, prima facie, is mostly negative. Nevertheless, he saw that scientific knowledge shared the dimension of pure experience. Even then, Nishida felt that the physical world treated by scientists presented merely a segment of the rich and colorful world. He elaborates on his view with an interesting remark:

> The independent, self-sufficient reality prior to bifurcation into subject and object is characterized by the unity of cognition, feelings, and the will. Contrary to popular belief, reality as such is not an object of cool ratiocination but it arises through our feelings and will. It is not mere something but it is reality with meaning. If we were to take away the feelings and the will from this actual world, it would no longer be a concrete reality but turns into an abstract concept. The world described by physicists is like a line without width and a plane without thickness, and is not something that actually exists. In this sense, I dare say artists, not scholars, are more the experts in articulating this reality.[3]

In privileging artists over scholars, Nishida suggests that our intellectual understanding of the world requires an everyday understanding. He emphasizes the importance of everydayness in Japanese culture—such as the mental-spiritual composure embodied in tea ceremony, because it possesses its own coherent worldview. Nishida considered the physical world described by physicists captured only one aspect of this vibrant reality. But because his goal was to give due recognition to the primacy of pure experience, he grounded scientific activities also in direct intuition.

Interestingly, Nishida's early view of science touches on the problem treated by the phenomenology of the lifeworld. Nishida does not use the word "phenomenology" or "lifeworld," but his notion of pure experience is similar to Husserl's concept of lifeworld, which is the basis of later Husserlian phenomenology. According to Husserl, the lifeworld is the real concrete world given to consciousness. In this lifeworld, our action is consciously registered and experienced, and it is where our whole life's activities take place. From this perspective, Husserl severely criticized "mathematical physics," that is, Galileo's mathematization of nature, which he characterized as forgetting the lifeworld. For both Nishida and Husserl, empirical knowledge based on scientific hypotheses had to be critically assessed in light of immediate concrete experience. In particular, they both wanted to begin their philosophy from the phenomena of consciousness as the true foundation without postulates. In this sense, Nishida's early position shares the phenomenological methodology in that it started out with the evidence of direct experience without presuppositions. Nishida had already paid attention to this problem some twenty-five years before Husserl reflected on this matter in *The Crisis of European Sciences and Transcendental Phenomenology*.

2. THE RISE OF PHILOSOPHY OF SCIENCE IN EUROPE

Natural science as the subject of study emerged in the mid-sixteenth- to seventeenth-century Europe, buttressed by the method of demonstration and experimentation, out of the fertile ground of philosophy of nature. This was the first period of "scientific revolution." In the mid-nineteenth century, the second scientific revolution took place when the discipline of natural science was established accompanied by the modern scientific methodology of the hypothetico-deductive method. The word "scientist" was coined in the 1830s by William Whewell, a Cambridge professor. Accordingly, "philosophy of science" that investigated into the purpose and the methods of science emerged around this time, heralded by such works as John Herschel's *A Preliminary Discourse on the Study of Natural Philosophy* (1831) and W. Whewell's *Philosophy of the Inductive Sciences* (1840). After these pioneering works, many important books on the philosophy of science were written by the leading mathematicians and physicists of the day. What may be unexpected is that Nishida actually kept abreast of many of these works with great interest. He was familiar with such works as J. C. Maxwell's *Matter and Motion* (1877), Ernst Mach's *The Analysis of Sensations and the Relation of the Physical to the Psychical* (1886), J. W. R. Dedekind's *What Are Numbers and What Should They Be?* (originally in German, 1888), and Henri Poincaré's *Science and Hypothesis* (originally in French, 1902).

The period from the end of the nineteenth century into the early twentieth century is known as the time of the "crisis of science," when the classical authority of Euclidian geometry and Newtonian physics came under close scrutiny. Non-Euclidean geometry, first proposed in around 1830 by Nikolai Lobachevsky and János Bolyai, was followed by a controversy as to its validity between Gottlob Frege and David Hilbert. Hilbert in his *Foundations of Geometry* (1899) demonstrated that non-Euclidean geometry is not an imaginary geometry but has its own foundation as sound as that of Euclidean geometry.

In 1902, Bertrand Russell shook the world of mathematics with his discovery of the paradox inherent in the set theory, which had been hitherto considered the foundation of mathematics. This discovery triggered debate among mathematicians, represented by the logicism of B. Russell and G. Frege, the formalism of D. Hilbert, and the intuitionism of L. E. J. Brouwer. Nishida in his last years of his life joined this debate coming from his own perspective of the "logic of action-intuition" (its brief explanation will follow shortly).

Not only in mathematics but in physics, too, the early twentieth century was an eventful time. Presently I only refer to the theory of relativity advanced by Albert Einstein (the theory of special relativity in 1905, and the theory of general relativity in 1915), and the discovery of the notion of quantum by Max Planck, which led to the establishment of quantum mechanics in the 1920s by Niels Bohr, Werner Heisenberg, Erwin Schrödinger, and Louis de Broglie. In 1927, concerning the concepts of reality and the Copenhagen interpretation of quantum mechanics, a heated controversy erupted between Bohr and Einstein. Nishida, enthusiastically embracing the paradoxical conclusion of quantum mechanics, attempted to give a philosophical foundation to it with his notion of action-intuition. Nishida, born in 1870 and died in 1945, indeed lived the period of the "crisis of science," and witnessed the traditional views of science crumble while new paradigms emerged. He unfolded his intellectual life in real time when the philosophy of science was developing in North America and Europe. In short, Nishida was a contemporary of Bertrand Russell and Ludwig Wittgenstein.

The following is a list, though not exhaustive, of Nishida's essays that refer to this paradigm shift in natural sciences:

1. "What is behind the Physical Phenomena" ("*Butsuri genshō no haigo ni aru mono*," 1924)
2. "Logic and Life" ("*Ronri to seimei*," 1936)
3. "Empirical Science" ("*Keiken kagaku*," 1939)
4. "On the Objectivity of Knowledge" ("*Chishiki no kyakkansei*," 1943)
5. "The World of Physics" ("*Butsuri no sekai*," 1944)
6. "Logic and Mathematics" ("*Ronri to sūri*," 1944)
7. "Space" ("*Kūkan*," 1944)
8. "Life" ("*Seimei*," 1944)
9. "A Philosophical Grounding of Mathematics" ("*Sūgaku no tetsugakuteki kisozuke*," 1945)

It is clear from this list that the bulk of Nishida's philosophical essays on natural sciences are heavily concentrated in his postretirement period from his university teaching position, which began in 1928. In the West, it was the time when the Vienna Circle of logical positivism was formed and dominated the field of philosophy of natural science. Interestingly, however, Nishida showed very little interest in this movement. As we shall see later, his attention was focused on the position far removed from the main stream of logical positivism. The position he assumed may be described "heterodox," but this peculiar feature of Nishida's thought merits further investigation, especially in relation to how philosophy of natural science was adopted and developed in modern Japan.

It was Tanabe Hajime who laid the foundation of philosophy of natural science in Japan. Still a graduate student, Tanabe was invited in 1913 to join the newly created Faculty of Science at Tohoku Imperial University in Sendai. His teaching duty included the outline of science. He published his lecture notes in book form soon after, entitled *Modern Natural Science* (1915) and *The Outline of Science* (1918), laying the corner stone for the future Japanese philosophy of science. *The Outline of Science* specifically grew out of his lectures given at Tohoku Imperial University. Although Tanabe adopted Neo-Kantian epistemology as the basis of his lectures, it was nevertheless a groundbreaking introductory book in Japan at that time.

In the 1930s, young thinkers, who organized the Society for the Study of Materialism (*Yuibutsuron kenkyūkai*), engaged in the study of philosophy of science from the Marxian perspective. Tosaka Jun's *The Scientific Method* (1929) and *The Discourse on Science* (1935) are representative works. Shimomura Toratarō, a disciple of Nishida Kitarō, established a philosophical study of science by applying the method of intellectual history; his works include *The Philosophy of Nature* (1939), *The Philosophy of the History of Science* (1941), and *Formation and Structure of the Theory of Infinity* (1944). Among these, the last work is especially noteworthy as the landmark achievement of Japanese philosophy of science in the pre-1945 period; in this work Shimomura discusses how mathematical foundation was established, extending to cover Wittgenstein's philosophy.

It is well known that Nishida was familiar with the works of his colleagues and students, such as Tanabe, Tosaka, and Shimomura. Moreover, in his last years, he was very well informed of the latest literature in the philosophy of science thanks to Shimomura. What renders Nishida's philosophy of natural science unique is that he did not adhere to Neo-Kantianism or Marxism, but approached mathematics, physics, and biology from his own philosophical perspective. For this reason, we actually have excellent clues in Nishida's philosophy of science that help us unravel the last phase of his seemingly rather recondite philosophical concepts.

3. LATER NISHIDA'S KEY PHILOSOPHICAL CONCEPTS

Before going any further, it is high time we examine Nishida's key concepts. The first is *action-intuition* (*kōiteki chokkan*), by which Nishida asserts that we obtain knowledge through our bodily interaction with external things. This working together of action and intuition is especially clear in *poiesis* (making or production of things). As Nishida states, "Every conceptual knowledge stems from the historical reality grasped by action-intuition and must be proven on this ground."[4] In October 1936, on the occasion of resetting the type, Nishida contributed a new preface to his first book, *An Inquiry into the Good*. Therein he sums up his philosophical development of the last twenty-five years as follows: "The world of direct or pure experience is what I now call the world of historical reality. This world of action-intuition, or the world of *poiesis*, is none other than the world of pure experience."[5] The term central in the earliest phase of his philosophy "pure experience" was no longer used after a while in his writings, because it could not fully account for the historical social reality. Instead, Nishida preceded his investigation into the structure of the world in terms of bodily action. We are actively and intuitively present in the world and give shape to it. The lifeworld as the basis of science is now identified as the world of *historical reality*. Nishida describes his philosophy of historical world as the "logic of historical formation."

Nishida explains that "to grasp a thing in an active-intuitive manner means to see a thing through the action of making it—it is to know the thing via *poiesis*."[6] Here, "poiesis" means skilled and artistic creative activities, which suggests a continuity of science and art. According to Nishida, both science and art belong to the praxes in the lifeworld.

Another key concept of Nishida's later philosophy is *historical body* (*rekishiteki shintai*), which is closely connected with the concept of action-intuition. In his talk entitled "The Historical Body," Nishida explains that "the historical body is a body that possesses language, tools, and so forth; it is a social 'life' (*shakaiteki seimei*)."[7] Language and tools are human cultural products, historically inherited from generation to generation. In other words, the whole wealth and memory of human experiences as well as praxes are accumulated and crystallized in the "historical body."

Scientific experiments make a good example of action-intuition performed by the historical body. In his essay, "Logic and Life," Nishida writes that "knowledge has its foundation in the action-intuition of the language-speaking body (*'logos'-teki shintai*). Scientific experiments, too, are the action-intuition of the body that possesses tools."[8] Though Nishida emphasizes the importance of experiment in scientific research, he does not commit himself to the view of verification developed by the logical positivists. Instead, he points out that experiments and theory are inseparably interwoven. On this point, he writes that "even if we know a thing by experiments with our external senses, experiments must have a certain theory," and again, "perception without a theory is blind."[9] As is well known, this kind of view came to be described in 1959 by N. R. Hanson as the "thory-ladeness of observation." Nishida's insight appears to be calling for a fresh revaluation from the perspective of contemporary philosophy of science.

4. INTUITIONISM AND THE FOUNDATION OF MATHEMATICS

As we touched on above, the debate over the foundation of mathematics, triggered by Russell's discovery of the paradox inherent in the set theory, took place among the three competing camps of logicism, formalism, and intuitionism. Those who adhered to logicism advanced by Frege and Russell tried to reduce mathematics to logic. In this attempt, Russell introduced "the theory of types" that distinguishes discrete levels of language in order to avoid contradictions. Hilbert, who shifted his position from axiomatism to formalism, considered mathematics as a kind of play of mathematical formulas ("*Formelspiel*") and attempted to secure the systems of formulas by proving the system of axioms to be free of contradictions. Finally, intuitionism advocated by Brouwer aimed at the reconstruction of mathematics from the standpoint of mathematical intuition. His strategy was to admit only those objects that can be manipulated by algorithm as mathematical entities, and attempted to prevent the rise of paradox by limiting the use of the law of excluded middle and proofs that are based on "reduction to absurdity."

Among these three positions, Nishida's position of action-intuition comes closest to Brouwer's intuitionism. There is no surprise then that Nishida's criticisms of logicism and formalism are pointed. Regarding logicism, Nishida writes: "I cannot agree with the position of reducing mathematics into mere logic, for at the foundation of mathematics, there has to be some sort of intuition."[10] Again, criticizing Russell's theory of types, he writes:

> Russell came up with the idea of different classes of propositional functions in order to avoid the paradox. I understand that this is what he means by the "predicative method." He considers the higher classes of predicative functions are reducible to the lower classes of predicative functions. Taking this as the essence of genus, he calls it the axiom of genus or axiom of reducibility (see his *Mathematical Logic as Based on the Theory of Types*). This is a cogent fine paper, but lacking at the foundation of the axiom of reduction is what I call "the self-determination of the individual many." ... Out of Russell's "logic of implication," such an axiom cannot be established. His logical theory is after all the logic of abstract universal. The axiom of reducibility must have at its foundation a dialectical logic that contains the self-determination of the individual many.[11]

This is how Nishida saw the shortcoming of Russell's theory of types. It is Nishida's contribution that he picked up the axiom of reducibility to be a problem-ridden axiom. In fact, the axiom of reduction, along with the axiom of choice, was hotly debated as the foundation of mathematics, especially its "ad-hoc" nature, and even R. Carnap, who otherwise endorsed the position of logicism, was critical of this point.

Along with logicisim, formalism too was problematic to Nishida. He writes on this point as follows:

> There is no denying that the axiomatic theory in mathematics that arose in response to Hilbert's geometric axiomatic system made tremendous contributions to the field of mathematics, but can one totally get rid of "intuition" from mathematics? Hilbert describes arithmetic as a model of one-to-one correspondence without contradictions. What is the basis of this non-contradiction? Can natural numbers be conceived, without the intuition of the conscious self-expressive self?[12]

I submit that this above observation, too, touches on the crucial weakness of formalism. It is because Hilbert's proof of noncontradiction was nothing more than a transposition of noncontradiction of Euclidian geometric axiomatic system to that of the axiomatic system of real numbers. That Hilbert eliminated spatial intuition from geometry was the decisive step that opened up the new field of the twentieth-century abstract mathematics. While Nishida acknowledges the significance of Hilbert's contribution, he nevertheless brings up his own view of action-intuition and writes:

> Since Hilbert, modern geometry left the so-called intuition and became axiomatic. Today, "axiom" no longer signifies self-evident intuitive truth but is understood as a mere postulate that determines the relationship among basic concepts necessary for the construction of scholarly inquiry. It does not matter if they are "dot," "line," or "plane" in geometry—they need not be what we intuitively think, and could be replaced with the "table," the "chair," and the "beer mug,"[13] for these things can be deduced from and constructed by a few geometric axioms. Truth, then, lies in the non-contradictory system of axioms. Certainly, I do not endorse a naïve view of "intuition" as the foundation of scholarship. The only thing I'm pointing out here is that even the axiomatic thinkers actually appeal to intuition, when they set out to prove that a system is non-contradictory. Hilbert proved the non-contradiction of geometric axioms by way of the non-contradiction of the axioms of real numbers. In short, for a number system to be established, there has to be the action-intuition of our simple cognition at its foundation.[14]

The first half of the above passage is Nishida's concise summary of Hilbert's view of geometry. It is clear that Nishida recognized the value of Hilbert's claim on axiomatic method, but he was not satisfied with it. It is because for Nishida "axioms are not things laying about out there to be picked up, but rather they are discovered through via action-intuition."[15] Moreover, the reason why Hilbert maintained the noncontradiction of the system of real numbers, which he placed at the basis of his proof of noncontradiction, is for Nishida nothing but the action-intuition that creates the very number system. For Nishida, "cardinal numbers are temporal individual many that are grasped spatially by action-intuition."[16] Therefore, even if one could eliminate spatial intuition from geometry, it is impossible to eliminate the activities of action-intuition that give rise to natural numbers as "the form of how we count things."[17] This is Nishida's objection. Thus, he states: "Axioms that form the foundation of scholarly inquiry must be all active-intuitive. Otherwise, even mathematics would degenerate into a mere game of numbers with a set of premises as the rules of the game."[18] This comment touches on the weakness of formalism, which considers mathematics in terms of a play of formulae of varying systems in which numbers are differently ordered.

Well then, is Nishida's position, which denies both logicism and formalism concerning the foundation of mathematics, to be classified as intuitionism? This is not easily determined. It is because Brouwer's definition of "logical intuition" and Nishida's "action-intuition" are quite far apart in content. It is at least safe to say that Nishida's evaluation of intuitionism is ambivalent. He says in one place that "I am not in agreement with intuitionism which constructs mathematics step by step by way of intuition, and rejects the rest,"[19] and yet at another place, he gives a high mark to intuitionism by saying, "Brouwer's fundamental intuition, understood as the self-determination of the *basho* (*topos*), is something like the action-intuition of the self-conscious self."[20] Certainly, this characterization by Nishida of Brouwer's position is perhaps distorting Brouwer's original view in Nishida's attempt to bring it closer to his own position. One thing is clear, however. It appears Nishida felt a certain affinity with mathematical intuitionism that discusses the existence of mathematical entities. We see this in the following statement, concerning the law of excluded middle:

> Even for the law of excluded middle to be meaningful and not just being tautology, a thing A has to have its own property and produces a certain result by an operation; on the other hand, if it has the property of non-A, then, it has to yield another result by another operation. In order to determine whether or not a thing has a certain property, it has to be tested by operation. If we cannot perform any operation, then there is nothing we can say about whether it has the property A or non-A.
>
> The law of excluded middle is very useful when we deal with mental constructs or mental activities. For instance, we can say that a positive number must be either even or odd—it has to be one or the other. But there are cases when we cannot easily say if the proposition is true or false. For instance, take Brouwer's example—the proposition that the sequence 0123456789 is possible at some point in the π-sequence. This proposition cannot be answered either positively or negatively. If someone comes upon this specific configuration of numbers, then the proposition is true. But no one can prove it. Again, if such a conjecture is to be proven to fall into logical contradiction, then it is false. But again, no one can prove it. Mathematicians might oppose my position that it cannot be proven. But those who are in opposition hold onto the view that things have their own property independent of operation.[21]

I submit that this is an apt summary of Brouwer's intuitionism, just as his summary of Hilbert's axiomatism was on the mark, as we saw above. The last sentence, "the position that things can have their own property independent of operation," refers to the claim of mathematical platonism, or "metaphysical realism," as Putnam put it. Those who adhere to this position take as their premise the law of excluded middle as valid and consider that all propositions are either true or false (the so-called binary principle). If we are to apply their position to the question of existence, the question of whether or not the consecutive numbers from 0 to 9 exist in the π-sequence is already predetermined from the perspective of God, regardless of the proof by mathematicians.

Nishida proposes that there is "yet another conception of existence," namely, "first of all, we conjecture the existence of a certain thing, i.e., we construct a concept of a certain thing. Insofar as this concept behaves according to our directions, it is true—that is, this thing exists." This is akin to C. S. Pierce's "pragmatic maxim." But Nishida bases his statement not on pragmatism but on P. W. Bridgman's concept of operation. Thus, Nishida calls it "the notion of existence from the standpoint of operation."[22] Nishida's standpoint concerning the foundation of mathematics is curiously close to Brouwer's intuitionism, but he is not utterly comfortable with Brouwer's position, and instead he tries to replace it with his own philosophical system to reformulate the position of intuitionism. The idea of "operation" captures Nishida's position concisely, as it is directly connected with his key concepts of "action-intuition" and "*poiesis*." For this reason, we need to examine Bridgman's operationism in relation to what forms the background of Nishida's view of reality.

5. OPERATIONISM OF MODERN PHYSICS

Just to reiterate, among the fields Nishida traversed in his last ten years as a philosopher of science were mathematics, physics, and biology. His thought on the philosophy of physics especially gives us wonderful tools to decode the crux of Nishida's later philosophy. In developing his philosophy of physics, he especially relied on the works of American experimental physicist, P. W. Bridgman (1882–1961). This is clearly stated by Nishida as follows:

> I consider even scientific experiences to be what I call action-intuition. What kind of knowledge is physical knowledge? Since I am not a physicist, I shall develop my thought on this point by drawing upon P. W. Bridgman, who appears to me to support my view. (The two books by Bridgman that I refer to are *The Logic of Modern Physics* and *The Nature of Physical Theory*.) According to Bridgman, the basic concepts of physics are all operational. This fact was clearly demonstrated by Einstein's principle of the special theory of relativity. Even physical concepts signify nothing but the physical operation by the active-self acting in this concrete world, but conventionally they have been considered as the property of things themselves, independent of the operation.[23]

Again, in another essay, he writes:

> Every conceptual knowledge comes into being from the historical reality grasped actively-intuitively, and must be proven on this ground. I cannot help but agree with Bridgman's statement that physical concepts are operational. Even the form of cognition came about through history. But it is not the same as approaching knowledge by way of pragmatic philosophy. What manifests itself existed prior to its appearance, but it existed in such a way as to manifest itself (*arawareru beku atta*), and what exists (*jitsuzai*) is that which forms itself as the contradictory self-identity. Apart from this, there is no other so-called "external world." I do not approach the question of truth from the subjective human standpoint like the pragmatic thinkers.[24]

Here, we see that Nishida's clarification of scientific knowledge based on the perspective of action-intuition shares the same track with Bridgman's operationism. Also to be emphasized here is that Nishida rejects his view to be identified with that of pragmatism. This is most likely based on Nishida's criticism of William James's anthropocentric definition of truth in terms of "practical utility" of the action.

What is to be especially noted here is Nishida's statement (in the first passage above) that "the physical concepts have been considered as the property of things themselves, independent of the operation." This is a reference to the physical platonism and metaphysical realism that are asserted independent of the operation.

This same point is reiterated in the second passage above as "what manifests itself existed prior to its appearance, but it existed in such a way as to manifest itself (*arawareru beku atta*)." In his words, "it existed in such a way as to manifest itself," Nishida suggests the inseparability of phenomenon and operation. I submit that this rather contorted phrasing reveals the very core intuition of Nishida's view on existence. To this point I shall return shortly.

Bridgman's operationism, which Nishida embraced warmly, took the basic idea from Einstein's definition of "synchronicity" in the special theory of relativity. That is, Bridgman warns against the notions such as "absolute time" and "absolute space" taken out of Newtonian mechanics that dominated the field as the independent major concepts; instead he attempts to base physical concepts on the concrete measuring operations. Describing this approach, Bridgman succinctly writes: "In general, we mean by any concept nothing more than a set of operations; *the concept is synonymous with the corresponding set of operations*."[25] As the word "synonymous" implies, operationism is fundamentally a semantic claim concerning how the meaning of a concept is to be defined. Nishida on his part ties the notion of "operation" with "action-intuition," and extends its scope to the world-formation by way of bodily activities, that is, "*poiesis*." Nishida writes:

> What does it mean by "operation"? It has to be approached from the activity of "making things." That is, it is *poietic*. The notion of *poiesis* is generally taken to mean something subjective. But it is not merely to create a mental image. Rather, it is to produce a thing outwardly in the objective world ... Even in designing an experimental apparatus to carry out a physical experimentation, it requires our physical action and technique. A physical phenomenon in turn manifests itself through this experimental apparatus ... According to Bridgman, basic physical concepts, such as Newton's absolute time, have been until now defined independently of physical operations, and in terms of the property of a thing. In the like manner, I maintain that in traditional philosophy the structure of the objective world has been postulated abstractly, without recourse to the form-producing activities, i.e., *poiesis*, in the historical world.[26]

As we see above, Nishida broadens the experimental operations in physics to cover the form-producing activities (*poiesis*) of the body in the concrete historical world. Thus Nishida maintains that "physical operations are originally history-forming bodily operations" (*rekishiteki shintaiteki*).[27] The "historical body" refers to the way we are physically present in this historical world and produce things creatively. Thus, the experimental apparatus that enables the experimental operations is considered as the extension of this historical body. He writes: "The world of physical experimentation is the world of activities of our bodily self (*shintaiteki jiko*). We know physical facts by way of activities of our bodily self, i.e., by way of physical experiments. There is no world of physics independent of the activities of the bodily self."[28] This passage nicely captures Nishida's view of reality, which stands on action-intuition and the historical body.

Just as the physical reality independent of experimental operations makes no sense to Bridgman, the abstract "structure of the objective world" that is independent of the production of history is but an empty notion to Nishida. For this reason, Nishida evaluates highly the field of quantum mechanics, in which the operation of measurement has a decisive place especially in "the reduction of wave packet," for "in today's quantum physics, the field of physics for the first time returned to the standpoint of the self-awareness of truly bodily self, to the uncompromising empirical standpoint of the demonstration of facts."[29] Concerning the uncertainty principle of Heisenberg, Nishida states as follows:

> In macroscopic physics, it was thought that the activity of measurement had no influence on the thing that was measured. In today's particle physics, however, this does not pertain any longer. Let us take a hydrogen atom, for instance. In order to measure the distance between two hydrogen atoms, the second hydrogen atom is used. But when this measuring atom touches the first atom, it already disturbs the position of the first atom. Thus, it is impossible to determine the position of the particles in terms of temporal-spatial coordinates. This is why the field crossed into quantum physics. What this reveals is that physics returned to its starting point of empirical facts. The world of classical physics is a world postulated objectively and logically; a continuous world is an ideal world. The actual world never leaves our empirical facts.[30]

The reason why quantum mechanics is described to have "returned to the empirical facts" in contrast to classical physics is that it is inseparable from the operation of measurement. In quantum mechanics, the position of particles is identified in terms of the value of wave function, that is, in terms of the probability of their existence, for it is not possible to determine the objective position independent of the measuring operation. The measuring operation is ultimately a physical action that takes place through the experimental apparatus. Nishida, agreeing with this point, notes "today's physics truly returned home to the intuition of the bodily self."[31]

If this is the case, the question is, is it meaningless to talk about the reality of the world prior to the disclosure by the measuring activities performed by the bodily self? Nishida answers this question both in yes and no. What is closely interwoven with this question is his statement I cited earlier: "What manifests itself existed prior to its appearance, but it existed in such a way as to manifest itself."[32] Moreover, what gives support to Nishida's position is de Broglie's question concerning the presence of seven colors in a colorless translucent ray of light prior to the analysis by prism (see his *Matter and Light*). De Broglie maintained that "Yes, seven colors exist . . . but they exist only as the possibility preceded by the actual event of manifestation. Only the actual event tells us whether or not that possibility was actually realized."[33] Nishida must have liked this example very much, for he quotes it repeatedly in several essays of his, not only in his "Logic and Life," but also in "Praxis and the Recognition of the Object," "The World of Physics," "Logic and Mathematics," and other scientific essays. Nishida's interpretation of de Broglie's position is as follows:

> With de Broglie, we can say that there were seven colors in the colorless translucent ray of light, prior to the analysis by prism. But these seven colors existed in

> such a way as to make themselves manifest, if we conducted an experiment. The question can be framed in this way: did these colors exist prior to the formation of "eyes"? Yes, colors existed, but they existed in such a way as to be visible, if "eyes" came into being. This does not mean, however, that eyes create color. What manifests themselves in the present moment has already been in existence. The "present moment" may be understood in terms of the result of the past, as the synthesis of infinitely latent elements. But however much we may pile up the latent elements, they do not become patent. Instead, it is possible to think of "*dynamis*" (potentiality) as the image of "*energeia*" (actuality).[34]

According to Nishida, the reason why we can say that the seven colors "existed" prior to the analysis by the prism, and that colors "existed" prior to the emergence of eyes, is because we project the revealed results back to their "prior state." We reconstruct the colors "after the fact" by "hindsight knowledge"; it is nothing to do with the "objective" mode of existence of the world prior to the experimental operation. Our view of how actuality should manifest is already implied therein. This is the reason why Nishida maintained that "potentiality (*dynamis*) is the image of actuality (*energeia*)" to counter the uncritical view.

Also, I would like to take a moment to consider what Nishida means by the "synthesis of infinitely latent elements." In quantum mechanics, the series of physical states (*kei*系) prior to an observational operation is considered a "pile" of innumerable state vectors—that is, they are in the state of "potentiality." But however many of these potential series are piled up, they do not become actuality. For them to become actual, it is necessary that the "wave packet" is triggered to reduce through the operation of measurement. In this sense, Nishida's ontology is in line with that of modern physics. Moreover, this is not a result of Nishida agreeing with Bridgman's operationalism, but rather his philosophical position of "action-intuition" and "historical body" necessitated him to choose Bridgman's operationalism, in his effort to establish an ontology, which happened to resonate with modern physics.

6. ORGANISM IN BIOLOGY

Thus far, we have covered Nishida's philosophy of science relating to mathematics and physic somewhat in detail. As for Nishida's philosophy of biology, since I have written on this topic elsewhere, let me just summarize the gist of my papers here below.[35]

For Nishida the question of "*life*" occupied from the very start the central importance in his scholarly and philosophical inquiry. Reflecting on the broad scope of the meaning of this word "life," and also taking into account the spiritual experience of "rebirth" to authentic self from inauthentic self, he comes to form his conviction that the significance of life should not be severed from cultural consciousness. Hence, the "will to life" has to have the dimension of the "will to cultural life."[36] He interprets Bergson's idea of *élan vital*, for instance, in his discussion as follows:

> What it means for us to fulfil our purpose of life is for us to move away from the abstract standpoint and proceeds towards the concrete root of life. We can

interpret Bergson's *élan vital* to be pointing to this direction. The move from logic to mathematics, for rational number to real number—these are all a kind of *élan vital*.[37]

As he refined his view of life, however, Nishida came to find that Bergson's view of inner duration emphasizes only the aspect of continuation of life and ignores its disjunctive aspect. In his essay "I and Thou" (1932), he writes:

> We must understand the real process of life not in terms of Bergson's creative evolution, which simply is a continuous inner development, but in terms of the continuation of the discontinuous. It has to have the significance of "to be born by dying." The *élan* of life has to be disjunctively continuous. In Bergson's life, there is no genuine moment of death. For this reason in his philosophy the foundation of spatial limitation is not clear. Actual life is conceptually defined as the self-determination of the absolute reality, in which death is part of life.[38]

Here, Nishida is speaking about life in terms of "personal life" (*jinkakuteki seimei*), in which each of us as a person encounters and faces our own death, because we as persons have the physical foundation. The body is the principle of individuation that distinguishes "I" from other persons. Again, here is Nishida on Bergson concerning the body:

> Life in Bergson's thought is neither concrete nor actual. His is a life without the body; the body in his thought is a mere instrument of life. It is not that I postulate matter at the foundation of life like some natural scientists, but rather I place the *irrational* at the foundation of life and regard life of living beings (*jitsuzaiteki seimei*) to be corporeal (*shintaiteki*). Without the body, there is no actual life. And if we allow the possibility of our being born to real life—to be resuscitated from absolute death—then we cannot seek the foundation of life in an "inner duration" (*naimenteki jizoku*) but in the actual practical action (*jissenteki kōi*). In action, we are not determined by the past but we determine ourselves in view of the future.[39]

Here we find Nishida's ideas of "historical body," "action-intuition," and "history-forming life" to be already in the making, although not yet clearly articulated as such. Also important is that in this essay Nishida places beings in the *environment* by advancing his view that "all that exist exist in some thing; concrete beings exist in the environment that determines the individuals, and which the individuals determine."[40]

Nishida returns to the inquiry into life for the last time in his essay "Life" (1944), a year before his death. Therein he begins his essay by referring to J. S. Haldane's *The Philosophical Basis of Biology*, by noting that he finds Haldane's theory of *organism* to come closest to his own philosophical position.[41] Organism is a biological theory that considers life in terms of interaction of organisms and environment. Haldane was a specialist of physiology of respiration; inhaling breath takes in the oxygen from outside, while exhaling breath releases carbon dioxide from inside the body into the external environment. This simple fact shows that the organism (i.e. inside) and its environment (i.e. outside) are inseparably bound to maintain life. (Nishida calls this manner of maintenance of life as "*katachi*" or form.)

This interactive interdependent paradigm of life was an alternative position in the field of biology to mechanism and vitalism. Mechanism reduces biological activities to mechanical processes, whereas vitalism postulates the mysterious entity of entelechy, which gives life an independent and autonomous status. But both positions substantialize life. Organism, in contrast, considers life in the fluid and dynamic manner, and that is Nishida's view as well.

Not only is life conditioned by its environment, but when it comes to the cultural life of human individuals, subject (*shutai*) conditions environment, and environment subject. Take, for instance, the activity of eating which is sine qua non for a living being in order to subsist. Eating food involves taking food from the external world, and here the external world must "negates itself" to provide food. Should the external world refuse to yield, it would simply remain an unfriendly matter and hence not an "environment." There would be no internal or external relationship with the matter. Our body takes in the environment, that is, it "homogenizes" the environment, which is for the body to organize the "matter" biologically into a system.[42] This kind of mutuality (here specifically of the body and the environment as an example) is what Nishida calls "the contradictory-self-identity" (*mujunteki jiko dōitsu*) which is the basic "form" or "shape" of actual reality. In this dynamic inter-determination, moreover, every concrete action has the potential to change or transform the world (i.e. the environment) as well as the subject itself, and this is why creativity beyond sheer environmental determinisms is possible. For Nishida "life" is essentially this dynamic unrepeatable one-time "occurrence" or "fact" (*koto*), and not static or abstract conceptual "matter" (*mono*).[43] Human existence is ultimately this history-forming life, which transforms biological life into that of culture-producing human presence in the world.

7. NISHIDA'S POSITION CONCERNING MODERN PHILOSOPHY OF SCIENCE

To summarize, Nishida sided with intuitionism in mathematics, operationism in physics, and organism in biology. These were positions that by no means constituted the main stream of natural sciences at the time he was philosophizing. From the present-day perspective, however, they offer ample room for philosophical reevaluation and reappraisal. It is quite remarkable that Nishida made such choices by following his hunch, during the period heading into the Second World War, when the flow of scholarly information from overseas was largely stopped.

How is Nishida's philosophy of science to be appraised today within the parameter of modern philosophy of science? There are two axes in modern philosophy of science—naturalism and anti-naturalism on the one hand, and realism and anti-realism on the other. Crossing the axes we obtain four quadrants, namely: (1) naturalism and realism, (2) naturalism and anti-realism, (3) anti-naturalism and realism, and (4) anti-naturalism and anti-realism. Among them, naturalism and realism (1, above) constitutes the main stream in today's philosophy of science. Naturalism upholds that human affairs are but natural phenomena and ultimately can be explained away by natural sciences. Realism maintains that the world has its objective structure, independent of our human cognition.

If this way of mapping is helpful to sort out the various philosophical positions, Nishida's philosophy of science falls in the fourth quadrant—that of anti-naturalism cum anti-realism. It is obvious that Nishida's position is incompatible with naturalism, and as for his view of physics, he stands by the anti-realist position of operationism, which sharply criticizes the traditional view of physics that regarded things to "have their own property independent of operations."[44] Further, another supporting evidence of Nishida's position to be anti-realist is that he found affinity with mathematical intuitionism.

In this context, let me cite M. Dummett (1925–2011), who assumes the anti-realist position based on intuitionism. He describes the difference between realism and anti-realism as follows:

> Realism I characterise as the belief that statements of the disputed class possess an objective truth-value, independent of our means of knowing it: they are true or false in virtue of a reality existing independently of us. The anti-realist opposes to this the view that statements of the disputed class are to be understood only by reference to the sort of things which we count as evidence for a statement of that class.[45]

It is a dense text, but what he means by "statements of the disputed class" refers to the act of statement-making concerning existence—it may be of the physical world, the mental state, the mathematical objects, or past events. Dummett calls the position of realism as the conviction that truth and falsity of these statements are objectively determined in terms of actual correspondence with reality, "independent of the means of knowing." In contrast, anti-realism stands for the conviction that the truth and falsity of these statements are determined only in the light of concrete evidence, that is, verification. According to this criterion, it is clear that Nishida's position of philosophy of science belongs to anti-realism, as his words we saw above amply make it clear: "We know physical facts by way of activities of our bodily self, i.e., by way of physical experiments. There is no world of physics independent of the activities of the bodily self."[46]

Another passage of Dummett also demonstrates that Nishida's position shares common features associated with anti-realism. Dummett asserts over against mathematical platonists that "we could have instead the picture of a mathematical reality not already in existence but as it were coming into being as we probe."[47] We may recall that Nishida criticized the platonist position, which considered things "to have their own property independent of operation."[48] Dummett's criticism continues further: "Our investigations bring into existence what was not there before, but what they bring into existence is not of our own making."[49] These words correspond to de Broglie's example of the prism, which caught Nishida's imagination so vividly. In my assessment, Nishida's philosophical claims should be accorded a due recognition in contemporary debates concerning the philosophy of science.

CONCLUSION

Nishida's philosophy of science is "anti-realism," as it presupposes no ideal scientific world independent of scientists' activities. To put it another way, reality (including the natural world) for Nishida is not a stiff reality furnished with unchanging everlasting structure, but it is malleable and reveals all kinds of faces according to varying scientific investigations. For Nishida, it also means that the structure of reality cannot remain untouched by the process of historical formation enacted by the historical body.

Nishida's philosophy of science occupies an integral part of his later philosophy, together with his philosophy of religion and history. To ignore this vibrant aspect of his thoughts is to shortchange Nishida's philosophical achievements. We will do well to shed light on his philosophy of science, which will in turn illuminate the early and middle phases of his philosophical thinking, and reevaluate his philosophy in its depth and scope, especially today when Nishida's philosophy is receiving much attention from various corners of the field.

NOTES

An earlier sketch of this chapter, "Nishida Kitarō as Philosopher of Science," appeared in FJP 4 (2009), 119–126. This present chapter is a translation of "*Kagaku tetsugakusha to shite no Nishida Kitarō*" [Nishida Kitarō as a philosopher of science], published in *Nishida Tetsugakukai nenpō* 6 (2009), 1–17, with additional materials from "*Rekishiteki seimei no ronri*" [The logic of historical life] (1996) and "*Shutai to kankyō no seimeiron*" [Philosophy of life concerning subject and environment] by the same author. The text has been edited into a coherent whole and translated into English by M. Yusa.

1. "*Aru kyōju no taishoku no ji*" ["A retirement speech of a professor"], NKZ 12.169–170. The English translation: M. Yusa, *Zen and Philosophy: An Intellectual Biography of Nishida Kitarō* (Honolulu: Hawaii University Press, 2002), 225.
2. "*Watakushi no ronri ni tsuite*" [Concerning my logic] (1945), NKZ 12.265.
3. *Zen no kenkyū* [An inquiry into the good] (1911), NKZ 1.60.
4. "*Kōiteki chokkan*" [Action-intuition] (1937), NKZ 8.565.
5. "Preface," *Zen no kenkyū* (1936), NKZ 1.7.
6. "*Zettai mujunteki jiko dōitsu*" [Absolutely contradictory self-identity] (1939), NKZ 9.194.
7. "*Rekishiteki Shintai*" [The historical body] (1937), NKZ 14.290.
8. "*Ronri to seimei*" [Logic and life] (1936), NKZ 8.326.
9. "*Jissen to taishō ninshiki*" [Praxis and the recognition of objects] (1937), NKZ 8.396.
10. "*Ronri to sūri*" [Logic and mathematics] (1943), NKZ 11.88.
11. Ibid., NKZ 11.101.
12. Ibid., NKZ 11.88.
13. This is what Hilbert reportedly said in the waiting room at the Berlin Train Station.

14. "*Kūkan*" [Space] (1944), NKZ 11.207.
15. "*Sūgaku no tetsugakuteki kisozuke*" [*A philosophical grounding of mathematics*] (1945), NKZ 11.254.
16. Ibid., 11.275.
17. Ibid., 11.272.
18. Ibid., 11.280.
19. "*Ronri to suūri*" [Logic and mathematics] (1944), NKZ 11.106.
20. Ibid., NKZ 11.110.
21. "*Keiken kagaku*" [Empirical science] (1939), NKZ 9.233–234.
22. Ibid., NKZ 9.234.
23. Ibid., NKZ 9.223.
24. "*Kōiteki chokkan*" [Action-intuition] (1937), NKZ 8.565.
25. P. W. Bridgman, *The Logic of Modern Physics* (New York: Macmillan, 1961), 5; emphasis in the original.
26. "*Keiken kagaku*" [Empirical science] (1939), NKZ 9.238–239.
27. Ibid., NKZ 9.259.
28. "*Butsuri no sekai*" [The world of physics] (1943), NKZ 11.31.
29. Ibid., NKZ 11.50.
30. Ibid., NKZ 11.41.
31. Ibid., NKZ 11.50.
32. "*Kōiteki chokkan*" [Action-intuition], NKZ 8.565.
33. Quoted in "*Ronri to seimei*" [Logic and life] (1936), NKZ 8.390.
34. "*Jissen to taishō ninshiki*" [Praxis and the recognition of objects] (1937), NKZ 8.438–439.
35. See Noe Keiichi, "*Rekishiteki seimei no ronri*," in *Kōza Seimei*, ed. Nakamura Yūjirō, Kimura Bin (Tokyo: Tetsugaku Shobō, 1996), 9–36. Also see Noe Keiichi, "*Shutai to kankyō no seimeiron*," *Japanese Philosophy* 3 (Japan Philosophy Forum, Kyoto) (Kyoto: Shōwadō, 2002), 29–51.
36. "*Batsu*" [Postscript], *Jikaku ni okeru chokkan to hansei* [Intuition and reflection in self-consciousness] (1917), NKZ 2.349.
37. Ibid., NKZ 2.348–49.
38. "*Watakushi to nanji*" [I and Thou] (1932), NKZ 6.356. This essay, in which Nishida clarifies the mutual relationship of individuals that are conceived as the self-determination of the *basho* (*topos*), forms the bridge to the later philosophy of life, and as such it is an important work.
39. Ibid., NKZ 6.360.
40. Ibid., NKZ 6.365.
41. "*Seimei*" [Life] (1944), NKZ 11.289.
42. Ibid., NKZ 11.315.
43. "*Butsuri no sekai*" [The world of physics] (1943), NKZ 11.8–9.

44. "*Keiken kagaku*," [Empirical science] NKZ 9.244.
45. Michael Dummett, *Truth and Other Enigmas* (Cambridge, MA: Harvard University Press, 1978), 146.
46. "*Butsuri no sekai*," [The world of physics] NKZ 11.31.
47. Dummett, *Truth and Other Enigmas*, 18.
48. "*Keiken kagaku*," NKZ 9.234.
49. Dummett, *Truth and Other Enigmas*, 18.

REFERENCES

Bridgman, P. W. *The Logic of Modern Physics*. New York: Macmillan, 1961.

Dummett, Michael. *Truth and Other Enigmas*. Cambridge, MA: Harvard University Press, 1978.

Nishida Kitarō. 西田幾多郎. *Zen no kenkyū* [An inquiry into the good] (1911). NKZ 1.1–200.

Nishida Kitarō. *Jikaku ni okeru chokkan to hansei* [Intuition and reflection in self-consciousness] (1917). NKZ 2.1–350.

Nishida Kitarō. "*Aru kyōju no taishoku no ji*" ["A retirement speech of a professor"] (1928). NKZ 12.168–171; English translation, "A Retirement Speech of a Professor." In *Zen and Philosophy: An Intellectual Biography of Nishida Kitarō*, ed. M. Yusa, 224–226. Honolulu: Hawaii University Press, 2002.

Nishida Kitarō. "*Watakushi to nanji*" [I and Thou] (1932). NKZ 6.341–427.

Nishida Kitarō. "*Ronri to seimei*" [Logic and life] (1936). NKZ 8.273–394.

Nishida Kitarō. "*Jissen to taishō ninshiki*" [Praxis and the recognition of the object] (1937). NKZ 8.395–499.

Nishida Kitarō. "*Kōiteki chokkan*" [Action-intuition] (1937). NKZ 8.565.541–571.

Nishida Kitarō. "*Rekishiteki Shintai*" [The historical body] (1937). NKZ 14.265–291.

Nishida Kitarō. "*Keiken kagaku*" [Empirical science] (1939). NKZ 9.223–304.

Nishida Kitarō. "*Zettai mujunteki jiko dōitsu*" [Absolutely contradictory self-identity] (1939). NKZ 9.147–222.

Nishida Kitarō. "*Ronri to sūri*" [Logic and mathematics] (1943). NKZ 11.60–113.

Nishida Kitarō. "*Butsuri no sekai*" [The world of physics] (1943). NKZ 11.5–59.

Nishida Kitarō. "*Kūkan*" [Space] (1944). NKZ 11.193–236.

Nishida Kitarō. "*Seimei*" [Life] (1944). NKZ 11.289–370.

Nishida Kitarō. "*Sūgaku no tetsugakuteki kisozuke*" [*A philosophical grounding of mathematics*] (1945). NKZ 11.237–284.

Nishida Kitarō. "*Watakushi no ronri ni tsuite*" [Concerning my logic] (1945). NKZ 12.265–266.

Noe Keiichi 野家啓一. "*Rekishiteki seimei no ronri*" 「歴史的生命の論理」 [The logic of historical life]. In *Kōza Seimei*『講座生命』 [Lecture on life], ed. Nakamura Yūjirō 中村雄次郎 and Kimura Bin 木村敏, 9–36. Tokyo: Tetsugaku Shobō, 1996.

Noe Keiichi. "*Shutai to kankyō no seimeiron*" 「主体と環境の生命論」 [Philosophy of life concerning subject and environment]. In *Japanese Philosophy* 『日本の哲学』 [Japanese philosophy] 3 (Japan Philosophy Forum, Kyoto), 29–51. Kyoto: Shōwadō, 2002.

Noe Keiichi. "*Kagaku tetsugakusha to shite no Nishida Kitarō*" [Nishida Kitarō as a philosopher of science]. *Nishida Tetsugakukai nenpō* 6 (2009), 1–17.

FURTHER READING

Hashi, Hisaki. "The Significance of Einstein's Theory of Relativity in Nishida's 'Logic of Field.'" *Philosophy East and West* 57.4 (2007), 457–481.

Nishida Kitarō 西田幾多郎. *Nishida tetsugaku Senshū* 『西田哲学選集』 [Selected works of Nishida Kitarō], vol. 2. "*Kagaku tetsugaku*" *Ronbunsyu* [Essays on the philosophy of science]. Kyoto: Tōeisha, 1998.

Noe Keiichi 野家啓一. "*Rekishi no naka no shintai: Nishidatetsugaku to genshōgaku*" 「歴史の中の身体：西田哲学と現象学」 [Body within history: Nishida's philosophy and phenomenology]. *Gendai shisō* 21.1 (Tokyo: Seidosha, 1993), 155–169.

Noe Keiichi. "*Rekisi no naka no kgaku: Nishida Kitarō no kagaku tetsugaku*," 「歴史の中の科学：西田幾多郎の科学哲学」 [Science in history: Nishida Kitarō's philosophy of science]. *Shisō* 857 (Tokyo: Iwanami Shoten, 1995), 38–55.

Noe Keiichi. "*Rekisiteki seimei no ronri: Nishida Kitarō no seimeiron*" 「歴史的生命の論理：西田幾多郎の生命論」 [Logic of historical life: Nishda Kitarō's philosophy of life]. *Kōza seimei* 1.1 (Tokyo: Tetsugaku Shobō, 1996), 9–36.

Noe Keiichi. "'*Kōiteki chokkan' no shatei: kagakuron kara mita Nishida tetsugaku*" 「＜行為的直観＞の射程：科学論から見た西田哲学」 [The parameter of "active intuition": Nishida's philosophy viewed from Sciences]. *Shisaku* 29 (Sendai: Tōhoku Daigaku Tetsugaku Kenkyūkai, 1996), 1–20.

Noe Keiichi. "*Rekisiteki jitsuzai no ronri: Nishida Kitarō to Bridgman*" 「歴史的実在の論理：西田幾多郎とブリッジマン」 [Logic of historical reality: Nishida Kitarō and P.W. Bridgman]. *Shisaku* 35 (Sendai: Tōhoku Daigaku Tetsugaku Kenkyūkai, 2002), 1–20.

Noe Keiichi. "*Shutai to kankyō no seimeiron: Nishida Kitarō and Imanishi Kinji*" 「主体と環境の生命論：西田幾多郎と今西錦司」 [Philosophy of life concerning subject and environment: Nishida Kitarō and Imanishi Kinji]. *Nihon no Tetsugaku* [Japanese philosophy] 3 (Kyoto: Shōwadō, 2002), 29–51.

Noe Keiichi. "Postmodernism and 'Overcoming Modernity.'" *POETICA* 56–57 (Tokyo: EICE, 2002), 1–20.

Ōhashi Ryōsuke大橋良介*Nishida tetsugaku no sekai*, 『西田哲学の世界』 [The world of Nishida's philosophy]. Tokyo: Chikuma Shobō, 1995.

Shimomura Toratarō 下村寅太郎. *Shimomura Toratarō Chosakusyu* 『下村寅太郎著作集』 [Collected writings of Shimomura Toratarō], vol. 12, *Nishida tetsugaku to Nihon no shisō* 「西田哲学と日本の思想」 ["Nishida's philosophy and Japanese thought"]. Tokyo: Misuzu Shobō, 1990.

Ueda Shizuteru上田閑照, ed. *Nishidatetsugaku* 『西田哲学』 [Nishida's philosophy]. Tokyo: Sōbunsha, 1994.

Yamagata Yorihiro 山形頼洋 and Mishima Masaaki 三島正明. *Nishidatetsugaku no hutatsu no hūkō: kagaku to Furansu tetsugaku*, 『西田哲学の二つの風光：科学とフランス哲学』 [Two scenes in Nishida's philosophy: Science and French philosophy]. Nara: Kizasu Shobō, 2009.

PART FIVE

Philosophical Dialogue on Gender and Life

CHAPTER THIRTEEN

Japanese and Western Feminist Philosophies: A Dialogue

ERIN A. McCARTHY

INTRODUCTION

This chapter builds on the works introducing Japanese feminist philosophers into the conversation about Japanese philosophy and Western feminist philosophy. I demonstrate that Japanese feminist philosophy has much to offer Western feminist philosophy. Drawing on recent translations, I introduce and analyze the work of Japanese feminist philosophers such as Yosana Akiko (1878–1942) and Hiratsuka Raichō (1886–1971), highlighting the themes of spirituality, embodiment, subjectivity, independence, and gender. I also investigate the ways in which Western feminist philosophy often struggles to find nondualistic frameworks for thinking about gender, and bring it into dialogue with Japanese feminist thought.

As it has been pointed out, "These [Japanese] women posed a radical challenge to the traditional boundaries of 'rational thinking' and cannot be dismissed as a mere 'proto-philosophy.' "[1] Indeed, their challenge to rational thought does not come into its own in the West until continental feminism raises questions about dualism of mind and body. In addition to developing their own accounts of women's subjectivity, feminist philosophers such as Luce Irigaray and Hélène Cixous, to name only two, question binary accounts of the world, the roots of which extend past Descartes to early Greek philosophy. Japanese philosophy likewise rejects a binary view of self. It does not separate mind from body in accounting for knowledge or selfhood. How has this nondualistic starting point affected the development of Japanese feminist philosophy and the concepts of self, body, and gender?

The view of self as relational which features not only in the philosophy of Japanese women but even in more "traditional" Japanese philosophy (i.e. Watsuji Tetsurō, Yuasa Yasuo, et al.[2]) is often characterized as "feminine" in Western philosophy—indeed it is similar to the concept of self characterized as feminine by defenders of Care Ethics.[3] But if such a view of self predates the development of feminist philosophy in Japan (and is taken to apply to all genders), it is worth asking what kind of female subjectivity develops when this very different conceptualization of the self is taken as a starting point?

Likewise, Sakiko Kitagawa notes that "as a cultural category by and large independent of the duality of the sexes, femininity has held an essential place in Japan's cultural self-understanding."[4] Femininity as a cultural category carries over and influenced feminist philosophy in Japan, particularly in its early days. I build on M. Yusa and Kitagawa's analyses to help Western philosophers understand how Japanese feminist philosophy manifests a polyphony[5] uniting Buddhist spiritual influences and a deep culture of femininity that developed independently of dualistic gender categorization into the recognition of the importance of embodied experience, while addressing such issues as the need or drive for economic independence and self-reliance, and the development of a female subjectivity.

Without denying, for example, that women had generally been given a very raw deal, that their liberation *as women* or *as the female sex* is of central importance, and that women need their own sense of self, Japanese feminist philosophers, at the same time, argue that gender has no essential nature. For example, Raichō argues for a concept of self that moves beyond gender entirely (influenced, as we will see, by her Zen practice), and Yosano Akiko, as Kitagawa notes: "speaking within the context of Heian literature and from the perspective of the rhythms of life, claims that infusing gender distinctions into morality is indeed an abuse of women's morality … *There could be no doubt that for both of them gender distinctions were not a matter of biology but of social and cultural categories.*"[6] Decades before the idea of the social construction of gender emerged in Western feminist thought, it was latent in the work of these Japanese feminist philosophers.

1. NONDUALISM AND GENDER

Questions raised by these philosophers are questions that feminist philosophers in the West are still asking today. Leah Kalmanson writes:

> Raichō and her colleagues faced two interrelated problems: (1) Are the categories of gender and sexual identity purely constructed, or are they at least partly rooted in biology or an innate nature? (2) Are members of the women's movement working toward a new understanding of both humanity and equality that cuts across, or possibly transcends, gender and sex distinctions? Or, are they working at least in part to showcase women's uniqueness, and hence to develop a vision of equality that prioritizes gender particularity?[7]

In her 1995 book *Space, Time, Perversion*, Elizabeth Grosz echoes these questions when she writes: "Are women to be attributed an identity and sociocultural position in terms that make it possible for them to be conceived as men's equals? Or are women's identities to be conceived in terms entirely different from those associated with and provided by men?"[8] In Western feminist philosophy, these views are often seen to be at least in tension with one another, if not outright at odds with each other. Very briefly put, equality feminists argue that society should treat women as persons equal to men—they should have equal rights. What has come to be called "difference" feminism, however, points out that the system that women need to embrace in this scenario of equality has been determined by and set up by men. Difference feminism argues that women need to embrace their own subjectivity, that which is not defined simply in opposition to men, but that which honors women's different values and perspectives.[9] In early Japanese feminist philosophy, however, we find models for how the choice between "difference" or "equality" feminism is not an issue in the same way. The nondualism at the root of Japanese feminist philosophy means that the philosophy that develops can hold both views at the same time without contradiction, particularly in its early days.

One of the most interesting examples of nondualism is the idea of gender reversibility or fluidity. In Japan, historically, gender has been a much more fluid concept than in the West. This is significant for the way that feminist philosophy has developed in Japan compared to Europe and North America. In fact, in the Japanese cultural imaginary, the "feminine" is more prevalent and powerful: "As a cultural category in Japan, femininity clearly holds sway over masculinity," writes Kitagawa, going on to say that "it is not enough to consider femininity as a principle on a par with masculinity, analogous to *yin* and *yang*."[10] She further states that "if we are to understand its place in premodern Japan, we need to disassociate the meaning of femininity from questions of biological and social dualism."[11] Citing Japanese aesthetics as her primary evidence, Kitagawa takes Baba Akiko's analysis of the polyphonic principle at work in the tradition of feminine poetry in conjunction with Sakabe Megumi's exploration of the "philosophical implications of this culture of femininity which sees it in the ground of the Japanese idea of the subject"[12] to lead to her conclusion that "in the Japanese context, femininity needs to be seen primarily as a principle of polyphony" and furthermore that we need to think about the reversibility of gender as a basic element of Japanese culture—something not terribly well understood or analyzed outside of Japan and which we can touch on only briefly here.[13]

In her 2002 book *Between East and West: From Singularity to Community*, French philosopher Luce Irigaray turns to Asian thought to find sources for a creative dimension to female subjectivity which is also central to the philosophies of Yosano and Raichō. While Irigaray identifies this female creative dimension of self as maternal, she turns to Asian traditions specifically because in them she finds an idea of the feminine that is not necessarily identified as maternal. She writes: "These traditions are feminine, which does not mean maternal. The accent put solely on the maternity of women is rather a masculine perspective in the evolution of the tradition."[14] The patriarchal appropriation of these traditions has created an identity between the feminine and the maternal but at the same time has stripped the maternal of its creative power. And yet as Irigaray points out, there remains in Asian traditions a concept of the feminine that is not defined solely as maternal. This holds true for the way in which the feminine is conceptualized in premodern Japan. Kitagawa claims that in Japan, femininity "was widely adopted without reference to women."[15] Citing Sakabe Megumi's thesis that there was "the dynamic crossover in the relation between masculinity and feminity," and giving the example of Prince Genji as "a typical example of a hero with 'delicate elegance,'" Kitagawa observes that this "reversibility of gender is clearly one of the basic elements of Japanese culture, suggesting a use of femininity completely different from that of sexual dichotomy."[16] This, in turn, suggests that the modern concept of the "subject," with its individualistic overtones and its clear distinction between the sexes, is largely alien to traditional Japanese modes of thought.[17] This means that there are resources within this tradition for reappropriating the feminine in a way that does not have to be restrictive or fall into the masculine/feminine binary opposition in which the feminine is almost always devalued. To be sure, simply the fact that the feminine was valued did not lead to women being any more valued than in the West. But the fact remains that there are resources for feminist thinkers to draw on and that also help explain the resistance of early Japanese feminist philosophers to importing dualistic models of liberation in the modern period.

2. INTIMACY AND THE FEMININE

This "feminine" orientation of Japanese philosophy and culture in general is what philosopher Thomas Kasulis has called an "intimacy" orientation and it is this which resonates most with strands of Western feminist thought.[18] Intimacy-oriented thinking stresses values which are indeed found in Asian philosophy, and in some versions, I believe, of Western feminist philosophy—Irigaray's among them—in other words, qualities we might normally be apt to call "feminine." Among these qualities are:

1. Intimacy, while objective, is personal rather than public.
2. In an intimate relation, self and other belong together in a way that does not sharply distinguish the two.
3. Intimate knowledge has an affective dimension.
4. Intimacy is somatic as well as psychological.[19]

By contrast, the dominant paradigm of modern Western philosophical culture is what Kasulis calls an "integrity based model," one which values qualities such as:

1. Objectivity as public verifiability
2. External as more fundamental than internal relations
3. Knowledge as ideally empty of affect
4. The intellectual and psychological as distinct from the somatic
5. Knowledge as reflective and self-conscious of its own grounds[20]

We see these integrity qualities emerge in the process of modernization in Japan, as Kitagawa notes above. Although Japanese culture may be more intimacy based or "feminine," it is still patriarchal because "[i]n a patriarchal society . . . men would be taught to focus on the dominant orientation and this would leave the other orientation for the women. In this way, the societal structure reinforces the patriarchy by giving the male-defined roles more cultural authority."[21] This is indeed what occurred in Japanese culture and makes possible the striking similarity, for example, between the way the self is described by philosophers such as Watsuji Tetsurō and his concept of human being as *ningen*—as relational, and fundamentally involving betweenness with other human beings—and the way self is described by Western feminist philosophers of care ethics, where, for example, Virginia Held describes the self as "relational," rather than as the self-sufficient independent individuals of dominant moral theories.[22]

Having this sense of intimacy or the feminine at the root of Japanese culture in general explains in part Yosano Akiko's resistance to the dualistic gender distinction that came along with modernity: "For Yosano, gender distinction is one more item in the list of regulations devised by a heteronomous morality that has forgotten the 'true countenance of life.' It has left people stuck in the mud and unable to move, fallen into the most dangerous position of yielding to the 'extinction of the will to life.'"[23] Perhaps not surprisingly, the reversibility of gender gets lost in the modernization of Japan and yet the nondualism that underlies it remains and gives Japanese feminist philosophy a style and approach quite different from Western feminists. And this is, I maintain, one of the richest resources for feminist philosophy today. Because we can, as Kitagawa suggests, understand the use of femininity in Japanese thought (before modernization) in a completely different way from that of sexual dichotomy,[24] thinkers like Yosano and Raichō were not, unlike most Western feminist philosophers until recently, bound by dualistic thinking. As Kitagawa writes,

> Modern women thinkers like Hiratsuka Raichō and Yosano Akiko, as representatives of prewar Japanese feminism, were greatly conscious of this dialectic of gender. They sought to recall the feminine line of Japanese cultural tradition to deconstruct modernity. In this sense, Japanese feminism may be seen as a kind of radical postmodernism, one that sought to overcome the rapid modernization and Westernization that had taken hold of the country.[25]

This also explains the resonance their work has with the continental feminist philosophers who are considered postmodern feminists.

3. FEMALE SUBJECTIVITY

At its root, feminism—whether Japanese or Western—aims to address injustice toward women. Simone de Beauvoir's groundbreaking work laid bare the issues that have arisen for women as a result of a dualistic system: women are seen as not-man, as a lack, as the opposite of man *and* inferior. Well before her famous claim that "one is not born, but rather becomes, woman,"[26] Beauvoir points out that humanity is in constant becoming and is not something static.[27] She indicates that even though the attempt has been made to deny woman the discovery or creation of her own subjectivity, she nonetheless has the potential to discover herself as a subjectivity that is not fixed, and certainly not static in the way she has traditionally been made out to be, namely, as an object defined by man. As Sara Heinämaa explains, the "uniting idea of her [Beauvoir's] treatise is the attempt to think about femininity in dynamic terms: to be a woman—to take part in the common feminine existence—is not to be subsumed under an exact concept or a general rule, and it is not to instantiate an eternal idea or a Platonic essence."[28] Beauvoir's analysis in *The Second Sex* shows us how patriarchy has prevented woman from fully living her dynamic subjectivity as concrete individuality.

Beauvoir's analysis also shows how woman is more often than not defined as her body—she is a womb, a thing, a vessel. As she sees it, however—much like Heidegger, Sartre, and Merleau-Ponty—"the body is not a *thing*, it is a situation: it is our grasp on the world and the outline for our projects."[29] Biology, as Beauvoir's analysis reveals in the "Biological Data" chapter of *The Second Sex*, only gives answers that take the body as a thing, rather than as situation, and thus severely limits our understanding of woman if taken as the place from which to define her. It is not the female body that is the cause in itself of woman's oppression, "but rather its interpretation and signification as 'a passive sexual object' at a particular historical moment, which is then accepted as destiny by the majority of both men and women."[30] As Fredrika Scarth explains,

> In *The Second Sex*, Beauvoir's focus on women led her to see that embodiment was not the same experience for women as it was for men. She began to see that the experience of embodiment was enmeshed in a web of social and material conditions. Indeed, she developed a very pointed thesis: that in patriarchal culture, men are very easily able to identify their bodies with freedom and transcendence and that women are led, almost inevitably, to identify their own bodies with immanence.[31]

Viewing their bodies as immanence tied women to a reproductive function and to the material demands of hearth and home.

As the devalued term in the man/woman dichotomy, woman's freedom is further limited by the conditions imposed upon it by man, for humanity "is male, and man defines woman, not in herself, but in relation to himself; she is not considered an autonomous being."[32] While woman may not be *considered* an autonomous being by man, or indeed, even by herself, Beauvoir clearly believes there is a way out of these conditions. Historically, as Beauvoir points out, women have been relegated to the immanence side of the equation—trapped in the definition they have been assigned by man, as the "Other" and not free to transcend this situation and to direct their own future, create their own meaning. Woman, she argues is not a fixed identity, stuck in immanence as the structure of patriarchy would have it, but she is a free, autonomous being, one that holds the possibility of transcendence, the freedom to make her own meaning, even as concrete expressions of it are systematically denied to her.[33]

Several years before Beauvoir made these observations, Japanese women thinkers were demonstrating a tendency to "think out of their own experience and reality," to reject borrowed thought and be critical of modern Japanese philosophy's tendency to borrow philosophy from the West. So, while inspired by groundbreaking Western feminists—such as Ellen Key, Olive Schreiner, Charlotte Gilman, and Mary Wolstonecraft—as well as work by the likes of John Stuart Mill and others—they held that, as S. Kitagawa puts it, "the failure to 'think for oneself' would turn whatever freedom and liberation they would gain into another form of servitude."[34] In other words, they realized that simply importing Western feminism into Japan would not actually liberate women. Rather, in refusing to simply import Western feminism wholesale, these thinkers were resisting the aspects of the modernization of Japan that like "modernization pretty much everywhere … was strongly dominated by masculinity."[35] One of the imports of Western modernization they resisted in their philosophies was dualism. While Japanese enlightenment thinkers appear quite liberal, advocating for and emphasizing equality for women,[36] at the same time,

> it is important to note that this liberal gender discourse focused on discrimination against women within the family, and reduced the whole of the women issues to the domain of the "household." Characteristically enough, these writers did not pay any attention to the social and political problems of women, among them the absence of political equality. Their liberal discourse served to limit women's issues on the family and to brand women's "liberation" as a revolt against the traditional structure and morals of the family.[37]

The view of women's embodiment in the period out of which Yosano and Raichō emerged was grim. As Sharon Sievers writes, "any 'education' a Tokugawa woman did get was likely to be limited to learning to read, or to memorize, didactic Confucian literature justifying her low status or dispensing practical information about the primary function of women: childbirth."[38] The Confucian *Great Learning for Women* suggested how and who women were meant to be: submissive, child bearing, and above all, obedient. In some cases, particularly in the case of samurai women, women were seen as nothing more than "borrowed wombs."[39] Raichō and Yosano were among those who sought to change this perception and reality.

The dualistic view that men belonged in the public sphere and women in the private one served to limit women, something that these early feminist philosophers recognized, much as Beauvoir realized decades later. Kitagawa explains that in Japanese culture and thought, "Feminine values had been something that reached beyond mere social norms, and indeed seemed to have had a social and cultural power enabling them to transcend normal social differences. But these were replaced by modern 'feminine virtues' like that of 'good wife and wise mother,' which served to tether women to the realm of home and children."[40] We see that we cannot then easily fit early Japanese feminist philosophy into the categories established in the West by Beauvoir, for while these philosophers share some concerns with Beauvoir, including her desire to free women from the tyranny of the home, their philosophies also resist the immanence/transcendence model at the heart of her philosophy.

Pursuing Beauvoir's idea of woman as becoming, Luce Irigaray maintains that the dualism of mind and body that permeates Western philosophy renders impossible an adequate view of both female subjectivity and ethics. The primary point of contention with dualism for Irigaray is that it leads to the subjugation of the less privileged term: mind is privileged over body; subject over object; man over woman; self over other. The second term in each dichotomy is subsumed under the first term; the first term becomes the norm and the second becomes the "other"; the first term is taken as "neutral" and either denies the second term its own subjectivity or makes it merely an aid to the flourishing of the first term. If woman is always the Other—on the devalued side of the binary; subsumed by the male subject which is presented in the guise of something gender neutral or even neuter; defined only as that which is not male—then she has no subjectivity of her own. The world which claims to be neuter—in the sense of being stripped of its identification with any gender—has in fact been man's alone.[41] Irigaray's vision of woman's subjectivity is one that is not built in opposition to man, but rather on openness to the other, to continual becoming and to challenging the meaning of woman, all the while retaining difference: "In order to become, it is essential to have a gender or an essence ... as *horizon*. Otherwise, becoming remains partial and subject to the subject. When we become parts or multiples without a future of our own this means simply that we are leaving it up to the other ... to put us together."[42] This is what Beauvoir so deftly demonstrates has happened—man has set up the conditions that have fixed in place the female subject as Other and up until now, woman has not been able to see the horizon toward which her becoming can strive.

On Irigaray's view, women have been denied their voice, in part, because their bodies have been denied their voice, relegated to mere object status and viewed as tools that reproduce while yet not themselves productive.[43] This hierarchy has led to both body and women being subordinated in philosophy. Irigaray finds woman's becoming and subjectivity in sexual difference rather than, with Beauvoir, through gender equality. She maintains that to "demand equality as women is ... a mistaken expression of a real objective. The demand to be equal presupposes a point of comparison. To whom or to what do women want to be equalized? To men? To a salary? To a public office? To what standard? Why not to themselves?"[44] Raichō, we will see, asks this same question regarding liberation of women, and insists that equality alone is not the answer. For Irigaray, woman's subjectivity is found in its difference from that of man. She argues throughout her work that before we can even move to a discussion of equality, we first need to establish woman's own subjectivity, for up to this point, woman has only been a lack, the Other. As she succinctly puts it: "The 'feminine' is always described as deficiency, atrophy, lack of the sex that has a monopoly on value: the male sex."[45]

Like the Japanese feminist philosophers with whom we engage here—Irigaray challenges the primacy and boundaries of rational thought. She suggests that philosophy instead take on a "plural" meaning. She argues that this

> possible interpretation would imply that philosophy joins together, more than it has done in the West, the body, the heart and the mind. That it not be founded on contempt for nature. That it not resort to a logic that formalizes the real by removing it from concrete experience; that it be less a normative science of the truth than the search for measures that help in living better: with oneself, with others, with the world.[46]

A framework like the one she seeks, I believe, is also be found in Raichō's work. As we will see, Raichō holds that a search for liberation is not just a search for equal rights or individual freedom. As Leah Kalmanson suggests, for these Japanese philosophers, "liberation is not freedom for a generic subject; a deeper sense of liberation empowers the particular, embodied person and enables the capacity to work actively on behalf of others in society. This commitment is seen across a spectrum of feminist voices in Japan, both in Raichō's lifetime and today."[47] Yosano also expresses this when she writes:

> My aim is consciously to effect a unity among the three sides of life: as a private individual, as a citizen of a country, and as a member of the wider world. All of us are constantly living in a unity of these three, but I would like to build a life for myself that is clearly conscious of this fact.[48]

4. YOSANO AKIKO

Yosano Akiko's work challenges the hegemony of reason—the dominance of the masculine discourse—whether in the process of modernization, or in the history of philosophy. In *To Speak Is Never Neutral*, Irigaray writes:

> the issue of the sexualization of discourse has never been broached. As animal endowed with language, as rational animal, man has always represented the only possible subject of discourse, the only possible subject. And *his* language appears to be the universal itself. The mode(s) of predication, the categories of discourse, the forms of judgment, the reign of the concept … have never been questioned with respect to their determination by a sexed being.[49]

The early feminist philosophers in Japan also encouraged women to find their own voices and their own subjectivity, and chose oftentimes not to write in what would be considered traditional academic philosophical style. Yosano Akiko, one of the best-known early Japanese feminists, and a supporter of *Seitō*, The Bluestocking Society, was primarily known for her poetry. In her poem, "Rambling Thoughts" ("*Sozorogoto*"), written for and published in the inaugural edition of the *Seitō* journal, she calls for women to find their "I."

"Mountain Moving Day"

The day when mountains move has come.
Or so I said. But no one believed me.
The mountains have simply been asleep for awhile.
In their ancient past,
the mountains blazed with fire and they moved.
If you don't believe that either, fine.
But trust me when I tell you this—
all the women who were sleeping
are awake now and moving.
"First Person"
I desire to write entirely in the first person.
I who am a woman.
I desire to write entirely in the first person.
I, I.[50]

Hiroko Tomida points out that

> Yosano uses the prounoun "*ware*" to express "I." Her statement is not exclusively about language, but has deeper implications. Even in 1911 when Yosano composed this, it was unusual for women to use the pronoun 'I' and write in the first person. Using "I" was very much a male privilege, and men could express their own views and feelings while women could not. Yosano ventured to use "I" to abandon this convention, speaking for herself and expressing her own feelings.[51]

While writing poetically and challenging the hegemony of reason, Yosano also reappropriates the male "I" to express her own female subjectivity. Yosano's poetry clearly seeks to liberate women, and to find the voice to express her feelings from her own perspective, and, like Raichō, as we will see, she thinks that women need time for reflection and meditation in this search for self—to turn inward, and to explore the spiritual as well. In "Women and Thinking" she writes:

> The most precious thing for humans is to think and imagine. To imagine is the most free and sublime thing. Our capacity for imagination allows us to understand, design, create, criticize, self-reflect, synthesize, and so forth. When we act on the basis of what we think, our work gains in significance and value . . .
>
> Those who know the pleasure of meditation and quiet thinking are blessed indeed… . It opens the eye of wisdom to help us reflect on ourselves, criticize our actions, and sharpen our capacity for understanding… . In a word, contrary to all the fears and worries of the conservatives, thinking creates a deeply ethical person.[52]

In her essay "Conditions for Reform," she begins with the first of these conditions:

> *The principle of ego development.* Instead of suppressing the personality by bending it in a certain direction, we should let it unfold and expand freely in all directions, as much as it wants and as much as it can stand. The inherent capacities of the human personality are unlimited … Women, especially, are an unopened treasure chest.[53]

We see in these passages how Yosano calls for equality and recognition of women's equal status as subject and also for recognition and cultivation of the unique qualities, circumstances, and conditions necessary for women to develop their own subjectivity. Yosano's poetry, particularly "*Sozorogato*," the first two verses of which I have quoted, and her essays are multilayered and polyphonous. Her work reveals the complexity of the struggle for finding a true woman's voice, the struggle, we might say, to find the *écriture feminine* that, decades later, Hélène Cixous advocates in the West. A recurrent theme running through both Yosano's and Raichō's work is that underlying the struggle is hope for the future—if only women can tap into that embryo of creativity. In the final verse of the poem, Yosano invokes the image of a moon flower which, Bardsely argues, "can signal an association among female creativity, genius and *Seitō*."[54]

5. HIRATSUKA RAICHŌ

Raichō is the pen name of Hiratsuka Haru (1886–1971).[55] She is perhaps best known for founding The Bluestocking Society or *Seitōsha* and the journal *Seitō* in Japan in the early twentieth century, and was also a practicing Zen Buddhist. While concerned with the practical elements of women's liberation and advocating better education, relief from the drudgery of housework, and from the sole responsibility for family, Raichō's more fundamental goals for women's liberation were, according to Jan Bardsley, metaphysical:

> Since Raichō imagines liberation in a metaphysical sense, what she most wants for women is the time for meditation—not career opportunities, not the vote, not the mundane advantages of this world that would put women on a par with their brothers, but the passionate desire to look deep within for a genuine self, a self that transcends gender boundaries altogether.[56]

But while Raichō's philosophy seeks to move beyond gender, it also seeks a firm foundation for female subjectivity. Only then is it able to move beyond the hierarchy of the male/female dichotomy. Raichō knew unequivocally that women need an identity of their own to be awakened—whether as feminists or as Buddhists—and argued passionately that the oppression of women needs to be ended. For her, to deny women full status as persons is to deny them the possibility of any awakening at all.

In her famous *Seitō* manifesto "In the Beginning, Woman Was the Sun," Raichō writes:

> Genius in itself embodies mystery. The authentic person.
>
> Genius is neither male nor female.
>
> Categories like "Man" and "Woman," which describe sexual differences, belong to a self that has reached only the middle or even the lower stratum in the hierarchy of spiritual concentration. They belong to a false self, a mortal self destined to perish. It is utterly impossible for such categories to exist as part of the self of the highest stratum, the true self that does not die, that never will perish.[57]

While a tireless advocate for women's rights, Raichō clearly does not think that equality is the only way for women to attain authentic personhood and here she states something very similar to what Irigaray put into question above: "Freedom and liberation! We have long been aware of the cacophony of voices calling for women's liberation. But what does that mean? As I think of it, hasn't the meaning of what we call freedom and liberation been enormously misunderstood?"[58]

Decades before Irigaray, Raichō questions the meaning of equality and liberation. She does not deny that women should be given equal opportunities in education, the workplace, the right to vote, a place in the public sphere and independence—all elements of what in the West is called "equality feminism," and which would be in line with what Beauvoir called for decades later. Still, Raichō questions whether these things will really liberate women, whether they are enough to make the kind of difference necessary for women to gain full status: "I can see that perhaps these would give the space and opportunity by which women could arrive at the stage of true liberation, but they are no more than expediencies. The means, but not the ends. They do not constitute the ideal."[59] Anticipating the objection that she may be siding with those who wish to deny education to women, she goes on to explain:

> Yet saying this does not by any means imply that I am one of those, like so many of Japan's intelligentsia, who advocate that higher education is unnecessary for women. Males and females are born not so much of "nature" as of a unified essence. Therefore, although it has been temporarily acceptable in some countries during certain time periods to believe that what is necessary for one sex is not necessary for the other, deeper consideration shows that there is really nothing quite so irrational as this.[60]

What Raichō is saying here is that women need education and the opportunities that men have, but that merely putting the structures into place that would allow women to avail themselves of these opportunities will not guarantee their liberation.

In the same manifesto, now sounding very much like the views of difference feminists many years later, she goes on to say, "I cannot bear to see those women who blindly envy men, who imitate men, and who, though lagging behind a bit, attempt to walk exactly the same road the men have walked."[61] Raichō recognizes something that difference feminists like Irigaray recognized decades later: that this kind of equality is only surface equality. For example, putting laws into place, or simply making educational opportunities for women available, is no guarantee that women are no longer oppressed and discriminated against—equality before the law does not guarantee justice in and of itself. So education is important (as she argues passionately in her 1913 article "To the women of the world") but it is not enough.

After her rebuke to women who emulate men she writes:

> Women! Rather than building a mountain of rubbish in your minds, empty the mountain and you shall know Nature in its entirety. Given what I have said, what is this true freedom and liberation for which I plead? Needless to say, it is none other than that which makes fully manifest both hidden Genius and latent Talent … When we separate ourselves from Self, we reveal our hidden Genius.[62]

I suggest that we can read "Self" here in two senses. First, it is the self that has been imposed on women by patriarchy. As she writes in 1913, for example, "Modern women who have more or less awakened as individuals can no longer feel any sense of appreciation for the so-called womanly virtues of submission, gentleness, chastity, patience, self-sacrifice, and so on that men, and that our society have thus far forced upon us."[63] Second, it is the self that manifests when women slavishly emulate men. In her call for true liberation, she argues that women need to develop their own subjectivity. In doing so, she claims, they can "again become the Sun of ancient times. An authentic person."[64] Raichō recognizes, three decades before Beauvoir, that women have not been defined as human beings in their own right, but rather as other to man, in terms of marriage and motherhood—as "good wife and wise mother," limited to the private sphere.

Raichō's work is intriguing and distinctive, for in her work we find both equality and difference arguments in the same philosophy, and while the emphasis tends to be on the side of what we would now term "difference feminism," it nonetheless has a different flavor from Western feminism—the two sides, equality and difference, are not presented as binaries as they often are in the West. Equality in education, for example, is seen as essential: "we demand as much liberal education as possible for women."[65] But at the same time, she argues for women to find their own spiritual path—to explore and determine what liberation would be for women, not as defined by man. M. Yusa explains Raichō's trajectory this way:

> In her manifesto, we notice already a variety of positions on gender—at times advocating the overcoming of constructed gender identities and at times celebrating the uniqueness of women's spiritual potential. . . . By elevating the 'true self' beyond all gender distinctions, she in fact refused to see any positive value in the sexed body, either male or female. She was not yet ready to see herself in the particular, and she stuck to the dimension of the universal.[66]

Raichō herself said:

> Rather than demand legal, political, and economic freedom, as Western feminist movements have done, we focused on awakening the spiritual freedom and spiritual independence of women. . . . In that sense, one could call it a kind of spiritual (or religious) movement, but not yet a social movement.[67]

Yusa argues that Raichō's "impetus for social action" was intimately linked to her practice of Zen Buddhism and specifically her *kenshō* experience—the first stage in Zen enlightenment.[68] For Raichō the two developed hand in hand and her *kenshō* experience was, we might say, the underpinning of her vision of the New Woman in Japan. As Yusa puts it: "Her habit of independent thinking nurtured by her Zen practice liberated her from the yoke of hackneyed conventional concepts and ready-made ideas. Her development as a critical thinker was sustained by her religious awareness of the place of the ego in view of the boundlessness of life."[69] This view permeates Raichō's feminism and gives it a distinctively Zen flavor.

Raichō's *Seitō* manifesto helps us to see better how her feminism is infused with Zen, with spirituality, in precisely the way Irigaray calls for decades later. Continuing on her theme of hidden genius, Raichō writes:

> What does it mean to "rid oneself of all worldly thoughts?" Isn't this the point at which one reaches a state where one is able to forget the self, a state obtained only by arriving at the farthest reaches of prayer and the most intense spiritual focus? Isn't it non-action, an ecstatic trance? Isn't it emptiness? Isn't it a void?
>
> In truth, this is the void, and yet precisely because it is so, this emptiness is the great storehouse that holds inexhaustible supplies of wisdom. It is the wellspring of all vital energy. It is the abundant field of all ability which has always passed through plants, animals, and human beings, and which must be transmitted for all eternity. . . . Ah, hidden Genius! It is the embryo of the wisdom of Nature at

the center of the flames burning deep within us. It is the child of omniscient and omnipotent Nature.[70]

Here Raichō unites her knowledge and practice of Zen with what was a common theme among these early Japanese feminist thinkers, namely, the importance of "women's awakening" over social reform. In other words, before embarking on meaningful social reform, women first needed to develop their own subjectivity, their own sense of self not determined by patriarchy. In this sense, women's thought may be classified as a "philosophy of self-awareness."[71] In the above passage, Raichō is referencing the idea that in Zen, emptiness of self or ego in this case is the ground for all being and that out of which wisdom arises—here, wisdom about what it is to be a female subject, free of demands and expectations placed upon her by patriarchy. In her claim about the wisdom of nature, we can also read Raichō as referencing the Mahayana doctrine of *tathāgatagarbha*, what Zen philosopher Dōgen calls Buddha-nature, the embryo or womb of the Buddha that is within all beings.[72] But, I claim, in this particular context, in the inaugural issue of *Seitō*, aimed at women, *tathāgatagarbha* takes on a double meaning. Following Dōgen's interpretation of Zen and Buddha-nature as something available to women as well as men,[73] Raichō is saying that women have the embryo of their own awakening, both spiritual and social, within themselves—they have the capacity to discover their own sense of self both as independent beings *and* as something greater—as something ultimately beyond gender. Often in Zen philosophy, however, the concept of *tathāgatagarbha* is read as universal and somewhat abstract. Even though it draws on the idea of the womb, an idea that comes directly out of women's embodiment, it is universalized and abstracted to a point where it has no philosophical connection to women's bodies. Here, however, I believe, in this inaugural issue of *Seitō*, Raichō deliberately attempts to unite the abstract idea of awakening of *tathāgatagarbha* as something that occurs within women's concrete bodies thus representing individual, spiritual, and social liberation.

Raichō also offers promising tools for the thought that arises out of the work of another continental feminist philosopher—Hélène Cixous—to draw on. Like Irigaray, Cixous's feminism incorporates the body. Her *écriture feminine* has been called "writing the body," "meaning that she does not rely mainly on rationality but incorporates the body's rhythms, humors and moods."[74] In "The Laugh of the Medusa," Cixous explains how *écriture feminine* challenges patriarchy and the way patriarchy has informed philosophy, literature, and the arts and affected women's lives. "Woman," she writes, "must write her self: must write about women and bring women to writing, from which they have been driven away as violently as from their bodies—for the same reasons, by the same law, with the same fatal goal. Woman must put herself into the text—as into the world and into history—by her own movement."[75] She later writes, "When I say 'woman', I'm speaking of woman in her inevitable struggle against conventional man; and of a universal woman subject who must bring women to their senses and to their meaning in history."[76] Cixous says she will not do this by becoming man, but by embracing her embodiment as woman: "A woman without a body, dumb, blind, can't possibly be a good fighter. She is reduced to being the servant of the militant male, his shadow."[77] Woman's writing, she proposes is an

> act that will also be marked by woman's *seizing* the occasion to *speak*, hence her shattering her entry into history, which has always been based *on her suppression*. To write and thus to forge for herself the anti-logos weapon. To become *at will* the taker and the initiator, for her own right, in every symbolic system, in every political process. It is time for women to start scoring their feats in written and oral language.[78]

Part of the anti-logos weapon as Cixous points out is not just reclaiming or creating language, but also including the body in philosophy. One way in which patriarchy has limited women's ability to self-determination is through the strict control of both individual women's virginity and the imposition of women's virginity as owned by men. While Raichō's views on virginity and chastity may strike us today as somewhat quaint or outdated, against the Tokugawa background we see that her call for women to take control of their bodies and sexuality is radical. She urges women to own their bodies (something, arguably, we have not attained even in 2017) to determine *for themselves*, for example, how long virginity is useful: "A virgin should preserve her virginity, which is hers to keep as she wishes, until the best time to lose it comes around. To throw it away at the wrong time is a waste, but so is not to lose it at the right moment."[79] Raichō also advocated that women should embrace their sexuality and find positive significance in sex:

> The most essential questions for women are whether or not they are able to pursue romantic love, which is so central to women's existence; whether or not they can develop a healthy and natural sexual life, which also belongs to the core of women's existence; and whether or not they can achieve happiness in life. In this sense, it is only natural for women to defend their virginity when it is threatened with violence. It is something that belongs to the individual, who must proclaim her rights to her own life and must respect the desires of a healthy individuality.[80]

She objects to women's virginity (and by extension, women themselves) being treated like things or objects—as if a woman's virginity (and sexuality in general) was something apart from the rest of her being—as something that can be owned by or taken away from one by a man—which was the view at the time. This view of Raichō's was even controversial among the members of *Seitō* (The Bluestocking Society) of the time, some of whom maintained that chastity was intimately related to women's dignity.[81]

Another aspect of women's embodiment discussed by and among these thinkers was motherhood. It is in the famous "Debate on Motherhood" or "Controversy over Motherhood," which came to a head in a series of articles back and forth, largely between Raichō and Yosano in 1918–19. By this point, Raichō's and Yosano's feminisms diverged, particularly on this issue. Much has already been written about the controversy,[82] in which we find parallels with the way Western feminism has seen the issue. Their contemporary, the feminist thinker Yamakawa Kikue, summarized the two sides as follows:

> Yosano Akiko's discussion of the protection of motherhood begins with her emphasis on women as individuals, advocates the need for women's freedom of education, for the extension of the scope of women's occupations, and for women's economic independence, and ends with the demand for women's suffrage. Yosano's discussion carries forward the tradition of the so-called *joken undō* [the women's rights movement] ... On the other hand, Hiratsuka values and emphasizes the gendered differences of women compared to men, explains the harmful effect which equal opportunities for both sexes would have on women, and advocated the right to be a mother and all the rights which will come with being a mother. Hirtasuka's ideas demonstrate that Hiratsuka is opposed to *joken undō*, and her emphasis on motherhood certainly belongs to the tradition of *boken undō* [the maternal rights movement].[83]

What is interesting is that whether one took the position that women as mothers should be revered and protected or, instead, that motherhood should not be the center of a woman's life, it was acknowledged that women were no longer to be seen merely as reproducing machines or borrowed wombs. The debate brought to the fore that women's embodied creative dimension—her ability to grow and give life—was significant and necessary to address in any model of liberation—to ensure that her biology no longer served to limit her ability to become a full human being.

CONCLUSIONS

In the introduction above, we asked: given a view of self that is considered "feminine" by Western standards predated the development of feminist philosophy in Japan, what kind of female subjectivity develops as a result of this different conceptualization of the (masculine) self? I have argued that what develops is a feminist consciousness that is, in its beginnings at least, distinctly nondualistic. The thought of these early feminist philosophers was firmly rooted in their embodied experience—their experience as individuals—and yet at the same time was taken to be essentially part of something greater, something beyond gender. This attitude continues to influence the development of Japanese feminist thought. In the early 1970s, for example, we can hear the echoes of Yosano and Raichō in the words of Tanaka Mitsu, one of the leaders of the early 1970s *ūman libu* (women's liberation) movement. She wrote: "Libbers are not simply cross with the general man society. What I want is not a man or a child. I want to have a stronger soul with which I can burn myself out either in heartlessness or in tenderness. Yes, I want a stronger soul."[84] Leaving aside what Tanaka meant by burning herself out, what is clear is that the idea that women's liberation involves self-awareness and self-discovery alongside a struggle for rights pervades Japanese feminist thought. Not able to neatly fit inside Western feminist philosophies, Japanese feminist philosophies are a rich resource for the continued development of feminist philosophies in a global age.

NOTES

1. M. Yusa, "Overview to Women Philosophers," JPS, 1116.
2. See Erin McCarthy, *Ethics Embodied: Rethinking Selfhood through Continental, Japanese, and Feminist Philosophies* (Lanham, MD: Lexington Books, 2010).
3. See McCarthy, "Towards a Transnational Ethics of Care," FJP (2008), 113–128.
4. S. Kitagawa, "Overview to Women Philosopher," JPS, 1126.
5. See S. Kitagawa, JPS; and "Living as a Woman and Thinking as a Mother in Japan: A Feminine Line of Japanese Moral Philosophy," FJP 6 (2009), 141–154.
6. S. Kitagawa, JPS, 1134; emphasis added.
7. L. Kalmanson, in Michiko Yusa and Leah Kalmanson, "Raichō: Zen and the Female Body in the Development of Japanese Feminist Philosophy," in Bret W. Davis, ed., *The Oxford Handbook of Japanese Philosophy* (online version, 2014), 10.
8. E. Grosz, *Space, Time, Perversion: Essays on the Politics of Bodies* (New York: Routledge, 1995), 50.
9. For an overview on equality and difference feminism, see Alison Stone, *An Introduction to Feminist Philosophy* (Cambridge: Polity, 2007), 131–132.
10. S. Kitagawa, JPS, 1126.
11. Ibid.
12. Ibid., 1127.
13. Ibid. Polyphony is originally a musical term, engaging the idea that "the echoes of the old voices contribute to the quality of sound of the new voices," creating new insights. http://www.timeshighereducation.co.uk/161898.article.
14. L. Irigaray, *Between East and West: From Singularity to Community*, trans. Stephen Pluhácek (New York: Columbia University Press, 2002), 60.
15. S. Kitagawa, JPS, 1127.
16. Ibid.
17. Ibid.
18. For more on this, see E. McCarthy, "Towards a Transnational Ethics of Care," in FJP 2 (2008), 113–128.
19. T. P. Kasulis, *Intimacy or Integrity: Philosophy and Cultural Difference* (Honolulu: University of Hawaii Press, 2002), 25.
20. Ibid.
21. Ibid., 138.
22. V. Held, *The Ethics of Care* (New York: Oxford University Press, 2006), 10. For more on Watsuji's concept of human being as *ningen* and its intersection with feminist philosophy, see Erin McCarthy, *Ethics Embodied: Rethinking Selfhood through Continental, Japanese, and Feminist Philosophies* (Lanham, MD: Lexington Books,

2010); and "Beyond the Binary: Watsuji Tetsuro and Luce Irigaray on Body, Self and Ethics," in *Japanese and Continental Philosophy: Conversations with the Kyoto School*, ed. Bret W. Davis, Brian Schroeder, and Jason M. Wirth (Bloomington and Indiana: Indiana University Press, 2011), 212–228.

23. S. Kitagawa, JPS, 1134.
24. S. Kitagawa, "Living as Woman and Thinking as a Mother in Japan: A Feminine Line of Japanese Moral Philosophy," FJP (2009),144.
25. Ibid., 142.
26. S. de Beauvoir, *The Second Sex*, trans. Sheila Malovany-Chevallier and Constance Borde (New York: Knopf Doubleday, 2010), 283.
27. Ibid., 73.
28. S. Heinämaa, *Toward a Phenomenology of Difference: Husserl, Merleau-Ponty, Beauvoir* (Maryland: Rowman and Littlefield, 2003), 83–84.
29. De Beauvoir, *The Second Sex*, 46; emphasis in the original.
30. A. Fell, *Liberty, Equality, Maternityin Beauvoir, Leduc and Ernaux* (Oxford: Legenda, 2003), 86.
31. F. Scarth, *The Other Within: Ethics, Politics, and the Body in Simone de Beauvoir* (Lanham, MD: Rowman and Littlefield, 2004), 8.
32. De Beauvoir, *The Second Sex*, 5.
33. For more on the immanence/transcendence distinction in Beauvoir, see Amy Allen, "Feminist Perspectives on Power," *The Stanford Encyclopedia of Philosophy* (Summer 2014 Edition); Edward N. Zalta, ed., http://plato.stanford.edu/archives/sum2014/entries/feminist-power/, particularly section 3.1; and "Transcendence and Immanence in the Ethics of Simone de Beauvoir," in *The Philosophy of Simone de Beauvoir: Critical Essays*, ed. Simons (Indiana University Press, 2006), 113–131.
34. Yusa, "Overview," JPS, 1130.
35. Kitagawa, "Living as Woman," 144.
36. Ibid., 145.
37. Ibid.
38. S. Sievers, *Flowers in Salt:The Beginnings of Feminist Consciousness in Modern Japan* (Stanford: Stanford University Press, 1983), 5.
39. Ibid., 4.
40. S. Kitagawa, "Living as Woman," 147.
41. L. Irigaray, *je, tu, nous: Toward a Culture of Difference* (New York: Routledge, 1993), 122.
42. L. Irigaray, *Sexes and Genealogies*, trans. Gillian C. Gill (New York: Columbia University Press, 1993), 61; emphasis in the original.
43. See Elizabeth Grosz, *Volatile Bodies Toward a Corporeal Feminism* (Indiana: Indiana University Press, 1994), 8–10.
44. Irigaray, *je, tu, nous: Toward a Culture of Difference*, 12.
45. L. Irigaray, *This Sex Which Is Not One*, trans. Catherine Porter and Carolyn Burke (Cornell: Cornell University Press, 1985), 69.

46. L. Irigaray, *Key Writings* (New York: Continuum, 2004), 2.
47. M. Yusa, in Yusa and Kalmanson, "Raichō: Zen and the Female Body," 6–7.
48. Yosano Akiko, "A Life of Unity in Three Dimensions" (1918), trans. M. Yusa, in *JPS*, 1142.
49. L. Irigaray, *To Speak Is Never Neutral* (New York: Routledge, 2002), 227.
50. Yosano Akiko, "Rambling Thoughts," trans. J. Bardsley, in Jan Bardsley, *The Bluestockings of Japan: New Woman Essays and Fiction from Seito, 1911–1916* (Ann Arbor: University of Michigan Press, 2007), 253–254.
51. H. Tomida, *Hiratsuka Raichō and Early Japanese Feminism* (Leiden and Boston: Brill, 2004), 155.
52. Yosano Akiko, "Women and Thinking" (1911), trans. M. Yusa, JPS, 1139.
53. Yosano Akiko, "Basic Thoughts on Women's Reform" (1919), trans. M. Yusa, JPS, 1143–1144.
54. Bardsley, *The Bluestockings of Japan*, 251.
55. Yusa, in Yusa and Kalmanson, "Raichō: Zen and the Female Body," 1.
56. Bardsley, *The Bluestockings of Japan*, 89–90.
57. Hiratsuka Raichō, "The Seitō Manifesto," in Bardsley, *The Bluestockings of Japan*, 95.
58. Ibid., 99.
59. Ibid., 100.
60. Ibid.
61. Ibid., 101.
62. Ibid.
63. Hiratsuka Raichō, "To the Women of the World," in Bardsley, *The Bluestockings of Japan*, 105.
64. Hiratsuka Raichō. "The Seitō Manifesto," in Bardsley, *The Bluestockings of Japan*, 102.
65. Hiratsuka Raichō. "To the Women of the World," in Bardsley, *The Bluestockings of Japan*, 104.
66. Yusa, in Yusa and Kalmanson, "Raichō: Zen and the Female Body," 4.
67. Hiratsuka Raichō, "The Mission of Women in Social Reform: In Lieu of a Foreword to the Inaugural Issue of *Women's League*" (1920), JPS, 1150.
68. Yusa, in Yusa and Kalmanson, "Raichō: Zen and the Female Body," 1; also Bardsley, *The Bluestockings of Japan*, 82.
69. Yusa, in Yusa and Kalmanson, "Raichō: Zen and the Female Body," 3–4.
70. Hiratsuka Raichō, "The Seitō Majifesto," in Bardsley, *The Bluestockings of Japan*, 98.
71. S. Kitagawa, JPS, 1132.
72. For more on this, see McCarthy, "Embodying Change: Buddhism and Feminist Philosophy," forthcoming in *Buddhist Philosophy: A Comparative Approach*, ed. Steven M. Emmanuel (Malden, MA: Wiley-Blackwell).
73. See Dōgen, *Shobogenzo*, "*Raihaitokuzui*" and McCarthy, "A Zen Master Meets Contemporary Feminism: Reading Dōgen as a Resource for Feminist Philosophy," in

Buddhist Responses to Globalization, ed. Leah Kalmanson and James Mark Shields (Lanham, MD: Lexington Books, 2014), 131–148.

74. M. Segarra, *The Portable Cixous* (New York: Columbia University Press, 2010), 12.
75. Ibid., 12.
76. Ibid., 27.
77. Ibid., 32.
78. Ibid., 32–33; emphases in the original.
79. Hiratsuka Raichō, "The Value of Virginity," JPS, 1158.
80. Ibid. (Raichō 2010, 1158).
81. H. Tomida, *Hiratsuka Raichō and Early Japanese Feminism*, 203.
82. For an excellent overview and detailed analysis of this issue, see Hiroko Tomida, *Hiratsuka Raichō and Early Japanese Feminism*, chapter 5, "Controversy over Motherhood."
83. H. Tomida, *Hiratsuka Raichō and Early Japanese Feminism*, 249.
84. Quoted in M. Matsui, "Evolution of the Feminist Movement in Japan," *NWSA Journal* 2 (1990), 435.

BIBLIOGRAPHY

Bardsley, Jan. *The Bluestockings of Japan: New Woman Essays and Fiction from Seito, 1911–1916*. Ann Arbor: University of Michigan Press, 2007.

de Beauvoir, Simone. *The Second Sex*, trans. Sheila Malovany-Chevallier and Constance Borde. New York: Knopf Doubleday, 2010.

Fell, Alison S. *Liberty, Equality, Maternityin Beauvoir, Leduc and Ernaux*. Oxford: Legenda, 2003.

Grosz, Elizabeth. *Volatile Bodies toward a Corporeal Feminism*. Bloomington: Indiana University Press, 1994.

Grosz, Elizabeth. *Space, Time, Perversion: Essays on the Politics of Bodies*. New York: Routledge, 1995.

Heinämaa, Sara. *Toward a Phenomenology of Difference: Husserl, Merleau-Ponty, Beauvoir*. Maryland: Rowman and Littlefield, 2003.

Held, Virginia. *The Ethics of Care*. New York: Oxford University Press, 2006.

Hiratsuka Raichō. "The Seitō Manifesto: 'In the Beginning, Woman Was the Sun,' " (1911), trans. J. Bardsley. In Bardsley, *The Bluestockings of Japan*, 94–103.

Hiratsuka Raichō. "In the Beginning, Woman Was the Sun: On the Inaugural Issue of Seitō," (1911), trans. T. Craig. JPS, 1148–1149.

Hiratsuka Raichō. "To the Women of the World," (1913), trans. J. Bardsley. In Bardsley, *The Bluestockings of Japan*, 103–107.

Hiratsuka Raichō. "The True Value of Virginity" (1915), trans. M. Yusa. JPS, 1157–1158.

Hiratsuka Raichō. "The Mission of Women in Social Reform: In Lieu of a Foreword to the Inaugural Issue of *Women's League*" (1920), trans. M. Yusa. JPS, 1149–1150.

Irigaray, Luce. 1985. *This Sex Which Is Not One*, trans. Catherine Porter and Carolyn Burke. Cornell: Cornell University Press, 1985.

Irigaray, Luce. *Sexes and Genealogies*, trans. Gillian C. Gill. New York: Columbia University Press, 1993.

Irigaray, Luce. *je, tu, nous: Toward a Culture of Difference*. New York: Routledge, 1993.

Irigaray, Luce. *Between East and West: From Singularity to Community*, trans. Stephen Pluhácek. New York: Columbia University Press, 2002.

Irigaray, Luce. *To Speak Is Never Neutral*. New York: Routledge, 2002.

Irigaray, Luce. *Key Writings*. New York: Continuum, 2004.

Kasulis, Thomas P. *Intimacy or Integrity: Philosophy and Cultural Difference*. Honolulu: University of Hawaii Press, 2002.

Kitagawa, Sakiko. "Living as a Woman and Thinking as a Mother in Japan: A Feminine Line of Japanese Moral Philosophy." ed. Raquel Bouso and James Heisig. FJP 6 (2009), 141–154.

Kitagawa, Sakiko. "Overview to Woman Philosophers." JPS (2011), 1126–1136.

Matsui, Machiko. "Evolution of the Feminist Movement in Japan." *NWSA [National Women's Studies Association] Journal* 2 (1990), 435–449.

McCarthy, Erin A. "Towards a Transnational Ethics of Care." In *Neglected Themes and Hidden Variations*, ed. Victor Sōgen Hori and Melissa Anne-Marie Curley, 113–128. Nagoya: Nanzan Institute for Religion and Culture, 2008.

McCarthy, Erin A. "A Zen Master Meets Contemporary Feminism: Reading Dōgen as a Resource for Feminist Philosophy." In *Buddhist Responses to Globalization*, ed. Leah Kalmanson and James Mark Shields, 131–148. Lanham, MD: Lexington Books, 2014.

McCarthy, Erin A. "Embodying Change: Buddhism and Feminist Philosophy." In *Buddhist Philosophy: A Comparative Approach*, ed. Steven M. Emmanuel. Malden, MA: Wiley-Blackwell, Forthcoming.

Scarth, Fredrika.*The Other Within: Ethics, Politics, and the Body in Simone de Beauvoir.* Lanham, MD: Rowman and Littlefield, 2004.

Segarra, Marta. *The Portable Cixous*. New York: Columbia University Press, 2010.

Sievers, Sharon. *Flowers in Salt.The Beginnings of Feminist Consciousness in Modern Japan*. Stanford: Stanford University Press, 1983.

Tomida, Hiroko. *Hiratsuka Raichō and Early Japanese Feminism*. Leiden and Boston: Brill, 2004.

Yosano Akiko. "Rambling Thoughts," trans. Jan Bardsley. In Bardsley, *The Bluestockings of Japan*, 253–256.

Yosano Akiko. "From a Corner" (1911), trans. M. Yusa. JPS, 1138–1140.

Yosano Akiko. "A Life of Unity in Three Dimensions" (1918), trans. M. Yusa. JPS, 1142–1143.

Yosano Akiko. "Basic Thoughts on Women's Reform" (1919), trans. M. Yusa. JPS, 1143–1145.

Yusa, Michiko. "Overview to Women Philosophers." JPS, 1115–1126.

Yusa, Michiko, and Kalmanson, Leah. "Raichō: Zen and the Female Body in the Development of Japanese Feminist Philosophy." In *The Oxford Handbook of Japanese Philosophy*, ed. Bret W. Davis (online version, 2014). DOI:10.1093/oxfordhb/9780199945726.013.36

FURTHER READING

Bardsley, Jan. *The Bluestockings of Japan: New Woman Essays and Fiction from Seito, 1911–1916*. Ann Arbor: University of Michigan Press, 2007.

de Beauvoir, Simone. *The Second Sex*, trans. Sheila Malovany-Chevallier and Constance Borde. New York: Knopf Doubleday, 2010.

Grosz, Elizabeth. *Volatile Bodies toward a Corporeal Feminism*. Bloomington: Indiana University Press, 1994.

Irigaray, Luce. *This Sex Which Is Not One*, trans. Catherine Porter and Carolyn Burke. Cornell: Cornell University Press, 1985.

Irigaray, Luce. *Sexes and Genealogies*, trans. Gillian C. Gill. New York: Columbia University Press, 1993.

Irigaray, Luce. *je, tu, nous: Toward a Culture of Difference*. New York: Routledge, 1993.

Irigaray, Luce. *Between East and West: From Singularity to Community*, trans. Stephen Pluhácek. New York: Columbia University Press, 2002.

Irigaray, Luce. *To Speak Is Never Neutral*. New York: Routledge, 2002.

Irigaray, Luce. *Key Writings*. New York: Continuum, 2004.

Kasulis, Thomas P. *Intimacy or Integrity: Philosophy and Cultural Difference*. Honolulu: University of Hawaii Press, 2002.

Kitagawa, Sakiko. "Living as a Woman and Thinking as a Mother in Japan: A Feminine Line of Japanese Moral Philosophy." FJP (2009), 141–154.

Kitagawa, Sakiko. "Overview" to "Woman Philosophers." JPS, 1126–1136.

Matsui, Machiko. "Evolution of the Feminist Movement in Japan." NWSA *[National Women's Studies Association] Journal* 2 (1990), 435–449.

McCarthy, Erin A. "Towards a Transnational Ethics of Care." In FJP, Victor Sōgen Hori and Melissa Anne-Marie Curley, eds, *Neglected Themes and Hidden Variations* (Nagoya: Nanzan Institute for Religion and Culture, 2008), 113–128.

McCarthy, Erin A. *Ethics Embodied: Rethinking Selfhood through Continental, Japanese, and Feminist Philosophies*. Lanham, MD: Lexington Books, 2010.

McCarthy, Erin A. "From Beauvoir to Irigaray: Making Meaning out of Maternity." In *Beauvoir and Western Thought from Plato to Butler*, ed. Shannon Mussett and William Wilkerson, 191–210. New York: SUNY Press, 2012.

McCarthy, Erin A. "A Zen Master Meets Contemporary Feminism: Reading Dōgen as a Resource for Feminist Philosophy." In *Buddhist Responses to Globalization*, ed. Leah Kalmanson & James Mark Shields, 131–148. Lanham, MD: Lexington Books, 2014.

McCarthy, Erin A. "Embodying Change: Buddhism and Feminist Philosophy." In *Buddhist Philosophy: A Comparative Approach*, ed. Steven M. Emmanuel, 189-203. Malden, MA: Wiley-Blackwell, 2017.

Segarra, Marta. *The Portable Cixous*. New York: Columbia University Press, 2010.

Tomida, Hiroko. *Hiratsuka Raicho and Early Japanese Feminism*. Leiden and Boston: Brill, 2004.

Yusa, Michiko. "Women Rocking the Boat: A Philosophy of the Sexed Body and Self-Identity." FJP 6 (2009), 155–169.

Yusa, Michiko. "Overview" to "Women Philosophers." JPS, 1115–1126.

Yusa, Michiko, and Kalmanson, Leah. "Raichō: Zen and the Female Body in the Development of Japanese Feminist Philosophy." In *The Oxford Handbook of Japanese Philosophy*, ed. Bret W. Davis (online version, 2014). DOI:10.1093/oxfordhb/9780199945726.013.36

CHAPTER FOURTEEN

Affirmation via Negation: Zen Philosophy of Life, Sexual Desire, and Infinite Love

MICHIKO YUSA

INTRODUCTION

In this chapter I will examine whether or not "Zen philosophy" is life affirming, and if so, how? Here "Zen" is understood as a path of spiritual awakening developed within the Mahayana Buddhist tradition, but also defined more broadly to include a certain nondualistic intellectual posture accompanied by the practice of mindfulness, meditation, and cultivation of compassion by embracing the insight into radical contingency, non-substantiality, and freedom of being. Moreover, this term "Zen philosophy" should be taken as an expedient grouping of thinkers and not as a rigid category.

I select three thinkers under the rubric of "Zen philosophers" or "Zen-inspired philosophers"—Hiratsuka Raichō (1886–1971), D. T. Suzuki (1870–1966), and Nishida Kitarō (1870–1945)—based on the common subject matters they addressed. It is my hope that this approach to bring them in "dialogue" with each other will deepen our understanding and appreciation of these thinkers. It is my hope, also, that the present approach adopted in this chapter crosses the tenuous boundaries that have separate religious thinking or feminist philosophy from "philosophy" in general. Nishida once wrote to a young philosophy student: "Daisetz is in the field of religion, and I in philosophy, but our views are the same."[1] Again, Suzuki and Raichō seem to overlap in their social and political concerns, especially the post–Second World War problems of how to secure peace, and the place of spiritual awakening needed for the reconstruction of the world, in order not to repeat the horrendous mistakes that had been committed in the last war. Sometimes Nishida's otherwise recondite expressions are made more concrete and accessible when we think of Raichō's experience as an example, especially in terms of the self-determination of the individual and the world.

To ask a question of if "Zen" teaching is life affirming may come as a surprise to some, for, after all, religious traditions should consist in their salvific message. But the popular perception of Zen (Buddhism) is sometimes associated with the way of the medieval Japanese *samurai*, for whom how to embrace death was the primary concern. Again, the images of austere monastic training, often portrayed in commercial films and documentaries, may show that Zen training extols strict discipline above everything else. Furthermore, in the philosophical writings of Nishida Kitarō and Nishitani Keiji, for instance, one finds such expressions as "absolute nothing" (*zettai mu*) and "emptiness" (*śūnyatā*) to occupy a significant place.

These impressions, however, must be placed under critical scrutiny, especially when we delve into the philosophical writings of Zen philosophers, that is, those thinkers whose worldviews and philosophical views are formed and informed by their awakening (*kenshō*) experience and fostered through their practice of *zazen* and their contemplative posture in life. Their philosophical views are usually holistic and nondual. Daisetz expressed it in terms of "*fuitsu funi*" (not one, not two), and Nishida "*mujunteki jiko dōitsu*" (contradictory self-identity), while Raichō preferred to employ poetic imageries, most famously the sun and the moon. We discover in their writings that the affirmation of life is as fundamental as "dying" to one's ego. Attainment of "satori" or spiritual awakening makes no sense unless "life" is fundamentally affirmed. But in what way?—this is the question.

When dealing with the writings of Zen philosophers, especially of those related to the "Kyoto School of philosophy," we need to exercise our hermeneutical caution as to the style of their discourse. Nishida for instance, repeatedly emphasized that what he designated by "absolute nothing" is at once "absolute being." What is behind in his adopting the negative expression, which I call "apophatic strategy,"[2] can be seen as an effort to defy the linguistic trappings that lead us to reify concepts into some objectified "thing," while dynamic and fluid reality ultimately eludes conceptual objectification. For this reason, "*zettai mu*" may be translated as the adverbial phrase "absolutely nothing" rather than into "absolute nothingness," which renders it into a substantive. The use of the negative expressions by Nishida, and the Kyoto School thinkers in general, has two aspects: (1) as a *linguistic device to point to the dynamic reality* (i.e. a symbolic use of the language), which is related to (2) the description of the unobjectifiable, non-substantializable nature of all things alive. On this point, the following statement by Nishida may be of interest:

> Because being *qua* eternal life that embraces all beings within it cannot be objectified as being, I called "the One" of Plotinus (which is "absolutely being") as "absolutely nothing" (*zettai mu*). The world of creative monads, that I have discussed in my most recent essay,[3] can be considered a world that contains the entirety of unlimited life.[4]

1. THREE ZEN THINKERS, A SHORT INTRODUCTION

Hiratsuka Haru, or better known by her penname of "Raichō," is generally considered a seminal pioneering figure in the women's rights movements in pre–Second World War Japan, and in the post–Second World War period she was known as the voice of the abolition of nuclear weapons. She called for the solidarity of women on a global scale to stand up for lasting peace. Roughly from 1906 to 1912, while in her twenties, she underwent serious Zen practice, first under Shaku Sōkatsu (1870–1954), the dharma heir of Shaku Sōen (1860–1919), at Ryōmō'an (a Zen practice place for university students and lay Buddhists led by Sōkatsu). When Master Sōkatsu left for the United States to disseminate Zen teaching, she continued her practice under a few different masters, before eventually settling on Nakahara Nantenbō (1839–1925). Both Sōkatsu and Nantenbō acknowledged her awakening (kenshō), at two different times—making her a unique case—which moreover testifies to the authenticity of her understanding. In her writings, however, she consciously avoided the mention of the word "Zen," based on her personal experience that "Zen" was generally misunderstood by the public. For this reason, most readers do not associate her writings with her Zen practice. Zen breakthrough, however, had a profound impact on her life. In fact, towards the very end of her life, reminiscing about her past, she uttered en passant these words which were duly recorded by her assistant: "Had I not practiced Zen, my life would have been something completely alien to social activism."[5] In her case, her spiritual awakening (kenshō) unleashed untapped energy that had been latent in the shy, reticent young woman. Her social activism was fueled by her self-awakening.

Suzuki Daisetz began his formal Zen practice under Master Imakita Kōsen at Engakuji in Kamakura in 1891, when he was twenty years old. After the master's sudden death in 1892, he continued his practice under Shaku Sōen, the dharma-heir of Master Kōsen. During Suzuki's sojourn in the United States and Europe, 1897–1909, Sōen remained his spiritual teacher, confidant, and close friend. After his return to Japan, he resumed his practice under Sōen until the latter's death in 1919. For Suzuki, his daily life was so deeply entrenched in his zazen practice that it is impossible to speak of his life as scholar-teacher divorced from it. Zen meditation was seamlessly integrated into his being. In one word, he lived to pursue the Zen ideal of bodhisattvahood, according to which a person dedicated himself or herself to saving all other sentient beings before entering into "*nirvāna*."

Nishida Kitarō sat zazen from his mid-twenties for a decade (1897–ca. 1906), at Senshin'an in Kanazawa, under Master Setsumon Genshō (1850–1915). His practice led him to curb his youthful selfish ambitions, and he became appreciative of the preciousness of most mundane everyday life. Nishitani Keiji, Nishida's student and a Zen adept, observed that "through Zen, Nishida's otherwise untamed life force became his finely honed will, and through this will he purified himself. This process culminated in a union between his self and the law of the universe."[6] Nishida early on resolved that his philosophical engagement had to be rooted in his life (*jinsei*), if it is to be relevant and meaningful at all. As the self-appointed "inquirer of life," he proceeded to build his philosophical system based on the concrete life-experience (rather than on abstract theories), as a "thoroughgoing empiricist." In his case, Zen practice added "agility" to his natural mental tenacity—what Dōgen called "*jūnan'shin*"—and aided him to "see reality as is" (*genjitsu chokushi*). He also said that Zen practice, if anything, would foster the attitude of "utter sincerity."

2. THE QUESTION OF RELIGION AND SEXUAL DESIRE

For these Zen philosophers their reflection on life naturally included sexual desire as its built-in aspect. For instance, Raichō in her autobiographical accounts took it as a theme of her self-development and wrote about her awakening as a woman in its several stages.[7] In her case, the reflection on sexuality was aided by her study of the Swedish thinker Ellen Key (1849–1926), who wrote on romantic love, marriage, and motherhood, among other issues.

Sexual desire, as D. T. Suzuki saw it, is closely connected with the primary instinct of the preservation of species, but it is also the source of creative human cultures, which, however, could easily tilt to destruction and aggression if the primary instincts are left unchecked by reason (*prajñā*).

Nishida's view on sexual desire is cast in the larger context of how an individual exists corporeally as a being-in-the-world. Desires arise as the individual "reflects" the outside world on its self-consciousness, which simultaneously means that the world is given shape by the individual's action elicited by desire. For Nishida, life is a "historical condition" and "history-making" at the same time, and it unfolds through the mutual reciprocal interactions of the individuals and the world.

Even from this short exposé, we see that these Zen thinkers bring different strengths to the discussion of life, sexual desire, and the body. This nicely demonstrates that "Zen philosophy" is not a monolithic entity but embraces a wide spectrum of approaches and interpretations. Moreover, Suzuki and Raichō spoke about the essential need for each person's self-awakening and self-transformation as the key to creating a fairer and more just and harmonious world, while Nishida engaged in a philosophical investigation into life. The present investigation into the philosophy of life may pave the path to sketching what "Zen philosophy" could contribute to the philosophy of peace, *philosophia pacis*, as this chapter shows.

3. THE SEMANTIC SCOPE OF "LIFE" AND THE RIVER AS ITS IMAGERY

Before going into the main body of this chapter, it may be good to have a cursory look into the meaning of the word "life," so that we are aware of its semantic scope.

In every language, I would imagine that there are many words for "life." Kimura Bin, who bridges the fields of philosophy and psychology, finds the distinction between "*zoe*" and "*bios*" as laid out by K. Kerényi, full of insight. Kimura summarizes that Kerényi viewed life in terms of the universal life-principle and individuated life represented by two Greek words, "*zoe*" and "*bios*." "*Zoe*" stands for the collective life of all living beings, and denotes life in general, without any particularity, while "*bios*" is an individuated, particularized form of life. The awareness of oneself as distinct from others belongs to the realm of "*bios*" and not to "*zoe*." "*Zoe*," according to Kerényi, is the immortal undying life force, rejecting *thanatos* (death) as antithetical to it. Whereas "*bios*," individuated in a physical body, does not exclude death; death is part of life.[8] (Note: Zen thinkers would voice their concern in the exclusion of death, *thanatos*, from life, *zoe*. They see life and death as inseparable—to cite Nishida: "death is essential to life."[9])

In the Japanese language, a similar but not complete distinction can be drawn between *zoe* and *bios*. "*Inochi*" (いのち, 命) and "*seimei*" (生命), both mean life force and correspond to "*zoe*,"[10] as they denote biological life force, both beyond births and deaths of individual beings, as well as one's very life. For instance, if someone says "*anata no ichochi wa mō nai*," it means, "You don't have much longer to live." In contrast, the word, "*jinsei*" (人生 life of an individual) nicely corresponds to "*bios*," laden with the inner significance of a personal life, which can be written into a "biography." Another word, "*shōgai*" (生涯), although similar to "*jinsei*," has an existential reflective connotation, as denoting one's "entire life," or "throughout one's life"—and thus slightly more universal in nuance than "*jinsei*." One can say "*jinsei no han'ryo*" or "*shōgai no han'ryo*" to refer to one's companion for life, but "*inochi*" or "*seimei*" cannot be used in that way, because they are not individuated life.

"*Isshō*" (一生) is a word that denotes "throughout one's life," and this corresponds to "*bios*" or "*zoe*"; this word can be used as an adverb, indicating "as long as I live." It can be used in a statement such as "I shall never forget your kindness *as long as I live*." ("*Shōgai*" can also be used in this sense, especially in its variant form, "*isshōgai*.") This word, *isshō*, could also occur with "companion" but more as an adverb as in "*isshō no han'ryo*" (a lifelong companion). The assumption behind the word *isshō* is that one's life has the beginning and the end; it refers to the duration of one's life.

The word "*seikatsu*" (生活) is the generic word that refers to "everyday life" or "daily living," and corresponds to *bios*. Interestingly, however, this word can be used to refer to the "lives of animals" as well, such as "*mori no dōbutsu no seikatsu*" (lives of animals in the forest). In this sense, the semantic scope of this word is probably wider than the Greek "*bios*." This word can occur in numerous phrase and compounds. For instance, "*seikatsu no chie*" means the "wisdom gained or accumulated in the experience of life," or "*seikatsu no shitsu*," the "quality of life." This word can be attached to another noun to form a compound, such as "student life" (*gakusei-seikatsu*), "married life" (*kekkon-seikatsu*), "dietary life" (*shoku-seikatsu*), "living environment" (*seikatsu-kankyō*), "ability to earn one's living" (*seikatsu-nōryoku*), and so on.

Other "functional equivalent" to "life" is "spirit" (Greek *pneuma*) or "breath" (*prāna* in Sanskrit), which sustains life. In Japanese it would be "*ki*" (気 as in "*genki*"—"in good spirits") and "*iki*" (息 breath). The Greek "*psyche*" (ψυχή), which signifies "vital principle," adds the intellectual and spiritual dimensions to the reality of "*zoe*" and "*bios*."[11] In Japanese it is "*tamashii*" (魂) or "*rei*" (霊 as in "*reisei*," spirituality). The semantic scope of Japanese "*inochi*" or "*seimei*" extends to contain the element of "*psyche*," the principle of animation. "*Eien no inochi*" or "*eien no seimei*"—"eternal life"—indeed has the religious connotation, bringing up the aspect of the "sacred and mysterious" quality of life. In this way, the copiousness of words indicating "life" reveals its complex multifaceted reality.

Among the contemporary Japanese philosophers, and not just among Zen-inspired thinkers, a philosophy of life has been a robust field, variously developed, especially in relation to the body and more recently in relation to the environment and the dire issue of care giving and care ethics in a society that is rapidly aging. Notable thinkers in this area are Washida Kiyokazu, Kimura Bin, Nakamura Yūjirō, and the late Yuasa Yasuo—just to name a few. The underlying framework of their investigation is that nature is experienced in its "nurturing" aspect (*natura naturans*). Nature gives birth to all things; the life-principle animates the entire cosmos—perhaps echoing the deep-seated sensitivity cultivated by the native religious tradition of Shintō in its emphasis on "*musubi*" ("fecundity" or "production" by the coming together of male and female sexes in nature). In any event, "life" is perceived as something far removed from a private possession or an object of human manipulation (and this is where a new set of problems arise in the present-day advancement of bio-technology).

A favorite traditional metaphor of life in Japanese literature is a river. The medieval Japanese author Kamo no Chōmei famously began his celebrated essay *An Account of My Hut* (or *Hōjōki*, written in 1212) with these words: "The flow of the river is ceaseless and its water is never the same. The bubbles that float in the pools, now vanishing, now forming, are not of long duration: so in the world are man and his dwellings."[12] The modern novelist, the late Endō Shūsaku (1923–96), also described the great Mother Ganges as the transcultural "deep river" that "swallows up the ashes of every person," rejecting no one, and flows along silently.[13] But the image of majestic river is more than a metaphor—from time immemorial, human civilizations sprang up along major rivers. Moreover, today we are painfully aware that these mighty rivers are essential arteries of the earth's ecosystem.

4. ZEN PHILOSOPHY OF LIFE: AFFIRMATION VIA NEGATION

In Zen philosophy, the affirmation of life must be mediated by the moment of "negation," the radical turnabout of the ego-consciousness toward its deeper root. This realization has at least two aspects: one is to see the essential importance of "religious practice" (*shugyō*) to transform one's base instinct into compassion, as Daisetz advocated; the other is the ontological recognition that negation and affirmation are built-in realities of life, as Nishida's thought most clearly demonstrates. Adding to this, the third aspect would be the one advanced by Raichō: one must affirm life in order to improve the plights of the poor and the underprivileged, to raise them out of negative conditions of life.

Unlike early Buddhism, which taught to annihilate "clinging" or "thirst" in order to stop suffering, D. T. Suzuki sees a positive reality in this blind life force (be it desire or libido). Instead of condemning it as something detrimental to spirituality, he sees in it the seed of great compassion, the infinite love. The originally crude but unfettered life force must be accepted and "purified" into compassionate love. When the Zen thinkers speak of "life" ("*inochi*") (Raichō), or the primordial driving force "*trishnā*" (D. T. Suzuki), or the "historical life" (*rekishiteki seimei*) (Nishida), they talk about this reality of life that animates all things, and is the very source of all "ex-istence."

Moreover, as briefly mentioned earlier, they do not see life to be antithetical to death, but life and death make up one unbreakable whole. Suzuki observes that to separate life from death and fear death is actually the cause of agony and anxiety. Moreover, to rejoice in life and abhor death came about as the result of the discriminating mind that divides life and death, the spirit and the flesh, the pure and the impure. Suzuki goes on to say, however, that the mind intuits beyond the discriminating mind itself and opens up our "mind's eye" to the eternal. This is the reason why human beings do not cease to long for the realm beyond life-and-death.[14] Life is "unborn" (*fushō*), and therefore undying, Zen Master Bankei said. This spiritual recognition of death is certainly not unique to Zen, as, for instance, St. Francis of Assisi has said it in his "Simple Prayer" that "it is in dying that we are reborn into eternal life."

5. PHILOSOPHY AND KENSHŌ, THE EXPERIENCE OF INITIAL AWAKENING

In and through the awakening experience of kenshō, one comes upon the greater source of "life" that is beyond the ego-centered attachment to life, and this kenshō experience is "life-changing." Moreover, each individual's kenshō experience differs in content from that of others. This "personal variance" seems to explain that the kind of kenshō experience is tied to the kind of philosophy each thinker espouses and develops. Be it zazen (seated meditation) or kōan practice (mediation coupled with working through a Zen "question" given by the master), it aims at freeing the mind from its habit of concept building.

Thomas Merton, although neither a Zen master nor a Zen student, aptly captured the essence of the kōan practice. Himself so deeply steeped in the Trappist life of contemplation, he seems to have understood the point of kōan practice very clearly. He observed as follows:

> [One] learns to "work through" the kōan, to live it as one's master has lived it. In fact, the heart of the kōan is reached, its kernel is attained and tasted, when one breaks through into the heart of life itself as the ground of one's own consciousness. It is then that one sees the "answer," or rather one experiences oneself as the question answered. The answer is the kōan, the question, seen in a totally new light. It is not something other than the question. The kōan is not something other than the self. It is a cryptic figure of the self, and it is interpreted insofar as the students can become so identified with the kōan that it revolutionizes and liberates their whole consciousness, delivering it from itself. . . .
>
> The Zen experience is first of all a liberation from the notion of "I" and of "mind"; yet it is not annihilation and pure consciousness (as Westerners sometimes imagine "nirvana" to be). It is, on the contrary, a kind of super-consciousness in which one experiences reality not indirectly or mediately but directly, and in which, clinging to no experience and to no awareness as such, one is simply

> "aware." This simple "awareness" or "awakeness" is in fact the true identity which the Zen student seeks.[15]

Merton does not fail to observe that this attainment of kenshō "is not the end but the serious beginning" for Zen students.[16]

As mentioned above, what constitutes the breakthrough experience of kenshō varies so much from individual to individual that it is best described as "to each his (her) own." Not only that, each individual's approach to kōan is also unique. Is there a prototypical "Zen awakening"? One must answer in the negative. In the following, we shall examine the kenshō experience of our three Zen philosophers.

5.1 Raichō's case

For Raichō, her kenshō took place as she immersed herself in intense sitting and the "study" of kōan given to her by Master Sōkatsu—"What is your original face before your parents were born?" Years later she wrote about her initial approach to kōan to be overly intellectual: "When I started zazen at Ryōmō'an, I had approached the kōan about 'my original face' as an intellectual problem. At every interview [with the Master], I had been scolded for giving a philosophical explanation. I had put tremendous effort and exertion to understand it."[17] Despite her "philosophical inclination," during the July *sesshin* (the intensive meditation training period) of 1906—several months into her Zen practice—she was suddenly seized by an extraordinary experience of "tears as large as hailstones" streaming down her face. Those tears were the outburst of her experience of having "broken free" of her "finite self" and reaching a "state of pure awareness." Her "whole being had exploded in a flood of tears," she wrote.[18] Master Sōkatsu was then expounding on *The Records of Linji* (J. *Rinzairoku*), which talks about "the real person of no fixed rank" (*mui no shin'nin*), the meaning of which directly spoke to her:

> The true source of the Buddha is none other than the person who is actually listening to this talk. Look at the person—the true man without rank—without shape or form, yet who truly exists. If you are able to discern this, you are no different from the Buddha. Do not ever release your grip on this. Everything that meets your eyes is this. There is no one among you who cannot attain enlightenment ... *Upon this lump of reddish flesh sits a true man with no rank.* Constantly he goes in and out of the gates of your face. If there is anyone here who does not know this for a fact, look, look![19]

The expression "the man of no fixed rank" (*mui no shin'nin* 無位の真人) became for Raichō the existential point of reference, which actually found its way into her inaugural essay for the *Seitō* magazine[20] as the "authentic person" (*shinsei no hito* 真正の人), in the opening line of her "manifesto": "In the beginning, woman was truly the sun, an authentic person."

Master Sōkatsu recognized her breakthrough and gave her the lay Buddhist name, "Ekun" (慧薫 fragrance of wisdom). Her kenshō took the form of a burst of deep consciousness breaking through the surface layers of conventional self; her philosophical thought bears the stamp of this warm, "affective" quality of elation, the joy that came with liberation. As mentioned earlier, the experience of kenshō radically liberated her from her introverted personality, transforming her into an audacious, energetic social activist.

Her kenshō was further confirmed in December of 1909 at Kaiseiji in Nishinomiya, where she attended the December *sesshin* led by Master Nantenbō.[21] The kōan she was given to work through was "*Mu-ji*" (The letter Mu), otherwise known as "Jōshū's Dog." At the end of the *sesshin*, Nantenbō, in the acknowledgment of her kenshō, took one character from his dharma name, Zenchū (全忠 utter fidelity), combined it with Raichō's given name "Haru" (明), and gave her the lay Buddhist name of Zenmyō (全明 utter lucidity). She never used these Buddhist names, however, preferring "Raichō" as her penname, for she found an affinity with the native wild mountain bird, ptarmigan (thunderbird), or "*raichō*."

5.2 D. T. Suzuki's case

Suzuki's kenshō took place during the year-end *sesshin* at Engakuji Temple in Kamakura in December 1896—in his sixth year of zazen practice. He was scheduled to depart for the United States to begin his career with the Open Court Publisher as Paul Carus's assistant in LaSalle, Illinois, in the February of the following year. Facing this "deadline," he had to, and did, attain his kenshō during the December *sesshin*—a few months before his departure. Once in America, he realized that it was his kenshō experience that sustained him, when he had to cope with an unfamiliar culture so different from his own. His commitment to Zen practice deepened in this way in the small North-American town, far away from Kamakura.

Several years later, on a sleepless night in LaSalle, he wrote a letter to Nishida, reminiscing about his kenshō experience, and described it for the first time:

> I had just finished my evening zazen and went out of the *zendō* (meditation hall) to return to my room in Kigen'in. It was a brightly moonlit night. As I descended the stone steps near the temple gate, suddenly I forgot myself. Ney, it was not that I forgot myself completely. The bright moonlight cast the shadow of tall trees on the ground like a painting. There, I found myself inside the painting, and there was no distinction between the trees and me. Trees were I, I the trees. This sensation pierced me through so vividly. It was crystal clear to me: "*This* is my original face!" Even after I returned to my quarter, my mind was limpid, clear, and there was not a cloud therein. I was filled with the sensation of joy.
>
> Tonight, as I was reading [sections of] Professor [William] James's Gifford Lectures, I felt as if he was describing my own kenshō experience, and it brought back my memory of it. I feel as if my mind is cleansed for the first time in a long while.[22]

In a much more colloquial manner, Suzuki also narrated this experience to an American friend of his years later: "I was taking the same old stone steps towards the temple gate, and all of a sudden, I had the conviction that I was the same as the trees on the side of the steps, and it wasn't that I had stopped being myself but I was the trees."[23] Suzuki's kenshō experience may be described as "natural," "poetic," and "visual." It was accompanied by the sense of dissolution of physical boundaries. His experience comes close to what has been traditionally described as "natural mysticism."

As for his Buddhist name, "Daisetz" (大拙 great simplicity), it was conferred on him by Master Shaku Sōen sometime in 1895; he soon began to use it to sign his writings, preferring it to his given name of Teitarō.

5.3 Nishida's case

For Nishida, zazen practice was by no means smooth going; he felt he was making two steps forward while retracting three backward. Earlier on, he resolved that merely passing one kōan after another was not the objective of his practice, and it was more important for him to get down to the bottom of Zen teaching. Master Setsumon, who guided him from the very beginning of his practice, recognized the maturity of his student's practice, and in 1901—the fifth year into his practice—he gave him the Buddhist name Sunshin (寸心 heart of an inch).[24] Nishida fondly used this name to sign his calligraphy pieces.

Receiving the lay Buddhist name did not lessen his difficulty with his kōan practice. Seeing his student struggle, Master Setsumon changed the kōan in 1902 from the "Letter Mu" (i.e. "Jōshū's Dog") to the "Sound of One-hand Clapping" (*sekishu no onjō*).[25] His attainment of kenshō came during the summer practice of 1903 under Master Kōjū at Daitokuji in Kyoto. When the master acknowledged his passing the kōan, Nishida was not elated; there was neither a burst of tears nor the sense of euphoria. He wrote about it to Setsumon and expressed his skepticism that perhaps Master Kōjū was too benevolent. To this Master Setsumon wrote back and said: "Trust what took place. Do not doubt [the validity of] Zen teaching and continue with your zazen practice."[26]

There is an interesting postscript to Nishida's kenshō. Following Master Setsumon's advice, he resumed his post-kenshō practice, and wrote about it to D. T. Suzuki, who in his typical candor observed a generic problem associated with overly intellectual minds (Suzuki seems to put Nishida in a different category, however, as he knew Nishida had a poetic mind):

> I am more and more inclined to think that the more intellectual a man is, the more mental efforts are needed to overcome the mind in order to reach the attitude as required by the *dhyāna* practitioners. Inasmuch as *dhyāna* practice is a sort of mysticism, it must be of great difficulty for a mind of predominantly intellectual turn. To such minds, what might be called poetic intuition or imagination does not appeal very much. They are always inclined to look at things intellectually, that is, in their abstract phase, while there is nowhere in this concrete world anything that exists in abstract. Well, what is necessary in the beginning is an actual experience, concrete personal experience felt in the deepest recess of our consciousness. This mystic incommunicable experience, once attained, you can give any explanation to it.[27]

Although it is a slight digression, it is of particular interest here to note that Suzuki actually uses the word "mysticism" and "mystic" to describe the kenshō experience, because later he came to deny it vehemently. For instance, in his 1965 review of Heinrich Dumoulin's *A History of Zen Buddhism*, Suzuki wrote somewhat pointedly:

> The major contention of this book … is that Zen is a form of mysticism. Unfortunately, some years ago, I too used the term in connection with Zen. I have long since regretted it, as I find it now highly misleading in elucidating Zen thought. Let it suffice to say here that Zen has nothing "mystical" about it or in it. It is most plain, clear as the daylight, all out in the open with nothing hidden, dark, obscure, secret or mystifying in it.[28]

Thomas Merton, acting as the arbiter between Suzuki and Dumoulin, who called Zen a kind of "natural mysticism," settled the disagreement by pronouncing it "more a matter of semantics than anything else."[29]

Going back to Nishida, his kenshō experience was something sober, and he was dissatisfied with it as his person was untouched by the experience of "passing" the kōan—or so it seemed to him at that time. This again, must be another kind of kenshō experience, and bespeaks Nishida's philosophical bent, with which he proceeded to "dig" the philosophical vein like a miner every inch of the way. One could argue that in Nishida's case the impact of kenshō matured slowly but steadily. His diary entry of July 3, 1927, reads that he "spent a quiet afternoon, alone, when a burst of jubilant experience of 'rebirth' came over" him. Indeed this is about a quarter of a century after his kenshō. From this we may surmise that a kenshō experience could continue to ferment and mature inside a person. Nishida's emphasis on the concrete action rather than abstract thinking, for instance, can be seen to have its roots in his Zen awakening. He steadfastly maintained the following position:

> The thinking self is not the real self. Even if I am thinking or feeling, it is not yet my self. My real self exists when and where I face the reality of taking action (*kōi*). The real self emerges in facing concrete situations (*ji* 事). The sense of the self we normally have is actually a "phantom" (or "imagined self," *kūsōteki jiko*). My real self is known to me in my self-awareness when I act (*jissenteki jikaku*) … I come to know my self in action. I become self-aware in action.[30]

The primacy of action that Nishida describes here seems to corroborate Raichō's decision to get involved in the women's liberation movement. Zen awakening can lead to a philosophy of action, rather than of indolence or armchair contemplation.

To conclude this section, I reiterate that each person's kenshō experience is indeed different, as it touches the core of the person concerned. It appears that there is no set formula of the kenshō experience, and that the kind of kenshō experience is an expression of each individual's psychological, intellectual, and emotional makeup. This is why Zen masters must wisely guide each student by taking into consideration the temperaments, the likes and dislikes, and so forth of the students who carry these things in their minds, before these notions and attachments are "voided."

6. ON LIFE AND SEXUAL DESIRE

The initial Zen awakening allows one to come face to face with "the real self," the source of one's true self-identity. The question of sexual desire being an integral component of life's experience, Zen thinkers do not eschew this aspect but rather work through it in order to "shed" the light of *prajñā*, or wisdom, onto it.

6.1 Raichō's view

In her initial phase of Zen practice Raichō came to learn that "Zen does not deny sexuality, and no one practices zazen in order to get rid of physical desires; many Zen priests remain uncompromisingly celibate, but they have chosen that way of life entirely on their own, after having first affirmed the reality of sexual desire."[31] In her effort to convince the incredulous, she brings up the kōan that has to be worked through for the advanced students before they can graduate from their kōan practice. It is called "*Basu shōan*" ("An old woman burning down the hut"), which directly deals with the question of sexual desire and spirituality. The kōan goes as follows:

> There was an old woman who supported a hermit. For twenty years she always had a girl of sixteen or seventeen years old to take to the hermit his food and wait on him. One day she told the girl to give the monk a close hug and ask, "What do you feel now?"
>
> The hermit responded, "An old tree on a cold cliff; Midwinter—no warmth."
>
> The girl went back and told this to the old woman.
>
> The woman said, "for twenty years I have supported this vulgar good-for-nothing!" So saying, she threw the monk out and burned down the hermitage.[32]

Now how are we to go about this kōan? First thing we learn from this kōan is that Zen practice does not aim at negating humanity, including sexual desire, so that the practitioner is not expected to become an insensible withered tree branch. How should the monk have responded to the girl's hug? When that happened, did not the old hermit feel a surge of warmth? He might have said to the girl to hug him even more tightly. He might have said, "Wow, it feels good to be hugged again. It's been a long time since I was hugged." Then he could have politely but warmly accepted the tray of food and gently dismissed the young girl. The old woman would not have burnt down his hermitage then—perhaps.

This kōan demonstrates that the spiritual practice should aim at increasing one's full humanity by purifying and elevating the base instincts into warm friendliness and compassion. Why did the old woman throw the hermit out of the hut and set it on fire? The point here seems to me that the old woman herself is "I," as much as the withered poor monk is "I." I must acknowledge the danger of wrong practice and also set on fire "my" comfortable hut, if "I" am becoming an old deadbeat monk with no human feelings left in "me." "I" as the old woman is not afraid of burning down the hut. Thanks to this "old woman," "I" can go back into the world with human warmth and treat others kindly, which is a way of sharing the benefit of "my" arduous religious practice of so many years. "Burning down the hut" means getting rid of any residue of "my" dichotomous thinking (i.e. attachment to concepts) of purity and impurity. The fire has to scorch the idea of sexual desire to be base or mean. Now this kōan makes better sense: for the old woman (who is I), the hermit's practice is inauthentic, consisted only of self-denial and repression of vital human nature, instead of working through it and to transform it. The monk (who is also I) may have failed to cultivate his compassion and wisdom, but now "I" am thrown out of my complacent comfort zone, and become aware that "I" must avoid falling into the pitfall of dichotomous conceptual thinking that "I" myself have create. How does *zazen liberate a person from sexual desire*? The key to the answer seems to be located in this very possibility of embracing it and working through it toward *transforming and channeling the sexual energy* into compassion. With this kind of practice, one will reach the state which Suzuki described as follows—*if a person has no "hang-up," there no "peg" to "hang" one's "hang-up's."*[33] That is the state of utter freedom.

Raichō admitted that it was premature for her to speak about this particular kōan, because she had yet to have the physical sensation of sexual desire. The *Seitō Manifesto*, "In the Beginning, Woman Was the Sun," was colored by her youthful, and not fully mature, view on sexual desire. The passages like the following must be interpreted accordingly:

> I shall seek my innate talent nowhere but in my mental-spiritual concentration.
>
> This innate talent is mystery; it is the authentic person.
>
> The innate talent has nothing to do with one being male or female.
>
> In terms of mental-spiritual concentration, this sexual distinction of male and female belongs to the sphere of intermediate or lower layer of the ego, to the tentative "ego" which ought to perish. Sexual distinction of male and female does not apply in the highest sphere of the ego, in the "true ego" (*shinga* 真我) that is immortal and non-perishing.[34]

She initially interpreted her kenshō experience to mean that "the original face" or the real self was "neither woman nor man; I transcend such distinctions."[35] This view was soon put to a test, which brought about much pain, confusion, fatigue, and self-reflection to Raichō.[36] In her resumption of zazen practice her sexed body may have become a kōan for herself. Even in her youthful reflection, however, she acknowledged that it was her own doing that created her suffering, and therefore it follow that she was in the position to rise above it. This Zen "affirmation" of subjectivity found itself into her manifesto, quoted above, wherein we read:

> Although I lamented, I also knew that I was the master of my agony, losses, bewilderment, mental confusion, and self-destruction.
>
> Thus, with the prerogative of the master of my own self, I came to settle on being satisfied as a free and independent person, in control of my own self. I no longer lamented over having allowed myself to plunge into self-destruction, and henceforth each time I faced challenges, I did not cringed. I have unflinchingly walked my own way.[37]

Raichō encountered an unexpected challenge when she found herself in a romantic love relationship, which eventually resulted in her cohabitation with Okumura Hiroshi and together creating their new family. At that critical moment, Ellen Key's work *Love and Marriage* came to her attention. She began translating it into Japanese as part of her study to learn new ideas. Key's conviction that marriage *should be based on romantic love* struck a novel cord. Years later she reflected on the significant impact of Key's philosophy on herself as follows: "If not for my encounter with Key, I would not have married my husband Okumura; instead I would have remained single and childless. The influence of Key on me was *that* revolutionary, even if not as fundamental as my *kenshō* experience."[38] In Raichō the traditional Zen teaching came to be blended with the philosophical outlook that affirmed romantic love, marriage, pregnancy, and motherhood. Perhaps unwittingly, Raichō opened a way for aspiring young contemporary Japanese women to embrace new possibilities of combining romantic love, spiritual life, and a career that may insure economic independence as much as circumstantially possible. In this way, she took Zen teaching into the arena of emancipation of women. Had he known about it, Thomas Merton would have appreciated her effort. Merton wrote in the 1960s of the dire need for traditional religions to shed their old shells to become relevant in the modern "secular" era. We read:

> Zen offers us a phenomenology and metaphysics of insight and of consciousness which has extraordinary value for the West. But the cultural accretions and trappings of Zen, the customs and mores of the *zendō*, while remaining a special interest, no longer have the living power they had in the Middle Ages. Like the Catholic liturgy, Zen practice calls for an *aggiornamento*.[39]

Raichō's thoughts on romantic love deepened as she underwent the experience of pregnancy and childbirth. In her struggle to have both "her private space of contemplation" and "a family life," she realized that the liberation of women has to take into account women's physical reality, and not just the disembodied abstract notion of "women." Four years have passed since she wrote the "manifesto" for the *Seitō* magazine. We read:

> Romantic love became something solemn and significant that I had to look at with completely different eyes. I had to think long and hard about what it means to live as a woman and what value there is for a woman to live a life of love. . . .
>
> In the process I came to see the need to *liberate women not only as human persons but also as sexed women*. This was a totally new philosophical problem for me.[40]

Through pregnancy and the delivery of her first baby, Raichō came to see that great life force permeated her body as a woman[41] and this recognition became the vehicle to overcome her fear and anxiety to accept motherhood. In her 1917 essay "A Year as a Mother," Raichō noted that horizon of her world was enlarging with the unfolding of life. Here we have a more mature and well-rounded thought of Raichō:

> It can be said that I lived the life of a mixture of "egoism" and "altruism" during the last year. I affirmed my romantic love initially in order to assert my individual

> ego and develop it. But my love rooted in self-affirmation and self-development turned out to be gateway to the love of others, to the other side of life. In no time the whole panorama of love of the other unfolded in front of me, first through the love I bore my lover, and then through my love for my child. I ended up experiencing all sorts of contradictions in my life, but I can no longer dismiss them as mere life's contradictions.
>
> I have rather come to think of them as gateway that opens out into a wider, larger, and deeper life. And the real harmonization of these two orientations [of private soul life and the family life] may well be the subtle and ultimate flavor of life itself.[42]

Her personal journey of wife and mother made her realize the lowly unprotected social status of young working mothers, which made her question whether such a treatment of women was just and justifiable in a modern nation.[43] In this way her feminist thought took shape, having her kenshō experience at the wellspring of her activism and Ellen Key's philosophy of social economic and political emancipation as the guide. She discovered the dialectic of love, in which her love for the others and her self-identity mutually interacted to ever more profound depths of altruistic love, which gave her the energy to tackle concrete social issues.

Raichō's postwar writing of "Know Thyself" (*Anata jishin o shire*, 1947), contains a cogent statement of her philosophy of life.[44] Therein she speaks to college age women about life (*inochi*), as the "original face," that is, the real self-identity, of the person. She explains that her kenshō experience consisted of coming face to face with the unquestionable presence of life force (*inochi*) that permeates the entire universe:

> In my youth, … I agonized over the question of religion and took up *zazen* for some time. Zen people speak of "one's original face before one's parents were born." It refers to the reality of the self as this unceasing life. It refers to one's coming to know the true nature of humanity that is divine—be it called God or Buddha… Probably you know that Christ said, "I am before Abraham was born" (John 8:58). This, too, speaks of the same intuition.[45]

Preceding the above passage is her exposition of life and the body. I quote this passage at length:

> We must acknowledge that human beings, just as trees and plants, insects, birds and animals, were born of this great *life* (*inochi*) that permeates this universe and gives rise to all beings and nurtures them all. Without this life, nothing comes into being. Religious people call this great life God—the great life that gives birth to all things—and maintain that God has created human beings, and that human beings are God's children.
>
> Just as this great *life* (*inochi*) that has given birth to you as a human being, permeates this universe; it also permeates you from within, although you may think that "you" are your own making. I suppose this all-permeating presence of life is the reason why sometimes it is said that the spirit of God dwells in each person. Yes, human beings originally reside in this confluence of inner and outer flows of

great life that plentifully fills the universe. You are embraced by God in the bosom of God; but God too is embraced by you and resides in your bosom.

You may think perchance that your young beautiful body is "you." But in fact, you already know that your body is just an "organ" created and animated by life (*inochi*). And this life is actually the real "you." Your organ may be young, beautiful, and looks very healthy right now. But soon in time, you will begin to have wrinkles on your face, just as they cover my face. Your jet-black hair will soon be mixed with grey streaks. Your eyesight will begin to dull, your mind will lose its sharpness, your limbs will start to become a little stiff, and whatever you will be doing, you will easily tire. However much you take good care of your body, it will not last for more than 90 or 100 years. This is because your body is but an organ and is not the same as this enduring life.

On the other hand, this life that is actually your real self lives on without fatigue or old age or death, regardless of what happens to your organ. It was there even before your body came into being from the womb of your mother; and even after your body perishes and only bones remain, life will continue to be. Life freely creates another body and gives birth to it. "You" are this eternal life.[46]

This in a nutshell is Raichō's view of life. For her the zazen meditation, which she continued to do even after her intensive Zen practice had petered out, allowed her to tap into the source of indefatigable life, and provided her with the immanently transcendent perspective in her everyday life.[47] She spoke about it in her essay of 1931, "On Zen Practice" (*Shūzen ni tsuite*):

I sit and meditate whenever I am tired. When I get writer's block, I sit. When my mind is not clear, I sit. When I am disappointed or at a loss as to how to come up with a solution to a critical situation or difficult problem, I sit. When I don't know to whom to vent my frustration or with whom to share my sadness, I sit. When I'm mentally and physically exhausted, I sit. When I'm at my wits' end as to how to get through a period of economic hardship, I sit. Whatever the situation may be, the more trying the circumstances, the more concentration I put into my lower belly, and sit, which has become my customary activity. Sometimes I may sit only for ten to twenty minutes, but sometimes I sit through several hours without stirring.

Indeed, have I never had done zazen, by now the well of my vitality (*seimei*) would have dried up, my strength would have been worn out, and I might have been suffocated by hackneyed and straitjacketed thinking. I am convinced that it is thanks to this activity of sitting that everyday my mind is refreshed; that hope, courage, and trust are bestowed on me; and that out of nature and my existence continue to well up abundant poems.[48]

6.2 *Suzuki's view*

D. T. Suzuki began to reflect seriously on the question of sexual life, when a romance bloomed between him and a young American woman, Beatrice Lane, his future wife. He wrote to Nishida, communicating his personal thoughts:

I am neither an adherent of asceticism or puritanism. I do not see anything wrong in so-called worldliness. Life consists of hopes, struggles, dreams, sorrows, etc. Let us not escape them, but let us live in the eternal whirlpool of passions and sufferings and hopes.

Thank you for your kind advice concerning my possible marriage with the American woman. The matter is not yet settled. I know many difficulties accompany this affair. She is not unaware of them, either. We have talked about interracial marriage from various angles, that is, socially, biologically, economically, as well as from the individual standpoint. . . .

In connection with this matter, I have lately paid a great deal of attention to sexual life. I have thought of it sociologically as it influences our civilization. One of the great differences that divide the East from the West is our sexual life. Some day I want to write an article or a booklet on this very interesting subject. I have many things I would like to talk with you concerning this and other kindred subjects, but I cannot do that very well in a letter.[49]

Nishida, already a married man who had fathered three daughters and two sons, and just recently had twin girls born in April, but also suffered the death of his beloved four-year-old daughter back in the January of the same year (1907), was certainly interested in what Daisetz had to say about sexual life. In response, he wrote:

I would like to hear your thoughts on sexual life. As you say, the Western view may differ greatly in this regard from the Japanese. In the collected letters of Lafcadio Hearn, we find a passage by him which says that the Japanese appreciate the beauty of nature as it is, but the Westerners tend to see nature's beauty through the feminine beauty embodied in women. He also maintained that because the Japanese do not have a strong sexual passion, great profound literature has not been produced. Is it an overstatement to say that in the West sexuality occupies the essential place in the culture, while in the East it is nature?[50]

It appears it was finally in 1948 when Suzuki found an occasion to write about sexual desire, but by then Nishida was no longer alive to read it. Suzuki's essay "Religion and Sexual Desire" (*Shūkyō to seiyoku*)[51] makes fuller sense when read together with his another essay on "desire" contained in the *Mysticism: Christian and Buddhist*, wherein he describes his view on the indispensability of "thirst" (*trishnā*) as the very driving force of this universe, as briefly mentioned earlier.

Suzuki maintains that the Mahayana understands "*trishnā*" (or *tanhā*, "thirst") as the first principle of the universe, while the earliest forms of Buddhism had considered it as *the* cause of suffering, and therefore had to be rid of.[52] The formation of the body is activated by *trishnā*, which causes things to come into being. Destruction of "thirst" surely means the "annihilation" of human beings.[53] Suzuki maintains that "thirst" is "our being itself. It is I; it is you; it is the cat; it is the tree; it is the rock; it is the snow; it is the atom."[54] "Thirst" is different from the will in that the will "strives to live against death, against destruction," and as such it implies dualism. *Trishnā*, however, "remains still dormant … as in the mind of God." It was *trishnā* that "made God give out his *fiat*, 'Let there be light.'"[55] Suzuki also notes that "in the beginning was *trishnā*," in contrast to John 1:1 "In the beginning was the Word." Let us turn to his writing:

> Buddhist philosophy considers *trishnā* or *tanhā*, or "thirst," the first principle of making things come into existence. In the beginning there is *trishnā*. It wills to have a form in order to express itself, which means to assert itself ... [W]hen it asserts itself it takes form. As *trishnā* is inexhaustible, the forms it takes are infinitely varied. *Trishnā* wants to see and we have eyes; it wants to hear and we have ears; it wants to jump and we have the deer, the rabbit, and other animals of this order; it wants to fly and we have birds of all kinds; it wants to swim and we have fish wherever there are waters; it wants to bloom and we have flowers; it wants to shine and we have stars; ... *Trishnā* is the creator of the universe.
>
> Being the creator, *trishnā* is the principle of individuation. It creates a world of infinite diversity.[56]

Furthermore, Suzuki maintains that the later Buddhists understood by *trishnā the power that transforms itself*. Here, Suzuki comes to the heart of the matter to unlock the oft-misunderstood equation of "*bonnō*" (delusion) and "*bodai*" (spiritual awakening)—an idea analogous to "*samsāra* is *nirvāna, nirvaāna samsāra*." He writes:

> The later Buddhist realized that *trishnā* was what constituted human nature—in fact, everything and everything that at all comes into existence; that to deny *trishnā* was committing suicide; to escape from *trishnā* was the height of contradiction or a deed of absolute impossibility; and that the very thing that makes us wish to deny or to escape from *trishnā* was *trishnā* itself. Therefore, all that we could do for ourselves, or rather all that *trishnā* could do for itself, was to make it turn to itself, to purify itself from all its encumbrances and defilements, by means of transcendent knowledge (*prajñā*). The later Buddhists then let *trishnā* work on in its own way without being impeded by anything else. *Trishnā* or "thirst" or "craving" then comes to be known as *mahākarunā*, or "absolute compassion," which they consider the essence of Buddhahood and Bodhisattvahood.
>
> This *trishnā* emancipated from all its encumbrances incarnates itself in every possible form in order to achieve a universal salvation of all beings, both sentient and non-sentient ... When *trishnā* comes back to itself, it is all-conquering, all-knowing, and also all-loving. It is this love or *karunā* or *maitri* [friendliness] that makes the Buddha or Bodhisattva abandon his eternally entering into a state of emptiness and subjects him- or herself to transmigrate [i.e. incarnate] through the triple world.[57]

The crucial point of Suzuki's view on the "thirst" is that "thirst turn to itself," and purifies itself of defilements by means of higher wisdom (*prajñā*). Put in another way, under the light of spiritual wisdom libido purifies itself and turns into the principle of loving compassion. (Here we may recall the kōan, "The old woman burning the hut.") Stating this more succinctly, he wrote: "The Buddhist training consists in transforming *trishnā* (*tanhā*) into *karunā*, ego-centered love into something universal, eros into agape."[58] Here again, we may recall Raichō's path of growth, which moved from ego-perpetuation to the life of altruistic love by entrusting herself to the voice of nature embodied in her female body.

Thus understood, we see why Suzuki considers *trishnā* the foundation of the doctrines of universal salvation, as well as the foundation of Amitābha Buddha's "vows" (*pranidhāna*) and the Bodhisattva's action of *parināmanā* ("turning over the merit to others").[59] Radical purification of sexual energy is the key to Buddhist transformation, into an altruistic social self, and as such is the prerequisite for bringing forth social harmony and peace.

Now let us turn to Suzuki's *Religion and Sexual Desire*. We recognize the basic theme is expounded in this essay on spirituality and sexual life. Suzuki calls for the healing of the split of the flesh and the spirit, and writes about how the body is indispensable in the creation of human cultures:

> It is precisely because of this physical body, despised and trampled [by some religious purists], that human beings have the opportunity to give birth to beautiful things. Consider, for instance, puppy love between young ones, or the feeling of oneness shared by a seasoned aged couple. These are the kinds of experiences reserved only for human beings. Romantic love by definition has a physical foundation, but for the young ones in love, this physical foundation is not within their purview. Theirs is a beautiful dream-like world. Again, the emotional bonding that grows in time between wife and husband is characterized by incomparable sense of inseparability so much so that when one of the partners dies the other often soon follows. This is why they say "the lotus flower, even though growing out of the mud, blooms beautifully." But actually, what is "beautiful" does not have its existence in the emotion (*kanjō*) of beautiful but in what gives rise to that emotion. A beautiful thing does not come into being by having something dirty as its source. A beautiful thing has something beautiful at its depth and simply reflects its beauty. A thing considered "dirty" gets purified by reflecting its source within it. A thing becomes "dirty" only when severed from this source.[60]

Suzuki's basic position is that the intellect in its discrimination dichotomizes life into two—the mind and the body, the spirit and the flesh, life and death. He sees that once the flesh is separated out of this primordial unity, everything becomes the source of constant worry and anxiety. In this dichotomized world an ideology such as dialectical materialism comes into being, claiming that consciousness emerge from the matter. But this claim is helpless in the face of the problems of human life. Again, if we were to give priority to the flesh as the principle of existence, we have nowhere else to turn to but to plunge into the abysmal void, for the flesh actually has no ground to stand on but the very edge of nihility. In such a world romantic love would disappear, and spiritual freedom, too, would vanish altogether.[61] For Suzuki the cause of various modern mental illnesses is rooted in this separation of the spirit and the flesh, which was brought about by the very workings of the conscious mind. He wonders if a diabolical element is at work in the biological evolutionary process. But contradictorily, it is out of the diabolical that the spiritual arises.[62] This is why the deep source of self-consciousness is ultimately a religious question, and no science can clarify it.

Out of his reflection Suzuki asserts that only by uncovering the full capacity of "reason and religion" can we save humanity and the world from utter destruction. By "reason" (*risei*) Suzuki means discerning wisdom (*prajñā*), and by "religion" (*shūkyō*) he refers to the dimension of religious practice that leads one to the self-discovery and self-transformation. Moreover, "religion" shares in common with the human capacity to imagine and to generate ideals.[63]

6.3 Nishida's view

Nishida spoke about his view on sexual life in his letter to Mr and Mrs Watsuji Tetsurō, who were involved in the search for a suitable wife-to-be for Nishida's second marriage (several years after the death of his first wife). He wrote:

> If I were a Zen monk or a Catholic priest, I suppose celibacy would be important, but for me, it is not so. Although I certainly have a deep-seated longing for a religious life, a merely formal religious life that denies humanity is not something that I would embrace. I don't even think that such is the ideal human existence. What I mean by "nothing" (*mu*) is more like the warm heart that Shinran possessed, which acknowledges everyone's freedom and embraces every sinner (although I don't know whether Shinran himself actually phrased it in this way).
>
> While I appreciate Eastern culture as profound and precious, I cannot deny my longing for Western culture, which is a great development of rich and free humanity. Just as I derive pleasure from Sesshū's paintings, or poetry in Chinese, so I cannot help but be moved by the paintings of Rembrandt or the poetry of Goethe. Instead of deriding the old Goethe who fell in love with young Ulrike von Levetzow and desired to marry her, I am touched by the greatness of his humanity.[64]

Here, we observe that Nishida's view on sexual life closely parallels that of D. T. Suzuki (as mentioned above in his letter of 1907); it is also closely associated with the cultural life at large. At around the time of his courtship that resulted in his remarriage in December 1931, Nishida's thought increasingly added a "personalistic" overtone. To cite a passage from his work of this period, we read:

> Love does not consist in the satisfaction of one's desire (*yokubō*), but it limits [i.e. curtails] such desire … Self-loving human beings are embraced in the absolute love of God and determined *qua* the self-determinations of absolute love. Absolute love is the Eternal Now, in which numerous moments are determined—it is the space that embraces numerous moments and establishes them.[65]

He distinguishes *yokkyū* (desire, demand) from *yokubō* (greed, including carnal desire), and locates the origination of desire (*yokkyū*) in the ontological mode of human beings existing as corporeal beings in the world of things.[66]

His reflection on deep inner life (*fukaki naiteki seimei*) occupied an important place in his writings from 1929 through 1932,[67] and out of this line of thinking such notions as action-intuition (*kōiteki chokkan*), historical body (*rekishiteki shintai*), and the overarching notion of historical life (*rekishiteki seimei*) were developed. In his last years, he also reflected on the religious aspect of life in terms of "eternal life" (*eien no seimei*).

In line with his basic philosophical stance of staying closely connected with concrete life, he came to identify the body (*shintai*) as a key philosophical problem.[68] He had already seen the body as the principle of individuation from the very beginning of his philosophical investigation, and therefore, this is to be understood as a deepening of his thought. For we have a fascinating "fragment" from the very early period of Nishida, perhaps even preceding his first book, *An Inquiry into the Good*, on the role of the body in relation to the arising of subject and object. It reads:

> A crow's call "*kah*!" constitutes pure objectivity. There is no distinction between the self and the thing. Unified reality alone is present. It is only when I turn my consciousness back to my *physical body* (*shintai*) and perceive that I am here, the distinction between the subject and the object arises. These various mental operations compose subjectivity. That is to say, when the idea occurs that "a thing is out there, and I am here hearing it," the subject-object dichotomy arises as something insurmountable.[69]

He came to see logic as the expression, or "logocization," of life, and the body that "speaks and understands" to partake the nature of the logos ("logos-*teki*").[70] As fascinating and intriguing an idea as it is, which guided his reflection and the formulation of the notion of "topos" (or *basho*), he rather paid close attention to the role of intuition in a bodily movement. He came to see that intuition and action always accompany the activity of making things (*poiesis*). He named this feature "action-intuition" or "*kōiteki chokkan*."[71] This action-intuition, as the mode of any creative action, is an invariant feature, extending from the humblest everyday activity of cooking, for instance, to creating a work of fine arts, literature, films, performing a musical instrument, and playing sport. In any of these activities, one usually envisions a hint of the end product, and the body works toward realizing that end in a coordinated manner.[72] In Nishida's "action-intuition" the body is being accorded the equal status with intuition; thereby it rehabilitates the original unity of the mind and the body. Far from referring to some esoteric action, the "action-intuition" refers to the fact that the mind and the body work together in the production of things in our everyday activities. Even writing a scholarly paper is a kind of action-intuition, as intuition (envisioning, thinking, musing) and the action of the body (holding a pen in a hand and writing, or typing, or dictating) are seamlessly coordinated. If one is hungry, one cannot concentrate on thinking or writing. If one lacks a good night sleep, one's mind is foggy, and it is impossible to carry out good thinking; lack of sleep does not help the blurring eyesight, either. So, even a highly cerebral activity of writing a philosophical paper still requires the physical preparedness and its "cooperation." Nishida usually gives the example of artistic production to explain the feature of action-intuition, because he finds this dynamism most pronounced in the artistic performance, such as making a calligraphy piece, playing a musical instrument, or playing sport, which requires a higher degree of physical and mental coordination as well as specialized skills developed and internalized over years of assiduous training.

By focusing on the reality of "life" (*seimei*), Nishida comes to advance his view that the primary mode of our being in the world is described in the movements of "from that which is created to that which creates" (*tsukurareta mono kara tsukuru mono e*)[73]—we are "born" into the world as that which is "created," and yet we move on to give birth to things, to "create" things, and thereby give shape to the world. A thing made belongs to the public domain, independent of the one who created it.[74] This created thing comprises various meanings and appeals to the wider audience, who are moved or influenced by what they encounter (or remain indifferent to it). In this way our action of making things shapes the world positively (i.e. constructively), neutrally, or negatively (i.e. destructively). The idea of "historical body" (*rekishiteki shintai*) refers to the same reality.

The adjective "historical" has a double connotation. Let us take the example of a newborn baby. It soon learns to respond "culturally," as it begins to emulate the behavior of those around it, responds to their emotions, and acquires a language spoken around it. Why is that? It is because our body is already a depository of past experiences of the countless generations of thousands of years. The body is "historical" in this sense. The other meaning of "historical" is that it pertains to the "making" of history. The salient example would be the athletic feats, as one witnesses in the Olympic Games, for instance, wherein athletes break the old world-records and establish new ones. The "historical body" is "history making" in this sense. Each of us as a historical body creates and changes the shape of the world. But this is only the half of the whole picture. In the mutually determining dynamic relationship, we are also changed and affected by the changes we make to the world. The changed world on account of our action further interacts with us—we may just think of the climate change, as an example. This mutually interacting process is in constant flux and never-ending (but how long can it be sustained?—we began to raise these questions). In his approach to "*poiesis* (making) and *praxis* (action)" Nishida paid attention to this mutually influencing dynamic reality of the human and the world—or the "dialectical world," for short.

In this dialectical world, "desire" (*yokkyū*) is "the demand of the self to fashion itself, i.e., to construct itself" (*jiko-keisei*) as an individual-in-the-world reflecting the external world. Moreover, the desire of the individual to fashion itself is contradictorily the desire of the world to form itself.[75] We can make sense of this statement of Nishida by referring to Raichō, who desired to establish herself as an independent authentic self in the world, while she was reflecting in her consciousness the predominantly androcentric social milieu of her time.

Nishida observed that in human beings biological instincts turn into desires.[76] The body has various aspects. As a biological body, consciousness is instinctive (*hon'nō-teki*); as a historical body, consciousness is mainly sensory (*chikaku-teki*), but consciousness becomes self-conscious (*jikaku-teki*) when the body finds itself being in the world, with which the body stands in the absolutely contradictorily self-identical relationship—that is, it is radically interacting.[77] Nishida says that in the recognition that without the body "I" cannot be, "I" become truly self-aware on the extreme edge of this recognition of the fact.[78] To summarize these points let us turn to Nishida's own words:

> In the world that moves on constantly "from that which is created to that which creates," the moment of "from that which is created" refers to the individual negating itself and entering into the world (a whole)—and in this direction the individual becomes "a thing" that belongs to the world. On the other hand, in the moment of "to that which creates," the individual gains its independence *qua* individual ... [In this radically mutual connectedness of the world and the individual], for an individual to "see" is to "work," and to "work" is to "see." To "see" means that the individual negates itself and enters into the world as a "whole," which, however, [contradictorily] signifies that the individual becomes a thing (*mono to naru*). By "that which creates" what is signified is that the individual works as one among the many [world constituting] individuals, by negating its being a "whole."
>
> An individual possesses desires by reflecting the world within itself. An individual is cognitive and constructive *qua* individual in the absolutely contradictorily self-identical world. The more the individual consciously defines itself as an individual, the more it works as a constitutive element of the world—in a contradictorily self-identical way. That is, the individual thinks, having become a thing, and it works, having become a thing. Hence, in the movement of "from that which is created to that which creates," the world is imbued with consciousness, and it is rational in its self-formation. Reason (*risei*) is not something that simply resides in the head of an individual but is thoroughly objective. Reason is the world-constructing power. In this sense, reason is thoroughly historical.[79]

In a nutshell, each of us as the "embodier" of historical life gives shape to the world in our *praxis* (action) and *poiesis* (thing-production), which transforms *both* the world *and* the self. To put it differently, each self, being self-conscious, determines itself in place and time, which has the signification of an "event" (or an occurrence) determining itself from the perspective of the world. When the individual self-expresses itself through action, it "negates" the world. Thus, the world arises with the "self-affirmation of the self." And yet, the self originally comes into being in accordance with the "law" of coming into being and going out of being (*jiko shōmetsu*—meaning, all things perish; no self abides forever).[80] So, the world ultimately "negates" the self in this sense. Herein, we cannot help but detect the fundamental Buddhist intuition of dependent co-origination (*pratītyasamutpāda*) of all things and the radical temporality of all things (*anityā*), as there is no eternally abiding self-substance (*ātman*). Nishida upholds that this is the radically objective picture of the world (i.e. the "one"), of which the individuals (i.e. the "many") are its constitutive elements. This is the dynamic way in which the historical world constantly takes its shape.

It is not surprising then that Nishida came to summarize his view of life in terms of the encompassing notion of "historical life" (*rekishiteki seimei*).[81] But, in its spiritual yearning, the individual is not satisfied without seeking "eternal life" (*eien no seimei*), as "love does not cease to long for eternal life."[82] Here, "love" is best understood to mean more than just romantic love or self-love, but as the principle that enables the interpersonal relations as well as the relationship to the entire universe. This is the culminating point of Nishida's reflection on life.

As noted at the outset of this chapter, Nishida resorted both to apophatic and kataphatic styles of discourse. While the analysis of consciousness renders itself more congenial to an apophatic style of discourse, the blood-flowing breathing body, a concrete and tangible existence, renders itself more readily to kataphatic discourse. Nishida does not seem to privilege one over the other, as his view is radically "contradictorily self-identical." Moreover, he writes that when the field of consciousness (*basho* or topos) determines itself, life is established.[83] This implies that the self-determination of self-consciousness and life "simultaneously arise" together. That is to say, unless we become self-aware, there is no "life." When we become self-aware, we are "alive."

What is the relationship of the body to eternal life? If the body were absolutely being, Nishida would argue that it makes no sense that it grows old, and eventually decays. If it were mere "nothing," then it could not come into being. The body, then, is a "relative being" partaking something of eternal life. Life force is absolutely-being-and-non-being, in that we cannot objectify it. Nishida finds this mode of being can be seen in the structure of time (*toki*): each "moment" comes into being and disappears in the next, but the "absolute present" or "eternal now," which determined itself as the moment, never ceases to be. He finds the same insight expressed by Heraclitus's view of "logos," which is in constant flux and yet remains "constant." Individuated lives are thus the independent "moments" of the "absolute present," and of the "eternal life." But in a religious consciousness, each individuated life, each moment, is eternal as the self-determination of the eternal life, the eternal now. We must leave behind such concepts as relative and absolute in the end.

CONCLUSION

The present exposition is an attempt to broaden the scope of the methodology of intercultural philosophy, while drawing on the Japanese thinkers. I had three guiding themes, which were:

1. By focusing on the topic of life, we can access the kataphatic dimension of Zen philosophy.
2. By bringing individual thinkers together in dialogue on a topic mutually shared, it can shed new light on the aspects of their thoughts that were formerly less obvious.
3. By introducing a woman thinker into the discourse, we may break down the artificial boundaries built around the kinds of "philosophies," and thereby we may obtain a more balanced picture of the issues under discussion. In this chapter, a conscious effort was made to bring in Hiratsuka Raichō as a convincing conversation partner with two other well-known "Zen" philosophers, Suzuki and Nishida.

The assessment of this present approach and investigation is left to the judgment of each reader.

At this time, one thing emerges to conclude this chapter. Raichō, Suzuki, and Nishida all talked about the importance of love (*ai*) (or compassion, *daihi, mahākarunā*) alongside insight or reason (*prajñā*). For Raichō, the life of romantic love unfolded into her life of altruistic love, which became the source of her energy to dedicate herself to the cause of women's movement. For Suzuki "eternal life (*eien no inochi*) was possible only where there is infinite love (*mugen no ai*)."[84] In his open letter of 1963, addressed to Gabriel Marcel, he noted that while "life" harbors the tendency to self-destruct as it individuates, love curbs that drive and rescues life from self-destruction.[85] He adds a cautionary remark that this faith in infinite love (*mahākarunā*) has to be backed by sustained hope, perseverance, and self-exertion, which constitute the bodhisattva path.[86] For Nishida love is nothing instinctive ("what is instinctive is not love but a selfish greed") but is that which enables and sustains the essential reciprocal relationship between individual persons, between "I" and "Thou."[87]

It appears it is here that the human responsibility comes in, as life is not a given or something "eternal" in itself, but we are radically related to it, although it is the ground of our being (in a "contradictorily self-identical way," Nishida would say). Just as we may neglect the health of the earth, we could play havoc on life. If Daisetz is right in holding that love curbs raw instincts, we will have to speak the language of love, friendliness, and gentleness. That is, if we want to see this world and humanity rehabilitate in such a way that the virtues—such as justice, equity, consideration for fellow beings, and magnanimity—can reclaim their places. Daisetz (and also Nishida) found in the following poem of Zen Master Shidō Munan a viable hint that can inform a new social principle. Infinite love is possible when we "die once while alive" (*ikinagara ni shinu*) and return to life as dynamic actors, not as ghosts. The poem reads:

ikinagara
shibito to narite
narihatete
kokoro no mama ni
suru waza zo yoki

While alive, I become a dead man
I die to my ego through and through
Then I act following my heart
Aren't these actions wonderful?

Daisetz wrote to Gabriel Marcel that he finds genuine "peace" in this experience of "dying and returning to life."[88] He illustrates this point with the same insight from the New Testament: "I died to the old Adam and live in Christ," while he also ponders the meaning of Christ having died on the cross before he was resurrected.[89]

Affirmation via negation, then, constitutes the vital key to the survival of every being and the hope for any chance for peace.

NOTES

In this chapter, all translations from Japanese into English are the author's, unless they are quotations from the English sources.

1. March 25, 1941, Letter #1564 to Kimura Michiko, NKZ 19.158: "*Kare wa shūkyō, watakushi wa tetsugaku da ga, mattaku onaji kangae desu.*"
2. This apophatic use of the language that grew out of the Christian mystical theology is very useful in interdisciplinary intercultural philosophy as well, and it is progressively being employed, independent of its theological origin, to uncover the dimensions of human experience otherwise difficult to "describe." See, for instance, William Franke, "Apophatic Paths: Modern and Contemporary Poetics and Aesthetics of Nothing," *Angelaki* 17.3 (2012), 7–16.
3. Nishida is referring to his essay "*Rekishiteki sekai ni okeru kobutsu no tachiba*" [On the individual's place in the historical world] (1938) (NKZ 9.69–146), which discussed Leibniz and the monad.
4. Letter #1284, September 25, 1938, to Miyake Gōichi, NKZ 19.47–48.
5. "Postscript" by Kobayashi Tomie, in HRJ 3.310. Raichō's autobiography is published in Japanese in four volumes (Tokyo: Ōtsuki Shoten, 1971–73). The first volume is fully translated into English together with the summary translation of the second volume by Teruko Craig, *In the Beginning Woman Was the Sun: The Autobiography of a Japanese Feminist* (New York: Columbia University Press, 2006). Volumes three and four are yet to be translated.
6. M. Yusa, *Zen and Philosophy: An Intellectual Biography of Nishida Kitarō* (Honolulu: University of Hawaii Press, 2002), xix. Original passage is in Nishitani Keiji, "Nishida, My Teacher," in *Nishida Kitarō*, trans. Yamamoto Seisaku and J. Heisig (Berkeley: University of California press, 1991), 27.
7. See M. Yusa, "Women Rocking the Boat: A Philosophy of the Sexed Body and Self-Identity," in FJP 6.155–169, for an initial treatment of this subject matter, as well as "Women Philosophers: Overview," in JPS 1115–1126.
8. See Kimura Bin, "*Seimeiron-teki sai no omosa*" [The weight of different theories of life], in *Nihon no tetsugaku* [*Japanese philosophy*] 3 (Kyoto, 2002), 19–20.
9. Nishida Kitarō, "*Ronri to seimei*" [Logic and life] (1936), NKZ 8.281.
10. *Zoe* (ἡ ζωή), meaning "life" as well as "a way of life," is derived from *zao* (ζάω), "to live," "to be in full life and strength," "to be fresh, be strong," with the connotation of "vitality." *Bios* (ὁ βίος) is life distinguished from "animal life" (ζωή), and denotes "a course of life, manner of living" (Latin *vita*); "life-time"; "a living," "means of living," "substance" (Latin *victus*); and "a life, biography." Bios is derived from *bioo* (βιόω), "to live," "pass one's life," whereas "*zao*" (ζάω) properly means "to live," "exist." "*Bios*" connotes a cultural dimension, laden with human values, as such words are derived from it as "*biosimos*" (βιώσιμος), meaning "worth living."
11. As opposed to *bios* (ό βίος), "way of living," and as opposed both to *bios* (ό βίος), and *zoe* (ή ζωή), meaning "existence," *psyche* (ή ψυχή) designates "vital principle," and the

compound, "to have psyche" or *psychen echon* (ψυχήν ἔχων), means to be "animated" or spirited.

12. Donald Keene, ed., *Anthology of Japanese Literature* (New York: Grove Press, 1994 (1960)), 197.
13. Shūsaku Endō, *Deep River*, Van Gessel, trans. into English (New York: New Directions, 1996), 189.
14. D. T. Suzuki, "On Death," in *Tōyōteki ichi* [The Eastern "nonduality"] (1942), SDZ 7.435–442.
15. Thomas Merton, "The Zen Kōan," in his *Mystics and Zen Masters* (New York: Farrar, Straus & Giroux, 1967 (1961)), 236–237. English slightly altered.
16. Ibid., 237.
17. Craig, trans., *In the Beginning Woman was the Sun*, 128.
18. Ibid., 92–93.
19. Ibid., 93; emphasis added.
20. It was the first journal of this kind, compiled, written, and sold by women for female readership in Japan. Its inaugural issue was published in September 1911.
21. Hiratsuka Raichō, "*Sanzen shite ita koro*" [Around the time when I was formally practicing Zen under Zen masters] (1924), HRC 4.83–84.
22. Suzuki Daisetz, #141, September 23, 1902, SDZ-N 36.222.
23. Narrated by Albert Stunkard, professor of Psychiatry at the University of Pennsylvania, in *A Zen Life*, DVD, directed by Michael Goldberg (2006). English slightly altered.
24. Could this name be connected with the notion of "*ātman*" in the *Upanishads*, where a small person, a size of a thumb, was thought to dwell in everyone's heart as the soul? There is no document to sustain this interpretation, but it is a charming association.
25. Nishida Kitarō, Letter #42 to D. T. Suzuki, October 27, 1902, NKZ 18.60. This letter is translated into English by M. Yusa, *Zen and Philosophy*, 73–75.
26. On Nishida's Zen practice, see M. Yusa, *Zen and Philosophy*, 45–75.
27. D. T. Suzuki, Letter #165, March 19, 1904, SDZ-N 36.248. This letter is originally in English. Suzuki's used the word "*dhyāna*" (i.e. "meditation") to refer to zazen. English slightly altered.
28. Suzuki, "Book review, Heinrich Dumoulin, *A History of Zen Buddhism*," *The Eastern Buddhist* (New Series) 1.1 (September 1965), 124.
29. Merton, *Mystics and Zen Masters*, 12.
30. Nishida Kitarō, "*Jitsuzai no kontei to shite no jinkaku gainen*" [The notion of the person as the ontological foundation of reality] (September 3–5, 1932), NKZ 14.152. This is a three-day lecture he delivered to the members of the Shinano Philosophy Association.
31. Craig, *In the Beginning Woman Was the Sun*, 133.
32. Thomas Yūhō Kirchner, trans., *Entangling Vines: Zen Kōans of the Shūmon Kattō-shū*, (Kyoto: Tenryūji Institute for Philosophy and Religion, 2004), Case 162, 84.

33. D. T. Suzuki, "*Shūkyō to seiyoku*" ["Religion and sexual desire"] (originally published in *Kokoro* 1.6, on December 1, 1948), SDZ 28.535/SDZ-N 33.300; emphasis added.
34. Hiratsuka Raicho7, "*Genshi josei wa taiyō de atta*," HRC 1.16.
35. Craig, *In the Beginning Woman Was the Sun*, 108.
36. On the "Shiobara incident" that broke down Raichō's youthful idealism, the circumstances leading up to it, and the aftermath, see ibid., 105–122.
37. Hiratsuka Raichō, "*Genshi josei wa taiyō de atta*," HRC 1.17.
38. Hiratsuka Raichō, *Jiden* [*Autobiography*], "*Fujin kaihō shisō*" [O the philosophy of liberation of women], HRJ 2.492–3. This section is omitted from Craig's translation.
39. Merton, *Mystics and Zen Masters*, 254.
40. Hiratsuka Raichō, "*Kojin to shite no seikatsu to sei to shite no seikatsu to no aida no sōtō ni tsuite*" [The conflict of life as an individual and as a gender] (August 1915), HRC 2.40–41. "Women Philosophers, Overview," JPS 1125; emphasis added.
41. Hiratsuka Raichō, "*Kojin to shite no seikatsu to sei to shite no seikatsu to no aida no sōtō ni tsuite*," HRC 2.49.
42. Hiratsuka Raichō, "*Haha to shite no ichinenkan*" [One year as a mother] (April 1917), HRC 2.274–275; JPS 1125–1126.
43. This led her to engage in debates on the need for the state protection of motherhood with Yosano Akiko, 1916–18. In 1919 together with Ichikawa Fusae she organized the New Women's Association (*Shin Fujin Kyōkai*), and initiated her activities for the women's suffrage movement.
44. Hiratsuka Raichō, "*Anata jishin o shire*" [Know thyself] (1947), HRC 7.18–22.
45. Ibid., HRC 7.21.
46. Ibid., HRC 7.19–20.
47. Hiratsuka Raichō, "*Shūzen ni tsuite*" [On Zen practice] (1931), HRC 5.274–276.
48. Ibid., HRC 5.275.
49. Suzuki Daisetz, Letter #211, May 21, 1907, from La Salle, SDZ-N 37.304–305. The letter is written in English.
50. Nishida Kitarō, Letter #55, dated July 13, 1907, NKZ 18.76.
51. Suzuki Daisetz, "*Shūkyō to seiyoku*," SDZ 28.522–537/SDZ-N 33.287–301.
52. Suzuki's reflections are tied with the notion of transmigration. To the question, what transmigrates?, Suzuki offers his understanding that "the soul is a principle, not an entity, and it creates a body suitable for its own habitation. Function determines form." See D. T. Suzuki, *Mysticism: Christian and Buddhist* (London and New York: Routledge, 2002 (1957)), 106.
53. Ibid., 109.
54. Ibid., 108.
55. Ibid.
56. Ibid., 106–107.
57. Ibid., 111.
58. Ibid., 63.

59. Ibid., 109.
60. Ibid., SDZ 28.525–526/SDZ-N 33.290.
61. Ibid., SDZ 28.532/SDZ-N 33.296–297.
62. Ibid., SDZ 28.537/SDZ-N 33.301.
63. Suzuki Daisetz, "*Heiwa no kakuritsu no tame ni warera wa nani o nasubeki ka*," [What should we—religionists—do to establish peace securely?] (1948), SDZ-N 33.203. This essay is compiled in the SDZ-N 33.198–204. See Moriya Tomoe, ed., *Zen ni ikiru* (Tokyo: Chikuma Shobō 2012), 358. On Suzuki's definition of "religion" to include the realm of imagination and ideal, see his essay "*Heiwa to sensō*" [Peace and war] (1947), SDZ 28.473/SDZ-N 33.158–159, in Moriya, *Zen ni ikiru*, 338, 341.
64. Nishida Kitarō, Letter #595, January 4, 1930, NKZ 18.396–398, trans. in Yusa, *Zen and Philosophy*, 246.
65. Nishida Kitarō, "*Jikanteki naru mono oyobi hi-jikanteki naru mono*" [That which is temporal and that which is a-temporal] (1931), NKZ 6.236.
66. Nishida Kitarō, "*Benshōhōteki ippansha to shite no sekai*" [The world as the dialectical universal] (1934), NKZ 7.340.
67. This line of investigation traces its beginning to the "*Ippansha no jiko gentei*" [The self-determination of the universal] (1929), NKZ 5.409.
68. One of the earliest mentions of the body in its philosophical significance is found in "*Hyōgenteki jiko no jiko gentei*" [The self-determination of the expressive self] (1930), NKZ 6.13–85; see, for instance, 6.77.
69. Nishida Kitarō, "*Junsui keiken ni kansuru danshō*" [Fragments on "pure experience"] (ca. 1900–1906), NKZ 16.348/NKZ-N 16.78. This passage strongly retains the flavor of Zen meditation, which was transiting into the field of philosophy.
70. Nishida Kitarō, "*Ronri to seimei*," NKZ 8.328.
71. The earliest mention of action-intuition is in "*Sekai no jikodōitsu to renzoku*" [The self-identity and continuation of the world] (1935), NKZ 8.7–106. Also he noted in "*Kōiteki chokkan no tachiba*" [The standpoint of action-intuition] (1935), NKZ 8.121: "Artistic intuition is no mere imagination; all intuition is something like action-intuition."
72. The exception to this is how the geniuses work. Nishida cites Mozart, to whom the entire score of symphonies would unfold first, which he subsequently would write down.
73. The first appearance of this phrase may be traced to "*Kōiteki chokkan*" [Action-intuition] (1937), NKZ 8.560.
74. See Nishida Kitarō, "*Rekishiteki shintai*" [The historical body] (1937). This was Nishida's two-day lecture, September 25–26, 1937, to the members of the Shinano Philosophy Association. NKZ 14.265–292.
75. Nishida Kitarō, *Nihon bunka no mondai* [The problem of the Japanese culture] (1940), NKZ 12.318. "Desire is the individual's demand for self-formation as it reflects the world inside itself; it is furthermore the demand of the contradictorily self-identical world that forms itself."

76. Ibid.
77. Nishida Kitarō, "*Jikaku ni tsuite*" [On self-consciousness] (1943), NKZ 10.523.
78. Nishida Kitarō, *Nihon bunka no mondai*, NKZ 12.318.
79. Nishida Kitarō, *Nihon bunka no mondai*, NKZ 12.324–325.
80. Cf. Nishida Kitarō, "*Butsuri no sekai*" [The world of physics] (1943), NKZ 11.9.
81. Noe Keiichi convincingly argues that Nishida's notion of action-intuition and the historical body were finally synthesized in the notion of historical life (*rekishiteki seimei*), which Noe finds as the culminating point of the later Nishida philosophy. See Noe Keiichi, "*Rekishiteki seimei no ronri*" [The logic of historical life], in *Kōza Seimei*, ed. Y. Nakamura and B. Kimura (Tokyo: Tetsugaku Shobō, 1996), 21.
82. "*Ai wa eien no inochi o motomeru no de aru*," Nishida Kitarō, "*Poieshisu to purakushisu*" [Poiesis and praxis], NKZ 10.125.
83. Nishida Kitarō, "*Ronri to seimei*," NKZ 8.284: "*Basho ga basho o gentei suru to iu koto kara seimei ga seiritsu suru no de aru.*"
84. D. T. Suzuki, "'*Mugen no ai' o shinjite, satori aru shūdan-shin o*" [Having faith in "Eternal love": Give rise to the communal spirit of awakening] (1963), SDZ-N 34.306; Moriya, *Zen ni ikiru*, 406. Suzuki's open letter to Gabriel Marcel, published in the *Yomiuri Newspaper*, April 28, 1963; SDZ-N 34.305–310; Moriya, *Zen ni ikiru*, 405–411.
85. Suzuki, "'*Mugen no ai' o shinjite, satori aru shūdan-shin o*," SDZ-N 34.306.
86. Ibid., SDZ-N 34.307; Moriya, *Zen ni ikiru*, 408.
87. Nishida Kitarō, "*Bashoteki ronri to shūkyōteki sekaikan*" [The logic of topos and the religious worldview] (1945), NKZ 11.437.
88. Suzuki, "'*Mugen no ai' o shinjite, satori aru shūdan-shin o*," SDZ-N 34.306, Moriya, *Zen ni ikiru*, 406–407. Nishida quotes this poem by Zen Master Shidō Munan in his last essay, "*Bashoteki ronri to shūkyōteki sekaikan*," NKZ 11.437.
89. Suzuki, SDZ-N 34.306.

BIBLIOGRAPHY

Craig, Teruko, trans. *Hiratsuka Raichō. In the Beginning, Woman Was the Sun: The Autobiography of a Japanese Feminist*. New York: Columbia University Press, 2006.

Endō Shūsaku 遠藤周作. *Deep River*, trans. Van Gessel. New York: New Directions, 1996.

Goldberg, Michael (executive producer). *A Zen Life, D. T. Suzuki* (DVD). Japan Inter-Culture Foundation, 2006.

Hiratsuka Raichō 平塚らいてう. "*Genshi josei wa taiyō de atta*" [In the beginning woman was the sun] (1911), HRC 1.14–27.

Hiratsuka Raichō. "*Kojin to shite no seikatsu to sei to shite no seikatsu to no aida no sōtō ni tsuite*" [The conflict of life as an individual and as a gender] (1915). HRC 2.36–52 (quoted in parts in "Women Philosophers, Overview," JPS 1124–1125).

Hiratsuka Raichō. *Sanzen shiteita koro* [Around the time when I was formally practicing Zen under Zen masters] (1924). HRC 4.83–84.

Hiratsuka Raichō. "*Haha to shite no ichinenkan*" [One year as a mother] (1927). HRC 2.266–275.

Hiratsuka Raichō. *Shūzen ni tsuite* [On Zen practice] (1931). HRC 5.274–276.

Hiratsuka Raichō. "*Anata jishin o shire*" [Know thyself] (1947). HRC 7.18–22.

Hiratsuka Raichō. *Jiden* [Autobiography], 4 vols. Tokyo: Ōtsuki Shoten, 1971–73.

Kamo no Chōmei 鴨長明. *An Account of My Hut*, trans. Donald Keene. In his *Anthology of Japanese Literature*, 197–212. New York: Grove Press, 1960.

Kimura Bin 木村敏. "*Seimeiron-teki sai no omosa*" [The weight of different theories on life]. In *Nihon no tetsugaku* [*Japanese philosophy*] 3 (Kyoto, 2002), 10–28.

Kirchner, Thomas Yūhō, trans. *Entangling Vines: Zen Kōans of the Shūmon Kattōshū* 宗門葛藤集. Kyoto: Tenryūji Institute for Philosophy and Religion, 2004.

Merton, Thomas. *Mystics and Zen Masters.* (New York: Farrar, Straus & Giroux, 1967 (1961).

Moriya Tomoe 守屋友枝, ed. *Suzuki Daisetsu: Zen ni ikiru* [D. T. Suzuki: Living by Zen]. Tokyo: Chikuma Shobō, 2012.

Nishida Kitarō 西田幾多郎. "*Junsui keiken ni kansuru danshō*" [Fragments on "pure experience"] (ca. 1902–1906). NKZ 16.267–572/NKZ-N 16.1–291.

Nishida Kitarō. "*Ippansha no jiko gentei*" [The self-determination of the universal] (1929). NKZ 5.353–417/NKZ-N 4.281–332.

Nishida Kitarō. "*Hyōgenteki jiko no jiko gentei*" [The self-determination of the expressive self] (1930). NKZ 6.13–85/NKZ-N 5.11–68.

Nishida Kitarō. "*Jikanteki naru mono oyobi hi-jikanteki naru mono*" [That which is temporal and that which is a-temporal] (1931). NKZ 6.233–259.

Nishida Kitarō. "*Jitsuzai no kontei to shite no jinkaku gainen*" [The ontological notion of person as the foundation of reality] (1932). NKZ 14.133–174/NKZ-N 12.213–254.

Nishida Kitarō. "*Benshōhōteki ippansha to shite no sekai*" [The world as the dialectical universal], (1934). NKZ 7.305–428/NKZ-N 6.239–334.

Nishida Kitarō. "*Sekai no jikodōitsu to renzoku*" [The self-identity and continuation of the world] (1935). NKZ 8.7–106/NKZ-N 7.5–82.

Nishida Kitarō. "*Kōiteki chokkan no tachiba*" [The standpoint of action-intuition] (1935) NKZ 8.107–218/NKZ-N 7.83–168.

Nishida Kitarō. "*Ronri to seimei*" [Logic and life] (1936). NKZ 8.273–394/NKZ-N 8.7–100.

Nishida Kitarō. "*Kōiteki chokkan*" [Action-intuition] (1937). NKZ 8.541–571/NKZ-N 8.215–238.

Nishida Kitarō. "*Jissen to taishō ninshiki*" [Praxis and the recognition of the object] (1937). NKZ 8.393–499/NKZ-N 8.101–182.

Nishida Kitarō. "*Rekishiteki shintai*" [The historical body] (1937). NKZ 14.265–292/ NKZ-N 12.343–367.

Nishida Kitarō. "*Poieshisu to purakushisu*" [Poiesis and praxis] (1940). NKZ 10.124–176/ NKZ-N 9.191–232.

Nishida Kitarō. *Nihon bunka no mondai* [The problem of the Japanese culture] (1940). NKZ 12.275–383/NKZ-N 9.3–85.

Nishida Kitarō. "*Rekishiteki keisei sayō to shite no geijutsuteki sōsaku*" [Artistic creation as the formation of history] (1941). NKZ 10.177–264/NKZ-N 9.233–300.
Nishida Kitarō. "*Jikaku ni tsuite*," [On self-consciousness] (1943). NKZ 10.477–564/ NKZ-N 9.465–532.
Nishida Kitarō. "*Butsuri no sekai*" [The world of physics] (1943). NKZ 11.5–59/NKZ-N 10.5–47.
Nishida Kitarō. "*Bashoteki ronri to shūkyōteki sekaikan*" [The logic of *topos* and the religious worldview] (1945). NKZ 11.371–464/NKZ-N 10.295–367.
Noe Keiichi 野家啓一. "*Rekishiteki seimei no ronri*" [The logic of historical life]. In *Kōza Seimei* [Lectures on life], ed. Y. Nakamura and B. Kimura, 9–36. Tokyo: Tetsugaku Shobō, 1996.
Suzuki, Daisetz T. 鈴木大拙 (貞太郎). "*Shi*" [Death]. In *Tōyōteki ichi* [The Eastern nonduality] (originally published by Daitō Shuppansha in 1942). SDZ 7.435–442.
Suzuki, Daisetz T. "*Heiwa to sensō*" [Peace and war] (1947). SDZ 28.466–473/SDZ-N 33.152–159.
Suzuki, Daisetz T. "*Heiwa no kakuritsu no tame ni warera wa nani o nasubeki ka*" [What should we—religionists—do to establish peace securely?] (1948). SDZ-N 33.198–204.
Suzuki, Daisetz T. "*Shūkyō to seiyoku*" [Religion and sexual desire] (1948). SDZ 28.522–537/SDZ-N 33.287–301.
Suzuki, Daisetz T. *Mysticism: Christian and Buddhist*. London and New York: Routledge, 2002 (1957).
Suzuki, Daisetz T. "'*Mugen no ai' o shinjite, satori aru shūdan-shin o*" [Having faith in "eternal love": Give rise to the communal spirit of awakening] (1963). SDZ-N 34.305–310.
Yusa, Michiko. *Zen and Philosophy: An Intellectual Biography of Nishida Kitarō*. Honolulu: University of Hawaii Press, 2002.

FURTHER READING

Craig, Teruko, trans. *Hiratsuka Raichō. In the Beginning, Woman Was the Sun: The Autobiography of a Japanese Feminist*. New York: Columbia University Press, 2006.
Merton, Thomas. *Mystics and Zen Masters*. New York: Farrar, Straus & Giroux, 1967 (1961).
Merton, Thomas. *Zen and the Birds of Appetite*. New York: New Directions, 1968.
Moriya Tomoe, ed. *Zen ni ikiru* [Living by Zen]. Tokyo: Chikuma Shobō, 2012. This volume contains selected essays of D. T. Suzuki especially addressing the topic of war, peace, and the problem of the social-political system.
Nishida Kitarō, his essays collected in NKZ, noted in the bibliography, above.
Suzuki, Daisetz. *Mysticism: Christian and Buddhist*. London and New York: Routledge, 2002.
Yusa, Michiko. *Zen and Philosophy: An Intellectual Biography of Nishida Kitarō*. Honolulu: University of Hawaii Press, 2002.
Yusa, Michiko, and Kitagawa Sakiko, "Women Philosophers." In JPS 1115–1137 (overview) and 1138–1164 (selected works by women philosophers translated into English).

APPENDIX: TWO ESSAYS BY NISHIDA KITARŌ

1. "THE BEAUTY OF CALLIGRAPHY" (*SHO NO BI* 書の美) (MAY 1930)[1]

西洋では書というものは美術の中へ入らないが、東洋では書は美術の大なる領分を占めて居ると云うことができる。書は如何なる種類の美術であろうか。美は主客の合一にあるのはいうまでもないが、芸術には客観的対象を写すということが主となって居るものと、主観的感情の発現ということが主となって居るものとがある。

絵画とか彫刻とかいうものは前者に属し、音楽という如きものは後者に属するのである。建築の如きも感情の発現とは云い難いが、それが何等かの対象を写すというのでなく、一種のリズムをあらわすという点に於て、寧ろ後者に属すると考うべきでもあろう。

右の如く芸術を分類して見ると、書というものも何等かの対象を模するというのではなく、全く自己の心持を表現するものとして、音楽や建築と同じく、全くリズムの美をあらわすものということができるであろう。その静的な形のリズムという点に於ては建築に似て居るが、建築の如く実用に捉われたものでなく、全く自由なる生命のリズムの発現である。そういう点に於ては音楽に似て居る。つまり建築と音楽との中間に位するとでも考うべきであろうか。「凝結せる音楽」とでもいうべきであろう。

Whereas in the West calligraphy may not be considered to belong to the genre of fine arts, in the East it occupies a significant place. What kind of art is calligraphy? It goes without saying that beauty resides in the unity of the subject (i.e. the viewer) and the object, but art is of two types—what mainly copies or imitates the appearance of objective things, and what mainly expresses subjective emotions and feelings.

Such art forms as painting and sculpture belong to the first type, while music belongs to the second type of art. Although it is difficult to characterize architecture as the "expression of emotions and feelings," it, too, belongs to the second type of art in that it expresses a certain rhythm, instead of copying some objective things out there.

If we classify art in this manner, calligraphy belongs to the second type, as what expresses the inner feelings rather than copies the appearances of things, and as such it expresses the beauty of the rhythm just as music and architecture. In its presenting the "static rhythm," calligraphy resembles architecture, but unlike architecture, calligraphy is not constrained by utility but is an utterly free expression of the rhythm of life itself. In this sense, it resembles music. Calligraphy then stands somewhere in between architecture and music. One could perhaps call it "congealed music."

ショーペンハウエルは音楽は物自体たる意志そのものを表現するものだから、最も深い芸術だと云った。リズムそのもの程、我々の自己そのものを表すものはない。リズムは我々の生命の本質だと云ってよい。音楽と書とは絵画や彫刻の如く対象に捕われることなく、直にリズムそのものを表現するものとして、我々の自己に最も直接した芸術と云ってよい。而もかかるリズムを静的に見る所に、芸術としての書の特殊的な点があるのである。

It was Schopenhauer who said that music, as expressing the will of the "thing in itself" (*Ding an sich*), is the profoundest form of art. Nothing expresses our being (*jiko*) better than rhythm. Rhythm *is* the essence of life. Music and calligraphy, without being confined by external objects and unlike paintings and sculptures, directly express the very rhythm of being, and as such they are the art forms most immediate to our being. Moreover, the unique feature of calligraphy qua art consists in how this dynamic rhythm is viewed in its stillness.

それで書の価値というものは、所謂技巧というよりも、多分にその人によるものでないかと思う。無論、如何なる芸術もその芸術家自身の人格の発現でないものはなかろう。併し絵画や彫刻の如きものはいうまでもなく、音楽の如きものであっても、客観的制約が多いと思う。然るに書に至っては、それが極めて少なく、筋肉感覚を通して、簡単なる線とか点とかより成る字形によって、自由に自己の生命の躍動を表現するのである。

This leads me to think that if we speak of such a thing as the value of calligraphy, it derives not so much from the technical merit as from the personality of the artist. Certainly, every art in one way or other is an expression of the artist as a person. In contrast to such art forms as paintings and sculptures, and even music, which are bound by many objective restrictions, in calligraphy such objective restrictions are quite few. Through the muscular sense, a calligrapher freely expresses one's dynamic impetus of life (*élan vital*) in letters that are composed of simple dots and lines.

2. "ON JAPANESE SHORT POETRY, *TANKA*" (*TANKA NI TSUITE* 短歌について) (JANUARY 1933)[2]

ベルグソンは『創造的進化』に於て、動物的生命から植物的生命、さては物体運動の如きものに至るまで、物質面を破って進展する飛躍的生命の種々なる形態なることを論じて、人間の生命は生命の大なる息吹であると云って居る。

In his *Creative Evolution*, Henri Bergson advanced his view that everything from animal life to plant life and even the material movements are but various modes of vital force (*élan vital*) that unfolds by piercing through the material crust; in this regard, he describes human life as the great emanation of this life force.

我々の生命と考えられるものは、深い噴火口の底から吹き出される大なる生命の焔という如きものでなければならぬ。詩とか歌とかいうものはかかる生命の表現ということが出来る、かかる焔の光ということができる。物質面に突き当たった生命の飛躍が千状万態を呈する如く、生命には無限の表現がなければならない。熹微たる暁の光も清く美しい。天を焦がす夕焼も荘厳だ。

Human life is like the flames of great life that erupt from the dark depths of a volcano. Poems of all kinds can be described as the expressions of such vibrant life—the radiant rays of the volcanic flames. Just as the leap of vital force that crashes into matter refracts and sparkles in myriad directions, so are infinite the expressions of life. The faint glow of the dawn is pure and beautiful; the evening sunset that scorches the heavens is solemn and majestic.

私は何でも西洋の文物が東洋のものに勝れると考えるものでもないが、さらばと云って何でも東洋のものでなければならぬと考えるものでもない。東洋の文化は東洋の文化として、西洋の文化は西洋の文化として、それぞれ他の有せない人間性の一面を現すものとして貴いのである。西洋画によって南画の美を現すことができないと共に、南画によって西洋画の美を現すことはできない。而も南画は南画として、西洋画は西洋画としてそれぞれに美しいのである。自由な豊富な偉大なる芸術として、我々は西洋画の前に頭を下げねばならないと共に、南画は南画として西洋画によって現すことのできない深い人間性の一面を現して居ると思う。

我国の短歌とか俳句とかいうものは、文学上如何なる意義を有し、他の文学に比して如何なる位置に置くべきかの論は別として、兎に角ユニークなものであるということができる。支那の五言絶句というものも、短詩の形式に於てよく発達したものと思うが、内容によっては俳句の如きものによって、同じ内容を一層よく言い表し得るとも考えることができる。

例えば、唐詩の

「反照入閭巷
憂来誰共語
古道少人行
秋風動禾黍」

という詩は

「この道や
行く人なしに
秋の暮」

という句と殆んどその内容を同じくするものと云い得るであろう。

I do not consider things Western to be indiscriminately superior to things Eastern, nor do I merely insist on the merit of things Eastern. Both Eastern and Western cultures are precious because each expresses the aspects of humanity that the other does not. Just as an artist cannot express the beauty of "*nanga*"[3] by a Western-style painting, so it is impossible to capture the essence of Western painting by the medium of *nanga*. Moreover, *nanga* drawings and Western paintings are each in their own way beautiful. While we admire Western paintings as the art form that embodies the free and great human spirit, we must also recognize the *nanga* drawings to reveal yet another profound dimension of humanity that cannot be depicted by Western paintings.

Putting aside the discussion of the literary merit of the Japanese *tanka* (the thirty-one-syllable poems) and haiku (the seventeen-syllable poems), or where they should belong in the genre of literature, we can nonetheless say that these poetic forms are unique. The Chinese poetic form of quatrain with five-characters per line (*gogon zekku*) is a nicely perfected short poetic form, but depending on the content, some of them can be more succinctly expressed by haiku. Take, for example, the poem of the Tang period:

"The evening sunlight shines upon a hamlet;
The sense of melancholy takes over me, but is there anyone to talk with?
Hardly a soul travels on the old country road.
Only the autumn wind moves the head of rice plants and millet leaves."[4]

The content of this poem comes very close to the *haiku*:

"Ah, this path!
not a soul is traversing—
the autumn dusk is falling."[5]

西洋でも二三行位の短詩というものはないではないが、多くは概念的であって、教訓的とか風刺的とかいうものが多い。短詩の形式によってのみ言い表される芸術的内容を言い表したものとして我国の短歌の如くそれ自身の芸術的領域を有つものは少ない。短詩の形式によって人生を表現するということは、単に人生を短詩の形式によって表現するということではなく、人生には唯、短詩の形式によってのみ掴み得る人生の意義というものがあることを意味するのである。

Certainly, there is the tradition of short poetry in the West consisting of two or three lines. But most of them are conceptual in tone, and many are didactic or satirical. Short poetic forms that can boast its own artistic merit, comparable to the Japanese *tanka*, which deftly expresses artistic contents possible only in short poetic form, are scarce. To express life-experience in a short poem does not simply mean to express it in short poetic form, but rather that there is a significance of our lives that can only be captured by short poems.

短詩の形式によって人生を掴むということは、人生を現在の中心から掴むということでなければならぬ、刹那の一点から見るということでなければならぬ。人生は固より一つである。併し具体的にして動き行く人生は、之を環境から見るということと、之を飛躍的生命の尖端から掴むということとは同一ではない。そのいずれより見るかによって、人生は異なった観を呈し、我々は異なった意義に於て生きるということとなるのである。

To grasp life-experience by way of short poetic form ("*tanshi*") is to grasp it from the center of the present moment. It is to view life from the very moment of experience. Life, surely, is one whole unity, but in grasping this concrete and vibrant life, it is one thing to look at it from the environment; it is quite another to grasp it at the very tip of a vividly pulsating life. Depending on which angle we take to view life, it presents a different vista, and we actually live a different significance of life.

過去を忘れ未来を思わず、現在に即して見、現在に即して行なうというのが我々日本人の特徴である様に思われる。そこに日本文化の長所もあれば、欠点もあるのであろう。俳句は短歌よりも更に短いものであるが、俳句には俳句の領域があり、短歌には短歌の領域がある。私は短歌によっては極めて内面的なるものが言い表されると思う。短歌は情緒の律動を現すものとして、勝義に於て叙情的というべきであろう。

To forget the past and not think about the future, but look at reality at the given moment and act accordingly appears to be characteristic of Japanese mentality. I suppose both the strengths and the weaknesses of the Japanese culture derive from this mentality. Haiku is even shorter than *tanka*, but it has its own domain as art form, just as *tanka* has its own. I think that one can express a very profound inner feeling in *tanka*. *Tanka*, as that which retains the rhythm of emotion, is essentially "lyrical."

* * *

嘗てホメロスを読んで、私はその素朴なる中に、能く深い人情の機微に触れ、且つ事物の描写の精緻なるに驚いた。ホメロス以来文学は如何程進んだのであろう。シルレルがホメロスは詩の海だと云ったのも尤もだと思った。

Years ago when I read Homer, I discovered that deep and subtle furrows of human feelings were so deftly described by his simple verses, and I was surprised by how precise and detailed his descriptions of things and events were. It makes me wonder how much progress literature has made since Homer. I fully see why Schiller called Homer "the sea of poetry."

万葉というものに就ても同様の感なきを得ない。その中には今日青年男女をして正にその心緒を述べしめるも、これ以上にはと思わしめるものもある。歌に於て万葉を師とすべきはいうまでもない。併し徒らに万葉を模倣することは真に万葉を学ぶものではない。万葉に学ぶべき所はその純真なる所になければならぬ。素朴的と云い客観的というも、既に一種の外殼たるに過ぎない。殊更らしい万葉調は却って非万葉的というべきである。

* * *

I cannot help but feel the same way about the *Man'yō* poetry collection. Some of the poems compiled in this collection perfectly capture the feelings of love between young men and women of today, and they can hardly be surpassed by today's poems. There is no question that the *Man'yō* collection should be considered the master teacher of poetry composition, but if we end up merely imitating the *Man'yō* style, we are actually not learning from it. What we must learn from the *Man'yō* poetry is the purity and sincerity of human heart that is at work behind the poetry composition. Just to praise the *Man'yō* tone as "simple" or "objective" is to miss its spirit, and we gain nothing but a dead husk. Overt imitation of the *Man'yō* style is actually to miss the spirit of the *Man'yō* poetry.

* * *

我国の短歌というものは形式が簡単であるだけに何人も容易に試み得る如くに考えられる、併しそれだけに却って内容の充実したもの、鍛錬せられたものでなければならぬ。

Many are under the impression that anyone can compose the Japanese *tanka* poem, because of the simplicity of its form. The truth is exactly the opposite. Precisely because of the brevity of the poetic form, its content has to be richly developed, thoroughly refined, and carefully wrought out.

NOTES

1 Collected in the *Zoku shisō to taiken* 『続思索と体験』 (*Contemplation and Experience II*], NKZ 12.150–151/NKZ-N 7.331-332. These two essays are translated by M. Yusa.

2 NKZ 13.130–132/NKZ-N 11.162–164.

3 It is also known as "*bunjinga*," the so-called amateur paintings drawn by the literati. This genre of painting became popular in the eighteenth century during the Edo period. Celebrated *bunjinga* artists included Ike no Taiga and Yosa no Buson.

4 This poem, "Autumn Day" 秋日, is by Geng Wei (J. Kōi) 耿湋 (734?–?).

5 Matsuo Bashō composed this verse on the lunar calendar, September 26, 1694, about a month before his death.

TIMELINE

Japanese historical period	*Names of Japanese thinkers, artists, and written works mentioned in this volume*	*Western, Chinese and Indian thinkers mentioned in this volume*
Jōmon 縄文 11,000–300 BCE Yayoi 弥生 300 BCE–200 CE Kofun (Tumuli) 古墳 200–500 CE		• Homer (10th century BCE) • Confucius (J. Kōshi) 孔子 (551–479 BCE) • Socrates (470/469–399 BCE) • Gautama Siddhārtha Buddha 仏陀 (463–383 BCE) • Plato (428/427 or 424/423–348/347 BCE) • Aristotle (385–323 BCE) • Marcus Tullius Cicero (106–43 BCE) • Jesus of Nazareth (4 BCE–30/33 CE) • Plotinus (204–70)
Asuka-Hakuhō 飛鳥・白鳳 500–710	• 538—the introduction of Buddhism to Japan • Prince Shōtoku 聖徳太子 (574–622)	• Fazang (J. Hōzō) 法蔵 (643–712)
Nara 奈良 710–84	• 712 *Kojiki* 『古事記』 *The Records of the Ancient Matters* • Ca. 759 *Man'yōshū* 『万葉集』 *The Man'yō Poetry Collection* • Kūkai 空海 (774–835)	• Tu Fu (or Du Fu) (J. Toho) 杜甫 (712–70) • Geng Wei (J. Kōi) 耿湋 (734?–?)

Japanese historical period	*Names of Japanese thinkers, artists, and written works mentioned in this volume*	*Western, Chinese and Indian thinkers mentioned in this volume*
Heian 平安 794–1192	• Sei Shōnagon 清少納言 (965?–ca. 1020) • Ca. 1000 *Makura no sōshi* 『枕草子』 *The Pillow Book* (994–1000) • Murasaki Shikibu 紫式部 (976/7?–1014?) • Ca. 1008 *Genji monogatari* 『源氏物語』 *The Tale of Genji* • Fujiwara no Shunzei 藤原俊成 (1114–1204) • Saigyō 西行 (1118–90) • Hōnen 法然 (1133–1212)	• Zhaozhou Congshen (J. Jōshū Jūshin) 趙州従諗 (778–897) • Linji Yixuan (J. Rinzai Gigen) 臨濟義玄 (?–866) • Yangshan Huiji (J. Kyōsan Ejaku) 仰山慧寂 (807–83) • Sansheng Huiran (J. Sanshō Enen) 三聖慧然 (n.d.) • Zhu Xi (J. Shuki) 朱熹 (1130–1200)
Kamakura 鎌倉 1192–1333 the military government, Shogunate, was established	• Kamo no Chōmei 鴨長明 (1153–1216) • 1212 Hōjōki 『方丈記』 *An Account of My Hut* • Shinran 親鸞 (1173–1262) • Fujiwara no Teika 藤原定家 (1162–1241) • Dōgen 道元 (1200–53) • Ca. 1250 *Heike monogatari* 『平家物語』 *The Tale of the Heike* • Yoshida Kenkō 吉田兼好 (ca. 1280–1352) • Daitō Kokushi (Shūhō Myōchō) 大燈国師 (宗峰妙超) (1282–1337) • Kyūsei (Kyūzai, or Gusai) 救済 (1283?–1376?) • Kitabatake Chikafusa 北畠親房 (1293–1354)	• St. Francis of Assisi (1181/82–1226) • Meister Eckhart (1260–1328) • Giotto di Bondone (1266/7–1337)

Japanese historical period	*Names of Japanese thinkers, artists, and written works mentioned in this volume*	*Western, Chinese and Indian thinkers mentioned in this volume*
Muromachi 室町 1336–1573 Ashikaga Shogunate ruled Japan	• Zeami 世阿弥 (1364?–1443) • Shinkei 心敬 (1403–75) • Sōgi 宗祇 (1421–1502) • Sesshū Tōyō 雪舟等楊 (1420–1506) • 1549 Francis Xavier introduces Christianity to Japan	• Nicholas of Cusa (1401–64) • Wang Yangming (J. Ō Yōmei) 王陽明 (1472–1529) • Baldassare Castiglione (1478–1529) • Giorgio Vasari (1511–74)
Azuchi-Momoyama 安土・桃山 1573–1603	• Sen no Rikyū 千利休 (1522–91)	• Francis Bacon (1561–1626) • Galileo Galilei (1564–1642)
Edo 江戸 1603–1867 Tokugawa Shogunate ruled Japan	• Shidō Munan 至道無難 (1603–76) • Nakae Tōju 中江藤樹 (1608–48) • Kumazawa Banzan 熊沢蕃山 (1619–91) • Bankei Eitaku (or Yōtaku) 盤珪永琢 (1622–93) • Itō Jinsai 伊藤仁斎 (1627–1705) • Matsuo Bashō 松尾芭蕉 (1644–94) • Ogyū Sorai 荻生徂徠 (1666–1728) • Hakuin Ekaku 白隠慧鶴 (1686–1768) • Bitō Nishū 尾藤二洲 (1745–1813) • Rai Shunsui 頼春水 (1746–1816) • Matsudai Sadanobu 松平定信 (1759–1829) • Satō Issai 佐藤一斎 (1772–1859) • Fujita Yūkoku 藤田幽谷 (1774–1826) • Ōshio Chūsai (or Heihachirō) 大塩中斎 (平八郎) (1793–1837) • Yamada Hōkoku 山田方谷 (1805–77)	• Thomas Hobbes (1588–1679) • René Descartes (1596–1650) • Rembrandt Harmenszoon van Rijn (1606–69) • Giambattista Vico (1668–1744) • Charles Batteux (1713–80) • Immanuel Kant (1724–1804) • Jeremy Bentham (1748–1832) • Johann Wolfgang von Goethe (1749–1832) • Mary Wollstonecraft (1759–97) • Johann Christoph Friedrich Schiller (1759–1805) • Johann Gottlieb Fichte (1762–1814) • Georg Wilhelm Friedrich Hegel (1770–1831) • Arthur Schopenhauer (1788–1860) • Nikolai Lobachevsky (1792–1856) • John Herschel (1792–1871)

Japanese historical period	*Names of Japanese thinkers, artists, and written works mentioned in this volume*	*Western, Chinese and Indian thinkers mentioned in this volume*
	• Okunomiya Zōsai 奥宮慥斎 (1811–78)	• William Whewell (1794–1866)
	• Kasuga Sen'an 春日潜庵 (1811–78)	• Auguste Comte (1798–1857)
	• Imakita Kōsen 今北洪川 (1816–92)	• János Bolyai (1802–60)
		• Max Stirner (1806–56)
	• Katsu Kaishū 勝海舟 (1823–99)	• John Stuart Mill (1806–73)
	• Saigō Takamori 西郷隆盛 (1828–77)	
	• Nishi Amane 西周 (1829–97)	• Johann Gustav Droysen (1808–84)
***	• Yoshida Shōin 吉田松陰 (1830–59)	
Meiji		• Søren Kierkegaard (1813–13)
明治	• Mishima Chūshū 三島中洲 (1830–1919)	
1868–1912		• Karl Marx (1818–83)
Emperor Mutsuhito's reign	• Fukuzawa Yukichi 福沢諭吉 (1835–1901)	• Gustave Émile Boissonade (1825–1910)
	• Katō Hiroyuki 加藤弘之 (1836–1916)	• J. C. Maxwell (1831–79)
	• Takasugi Shinsaku 高杉晋作 (1839–67)	• J. W. R. Dedekind (1831–1916)
	• Nakahara Nantenbō 中原南天棒 (1839–1925)	• Wilhelm Dilthey (1833–1911)
	• Kōjū Sōtaku 広州宗澤 (1840–1907)	• Ernst Mach (1838–1916)
		• Franz Brentano (1838–1917)
	• Shibusawa Eiichi 渋沢栄一 (1840–1931)	• C. S. Pierce (1839–1914)
	• Nakae Chōmin 中江兆民 (1847–1901)	• Konrad Fiedler (1841–95)
	• Setsumon Genshō 雪門玄松 (1850–1915)	• William James (1842–1910)
	• Inoue Tetsujirō 井上哲次郎 (1855–1944)	• Friedrich Nietzsche (1844–1900)
	• Ikegami Shōsan 池上湘山 (1856–1928)	• Josiah Royce (1855–1916)
		• Gottlob Frege (1848–1925)
	• Inoue Enryō 井上円了 (1858–1919)	
		• Ellen Key (1849–1926)
***	• Hōjō Tokiyuki 北条時敬 (1858–1929)	• Lafcadio Hearn (1850–1904)
Taishō		• Jane E. Harrison (1850–1928)
	• Shaku Sōen 釈宗演 (1860–1919)	
大正		• Paul Carus (1852–1919)
	• Miyake Setsurei 三宅雪嶺 (1860–1945)	
1912–1926		• J. Henri Poincaré (1854–1912)

Japanese historical period	*Names of Japanese thinkers, artists, and written works mentioned in this volume*	*Western, Chinese and Indian thinkers mentioned in this volume*
Emperor Yoshihito's reign	• Nitobe Inazō 新渡戸稲造 (1862–1933)	• Olive Schreiner (1855–1920)
	• Kiyozawa Manshi 清沢満之 (1863–1903)	• Alois Riegl (1858–1905)
	• Okakura Tenshin (Kakuzō) 岡倉天心 （覚三） (1863–1913)	• Georg Simmel (1858–1918)
	• Tokutomi Sohō 徳富蘇峰 (1863–1957)	• Max Planck (1858–1947)
	• Hiroike Chikurō 廣池千九郎 (1866–1938)	• Edmund Husserl (1859–1938)
***	• Hattori Unokichi 服部宇之吉 (1867–1939)	• Henri Bergson (1859–1941)
Shōwa 昭和 1926–89 Emperor Hirohito's reign	• Natsume Sōseki 夏目漱石 (1867–1916)	• Charlotte Perkins Gilman (1860–1935)
	• Matsumoto Bunzaburō 松本文三郎 (1869–1944)	• John Scott Haldane (1860–1936)
	• Takase Takejirō 高瀬武次郎 (1869–1950)	• David Hilbert (1862–1943)
	• Fujioka Sakutarō 藤岡作太郎 (1870–1910)	• Max Weber (1864–1920)
	• Nishida Kitarō 西田幾多郎 (1870–1945)	• Paul Valéry (1871–1945)
	• Shaku Sōkatsu 釈宗活 (1870–1954)	• Bertrand Russell (1872–1970)
	• Suzuki Daisetz 鈴木大拙 (1870–1966)	• Max Scheler (1874–1928)
	• Ishizaki Tōgoku 石崎東国 (1873–1931)	• Rainer Maria Rilke (1875–1926)
	• Yanagita Kunio 柳田國男 (1875–1962)	• Beatrice Lane Suzuki (1878–1939)
	• Hatano Seiichi 波多野精一 (1877–1950)	• Martin Buber (1878–1965)
	• Kubota Utsubo 窪田空穂 (1877–1967)	• Albert Einstein (1879–1955)
	• Yosano Akiko 与謝野晶子 (1878–1942)	• Robert Musil (1880–1942)
	• Sōda Kiichirō 左右田喜一郎 (1881–1927)	• Wilhelm Worringer (1881–1965)
	• Abe Jirō 阿部次郎 (1883–1959)	• L. E. J. Brouwer (1881–1966)
	• Tanabe Hajime 田辺元 (1885–1962)	• P. W Bridgman (1882–1961)
		• Karl Jaspers (1883–1969)
		• Niels Bohr (1885–1962)
		• Erwin Schrödinger (1887–1961)

Japanese historical period	Names of Japanese thinkers, artists, and written works mentioned in this volume	Western, Chinese and Indian thinkers mentioned in this volume
	• Takahashi Satomi 高橋里美 (1886–1964)	• Ludwig Wittgenstein (1889–1951)
	• Hiratsuka Raichō 平塚らいてう (1886–1971)	• Oskar Becker (1889–1964)
	• Ueda Juzō 植田寿蔵 (1886–1973)	
	• Orikuchi Shinobu 折口信夫 (1887–1953)	• Gabriel Marcel (1889–1973)
	• Kuki Shūzō 九鬼周造 (1888–1941)	• Martin Heidegger (1889–1976)
	• Watsuji Tetsurō 和辻哲郎 (1889–1960)	• Louis-Vietor de Broglie (1892–1989)
	• Hisamatsu Shin'ichi 久松真一 (1889–1980)	• Max Horkheimer (1895–1973)
	• Mutai Risaku 務台理作 (1890–1974)	• Károly Kerényi (1897–1973)
	• Yamanouchi Tokuryū 山内得立 (1890–1982)	• Friedrich Hayek (1899–1992)
	• Ishida Yoshisada 石田吉貞 (1890–1987)	• Werner Heisenberg (1901–76)
	• Yasuoka Masahiro 安岡正篤 (1892–1983)	• Linus Carl Pauling (1901–94)
	• Hisamatsu Sen'ichi 久松潜一 (1894–1976)	• Karl Popper (1902–94) • Theodor W. Adorno (1903–69)
	• Miyake Gōichi 三宅剛一 (1895–1982)	
	• Miki Kiyoshi 三木清 (1897–1945)	• Mark Rothko (1903–70) • Hans Jonas (1903–93)
	• Uehara Senroku 上原専禄 (1899–1975)	• Eugen Fink (1905–75) • Jean-Paul Sartre (1905–80)
	• Tosaka Jun 戸坂潤 (1900–45)	• Hannah Arendt (1906–75)
	• Moritaki Ichirō 森瀧市郎 (1901–94)	• Emmanuel Levinas (1906–95)
	• Nakai Masakazu 中井正一 (1900–52)	• Rachel Carson (1907–64) • Maurice Merleau-Ponty (1908–61)
	• Kōsaka Masaaki 高坂正顕 (1900–69)	• Simone de Beauvoir (1908–86)
	• Nishitani Keiji 西谷啓治 (1900–90)	• Jorge Oteiza (1908–2003)

Japanese historical period	*Names of Japanese thinkers, artists, and written works mentioned in this volume*	*Western, Chinese and Indian thinkers mentioned in this volume*
	• Kobayashi Hideo 小林秀雄 (1902–83)	• Claude Lévi-Strauss (1908–2009)
	• Shimomura Toratarō 下村寅太郎 (1902–95)	• Marshall McLuhan (1911–80)
	• Karaki Junzō 唐木順三 (1904–80)	
	• Kōyama Iwao 高山岩男 (1905–93)	• Paul Ricoeur (1913–2005)
		• Thomas Merton (1915–68)
	• Tomonaga Shin'ichirō 朝永振一郎 (1906–79)	• Raimon Panikkar (1918–2010)
	• Yukawa Hideki 湯川秀樹 (1907–81)	
	• Suzuki Shigetaka 鈴木成高 (1907–88)	• John W. Gofman (1918–2007)
	• Takeuchi Yoshimi 竹内好 (1910–77)	• Paul Celan (1920–70)
		• Cornelius Castoriadis (1922–97)
***	• Mori Arimasa 森有正 (1911–76)	• Antoni Tàpies (1923–2002)
Heisei	• Izutsu Toshihiko 井筒俊彦 (1914–93)	• Norwood Russell Hanson (1924–67)
平成	• Maruyama Masao 丸山真男 (1914–96)	
1989–	• Katō Shūichi 加藤周一 (1919–2008)	• Arthur Danto (1924–2013)
Emperor Akihito's reign		• Michael Dummett (1925–2011)
	• Taketani Mitsuo 武谷三男 (1911–2000)	
	• Ōmori Shōzō 大森荘蔵 (1921–97)	
	• Setouchi Jakuchō 瀬戸内寂聴 (1922–)	
	• Endō Shūsaku 遠藤周作 (1923–96)	
	• Yuasa Yasuo 湯浅泰雄 (1925–2005)	
	• Nakamura Yūjirō 中村雄二郎 (1925–)	• Hilary Putnam (1926–2016)
	• Izutsu Toyoko 井筒豊子 (1925–)	• Robert Bellah (1927–2013)
	• Ueda Shizuteru 上田閑照 (1926–)	• Arthur R. Tamplin (1926–2007)
	• Takiura Shizuo 滝浦静雄 (1927–2011)	• José Ángel Valente (1929–2000)

Japanese historical period	*Names of Japanese thinkers, artists, and written works mentioned in this volume*	*Western, Chinese and Indian thinkers mentioned in this volume*
	• Kida Gen 木田元 (1928–2014) • Nitta Yoshihiro 新田義弘 (1929–) • Tatematsu Hirotaka 立松弘孝 (1931–2016) • Kimura Bin 木村敏 (1931–) • Kubota Jun 久保田淳 (1933–) • Hiromatsu Wataru 廣松渉 (1933–94) • Ōe Kenzaburō 大江健三郎 (1935–)	• Alasdair MacIntyre (1929–) • Amitai Etzioni (1929–) • Jacques Derrida (1930–2004) • Michel Serres (1930–) • Luce Irigaray (1930–) • Richard Rorty (1931–2007) • Charles Taylor (1931–) • Shlomo Avineri (1933–)
	• Sakabe Megumi 坂部恵 (1936-2009) • Hase Shōtō 長谷正當 (1937–) • Ōhashi Ryōsuke 大橋良介 (1944–) • Karatani Kōjin 柄谷行人 (1945–) • Murata Jun'ichi 村田純一 (1948–) • Fujita Masakatsu 藤田正勝 (1949–) • Washida Kiyokazu 鷲田清一 (1949–) • Noe Keiichi 野家啓一 (1950–)	• Alois M. Haas (1934–) • William LaFleur (1936–2010) • Gianni Vattimo (1936–) • Hélène Cixous (1937–) • Helen Caldicott (1938–) • Augustin Berque (1942–) • Pataricia Lindop (1943–2002) • Giangiorgio Pasqualotto (1946–) • Thomas Kasulis (1948–) • Michael J. Sandel (1953–) • Amador Vega Esquerra (1959–)

INDEX: JAPANESE TEXTS CITED

For the collected works, the volume number is followed by a period and page number(s).

HRC 『平塚らいてう著作集』 *Hiratsuka Raichō Chosakushū* (Collected works of Hiratsuka Raichō), Hiratsuka Raichō Chosakushū Iinkai, ed. (Tokyo: Ōtsuki Shoten, 1983–84).

- 1.14–27. "*Genshi josei wa taiyō de atta*" 「原始女性は太陽であった」 [In the beginning woman was the sun] (1911).
- 2.36–52. "*Kojin to shite no seikatsu to sei to shite no seikatsu to no aida no sōtō ni tsuite*" 「個人としての生活と性としての生活との間の争闘について」 [On the conflict/struggle between the life as an individual and the life as a sexed woman] (1915).
- 2.266–275. "*Haha to shite no ichinenkan*" 「母としての一年間」 [One year as a mother] (1917).
- 4.81–85. "*Sanzen shiteita koro*" 「参禅していた頃」 [When I was formally practicing Zen] (1924).
- 5.274–276. "*Shūzen ni tsuite*" 「修禅について」 [On Zen practice] (1931).
- 7.18–22. "*Anata jishin o shire*" 「あなた自身を知れ」 [Know thyself] (1947).

HRJ 『平塚らいてう自伝、原始女性は太陽であった』 *Hiratsuka Raichō Jiden: Genshi josei wa taiyō de atta* [Autobiography: In the beginning woman was the sun], 4 vols (1971–73).

HSC 『久松真一著作集』 *Hisamatsu Shin'ichi Chosakushū* [Works of Hisamatsu Shin'ichi] (Tokyo: Risōsha, 1970–73). Vol. 4. *Chadō no tetsugaku* 『茶道の哲学』 [Philosophy of the art of tea ceremony]. 5.246–248. "*Koshō*" 「己象」 [Self-image].

MKZ 『三木清全集』 *Miki Kiyoshi Zenshū* [Collected works of Miki Kiyoshi] (Tokyo: Iwanami Shoten, 1966–) 20 vols.

- 1.204–212. "*Kōfuku ni tsuite*" 「幸福について」 [On happiness], later compiled in his *Jinseiron nōto* [Essays on life] (1938–41).
- 1.353–368. "Waga seishun" 「我が青春」 ["My youth"] (1942).
- 6.1–288. *Rekishi tetsugaku* 『歴史哲学』 [*The philosophy of history*] (1932).
- 7.195–329. "*Gijutsu tetsugaku*" 「技術哲学」 [Philosophy of technics] (1941–42).

INDEX: NAMES AND TERMS

CPSIA information can be obtained
at www.ICGtesting.com
Printed in the USA
LVHW050825190419
614807LV00007B/92/P

9 781350 096950